Managing Crises in the Academic Library

Past, Present, and Future

Edited by
Doris Van Kampen-Breit

Association of College and Research Libraries
A division of the American Library Association
Chicago, Illinois 2023

The paper used in this publication meets the minimum requirements of American National Standard for Information Sciences–Permanence of Paper for Printed Library Materials, ANSI Z39.48-1992. ∞

Library of Congress Control Number: 2023938818

Copyright ©2023 by the Association of College and Research Libraries.

All rights reserved except those which may be granted by Sections 107 and 108 of the Copyright Revision Act of 1976.

Printed in the United States of America.

27 26 25 24 23 5 4 3 2 1

Contents

VII INTRODUCTION

1 CHAPTER 1. Managing Library Units in Times of Crisis and Change
David Schuster and Caryl Ward

9 CHAPTER 2. The Impact of COVID-19 on HBCU Libraries: Trend Forecasting for a Post-pandemic World
Jessica Epstein

21 CHAPTER 3. Academic Library Budgets in Perpetual Crisis: Managing Vocational Grief from the Great Recession to the COVID-19 Pandemic and Beyond
Stephen Patton and Kristina Keogh

35 CHAPTER 4. Transformative Teamwork: Managing Change before, during, and beyond the COVID-19 Pandemic at Moraine Valley Community College
Marie M. Martino and Terra B. Jacobson

47 CHAPTER 5. Budgeting in Crisis: Responsive Decision-Making in Academic Library Collections
Braegan Abernethy

59 CHAPTER 6. The Human Factor: Managing Chaos and Change in Times of Uncertainty
Stephanie Sterling Brasley, Adriana Popescu, Alicia Virtue, and Delritta Hornbuckle

73 CHAPTER 7. Solidarity in Isolation: Shared Pandemic Experiences of Medical and Academic Middle Manager Librarians
Laureen P. Cantwell-Jurkovic, John Mokonyama, Christine F. Smith, Christina Prucha, and Marlowe Bogino

97 CHAPTER 8. Side Effects: How the COVID Pandemic Helped Us Build a Healthier Library Organization
Amanda Nash, Joy Bolt, Timothy Daniels, and Austina Jordan

111 CHAPTER 9. Managing Stakeholder Expectations during a Crisis
Jocelyn T. Tipton

iv Contents

119 CHAPTER 10. When Change Management Is Not Enough
Cinthya Ippoliti

131 CHAPTER 11. When the World Shuts Down: Perspectives of Leading through Crisis and Strategies for Wellness, a Case Study
Kayleen Lam and Michele Whitehead

145 CHAPTER 12. More Change?!? Developing a Strategic Plan during a Time of Crisis and Uncertainty
Bethany Wilkes

155 CHAPTER 13. Continuity of Operations Planning (COOP) for Academic Library Crisis Management: A Case Study
Nancy Falciani-White and Kevin Butterfield

167 CHAPTER 14. Professional Identity during COVID-19: Experiences of Academic Library Leaders in the United States
Erik Nordberg

175 CHAPTER 15. Overall Experience of Library Employees Working from Home during the COVID-19 Pandemic
Renee Gould, Amy Harris, Audrey Koke, Marissa Smith, Michelle Joy, and Delaney Rose

199 CHAPTER 16. Crisis Management in Brazilian Libraries: Management Lessons Learned from the Pandemic of the Novel Coronavirus
Danielly Oliveira Inomata and Célia Regina Simonetti Barbalho

213 CHAPTER 17. Helping Readers Imagine the Past and Remember the Future: Calming Anxieties and Fostering Literacies during Crises
Lynn D. Lampert

233 CHAPTER 18. Quick and Precise: A Case Study of Flexibility and Strategy in the Time of COVID
Matthew Shaw, Michael Szajewski, and Suzanne Rice

245 CHAPTER 19. Testimony and Tenacity: Rapid-Response Collecting the Pandemic
Sean D. Visintainer, April W. Feldman, Pamela Nett Kruger, and Christopher B. Livingston

261 CHAPTER 20. Libraries Making Lemonade: Technical Services Work Roles
Emily Szitas and Melissa Brooks

277 CHAPTER 21. Planning through a Pandemic: A Case Study of Miami University
Kimberly Hoffman, Rachel Makarowski, and William Modrow

291 CHAPTER 22. Hunker Down, Anchor Town! How the University of Alaska Anchorage Consortium Library Responded to COVID-19, March 2020 to May 2021
Lorelei Sterling

Contents   v

301   CHAPTER 23. Mold Mitigation during a Pandemic: Accessible Strategies for Archivists
Kayla Van Osten and Jill M. Borin

311   CHAPTER 24. Utilizing Library Storage Facilities in Crises and Disasters
Charlotte M. Johnson and Sharon Jasneski

321   CHAPTER 25. Task Sharing in Academic Libraries: Creating Opportunities for Professional Growth and Community during Times of Crisis
Yuki Hibben, Laura Westmoreland Gariepy, and M. Teresa Doherty

335   CHAPTER 26. Deconstructing the Team: Using Documentation and Cross-training to Maintain Coverage during Times of Crisis
Renna T. Redd and Mason Smith

345   CHAPTER 27. Difficult Decisions in Downsizing: A Library Management Perspective and Case Study
Alison S. Gregory

357   CHAPTER 28. Saying No to Say Yes: Mediating Student Technology Needs in Times of Crisis
Catherine Fonseca, Rita Premo, and Hilary Smith

371   CHAPTER 29. Interim Leadership in a Crisis
Livia Piotto

383   AUTHOR BIOS

Introduction

Academic libraries can most effectively respond to existential threats and crises by engaging with their teams and their communities. Untapped resources and opportunities for collaboration await if we can look past our current frameworks.

There have been many crises that have confronted academic libraries, such as the Great Depression and the Great Recession, though almost none have been as widespread nor as profoundly impactful on libraries as the COVID-19 pandemic. As has been the case in other crises, the pandemic forced academic library teams to confront change and make difficult decisions, many of which were not of their choosing. The cost in team productivity, library effectiveness, and the mental and emotional toll on the people who serve their academic community has been enormous, and the consequences will be felt long after the pandemic is endemic.

The Covid-19 pandemic accelerated the pace of change, altered the library landscape, and greatly influenced user expectations. The changes for many people and institutions were outside their realm of experience and they were caught up in a maelstrom. Despite the enormous and rapid onset of this crisis and its effects on user expectations, staffing, and budgets, library leaders and their teams rose to the challenges presented and found stakeholder-centered solutions. As each month brought increasing uncertainty for students, faculty, and staff, library teams focused on supporting each other while also adjusting to the "new normal." This new normal created challenges and opportunities in rethinking many aspects of academic libraries. It also forced some very painful and rapid decision making. Layoffs, budget cuts, and reorganization were part of the fallout from the pandemic. Many institutions will feel the effects for years to come in staffing models and levels and their ability to respond rather than react.

Organizations' resiliency and effectiveness are driven by their employees. When a crisis occurs, it is their response to the crisis at a personal and professional level and their ability to plan for contingencies and emergencies that can mean the difference between organizational success and failure. Clear channels of communication, courage to confront the crisis, and the authority to act in ways that do not damage the mission and purpose of the library are essential.

As you read this book, take time to digest and process what you read. Several chapters provide insight into theoretical frameworks and advise against casting library employees as either heroes or saviors; other authors speak from the heart and open up their lived experiences in order to help make sense of this time in history. All provide food for thought. This book is best read in parts, in groups, and in reflective response. At times both poignant and strong, it reflects the reality of the times we are living in and living through. The reflections, case studies, and management experiences in this book cover a broad range of topics and institutions from the United States and abroad; they speak to the resilience and tenacity of the people who work in academic libraries, their love of and passion for their chosen profession, and in many cases, the compassion and care for others demonstrated in the midst of crisis.

Some library leaders and their teams had to make very difficult decisions in the last several years, implementing transformative activities to align with new institutional norms and budgets. All of the authors share their insight into how they and their teams dealt with each new challenge or constraint. What can we learn from their stories? We can learn to be agile, and entrepreneurial; we can learn to be OK with being human; we can learn to let go of being the rescuer at the expense of our identity; we can remember to embrace our unique differences and support one another when things get tough and employee morale is decimated. Many library teams have also been left terribly wounded by decisions beyond their control, causing employees to wonder whether the cost of their institutional service was appreciated or even noticed.

Each vignette in this book speaks to that creativity and mental toughness the individuals and teams harnessed in the midst of their own unique crises. From each of these stories we can reflect, foster, and strengthen our own resilience. The future of academic libraries and the profession itself is becoming unclear as it is rapidly evolving, disrupted by the technologies implemented to serve our communities. Resources, services, and processes once thought to be at the core of the academic library may have been inalterably changed, yet the mission, vision and values of academic libraries are at the heart of our service to others. That forum for ideas and discourse may be altered but it is not destroyed. Lean into the change, embrace it if possible, and find strength in the new opportunities it brings.

Reading this book will prepare current and future library leaders to be ready for the next crisis. Being better prepared for the next unexpected event, whether it be political, monetary, man-made, or natural, can help academic libraries create their own path forward, moving with the tides of change instead of being overwhelmed by them. At the end, we must think about our mission, purpose, and potential new directions, and why academic libraries will continue to be an essential part of academe in some new and wonderful ways, full of opportunity and potential.

Preparing for the future means examining what academic libraries are moving toward and what they're moving away from. Students have grown ever more comfortable accessing resources and learning from their places of residence. Hybrid models of campus-based courses are being developed to align with demand, with students being able to select from a menu of online, in person, and blended courses. Online degrees and certificates will continue to grow. Virtual reality, artificial intelligence (AI), AI chatbots such as ChatGPT, and other alternatives to traditional learning technology and tools will potentially replace some processes and employee roles as academic units vie for funding, placing even greater pressure on strained budgets and personnel in reference services, collection development, and cataloging. The effects and uncertain future have led to burned out employees, low morale, and stressed-out students—all will need to be addressed.

What does that mean for the library? Students will continue to want physical spaces to collaborate, socialize, and study in, but they will also want more streaming video resources, more individual and group study rooms, and many (but not all) are increasingly less interested in traditional print resources and even online text-based information. Students want more freedom to choose the time and place of learning, the means and ways of learning, and fewer restrictions on their time as they strive to find balance in their lives. How can libraries help create this desired future? Library teams and leaders need to examine their unique organizational structure and advocate for the freedom necessary to address their students' and employees' needs. As a customer-focused entity, libraries develop and implement services that meet the needs and expectations of the current generation of students and faculty.

Foot traffic and circulation statistics are starting to bounce back, but budgets have fallen and the demand to do more with less is increasing. For institutions who have weathered the storm with sufficient funds, rethinking the library spaces and building to meet user needs will re-energize the space and provide that third place. People want safe nurturing spaces with a communal feel; libraries can and should be one of those spaces.

All is not gloom and doom: While the pandemic has acted as an accelerant to change, it has also provided academic library teams with many opportunities to re-energize and engage with their primary constituents—students and faculty. Crises create times in which its necessary to innovate and keep focused on the relationships we form with faculty, students, and other departments, including those which may have been overlooked—for example, student affairs and athletics—for that is where our power to transform libraries will be best used. Focus on building strong relationships with faculty to increase use of library resources and services by collaborating on instructional supports and academic resources that hone and enhance critical thinking and increase students' academic competency. The people matter more than the format.

Library teams can be the bridge for academic excellence and improved retention. Students who use the library have been proven to be more engaged and more likely to graduate. Now is the time to draw more students and faculty into meaningful conversations and build real relationships. Help them become comfortable asking for help online and in person. They are at the core of our mission. Get involved and embedded in course development and courses, where it is more likely librarians will be able to develop deeper and more meaningful relationships with our students, faculty, and course designers.

Reference services can be a lifeline for academic success by building personal relationships that students will return for, not just study spaces and makerspaces and coffee shops (although those do help!). Students and faculty need a friendly face and supportive person to reduce their cognitive overload and anxiety. Be resilient, friends; be strong; as you read these chapters, reflect on the underlying currents driving the tides of change, and prepare yourself and your team now for the next storm. This book is not simply for academic library leaders; it is for anyone interested in resiliency and the future of the academy, as seen through the lens of the academic library. Even if you are not in a leadership position, you can make a difference.

The next crises confronting higher education and academic libraries are likely to be almost as impactful as the pandemic. The coming enrollment cliff will place added strain on budgets and staffing levels, while artificial intelligence and chatbots such as ChatGPT will create new and different expectations in students and faculty. Other crises are also likely to appear on the horizon. Academic library teams can stay abreast of the currents in society, spot the trends ahead, and prepare for the next crisis.

Libraries and library employees are deeply sustaining lifelines for many students. Proving our worth and marketing to our audiences is frequently overlooked. It is time we demonstrated the need for, and value of, academic libraries and the profession committed to making a difference in our users' lives. This is not the time to be fearful of change. This is the time to leverage and embrace it, trumpeting our successes and learning from failures.

CHAPTER 1

Managing Library Units in Times of Crisis and Change

David Schuster and Caryl Ward

Empowering staff by trusting in their knowledge, skills, and abilities reduces their stress, enabling them to be successful regardless of the situation. To successfully lead others in an organization it is imperative that managers understand themselves and the importance of their own leadership.

Event Planning for Crisis 101 vs. No Road Map

Managing a library and its personnel at any time is challenging; managing during a time of crisis and the changes it precipitates is demanding and exhausting. Nevertheless, administrators can usually look to their team, along with best practices and a knowledgeable librarian network of support, when confronted with a crisis. While recovery from natural disasters such as floods and fires or the way to represent the institution with the media has been covered in the professional literature, other contingencies have not. Previous research about managing libraries in times of crisis alludes to wars and acts of terrorism with a focus on how the libraries continue to provide service to patrons rather than how to continue internal operations and support one's team while meeting the needs of the other stakeholders. Robertson's 2014 *Disaster Planning for Libraries* did acknowledge the seriousness of a pandemic (with nods to 1918 flu and 2003 SARS outbreaks) and anticipated lengthy closures of libraries, but with staff relocation to alternate worksites, not a pivot to working from home.[1] COVID's mandatory shutdowns did not closely follow this model.

The 2020 COVID outbreak left many library teams unprepared for the sudden and sustained disruption, as its impact reached far beyond the workplace and into virtually every home and business on Earth. In a constantly evolving situation without a playbook or an end in sight, managers were tasked with reacting to ambiguity concerning the length of the disruption and uncertainty over much of the future that created significant anxiety and emotional stress.

This chapter will consider the first three domains of "Six Domains of Knowledge for College Leaders during Crisis Times" by Jason Lane—know yourself, know your Skills, know your Team[2]—as applied to the 2020 COVID crisis. It will outline how library leaders at Binghamton University were able to ensure staff engagement, continue moving forward, and gauge success.

Binghamton University is one of the four university centers in the State University of New York (SUNY) system, and is classified as an R1 research intensive university. About 18,000 undergraduate and graduate students are served by three libraries and an annex. Telecommuting by library staff had never even been explored, so as the 2020 crisis began, the logistics of the abrupt closure of the university and the shift to work from home were overwhelming for many. The overnight pivot to a telecommuting environment involved brainstorming solutions to provide staff with assignments, equipment, software, and technical support. Operations often took a back seat to wellness.

While it was unclear when a return to normal workflows would happen, it was also unclear when staff would see each other in person again. Of great concern to many managers was COVID's impact on mental health and ensuring the well-being of every member of the library staff now balancing at-home work and their personal lives. With the water cooler emptied, the coffee pot turned off, doors closed and locked, and limited in-person interactions at most institutions, it was necessary to find new ways to engage remotely.

How Did We Manage in Times of Crisis and Change?

Lane describes high performing teams in this way:

> High performing teams have a commitment to each other as well as the larger goals and challenges confronting the team. They share a collective responsibility to advance the collective work and interests of the team, as well as to look out for the success and well-being of each other. They understand the shared norms and values of the team (e.g., rules of engagement) and adhere to those principles particularly when tensions arise. Moreover, they engage in extensive dialogue and manage conflict through a collaborative lens where critical feedback can be constructive.[3]

Effective leaders plan, communicate, and execute when challenges arise. Although unit heads at Binghamton University Libraries had little opportunity to prepare before COVID forced the workplace shutdown, they effectively responded to the immediate obstacle: the lack of equipment and internet access for all library employees. Without an existing telecommuting plan in place, a lot of anxiety was created for those lacking a home setup. The technical support staff were empowered with the knowledge and authority to adapt and make changes during these unusual times so that everyone could continue working and be successful in their jobs. Getting the technology right by shipping printers, mice, webcams, and headphones directly to people's homes was critical. Having tools for a very patient technical support team to view others' screens and even control the desktop remotely made library staff feel more at ease and that it was OK to ask for help.

Once equipment and remote access needs were met, there still remained a need to address and support not only the logistics of technology but also the emotional needs of staff. Leaders had to ensure that people had what they needed, be understanding of their concerns, and encourage their participation in discussions. Communication in libraries is enabled by face-to-face meetings as well as informal hallway discussions. In-person contact was impossible during the first few months of the COVID pandemic, while informational needs increased dramatically. In order to rethink in-person interactions, exploring new ways of communicating and engaging with one another had to be addressed. Three strategies used during the pandemic by library managers were know yourself, know your skills, and know your staff.

Know Your Staff

Knowing your staff includes
- how staff members generally react
- useful knowledge for guiding staff through any new crisis

Understanding one's team and each individual in the team is important to understanding what they may be going through or the challenges they may be having technologically or personally. Empowering staff by trusting in their knowledge, skills, and abilities reduces their stress, enabling them to be successful regardless of the situation. Knowing they can suggest and initiate workflow improvements, tackle the challenge of doing things differently, and find alternative solutions to daily work demonstrates empowerment. During the first weeks of the shutdown, it was imperative to communicate that staff members could ask for anything needed to change or complete a job and to emphasize that implementing workflow improvements makes work easier.

Supervisors also had to ensure people had meaningful work at home, at first envisioning the changes as just a few weeks' disruption. As early spring moved toward early summer, it became obvious the extended crisis would necessitate longer term projects and arrangements. Short-term absence from the physical workplace is easily covered, but when it extended for almost a year, the leader's emotional intelligence, knowledge, and skills become critical for continued success during the crisis. This library's long-term response for continued success included continuing the quarterly all-staff meetings and focusing more on the human side of operations. Spending money on what staff really needed to do their job was not questioned. The message: just give it to them now.

Individuals with families have a different need for support than those who are alone. During this crisis we needed to make staff feel connected with their work and each other, even though they were not sitting next to someone in a cubicle or office. Each online meeting offered time before getting down to business to chat about home life or share a funny anecdote. This served to help staff connect at the personal level and became a critical opportunity to listen for signs of concern; signals included cameras turned off, aloofness, and lack of engagement at the usual level. Open-ended "getting to know you" questions asked at the beginning of online meetings were engaging and set a tone for how conversations that used to happen informally in the office could continue in the online environment. A quality leader should engage by learning about people's home life, how they cope, their pets, and other likes or dislikes while still carefully respecting personal comfort levels concerning privacy.

Know Yourself

Knowing yourself includes how you react:
- skills needing improvement
- techniques that will be challenging to master

While it was immediately apparent that there was no playbook for managing the COVID crisis, it is always true that managers who know their team and have a solid foundation of leadership skills and knowledge of their own personal strengths are more able to thrive in a constantly evolving, stressful environment. The dean and his administrative staff were overwhelmingly supportive of managers and sensitive to their stressors. Managers were free to take action and direct by their own style as much as possible under the directives of the university and the state. The message was, "We support you, you know what you're doing, we've got your back."

To successfully lead others in an organization it is imperative that managers understand themselves and the importance of their own leadership. Guiding a team can be exhilarating as well as exhausting under routine circumstances, and situations like the COVID pandemic can amplify those feelings and others. The leadership process in a crisis involves knowing how to respond to individual events as well as knowing how the team generally reacts to sudden and unexpected change. The COVID pandemic of 2020 demonstrated the benefits of new managers assessing their strengths and weaknesses in order to prepare for any situation. Seasoned managers can also benefit from ongoing self-evaluation, which provides insight and allows staff to know the kind of emotional, mental, and physical support they can expect from their supervisor. Knowing yourself is more than superficial understanding. It means using self-reflection and an honest look at one's own behaviors, including deeply evaluating past workplace situations and staff and peer reactions, how others perceived those reactions, and considering if there might have been a better response.

The 2020 pandemic challenged all traditional skills of knowing yourself as a manager. Managing a library unit in this situation required modifying emotional intelligence and listening skills. While working remotely, it was paramount to meet regularly to stay connected to colleagues. During the first months of the COVID crisis, managers at Binghamton made great efforts to make themselves available to the staff in their respective units. There is a greater impact when leaders have already established a practice of holding scheduled meetings as well as being available outside of formal meetings. With these routines already in place we were easily able to transition to an online format.

Keeping the computer camera on so that others could see the manager's face offered reassurance as changes and new practices were communicated. Managers should be aware of emotional and visual cues as they become amplified on screen. While observing oneself on video, watching facial expressions can demonstrate true emotions sending an unintended message. It is helpful to practice calming one's body so as to not appear agitated or unfocused during a discussion and to consider the impact of the actual or virtual background. *Be calm, keep voices low and slow, and focus on the individual.* All of these things set a tone for the conversation.

Know Your Skills

Knowing your skills includes
- unique skills that have been mastered
- how these skills can be used to your advantage

Emotional intelligence skills, such as reading body language, facial expressions, and tone of voice, as well as noticing when someone doesn't participate in a meeting, are important keys to understanding individuals. Active listening skills include being able to sit and listen while gently asking probing questions to get at the heart of someone's concern. During times of crisis, leaders will find themselves communicating with individuals under stress who just need someone to listen. How can one practice reactions to a situation? One tactic is to think through past situations and potential issues and consider alternate responses. Or, at a meeting with someone, indicate you are going to practice listening skills so they understand you are changing styles. After a conversation ask the other individual how they perceived your openness and their ability to truly communicate. Afterward, reflect how it went and how to improve as a listener. It takes practice to change and to continue the reflection on how to handle new situations.

During a crisis watching and noticing out-of-ordinary situations or reactions can be crucial to identifying problems. While observing uncharacteristic behavior we need to gently ask questions in order to pinpoint the root cause. If the observation happens during a larger group meeting, it should be addressed privately, with open-ended questions to get to the root of any concerns. The work-from-home setting during the COVID shutdown collided with personal lives. Some staff faced increased family responsibility and conflict, while some individuals were isolated, and many had severe anxiety about the future. Reaching out to staff and following up on observations can let individuals know they are supported and valued by this single act of kindness. It is important to know what services are at a manager's disposal—for example, referrals to EAP (Educational Assistance Program) or other counseling resources—and how to deploy them for staff in a traumatic time. If someone becomes overbearing during a meeting or begins to act out, we need to calmly work to close the meeting and then work with that individual. We all want to know about personal situations in the workplace, but with privacy and Health Insurance

Portability and Accountability Act (HIPAA) rules and regulations, managers need to be very conscientious about keeping confidentiality. In a virtual workplace however, employees may sense coworkers are struggling and may be concerned about each other. Managers cannot divulge information about those who put their trust in us.

Working together in an office provides the opportunity to learn and share skills through demonstration. Working remotely, we learn new skills to demonstrate and share information with others, such as sharing screens, providing remote control of the cursor, and collaborating on a shared document virtually. Having clear documentation on workflows and processes is a prerequisite, and documentation should be easily adaptable if necessary. In virtual situations having the ability to share screens is a solution allowing everyone literally to be on the same page, and potentially even to share the control of the screen to demonstrate how to do something. Working with cloud-based software, rarely did we need to have software installed for individuals to do their work. If software was required, we also had to navigate through virtual private network (VPN) access with each employee to ensure they could connect to the appropriate servers on campus while working remotely.

Empowered staff can modify the workflows as needed to ensure work is accomplished. For example, printed invoices are required by campus. During the first months of the shutdown, staff devised a temporary scanning work-around to ensure that invoices were processed when possible.

Knowing they can suggest and initiate workflow improvements, tackle the challenge of doing things differently, and find alternative solutions to daily work demonstrates staff empowerment. Knowing they can ask for anything they need to change or complete a job was key, and implementing workflow improvements makes work easier.

What We Learned

During the COVID crisis it was observed that quality work was getting done, despite a range of work-from-home mandates followed by transition to a socially distanced office. In this chapter we suggested several ways we worked with staff to ensure management was listening and cared about them, through emotional intelligence skills, observation, providing needed equipment, and listening.

Staff who are able to adapt to change in normal times are valuable in times of crisis. We learned that flexibility and the feeling of empowerment are tremendous assets. Throughout the library there are many problem solvers who were able to function effectively amid the COVID chaos and challenges: indeed, the propensity for problem-solving served them well. Finding a balance between engagement and staff well-being rose in importance during the pandemic. Keeping them informed and ensuring they were aware of the big picture provided staff with tools to change and move forward, while continuing the dialogue of daily work and feelings of accomplishment. Keeping engaged with each other helps to provide a continued sense of teamwork and accomplishment.

Some interim changes will have an impact on future operations as they are considered for long-term adoption. For example, in the early days of COVID we operated in a paperless environment by necessity. How much printing and paper shuffling can be eliminated forever, and how much is required for campus and state record keeping? Asking staff to evaluate temporary workflows invites them to provide meaningful feedback and demonstrates their value to the organization.

Setting clear expectations and encouraging discussion about what is or is not working helps with engagement, empowerment, and staff well-being. In preparation for the future, managers will reflect with the team on what went well, what did not, and what needs to change that would allow them the flexibility and empowerment to do their jobs and build confidence and comfort for tackling future challenges.

In the workplace, having plans and a process in place for hybrid work makes it easier to shift to work-from-home scenarios. The complete work-from-home situation may never arise again, but having staff ready to shift with appropriate workspace and equipment at their homes is as important as a regular work schedule. It was demonstrated that we can be successful, and staff want this option for alternate work locations. Management needs to reflect on how it can be facilitated in the future.

We also learned the benefits of getting to know one's management style, knowing the skills that have been mastered, and the benefit of working on those that need improvement—for example, the importance of staying abreast of technology options available to the team for immediate off-site deployment (and hope that they will never be used), and also getting to know your staff, how they interact, and the personal or technological skills they need help refining.

We are also learning that postcrisis is the time to help staff at all levels grow and master new skills. Encouraging professional development will provide opportunities for staff to thrive in or out of a crisis. It is a job, but we are all people; treating each other with respect, and providing encouragement and opportunities, makes for great leaders and even better staff.

Notes

1. Guy Robertson, *Disaster Planning for Libraries* (Waltham, MA: Chandos, 2014), ProQuest Ebook Central.
2. Jason E. Lane, "Six Domains of Knowledge for College Leaders during Crisis Times," Inside Higher Ed, April 14, 2020, https://www.insidehighered.com/advice/2020/04/14/advice-how-college-leaders-can-best-respond-during-times-crisis-opinion.
3. Jason E. Lane, "Six Domains of Knowledge for Higher Education Leaders," SAIL Institute, State University of New York, December 13, 2017, https://sunysail.org/2017/12/13/six-domains-of-knowledge-for-higher-education-leaders/.

Bibliography

Lane, Jason E. "Six Domains of Knowledge for College Leaders during Crisis Times." Inside Higher Ed, April 14, 2020. https://www.insidehighered.com/advice/2020/04/14/advice-how-college-leaders-can-best-respond-during-times-crisis-opinion
———. "Six Domains of Knowledge for Higher Education Leaders." SAIL Institute, State University of New York, December 13, 2017. https://sunysail.org/2017/12/13/six-domains-of-knowledge-for-higher-education-leaders/.

Robertson, Guy. *Disaster Planning for Libraries: Process and Guidelines*. Waltham, MA: Chandos, 2014. ProQuest Ebook Central.

CHAPTER 2

The Impact of COVID-19 on HBCU Libraries

Trend Forecasting for a Post-pandemic World

Jessica Epstein

The library is one of the most popular campus locations for many students, and ...when compared to their white peers at PWIs, Black students more actively engage in a variety of activities when in the library. A further inference is that, for Black students at PWIs, the library might be a location somewhat less fraught than other spaces.

Introduction

The loss of community and normality was swift and dramatic. Once the decision was made to close the university campus, U-Hauls appeared everywhere as students loaded up their things and headed home or to other off-campus locations in March 2020. Dining services were shuttered. Classes moved online. Staff members were given laptops and sent home as campus buildings closed. New computer applications became commonplace, and certain words became part of the communal vocabulary: Zoom, Teams, asynchronous, virtual background, mute, pivot. For those students set to graduate in 2020, the conclusion of their senior year would be spent away from peers and friends cultivated over the previous three-plus years. Many juniors who graduated in 2021 spent their final fifteen months of college away from campus. Freshmen who may have spent their first semester away from home returned almost as if they'd never left. Faculty members who had never before taught online needed to shift assignments to adapt them for an entirely different mode of learning and ensure their readings now complied with copyright restrictions. Students relying on campus libraries and computer labs for internet access and hardware devices had to figure out alternate ways of accessing course materials, attending class, and writing papers. In some cases, for students who did not stray far from campus, this meant accessing Wi-Fi from campus parking lots or other locations converted into internet hot spots by some institutions during the pandemic.[1]

The impact of COVID-19 on the campus environment was keenly felt by those working in academic libraries. Staff regularly collaborate with faculty on collection development, course reserves, instruction, and so on, or provide research assistance, and also engage with students on consultations and the use of library resources. Phone, e-mail, and chat have existed for years as avenues of virtual service, but they always supplemented more traditional face-to-face options; campus constituents could typically enter a physical building—to use a computer, find a book, or speak to their subject librarian. As many libraries began acquiring online collections and e-books decades ago,[2] faculty and students were able to maintain access to much of the collection and continue research during the pandemic. Built in 1982, the Atlanta University Center (AUC) Robert W. Woodruff Library serves four separate HBCUs (historically Black colleges and universities): Clark Atlanta University, the Interdenominational Theological Center, Morehouse College, and Spelman College. Founded in the 1860s, Clark College and Atlanta University merged in 1998 to become Clark Atlanta University. Morehouse College was also founded in the 1860s, Spelman College in the 1880s, and the Interdenominational Theological Center in the 1950s.[3] Together, the campuses constitute the world's largest consortium of HBCUs.[4] Prior to 1982, each institution had its own campus library, but following the building's construction, individual campus collections were all relocated to the AUC Woodruff Library, which, during the pandemic, enacted services similar to those offered by other academic institutions during campus shutdown, including parking lot pickup. Staff, faculty, and students could place items on hold, and one designated day each week, users could drive to the building and a staff member would bring items to their car.

The overarching impact of COVID-19 on students is difficult to assess as the pandemic remains ongoing. Disparities in access to technology and the internet, information and computer literacy, and help-seeking differences are all likely to have been exacerbated during this crisis. Discussions of a return to normal shift as *normal* is continually redefined. The importance of campus libraries as physical spaces has been long established,[5] but that could potentially change in the months and years following the pandemic. Are there things libraries might do differently once the pandemic ends? Are there specific initiatives HBCU libraries should undertake as a result of the pandemic, and if so, how and why might those initiatives differ from any enacted at PWIs (predominantly white institutions)? Black students at HBCUs are generally more engaged in campus life than Black students at PWIs,[6] so the loss of campus clubs, activities, and face-to-face interactions were especially missed. Not only did incoming students at HBCUs experience the generic disruption and trauma that all in-person learners did, but they also missed out on forging in-person relationships with Black faculty members, who often serve as significant role models for student development.[7]

Given these factors, how can HBCU libraries best position themselves to serve students and faculty members as campuses across the country reopen in various capacities and to varying degrees? What follows is a review of the significant position libraries continue to hold on campuses, how community on HBCU campuses extends beyond the library, and also how, by the cultural nature of HBCUs, the library remains a central campus location for individual and group study, as well as socializing and support. Inquiries to staff members at HBCU libraries for statistics comparing student utilization trends from the fall 2019 semester before COVID-19 through October 2021 reveal that most libraries continue to see downward trends in in-person use.[8] Historically, library closures have precipitated notable drops in services generally accessed in person, including circulation, as well as requests for interlibrary loan and library instruction. The longer the building stays closed, the more precipitous the declines become.[9] Will downward trends in usage and services continue to be the case even when more students return to campus and in-person learning and as libraries reopen more fully or to higher numbers of patrons? What should staff and administrators at HBCU libraries plan for in terms of future collection development, building hours, library instruction, and division of space for individual or group study?

Libraries as "Third Places"

Numerous articles exist on the importance of campus libraries as physical spaces sought out by students for reasons as varied as quiet study, group study, socialization, computer access, or research assistance.[10] Other factors contributing to the amount of foot traffic in a campus library include a centralized location, Wi-Fi, convenience as a meeting place with peers, a place to access and check out physical materials, and in some cases a place to purchase food and drink.[11] Over the decades, libraries have adapted to provide services and resources to students. These changes may be to the building itself in the form of renovations, to the building's interior design through the creation of more communal work spaces or study rooms, or via the purchase of newer, more comfortable furniture. Some libraries have expanded their hours of operation. Still others have hired staff dedicated to distance learning, public outreach and engagement, digital services, data visualization, or other avenues in order to broaden the library's reach. Libraries have also upgraded technological infrastructures by installing charging stations or stronger internet service. Some have relaxed their policies around eating and drinking, including adding vending machines or cafes in the libraries themselves.[12]

Much like the prematurely reported death of Mark Twain,[13] reports of campus library decline are an exaggeration. In his article on usage during the recession years of 2008–2010, Long Island University librarian John Regazzi determined that at most of the more than 3,000 university libraries examined, reference and circulation statistics dropped significantly, while physical visits in this same period were essentially unchanged.[14] The implication, then, is that students may have moved away from heavy usage of physical library materials like books, DVDs, and other media in favor of those resources accessible online, yet still use the physical space of the library. Students continue to view campus libraries as safe places in which to study, congregate with peers, and use computers and internet for both library and nonlibrary purposes. This has led some researchers to posit that in the world of academia, campus libraries may qualify as examples of what sociologist Ray Oldenburg termed "third places." Oldenburg designates home and work as a person's first and second places, respectively; that is, those places where a person spends the majority of their time.[15] Third places are those establishments people choose to patronize outside of home and work, like coffee shops, bookstores, salons, and, yes, libraries. In an analysis examining academic library use and perception, findings showed the most preferred campus location to spend time outside of class was the library (at 33.3%).[16] Though that study was conducted at an institution where most students lived off campus, other studies have demonstrated the popularity of campus libraries as a place to learn and socialize.[17] A national survey of Black students at non-HBCUs conducted over 2016–2018 reinforced this idea and indicated that Black students may view the campus library specifically as a "third place" on their respective campuses.[18]

Though all students conduct similar activities in campus libraries, there may be differences in how the library is viewed by Black students and white students at PWIs, or how libraries are utilized by racially different groups of students. If engagement or perception varies by racial group, then the meaning of the library potentially changes from institution to institution and, by extension, so does the library's responsibility to its constituents.

The HBCU Effect

In a study conducted at North Carolina State University in 2013, library users were asked to rate activities conducted in the library on a seven-point scale. Researchers found that, in general, activities were rated higher by Black students than other groups of respondents, meaning they always or almost always engaged in those activities while in the library. Those activities most highly rated included "doing assignments (6.6), computer/lab use (6.3), library technology use (6.0), electronic resources use (5.8), and group study (5.6)."[19]

Duke University Libraries conducted a study in 2019 to assess the experience of Black students in campus libraries. Students commented broadly on their experience of being Black at a PWI, which included stories of students being profiled by campus security, being mistaken for staff members by white students, and microaggressions at the hands of some faculty members. Students did express issues with the library as well, including the lack of visual representations of Black life and culture in library displays and artwork. One undergraduate student, however, when discussing the library and campus life, said, "The library is the least of our problems, if I'm being honest. Like, the *least*."[20]

The two aforementioned studied, if taken together, suggest the library is one of the most popular campus locations for many students, and that when compared to their white peers at PWIs, Black students more actively engage in a variety of activities when in the library. A further inference is that, for Black students at PWIs, the library might be a location somewhat less fraught than other spaces. If Black students at PWIs view the library as a place they are less likely to encounter prejudice, the library may lend itself to being an informal gathering place, adding another layer to its importance as campus physical space. In this case, the library becomes not only a place for students to study, to make use of reliable internet access, or to find and use course materials, but also a semi-refuge from other, more potentially hostile campus spaces.

HBCUs are yet another consideration. Students at HBCUs also view the campus library as a place to gather, study collaboratively, and socialize. While campus libraries or multi-cultural spaces—like Duke University's Mary Lou Williams Center for Black Culture—may serve as havens for Black students at PWIs, entire campuses at HBCUs can serve this same purpose. Indeed, many Black students weigh issues of race, identity, and a sense of belonging in their college choice,[21] and for those students who choose to attend an HBCU, the idea of matriculating at an institution populated mostly by other Black students is a key factor.[22] Given that many students attend HBCUs to explore and develop their identity,[23] the sudden loss of regular in-person interaction with other Black students and faculty members during the height of the pandemic must have been particularly detrimental in several ways.

When the Pandemic's Over

Queries asking for a comparison in library usage from the fall of 2019 to the fall of 2021 were e-mailed to library staff members at ninety HBCUs in the fall of 2021. Of the eighteen responses received, twelve libraries indicated that the number of students in their library, as well as the number of reference inquiries and study room bookings—in libraries where study rooms are available—continued to be down in the fall 2021 term, despite having reopened. Four libraries, on the other hand, including AUC Woodruff Library, showed an increase in at least one of these measures.

Librarians whose institutions have seen an increase in study rooms bookings believe this stems from a combination of factors. These include fewer spaces from before the pandemic in which to gather as groups on campus, fewer off-campus spaces where students can meet and remain for multiple hours at a time, the ability to remove masks while in library study rooms, and specifically in the case of AUC Woodruff Library, the ability to congregate with students from other AUC campuses. In order to limit potential spread of COVID-19, since the beginning of the pandemic through at least December 2021, AUC students were not allowed on each other's campuses, leaving the library as the only indoor campus space in which to engage with students attending another AUC institution.

HBCU library respondents were also asked to reflect on what library trends—if any—they anticipate once the pandemic ends. Several articles have addressed this question for academic libraries broadly, though the trend forecasting doesn't necessarily differ from HBCUs to PWIs. Nearly all HBCU respondents noted they expect e-book purchases to continue at higher rates than pre-pandemic e-book ordering, as has also been postulated in a recent study conducted across three academic institutions.[24] Other projected trends included the use of fewer course reserves, the purchase of fewer print books—which is not necessarily as a result of buying more e-books, although budgetary constraints would likely make that so—increased collaboration with other campus departments to broaden outreach, a shift to longer opening hours, and increased digitization initiatives. Other noted potential impacts less focused on library projects but still impacting libraries are those of greater numbers of students opting to live off campus and reconfigurations of library staffing models as some retirements have been hastened by the pandemic.[25]

One respondent commented they believe that while virtual instruction is not a substitute for in-person instruction, the utilization of technology in library instruction would continue after the pandemic. The literature has also suggested that library users—particularly students—will want not only in-person services to resume, but also for virtual services to continue after the pandemic.[26] The same article suggests some users might want libraries to simultaneously offer programs and workshops both in person and virtually. This could broaden the reach of library events, enabling multiple audiences to attend without having to commute: any students uncomfortable with in-person attendance; students who are local, but not on campus; distance students, and so on.

In her article on a 2020 student library survey conducted by the University of Illinois Chicago, Jung Mi Scoulas recommends reviewing chat transcripts to leverage virtual services to the library's advantage.[27] These transcripts can highlight areas of library access or resource seeking where students encounter problems as well as areas of weakness librarians may have in virtual reference. Once these areas are known, the library can proactively create workshops, guides, or tools to remedy these issues.

Assuming virtual services continue, it will be crucial to consider how best to increase awareness of resources and services and to reach out to students who continue to access the library only virtually. This is especially true given the fact that lack of high-speed internet access often disproportionately impacts minority communities.[28] Though primarily beyond the control of academic libraries and librarians, this issue may create unintended consequences, including that of connectedness with the university and library. The University of Illinois Chicago survey, which assessed students' feelings on belonging and inclusion in the library, found that students who used both the physical and online libraries were the group most likely to feel a sense of belonging. Students who used only the physical library felt a greater sense of inclusion and belonging than students who used only the virtual library.[29]

This is important because it suggests that, while a university's physical and virtual libraries may in tandem offer the ideal research experience and environment for students, the virtual library by itself lags behind the physical in terms of creating stronger community and a sense of fitting in, or belonging. HBCU students unable to access the physical library because of a pandemic closure or other reasons may also have less reliable access to high-speed internet,[30] which would in turn leave them less able to interact with virtual library resources. Besides being likelier to have poorer internet or less reliable access to high-speed internet, lower-income students and families are likelier to rely on smartphones for internet access. This could mean a household has internet access but no laptop or desktop computer from which to access it, or that the household lacks internet access and members use phone plan data to access the internet.[31] While students are proficient at using smartphones and might even prefer them for certain activities, it is difficult to imagine smartphones being ideal for academic-level research and paper writing.

The same University of Illinois Chicago survey on students' sense of belonging noted unsurprisingly, that students who did not interact with either library were the group most likely to not feel a sense of inclusion. Given the increased importance of community at HBCUs, a situation where students cannot access the physical library and also have intermittent or erratic access to the virtual library is untenable for fostering a sense of belonging and for facilitating positive student learning outcomes.

Both a lack of belonging and poor grades are factors known to contribute to distress among college students, who are more susceptible to mental health problems than the general population.[32] Minorities are also a higher risk population. This indicates that Black college students have multiple risk factors associated with poor mental health. Some research, however, has shown that Black students attending HBCUs are less likely to experience as high a level of mental health distress as Black students attending PWIs.[33] This again highlights the importance for HBCU libraries of maintaining connection with students, of ensuring virtual outreach is dependable, and ensuring that online resources are optimal. One way of ensuring contact, suggested by Gerardo E. de los Santos and Wynn Rosser in their article about COVID-19 and the digital divide, is to assign each student a campus faculty or staff member who is digitally connected to them.[34] Just as students have an academic advisor, they could be given an outreach advisor, whose job it is to communicate regularly with a student if an extended campus closure occurs, if the student takes a leave of absence, or one semester enrolls in only online courses. This could also help to maintain some of the personal connection—albeit, not in person—between HBCU students and potential campus role models.

The concept of "library as place" at HBCUs is crucial for the reasons outlined above, including access to high-speed internet and devices, positive academic and social experiences with peers, opportunities to hone information-seeking behaviors with library staff, and the ability to regularly be in spaces with exhibits, displays, and artwork representative of the Black community.

There are several areas in which libraries can try to best position themselves in the post-COVID environment. One involves reviewing pre-COVID policies on building hours, room reservations (including the spaces available for booking), and other aspects of the physical space. For institutions like the AUC Woodruff Library—which saw an increase in study room bookings during the fall 2021 semester over pre-COVID bookings—there may be a need to reevaluate whether the building has enough available study rooms. Revamping preexisting policies related to the library's physical space could foster a more welcoming environment for students while taking into account ways that use of physical space has changed since the pandemic.

Libraries may also want to consider those policies adopted during COVID that can be kept or adapted as buildings fully reopen. Services like parking lot pickup, grab-and-go stations, enhanced virtual services, extended hours for virtual services, and remote work for staff are all things that could be continued or integrated to broaden the library's reach and to create avenues of greater convenience for students, faculty, and staff.

Finally, there are the more amorphous issues of how to make the library feel welcoming and ensure that it contributes positively to a students' sense of belonging, as well as how to help students facilitate reliable, high-speed internet and devices appropriate to the pursuit of their studies. Some low-tech ideas might include free drink and snack distribution by library staff to students during orientation week, midterms, and finals. Another might be library displays related to campus history or student life. Higher tech options could include welcome messages and information about library events or programs displayed on a large LCD display screen or other visual technology.

Libraries might investigate the purchase of some devices like tablets or Wi-Fi hot spots that could be circulated. Grant programs might be available to help fund the purchase of tablets or laptops for incoming students. Beyond the purview of just the library, some initiatives would need support from campus administrations. Finally, libraries may choose to adopt new initiatives like that of assigning outreach advisors to students as a method of facilitating better communication with students.

As students return to campus libraries, clad in school apparel, side-by-side with new friends, they will ask how to reserve study rooms, and gather in them with dry-erase markers, scribbling mathematical formulas or foreign language vocabulary on whiteboards. They will ask for help finding a title in the stacks and smile in wonderment when told they can check out twenty items at a time. They will inquire how to print an article found in a research database that exactly addresses the question of their senior thesis proposal. In short, students will still want to do all the things in the library they did before the pandemic, and likely more. The job of libraries and librarians will be to proactively and with intentionality address student needs with flexibility, creativity, and empathy. This is because, whatever student needs are and however they change with time and technologies, students always want to be seen and heard, whether across the reference desk or via computer monitor.

Notes

1. Gerardo E. de los Santos and Wynn Rosser, "COVID-19 Shines a Spotlight on the Digital Divide," *Change: The Magazine of Higher Learning* 53, no. 1 (2021): 22–25, https://doi.org/10.1080/00091383.2021.1850117.
2. Michael Levine-Clark, "Access to Everything: Building the Future Academic Library Collection," *portal: Libraries and the Academy* 14, no. 3 (July 2014): 425–37, https://doi.org/10.1353/pla.2014.0015.
3. Atlanta University Center Consortium, "History," accessed December 6, 2021, https://aucenter.edu/history.
4. Robert W. Woodruff Library, "About Our Library," Atlanta University Center, accessed December 6, 2021, https://www.auctr.edu/about/overview/about-our-library.
5. Rachel Applegate, "The Library Is for Studying: Student Preferences for Study Space," *Journal of Academic Librarianship* 35, no. 4 (July 2009): 341–46, https://doi.org/10.1016/j.acalib.2009.04.004; Martin Garnar and Joel Tonyan, "Library as Place: Understanding Contradicting User Expectations," *Journal of Academic Librarianship* 47, no. 5 (September 2021): article 102391, https://doi.org/10.1016/j.acalib.2021.102391; Jong-Ae Kim, "User Perception and Use of the Academic Library: A Correlation Analysis," *Journal of Academic Librarianship* 43, no. 3 (May 2017): 209–15, https://doi.org/10.1016/j.acalib.2017.03.002; Robbin McGinins and Larry Sean Kinder, "The Library as a Liminal Space: Finding a Seat of One's Own," *Journal of Academic Librarianship* 47, no. 1 (January 2021): article 102263, https://doi.org/10.1016/j.acalib.2020.102263; Susan Montgomery and Jonathan Miller, "The Third Place: The Library as Collaborative and Community Space in a Time of Fiscal Restraint," *College and Undergraduate Libraries* 18, no. 2–3 (2011): 228–38, https://doi.org/10.1080/10691316.2011.577683; Harold B. Shill and Shawn Tonner, "Does the Building Still Matter? Usage Patterns in New, Expanded, and Renovated Libraries, 1995–2002," *College and Research Libraries* 65, no. 2 (2004): 123–50, https://

doi.org/10.5860/crl.65.2.123; Wayne A. Wiegand, "Library as Place," *North Carolina Libraries* 63, no. 3 (Fall/Winter 2005): 76–81, https://doi.org/10.3776/ncl.v63i3.70.

6. Pamela R. Bennett and Yu Xie, "Revisiting Racial Differences in College Attendance: The Role of Historically Black Colleges and Universities," *American Sociological Review* 68, no. 4 (August 2003): 567–80, https://www.jstor.org/stable/1519739.

7. Debbie Van Camp et al., "Choosing an HBCU: An Opportunity to Pursue Racial Self-Development," *Journal of Negro Education* 78, no. 4 (Fall 2009): 457–68, https://www.jstor.org/stable/25676099.

8. Multiple e-mail messages to author, October 25–November 11, 2021.

9 Walter M. Fontane, "Assessing Library Services during a Renovation," *Journal of Access Services* 13, no. 4 (2016): 223–36, https://doi.org/10.1080/15367967.2016.1250643.

10. Kim, "User Perception," 210.

11. Kim, "User Perception," 213.

12. Montgomery and Miller, "Third Place."

13. Emily Petsko, "Reports of Mark Twain's Quote about His Own Death Are Greatly Exaggerated," Mental Floss, November 1, 2018, https://www.mentalfloss.com/article/562400/reports-mark-twains-quote-about-mark-twains-death-are-greatly-exaggerated.

14. John J. Regazzi, "U.S. Academic Library Spending, Staffing and Utilization during the Great Recession 2008–2010," *Journal of Academic Librarianship* 39, no. 3 (May 2013): 217–22, https://doi.org/10.1016/j.acalib.2012.12.002.

15. Montgomery and Miller, "Third Place."

16. Kim, "User Perception."

17. Shill and Tonner, "Does the Building Still Matter?"

18. Brenton Stewart, Boryung Ju, and Kaetrena Davis Kendrick, "Racial Climate and Inclusiveness in Academic Libraries: Perceptions of Welcomeness among Black College Students," *Library Quarterly* 89, no. 1 (January 2019): 16–33, https://doi.org/10.1086/700661.

19. EunYoung Yoo-Lee, Tae Heon Lee, and LaTesha Velez, "Planning Library Spaces and Services for Millennials: An Evidence-Based Approach," *Library Management* 34, no. 6/7 (2013): 498-511, https://doi.org/10.1108/LM-08-2012-0049.

20. Joyce Chapman et al., *Understanding the Experiences and Needs of Black Students at Duke* (Durham, NC: Duke University Libraries, April 2020), 1-39, https://hdl.handle.net/10161/20753.

21. Debbie Van Camp, Jamie Barden, and Lloyd R. Sloan, "Predictors of Black Students' Race-Related Reasons for Choosing an HBCU and Intentions to Engage in Racial Identity–Relevant Behaviors," *Journal of Black Psychology* 36, no. 2 (2010): 226–50, https://doi.org/10.1177/0095798409344082.

22. Van Camp et al., "Choosing an HBCU."

23. C. Adrainne Thomas and Trina L. Spencer, "Navigating the Effects of Covid-19 at a Southeastern American HBCU," *Virginia Social Science Journal* 53 (2020): 94–101.

24. Ruth Sara Connell, Lisa C. Wallis, and David Comeaux, "The Impact of COVID-19 on the Use of Academic Library Resources," *Information Technology and Libraries* 40, no. 2 (June 2021): 1–20, https://doi.org/10.6017/ital.v40i2.12629.

25. Multiple e-mail messages to author, October 25–November 11, 2021.

26. Christopher Cox and Elliot Felix, "Visions of Success: Academic Libraries in a Post COVID-19 World," *Library Journal*, December 16, 2020, https://www.libraryjournal.com/?detailStory=Visions-of-Success-Academic-Libraries-in-Post-COVID-19-World.

27. Jung Mi Scoulas, "College Students' Perceptions on Sense of Belonging and Inclusion at the Academic Library during COVID-19," *Journal of Academic Librarianship* 47, no. 6 (December 2021): article 102460, https://doi.org/10.1016/j.acalib.2021.102460.

28. Alanna Gillis and Laura M. Krull, "COVID-19 Remote Learning Transitions in Spring 2020: Class Structures, Student Perceptions, and Inequality in College Courses," *Teaching Sociology* 48, no. 4 (2020): 283–99, https://doi.org/10.1177/0092055X20954263.

29. Scoulas, "College Students' Perceptions."

30. Dania V. Francis and Christian E. Weller, "Economic Inequality, the Digital Divide, and Remote Learning during COVID-19," *Review of Black Political Economy* 49, no. 1 (2022): 41–60, https://doi.org/10.1177/00346446211017797; James E. Wright II and Cullen C. Merritt, "Social Equity and COVID-19: The Case of African Americans," *Public Administration Review* 80, no. 5 (September/October 2020): 820–26, https://doi.org/10.1111/puar.13251.

31. Nicole A. Buzzetto-Hollywood et al., "Addressing Information Literacy and the Digital Divide in Higher Education," *Interdisciplinary Journal of e-Skills and Lifelong Learning* 14 (2018): 77–93, https://doi.org/10.28945/4029.

32. Sharron Xuanren Wang and Jarid Goodman, "Mental Health of HBCU Students during the COVID-19 Pandemic," preprint medRxiv, 2020, https://doi.org/10.1101/2021.07.22.21260878.

33. Dawnsha R. Mushoga and Angela K. Henneberger, "Protective Factors Associated with Positive Mental Health in Traditional and Nontraditional Black Students," *American Journal of Orthopsychiatry* 90, no. 1 (2020): 147–60, https://doi.org/10.1037/ort0000409.

34. de los Santos and Rosser, "COVID-19 Shines a Spotlight."

Bibliography

Applegate, Rachel. "The Library Is for Studying: Student Preferences for Study Space." *Journal of Academic Librarianship* 35, no. 4 (July 2009): 341–46. https://doi.org/10.1016/j.acalib.2009.04.004.

Atlanta University Center Consortium. "History." Accessed December 6, 2021. https://aucenter.edu/history.

Bennett, Pamela R., and Yu Xie. "Revisiting Racial Differences in College Attendance: The Role of Historically Black Colleges and Universities." *American Sociological Review* 68, no. 4 (August 2003): 567–80. https://www.jstor.org/stable/1519739.

Buzzetto-Hollywood, Nicole A., Hwei C. Wang, Magdi Elobeid, and Muna E. Elobeid, "Addressing Information Literacy and the Digital Divide in Higher Education." *Interdisciplinary Journal of e-Skills and Lifelong Learning* 14 (2018): 77–93. https://doi.org/10.28945/4029.

Chapman, Joyce, Emily Daly, Anastasia Forte, Ira King, Brenda W. Yang, and Pamela Zabala. *Understanding the Experiences and Needs of Black Students at Duke.* Durham, NC: Duke University Libraries, April 2020. https://hdl.handle.net/10161/20753.

Connell, Ruth Sara, Lisa C. Wallis, and David Comeaux. "The Impact of COVID-19 on the Use of Academic Library Resources." *Information Technology and Libraries* 40, no. 2 (June 2021): 1–20. https://doi.org/10.6017/ital.v40i2.12629.

Cox, Christopher, and Elliot Felix. "Visions of Success: Academic Libraries in a Post COVID-19 World." *Library Journal*, December 16, 2020. https://www.libraryjournal.com/?detailStory=Visions-of-Success-Academic-Libraries-in-Post-COVID-19-World.

de los Santos, Gerardo E., and Wynn Rosser. "COVID-19 Shines a Spotlight on the Digital Divide." *Change: The Magazine of Higher Learning* 53, no. 1 (2021): 22–25, https://doi.org/10.1080/00091383.2021.1850117.

Fontane, Walter M. "Assessing Library Services during a Renovation." *Journal of Access Services* 13, no. 4 (2016): 223–36. https://doi.org/10.1080/15367967.2016.1250643.

Francis, Dania V., and Christian E. Weller. "Economic Inequality, the Digital Divide, and Remote Learning during COVID-19." *Review of Black Political Economy* 49, no. 1 (2022): 41–60. https://doi.org/10.1177/00346446211017797.

Garnar, Martin, and Joel Tonyan. "Library as Place: Understanding Contradicting User Expectations." *Journal of Academic Librarianship* 47, no. 5 (September 2021): article 102391. https://doi.org/10.1016/j.acalib.2021.102391.

Gillis, Alanna, and Laura M. Krull. "COVID-19 Remote Learning Transitions in Spring 2020: Class Structures, Student Perceptions, and Inequality in College Courses." *Teaching Sociology* 48, no. 4 (2020): 283–99. https://doi.org/10.1177/0092055X20954263.

Kim, Jong-Ae. "User Perception and Use of the Academic Library: A Correlation Analysis." *Journal of Academic Librarianship* 43, no. 3 (May 2017): 209–15. https://doi.org/10.1016/j.acalib.2017.03.002.

Levine-Clark, Michael. "Access to Everything: Building the Future Academic Library Collection." *portal: Libraries and the Academy* 14, no. 3 (July 2014): 425–37, https://doi.org/10.1353/pla.2014.0015.

McGinins, Robbin, and Larry Sean Kinder. "The Library as a Liminal Space: Finding a Seat of One's Own." *Journal of Academic Librarianship* 47, no. 1 (January 2021): article 102263. https://doi.org/10.1016/j.acalib.2020.102263.

Montgomery, Susan, and Jonathan Miller. "The Third Place: The Library as Collaborative and Community Space in a Time of Fiscal Restraint." *College and Undergraduate Libraries* 18, no. 2–3 (2011): 228–38. https://doi.org/10.1080/10691316.2011.577683.

Mushoga, Dawnsha R., and Angela K. Henneberger. "Protective Factors Associated with Positive Mental Health in Traditional and Nontraditional Black Students." *American Journal of Orthopsychiatry* 90, no. 1 (2020): 147–60. https://doi.org/10.1037/ort0000409.

Petsko, Emily. "Reports of Mark Twain's Quote about His Own Death Are Greatly Exaggerated." Mental Floss, November 1, 2018. https://www.mentalfloss.com/article/562400/reports-mark-twains-quote-about-mark-twains-death-are-greatly-exaggerated.

Regazzi, John J. "U.S. Academic Library Spending, Staffing and Utilization during the Great Recession 2008–2010." *Journal of Academic Librarianship* 39, no. 3 (May 2013): 217–22. https://doi.org/10.1016/j.acalib.2012.12.002.

Robert W. Woodruff Library. "About Our Library." Atlanta University Center. Accessed December 6, 2021. https://www.auctr.edu/about/overview/about-our-library.

Scoulas, Jung Mi. "College Students' Perceptions on Sense of Belonging and Inclusion at the Academic Library during COVID-19." *Journal of Academic Librarianship* 47, no. 6 (December 2021): article 102460. https://doi.org/10.1016/j.acalib.2021.102460.

Shill, Harold B., and Shawn Tonner. "Does the Building Still Matter? Usage Patterns in New, Expanded, and Renovated Libraries, 1995–2002." *College and Research Libraries* 65, no. 2 (2004): 123–50. https://doi.org/10.5860/crl.65.2.123.

Stewart, Brenton, Boryung Ju, and Kaetrena Davis Kendrick. "Racial Climate and Inclusiveness in Academic Libraries: Perceptions of Welcomeness among Black College Students." *Library Quarterly* 89, no. 1 (January 2019): 16–33. https://doi.org/10.1086/700661.

Thomas, C. Adrainne, and Trina L. Spencer. "Navigating the Effects of Covid-19 at a Southeastern American HBCU." *Virginia Social Science Journal* 53 (2020): 94–101.

Van Camp, Debbie, Jamie Barden, and Lloyd R. Sloan. "Predictors of Black Students' Race-Related Reasons for Choosing an HBCU and Intentions to Engage in Racial Identity–Relevant Behaviors." *Journal of Black Psychology* 36, no. 2 (2010): 226–50. https://doi.org/10.1177/0095798409344082.

Van Camp, Debbie, Jamie Barden, Lloyd Ren Sloan, and Reneé P. Clarke. "Choosing an HBCU: An Opportunity to Pursue Racial Self-Development." *Journal of Negro Education* 78, no. 4 (Fall 2009): 457–68. https://www.jstor.org/stable/25676099.

Wang, Sharron Xuanren, and Jarid Goodman. "Mental Health of HBCU Students during the COVID-19 Pandemic." Preprint, medRxiv, 2020. https://doi.org/10.1101/2021.07.22.21260878.

Wiegand, Wayne A. "Library as Place." *North Carolina Libraries* 63, no. 3 (Fall/Winter 2005): 76–81. https://doi.org/10.3776/ncl.v63i3.70.

Wright, James E., II, and Cullen C. Merritt. "Social Equity and COVID-19: The Case of African Americans." *Public Administration Review* 80, no. 5 (September/October 2020): 820–26, https://doi.org/10.1111/puar.13251.

Yoo-Lee, Eun Young, Tae Heon Lee, and LaTesha Velez. "Planning Library Spaces and Services for Millennials: An Evidence-Based Approach." *Library Management* 34, no. 6/7 (2013): 498–511. https://doi.org/10.1108/LM-08-2012-0049.

CHAPTER 3

Academic Library Budgets in Perpetual Crisis

Managing Vocational Grief from the Great Recession to the COVID-19 Pandemic and Beyond

Stephen Patton and Kristina Keogh

> *How can library leaders best prepare themselves, their staff, and their communities in order to effectively and sustainably shepherd library budgets for the next crisis to come?*

Introduction

A reality that all academic library managers face is having to cope with budget reductions. Although *uncertainty and uneasiness* arise whenever budget reductions occur, they will nonetheless eventually happen. At some point in a library manager's career, that person encounters a budget reduction from one fiscal year to the next, or worse, an approved allocation is reduced (rescinded) after the fiscal year has begun.[1] Budget reductions are such an expected phenomenon in libraries that Robert Dugan and Peter Hernon preface a chapter of advice and best practices for budget reduction strategies, from their 2017 text on academic library financial management, with a statement summarizing the inevitability of such an event, as well as the anxiety that follows it. In fact, the negative emotions associated with these occurrences have permeated library operations for several decades.

When the world shut down in spring 2020 due to the emerging COVID-19 pandemic, academic library administrators (and everyone else) were faced with numerous challenges, and a wide variety of emotional responses, as they endeavored to maintain services and access to resources while also prioritizing staff and patron safety during a time of uncertainty. Although many of the issues academic libraries have confronted during this period were nearly unprecedented, including the sudden transition of students, faculty, and library employees to online and very limited operations continuing on most college and university campuses, declining finances during times of economic crises are not new to college and university libraries.

Following the Great Recession of 2008, most libraries were forced to cut collections, operations, and personnel expenditures, while also often facing pressure to maintain services at the same levels, despite freezes, cuts, and consolidations of budgets, as well as reductions in overall personnel.[2] In many cases, higher education in general and academic library budgets in particular have still not recovered completely from that event.[3] Likewise, and even as institutions begin to open up and return to at least partial pre-pandemic operations, many academic library deans and directors expected the financial effects of the COVID-19 crisis to be felt for years to come.[4] Even now, budgetary constraints driven by the pandemic's rapid enrollment declines of 3.5 percent in 2020–2021 make clear that for many academic libraries the associated budget reductions will continue to have an impact.[5]

What can academic library administrators and budget managers learn from these seemingly back-to-back crises? How can library leaders best prepare themselves, their staff, and their communities in order to effectively and sustainably shepherd library budgets for the next crisis to come? While most library leaders would certainly acknowledge a need to reduce expenditures from time to time, academic library administrators may also consider diminishing or flat budgets in the face of inflationary pressures and declining enrollments as a new operational and emotional paradigm affecting all aspects of library personnel and operations.[6]

The present analysis seeks to first make a temporal determination of budget impacts through a literature review and summary of previously published data with a particular focus on the period from the Great Recession forward. The authors will then investigate recent academic library budget practices and operational responses at the intersection of crisis management, change management, and what we will call *vocational grief*. To that end, the remainder of the chapter will turn to an examination of shared academic library responses to budget reductions through the lens of the five stages of grief, as codified by Elisabeth Kübler-Ross.[7] The authors will discuss how fundamental changes to the way an organization operates can be identified, experienced, and managed as vocational grief, and specifically how incessant budget declines within academic libraries have caused grief within our operations and profession as a whole.[8]

Vocational grief will further be posited as a conceptual model and framework that will allow library leaders to work toward organizational communication strategies and come to acceptance under a forecast "new normal" for library budget austerity as academic libraries move to a future beyond the COVID-19 pandemic with anticipation that academic library finances will continue to contract or remain stagnant for years to come. The authors argue that by moving their organizations to a frame of acceptance, academic library leaders may work together with stakeholders to clarify and preserve their library's mission, purpose, and human capital for the next crisis to come.

Literature Review: Academic Library Budgets in Crisis

How has academic library funding changed or not changed over the last few decades? Can one establish that academic library budgets have indeed fallen into a state of crisis, or a period of decisive change from the past?[9] There is ample evidence in the professional literature that academic libraries, as a group, have received shrinking percentages of overall university budgets particularly in comparison with the post–World War II era, as well as their record highs in the 1980s and 1990s.[10] Following the global economic downturn in 2007–2008, now commonly known as the Great Recession, academic libraries increasingly faced pressure to make cuts across different expenditure types, while also simultaneously facing pressures of increasing costs for materials and services.[11]

A trio of studies by John J. Regazzi that analyzed longitudinal data collected from a period prior to and up through the Great Recession also establish shifts in spending beginning in that period. As Regazzi reports, the slowdown in the US economy that began in 2007 brought library spending down from its "historic highs" in the decade prior.[12] From 1998 through 2008, and despite anecdotal discussions of "eroded and constrained" budgets prior to that time, academic library budgets grew almost 12 percent above inflation.[13] However, in comparison with the growth overall in higher education during that same period, in a subsequent study Regazzi found that the "share of expenditures on Academic Libraries relative to the total [spent on higher education] …declined over this time period [1998–2008] by 24%."[14] Likewise, statistics collected by the Association of Research Libraries (ARL) illustrate an undeniable downward trend in library expenditures as a share of total university expenditures well prior to, and continuing after, the Great Recession during the time period of 1982–2017.[15] As ARL institutions' overall university budgets were trending upward, these same institutions, which have a focus on research, were reducing their financial support of their libraries. In comparison, teaching institutions may be in an even more difficult position from which to argue for increased or adequate collections, operating, and personnel budgets.

Regazzi also underscores that academic libraries are not a "homogenous" group, with his analyses indicating variable impacts on small-to-medium versus large doctoral-granting institutions, with the former showing greater economic stress compared to the latter, particularly over the period from 2008 to 2010.[16] Smaller institutions, according to Regazzi's findings, were more likely to experience both staff and overall spending reductions than their larger counterparts.[17] A more recent study by Starr Hoffman and Samantha Godbey that specifically looked at staffing changes and staffing expenditure trends across all types of academic libraries from the period of 1996–2016 found that staffing expenditures (salaries and benefits) in particular have declined, when adjusted for inflation, since 2010, showing a drop following the Recession from which most academic libraries, including doctoral, master's, and baccalaureate institutions, had not recovered through the examined period in 2016.[18]

The long-term financial and human impacts of COVID-19 are not yet known, but after more than a year of operations under conditions brought about by the pandemic some overall changes and expectations of changes to library budgets and associated operations can be tracked. An Ithaka S+R survey from December 2020 found that plans by the majority of the 600 respondents encompassed modeled cuts of either 5 to 9 percent or 10 to 14 percent.[19] While actual cuts for the 2021 fiscal year fell below the most extreme expectations, cuts of some measure did happen across all expenditures in the majority of cases of the respondents, with doctoral and public institutions feeling the most impact, particularly in comparison with private baccalaureate institutions.[20] Many respondents to the Ithaka S+R survey also reported that they had been anticipating a need to make cuts even prior to the pandemic, suggesting that the financial impacts of COVID-19 may have simply accelerated conditions already in place and continued the financial impacts on academic libraries' budgets from prior years.[21]

The Ithaka S+R report also underscores the unpredictable nature of library budgets during the current crisis. "For academic libraries, 'the main theme is uncertainty,'" stated an Ithaka S+R administrator, regarding library operations and planning in the midst of the COVID-19 pandemic.[22] Uncertainty as a mode of operation naturally impacts a budget manager's ability to effectively shepherd budgets and plan for the future, which can provoke a feeling of grief in leaders and library staff alike.[23] This is particularly true in the midst of the pandemic as access takes precedence over planning and contemplations of fiscal impact are put off to another day.[24]

Vocational Grief amid Academic Library Budget Crises

While library leaders may employ a variety of practical strategies to manage budgets when reductions occur, they may also respond in a particularly human way that can manifest as grief. In this section, an examination of examples of how libraries may operate through budget crises as a spectrum of the grief process is provided.

The authors propose that grief in the organizational context, and in the library context in particular, presents its own unique challenges to those in the profession. Fobazi Ettarh argues that "vocational awe" equates the work of librarians and libraries with a sacred calling, or vocation, rather than that of a profession or discipline, which resists criticism and commands "absolute obedience to a prescribed set of rules."[25] Here, the present authors build on Ettarh's conception of vocational awe as a way of calling attention to negative behaviors and ideals around the work of libraries and propose a related term—*vocational grief*—to denote the impact of negative emotions as libraries experience changes to long-time processes, positions, and expectations amid an uncertain and shifting economic and societal status for academic libraries. Such negative emotions are experienced in particular by library employees inside the profession when their professional identities and satisfaction with their work are intrinsically tied to their vocational calling.

Such negative emotions are also closely tied to "resilience narratives," as library employees may be counseled to "do more with less" as the blame for systemic problems, such as flat or reduced budgets, is shifted to individuals rather than institutions and structures.[26] Moreover, the implicit vocational status that permeates library work can also have a negative impact on users (including students and faculty) outside the organization, as the library may be perceived to have failed those who are served by that library.[27] Vocational grief may also affect how managers are approaching necessary budget cuts and how they are communicating (or at times, not communicating) those changes to all stakeholders as to how budgets are evaluated for reductions and reallocated following austerity measures.

Elisabeth Kübler-Ross argues that a terminal patient will undergo various coping strategies as they work to understand the process of death and dying.[28] While not suggesting that academic libraries are terminal or experiencing death as a field or organization writ large, through the coping activities within the stages of grief described below, the authors argue that academic libraries are entering a new model of operating that is akin to the transition which the process of dying evokes.[29] Through this transition, academic libraries and their staffs have the opportunity to become more cognizant of ongoing changes, and therefore resist destructive tendencies and structures and instead endeavor to revitalize their operations, work, and status within their communities.

Denial, or Maximizing Efficiencies

> Denial functions as a buffer after unexpected shocking news. [It] allows the patient to collect himself and, with time, mobilize other, less radical defenses.[30]

Library budget managers may first greet the need to cut budgets, or maximize efficiencies, with the idea the budget will eventually be restored and continue to grow as necessary. One initial response to budget cuts is to tell staff, users, and even oneself that the cuts are only temporary.[31] Libraries have also become specialists in analyzing data in order to trim the fat and to get rid of, for example, journal titles with less usage, another common tactic that can be tied to the time of the Great Recession.[32]

During the COVID-19 crisis, as funds continue to be realigned to prioritize online collections, many libraries have ceased purchases of physical materials, an easy cut that does not require much thought or planning and that prioritizes both patron and staff safety.[33] As academic libraries emerge from the pandemic and perhaps look to restore their practice of print purchases, they may find that budget realignments and evolving patron needs also do not allow for that type of restoration.

The period immediately following the Great Recession also saw a similar reduction in print purchasing as budgets were consolidated. At that time, library vendors worked with libraries to consolidate subscriptions and negotiate multiyear deals. Simultaneously, as they helped libraries to develop cost-saving and advocacy strategies, these same vendors began increasing pricing at unsustainable rates.[34] Years later, many libraries may have found they had reduced their unique and high-impact practices in order to purchase (or rent) collections content from these same vendors.

Anger, or the Deepest Cut

> When the first stage of denial cannot be maintained any longer, it is replaced by feelings of anger, rage, envy, and resentment.[35]

As an organization, staff, or leader moves from denial, they may enter a phase expressed as anger. This stage may be best characterized by the so-called Washington Monument Strategy, which is named for a reaction to federal budget cuts.[36] Through this strategy, a library might undertake seemingly dispassionate decisions to cut popular collections and services in a way that may hurt patrons while also specifically targeting higher education administrators and decision makers. In addition to overall collections budget reductions, library leaders may also respond to cutbacks by reducing building hours or limiting the availability of services such as interlibrary loan. This tactic may be categorized as a lashing out so that others feel the library's pain in order to force the restoration of slashed budgets. Here, library leaders may also hope to incite their users to argue for the reinstatement of financial support from higher education administrators. In the midst of the anger stage, there also may be a difference between making strategic changes that are necessary in the face of budget reductions and making those that are purely retaliatory. Change needs to come from a strategic state of mind rather than from a position of nonacceptance and resentment. In the anger stage, library managers may make changes, but are not necessarily providing solutions.[37] As argued further below, strategic changes may be possible only after an organization has moved through the stages of vocational grief and come to a stage of acceptance.

Bargaining, or the Value Argument

> If we have been unable to face the sad facts in the first period and have been angry at people and God in the second phase, maybe we can succeed in entering into some sort of an agreement which may postpone the inevitable happening.[38]

In the bargaining phase, we wish to buy more time. In libraries, this may be the point when we begin to communicate and even to collaborate with users who may themselves resist inevitable cuts to budgets.[39] As more cuts are needed, libraries have also turned to attempts to break up Big Deal journal packages.[40] The bargaining phase is also where libraries may turn to marketing and value statements to external audiences as a response to austerity measures. These efforts acknowledge that libraries have learned they need to continuously strive to argue for their status as an irreplaceable resource that is worthy of continuing financial support.[41] One might acknowledge here that academic library managers are in a constant state of having to argue for their relevance. Librarians are straddling a line encompassing the vocational awe that Ettarh argues is inherent in the profession and wherein they endeavor to effectively deliver services while also simultaneously arguing for the library's value to their institutions.

If academic library managers are working through the stages of grief to bring their libraries to acceptance, one part of that may be the realization that institutional funds will continue to be inadequate. At this point, leaders will begin looking for alternative sources of funding, such as grants, donations, and other means of generating revenue. Such well-established methods illustrate that libraries do recognize the reality of local budgetary pressures and can also acknowledge that state and institutional funding sources are likewise diminished.[42] Nevertheless, and despite successes in fundraising across various types of libraries, outside donor funds do not necessarily address systemic inadequacies in academic library funding and support.[43] In some cases, fundraising as a bargaining tactic may only temporarily allay reductions and may prove to higher education administrators that libraries do not need adequate institutional support.[44] Therefore, in this scenario, institutional funding may not be restored because libraries have found funding from other inconsistent or temporary sources.

Depression, or the Good Old Days

> When the terminally ill patient can no longer deny his illness, when he is forced to undergo more surgery or hospitalization, when he begins to have more symptoms or becomes weaker and thinner, he cannot smile it off anymore. His numbness or stoicism, his anger and rage will soon be replaced with a sense of great loss.[45]

A relationship between the stage of depression and mourning over better days or a nostalgia for past times and processes may be recognizable to many library leaders, particularly those who manage staff with long institutional memories and genuine recollections of the good old days. While a loss is recognized during this phase, it may also present an opportunity to think about change.

A lack of a clear direction going forward, and a manager feeling that depression, may lead to a call to an outside consultant or coach. Consultants may allow a library to escape negative thinking; yet it is important to realize that they may push the organization toward acceptance before it is ready.[46] If a library leader tries to force staff and other stakeholders through these stages, they run the risk of falling back into a state of nonacceptance. In these cases, an organization may retreat further into depression and perhaps even return to denial.[47] It might be proposed that no stages of grief can be avoided. For an organization, the stages should be embraced so all stakeholders can progress to acceptance, strive to self-care, and look forward to a new future for academic libraries.

Acceptance, Library Leaders as Grief Counselors, and Next Steps

> Acceptance should not be mistaken for a happy stage. It is almost void of feelings. It is as if the pain had gone, the struggle is over....[48]

Academic libraries as a group have grappled with near relentless budget reductions or flat budgets in the face of inflationary pressures over more than a decade, and through multiple global catastrophes. While it is difficult to argue that library administrators and budget managers—who track their spending so diligently—could possibly be in denial about the health, or lack thereof, of library budgets, the authors' review of the data and sample responses to budget compressions suggests otherwise. Furthermore, it is necessary for the library profession to recognize—and accept—such disruptions to operations and move forward with a renewed sense of hope within changing environments.[49] As academic libraries move into a post-COVID world and beyond the current disaster where many have experienced actual personal loss due to layoffs, illness, and death, many will come to accept that the day-to-day operations and what libraries can and cannot provide to their stakeholders will not emerge unscathed. Once academic libraries as a profession move to that stage of acceptance, then they will be in a better place to strategically realign the mission and goals of the academic library.

A recognition of vocational grief can allow libraries, the people who work in them, and those who use their services to move through necessary stages within a grieving process in order to accept the reality of fundamental changes in (at the very least) operations. A review of the literature provides evidence of the past, present, and likely future state of collective academic library budgets. The overarching data for academic libraries is also offered as a model for an internal historical review of one's own library finances, which can be part of the process of bringing a library and the community it serves to acceptance. Open communication, and particularly transparency, may also allow all involved to take part in collective mourning practices, during which individuals can share their feelings and ideas and communally let go of unnecessary and unsustainable tasks, processes, and workloads.[50] While no library is exactly like the others, all libraries will be faced with determining their future. An honest evaluation of current and possible future budgetary trends, along with an evaluation of services and resources at the core of each library's mission will be essential. Ongoing, iterative, and positive-change management practices, such as appreciative inquiry, which examine whole systems and provide a constructive approach to managing organizational change, may be proposed as one method to consider in the midst of ongoing fundamental and structural changes to the work and missions of academic libraries.[51]

While so-called once-in-a-generation events such as recessions and a pandemic seem compartmentalized, they make up a tapestry of impacts that result in the changing of our personal and professional processes and identities. The ongoing COVID-19 pandemic is certainly one part of this, as was the Great Recession before it; next, we can look toward the declining high school graduation rates and college-age population decline that is expected to impact higher education enrollments before the end of the decade. For many academic library administrators and budget managers, these supposedly singular events will continue to drive change for all libraries. Library leaders must move with their staff and communities through the stages of vocational grief and come together to acceptance, forging a hopeful path forward.

Notes

1. Robert E. Dugan and Peter Hernon, "A Smorgasbord: Budget Reduction Strategies, Fraud, and Best Practices," in *Financial Management in Academic Libraries: Data-Driven Planning and Budgeting* (Chicago: Association of College and Research Libraries, 2017), 148.
2. Dugan and Hernon, "Smorgasbord," 148.
3. Charles B. Lowry, "ARL Library Budgets after the Great Recession, 2011–2013," in *Research Library Issues: A Report from ARL, CNI, and SPARC*, no. 282 (2013): 9, https://doi.org/10.29242/rli.282.2. See also Audrey Williams June, "State Funding for Higher Ed Increased in 2020 for the 8th Straight Year. It Won't Make Up for Past Cuts," *Chronicle of Higher Education*, May 28, 2021, https://www.chronicle.com/article/state-funding-for-higher-ed-increased-in-2020-for-the-8th-straight-year-it-wont-make-up-for-past-cuts.
4. Jennifer K. Frederick and Christine Wolff-Eisenberg, *Academic Library Strategy and Budgeting during the COVID-19 Pandemic* (New York: Ithaka S+R, December 9, 2020), https://doi.org/10.18665/sr.314507.
5. See "Spring 2021: Current Term Enrollment Estimates," National Student Clearinghouse Research Center, June 10, 2021, https://nscresearchcenter.org/current-term-enrollment-estimates/ (page content changed).
6. Mark S. LeClair, "For College Finances, There's No 'Return to Normal,'" *Chronicle of Higher Education*, June 15, 2021, https://www.chronicle.com/article/for-college-finances-theres-no-return-to-normal.
7. Elisabeth Kübler-Ross, *On Death and Dying* (New York: Routledge, 1969; repr. New York: Scribner Classics, 1997).
8. Grief, in general, has been well explored in organizational contexts, though less so in the professional library context. For a previous essay particularly relevant to the present discussion, that of facing and accepting the reality of changes within the cultural heritage profession, see Michael Fox, "The Psychology of Letting Go," *RBM: A Journal of Rare Books, Manuscripts, and Cultural Heritage* 12, no. 2 (2011): 104–9, https://doi.org/10.5860/rbm.12.2.357. For a discussion of grief in libraries following a catastrophic event, such as a mass shooting, and the "grief archives" that are collected, see Ashley R. Maynor, "Libraries and Librarians in the Aftermath: Our Stories and Ourselves," *Collaborative Librarianship* 11, no. 1 (2019): article 10, https://digitalcommons.du.edu/collaborativelibrarianship/vol11/iss1/10. Finally, see an analysis of loss in the instance of library colleague retirements in Elena Romaniuk, "Losing Staff: The Seven Stages of Loss and Recovery," *Serials Librarian* 66 (2014): 241–47.
9. We are employing here the definition of *crisis* that encompasses a "vitally important stage in the progress of anything; a turning-point; a state of affairs in which a decisive change for better or worse is imminent…." See *Oxford English Dictionary*, s.v. "Crisis, n.," June 2021, Oxford University Press, https://www.oed.com/.
10. Phil Davis, "Libraries Receiving a Shrinking Piece of the University Pie," *Scholarly Kitchen* (blog), February 15, 2012, https://scholarlykitchen.sspnet.org/2012/02/15/a-shrinking-piece-of-the-university-pie/.
11. Charles B. Lowry, "Year 2 of the 'Great Recession': Surviving the Present by Building the Future," *Journal of Library Administration* 51, no. 1 (2010): 44, https://doi.org/10.1080/01930826.2011.531640. See also Charles B. Lowry, "Three Years and Counting—The Economic Crisis Is Still with Us," *portal: Libraries and the Academy* 11, no. 3 (2011): 763; Charles I. Guarria and Zhonghong Wang, "The Economic Crisis and Its Effect on Libraries," *New Library World* 112, no. 5/6 (2011): 200.

30   Chapter 3

12. John J. Regazzi, "Constrained? An Analysis of U.S. Academic Library Shifts in Spending, Staffing, and Utilization, 1998–2008," *College and Research Libraries* 73, no. 5 (2012): 450, https://doi.org/10.5860/crl-260.

13. Regazzi, "Constrained?" 466.

14. John J. Regazzi, "Comparing Academic Library Spending with Public Libraries, Public K–12 Schools, Higher Education Public Institutions, and Public Hospitals between 1998–2008," *Journal of Academic Librarianship* 38, no. 4 (2012): 206 and table 2, 210.

15. "Library Expenditures as a Percent of Total University Expenditures, 1982–2017," ARL Statistics Survey Statistical Trends, Association of Research Libraries, https://www.arl.org/wp-content/uploads/2020/03/ARL-Library-Expenditures.pdf.

16. John J. Regazzi, "U.S. Academic Library Spending, Staffing and Utilization during the Great Recession 2008–2010," *Journal of Academic Librarianship* 39, no. 3 (2013): 218.

17. Regazzi, "U.S. Academic Library Spending," 220.

18. Starr Hoffman and Samantha Godbey, "US Academic Libraries' Staffing and Expenditure Trends (1996–2016)," *Library Management* 41, no. 4/5 (2020): 261.

19. Frederick and Wolff-Eisenberg, *Academic Library Strategy and Budgeting*, 15.

20. Frederick and Wolff-Eisenberg, *Academic Library Strategy and Budgeting*, 15–16.

21. Frederick and Wolff-Eisenberg, *Academic Library Strategy and Budgeting*, 19–20.

22. Roger Schonfeld (director of Ithaka S+R's Libraries, Scholarly Communication, and Museums program), quoted in Lisa Peet, "Budgeting for the New Normal: Libraries Respond to COVID-19 Funding Constraints," *Library Journal*, September 24, 2020, https://www.libraryjournal.com/?detailStory=budgeting-for-the-new-normal-libraries-respond-to-covid-19-funding-constraints.

23. "Emotions affect decision-making if leaders perceive an issue as a threat or opportunity. Grief is often triggered by a loss or impending loss." Elmar Friedrich and Rolf Wüstenhagen, "Leading Organizations through the Stages of Grief: The Development of Negative Emotions over Environmental Change," *Business and Society* 56, no. 2 (2017): 187.

24. Uncertainty may also manifest as anticipatory grief, which occurs when the future is unknown. Scott Berinato, "That Discomfort You're Feeling Is Grief," *Harvard Business Review*, March 23, 2020, https://hbr.org/2020/03/that-discomfort-youre-feeling-is-grief.

25. According to Ettarh, this status given to librarianship has led to historical, contemporary, and institutional flaws in the profession. Fobazi Ettarh, "Vocational Awe and Librarianship: The Lies We Tell Ourselves," *In the Library with the Lead Pipe*, January 10, 2018, https://www.inthelibrarywiththeleadpipe.org/2018/vocational-awe/.

26. "Resilience is repackaged trauma for organizations in a state of perpetual recovery." Jacob Berg, Angela Galvan, and Eamon Tewell, "Responding to and Reimagining Resilience in Academic Libraries," *Journal of New Librarianship* 3, no. 1 (2018): 1, https://doi.org/10.21173/newlibs/4/1.

27. Appropriately, the term *vocational grief* has been used in a religious context during the pandemic and defined as referring "to the emotions and losses people experience when significant callings in their lives become difficult, burdensome, or lost." Jessie Bazan, "Six Stories of Vocations Interrupted by the Pandemic," *U.S. Catholic*, May 26, 2021, https://uscatholic.org/articles/202105/six-stories-of-vocations-interrupted-by-pandemic/.

28. Kübler-Ross, *On Death and Dying*, 49.

29. Deone Zell argues that "viewing the process of change in a professional bureaucracy as a process of death and dying may broaden understanding of resistance to change in these unique types of organizations…." Deone Zell, "Organizational Change as a Process of Death, Dying, and Rebirth," *Journal of Applied Behavioral Science* 39, no. 1 (2003): 75, https://doi.org/10.1177/0021886303039001004.

30. Kübler-Ross, *On Death and Dying*, 52.

31. Guarria and Wang conclude their article by assuring their readers that the economy cannot contract forever despite the fact that the recession had already lasted almost twice as long as average economic retractions during the twentieth century. Guarria and Wang, "Economic Crisis and Its Effect on Libraries," 212.

32. For a recent proposed method, see Shea-Tinn Yeh, Marne Arthaud-Day, and Michelle Turvey-Welch, "Propagation of Lean Thinking in Academic Libraries," *Journal of Academic Librarianship* 47, no. 3 (2021): article 102357, https://doi.org/10.1016/j.acalib.2021.102357.

33. After so many years and such a great deal of experience with trimming the fat, libraries can almost make these cuts by rote. In the organizational context, denial is also characterized as a passive phase. See Friedrich and Wüstenhagen, "Leading Organizations through the Stages of Grief," 198.

34. Vendors have also contributed to the library literature, offering advice on how libraries should deal with budget reductions. See Tim Collins, "The Current Budget Environment and Its Impact on Libraries, Publishers and Vendors," *Journal of Library Administration* 52, no. 1 (2012): 18–35; and Allen Powell, "Times of Crisis Accelerate Inevitable Change," *Journal of Library Administration* 51, no. 1 (2010): 105–29. Both of these authors worked for EBSCO at the time of publication.

35. Kübler-Ross, *On Death and Dying*, 63.

36. Dugan and Hernon, "Smorgasbord," 149–50.

37. Friedrich and Wüstenhagen note that "managers tend to show active reactions in this phase, but their emotional energy is not yet directed toward solutions." Friedrich and Wüstenhagen, "Leading Organizations through the Stages of Grief," 199,

38. Kübler-Ross, *On Death and Dying*, 93.

39. Friedrich and Wüstenhagen note that at this stage managers try to "influence the increasingly inevitable changes in the institutional environment to their favor." Friedrich and Wüstenhagen, "Leading Organizations through the Stages of Grief," 199. For resistance by teaching faculty to necessary collections cuts, see, for instance, Mary Ann Trail, "Evolving with the Faculty to Face Library Budget Cuts," *Serials Librarian* 65, no. 2 (2013): 213–14.

40. David Nicholas et al., "The Impact of the Economic Downturn on Libraries: With Special Reference to University Libraries." *Journal of Academic Librarianship* 36, no. 5 (2010): 380. See also George Machovec, "From Your Managing Editor: Licensing for Libraries during the Pandemic," *Charleston Advisor* 22, no. 2 (October 2020): 3, https://doi.org/10.5260/chara.22.2.3, for a current discussion around new tools and technology, such as Unsub (https://unsub.org), that help librarians make "better decisions on how to cancel or cut back on big deal journal packages."

41. Betsy Kelly, Claire Hamasu, and Barbara Jones, "Applying Return on Investment (ROI) in Libraries," *Journal of Library Administration* 52 (2012): 669.

42. Cheryl Cuillier and Carla J. Stoffle, "Finding Alternative Sources of Revenue," *Journal of Library Administration* 51 (2011): 778. The authors also note that "with state/institutional funding unlikely to ever return to previous levels, fundraising will be a permanent fact of life for libraries" (p. 801).

43. See also Berg, Galvan, and Tewell, "Responding to and Reimagining Resilience," which argues that our organizations require "adequate institutional funding of services and appropriate staffing levels"1

44. While one could argue that libraries that look for outside sources of funding have entered the acceptance stage, we have placed it within bargaining, as such activities are sometimes carried out in order to prove to administrators that libraries can effectively shepherd available funds and in hopes of continuing institutional support. See, for instance, Cuillier and Stoffle, "Finding Alternative Sources of Revenue," 801, which notes that "well-run libraries that collaborate, streamline, leverage resources, and outsource work when possible will be best placed to receive maximum organizational support."

45. Kübler-Ross, *On Death and Dying*, 97.

46. Zell, "Organizational Change," 95, argues that individual or groups cannot "simply be hurried or 'herded' through the stages."

47. Friedrich and Wüstenhagen, "Leading Organizations through the Stages of Grief," 202: "Collective denial …could extend or even intensify the grieving process."

48. Kübler-Ross, *On Death and Dying*, 124.

49. Friedrich and Wüstenhagen, "Leading Organizations through the Stages of Grief," 200, argues that "the acceptance stage is marked by an adaptation toward the new environment and more positive feelings toward it."

50. Zell, "Organizational Change," 90.

51. For examples of the use of appreciative inquiry in libraries, see Tricia Kelly, "A Positive Approach to Change: The Role of Appreciative Inquiry in Library and Information Organizations," *Australian Academic and Research Libraries* 41, no. 3 (2010): 165–66, and Katherine Dabbour and Katherine Kott, "Dialogic Approaches to Strategic Planning in Academic Libraries: An Appreciative Inquiry Case Study at Oviatt Library," *Journal of Library Administration* 57, no. 4 (2017): 471.

Bibliography

Association of Research Libraries. "Library Expenditures as a Percent of Total University Expenditures, 1982–2017." ARL Statistics Survey Statistical Trends. https://www.arl.org/wp-content/uploads/2020/03/ARL-Library-Expenditures.pdf.

Bazan, Jessie. "Six Stories of Vocations Interrupted by the Pandemic." *U.S. Catholic*, May 26, 2021. https://uscatholic.org/articles/202105/six-stories-of-vocations-interrupted-by-pandemic/.

Berg, Jacob, Angela Galvan, and Eamon Tewell. "Responding to and Reimagining Resilience in Academic Libraries." *Journal of New Librarianship* 3, no. 1 (2020): 1–4. https://doi.org/10.21173/newlibs/4/1.

Berinato, Scott. "That Discomfort You're Feeling Is Grief." *Harvard Business Review*, March 23, 2020. https://hbr.org/2020/03/that-discomfort-youre-feeling-is-grief.

Collins, Tim. "The Current Budget Environment and Its Impact on Libraries, Publishers and Vendors." *Journal of Library Administration* 52, no. 1 (2012): 18–35.

Cuillier, Cheryl, and Carla J. Stoffle. "Finding Alternative Sources of Revenue." *Journal of Library Administration* 51 (2011): 777–809.

Dabbour, Katherine, and Katherine Kott. "Dialogic Approaches to Strategic Planning in Academic Libraries: An Appreciative Inquiry Case Study at Oviatt Library." *Journal of Library Administration* 57, no. 4 (2017): 468–80.

Davis, Phil. "Libraries Receiving a Shrinking Piece of the University Pie." Scholarly Kitchen, February 15, 2012. https://scholarlykitchen.sspnet.org/2012/02/15/a-shrinking-piece-of-the-university-pie/.

Dugan, Robert E., and Peter Hernon. "A Smorgasbord: Budget Reduction Strategies, Fraud, and Best Practices." In *Financial Management in Academic Libraries: Data-Driven Planning and Budgeting*, 147–58. Chicago: Association of College and Research Libraries, 2017.

Ettarh, Fobazi. "Vocational Awe and Librarianship: The Lies We Tell Ourselves." *In the Library with the Lead Pipe*, January 10, 2018. https://www.inthelibrarywiththeleadpipe.org/2018/vocational-awe/.

Fox, Michael. "The Psychology of Letting Go." *RBM: A Journal of Rare Books, Manuscripts, and Cultural Heritage* 12, no. 2 (2011): 104–9. https://doi.org/10.5860/rbm.12.2.357.

Frederick, Jennifer K., and Christine Wolff-Eisenberg. *Academic Library Strategy and Budgeting during the COVID-19 Pandemic: Results from the Ithaka S+R US Library Survey 2020*. New York: Ithaka S+R, December 9, 2020. https://doi.org/10.18665/sr.314507.

Friedrich, Elmar, and Rolf Wüstenhagen. "Leading Organizations through the Stages of Grief: The Development of Negative Emotions over Environmental Change." *Business and Society* 56, no. 2 (2017): 186–213.

Guarria, Charles I., and Zhonghong Wang. "The Economic Crisis and Its Effect on Libraries." *New Library World* 112, no. 5/6 (2011): 199–214.

Hoffman, Starr, and Samantha Godbey. "US Academic Libraries' Staffing and Expenditure Trends (1996–2016)." *Library Management* 41, no. 4/5 (2020): 247–68.

Kelly, Betsy, Claire Hamasu, and Barbara Jones. "Applying Return on Investment (ROI) in Libraries." *Journal of Library Administration* 52 (2012): 656–71.

Kelly, Tricia. "A Positive Approach to Change: The Role of Appreciative Inquiry in Library and Information Organizations." *Australian Academic and Research Libraries* 41, no. 3 (2010): 163–77.

Kübler-Ross, Elisabeth. *On Death and Dying*. New York: Routledge, 1969. Reprinted New York: Scribner Classics, 1997.

LeClair, Mark S. "For College Finances, There's No 'Return to Normal.'" *Chronicle of Higher Education*, June 15, 2021. https://www.chronicle.com/article/for-college-finances-theres-no-return-to-normal.

Lowry, Charles B. "ARL Library Budgets after the Great Recession, 2011–2013." In *Research Library Issues: A Report from ARL, CNI, and SPARC*, no. 282 (2013), 2–12. https://doi.org/10.29242/rli.282.2.———. "Three Years and Counting—The Economic Crisis Is Still with Us." *portal: Libraries and the Academy* 11, no. 3 (2011): 757–64.

———. "Year 2 of the 'Great Recession': Surviving the Present by Building the Future." *Journal of Library Administration* 51, no. 1 (2010): 37–53. https://doi.org/10.1080/01930826.2011.531640.

Machovec, George. "From Your Managing Editor: Licensing for Libraries during the Pandemic." *Charleston Advisor* 22, no. 2 (October 2020): 3. https://doi.org/10.5260/chara.22.2.3.

Maynor, Ashley R. "Libraries and Librarians in the Aftermath: Our Stories and Ourselves." *Collaborative Librarianship* 11, no. 1 (2019): article 10. https://digitalcommons.du.edu/collaborativelibrarianship/vol11/iss1/10.

National Student Clearinghouse Research Center. "Spring 2021: Current Term Enrollment Estimates," June 10, 2021, https://nscresearchcenter.org/current-term-enrollment-estimates/ (page content changed).

Nicholas, David, Ian Rowlands, Michael Jubb, and Hamid R. Jamali. "The Impact of the Economic Downturn on Libraries: With Special Reference to University Libraries." *Journal of Academic Librarianship* 36, no. 5 (2010): 376–82.

Peet, Lisa. "Budgeting for the New Normal: Libraries Respond to COVID-19 Funding Constraints." *Library Journal*, September 24, 2020. https://www.libraryjournal.com/?detailStory=budgeting-for-the-new-normal-libraries-respond-to-covid-19-funding-constraints.

Powell, Allen. "Times of Crisis Accelerate Inevitable Change." *Journal of Library Administration* 5, no. 1 (2010): 105–29.

Regazzi, John J. "Comparing Academic Library Spending with Public Libraries, Public K–12 Schools, Higher Education Public Institutions, and Public Hospitals between 1998–2008." *Journal of Academic Librarianship* 38, no. 4 (2012): 205–16.

———. "Constrained? An Analysis of U.S. Academic Library Shifts in Spending, Staffing, and Utilization, 1998–2008." *College and Research Libraries* 73, no. 5 (2012): 449–68. https://doi.org/10.5860/crl-260.

———. "U.S. Academic Library Spending, Staffing and Utilization during the Great Recession 2008–2010." *Journal of Academic Librarianship* 39, no. 3 (2013): 217–22.

Romaniuk, Elena. "Losing Staff: The Seven Stages of Loss and Recovery." *Serials Librarian* 66 (2014): 241–47.

Trail, Mary Ann. "Evolving with the Faculty to Face Library Budget Cuts." *Serials Librarian* 65, no. 2 (2013): 213–20.

Williams June, Audrey. "State Funding for Higher Ed Increased in 2020 for the 8th Straight Year. It Won't Make Up for Past Cuts." *Chronicle of Higher Education*, May 28, 2021. https://www.chronicle.com/article/state-funding-for-higher-ed-increased-in-2020-for-the-8th-straight-year-it-wont-make-up-for-past-cuts.

Yeh, Shea-Tinn, Marne Arthaud-Day, and Michelle Turvey-Welch. "Propagation of Lean Thinking in Academic Libraries." *Journal of Academic Librarianship* 47, no. 3 (2021): article 102357. https://doi.org/10.1016/j.acalib.2021.102357.

Zell, Deone. "Organizational Change as a Process of Death, Dying, and Rebirth." *Journal of Applied Behavioral Science* 39, no. 1 (2003): 75–96. https://doi.org/10.1177/0021886303039001004.

CHAPTER 4

Transformative Teamwork

Managing Change before, during, and beyond the COVID-19 Pandemic at Moraine Valley Community College

Marie M. Martino and Terra B. Jacobson

During the COVID-19 health crisis, the library and MVCC put people first. Indeed, teaching and learning are an essential part of the mission of the college, but when the pandemic took hold, ensuring students, faculty, and staff were safe became the primary focus. While this might run contrary to the operational and financial success of the institution, it was a decision that revealed the organization's values and overall character.

Introduction

COVID-19's impact on higher education resulted in record declines in student enrollments for many colleges across the United States. The remaining student base was unsure about their future and wondering if pursuing their degree was the right choice, right now. Community colleges in particular suffered a sizable enrollment decline, with first-time freshman enrollments dropping by an average of 21 percent.[1] Institutions had to make swift, sweeping decisions, adopt new policies, and implement programs and tools that allowed them to maintain the health and safety of their community, while still fulfilling their missions of teaching and learning.

35

Library staff members across states and institutions scrambled to modify services to meet their users' needs as they evolved in the moment, all while coping with school closures, staff and budget reductions, and overwhelming uncertainty.[2] Many academic libraries embraced their existing role to support their communities and worked to find new and innovative solutions to help mitigate the effects of the pandemic on their users.[3] The Moraine Valley Community College (MVCC) Library aspired to be one of those libraries. Located in Palos Hills, Illinois, just outside Chicago, the library serves a diverse community of over 13,000 students, as well as in-district community members. The MVCC Library staff consists of six full-time faculty-librarians, ten adjunct librarians, eight full-time staff, seven part-time staff, four part-time student employees, and a library dean. For several years now, the library has been building a change-ready culture with substantial intention. Not only does being change-ready enable the library to support users and develop new projects to quickly meet their ever-evolving needs, but it also builds up crisis preparedness. While traditional change management is a reactive approach where change might feel unsettling, change readiness embraces change and integrates it into daily work. The success of Moraine Valley Library's change-ready culture is predicated on the library teams' role in the organization. Members are highly valued for their knowledge, skills, and service. Library leaders actively encourage team members to communicate openly, learn while on the job, and collaborate with each other. By using these team-centered strategies, staff are equipped with the mindset, capacity, and resources necessary not only to bring about controlled change, or change that is managed systemically, but also to cope more effectively in times of unplanned change, including that which can be created by crisis. When the COVID-19 pandemic and its effects took hold, the Moraine Valley Library's approach to change and crisis management allowed the library to shift library services and user expectations, find resilience, and create opportunities for the library's growth.

Managing the COVID-19 Crisis

In March of 2020, the pandemic, as well as the uncertainty that accompanied it, was a clear threat, not only to the health and safety of the MVCC community, but also to the overall mission and goals of the college. Students struggled with a number of issues directly related to COVID-19, including how it impacted their educational plans. The shift to online learning was rough and rife with a variety of challenges for most students, including some of the most basic needs for being successful in college. A number of those students lacked required textbooks; a quiet, safe space to study; or the technology required to facilitate this transition. As with many other institutions, the socioeconomic and digital divides among the student population became highly visible.[4]

Additionally, faculty and staff had to scramble to prepare for the upcoming closures of the physical spaces, as everyone waited for the issuance of official state mandates and health agency guidelines to make smart decisions about how to proceed. An overwhelming sense of both urgency and ambiguity flooded campus communications. Not long after, there were also staffing and budget reductions. Collectively, stress and emotions ran high campus-wide. While no one on staff was using the verbiage just yet, this situation had all the characteristics of a crisis and needed to be managed deliberately, positively, and ethically.

Transformative crisis management (TCM) is defined as "being positively resilient where individuals and organizations can thrive before, during, and after experiencing adversity but do so without incurring unfair costs on others."[5] The ability to be transformative hinges on the organization's preparedness, to have organizational resources and capacity built up before a crisis ever surfaces. Then, if and when a crisis materializes, the goal becomes to minimize its impact as much as possible and heal from the experience. While it is perhaps difficult to grasp from within the eye of the storm, organizations may even find unexpected opportunities that can allow for growth or even some form of gain.[6]

During the COVID-19 health crisis, the library and MVCC put people first. Indeed, teaching and learning are an essential part of the mission of the college, but when the pandemic took hold, ensuring students, faculty, and staff were safe became the primary focus. While this might run contrary to the operational and financial success of the institution, it was a decision that revealed the organization's values and overall character. Unsurprisingly, a crisis truly is "a test of the capacity and character of the organization,"[7] and the pandemic certainly tested both of these within the library. But library leadership committed to its core values by prioritizing staff, their health, and their families by acting from an ethically minded and people-centered position.

Because the library put people first, trust in the organization and leadership was reinforced among team members as they worked diligently to meet organizational goals in new ways. Safety initiatives were made a priority. Personal protective equipment was made widely available, plexiglass was installed at service desks, masks and social-distancing protocols were mandated campus-wide. Additionally, the library held (and continues to hold) periodic all-staff meetings to solicit input and hear feedback related to safety concerns as we reopened with greater access to library services and increased numbers of patrons. Library leadership welcomed questions and weighed opposing opinions, and employee voices drove decision-making, which ultimately resulted in a library plan. In exchange, leadership offered transparent and honest answers, even acknowledging when they themselves were unsure of what the next steps would be.

In mid-March 2020, the library was still unsure about how academic institutions would handle the crisis. Using the best information available at the moment, the library advocated for closure due to the unknown health factors surrounding the virus. Anticipating that there could be additional sudden changes, the library also developed an extensive and phased return-to-work plan prior to the campus's decision-making. This plan allowed the library to move services fully online and to reimagine what library resources and services would look like at each stage, as well as advocate for the library team's needs while living and working through a pandemic. The plan was submitted to the campus administration, and eventually the administrators used the library plan as a model for other units in the college, distributing it as an example to others.

From Kovoor-Mishra's definition of TCM, it is clear that the ability to be prepared and act transformatively while managing a crisis demands that an organization be change-ready. Change readiness can be viewed as "a constant opportunity to evolve."[8] Rather than change in libraries being perceived as a series of manageable, stand-alone, isolated incidents, it is understood as an ongoing phenomenon. For libraries, Steven Bell has likened it to "a holistic process, a cycle of activities with which we stay engaged."[9] Being change-ready allows libraries to be flexible and address their users' needs, which was critical in the early days of remote learning and work imposed by the pandemic.

As official COVID-19 guidelines were released both nationally and locally, the college began its process of closing the physical spaces. In the last few days of March, library operations wound down with only the dean and departmental supervisors remaining on campus to provide vital services for students, such as technology acquisition, checkout, and distribution. Other staff members worked safely, diligently, and collaboratively online from their homes to support students and develop new ways to connect with and best serve the MVCC community.

Within the span of just a couple of days, the circulation department made alterations to its business rules that extended item due dates, turned off overdue and billing notices, and waived minor fines and other billing fees for patrons. Alternatives were put in place in lieu of physical item interlibrary loan requests while intra- and inter-campus delivery services were temporarily shut down. The library circulation department quickly became an indispensable part of the campus's efforts to address the technological needs of students, working collaboratively with campus IT to track all of the devices that were distributed to students within the integrated library system remotely. As COVID-19 relief funding was distributed to the college, the library became the place on campus for student laptop and technology distribution, with a final collection of 400 laptops and 200 hot spots provided for students. The library was able to furnish a device for any Moraine Valley student who expressed a need for one.

Librarians shifted their focus to electronic resources and expanded research and library help guides. Staff adopted new communication methods for day-to-day operations, shifting to workplace collaborative communication tools, giving employees a way to connect on both an interpersonal and an intra-organizational level. Various teams within the library began to plan for larger and more sustained projects moving further into 2020 as it became clear that COVID-19 was going to affect future terms at the college and services would continue to be primarily virtual.

Embracing Change Readiness

An organization's approach to change readiness is often analyzed in two ways: first, by reviewing an organization's resources (financial, material, human, etc.), and second, by examining the culture or mindset, the psychological disposition to cooperatively foster change collectively or individually.[10] To employ a change-ready approach, libraries must tend to both aspects of change readiness.

When assessing an organization's ability to be change-ready, Combe identifies three interlocking drivers: capacity, commitment, and culture.[11] *Capacity* can be defined as the extent to which an organization can maximize, mobilize, and shift its systems, people, processes, technology, and physical resources.[12] In libraries, the budget and staffing are the key resources, and it is helpful to have space in your budget and your rules and policies for change. Having flexible policies and committing funds for new and unknown technology can ensure you utilize those funds to plan for innovation.

Commitment refers to elements such as value alignment, time, skill, involvement, and perceived value among teams and individuals in the organization.[13] Teams require time and space to plan for and adjust to change. Building free time into employee schedules or time off of a service desk allows staff to have the mental space to think about taking risks and innovation. At Moraine Valley Library, gathering to get coffee is something staff members would do, pre-pandemic, to take a break, build comradery, and discuss or brainstorm ideas.

Culture is the third driver of change readiness and consists of shared norms, values, and beliefs of the members within the organization.[14] Shaping a culture is an intentional effort and must be modeled by library leadership. They must be the change if they want to see the change. If the goal is to develop a better work-life balance, leadership cannot message other staff after work hours. Team leaders have to model the cultural norms. No matter how inclusive leadership may feel their culture is, they still need to ask, In what ways is the culture restrictive to some employee groups?

Because commitment and culture are related to mindset, they are more difficult to assess, but are equally as important to being change-ready as the hard resources outlined under capacity.[15] The elements of these three drivers are overlapping and interdependent, and the individuals, teams, and collective body of the library organization play key roles in each of these drivers.

The very notion of change and adaptability is built into both Moraine Valley Library's mission and vision statements,[16] which were crafted through an iterative process that involved employees at all levels. These statements guide the library strategically, as well as philosophically, prioritizing the evolving needs of patrons and the library's obligation to be adaptive and responsive to them. The capacity, commitment, and culture of Moraine Valley Library for change has been intentionally fostered; by explicitly acknowledging that users' needs are an always-moving target within a dynamic information landscape, staff are positioned to adapt and empowered to act.

The Transformative Team

The primary role of the team and its individual members is evident in a change-ready strategy, as they are at the heart of each driver of change readiness. It is people who determine the success or failure of any project, especially in a high-stakes situation or crisis. Musselwhite and Plouffe posit that "the continuous and integrated approach to change requires the coordinated participation of everyone in the company, not just a few change agents or change leaders."[17] Moraine Valley Library uses the following change-ready and team-centered strategies to build and reinforce organizational capacity, commitment, and culture:

- Create and maintain a culture of change.
- Communicate often and openly.
- Support learning and professional development.

- Encourage collaboration.
- Commit to trying new ideas.

Library leaders can foster these team-focused strategies to help team members develop the mindset, capacity, and resources necessary not only to bring about thoughtful change, but also to cope more effectively in times of unplanned change, thus facilitating inherently transformative behaviors among staff.

Create and Maintain a Culture of Change

Change can be difficult and stressful for organizations and their employees. Resistance to change often stems from individuals associating change with various types of loss and uncertainty.[18] Thus, it is no surprise that the mere notion of change can be scary for employees and organizations. But team leaders *at all levels* can help make change feel like an exploration of something new and beneficial rather than a terrifying unknown by normalizing and demystifying it. To develop and maintain a culture of change is to nurture the collective mindset and integrate change into the shared norms and values of library staff. This takes time to accomplish and requires trust to build throughout the organization.

Therefore, it is crucial to construct a culture that works for the *entire* team. It is important to listen to team members' needs, fears, and past experiences that impact the way they personally feel about change and other issues. Each individual needs to feel safe and secure coming to their supervisors with any question or issue they may have, no matter how big or how small. Team leaders must be reliable and consistently cultivate an environment where the team can trust that they will be led and supported, but especially when they pursue continuous improvement measures, change, and innovation. The team should feel confident that their leadership is comfortable with the uncertainty that comes with the unknown.

Nevertheless, spontaneous change is certainly more difficult to tackle and is not something library staff members will be able to handle alone. Library leadership needs to play a significant role in addressing the crisis and managing expectations, offering guidance to contain the crisis internally and within the context of the larger organization and control the new culture that this sudden change will create. The pandemic forced Moraine Valley, like many libraries, to completely alter its service models, to expand access to technology for the benefit of the students and employees, and teams were asked to pivot very quickly. Organizations that operate in a culture of change may definitely feel challenged in these moments, but not severely threatened. Teams that engage in transformative behaviors will find they can better perform, cope, and learn from their experiences during a crisis.[19]

Communicate Often and Openly

Good communication among staff is an essential process at all times. Having an effective system for communication helps build internal resources and capacity, thus augmenting the organization's crisis preparedness. Information needs to be communicated clearly, calmly, transparently, and regularly.[20] That information must be received by the appropriate people, at a well-appointed time and through all pertinent channels, especially during moments of crisis.[21] Transparency can be modeled by leaders.[22] Library leadership should be as open as possible with regard to budget figures, plans for projects, risks and failures, and imparting all the information about what can be realistically done or not. Staff will use this information to create goals for changes that are achievable. This has been especially important during the pandemic. MVCC Library leadership started by providing daily communication updates at the beginning of the pandemic and transitioned to weekly library updates for all staff. In feedback sessions, library employees noted that they valued this frequent communication and had hoped that it would continue indefinitely. Withholding information to retain power is detrimental to the collective body.[23] Employing solid communication practices such as those listed above helps staff solve problems, distribute knowledge, and build relationships, ultimately making teams stronger.

Additionally, having suitable tools to get the job done can be essential. Before the pandemic, the MVCC Library's methods for communication sufficed and often involved face-to-face conversations and quick check-ins, but once the pandemic hit and most staff were working from home, the library clearly needed a better way for staff to connect. Initially, the staff adopted the free version of Slack for a few months, but eventually chose to become an early on-campus adopter of Microsoft Teams, which provided a more robust and customizable solution for its communication needs. Overall, the adoption rate has been high. Team members log in daily for updates and operational information, have informal meetings, participate in asynchronous committee work, celebrate personal milestones, and visit the ever-popular "Work-from-Home Animals" channel. The value of implementing this tool will extend far beyond the pandemic.

Support Learning and Professional Development

There is a clear connection between learning and forming a team that can act in a transformative manner. Peter Senge, the prominent MIT scholar whose research centers around leadership, systemic change, and the learning organization, argues that "deep change comes only through real personal growth—through learning and unlearning,"[24] rather than from acting out of a need to simply comply with management's desires. In this case, the impetus for change stems from an individual's genuine care for and interest in their work. This phenomenon is a clear example of commitment, which is a mindset-dependent change-ready driver worth cultivating. At Moraine Valley Library, making time and space for team member learning has helped improve cross-departmental communication, boosted project development, and fortified team members' confidence. Doing so may require the adjustment of strategic priorities and the mutual flexibility among team members. Professional development can be situated among current staff duties, especially during lulls in the workday.

As part of being change-ready, a growth mindset is needed; all levels of staff are encouraged to pursue professional development and learning opportunities as part of their workday. This has been especially true during the pandemic when virtual programs were plentiful, free, or discounted. Many staff took advantage of professional development opportunities individually or as groups. Additionally, library staff regularly run a number of internal workshops, training sessions, and article discussions. From the beginning of 2020 through the summer of 2021, library staff conducted over twenty-five employee training events, including a scaffolded, eight-week, multimodal MS Teams training for all levels of library staff. Whether folks are learning how to use a new tool for cataloging or discussing an article on critical pedagogy, these efforts are run with the intent of establishing various communities of practice and a built-in support network inside the library. In addition to sharing knowledge and helping each other solve problems, when team members become part of a community of practice, they may also "…develop personal relationships and established ways of interacting …even …a common sense of identity,"[25] which contribute to the development of both commitment and culture.

Encourage Collaboration

Teamwork is a type of collaboration, and making collaboration part of the culture encourages idea generation and a feedback system. It eliminates silos, brings in multiple perspectives, and can help build trust among team members throughout the organization. Collaboration can occur within the library or across the campus and community. Within the MVCC Library, individuals and teams collaborate across departments, employee classification types, and interest areas on various projects. Library leadership promotes this type of collaboration regularly by forming diverse teams and committees. It is customary to get feedback from teammates at different project milestones in a variety of ways—public forums, surveys, one-on-one meetings, and brainstorming sessions when working on new projects.

By working with other areas on campus or in the community, the library can garner useful information about stakeholders' needs and priorities. This also creates valuable connections throughout the campus community to assist when sudden shifts like those brought about by COVID-19 pandemic need to happen. By understanding campus communities' various needs and collaborating with other departments like Student Life, Information Technology, the Center for Teaching and Learning, and teaching faculty, the library has been able to quickly poll students and faculty and staff to understand their needs during this time. Even in this crisis situation, the library was able to draw from its connections and past collaborations to quickly solve problems and address emerging student needs. For example, the library has been able to offer safe and secure virtual study spaces for students in partnership with IT, utilizing an available integration of the library's scheduling software and MS Teams. While the library was not the department tasked with this effort, library team members saw an opportunity to respond to the request and worked with IT to implement this service.

Commit to Trying New Ideas

Being change-ready involves thoughtfully taking risks, allowing for potential failure, and celebrating success. It is important that library leaders commit resources to new projects and ideas. The shape that risk takes depends on the institution's resources, the project being considered, and stakeholder buy-in. Resources will certainly vary among institutions, but staff may be provided with time, connections with other departments, community resources, or additional funding if available. Change will not happen without this commitment.

Innovation and exploration require risk-taking and a willingness to accept the possibility of failure. No matter how well supported a team is, success is not guaranteed. Ensuring the team knows that even unsuccessful endeavors may still be fruitful will allow for the risk-taking that leads to innovation. Developing a time line replete with check-in meetings, goals, clear expectations and providing the team with accurate and honest information about the resources available to them will help to ensure that a team is set up for success. This allows for more communication and for team leaders to provide feedback so projects stay on mission and on time. Finally, it is important that library leadership communicate results to the rest of the library to ensure the entire staff is informed of the status and outcomes of each project.

Additionally, leadership needs to stay involved with the process but not get in the way of innovation by being overly involved. Sometimes the presence of leadership at a meeting can affect team dynamics and limit more authentic interactions of the group. For example, the library's marketing committee operates as an independent library committee with members from various library departments. This team has recently expanded MVCC Library's social media presence into new platforms. The team was not sure if a foray into new online spaces like TikTok would be successful, but they developed a small presence to test the waters and advertised this tool first to library employees and then campus-wide after a trial run. The team was able to work independently without administrative approval for campaign ideas and was more creative and experimental since they knew they had the freedom and support to try something new. Although it has had limited success thus far, getting started on a new platform has expanded how the library looks at our marketing ideas and allowed room for innovation.

Challenges

Engaging in transformative crisis management is certainly not without challenges. Even the most integrated team will run across issues that may be unresolved or difficult to traverse. The transformative team-centered model used at the Moraine Valley Library is beneficial, but there have been obstacles that make navigating the crisis difficult at times. There will always be institutional barriers, external factors, and team members' personal preferences that may change the library leadership's desired response.

The library did not receive additional funding or support directly from the college for many of the needed changes during the pandemic. The uncertainty of enrollment and the overall crisis left the college with a flat budget for student resources, and the library's staffing budget was reduced by roughly 25 percent. Due to these restrictions the library was asked to furlough some part-time, non-benefited staff. Unsurprisingly, this was not great for morale and a very painful task for library leadership. In addition to the impact it had on those to whom the library had to say goodbye, the loss was devastating for many team members who were close with their colleagues. Due to the loss of staffing, the library also had to decrease the services that it could offer.

Additionally, instruction numbers dropped from 251 librarian-led in-person sessions in fall 2019 to 132 librarian-led online sessions in fall 2020 because of campus restrictions. Many college faculty members who often sought out library instruction sessions for their classes were overwhelmed with the immediate transition to online teaching, making library instruction less of a priority for a number of classroom faculty as they shifted their attention to altering their own course materials to be more engaging for students in a virtual format. Concern that the library will have a difficult time persuading instructors to bring their classes back for information and digital literacy sessions in the future still persists.

As many organizations experienced, COVID-19 brought many changes, restrictions, and rules with regard to handling materials. As there were a variety of unknowns early on about the spread of the disease and how it transferred, many of the library's physical resources became inaccessible for a time. Many MVCC students have relied on the library's textbook collection as a stopgap as they awaited financial aid funding for course materials or as a way to get resources they could not afford. The library was unable to provide access to short-term checkouts due to quarantine guidelines. But the library worked with the college foundation and faculty across campus to develop a way for students to access emergency funds to help them purchase their textbooks, since they could not rely on this shared resource.

Personally, staff had to deal with learning many new skills all at once. Some staff struggled with new technology adoption, and others were not interested in participating in the use of new communication modes. While many team members jumped in and enjoyed the opportunity to connect online, those who lacked personal devices or had less experience using computer-mediated communication felt the greatest impact of the digital divide. Due to the limited amount of campus technology available for staff to take home, some were left behind in our workflows and had to catch up as resources became available.

Dealing with the impact of the sudden changes and institutional requests, the library's leadership was required to rebuild schedules last minute and adjust and readjust workflows to match ever-changing campus, state, and national guidelines. When coping with these challenges, it was helpful to have the library mission as a guide. The library's priorities were defined by its goals to help students succeed, and this overall mission was a force that drove many library staff members in their work, despite challenges.

Conclusion

While libraries cannot predict when an event like the COVID-19 pandemic will occur, they can prepare for crises by planning for constant change using a transformative approach to crisis management. This requires understanding that change is ongoing and must it be expected by leadership and team members alike. Strategies for library leaders include instituting a culture of change, promoting good communication practices, supporting learning and professional development, and making space for collaboration and risk-taking. While there will always be external forces and institutional barriers to contend with, libraries can implement these practices to build capacity, commitment, and culture. Developing a transformative team takes time, but its pursuit allows staff to feel prepared for challenges and builds trust within the organization. Transformative teams are more agile and able to adapt quickly in moments of crisis.

Notes

1. National Student Clearinghouse Research Center, "Current Term Enrollment Estimates: Fall 2020," accessed September 1, 2021, https://nscresearchcenter.org/wpcontent/uploads/ CTEE_Report_Fall_2020.pdf.
2. Melissa Blankstein and Christine Wolff-Eisenberg, *Library Strategy and Collaboration across the College Ecosystem* (New York: Ithaka S+R, September 9, 2021), *https://doi.org/10.18665/sr.315922*.
3. Ellysa Stern Cahoy and Maribeth Slebodnik, "Exploring Innovative Strategies and Services in a Pandemic Era," *portal: Libraries and the Academy* 22, no. 1 (January 2022): 1–6, https://doi.org/10.1353/pla.2022.0006.
4. Lindsay McKenzie, *Bridging the Digital Divide* (Washington, DC: Inside Higher Ed, February 2, 2021), https://www.insidehighered.com/content/bridging-digital-divide-lessons-covid-19.
5. Sarah Kovoor-Misra, *Crisis Management* (Los Angeles: Sage, 2020), 42.
6. Kovoor-Misra, *Crisis Management*, 58.
7. Kovoor-Misra, *Crisis Management*, 5.
8. Chris Musselwhite and Tammie Plouffe, "Four Ways to Know Whether You Are Ready for Change," *Harvard Business Review*, June 2, 2010, https://hbr.org/2010/06/four-ways-to-know-whether-you.
9. Steven Bell, "From Change Management to Change-Ready Leadership: Leading from the Library," *Library Journal*, March 1, 2018, https://www.libraryjournal.com?detailStory=change-management-change-ready-leadership-leading-library.
10. Marge Combe, *Change Readiness*, white paper, PMI, July 2014, https://www.pmi.org/learning/library/change-readiness-11126.
11. Combe, *Change Readiness*.
12. Combe, *Change Readiness*.
13. Combe, *Change Readiness*.
14. Jason Martin, "Organizational Culture and Organizational Change: How Shared Values, Rituals, and Sagas Can Facilitate Change in an Academic Library," in *Imagine, Innovate, Inspire: The Proceedings of the ACRL 2013 Conference*, ed. Dawn M. Mueller (Chicago: Association of College and Research Libraries, 2013), 460–65, http://hdl.handle.net/11213/18122.
15. Combe, *Change Readiness*.
16. Moraine Valley Community College Library, "Mission Statement," accessed September 1, 2021, https://lib.morainevalley.edu/policies/missionstatement; Moraine Valley Community College Library, "Vision Statement," accessed September 1, 2021, https://lib.morainevalley.edu/policies/visionstatement.
17. Musselwhite and Plouffe, "Four Ways to Know."
18. Rosabeth Moss Kanter, "Ten Reasons People Resist Change," *Harvard Business Review*, September 25, 2012, https://hbr.org/2012/09/ten-reasons-people-resist-chang.
19. Kovoor-Misra, *Crisis Management*, 45–47.
20. Sue Erickson, "Communication in a Crisis and the Importance of Authenticity and Transparency," *Journal of Library Administration* 61, no. 4 (2021): 476, https://doi.org/10.1080/01930826.2021.1906556.
21. Laura Blessing, "The Transparent Organization: Keeping Staff in the Loop," in *Workplace Culture in Academic Libraries: The Early 21st Century*, ed. Kelly Blessinger and Paul Hrycaj (Oxford: Chandos, 2013), 331.
22. Blessing, "Transparent Organization," 326.
23. Zhou (Joe) Jiang, "Why Withholding Information at Work Won't Give You an Advantage," *Harvard Business Review*, November 26, 2019, https://hbr.org/2019/11/why-withholding-information-at-work-wont-give-you-an-advantage.
24. Peter Senge, quoted in Alan M. Webber, "Learning for a Change," *Fast Company*, April 30, 1999, https://www.fastcompany.com/36819/learning-change.

25. Etienne Wenger, Richard McDermott, and William M. Snyder, *Cultivating Communities of Practice* (Boston: Harvard Business School Press, 2002), 4.

Bibliography

Bell, Steven. "From Change Management to Change-Ready Leadership: Leading from the Library." *Library Journal*, March 1, 2018. https://www.libraryjournal.com?detailStory=change-management-change-ready-leadership-leading-library.

Blankstein, Melissa, and Christine Wolff-Eisenberg. *Library Strategy and Collaboration across the College Ecosystem: Results from a National Survey of Community College Library Directors*. New York: Ithaka S+R, September 9, 2021. https://doi.org/10.18665/sr.315922.

Blessing, Laura. "The Transparent Organization: Keeping Staff in the Loop." In *Workplace Culture in Academic Libraries: The Early 21st Century*, edited by Kelly Blessinger and Paul Hrycaj, 323–33. Oxford: Chandos, 2013.

Cahoy, Ellysa Stern, and Maribeth Slebodnik. "Exploring Innovative Strategies and Services in a Pandemic Era." *portal: Libraries and the Academy*, 22, no. 1 (January 2022): 1–6. https://doi.org/10.1353/pla.2022.0006.

Combe, Marge. *Change Readiness: Focusing Management Where It Counts*. White paper, PMI, July 2014. https://www.pmi.org/learning/library/change-readiness-11126.

Erickson, Sue. "Communication in a Crisis and the Importance of Authenticity and Transparency." *Journal of Library Administration* 61, no. 4 (2021): 476–83. https://doi.org/10.1080/01930826.2021.1906556.

Jiang, Zhou (Joe). "Why Withholding Information at Work Won't Give You an Advantage." *Harvard Business Review*, last updated November 26, 2019. https://hbr.org/2019/11/why-withholding-information-at-work-wont-give-you-an-advantage.

Kanter, Rosabeth Moss. "Ten Reasons People Resist Change." *Harvard Business Review*, September 25, 2012. https://hbr.org/2012/09/ten-reasons-people-resist-chang.

Kovoor-Misra, Sarah. *Crisis Management: Resilience and Change*. Los Angeles: Sage, 2020.

Martin, Jason. "Organizational Culture and Organizational Change: How Shared Values, Rituals, and Sagas Can Facilitate Change in an Academic Library." In *Imagine, Innovate, Inspire: The Proceedings of the ACRL 2013 Conference*, edited by Dawn M. Mueller, 460–65. Chicago: Association of College and Research Libraries, 2013. http://hdl.handle.net/11213/18122.

McKenzie, Lindsay. *Bridging the Digital Divide: Lessons from COVID-19*. Washington, DC: Inside Higher Ed, February 2, 2021. https://www.insidehighered.com/content/bridging-digital-divide-lessons-covid-19.

Moraine Valley Community College Library. "Library Vision Statement." Accessed September 1, 2021. https://lib.morainevalley.edu/policies/visionstatement.

———. "Mission Statement." Accessed September 1, 2021. https://lib.morainevalley.edu/policies/missionstatement

Musselwhite, Chris, and Tammie Plouffe. "Four Ways to Know Whether You Are Ready for Change." *Harvard Business Review*, June 2, 2010. https://hbr.org/2010/06/four-ways-to-know-whether-you.

National Student Clearinghouse Research Center. "Current Term Enrollment Estimates: Fall 2020." Accessed September 1, 2021, https://nscresearchcenter.org/wp-content/uploads/CTEE_Report_Fall_2020.pdf.

Webber, Alan M. "Learning for a Change." *Fast Company*, April 30, 1999. https://www.fastcompany.com/36819/learning-change.

Wenger, Etienne, Richard McDermott, and William M. Snyder. *Cultivating Communities of Practice: A Guide to Managing Knowledge*. Boston: Harvard Business School Press, 2002.

CHAPTER 5

Budgeting in Crisis
Responsive Decision-Making in Academic Library Collections

Braegan Abernethy

A key takeaway for library managers encountering similar fiscal realities is the intrinsic value of flexibility and creative-problem solving when faced with seemingly devastating budget reductions. This spirit of ingenuity will be needed as the ongoing economic impact to libraries from the COVID-19 pandemic is realized in the coming years.

Introduction

When faced with a crisis that impacts academic library budgets, libraries must by necessity reduce expenditures. Frequently targeted areas for reduction are operations, staffing, and collections. Some libraries are mandated to cut across the board, while others are given more latitude in selecting how the reductions are distributed.[1] Collections budgets often take a sizable cut during such times, as library administrators look to align spending priorities with strategic plans.[2] The Great Recession, occurring between 2007 and 2009, particularly impacted academic libraries, as "library budgets as a percentage of total institutional spending shrank, and in some places never fully recovered."[3] Reduction and stagnation in collections budgets continued years after the recession's economic downturn.[4] In early 2020, just prior to the beginning of the global COVID-19 pandemic, *Library Journal* reported:

> Although spending on higher education has improved since the Great Recession, many institutions are not funding their libraries to the same extent as in previous years, and many libraries are opting to allocate their moderate budget increases to new services rather than collections.[5]

47

Facing this reality and encountering a new crisis, the global COVID-19 pandemic, the library collections budget at Georgia State University (GSU) began fiscal year 2021 (FY21) with an overall 12 percent budget reduction and a one-time reduction of an additional 19.5 percent for a total 31.5 percent budget cut. In the years prior to the pandemic, the GSU Library experienced stagnant or reduced collections budgets, but this cut was an unprecedented reduction. Not even the Great Recession had dealt such a severe blow to budget planning and implementation at GSU. COVID-19 prompted a reexamining of the acquisitions and collections processes and required cross-departmental collaboration. This collaboration led to the ongoing development of a responsive collections strategy to meet users' needs while confronting a historically overstretched budget. Tactical rather than strategic decision-making took precedence as the library navigated urgent research and resource demands alongside fiscal responsibility. This chapter explores the recent history of crisis-led collections budget management in academic libraries, examining specifically how the GSU Library responded during the Great Recession and COVID-19 pandemic and revealing insights and implications for future collections management in crises.

The Great Recession and Academic Libraries

The COVID-19 pandemic is the largest mass-scale public health crisis since the Spanish flu pandemic of 1918. The building of academic library collections, however, did not begin to increase to modern scales until the 1960s.[6] An accurate comparison of library collections budget management during crises can be made only by studying more recent examples. Thus, the most relevant event of financial upheaval in recent history is the Great Recession, with effects that lasted much longer. Academic libraries across the United States experienced budget cuts and stagnation for years during and after the recession. An Association of Research Libraries (ARL) study conducted in 2009 showed that 70 percent of respondents anticipated budget cuts for their 2009–2010 fiscal year, and 60 percent of those expected a cut of 5 percent or more.[7] Articles published amid this economic crisis were generally pessimistic in their outlook, with one author commenting on the "more subsequent and longer-lasting impact" the recession would have on library collections budgets.[8] This prediction proved accurate, as shown in a follow-up ARL study, where 52 percent of responding members reported flat or declining acquisitions budgets. In the fiscal year 2011–2012, 89 percent of reporting libraries had budgets that did not keep up with inflation—meaning they "increased less than 3%, remained static, or were reduced from the previous year."[9]

Academic libraries responded in various ways to the deep cuts of the Great Recession. Some turned to collaboration with peer institutions, forming consortia to leverage purchasing power.[10] Many libraries drastically accelerated their shift from acquiring print to prioritizing electronic resources.[11] Library professionals during this time argued that libraries were already operating under a "value deficit" prior to the recession. Thus, they needed to begin an urgent analysis of their specific users while employing targeted marketing and more effective delivery of resources to stay relevant in the post-recession landscape.[12]

To respond to this urgency, many libraries began focusing on a just-in-time (JIT) collection development approach, concentrating on prioritizing resources with high use "that more closely matched local research and teaching needs."[13] Forced by severe budget cuts and emerging methods of acquisition, librarians at the University of North Texas (UNT) adopted this strategy. They established the Access-Based Collection Development model, which, "views the collection as a service designed to meet user needs at the point of service."[14] Adopting JIT collection development and budget measures allowed UNT librarians to be nimble in their ability to adjust and redeploy funds as necessary to support their service expectations. These examples are just a few of the many types of quick, tactical decision-making and innovative solutions that sustained libraries through the lean years of the recession and subsequent, albeit weak, recovery.

The GSU Library experienced similar measures during the Great Recession. Although the collections budget did not suffer a significant cut in FY09, it remained stagnant. Between FY10 and FY16, the budget had received a total increase of only approximately 2.7 percent. In response, GSU conducted annual serials reviews and cancellations to try to combat the effects of rising inflation and price increases. Librarians also drastically reduced the firm orders budget, with an overall 28 percent reduction in allocations from FY08 to FY13. The image in figure 5.1 represents the breakdown of allocations between firm (one-time) orders, approval plans, and continuing resources allocations (the majority of which include electronic and database resources). Like many peer institutions, GSU accelerated commitments to electronic rather than monographic resources during this period.

Figure 5.1
Firm vs. continuing allocations

Background

Understanding the library's budget circumstances requires some knowledge of the institution it serves. GSU is an urban, public research institution originally founded in 1913 as an evening school of the Georgia Institute of Technology and becoming a fully independent college by 1955. It is one of twenty-six institutions in the University System of Georgia (USG) governed by the Georgia Board of Regents, a body appointed by the state's governor. GSU has six campuses, with its main campus located in downtown Atlanta, Georgia. With an approximate enrollment of 54,000 students, it is the largest USG institution. The Georgia General Assembly allocates funds to the USG each fiscal year. State appropriations make up approximately 30 percent of the USG budget, with the remaining 70 percent comprising tuition, institutional fees, and federal funding.[15]

The University Library encompasses six libraries, with its central library located on the Atlanta campus. Average weekly visits to the libraries in October of 2019 topped a combined 59,000.[16] Similarly, library users retrieved over two million full-text downloads from library-provided electronic resources in 2018–2019, with an average of one million visits to the library website.[17] These numbers demonstrate how vital the library is to the university community, both as a place and as a provider of valuable resources and materials.

In the summer of 2016, the library underwent a planning initiative to align the library's priorities more closely with the university's strategic plan. This initiative resulted in a document outlining a five-year intentional focus on student success, the research life cycle, content, community engagement, culture, and space. Collections were explicitly highlighted within the "Content" section of the document, emphasizing a goal to "develop, manage, and provide access to collections in support of teaching, learning, and research."[18] A new collection development policy was also created, with policies established for individual programs at GSU, all emphasizing support for the research and curricular needs of the university's faculty and students. This outward shift toward emphasizing student success in collections mirrored measures taken by other libraries in the years following the Great Recession, an essential action for demonstrating the value and worth of library purchases and how they correlate to specific research and curricular requirements.

In the years following the adoption of the library's new strategic intentions, the materials budget remained flat. There was no increase to take inflation into account between FY17 and FY19. Comparatively, in an EBSCO Information Services document detailing five-year journal price increases, the total increase for those three years averaged 5.67 percent, with a combined total of approximately 17 percent.[19] In 2018, the library conducted another serials review and canceled 280 journal titles (4 percent of the continuing resources budget) to respond to this stagnation. In FY20, the collections budget received a modest increase of 3.7 percent, but that marginal gain was lost in the coming fiscal year as the COVID-19 pandemic developed.

Like many academic libraries, the GSU Library has, for many years, worked with subscription agents to manage serials and large package deals with publishers. GSU began prepaying for these subscriptions before 2000 and still prepays a significant portion of annual serials costs. Figure 5.2 shows the library's collections budget compared to the amount spent on continuing resources for 2013 through 2021.

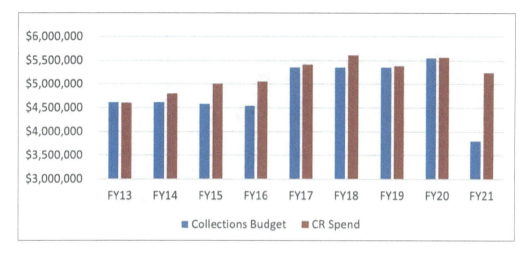

Figure 5.2
Collections budget versus continuing resources spend

As the chart reveals, the cost of continuing resources is more than the library's entire collections budget, leaving no excess for monographs or other materials purchases. Prepaying for continuing resources frees up money within the current fiscal year for monographs and other firm order spending. Typically, year-end funds from both the collections and operating budgets of the library are combined to form the basis of the prepayment for the next fiscal year's continuing resources costs. The library implemented this prepayment process to combat the generally stagnant and often reduced collections budget that could not keep pace with annual price increases. While prepaying allows the library to maintain collections at an acceptable level to meet users' needs, it requires a complicated budget planning and forecasting process to predict spending in the upcoming fiscal year. With the upheaval wrought by the COVID-19 pandemic and past economic crises, the sustainability of this method of budgeting is questionable and requires developing a more nuanced collections strategy.

COVID-19 and the GSU Library

When it became apparent that COVID-19 would impact the state of Georgia in early 2020, the GSU Library began an urgent planning process. Teams of librarians and administrators met weekly to develop contingency plans for maintaining as many services as possible in a closure scenario. During spring break, which occurred March 16–22, 2020, university officials decided to close campuses and finish the spring semester online. The library closed its physical locations to all but university employees. Many library faculty and staff with compatible positions transitioned to remote work. In contrast, others continued to work in the libraries under an essential employee authorization that allowed state employees to complete in-person work during the early days of the pandemic.

Fears emerged over the economic impact of the virus on the state's revenue going into FY21. Georgians faced record unemployment, peaking at 12.5 percent in April 2020.[20] The state experienced decreased revenue as businesses closed and residents reduced spending during shelter-in-place orders. In April 2020, as reported in an article in the *Atlanta Journal-Constitution*, local lawmakers feared a $4 billion shortfall due to the decrease in income and sales tax.[21] The state responded to these dire financial predictions by passing a budget for FY21 that included a 10 percent appropriation reduction to the USG.[22] Subsequently, GSU received an equivalent 10 percent reduction of state appropriations for FY21.[23]

As noted in the introduction, GSU administration mandated a 12 percent overall reduction to the library collections budget in FY21. In August 2020, the library returned an additional 19.5 percent in collections allocations to help fund a university-wide early retirement initiative. The university took this action to maximize personnel savings and address the state appropriations reductions impacting the entire university budget.[24] This additional cut resulted in the previously mentioned overall 31.5 percent reduction for the collections budget.

Budgeting through Crisis

Before the library received its final budget for FY21, planning began between the library's Resource Acquisitions and Collection Development and Discovery departments. Estimated cuts as high as 20 percent were part of the planning scenarios as early as May 2020. Because of the slight increase and some year-end funds received in late FY20, the library provided a significant prepayment to its subscription agent to ensure access to its continuing resource commitments through FY21. With a substantial portion of serials subscriptions protected, librarians looked at ways to maximize actual FY21 funds available for spending while also looking toward FY22. Because the library relies on current funds for the next fiscal year prepayment, the significant reduction in FY21 funds caused by the pandemic and resultant revenue reductions for the state of Georgia would reduce the year-end money available to prepay for FY22 resources. If the library could not prepay for its continuing resource commitments for FY22, that fiscal year would see severe cuts across the library's budget that would have harmful effects on research and curricular needs.

In light of concerns regarding the FY22 prepayment, the library enacted a series of actions. Responsive decision-making, with an emphasis on preserving resources most needed by the university community, took precedence. The library was already over a month into the fiscal year when it received its final budget for the year. Librarians made decisions quickly but prudently, always keeping the values of student success in mind. The first action required a goal of cutting 12 percent from non-prepaid databases. Cuts had been made to the monographs budgets for years while the continuing resources budget progressively increased. During the lean years of the Great Recession, only minimal cuts had been made to continuing resources when the library was faced with budget stagnation. However, with such a considerable reduction in funds for FY21, the library began cutting more from its electronic resources lines out of necessity. Usage statistics, impact on program of study, and availability of content in other resources were significant factors in those databases chosen for cancellation. Second, monographs also received a 12 percent cut from its FY20 allocation. Most of that amount was allocated to the approval plan and demand-driven acquisitions (DDA), with only 5 percent allocated to firm orders. In previous years, firm orders made up 30 percent of the monographs budget. With the expectation that many classes would remain online, maintaining e-book purchases through approval and DDA was crucial for supporting faculty and student resource requirements.

Finally, the library's Big Deal agreement with SpringerNature was up for renegotiation for the calendar year 2022. The library decided to unbundle this subscription, choosing a more selective approach with a collection of titles that would most benefit the university community. Selection and negotiation of the new title-by-title package was completed by librarians in the Collection Development and Discovery department using various criteria including "download data, article citations by institutional authors, open access availability of articles, articles published by institutional authors, and the projected costs of alternative access to those titles."[25] While this process did reduce GSU's overall spend with SpringerNature by 45 percent, future considerations for unbundling Big Deals include gathering more faculty input about cancellations and working with vendors to negotiate custom title-by-title packages that include multiyear price increase caps.

With an established practice of evaluating resources for cancellation, reduction, or replacement begun during the years following the Great Recession, accelerating these actions represented an approximate 8 percent decrease to FY21 collections spending. This ensured less drastic cuts in FY22 and helped reduce the impact of the 31.5 percent budget cut. Furthermore, it prompted the urgent need for a more responsive collections strategy to deal with the unpredictable fiscal reality brought on by the COVID-19 pandemic.

Figure 5.3
GSU New Collections Strategy

After formulating the plan for surviving FY21, a cross-departmental group gathered to reconsider the library's collections strategy. As illustrated in figure 5.3, four core themes emerged from an initial meeting. These included beginning a strategic dissection of large publisher packages to support a more specialized and nuanced grouping of titles that closely match faculty and student needs and usage. The library could no longer support Big Deal agreements that provide access to thousands of titles but at an unsustainable cost. This strategy closely aligns with an ongoing trend in academic libraries, as a 2019 survey revealed: "Of the 65% of respondents who indicated they had already broken up a Big Deal, 53% indicated it was because they could no longer sustain journal inflation, almost 23% because of a mandated budget reduction."[26]

Data gathering is another area of focus, with ideas for creating focus groups of librarians and university faculty and using surveying and other tools for analyzing library collections. Comprehensive reporting of trends in collections would also help decide what to retain and what is no longer needed to support collections goals. Education of the university community about the library's budget and collections would be a priority moving forward. Ideas included a faculty discussion series, a LibGuide specifically focused on collections, and a generally more open and active push of collections strategies outside of the siloed library environment. This tactic is vital for university constituents to be more involved in the process and gain a deeper understanding and appreciation for library collections and their numerous benefits.

New collections analysis tools have emerged in the past several years, many of which the library has utilized. These include evidence-based acquisitions, collections analysis software, and streaming video platforms that utilize patron-driven acquisitions. Finding space in the budget for supporting these developing tools is an important goal for the library in its pursuit to remain relevant in a rapidly changing industry. Formulating a sustainable collections strategy is an ongoing process at the GSU Library, requiring continuous reevaluation as the library shifts to a more effective budget model.

The Future of the Library Collections Budget

A key takeaway for library managers encountering similar fiscal realities is the intrinsic value of flexibility and creative problem-solving when faced with seemingly devastating budget reductions. This spirit of ingenuity will be needed as the ongoing economic impact to libraries from the COVID-19 pandemic is realized in the coming years. In a survey of periodical pricing for 2021, the authors wrote, "Many institutions are seeing or planning for permanent cuts between 9 and 13 percent to their base budget, a key difference from temporary cuts made after the Great Recession."[27] Planning at the GSU Library will move forward with that possibility, likely requiring continued use of responsive decision-making to combat budget disparities while supporting university research and curriculum. One article describes this as an "agile development model …not a strategic planning process, but instead a tactical method libraries can use to quickly identify what works for users."[28]

As predicted after the Great Recession, increased electronic and digital collections usage over physical collections will continue. Some favorable aspects may emerge from this acceleration, including "overcoming publishers' limits on library access to ebooks and resolving user privacy concerns."[29] Concurrently, a shift in budget priorities from the library as a physical repository to embracing an open, scholarly communications hub will significantly benefit the university community and help sustain academic libraries post-pandemic.

Characterizing the "most energized businesses," one author analyzes the future of forecasting in the for-profit business world, explaining, "instead of reverting to plan, they have assessed their assets and resources and asked what will make them most relevant and valuable now.... They've quickly cancelled what now feels obsolete and accelerated what has become urgent."[30] Going forward, academic librarians will need to draw upon this model of business in their own forecasting, as they develop criteria for improved collections strategies and responsible budget and resource management. Executing this flexibility is what allowed libraries and librarians to meet the economic and public health challenges of the recent past, and utilizing this ingenuity will reveal they can continue to respond effectively to the crises of the future.

Notes

1. Jennifer K. Frederick and Christine Wolff-Eisenberg, *Academic Library Strategy and Budgeting during the COVID-19 Pandemic* (New York: Ithaka S+R, December 9, 2020): 19–20.
2. Robert E. Dugan and Peter Hernon, *Financial Management in Academic Libraries* (Chicago: Association of College and Research Libraries, 2018), 148.
3. Lindsay McKenzie, "Libraries Brace for Budget Cuts," Inside Higher Ed, April 17, 2020, https://www.insidehighered.com/news/2020/04/17/college-librarians-prepare-looming-budget-cuts-and-journal-subscriptions-could-be#.
4. Charles B. Lowry, "ARL Library Budgets after the Great Recession, 2011–13," *Research Libraries Issues: A Report from ARL, CNI, and SPARC*, no 282 (2013): 5, http://publications.arl.org/rli282/.
5. Stephen Bosch, Barbara Albee, and Sion Romaine, "Costs Outstrip Library Budgets: Periodical Price Survey 2020," *Library Journal*, April 14, 2020, https://www.libraryjournal.com/?detailStory=Costs-Outstrip-Library-Budgets-Periodicals-Price-Survey-2020.
6. Arlene Sievers-Hill, "Building Library Collections in the 21st Century—It's the Economy, People," *Against the Grain* 21, no. 1 (February 2009): 72.
7. Allen Powell, "Times of Crisis Accelerate Inevitable Change," *Journal of Library Administration* 51, no. 1 (January 2011): 106, https://doi.org/10.1080/01930826.2011.531644.
8. Sievers-Hill, "Building Library Collections," 72.
9. Lowry, "ARL Library Budgets," 7.
10. Lizabeth A. Wilson, "Creating Sustainable Futures for Academic Libraries," *Journal of Library Administration* 52, no. 1 (January 2012): 86, https://doi.org/10.1080/01930826.2012.630241.
11. George Stachokas, *The Role of the Electronic Resources Librarian* (Cambridge, MA: Chandos, 2020), 92.
12. Michael Germano, "The Library Value Deficit," *Bottom Line* 24, no. 2 (August 2011): 102–5.
13. Stachokas, *Role of the Electronic Resources Librarian*, 93.
14. Laurel Sammonds Crawford et al., "Implementing a Just-in-Time Collection Development Model in an Academic Library," *Journal of Academic Librarianship* 46, no. 2 (March 2020): article 102101, https://doi.org/10.1016/j.acalib.2019.102101.
15. "All Budgets for Fiscal Year 2022," University System of Georgia, May 11, 2021, https://www.usg.edu/fiscal_affairs/assets/fiscal_affairs/documents/usg_budget_2022.pdf.
16. "Annual Report 2020: 2019–20 Year in Review," Georgia State University Library, accessed July 23, 2021, https://library.gsu.edu/files/2020/12/Annual-Report-FY19-20.pdf.
17. "Annual Report: 2018–19 Year in Review," Georgia State University Library, accessed July 23 2021, https://library.gsu.edu/files/2020/01/Annual-Report-FY18-19-DECEMBER2019.pdf.
18. "Strategic Intentions, 2017–2021," Georgia State University Library, accessed July 23, 2021, https://library.gsu.edu/wp-content/blogs.dir/640/files/2019/04/stategic-intentions-2017-05-15.pdf.
19. "Five Year Journal Price Increase History (2016–2020)," EBSCO Journal and e-Package Services, accessed July 23, 2021, https://www.ebsco.com/sites/g/files/nabnos191/files/acquiadam-assets/Five-Year-Journal-Price-Increase-History-EBSCO-2016-2020.pdf.

Chapter 5

20. "Unemployment Rate Drops to 4 Percent in June," news release, Georgia Department of Labor, July 15, 2021, https://dol.georgia.gov/press-releases/2021-07-15/unemployment-rate-drops-4-percent-june.

21. James Salzer, "Report: Ga. Budget Shortfall May Top $4 Billion over Next 15 Months," *Atlanta Journal-Constitution*, April 20, 2020, https://www.ajc.com/news/state--regional-govt--politics/report-budget-shortfall-may-top-billion-over-next-months/bCh9sdsuYVJupfCivsTDbJ/.

22. Eric Stirgus and James Salzer, "Pressure to Move Ga. College Courses Online, but Revenue Losses Could Be High," *Atlanta-Journal Constitution*, July 23, 2020, https://www.ajc.com/education/pressure-to-move-ga-college-courses-online-but-revenue-losses-could-be-high/54X7C77I6FEKDM-7MQRP3KM2RPI/.

23. "All Budgets for Fiscal Year 2021," University System of Georgia, July 1, 2020, https://www.usg.edu/fiscal_affairs/assets/fiscal_affairs/documents/usg_budget_2021.pdf.

24. "Voluntary Separation Program," Georgia State University Human Resources, accessed July 23, 2021, https://hr.gsu.edu/voluntary-separation-program/.

25. Laura Burtle, "Springer Journals," *University Library News* (blog), March 4, 2021, https://blog.library.gsu.edu/2021/03/04/springer-journals/.

26. L. Angie Ohler and Joelle Pitts, "From Peril to Promise: The Academic Library Post-COVID-19," *College and Research Libraries News* 82, no. 1 (January 2021): 42, https://doi.org/10.5860/crln.82.1.41.

27. Stephen Bosch, Barbara Albee, and Sion Romaine, "The New Abnormal: Looking Past the Pandemic to the New Periodicals Landscape," *Library Journal* 146, no. 4 (April 2021): 21, Gale Literature Resource Center.

28. Ohler and Pitts, "From Peril," 43.

29. Dave Shumaker, "The Next Normal: The Post-pandemic Future of Library Services." *Information Today* 38, no. 4 (May 2021): 14, MasterFILE Elite, EBSCOhost.

30. Margaret Heffernan, "Prepare for Surprises: Predicting and Planning for the Future in a Complex World Requires Leaders to Embrace New Skills around Flexibility, Open Mindedness, Responsiveness and Curiosity," *People and Strategy* 44, no. 1 (Winter 2021): 13, Business Source Complete, EBSCOhost.

Bibliography

Bosch, Stephen, Barbara Albee, and Sion Romaine. "Costs Outstrip Library Budgets: Periodical Price Survey 2020." *Library Journal*, April 14, 2020. https://www.libraryjournal.com/?detailStory=Costs-Outstrip-Library-Budgets-Periodicals-Price-Survey-2020.

———. "The New Abnormal: Looking Past the Pandemic to the New Periodicals Landscape." *Library Journal* 146, no. , (April 2021): 20–25. Gale Literature Resource Center.

Burtle, Laura. "Springer Journals." *University Library News* (blog), March 4, 2021. https://blog.library.gsu.edu/2021/03/04/springer-journals/.

Crawford, Laurel Sammonds, Coby Condrey, Elizabeth Fuseler Avery, and Todd Enoch. "Implementing a Just-in-Time Collection Development Model in an Academic Library." *Journal of Academic Librarianship* 46, no. 2 (March 2020). https://doi.org/10.1016/j.acalib.2019.102101.

Dugan, Robert E., and Peter Hernon. *Financial Management in Academic Libraries: Data-Driven Planning and Budgeting*. Chicago: Association of College and Research Libraries, 2018.

EBSCO Journal and e-Package Services. "Five Year Journal Price Increase History (2016–2020)." Accessed July 23, 2021. https://www.ebsco.com/sites/g/files/nabnos191/files/acquiadam-assets/Five-Year-Journal-Price-Increase-History-EBSCO-2016-2020.pdf.

Frederick, Jennifer K., and Christine Wolff-Eisenberg. *Academic Library Strategy and Budgeting during the COVID-19 Pandemic: Results from the Ithaka S+R US Library Survey 2020*. New York: Ithaka S+R, December 9, 2020. https://doi.org/10.18665/sr.314507.

Georgia Department of Labor. "Unemployment Rate Drops to 4 Percent in June." News release, July 15, 2021. https://dol.georgia.gov/press-releases/2021-07-15/unemployment-rate-drops-4-percent-june (page discontinued).

Georgia State University Human Resources. "Voluntary Separation Program." Accessed July 23, 2021. https://hr.gsu.edu/voluntary-separation-program/.

Georgia State University Library. "Annual Report: 2018–19 Year in Review." Accessed July 23, 2021. https://library.gsu.edu/files/2020/01/Annual-Report-FY18-19-DECEMBER2019.pdf.

———. "Annual Report 2020: 2019–20 Year in Review." Accessed July 23, 2021. https://library.gsu.edu/files/2020/12/Annual-Report-FY19-20.pdf.

———. "Strategic Intentions, 2017–2021." Accessed July 23, 2021. https://library.gsu.edu/wp-content/blogs.dir/640/files/2019/04/stategic-intentions-2017-05-15.pdf.

Germano, Michael. "The Library Value Deficit." *Bottom Line* 24, no. 2 (August 2011): 100–106. https://doi.org/10.1108/08880451111169124.

Heffernan, Margaret. "Prepare for Surprises: Predicting and Planning for the Future in a Complex World Requires Leaders to Embrace New Skills around Flexibility, Open Mindedness, Responsiveness and Curiosity." *People and Strategy* 44, no. 1 (Winter 2021): 10–13. Business Source Complete, EBSCOhost.

Lowry, Charles B. "ARL Library Budgets after the Great Recession, 2011–13." *Research Libraries Issues: A Report from ARL, CNI, and SPARC*, no 282 (2013): 2–12. http://publications.arl.org/rli282/.

McKenzie, Lindsay. "Libraries Brace for Budget Cuts." Inside Higher Ed, April 17, 2020. https://www.insidehighered.com/news/2020/04/17/college-librarians-prepare-looming-budget-cuts-and-journal-subscriptions-could-be#..

Ohler, L. Angie, and Joelle Pitts. "From Peril to Promise: The Academic Library Post-COVID-19." *College and Research Libraries News* 82, no. 1 (January 2021): 41–44. https://doi.org/10.5860/crln.82.1.41.

Powell, Allen. "Times of Crisis Accelerate Inevitable Change." *Journal of Library Administration* 51, no. 1 (January 2011): 105–29. https://doi.org/10.1080/01930826.2011.531644.

Salzer, James. "Report: Ga. Budget Shortfall May Top $4 Billion over Next 15 Months." *Atlanta-Journal Constitution*, April 20, 2020. https://www.ajc.com/news/state--regional-govt--politics/report-budget-shortfall-may-top-billion-over-next-months/bCh9sdsuYVJupfCivsTDbJ/.

Shumaker, Dave. "The Next Normal: The Post-pandemic Future of Library Services." *Information Today* 38, no. 4 (May 2021): 14–16. MasterFILE Elite, EBSCOhost.

Sievers-Hill, Arlene. "Building Library Collections in the 21st Century—It's the Economy, People." *Against the Grain* 21, no. 1 (February 2009): 72–73.

Stachokas, George. *The Role of the Electronic Resources Librarian*. Cambridge, MA: Chandos, 2020.

Stirgus, Eric, and James Salzer. "Pressure to Move Ga. College Courses Online, but Revenue Losses Could Be High." *Atlanta-Journal Constitution*, July 23, 2020. https://www.ajc.com/education/pressure-to-move-ga-college-courses-online-but-revenue-losses-could-be-high/54X7C77I6FEKDM-7MQRP3KM2RPI/.

University System of Georgia. "All Budgets for Fiscal Year 2021." July 1, 2020. https://www.usg.edu/fiscal_affairs/assets/fiscal_affairs/documents/usg_budget_2021.pdf

———. "All Budgets for Fiscal Year 2022." May 11, 2021. https://www.usg.edu/fiscal_affairs/assets/fiscal_affairs/documents/usg_budget_2022.pdf.

Wilson, Lizabeth A. "Creating Sustainable Futures for Academic Libraries." *Journal of Library Administration* 52, no. 1 (January 2012): 78–93. https://doi.org/10.1080/01930826.2012.630241.

CHAPTER 6

The Human Factor

Managing Chaos and Change in Times of Uncertainty

Stephanie Sterling Brasley, Adriana Popescu, Alicia Virtue, and Delritta Hornbuckle

> The unrelenting, unabating organizational, political, and human resource stressors library managers faced pushed the boundaries of their capacity to keep pace with the longer-term demands of this catastrophic time; however, their dedication and resilience, bolstered by wisdom from the models and theories discussed here, hold promise for a positive future.

Introduction

The California State University system (CSU) is the nation's largest four-year public university. Geographically spanning the entire state, from Humboldt in the north to San Diego in the south, it consists of twenty-three universities, enrolls approximately 486,000 students, and employs approximately 56,000 staff and faculty. The spring 2021 commencement brought the number of CSU living alumni to four million. CSU is recognized as having the most ethnically, economically, and academically diverse student body, although significant differences are present, as each university has its own culture. The CSU libraries support their local campus communities but are guided also by a common strategic plan and a unified commitment to student success.

The year 2020 was a zeitgeist year that brought into sharp focus deep systemic problems residing at various levels of our national, state, and local ecosystems; occurrences included a global health pandemic, a strident election process, and social and racial upheavals that highlighted severe chasms within the nation. These occurrences, which brought about major angst and uncertainty among employees, revealed the critical need for a bold leadership agenda among academic library leaders moving forward. The CSU libraries relied on a system-wide approach to the COVID-19 pandemic, guiding their respective organizations through hiring freezes, budget cuts, a rapid pivot to online services and programs, and staff and faculty well-being, using a strong existing foundation of collaboration and mutual support. The four deans talked informally and consulted one another on challenges that arose; these conversations reflected leadership styles that were being employed. However, the formal leadership theories and models surfaced much later as they began a debriefing process of their experiences over the first eighteen months of the pandemic.

At the writing of this manuscript, the COVID-19 pandemic challenges, political struggles, and racial tensions continue. However, it is with shifting narratives. This chapter focuses on the foundational eighteen-month time frame from the beginning of the pandemic in March 2020 to August 2021. The strategies, experiences, practices and lessons learned are shared in this chapter by four CSU library deans; they are grounded in common frameworks that connect the libraries, while at the same time reflecting campus-specific organizational structures and cultures, as well as geographic, demographic, and political factors.

Leading in Uncertain Times Using the Four-Frame Model, Crisis Leadership, and Reflective Leadership

The pandemic years will undoubtedly generate numerous leadership and organizational change studies that will affirm well-established models and theories or generate new ones. The four CSU library deans were familiar with and utilized several leadership models and theories as they navigated pandemic-related situations. Although the experiences described in this section primarily affirm the four-frame leadership model applied to academic library leadership, as well as tenets of reflective leadership and lessons on leading through crisis from leadership guru John Maxwell,[1] the four library deans also favored and called upon Blanchard and Hersey's Situational Leadership model, which emphasizes an adaptive leadership style based on operational needs and circumstances. Situational Leadership encourages managers to look at the developmental needs of employees and to pivot flexibly. This leadership approach asks the leader to adjust her style to the competence and commitment levels of the employees. This leadership style worked well operationally because it allowed each dean to assess employees' competency and readiness levels for taking on similar or different work roles and duties, while working remotely, and to plan and execute accordingly. The four-frame leadership model was prioritized in these narratives because it allowed each dean to capture the multifaceted levels on which they worked in order to respond to the crises they faced.

The four-frame model, first introduced into organizational theory literature in 1984 by Bolman and Deal, invites leaders to view work-related situations from four unique perspectives, or frames. The structural frame explores organizational architecture, with focus on institutional goals and objectives, roles, responsibilities, and processes. The human resource frame views situations from the vantage point of relationships, exploring the organizational interplay among personnel and the workplace and how this influences employee motivation and productivity. The political frame addresses resource allocation and decision-making, acknowledging the presence of elements such as power and conflict as components to be considered when formulating a leadership response. Finally, the symbolic frame invites leaders to recognize the beliefs and tenets common to an organization, taking into account the powerful role that culture plays as participants make sense of and assign meaning to work situations. Awareness of these diverse perspectives invited the authors of this chapter to reframe organizational situations in adaptive and creative ways.

Seminal leadership author John Maxwell proffers key considerations for effective general and crisis leadership: putting people first, being flexible, practicing adaptability, educating yourself, being authentic, and communicating judiciously more than continually.[2] Reflective leadership finds its roots in reflective learning, which emanated from frameworks grounded in transformational leadership and change management.[3] Defined as "the consistent practice of reflection, which involves conscious awareness of behaviors, situations and consequences with the goal of improving organizational performance," reflective leadership also "helps leaders make sense of uncertain, unique or conflicted situations."[4] This theory shares the common theme posited by Maxwell, Bolman, Deal, and Gallos of placing people, their needs, and their growth at the center at all times, while also exercising self-awareness and flexibility when confronting problems. The urgency of formulating and mobilizing responses while operating in highly uncertain circumstances called upon library leaders to view arising situations using the four frames, along with crisis and reflective leadership, to inform their decision-making, as their narratives will reveal.

The Dominguez Hills Experience

California State University, Dominguez Hills (CSUDH), designated as a minority-serving and Hispanic-serving institution, was established in 1960 and later, following the Watts Rebellion, intentionally relocated to Carson, a city in the South Bay of Los Angeles County, to provide educational opportunities for communities residing in the area, principally people of color. CSUDH educates more first-generation students than any other campus in the California State University system and, with a student body at 87 percent students of color, also has the distinction of serving the most ethnically diverse student body in the CSU system.

Early in 2020, academic library managers were thrust into an environment punctuated by a cataclysmic global health pandemic, national political theater, and devastating racial upheaval, while also being hampered by the slow pace of change pervading higher education. Reflecting on leadership and management situations through the four-frame, crisis, and reflective leadership lenses facilitated this academic leader's examination of activities that advanced the goals of the library and those that warranted revisions to thought and practice. Prior to the COVID-19 pandemic, 90 percent of courses were on premises; absent a telecommuting policy, all library faculty and staff were required to work on campus. The campus transitioned to remote learning and work following the COVID-19 surge in California.

Many of the activities in the pandemic pre-vaccine era necessarily focused on structural leadership for new or revised structures, policies, and procedures at the library and campus levels. This dean's leadership preferences gravitated toward Bolman and Deal's human resource, symbolic, and political frames and were embraced by campus leaders as well, resulting in synergies as managers navigated the myriad challenges arising from the multiple crises at play. This approach was driven by a keen awareness of the disproportionate negative impacts of COVID-19 on communities of color[5] and two preeminent "North Stars"—health and safety and student success—that guided planning and implementation.

The structural frame dominated the early months of the pandemic. With the North Stars front and center in decision-making for the library's plan of action, library faculty and staff pivoted quickly to planning and implementing virtual services to promote student success. The entire library team engaged in activities included in the structural frame to maintain core library academic support activities. Library faculty transitioned information literacy instruction to synchronous and asynchronous online modalities. Also, they worked efficiently and effectively to increase offerings of general and course-specific tutorials and instructional videos available. Staff professionals worked to make print course reserves materials available to students. The User Services team planned and implemented resource-sharing and course list management solutions and a safe and efficient curbside service. The implementation of a contactless locker system was a crowning achievement that furthered campus safety and student goals.

The political frame centers advocacy and negotiation as crucial traits for academic leaders as they advance their agendas among stakeholder groups. With resource-constrained budgets being reduced further by the pandemic, this library leader prioritized this frame, working with the library's advisory and faculty councils, which successfully wrote funding requests for the Coronavirus Aid, Relief, and Economic Security (CARES) Act, reviewed the library's budget for cost-saving measures, negotiated partnerships with information technology for equipment, and ratcheted up advocacy efforts for much-needed electronic resources.

Centering people, aligning employees' basic needs with organizational requirements, and enabling their agency in order to work at their highest capacity are vital components of the human resource frame as articulated by Bolman and Deal[6] and a critical tenet embraced by John Maxwell. The hallmarks of this frame include "open communication and transparency, empowerment, support, coaching, and care, and effective teams for collective action."[7] Utilizing the symbolic frame, characterized by communicating a vision, providing purpose, articulating values, and elevating the organization's culture, the provost and other campus leaders immediately conveyed the need to embrace the student-centered, faculty-driven, administrator-supported, policy-enabled, and community-relevant philosophy of the campus to address operational and structural fissures and to embrace opportunities. The CSUDH president, Dr. Thomas Parham, set the tone for campus activities, asserting that "crisis reveals character, crisis exposes weaknesses, and crisis creates opportunities."[8]

From this library leader's perspective, the unrelenting, unabating organizational, political, and human resource stressors library managers faced pushed the boundaries of their capacity to keep pace with the longer-term demands of this catastrophic time; however, their dedication and resilience, bolstered by wisdom from the models and theories discussed here, hold promise for a positive future. The strong character of the library team was illuminated by the cohesive teamwork displayed and the support they offered to each other as individuals dealt with family or community challenges. This library dean held virtual wellness and self-care check-in sessions with departments to communicate her concern for their well-being and that of their families. The Social and Racial Justice Action and Education Taskforce hosted a mini-retreat, "Breathe ... Relax, Relate, Release" as a self-care engagement session to acknowledge the challenges people had faced and to celebrate the team's resilience and thriving attitudes. The library's evolving work related to communication, transparency, policies, and procedures prior to the pandemic surfaced weaknesses in each of these areas that were highlighted among the chaos. Though uncomfortable at times, recognition of these deficiencies resulted in cultivation of the operational infrastructure, of stronger shared governance, and of relationship-building opportunities among staff professionals, library faculty, and managers. Seizing opportunities afforded by the multiple crises, following the racially motivated murder of George Floyd and resulting racial inequities highlighted by this event, provided the opportunity for the formation of a task force to address anti-racism and social and racial justice issues, as well as the completion of a diversity, equity, and inclusion (DEI) audit. Furthermore, the pandemic provided an opportunity to foster and improve confidence and competency teaching online in multiple modalities; improve cross-departmental teamwork; and, importantly for both crises, generate more empathy and compassion for others—the human factor at work.

Crisis indeed reveals character and spotlights inflection points. A crisis, according to John Maxwell "reveals what is inside of us."[9] This library leader's commitment to acting upon principles undergirded by emotional intelligence, integrity, empathy, and compassion won the day. Over the course of the last eighteen months, the library team at CSUDH has emerged stronger for weathering the crises and thriving during significant change and stress.

The Fresno State Experience

Fresno is the fifth largest city in California. California State University, Fresno (known as Fresno State), is the largest and the most centrally located of the three San Joaquin Valley (Central Valley) CSU campuses, which also include Bakersfield and Stanislaus. The Central Valley is an agricultural region in California, less than 1 percent of the total US farmland, yet producing 8 percent of the nation's agricultural output. Eighty-five percent of Fresno State students come from the Central Valley (mainly Fresno, Madera, Kings, and Tulare Counties), 70 percent are first-generation students, and 80 percent of graduates remain in the Central Valley. With an emphasis on education for the future leaders of the Central Valley, Fresno State has three distinct values—discovery, distinction, and diversity—that underscore a bold agenda of service, strengthening the Central Valley's economy and expanding employment opportunities for Fresno State graduates. The motto Learning by Serving is a core value in the Central Valley. Fresno State is a Hispanic-serving institution (HSI) and an Asian American and Native American Pacific Islander-Serving Institution (AANAPISI), with 89 percent of full-time undergraduates receiving some type of need-based aid.

Fresno State's Henry Madden Library underwent a $105 million renovation in 2009 with a generous gift of $10 million from the Table Mountain Rancheria that allowed completion of the renovation. Consequently, there is a very close relationship with the tribe, and the gift celebrates the Native American cultures prominent in the Central Valley; the architects worked closely with the local tribes and integrated traditional Native American patterns into the exterior and interior design of the building itself.

Fresno State's president, Saúl Jiménez-Sandoval, stated that "The Henry Madden Library is where knowledge, technology, ideas, belonging and becoming converge"[10] (August 2021), and the library is the largest and most central knowledge center and archival resource in the Central Valley. It is a substantial community resource for preservice teachers, current educators, and small businesses. The library has two internationally recognized centers housed in the library: the Arne Nixon Center for the Study of Literature and the Teacher Resource Center, which is a critical educational resource aligned with the Kremen School of Education for teacher candidates, preservice professionals, and Central Valley educators. The Henry Madden Library is an established home away from home for most Fresno State students; many students have long commutes to campus, and for others, the library is a quiet study space not available at home. Thus, the initial CSU system-wide COVID-19 lockdown in March 2020 had a severe impact on students' access to technology, campus resources, and study spaces. As a result, campus administration faced considerable pushback from parents, the local community, regional partners, and donors when the campus was shut down. As a result later that same month, the Henry Madden Library distinguished itself by becoming the sole library in the CSU system to reopen its doors during the pandemic and offer services, starting with curbside delivery of library material, followed by staff and administrators working in the building daily and providing services, with safety procedures in place.

Bolman and Deal's political frame surfaced prominently in the decision-making process.[11] Fresno, like many communities in the Central Valley, is very conservative, and the rate of COVID-19 infection and hospitalization was very high, keeping the entire region in the purple tier (more than seven daily new cases per 100,000 people and a more than 8 percent positivity rate). The disruption in services and the closing of businesses in Fresno were very controversial actions; many in the community denied the truth of the pandemic and the need to wear masks as a preventive measure. Campus administration faced the challenge of balancing messaging, planning and safety, and public health—listening to the concerns of an active conservative donor and community base while juggling the pressures of maintaining the teaching and learning functionality as faculty and students adjusted to an abrupt classroom change and a new teaching modality. The library remained open for staff, with faculty and students allowed to enter by appointment to receive checked-out materials.

Aligning with the structural frame, library leadership focused its efforts on developing a contingency plan that included detailed internal procedures for staff safety and security, for rearrangement of the physical space to enforce social distancing, and for considerable investment in staff training around safety awareness and protocols. The contingency plan was based on the following:

- self-service lockers
- an e-reserves platform
- curricular materials
- hiring of student assistant staff

This plan evolved as the library remained operational throughout the pandemic.

There was a clear awareness that the pandemic would propel the library forward in terms of service delivery. With the campus transition to online instruction, the library was faced with a sudden demand for virtual resources from faculty and, like many other CSU libraries, applied for CARES Act funding to purchase these resources. Providing affordable resources to students is a campus priority that aligns with the CSU system-wide Affordable Learning Solutions Initiative, which promotes low-cost or no-cost open educational resources to enable student success. Consequently, library leadership also accelerated its efforts to enhance students' educational experiences by expanding equitable access to free or affordable resources. Overall, the mobilization of these measures reflected library leadership's use of the structural frame to concentrate materials and focused energy on addressing logistical and operational needs.

The emotional toll on library faculty and staff who were required to work throughout the pandemic was significant and lingers to this day. Adding to this stress, 2020 was a year of tremendous civil and political unrest and a marked global awareness of social justice issues. Library administration relied on significant support from library deans and associate deans throughout the CSU to navigate mental well-being activities for support staff, crisis leadership strategies, external campus resources requests, and moral support during such an uncertain time. Consequently, library administrators prioritized the human resource frame, working closely with the employee engagement team and the library diversity committee to establish monthly virtual brown bag events, virtual fun activities to keep staff engaged and connected, and a meeting-free Tuesday afternoon to give everyone a break from Zoom meetings. Overall, the Henry Madden Library team rose to the challenge, embracing an agile management approach while facing the most challenging year in its history. The Henry Madden Library balanced the concerns of the surrounding community while making its services and resources accessible to students and faculty.

The Cal Poly Experience

California Polytechnic State University (Cal Poly) is situated on California's scenic central coast, in San Luis Obispo, roughly halfway between San Francisco and Los Angeles. The university's motto is Learn by Doing, reflecting a pedagogical focus on project-based curriculum. Cal Poly is considered to be the only predominantly white institution within the CSU. Based on fall 2020 data, 54 percent of the undergraduate population is white and only 10 percent of Cal Poly undergraduates identify as first-generation.[12] The faculty and staff demographics mirror the student population, with most employees identified as white.[13] Kennedy Library has forty full-time-equivalent employees and is guided by the school's ethos of Learn by Doing; with its studios, collaborative spaces, and specialized instructional programs, the library's space is an extension of the classroom, and its programs are supplemental to the curricular experience.

In early 2020, Kennedy Library was positioned to start a much-anticipated building renovation. An organizational restructuring was also expected, to align with the building transformation. However, March 17, 2020, marked the moment when planning for the future came to a standstill for most of the world: all focus, resources, and energy were diverted to respond to COVID-19. For Kennedy Library, the pandemic brought forward challenges that required a highly unexpected transformational change, more profound than simply adapting to serve a residential campus in an entirely different mode: the library's transformational change was driven by the social and racial justice awakening experienced nationwide in 2020.

In March 2020, when the university switched all courses to virtual modality, the library closed its doors and began transitioning its programs and services online. The uncertain and novel situation that the organization found itself navigating at the onset of the pandemic required that library leaders utilize a structural approach.[14] First, it was important that library leadership understand the university's strategy for continuing its educational mission in the new environment, while also understanding the challenges faced by instructional faculty and students. Restructuring and adapting traditional face-to-face programs to virtual delivery proved to be seamless. Over the past ten years, the library had invested heavily in electronic collections and engaged in sustained efforts to digitize materials from special collections and archives, especially those integrated into the curriculum; it also had online instructional modules developed for the General Education curriculum, which could be quickly modified to specialized upper-level curricula, and the library's participation in a twenty-four-hour chat cooperative service provided a high return on investment and quality service to the campus, particularly at this time. An additional benefit for the library was the university's investment in virtual computing, which had replaced the physical computer labs with virtual computer labs accessible via a web browser to any Cal Poly user from anywhere.

In the early months of the pandemic, small and nimble decision-making teams were formed to respond to the changing conditions; at the onset, this decentralized approach was successful, but later resulted in reduced transparency and limited inclusion of a broader range of stakeholders. It was clear that communication was crucial, and it had to be two-way, not just e-mail updates. Brief but frequent all-staff meetings where questions could be asked and answered, along with a weekly Chat with the Library Dean hour, all conducted via Zoom, helped address the reduced transparency. The structural approach proved effective during the transition and first months of virtual operation. However, the uncertainty of the pandemic's evolution, coupled with burnout, stress and "Zoom fatigue" brought to the forefront the real and critical issue of mental health.[15]

As these issues emerged, the murder of George Floyd on May 25, 2020, reverberated across the nation, and its ripples reached the university and library community. Feelings ranging from disbelief to anger engulfed the library team, and it soon became clear that leading the organization through this new challenge would require a different approach. Ensuring the health and well-being of the organization demanded more than creating structure or reaffirming a vision; it required empathy, care, and attending to people. It required a human resources approach to leadership.[16] At the height of the national movement for social and racial justice and throughout the contentious election process, library leadership focused on three key areas: listening with humility, learning and understanding the issues, and creating safe spaces for the very few underrepresented voices to be heard. Initially, these actions may appear disconnected from the operational and programmatic functions of the library; yet, in fact, they have been integral to the work of organizational transformation. Examples of actions taken by the leadership include acknowledging their own lack of lived experiences with racism; being open and listening to the critical voices while being ready to change plans; promoting and actively participating in diversity, equity, and inclusion (DEI) training; initiating a DEI audit, followed by an action plan based on the audit; and encouraging and supporting community spaces for safe discussions about whiteness in libraries and librarianship. When weathering a crisis requires a shift in the organizational culture, activating the Three Ps of Change—patience, persistence, and process—is crucial.[17] Patience is needed to bring the entire organization along; persistence is required when negotiating with stakeholders to gain buy-in and support for the change sought; and process is key in outlining the path to be taken to reach the end goal. For Kennedy Library, the end goal was to withstand the COVID-19 crisis while planning for the future and to emerge from it as a more culturally aware and competent organization.

Much of what was learned during the pandemic will be used to improve, innovate, and recalibrate the library's physical space, services, and programs,[18] as envisioned by the building transformation study.[19] However, the work of organizational culture transformation will continue for years, and it demands of this leader "personal courage to *break frame*—to step out of one's comfort zone and away from the crowd in seeking new options, proposing new explanations, or testing alternative responses."[20]

The outcomes may not be immediately evident, but with continued strong leadership commitment, an effective leadership tool kit (crisis and reflective leadership strategies and the four frames adapted by Gallos and Bolman), activation of the Three P's of Change, and an unfailing focus on people, the library will continue to inspire learning and connect people to knowledge, regardless of the crises that may lie ahead.

The Channel Islands Experience

As different California counties enacted mandatory stay-at-home orders during early 2020, CSU Channel Islands began a rapid shutdown of on-campus services. Students returned to their homes, and faculty quickly switched to online instruction. The pandemic exacerbated existing inequities experienced by students, who faced fiscal hardship and life pressures. Channel Islands serves diverse student populations: 83 percent are eligible for financial aid, and 62 percent are the first generation in their families to attend university.[21] The need for equitable access to internet connectivity, computer technology, and course-required software applications quickly became apparent. As a result, organizational staffing and services rapidly shifted and temporary cross-divisional coalitions were mobilized. Shaped by a common sense of purpose while working amid uncertain and evolving external conditions, these newly formed teams provided opportunities for adaptive leadership.

Library personnel became important partners in the university's response to provide critical resources needed for academic continuity, working closely with information technology and student services colleagues. The challenges these team members faced were operational rather than conceptual because they had clarity of mission and sense of purpose. Their mission aligned with well-established ethical underpinnings of academic libraries. The American Library Association calls upon libraries to provide services with "equitable service policies [and] equitable access" noting that equity "extends beyond equality—fairness and universal access—to deliberate and intentional efforts to create service delivery models that will make sure that community members have the resources they need."[22] However, at the same time, libraries share a firm commitment to the right to privacy and protection of confidentiality,[23] which required careful consideration as the team began to establish procedures to identify students in greatest need of support. While libraries have a strong and lasting commitment to equitable access, the library model of delivery rarely translates to one that offers services based on individualized patron circumstances, as was being called for in this unique situation. The circulation of key technology resources (primarily hot spots and laptops) could not easily be limited to any specific student population, nor could the library personnel look up circulation records of past users of laptops to identify students with tech-equity vulnerabilities. How could the library provide targeted services to historically underrepresented groups with the greatest need for equitable access without compromising privacy and service delivery models not designed to address this unique circumstance?

Reframing this challenge through the Bolman and Deal frames-based organizational model offered the ability to address the complexities of the situation from different perspectives of leadership.[24] The structural frame encouraged discussions about the operational aspects at hand, with focus on strategy formation, task completion, and the creation of processes to complete the team's objectives. The human resource frame placed emphasis on the significant contribution of each individual as a key element to organizational success, recognizing the specific work knowledge of each team member and the importance of individual empowerment. The political frame lent support to emphasizing the value of building a strong coalition and acknowledging the presence of divergent perspectives. For example, some political tensions existed since some members who provide individualized student service programs based on personal data points hoped to use the library to identify and deploy these selective need-based services. This was juxtaposed against library members who work in a context that purposely does not gather student personal data or shape services along individualized models in order to uphold commitments to student privacy. Recognizing these divergent perspectives from the political frame opened a way to approach this through a structural lens, which invited the coalition to be solutions-oriented and work together toward creative resolution. Viewing this from the human resources frame provided added support for recognizing and valuing the skills and perspectives each member brought to the conversation.

Gallos and Bolman note that the "architecture of disconnection in higher education" makes it difficult to manage change.[25] Fortunately, in this circumstance, team members operated in lateral team coordination, where representatives from each division worked as equal partners seeking to achieve well-defined common goals. The value of each member's role and contribution was clearly recognized. The information technology team members facilitated the daunting task of gathering and reimaging large numbers of classroom laptops for long-term circulation and facilitated new contractual negotiations with telecom vendors for hot spots and data plans. The student services team members contributed funding to support some of the new internet hot spot services and took responsibility for identifying and working directly with those students facing the greatest hardships and in significant need of immediate assistance. The library partners quickly mobilized staff and services to deploy these resources and carried the full weight of equipment distribution. They reconfigured the library's unified library management system to ingest all the laptops pulled from campus classrooms, configured and ingested the new Wi-Fi hot spots, and developed a workflow to circulate these resources by mail or through a new contactless locker delivery system. Each team member was empowered to communicate the boundaries of what could be accomplished through their operational framework. Through high-functioning effective team practices, including robust question asking, listening, and compromise, the group devised strategies that ensured success.[26]

This historic time called for extraordinary organizational and personal resilience. By creating a coalition with an adaptive structure that recognized the value of lateral coordination among equally empowered members, the participants were able to focus on the mission at hand. The group benefited from shared rather than hierarchical leadership, emphasis on common goals, open communication that publicly tested assumptions, and a willingness to discuss positions and perspectives not previously shared due to organizational silos—all components of group dynamics noted by Gallos and Bolman as indicators of organizational effectiveness.[27] These factors added to the active listening and learning practiced by the equally invested members of the group and fostered a healthy focus on positive discussions and successful outcomes. By working out of the normal silos, the library and all of its partners were able to meet the needs of the dispersed students for equitable access to resources, while also accomplishing the library's core mission.

Competencies for Future Academic Library Leaders

The unprecedented situations reflected in these four narratives, while historic in nature, foreshadow the future uncertainties that library leaders will likely navigate for the foreseeable future as they serve in a rapidly changing and highly disruptive global environment.

Developing the capabilities to effectively lead through ambiguous and evolving situations calls for active reflection and continuous situational and personal awareness. Leadership competencies that foster compassionate understanding, invite open communication, and place high value on gathering multiple perspectives will establish an operating framework for effective action. Practicing an adaptive leadership style that recognizes the importance of integrating divergent stakeholder perspectives into rapid decision-making will be critical for effective operation in highly complex situations.

The volatile and unpredictable challenges brought about by the pandemic created stressful operating environments that exacted an emotional toll on library personnel and required leaders to acknowledge and manage conflict. Being ready for resistance and developing the ability to lean into conflict as an opportunity to solve problems and embrace change is a key competency for leadership navigation of uncertainty. Leaning into conflict invites library leaders to approach workplace discord as an indication of differences of perspective. Developing competencies to fully assess the situation by reaching out to all involved and listening closely to the elements of the conflict allows library leaders to expose blind spots and previously hidden barriers. Recognizing and acknowledging all factors at play helps to move those involved toward common ground and creates a framework for shifting to solutions-oriented thinking. Providing opportunities for dialogue so that all stakeholders understand that their voices are valued and heard is an important component to building empowered teams that are capable of effective and strategic performance. Additionally, library leaders need to encourage and foster organizational teams and networks that clearly reflect core values of inclusivity and are living models of social integration and transparency. The library leaders in these narratives drew upon established and emerging management theories to bolster their ability to lead in times of crisis. Formal and information meetings with fellow library deans increased during the pandemic as colleagues shared emerging situations and offered reflections and strategies in response that often drew upon management frameworks that were newly applied to these unprecedented circumstances. The ability to quickly assess evolving situations and to engage with the broader contextual challenges of organizational culture requires library leaders of the future to be multifaceted in approach and perspective. Having the capacity to address rapid change by integrating known management skills with newly acquired adaptive leadership practices will be a core competency for leadership success in fast-changing environments. The pandemic was a call to leadership that invited resilience, empathy, and compassion. Realizing that encounters with crisis situations will be common for the foreseeable future, academic library leaders will need to reckon with and adjust to this new reality. Times of crisis reveal individual and collective character. How leaders view these experiences will determine the strength of their effectiveness in the certainty of rising to and leading through the challenges ahead.

Notes

1. John C. Maxwell, "Leading through Crisis: A Virtual Leadership Summit with John C. Maxwell (Day 1)," recorded March 22, 2020, YouTube video, 1:27:05, https://www.youtube.com/watch?v=H7MGO6C5r18.

2. Maxwell, "Leading through Crisis."
3. Castelli, "Reflective Leadership Review." P.217
4. Bolman and Deal, Reframing Organizations, XXX–XXX.
5. Florence C. Lee et al., "Counties with High COVID-19 Incidence and Relatively Large Racial and Ethnic Minority Populations—United States, April 1–December 22, 2020," Morbidity and Mortality Weekly Report 70, no. 13 (April 2, 2021): 483–89, https://doi.org/10.15585/mmwr.mm7013e1; Don Bambino Geno Tai et al., "The Disproportionate Impact of COVID-19 on Racial and Ethnic Minorities in the United States," Clinical Infectious Diseases 72, no. 4 (February 2021): 703–6, https://doi.org/10.1093/cid/ciaa815.
6. Bolman and Deal, Reframing Organizations.
7. Gallos and Bolman, Reframing Academic Leadership, 106.
8. Thomas A. Parham, "CSUDH Budget Update," University Statements, California State University, Dominguez Hills, July 21, 2020, https://www.csudh.edu/together/university-statements/.
9. Leading Through Crisis – Lesson 1. Maxwell says this quote is at 46:34 on the video. Recorded April 9th 2020. https://www.youtube.com/watch?v=8gqelNJgI8A
10. Anderson, N. "Fresno State's library named for a man who expressed 'clear antisemitic hate' and Nazi sympathies, university says" Washington Post. Nov. 30, 2021
11. Bolman and Deal, Reframing Organizations.
12. California Polytechnic State University, "2020 Student Enrollment Profiles," Institutional Research, accessed October 8, 2021, https://ir.calpoly.edu/2020-enrollment-profile.
13. California Polytechnic State University, "2020 Employee Profiles," Institutional Research, accessed October 8, 2021, https://ir.calpoly.edu/2020-employee-profile.
14. Gallos and Bolman, Reframing Academic Leadership.
15. World Health Organization, The Impact of COVID-19 on Mental, Neurological and Substance Use Services (Geneva, Switzerland: World Health Organization, 2020), https://apps.who.int/iris/handle/10665/335838.
16. Gallos and Bolman, Reframing Academic Leadership, 106.
17. Gallos and Bolman, Reframing Academic Leadership, 72.
18. Kate Ganim, Sofia Melian-Morse, and Kelly Sanford, "Beyond 'Welcoming and Inclusive': Designing Anti-racist Experiences," Brightspot Strategy (blog), December 15, 2020, https://www.brightspotstrategy.com/design-anti-racist-experiences/.
19. California Polytechnic State University, "Kennedy Library Renovation," Facilities Management and Development, accessed ,January 15, 2023 https://afd.calpoly.edu/facilities/planning-capital-projects/project-news/kennedy-library/.
20. Gallos and Bolman, Reframing Academic Leadership, 32.
21. California State University, Channel Islands, The Undergraduate Viewbook 2021 (Camarillo: California State University, Channel Islands, August 24, 2021), posted on Issuu, https://issuu.com/csu-channel-islands/docs/viewbook_2021_final_issuu2/1.
22. American Library Association, "Access to Library Resources and Services," October 23, 2015, https://www.ala.org/advocacy/intfreedom/access.
23. American Library Association, "Professional Ethics," May 19, 2017, https://www.ala.org/tools/ethics.
24. Bolman and Deal, Reframing Organizations.
25. Gallos and Bolman, Reframing Academic Leadership, 67.
26. Thomas R. Harvey and Bonita Drolet, Building Teams, Building People, 2nd ed. (Lanham, MD: Rowman & Littlefield Education, 2005).
27. Gallos and Bolman, Reframing Academic Leadership.

Bibliography

American Library Association. "Access to Library Resources and Services." October 23, 2015. https://www.ala.org/advocacy/intfreedom/access.

———. "Professional Ethics." May 19, 2017. https://www.ala.org/tools/ethics.

Bolman, Lee G., and Terrence E. Deal. Reframing Organizations: Artistry, Choice, and Leadership, 5th ed. San Francisco: Jossey-Bass, 2013.

Chapter 6

California Polytechnic State University. "Kennedy Library Renovation." Facilities Management and Development. Accessed January 15, 2023 . https://afd.calpoly.edu/facilities/planning-capital-projects/project-news/kennedy-library/ .

———. "2020 Employee Profiles." Institutional Research. Accessed October 8, 2021. https://ir.calpoly.edu/2020-employee-profile.

———. "2020 Student Enrollment Profiles." Institutional Research. Accessed October 8, 2021. https://ir.calpoly.edu/2020-enrollment-profile.

California State University, Channel Islands. *The Undergraduate Viewbook 2021*. Camarillo: California State University, Channel Islands, August 24, 2021. Posted on Issuu. https://issuu.com/csu-channel-islands/docs/viewbook_2021_final_issuu2/1.

Castelli, Patricia Ann. "Reflective Leadership Review: A Framework for Improving Organisational Performance." *Journal of Management Development* 35, no. 2 (2016): 271–36. https://doi.org/10.1108/JMD-08-2015-0112.

Gallos, Joan V., and Lee G. Bolman. *Reframing Academic Leadership*, 2nd ed. San Francisco: Jossey-Bass, 2021.

Ganim, Kate, Sofia Melian-Morse, and Kelly Sanford. "Beyond 'Welcoming and Inclusive': Designing Anti-racist Experiences." *Brightspot Strategy* (blog), December 15, 2020. https://www.brightspotstrategy.com/design-anti-racist-experiences/.

Harvey, Thomas R., and Bonita Drolet. *Building Teams, Building People: Expanding the Fifth Resource*, 2nd ed. (Lanham, MD: Rowman & Littlefield Education, 2005).

Lee, Florence C., Laura Adams, Sierra J. Graves, Greta M. Massetti, Renee M. Calanan, Ana Penman-Aguilar, S. Jane Henley, et al. "Counties with High COVID-19 Incidence and Relatively Large Racial and Ethnic Minority Populations—United States, April 1–December 22, 2020." *Morbidity and Mortality Weekly Report* 70, no. 13 (April 2, 2021): 483–89, https://doi.org/10.15585/mmwr.mm7013e1.

Maxwell, John C. "Leading through Crisis: A Virtual Leadership Summit with John C. Maxwell (Day 1)," Recorded March 22, 2020. YouTube video, 1:27:05. https://www.youtube.com/watch?v=H7MGO6C5r18.

Parham, Thomas A. "CSUDH Budget Update." University Statements, California State University, Dominguez Hills, July 21, 2020. https://www.csudh.edu/together/university-statements/.

Tai, Don Bambino Geno, Aditya Shah, Chyke A. Doubeni, Irene G. Sia, and Mark L. Wieland. "The Disproportionate Impact of COVID-19 on Racial and Ethnic Minorities in the United States." *Clinical Infectious Diseases* 72, no. 4 (February 2021): 703–6, https://doi.org/10.1093/cid/ciaa815.

World Health Organization. *The Impact of COVID-19 on Mental, Neurological and Substance Use Services: Results of a Rapid Assessment*. Geneva, Switzerland: World Health Organization, 2020. https://apps.who.int/iris/handle/10665/335838.

CHAPTER 7

Solidarity in Isolation

Shared Pandemic Experiences of Medical and Academic Middle Manager Librarians

Laureen P. Cantwell-Jurkovic, John Mokonyama, Christine F. Smith, Christina Prucha, and Marlowe Bogino

> *While not at all an easy time to start and develop as managers and leaders, the pandemic did in fact prove to be a training ground for leadership in many ways. This was a lesson in tenacity.*

Introduction

Transitioning to a leadership role can be difficult in the best of times. Internal or external turmoil increases the difficulty of the transition. With more time on the job, and more experience as well as stronger relationships with stakeholders, the means to confront and respond to a crisis are clearer. However, these tools are not available to all entering leadership roles. This chapter takes a, perhaps, unusual approach by having librarians reflectively interview themselves; the five librarians authoring this chapter are in leadership and middle management roles, and most had been hired or promoted to that role not long before the COVID-19 pandemic. The structure of the chapter is in two sections: First, two librarian-authors in library director–type roles at hospital libraries reflect on the pandemic's effects on their role and work (both positive and negative), on communication, and on

73

operations at their libraries; then three librarian-authors placed in middle management roles shortly before the pandemic reflect using a questionnaire posed to middle managers in the nursing field with regard to the COVID-19 pandemic as outlined in a 2021 study.[1] This structure allowed the authors to respond to the same queries and concepts. The chapter discusses the similarities and themes in varied experiences while confronting aspects of uniqueness in each circumstance. While these experiences are a small sampling of a larger population, they present a lens into library leadership during an unprecedented, exhausting, and change-intensive time.

Hospital Library Leadership during COVID-19: Two Leaders Share Their Experiences

When considering the concept of library management during a crisis, solo librarianship within a medical or hospital library presents a unique opportunity for reflection, analysis, and discussion. Within this section, two medical library leaders document their experiences, one a medical librarian at a community hospital and the other a librarian director at a leadership institute and hospital library. Both librarians began in their roles relatively recently: the former in 2016, and the latter in the summer of 2019. They both reflected on their library's functions, priorities, and operations during the COVID-19 pandemic and the overall effects that COVID-19 had on their work.

Overview of the Libraries and Staffing

Penn Medicine, Chester County Hospital, is Mokonyama's 129-year-old community hospital library that serves the biomedical and health-care research needs of physicians, nurses, students, and the community in the region. Since 2016, Mokonyama has been the sole medical librarian at the hospital, and he has assistance from one part-time volunteer. In addition to performing his daily tasks and library management at the hospital, he provides services to patrons in the hospital, collaborates with about twenty other librarians in the health-care system, and represents the library on numerous hospital and system committees. The other librarian-author, Bogino, a hospital library director who started her position in summer 2019, has a small staff—two full-time assistants and a part-time reference librarian in addition to her own director role—and three locations to serve. When Bogino accepted her role as director of the library just a little over two years ago, she too had set out in her mind a plan for getting to know the library, the organization, and the staff; for fine-tuning the library resources and offerings; and then for expanding out to internal and external neighbors to try to establish the medical library as a health information resource for the medical professionals and also the local community. Little did she know that, on top of trying to accomplish these goals, she would encounter a worldwide pandemic that would change everything. Everything from the resources her library had to offer to the way her team worked together and their library patrons would need to be examined and changed. Reflecting on the question "In what ways did the pandemic change how I thought I would be working as a new manager?" provided her with the opportunity for retrospection.

Leading with Compassion and Empathy

During her first year as a manager, Bogino looked for guidance for her new role as a manager director and discovered James Downton's idea of transformational leadership, which notes that the transformational leader can inspire others by their vision or personal mission.[2] This idea of a mission-led leader was enlightening for Bogino, and it provided the guidance she needed to help her lead her library and staff because it allowed her to use her personal mission statement to guide the work of her team and what they tried to accomplish.[3] For Bogino, within libraries, she had learned that her mission was to support others with the information within the library. The way she knew to best support others—including her staff, their patrons, and their partners and stakeholders—was with communication, accountability, and compassion. With the onset of the pandemic, she was able to see the vision of her personal mission come to fruition. Though the pandemic brought about change quickly for the entire world, it also helped establish the refinement of Bogino's personal mission as she encountered the varied and widespread changes caused by the pandemic.

During the pandemic, Mokonyama's library continued to provide research services to health-care practitioners and hospital management as well as providing health information to the public. Mokonyama in particular helped health-care professionals with locating current COVID-19–related research in line with each professional's specialty. The library saw an increase of about 20 percent in the number of reference questions asked by patrons. The difficulty level of the searches ranged from medium to complex. Many of the more complex, COVID-19–related questions were made more complex simply by the lack of readily available information about the virus itself. COVID-19 questions were also complex due to the rapid speed with which information was changing as additional COVID-19–related information emerged in various medical fields. In addition, some of the library patrons from minority groups (e.g., African American, Hispanic, etc.) were more interested in COVID-19 information as it specifically related to their ethnic and racial groups. Such information was not broadly available at that time. Overall, Mokonyama's patrons' common COVID-19 searches were focused on diagnosis, treatment, infection control, PPE (personal protective equipment), testing, vaccines, adverse effects and safety, and transmission. Providing responsive and supportive reference services can be essential during and immediately following a crisis—whether the crisis is environmental, such as a hurricane, or natural, such as a pandemic. Information that is relevant and accurate is paramount at such a time when individuals in crisis need to support each other.[4]

Indeed, taking center stage in Bogino's personal mission of supporting others through library information and resources was the idea that it must be done with compassion and empathy for others. During COVID-19, the need to acknowledge that we all are human and require a little grace and compassion was made even more evident.

The pandemic experience brought about continued exposure to trauma for everyone.[5] The need for the library as a workplace to also be a psychologically safe place for employees was crucial to maintaining a sense that all was going to be OK as they worked together through the pandemic. Kahn introduced the idea of psychological safety in 1990 and defined it as the act of allowing a person to feel safe in expressing themselves and to be themselves without a fear of punishment or retaliation.[6] The library could play a crucial role in providing supportive resources for employees, while also providing instruction and research support for its patrons and organizational support for its own employees. Bogino's library worked to create this type of environment for the library team on a weekly basis with the support and wellness training provided by hospital administration. Building this trusting environment involved Bogino conveying to the team that they, at any time, could come to her to ask questions, express their concerns about work, or even discuss the current environment the world was experiencing.

Mokonyama noted that challenging questions arose at his library, including ones about the efficacy, efficiency, and side effects of the vaccine, especially regarding pregnancy and fertility. In addition to doing research as a regular job for the hospital community, he found research questions to be personal because five of his colleagues had contracted COVID-19 while treating patients. He had two pregnant coworkers who were in search of credible information, and three of his friends had lost the battle with COVID-19. The biggest challenge was to sift through a spectrum of opinions and circulating misinformation about COVID-19. It was important for him to provide information that would not hurt the user. The biggest challenge was knowing what the evidence was behind the information being provided. Another challenge involved determining how the information might be helpful to the user's well-being and decision-making process. Mokonyama wanted to provide the best available information to help users and for the administration to use the information for making good decisions.

During the pandemic, Mokonyama's library experienced a 15 to 20 percent increase in the number of patrons who requested searches on stress, mental health, physical fitness, and self-care. He reasoned that perhaps many of the patrons were feeling the stress and fatigue caused by living through a pandemic. Health-care professionals specifically may have unmet information needs concerning their own self-care; it is necessary to be more proactive in providing information resources to this population.[7] Prior to the pandemic outbreak, Mokonyama completed a workshop at the hospital entitled Verbal Judo. In this workshop, he learned about self-care methods, mental health assessment, and applying Verbal Judo to influence others to come around to your way of thinking. He perceived a need for a light community-engagement event, and so he started a pleasure reading library book club, with Jodi Picoult's novel *Plain Truth* as the first selection. Initially, he expected to enroll twelve to fifteen book club members. Surprisingly, over 100 employee-patrons had joined by the third day of book club enrollment and the library needed to pause sign-ups. Fortunately, Mokonyama was able to modify the format of the book club to accommodate all patrons enrolled. To make the book club run smoothly, he recruited five other hospital staff members (a nursing informatics specialist, a physical therapist, the chief financial officer, a quality analyst, and the manager of interpreter services) to help with the book club facilitation. Based on patrons' input and discussions in the book club meetings, Mokonyama communicated with the department of human resources about the potential need for self-help training and workshops. Within a short time, human resources planned workshops and sessions on various topics that related to self-care, and they were all well attended.

Transitioning to Off-Site

Due to the lockdown, many of Mokonyama's university partner libraries were closed and not offering document delivery services. Other libraries scaled down their document exchange services. Library service changes slowed borrowing and the efficiency of information-sharing processes. The changes were fueled by different factors such as staffing, concerns about the spread of the virus, and uncertainty as to whether the shared physical resources had been disinfected or sanitized properly. Mokonyama's health care library at Penn Medicine, Chester County Hospital, also restricted materials that could be loaned out to other libraries. Only requests for periodical articles were processed; no books were allowed to be circulated from the middle of March 2020, and the policy is still in effect.

Beyond materials, practices also needed to change to accommodate the pandemic; Bogino's staff relied on open and clear communication to maintain the same level of services and accessibility for their patrons throughout the pandemic, as well as to maintain a bond between coworkers. The medium-size hospital library currently has three branches, two that support the clinical staff and one consumer health library to support patients and the larger community. Maintaining adequate coverage at each of these sites became instantly difficult with the onset of the pandemic, given the strict closures and restrictions on access to the physical campus. Staff worked through varied remote schedules ranging from completely off-site to a combination of on-site and remote. The latter involved rotating among each of the locations to ensure coverage. Throughout all this change, their daily e-mail and telephone call checks-ins and weekly team video calls helped them maintain their level of service to their patrons and to ensure accessibility. These communication efforts also helped Bogino and her staff maintain a sense of teamwork and commitment to the library patrons and to each other, increasing their flexibility for scheduling coverage of the library sites and handling the various library tasks. Bogino was proud of the team's all-hands-on-deck approach to managing and accomplishing the daily library tasks.

For Mokonyama, the library stayed open on a regular schedule (Monday through Friday, 8:00 a.m. to 4:30 p.m.), and he shifted from in-person work to a hybrid remote-and-in-person work model. A library volunteer came to work in the building on the two weekdays Mokonyama worked remotely. During the pandemic, the library continued to receive literature search requests via regular methods (e-mail, phone, walk-in, and the literature request form). Since the beginning of the COVID-19 pandemic, the library has opened a Zoom account. In addition to the regular methods mentioned, the library's Microsoft Teams and Zoom accounts have allowed it to conduct virtual meetings, reference service, and patron literature search consultations.

Bogino too used virtual meeting platforms such as Microsoft Teams and Zoom to maintain a sense of team for herself and her library team members. The physical access point of her office door turned into virtual access points via weekly Teams meetings and daily e-mails to keep communication flowing as if they all still occupied the same working space. This helped maintain positive morale for the team, which faced, like everyone in the world, days of uncertainty about health and security. As would be expected within a hospital, the work never stopped, though Bogino and her staff members had commenced working off-site. Introduction of the virtual tools mentioned ensured their patrons would continue to have the ready presence of a library staff member even if that person could not be there physically. With these tools, their reference and library instruction, research assistance, and interlibrary loan services continued allowing the library team to provide seamless support even from a distance.

Mokonyama's library was fortunate to have off-campus library access to research resources prior to the pandemic. Before 2020, the library had been providing online services that included article, book, and media content as well as e-mail and chat reference. The remotely accessible resources were essential in keeping the library connected to its patrons. Patrons were given access to temporarily free and open electronic resources as well to links to subscribed e-books. During COVID-19, health issues became one of the key concerns that Mokonyama considered regarding patrons; library safety upkeep was important to protect library patrons and staff. This became a concern because the library was potentially more vulnerable than before the pandemic to contamination from resource exchange and high foot traffic. To address the health issue, Mokonyama regularly disinfected high-volume library space; furniture and books were quarantined upon return before items could be checked out to the next user. He focused on infection prevention by following the CDC guidelines of handwashing, mask wearing, and using sanitizers and disinfectants. The library was able to open for in-person assistance five days per week (Monday through Friday).

The pandemic taught Mokonyama three things about library workflows and working off-site. Prior to the pandemic, the public view was that library work can be completed most efficiently and effectively inside a library's physical confines, such as the building. He learned, to the contrary, that work can be just as efficiently carried out remotely. Second, he discovered that it is easy to do both short-term and long-term projects when working remotely, prior to this time it was a challenge to focus on long-term projects—short-term daily activities and service fulfilment efforts were too time-consuming or distracting. Being on-site actually often makes it harder to switch tasks around on one's list of short- and long-term projects due to the nature of in-person work. One is more frequently interrupted when on-site; other priorities may take precedence over what one had in mind for the day. When working on-site, Mokonyama's practices had been to focus mostly on short-term, day-to-day operations and patron requests. Longer-term projects and planning were frequently shifted to the back burner, or they became summer projects. When he was working off-site, it became apparent that he could spend the time and attention needed for concentrated planning and focus for long-term projects. It was easier to focus on long-term projects because there were fewer interruptions and unexpected visits, and he could closely follow the daily checklist. Finally, the pandemic taught Mokonyama to be open to trying new things. For example, using Zoom for consultations proved to be helpful to patrons *and* to Monkonyama himself. While Mokonyama believes that on-site work is optimal for relationships and in-person support and that it will continue to thrive, he is also convinced about the need to be more flexible in one's schedule and that working virtually as an individual and with colleagues and patrons may be needed at different times and under different conditions, not just as a reaction to a pandemic.

Setting Up Expectations and Accountability

As part of working through her personal mission of supporting others with the information within the library, Bogino knew accountability for her actions would be paramount as she worked to set an example for the team members she led (and continues to lead). With COVID-19 invading the way everyone now had to work, the idea of accountability had spread to the way Bogino had to manage her team, the library budget for which she is responsible, and the way library instruction sessions were provided, shared, and taught.

With the normal workflow occurring completely off-site, it was imperative to create a flexible schedule that met everyone's working restrictions while also maintaining access to library services and resources for patrons. This required effectively communicating the organization's work ethic standards for working remotely and enforcing them, which proved to be a challenge. At the start of the pandemic, the library quickly pivoted to a completely remote schedule for support staff. This move required the creation of additional workflow process checks—such as listing the individual tasks each staff member could perform in a virtual environment—to ensure that the remote working schedule could be justified. This quick move to remote working also required Bogino to introduce special longer-term library work projects, such as electronic resource link checking and cataloging tasks that could be performed in the library service platform.

Bogino's original thought, when taking on the manager's role, was that she would have an opportunity to focus on learning about the resources the library had to offer. The pandemic changed this focus completely. With the costs associated with remaining open and serving the community increasing at the hospital because of the pandemic, nonessential or less essential budget items were eliminated. This caused Bogino to look closely at what could be maintained within the library offerings while also working with a smaller budget.

The expectation within a teaching hospital is that patients continue to receive care and care providers continue to learn how to best provide it. With thirty resident and fellowship programs, and visiting undergraduate nursing program students rotating through the hospital, the library is a busy place and is an integral part of supporting the educational programs. The library instruction sessions staff conduct—teaching about the library resources and how to use them—had to make a quick pivot from regularly scheduled, in-person classroom trainings to online, whenever-needed sessions to accommodate the changing patterns in which the students and residents would arrive back on the hospital campus during the pandemic. The undergraduate nursing students were not permitted on campus during height of the pandemic, and the medical residents, though on campus, had limited availability in their schedules for library instruction; all of this was dictated by the changing rules of engagement for addressing the pandemic. This was a lesson in tenacity for the small staff of research librarians, who also juggled an on-site/off-site remote working schedule.

While Mokonyama and Bogino addressed pandemic-induced challenges and changes to their library workflows, processes, and leadership styles, the academic librarians in the next section discuss how the pandemic impacted them. As middle managers, these academic librarians were faced with their own, often similar, issues, opportunities, and leadership development hurdles, yet, in their roles as recently promoted or hired individuals, they also have unique shared experiences.

Academic Library Leadership during the Pandemic: Shared Middle Manager Experiences

Academic librarians and their libraries were also certainly impacted by the COVID-19 pandemic in similar ways to their medical library colleagues. This section of the chapter strives to address the question "How does a manager learn to lead a new group, from the middle, during a pandemic situation?" by highlighting the experiences of three librarians in academic settings. All three librarians entered middle-management roles in North American academic libraries. For two of these librarians, the leadership role was a promotion within an organization where they had already been working; for the third, the adjustment involved a relocation and a position at an entirely new institution. Cantwell-Jurkovic was promoted from reference and distance services librarian, a nonsupervisory role, to head of access services and outreach, supervising four classified staff, at a regional university located in western Colorado in fall 2019. Smith was promoted from a limited-term appointment to a tenure-track unit head position within the collection services department of an urban Canadian university in early 2020. Prucha left a job as a director at a small Midwestern two-year college in fall 2019 to assume the position of head of collection services at a small four-year liberal arts university in the Pacific Northwest. This portion of the chapter provides a synthesis of their responses. (A complete listing of the nineteen questions to which they responded can be found in the appendix.)

After finding a journal article exploring nurses in middle-management roles in Switzerland during the COVID-19 pandemic, the authors decided to approach this section by using the questions of that survey as reflective inspiration.[8] Each person independently answered the questions, and the responses were then analyzed to identify common traits. This exercise led to the emergence of several themes, including challenges, pivots, opportunities, and realities. The themes, while rooted in a specific situation, will resonate with the reader in whatever role they currently have or aspire to in academic libraries.

Challenges

It is perhaps easiest to first approach what it was like for recently hired and recently promoted academic librarians to learn to lead from the middle during COVID-19 from the challenges they faced. One important challenge throughout their peak pandemic experience was the difficulty they faced in learning their jobs. As middle managers, all three found themselves in meetings related to organizational planning, some of which were within the typical scope of their job and others of which were solely due to COVID-19's arrival. The plans discussed at these meetings were also impacted by the pandemic, as seen in difficulties with budgets and forecasting. Furthermore, pre-pandemic concerns like the reality that students may be dealing with housing, financial, and food security issues did not vanish. Instead, they had to coexist with social distancing, sanitizing, occupancy limitations, decreased and canceled programming, staffing shortages, furloughs, retirements, stress, and more. Each author had a difficult time expressing what had changed about their jobs, in part because everything about their positions changed radically shortly after they arrived, but also because the changes just kept happening. Campus, local, and federal guidelines, employment and unemployment options: all of it changed as a result of the pandemic and kept changing as the pandemic went on.

The three middle managers faced other challenges when learning their new roles. They struggled to develop a sense of routine, which affected productivity, focus, feelings of belonging, and change uptake. In addition to difficulties setting and maintaining routines, librarians noted feelings of being Jills-of-all-trades[9] and task derailment, prioritizing the needs of others ahead of themselves, the need to upskill and cross-train, and very much the understanding that their roles were not limited to standard workweek hours. Most of the responsibilities they faced fell into the "other duties as assigned" areas of a job description, and those duties kept evolving as the pandemic progressed. As a result of the additional responsibilities, all three reported a sense of stress related to wanting to learn their new role while also attending to other equally pressing needs. Smith said that it was "evident that the role that existed pre-pandemic was vastly different from what [I] was doing in the early pandemic period." As a result, it took significantly longer for the author-respondents to learn their actual jobs, and they each understood that that adjustment, under more normal circumstances, would have most likely occurred more quickly. A flexible mindset, rather than specific rigid guidelines and protocols, and the value of self-trust, active listening, and addressing and accepting stress, represented the skill set needed for success as newly minted middle managers during a crisis.[10]

The employment circumstances of staff who reported to the author-respondents were also a concern—shifting to remote hiring processes for any openings they could fill, followed by remote onboarding efforts; campus and library discussions of staff redeployment or furloughs (voluntary or otherwise); positions vacated by retirements during a time of deep financial upheaval in the higher education context; and issues of accountability during work from home (WFH) as well as potential ongoing WFH accommodations. Overall, taking on a new role and responsibilities—and, for one of these librarians, a new organization entirely—while also supporting others within a pandemic situation created a wealth of challenges for these individuals. But the situation also created pivot points: moments that fostered change. Indeed, managing during the COVID-19 pandemic was very much about navigating change.

Within a clearly un-ideal situation, the ability of an organization and the individuals within it to pivot—to shift direction, mentally, behaviorally, emotionally, and functionally—is important to facilitating a strong, productive work environment. For new appointees, like the authors of this section, there have been three (at least) phases to their new positions—pre-pandemic, during peak pandemic/emergent circumstances, and the back-to-campus period. These phases are similar for many workers and created especially distinct pivot points in the job learning curve that these new managers faced during COVID-19. While each had the same job, technically, throughout the pandemic, the shifting realities of responding to the pandemic made the nature of their jobs shift within these phases and underscored the difficulties of learning the actual job.

Prucha's expectation prior to arrival was to perform the work of a long-standing previous department head who had retired and to create new programs and initiatives that would build upon that person's work. However, the pandemic quickly derailed these plans as Prucha soon found herself "covering four other positions in addition to learning [her] own [job]." She wrote:

> Due to a hiring freeze and furloughs, we lost several staff members. My Collections Technology librarian and I covered those positions. We dropped all other goals in favor of one over-arching commitment: We made sure materials became and remained accessible in a timely manner without inconveniencing our users. This meant that learning my job became second to mastering our staff's jobs. It also meant that my priorities constantly shifted or got pushed to the back burner in favor of everyone else's needs.

Similarly, Smith recalled that

> [she had] seen four of the roles in [her] unit vacated by retirements during the pandemic, which ...added more challenges including remote hiring, onboarding, etc. [and that these human resource changes] coupled with the complexities that arose due to the vast changes in Collections [i.e., great increase in more complex e-resource requests] made difficulties multifold.

While there is some evidence to suggest that a silver lining to the pandemic may be the uptick in free or low-cost professional development opportunities,[11] the realities of these managers—trying to develop in a new role, grow skills, and establish themselves—reflect the day-to-day challenges of professionally developing *in their jobs*, while *on the job*.[12]

While retirements, furloughs (voluntary or otherwise), and the like are often strains on and for organizations, for new managers they may prove even more difficult; the priorities of the department, its personalities, and its level of flexibility become so significant that each day holds multiple potential pivot points on which the manager may need to adjust. For Prucha, this flexibility also involved being real: she stated that she is not the kind of boss who puts on a fake and utterly cheerful face for faculty and staff, and

> [that this outlook allowed others to] ...know when [she is] stressed out and working through backlogs of work. That's when [she realizes] how lucky [she is] because they will step up and say, "I don't want to add any more to your plate" and "How can I help you?"

In some ways, this perspective reinforces the importance of remembering supervisors are humans, too; they, like all members of an institution, have goals, priorities, roadblocks, frustrations, energy boosts, and energy drains. But Prucha's statement also notes a way that she allows herself to find opportunities in challenging situations: by allowing those around her to *see* her humanity. The transparency she demonstrates also allows others to step away from their own stressors, if just for a moment, in order to show parts of their humanity in return—their understanding, their empathy, and their acknowledgement.[13] In a similar vein to acknowledging in-the-moment humanity, another mental pivot point uncovered by the authors was that of looking forward. Prucha discussed the fact that

> there are still days when I can't see a light at the end of the tunnel, and I worry that I don't have time to do the professional development and planning that needs to be done. Until the summer of 2021, those days were very frequent. Now, I see pinpoints of light as others are able to do their jobs without so much help, or when I can actually spend two hours with a staff member who needs it.

A typical role of a manager involves being forward-thinking and engaging in planning. However, these newly placed managers found planning very difficult not just because of the pandemic situation, but *also* due to the fact that they were also acclimating to their new positions. The struggle of Prucha and others to see the light ahead speaks to the discouraging nature of the pandemic and the need for self-motivation, self-encouragement, and self-care.

Cantwell-Jurkovic's reflection on her feelings and emotions during peak pandemic months and her institution's in-person 2020–2021 academic year involved oscillation between supportiveness and gratitude, and fatigue, overwhelm, and resentment. Cantwell-Jurkovic noted specific feelings of resentment at how thoroughly COVID-related tasks could take over, overwhelm from other job functions and priorities, and fatigue related to the exhaustion of focusing on all the (ever-changing) guidelines, concerns, time lines, and so forth set out by the institution and the government.[14] Like individuals around the world, librarians confronted the same information overload and ever-changing guidelines set by their local, regional, and national governments, which were then addressed and implemented by their organizations. That said, Cantwell-Jurkovic found helpful ways to pivot her mindset stating, that she

> could go back to the important reality that [she] was getting to work [her] job, on site, and that [she] was less isolated than so many others and that [they] were trying to stay safe and strong so that [their] institution could *also* stay strong. That was an important motivator and an enduring focal point for [them] all, even on the bad days.

This is a pivot point with which many supervisors can connect—the institutional, greater-good mindset as a form of motivation and energy and encouragement.[15] While the authors here highlight the various challenges they had with these transitions, they all found pathways to reconnect their minds and emotions in meaningful, honest, and motivating ways. It is important to note that the authors decidedly did not opt to focus on their lives outside work in their interviews. However, they all expressed an enhanced awareness that, for staff they managed, personal and professional lives were inextricably intertwined during the pandemic. Prucha noted the fact that, given that heightened awareness, managers may also find themselves in positions of negotiating rocky paths with their staff. Though traditional guidance has advised keeping one's personal and professional lives separate, there is much to indicate that managers must strive to understand that staff's personal life can very much, and very understandably, bleed into their professional. Within reason, managers must seek to help their staff through difficult times or help them connect with resources to do so.[16]

Remaining change-agile is not always easy, mentally or emotionally, for one's own benefit or the benefit of one's staff. Perhaps one of the ways to maintain a level of flexibility toward change is to lean into the feelings of possibility, of newness, of forward-moving change, of opportunity, and of empathy.[17]

Opportunities

The COVID-19 pandemic has been difficult for many; it has been heartbreaking, polarizing, scary, financially precarious, destructive, and extremely exhausting.[18] But it has not been without opportunity. Libraries as organizations are known for their adaptability to change, as a thing of circumstantial necessity, a quality desirable for managers and other leaders, and a key element of retained relevance.[19] Libraries and their workforces, as service-driven organizations and individuals, were able to embrace a number of changes when faced with the COVID-19 pandemic, and these adaptations allowed them to glimpse through windows of opportunity

As in many organizations, process adaptations and new technology implementations became a focal point of daily agendas for librarians during the pandemic.[20] Cantwell-Jurkovic's and Prucha's organizations had not previously supported remote access to work computers, but, within moments of the WFH order, it seemed, options were put into place that would allow employees to work off-site. All the middle manager librarians in this section experienced expedited institutional uptake and adoption of tools like Microsoft Teams and Zoom. Many already had access to these tools at their institutions, but the degree of use, user permissions, settings, and level of necessity all shifted. From staff meetings and quick messages to programming, outreach, and research consultations, new software came to the forefront of the author-respondents' work. Cantwell-Jurkovic also indicated additional uses of Teams implemented at her institution, which included task tracking for electronic resource renewals, bestseller collection suggestions, and committee project management (such as committee tasks underway at her institution's institutional review board). She is also currently using it as a drafting and source depository for an article she's coauthoring with institutional colleagues.

Many libraries were already collecting resources in electronic format prior to the pandemic. As a result, these libraries were well positioned to focus the remainder of

2019–2020's acquisitions budgets to enhance these electronic collections, which was facilitated by publisher COVID-19 open access offerings. Alongside these investments, libraries challenged with limitations to their interlibrary loan service turned to services like RapidILL, a consortium assisting libraries all over the world (members and nonmembers of the Rapid system) in gaining access to materials. Cantwell-Jurkovic's team was proud to be able to assist so many students, faculty, and researchers and to secure sufficient workloads in their now-limited daily spheres of work (without students and faculty on campus). While working to ensure that staff had a steady flow of responsibilities and continue as many patron services as possible, many public services middle managers also developed curbside pickup process for patrons,[21] or enhanced book chapter scanning services, allowing students working at a distance to access to print-only materials. At Prucha's library, ILL and collections services collaborated to purchase and send books requested through ILL directly to library users. Physical books were received and checked out as if they had been delivered to the library. Books were due when the library reopened, and when returned, more deliberate cataloging work and physical processing was done with each book. E-books were also purchased based on ILL requests and were made available as quickly as possible to ensure timely access. Some of these concepts will not be new to all libraries, but these opportunities nonetheless demonstrate that libraries and librarians chose not to resist change and upheaval, but rather to embrace the tumult in order to benefit their communities.

And the tumult within library communities was not always on the other side of the service desk—these three librarians who were new to their middle-management positions also sought ways to stabilize their staff during times when in-person meetings were impossible (i.e., while working from home) and when in-person meetings felt less personal than in pre-pandemic times (e.g., using masks, social distancing). But there were now new or more overt benefits to finding ways to meet—meetings proved beneficial for both individual and collective morale. Additionally, meetings now required a new sense of intentionality. According to Smith,

> My daily activity was very reactive; we were in a global crisis. However, we were all experiencing this crisis alone, working in a way that was so isolated from each other. The brief, recurring team and one-on-one meetings were not something that existed in our unit before the pandemic, but they are something that will not disappear after it. [They have] helped deepen relationships and make intentional moments to touch base with each other.

For Prucha, being entirely new to her institution, meetings provided an opportunity for new coworkers to get to know her, and her them. For Smith and Cantwell-Jurkovic, meetings offered the opportunity for coworkers to get to know them in their new role while also adjusting to a colleague in a new capacity (alongside all the other newness). Even instances of remote hiring procedures were new, but established an opportunity for institutions in higher education, including their libraries, to step away from the well-established—but time-consuming and expensive—hiring processes that have long been in place within academia. Learning from these experiences, institutions can at least consider alternative hiring process models with many now having experienced alternatives.

Additionally, given the then-recent hires and promotions of the contributors to this section, there were opportunities to mitigate the feeling of upheaval by engaging in cross-training and upskilling efforts. For all these middle managers, this allowed for increased fluency (potentially at a faster rate than would have occurred otherwise) with the daily operations and needs of the staff and services under their purview, and possibly faster buy-in from supervisees given this situation required a from-the-trenches approach to departmental work. In normal times, understanding the work done in one's area or library occurs naturally over time as people work together. Social distancing and remote work meant these newly-hired or -promoted managers did not learn their staff members' positions by working together in-person. However, the managers were able to mitigate feelings of upheaval by engaging in cross-training and upskilling. The professional development opportunities increased their knowledge of daily operations (potentially at a faster rate than would have occurred otherwise) and exposed them to the roles played by the staff they managed in ways that may not have happened before or after the pandemic. Quick upskilling and cross-training resulted in disassembling existing divisions of labor as the managers developed the skills needed to cover other positions under their direction, and sharing the labor may have created a sense of camaraderie between managers and staff that made it easier for staff to respond positively to change.

Lessons on Leadership

Despite the challenges faced by these middle managers in order to maintain library services during a tremendously difficult and stressful time, there were some long-lasting impacts from the additional responsibilities undertaken during the peak months of the pandemic. One such impact was the development of leadership styles that may not have been their initial approach prior to the pandemic, but that became appropriate as the circumstances unfolded. During this time, Prucha "learned [that] leadership is about …[establishing] a path forward and bringing everyone with you" and noted that this "has meant different things to different people. It's meant firmly insisting that we are a community that works together and that's why we are back in person when so many are not; but it's also meant realizing other people bring real concerns that require flexibility on [her] part."

Similarly, Smith noted that the "pandemic has made [her] more aware of human-centered leadership" to the extent that she adopted what she considers a user-centered design into her leadership practice, where the users would be her staff. Likewise, Cantwell-Jurkovic highlighted the role that dedication and commitment to the library and university played in her promotion and how those relate to her current leadership role:

> I also make sure I reinforce that my institution, our library, and my staff and coworkers come first [despite also starting a PhD program in Fall 2020] ...to reinforce [that I am] interruptible and show commitment to them and to [her] ability to prioritize.

While these realizations do not come without challenges, these realizations became opportunities for the authors to grow as leaders, to better understand the needs of their staff and colleagues, and to maintain a flexible, unity-focused mindset. Overall, the contributors' management and leadership styles became community-focused out of necessity.

In another relationship-building context, the pandemic caused Prucha had to develop a stronger relationship with her dean, while between March 2020 and August 2021 their interactions were wholly online. While Prucha noted uncertainty regarding how exclusively virtual interaction affected her relationship with her supervisor, she found that this "increase[d] her [Dean's] trust in both [her and] the Head of Public Services," stating:

> My counterpart and I returned to campus much earlier and were the boots on the ground who ran the library. We communicated a lot so [our Dean] was in the loop, and we successfully shut down and reopened the library.

Not only would these dynamics and dutiful communications have built trust,[22] but Prucha also gained appreciation for her dean's leadership both on- and off-site, stating that her library "successfully closed and reopened because of her [the dean's] direction, and because of the trust she placed in us." Smith and Cantwell-Jurkovic found that their previous roles within their respective organizations benefited relationship building with their supervisors and others when the pandemic hit. Cantwell-Jurkovic in particular noted her preexisting, strong working relationship with her supervisor facilitated more frequent interactions when forced to work from home:

> We talked a lot over text, Teams, phone, and email—likely daily and often involving lengthy planning meetings and back-and-forth calls and such. I think our faith in each other has already been well-placed, but nonetheless we have maintained a strong working relationship.... I think she [the supervisor] now has a clearer understanding of her limitations and her strengths, and that's allowed her to better leverage staff skills and roles.

The recurring theme of library leaders with strength in planning coupled with the involvement of middle managers in emergency planning efforts created a tremendous amount of work for all involved, but provided an important opportunity for top-level library leaders to train, mentor, and delegate to their middle managers.[23] This provides an excellent learning opportunity for those middle managers, which breeds appreciation, trust, and leadership bonds.

While the peak months of the COVID-19 pandemic were intensely change-heavy, some good changes permeated the frustration, challenges, and losses that occurred. However, independent of the challenges and opportunities caused by the pandemic realities, other challenges and opportunities continued to exist; the human realities faced by the librarian-authors did not stop when the pandemic hit. Prucha, in particular, highlighted the co-occurring social unrest going on in her city during the pandemic. She wrote, "This led to an increased awareness of building diverse, equitable, and inclusive collections"; her library was simultaneously impacted by COVID-19 and a heightened sense of social responsibility. Further, Cantwell-Jurkovic and Prucha were both involved in PhD programs during the pandemic; for Prucha, this meant that "[she] had to make a commitment to ending [her] weekend work in favor of finishing [her] dissertation.

[She] did that at the expense of library projects." She recognized a certain amount of "reverberation" from that choice, but also recognized its necessity. For Cantwell-Jurkovic, the addition of the doctoral program added weight in the form of additional tasks and responsibilities, but she too recognized her role must come first, which made juggling multiple conflicting responsibilities quite difficult. This became especially true as she oversaw staffing of the opening and closing of the building, including all open hours of checkout and reserves services. With three staff managing over ninety building hours each week, Cantwell-Jurkovic recognized that the pace, plans, and goals set for her day could quickly get off track. This challenge, present regardless of the pandemic, became nearly a full-time job in itself.

Beyond external factors, at least two of the mid-level managers voiced new anxieties with their new roles and responsibilities. Both Prucha and Cantwell-Jurkovic noted feeling that they must constantly stay connected to work communication during the pandemic, with Cantwell-Jurkovic noting that "no matter how tired [she] may be, it is critical that [she] check texts and emails during [her] wake-up process each day, and before the lights-out process each night," and Prucha described the anxiety in the hours when she is not with her team:

> I find it difficult to stay asleep. I wake up with rushing thoughts about everything I need to do and everyone I need to email. I sometimes feel dread, particularly on Sunday evenings because I don't know what is going to hit me when I get back on Monday morning.

While issues of insomnia have been documented among health-care workers during the COVID-19 pandemic,[24] clearly this issue arose in other industries as well. Smith, too, acknowledged a strong mix of anxiety and fatigue, even outside of work, despite having historically strong work-life separation abilities. For her, too, these feelings have abated, but, in her terms, due to "finding that balance" and, now, "after many months of practice [she has] been more or less successful keeping outside-of-work emotions separate from [her] work." These emotional ups and downs identified by all three author-librarians compounded overall anxiety, stress, and fatigue during the pandemic, with the additional factors of new jobs, new responsibilities, and complex, awkward learning curves.

The staff managed by the three librarian-authors too were tasked with coping with their own internal and external realities, and this added a layer of complexity to the management of these individuals. Prucha noted that staff exhibiting tendencies toward introversion "flourished" in the COVID work environment,[25] stating,

> They were less stressed because of the lack of interaction and have become more stressed as we have become required to work together again in our shared space. Other more extroverted people have benefitted from returning to a more communal environment. [Their] productivity and engagement have increased.

Beyond introvert versus extrovert needs and challenges, Smith also began to consider the role of Maslow's hierarchy of needs in staff since the pandemic began.[26] She believes that before the pandemic, the needs of her staff would have fallen higher on that hierarchy—for example, self-actualization, esteem, and so on. However, she emphasized that as "the pandemic shook us all in a variety of ways.... People have been bringing up needs that [now] range the spectrum of Maslow's hierarchy." This observation requires a certain amount of emotional intelligence on the part of the manager, particularly in the case of managers who are new to their staff[27]—not only must they meet staff, get to know job functions, and start building relationships, but in crises like the COVID-19 pandemic, managers must be all the more ready and able to understand the emotional contexts of their supervisees, within and even outside of work.[28]

Conclusion

In many ways, the overarching themes of managing during a crisis like the COVID-19 pandemic—and likely other crises—can be summarized by resilience, communication, patience, flexibility, and determination, as well as the value of self-care, listening, and openness. While this chapter is not without its limitations, it strives to share key stories of those who needed to rise to library leadership challenges, particularly within the context of a new position, in the midst of a global pandemic. This chapter also seeks to draw attention to the important roles of library leaders working primarily alone and who needed to do so in a circumstance that created even more aloneness and isolation. Medical librarians have long played a crucial role in providing research information to their constituents. Their role was even more critical during COVID-19 as the pandemic severely affected all human activity, up-to-date and accessible information was paramount, and the activities surrounding information sharing had grown in their complexity.

This pandemic has highlighted the need for librarians to be agile and nimble and to have and provide access to current, reliable, and high-quality research resources. For both Mokonyama and Bogino, workflow changes were made—like the increased need to shift some acquisitions from print to electronic resources, while also supporting the print collections—but such needs and shifts were not exclusive to medical and hospital libraries; all libraries and their staff needed to find pathways toward providing resources and continue outreach to patrons, no matter the context. Thus, more than anything, the pandemic reinforced the need to support others with information, and the strong positioning and commitment of library leaders and staff to providing exactly that support. This was evident across all managers involved in this chapter, not only for themselves but also for their reflections on the work of their entire libraries during the pandemic. While not at all an easy time to start and develop as managers and leaders, the pandemic did in fact prove to be a training ground for leadership in many ways, even if not ideal, as well as a time and space for deep reinforcement of leaders' commitments to their organizations and, above all, to their patrons.

Appendix A: Self-Interview Questions Used by Cantwell-Jurkovic, Prucha, and Smith

1. Can you tell me what role you have, in what department/context you work, and how many years of professional experience you have?
2. Focusing on this pandemic period and your daily work activity, can you tell me how this has changed from the point of view of the contents of the activity?
3. What has changed?
4. What is new?
5. What is no longer there?
6. How has your forecasting and planning activity changed?
7. What aspects did you find difficult in this period?
8. Thinking again about your daily activity, can you tell me how it has changed compared to the relationships you have with the people you manage?
9. Thinking about the people you manage, have you been able to observe changes in their needs and requests in this last period?
10. What have you put in place to meet them?
11. And with respect to the ways they related to you, has anything changed?
12. If you think about how you relate to them, do you notice any changes in your way you pose yourself during this time?
13. Thinking about your leadership style, do you think it has changed in this period? If so, in what way?
14. Thinking about the management team in which you are part of and its way of functioning, can you tell me if and how the relationship with the different professionals of the team has changed?
15. Have you changed the way you proceed in your daily work? And what about decision-making and planning?
16. Thinking about your supervisor …has your relationship changed during this period? If so, in what way?
17. If you were to identify a person you are referring to in this period to seek help or to seek someone who will listen to you, who would that be?
18. Now think about yourself during your workdays. Tell me how you feel and what are the feelings and emotions you experience during your work shifts?
19. If you think about the period between one shift and the next and the journey that takes you to your workplace, what feelings/emotions do you experience in these moments?

Notes

1. Monica Bianchi, Cesarina Prandi, and Loris Bonetti, "Experience of Middle Management Nurses during the COVID-19 Pandemic in Switzerland: A Qualitative Study," *Journal of Nursing Management* 29, no. 7 (October 2021): 1956–64, https://doi.org/10.1111/jonm.13339.
2. Alexander Newman, Ross Donohue, and Nathan Eva, "Psychological Safety: A Systematic Review of the Literature," *Human Resource Management Review* 27, no. 3 (2017): 521-535.
3. Bernadette Dillion and Juliet Bourke, *The Six Signature Traits of Inclusive Leadership* (New York: Deloitte University Press, 2016), https://www2.deloitte.com/content/dam/Deloitte/au/Documents/human-capital/deloitte-au-hc-six-signature-traits-inclusive-leadership-020516.pdf.
4. Robin M. Featherstone et al., "Provision of Pandemic Disease Information by Health Sciences Librarians: A Multisite Comparative Case Series," *Journal of the Medical Library Association* 100, no. 2 (2012), 104–12, https://doi.org/10.3163/1536-5050.100.2.008.
5. Lara Guedes de Pinho et al., "Portuguese Nurses' Stress, Anxiety, and Depression Reduction Strategies during the COVID-19 Outbreak," *International Journal of Environmental Research and Public Health* 18, no. 7 (2021): 3490, https://doi.org/10.3390/ijerph18073490.
6. Newman, Donohue, and Eva, "Psychological Safety," 523.
7. Guedes de Pinho et al., "Portuguese Nurses."
8. Bianchi, Prandi, and Bonetti. "Experience of Middle Management Nurses."
9. Melissa Aho, "Circulation Supervisor Superstar or Jill of All Trades, Mistress of None," in *The New Academic Librarian: Essays on Changing Roles and Responsibilities*, ed. Rebecca Peacock and Jill Wurm (Jefferson, NC: McFarland, 2014), 9–17.
10. Ciara Smyth, Natasha Cortis, and Abigail Powell, "University Staff and Flexible Work: Inequalities, Tensions, and Challenges," *Journal of Higher Education Policy and Management* 43, no. 5 (2021): 489–504, https://doi.org/10.1080/1360080X.2020.1857504; Caryl Goodyear, "Overcoming the Overwhelming," *Nursing Management* 52, no. 2 (2021): 56, https://doi.org/10.1097/01.NUMA.0000731960.67612.ef; Gerald C. Kane et al., *The Transformation Myth* (Cambridge, MA: MIT Press, 2021).
11. John M. Levis and Sinem Sonsaat Hegelheimer, "COVID Silver Linings: Accessible and Affordable Professional Development," *Journal of Second Language Pronunciation* 7, no. 1 (May 2021): 1–9, https://doi.org/10.1075/jslp.21001.lev.
12. Katarzyna Mikołajczyk, "Changes in the Approach to Employee Development in Organisations as a Result of the COVID-19 Pandemic," *European Journal of Training and Development* 46, no. 5/6 (2021): 544–62, https://doi.org/10.1108/EJTD-12-2020-0171.
13. Cen April Yue, Linjuan Rita Men, and Bruce K. Berger, "Leaders as Communication Agents," in *Current Trends and Issues in Internal Communication: Theory and Practice*, ed. Linjuan Rita Men and Ana Tkalac Verčič (Cham, Switzerland: Palgrave Macmillan, 2021), 29–38; Steve Kempster, Marian Iszatt-White, and Matt Brown, "Authenticity in Leadership: Reframing Relational Transparency through the Lens of Emotional Labour," *Leadership* 15, no. 3 (2019): 319–38.
14. Jerel E. Slaughter et al., "Getting Worse or Getting Better? Understanding the Antecedents and Consequences of Emotion Profile Transitions during COVID-19-Induced Organizational Crisis," *Journal of Applied Psychology* 106, no. 8 (2021): 1118–36, https://doi.org/10.1037/apl0000947; Anatoly Oleksiyenko, "Global Higher Education and COVID-19: A Virtual Autoethnography Experience from a Faculty," in *Online Teaching and Learning in Higher Education during COVID-19: International Perspectives and Experiences*, ed. Roy Y. Chan, Krishna Bista, and Ryan M. Allen (New York: Routledge, 2021), 167–80.
15. Cătălin Pîrvu, "Emotional Intelligence—A Catalyst for Sustainability in Modern Business," *Theoretical and Empirical Researches in Urban Management* 15, no. 4 (2020): 60–69.
16. John Mullins, "People-Centred Management in a Library Context," *Library Review* 50, no. 6 (August 2001): 305–9, https://doi.org/10.1108/EUM0000000005599.
17. Paul Swanson, "Building a Culture of Resilience in Libraries," *Information Technology and Libraries* 40, no. 3 (September 2021), https://doi.org/10.6017/ital.v40i3.13781; Talha Khan et al., "'Back to Human': Why HR Leaders Want to Focus on People Again," *McKinsey & Company*, June 4, 2021,

https://www.mckinsey.com/business-functions/people-and-organizational-performance/our-insights/back-to-human-why-hr-leaders-want-to-focus-on-people-again.

18. Alison Abbott, "COVID's Mental-Health Toll: How Scientists Are Tracking a Surge in Depression," *Nature* 590 (February 3, 2021): 194–95, https://www.nature.com/articles/d41586-021-00175-z; Sandro Galea, Raina M. Merchant, and Nicole Lurie, "The Mental Health Consequences of COVID-19 and Physical Distancing: The Need for Prevention and Early Intervention," *JAMA Internal Medicine* 180, no. 6 (2020): 817–18, https://doi.org/10.1001/jamainternmed.2020.1562; Colleen Flaherty, "Faculty Pandemic Stress Is Now Chronic," Inside Higher Ed, November 19, 2020, https://www.insidehighered.com/news/2020/11/19/faculty-pandemic-stress-now-chronic; Walter Leal Filho et al., "Impacts of COVID-19 and Social Isolation on Academic Staff and Students at Universities: A Cross-sectional Study," *BMC Public Health* 21 (2021): article 1213, https://doi.org/10.1186/s12889-021-11040-z.

19. Gail Munde and Kenneth Marks, *Surviving the Future* (Oxford: Chandos, 2009).

20. Christopher Cox et al., "Looking through the COVID Fog: Toward Resilient, Reimagined Libraries," *College and Research Libraries News* 82, no. 8 (2021): 362–63, 368, https://doi.org/10.5860/crln.82.8.362; M. Wynn Tranfield, Doug Worsham, and Nisha Mody, "When You Only Have a Week: Rapid-Response, Grassroots Public Services for Access, Wellness, and Student Success," *College and Research Libraries News* 81, no. 7 (2020): 326–29, 336, https://doi.org/10.5860/crln.81.7.326.

21. Laureen P. Cantwell, "Developing a Curbside Pickup Scheduling Tool on the Fly Using Springshare's LibCal," *Marketing Libraries Journal* 5, no. 1 (Summer 2021): 42–66, https://journal.marketinglibraries.org/summer2021/04_MLJv5i1.pdf.

22. Helena Bulińska-Stangrecka and Anna Bagieńska, "The Role of Employee Relations in Shaping Job Satisfaction as an Element Promoting Positive Mental Health at Work in the Era of COVID-19," *International Journal of Environmental Research and Public Health* 18, no. 4 (2021): article 1903, https://doi.org/10.3390/ijerph18041903; Noel Carroll and Kieran Conboy, "Normalising the 'New Normal': Changing Tech-Driven Work Practices under Pandemic Time Pressure," *International Journal of Information Management* 55 (2020): article 102186, https://doi.org/10.1016/j.ijinfomgt.2020.102186; Jennifer Schulte, "Professional Development for Communication Skills, Collaboration Skills, and Fostering Positive Connections in the Workplace" (EdD diss, Arizona State University, 2021), ProQuest Dissertations and Theses (28410670).

23. Janka I. Stoker, Harry Garretsen, and Joris Lammers, "Leading and Working from Home in Times of COVID-19: On the Perceived Changes in Leadership Behaviors," *Journal of Leadership and Organizational Studies* 29, no. 2 (2021): 208–18, https://doi.org/10.1177/15480518211007452; Jennifer Matthews, "When Does Delegating Make You a Supervisor?" *Online Journal of Issues in Nursing* 15, no. 2 (2020): manuscript 3, https://doi.org/10.3912/OJIN.Vol15No02Man03.

24. Sofia Poppa et al., "Prevalence of Depression, Anxiety, and Insomnia among Healthcare Workers during the COVID-19 Pandemic: A Systematic Review and Meta-analysis," *Brain, Behavior, and Immunity* 88 (2020): 901–7, https://doi.org/10.1016/j.bbi.2020.05.026; Knar Sagherian et al., "Insomnia, Fatigue and Psychosocial Well-Being during COVID-19 Pandemic: A Cross-sectional Survey of Hospital Nursing Staff in the United States," *Journal of Clinical Nursing*, online version of record, November 20, 2020, https://doi.org/10.1111/jocn.15566.

25. Anthony M. Evans et al., "Extroversion and Conscientiousness Predict Deteriorating Job Outcomes during the COVID-19 Transition to Enforced Remote Work," *Social Psychological and Personality Science* 13, no. 3 (2021): 1–11, https://doi.org/10.1177/19485506211039092; Devalina Nag, "Enhancing Work Engagement in Diverse Employees via Autonomy: Acknowledging Introversion and Extroversion Workspace Preferences," in *Work from Home: Multi-level Perspectives on the New Normal*, ed. Payal Kumar, Anirudh Agrawal, and Pawan Budhwar (Bingley, UK: Emerald Publishing, 2021), 131–46; H. Deniz Günaydin, "Impacts of Personality on Job Performance through COVID-19 Fear and Intention to Quit," *Psychological Reports* 124, no. 6 (2021): 2739–60, https://doi.org/10.1177/00332941211040433.

26. Hasaranga Dilshan Jayathilake et al., "Employee Development and Retention of Generation-Z Employees in the Post-COVID-19 Workplace: A Conceptual Framework," *Benchmarking: An International Journal* 28, no. 7 (2021): 2343–64, https://doi.org/10.1108/BIJ-06-2020-0311; Eugene W. Mathes, "Maslow's Hierarchy of Needs as a Guide for Living," *Journal of Humanistic Psychology* 21, no. 4 (Fall 1981): 69–72.

27. Steve Langhorn, "How Emotional Intelligence Can Improve Management Performance," *International Journal of Contemporary Hospitality Management* 16, no. 4 (2004): 220–30, https://doi.org/10.1108/09596110410537379.

28. Veronika Koubova and Aaron A. Buchko, "Life-Work Balance: Emotional Intelligence as a Crucial Component of Achieving Both Personal Life and Work Performance," *Management Research Review* 36, no. 7 (2013): 700–19, https://doi.org/10.1108/MRR-05-2012-0115; Rangarajan Parthasarathy, "Emotional Intelligence and the Quality Manager: Beauty and the Beast?" *Journal for Quality and Participation* 31, no. 4 (2009): 31–34; Chaoying Tang and Yunxia Gao, "Intra-department Communication and Employees' Reaction to Organizational Change: The Moderating Effect of Emotional Intelligence," *Journal of Chinese Human Resource Management* 3, no. 2 (2012): 100–17, https://doi.org/10.1108/20408001211279210.

Bibliography

Abbott, Alison. "COVID's Mental-Health Toll: How Scientists Are Tracking a Surge in Depression." *Nature* 590 (February 11, 2021): 194–95. https://www.nature.com/articles/d41586-021-00175-z.

Aho, Melissa. "Circulation Supervisor Superstar or Jill of All Trades, Mistress of None." In *The New Academic Librarian: Essays on Changing Roles and Responsibilities*, edited by Rebecca Peacock and Jill Wurm, 9–17. Jefferson, NC: McFarland, 2014.

Bianchi, Monica, Cesarina Prandi, and Loris Bonetti. "Experience of Middle Management Nurses during the COVID-19 Pandemic in Switzerland: A Qualitative Study." *Journal of Nursing Management* 29, no. 7 (October 2021): 1956–64. https://doi.org/10.1111/jonm.13339.

Bulińska-Stangrecka, Helena, and Anna Bagieńska. "The Role of Employee Relations in Shaping Job Satisfaction as an Element Promoting Positive Mental Health at Work in the Era of COVID-19." *International Journal of Environmental Research and Public Health* 18, no. 4 (2021): article 1903. https://doi.org/10.3390/ijerph18041903.

Cantwell, Laureen P. "Developing a Curbside Pickup Scheduling Tool on the Fly Using Springshare's LibCal." *Marketing Libraries Journal* 5, no. 1(Summer 2021): 42–66. https://journal.marketinglibraries.org/summer2021/04_MLJv5i1.pdf.

Carroll, Noel, and Kieran Conboy. "Normalising the 'New Normal': Changing Tech-Driven Work Practices under Pandemic Time Pressure." *International Journal of Information Management* 55 (2020): article 102186. https://doi.org/10.1016/j.ijinfomgt.2020.102186.

Cox, Christopher, Elliot Felix, Greg Raschke, and Mary Ann Mavrinac. "Looking through the COVID Fog: Toward Resilient, Reimagined Libraries." *College and Research Libraries News* 82, no. 8 (2021): 362–63, 368. https://doi.org/10.5860/crln.82.8.362.

Dillion, Bernadette, and Juliet Bourke. *The Six Signature Traits of Inclusive Leadership: Thriving in a Diverse New World*. New York: Deloitte University Press, 2016. https://www2.deloitte.com/content/dam/Deloitte/au/Documents/human-capital/deloitte-au-hc-six-signature-traits-inclusive-leadership-020516.pdf.

Evans, Anthony M., M. Christina Meters, Philippe P. F. M. van de Calseyde, and Olga Stavrova. "Extroversion and Conscientiousness Predict Deteriorating Job Outcomes during the COVID-19 Transition to Enforced Remote Work." *Social Psychological and Personality Science* 13, no. 3 (2021): 1–11. https://doi.org/10.1177/19485506211039092.

Featherstone, Robin M., R. Gabriel Boldt, Nazi Torabi, and Shauna-Lee Konrad. "Provision of Pandemic Disease Information by Health Sciences Librarians: A Multisite Comparative Case Series." *Journal of the Medical Library Association* 100, no. 2 (2012), 104–12. https://doi.org/10.3163/1536-5050.100.2.008.

Filho, Walter Leal, Tony Wall, Lex Rayman-Bacchus, Mark Mifsid, Diana J. Pritchard, Violeta Orlovic Lovren, Carla Farinha, Danijela S. Petrovic, and Abdul-Lateef Balogun. "Impacts of COVID-19 and Social Isolation on Academic Staff and Students at Universities: A Cross-sectional Study." *BMC Public Health* 21 (2021): article 1213. https://doi.org/10.1186/s12889-021-11040-z.

Flaherty, Colleen. "Faculty Pandemic Stress Is Now Chronic." Inside Higher Ed, November 19, 2020. https://www.insidehighered.com/news/2020/11/19/faculty-pandemic-stress-now-chronic.

Galea, Sandro, Raina M. Merchant, and Nicole Lurie. "The Mental Health Consequences of COVID-19 and Physical Distancing: The Need for Prevention and Early Intervention." *JAMA Internal Medicine* 180, no. 6 (2020): 817–18. https://doi.org/10.1001/jamainternmed.2020.1562.

Goodyear, Caryl. "Overcoming the Overwhelming." *Nursing Management* 52, no. 2 (2021): 56. https://doi.org/10.1097/01.NUMA.0000731960.67612.ef.

Guedes de Pinho, Lara, Francisco Sampaio, Carlos Sequeira, Laetitia Teixeira, César Fonseca, and Manual José Lopes. "Portuguese Nurses' Stress, Anxiety, and Depression Reduction Strategies during the COVID-19 Outbreak." *International Journal of Environmental Research and Public Health* 18, no. 7 (2021): 3490. https://doi.org/10.3390/ijerph18073490.

Günaydin, H. Deniz. "Impacts of Personality on Job Performance through COVID-19 Fear and Intention to Quit." *Psychological Reports* 124, no. 6 (2021): 2739–60. https://doi.org/10.1177/00332941211040433.

Jayathilake, Hasaranga Dilshan, Dazmin Daud, Hooi Cheng Eaw, and Nursyamilah Annuar. "Employee Development and Retention of Generation-Z Employees in the Post-COVID-19 Workplace: A Conceptual Framework." *Benchmarking: An International Journal* 28, no. 7 (2021): 2343–64. https://doi.org/10.1108/BIJ-06-2020-0311.

Kane, Gerald C., Rich Nanda, Anh Nguyen Phillips, and Jonathan R. Copulsky. *The Transformation Myth: Leading Your Organization through Uncertain Times.* Cambridge, MA: MIT Press, 2021.

Kempster, Steve, Marian Iszatt-White, and Matt Brown. "Authenticity in Leadership: Reframing Relational Transparency through the Lens of Emotional Labour." *Leadership* 15, no. 3 (2019): 319–38.

Khan, Talha, Asmus Komm, Dana Maor, and Florian Pollner. "'Back to Human': Why HR Leaders Want to Focus on People Again." McKinsey and Company, June 4, 2021. https://www.mckinsey.com/business-functions/people-and-organizational-performance/our-insights/back-to-human-why-hr-leaders-want-to-focus-on-people-again.

Koubova, Veronika, and Aaron A. Buchko. "Life-Work Balance: Emotional Intelligence as a Crucial Component of Achieving Both Personal Life and Work Performance." *Management Research Review* 36, no. 7 (2013): 700–19. https://doi.org/10.1108/MRR-05-2012-0115.

Langhorn, Steve. "How Emotional Intelligence Can Improve Management Performance." *International Journal of Contemporary Hospitality Management* 16, no. 4 (2004): 220–30. https://doi.org/10.1108/09596110410537379.

Levis, John M., and Sinem Sonsaat Hegelheimer. "COVID Silver Linings: Accessible and Affordable Professional Development." *Journal of Second Language Pronunciation* 7, no. 1 (May 2021): 1–9. https://doi.org/10.1075/jslp.21001.lev.

Mathes, Eugene W. "Maslow's Hierarchy of Needs as a Guide for Living." *Journal of Humanistic Psychology* 21, no. 4 (Fall 1981): 69–72.

Matthews, Jennifer. "When Does Delegating Make You a Supervisor?" *Online Journal of Issues in Nursing* 15, no. 2 (2020): manuscript 3. https://doi.org/10.3912/OJIN.Vol15No02Man03.

Mikołajczyk, Katarzyna. "Changes in the Approach to Employee Development in Organisations as a Result of the COVID-19 Pandemic." *European Journal of Training and Development* 46, no. 5/6 (2021): 544–62. https://doi.org/10.1108/EJTD-12-2020-0171.

Mullins, John. "People-Centred Management in a Library Context." *Library Review* 50, no. 6 (August 2001): 305–9. https://doi.org/10.1108/EUM0000000005599.

Munde, Gail, and Kenneth Marks. *Surviving the Future: Academic Libraries, Quality, and Assessment.* Oxford: Chandos, 2009.

Nag, Devalina. "Enhancing Work Engagement in Diverse Employees via Autonomy: Acknowledging Introversion and Extroversion Workspace Preferences." In *Work from Home: Multi-level Perspectives on the New Normal,* edited by Payal Kumar, Anirudh Agrawal, and Pawan Budhwar, 131–46. Bingley, UK: Emerald, 2021.

Newman, Alexander, Ross Donohue, and Nathan Eva. "Psychological Safety: A Systematic Review of the Literature." *Human Resource Management Review* 27, no. 3 (2017), 521–35.

Oleksiyenko, Anatoly. "Global Higher Education and COVID-19: A Virtual Autoethnography Experience from a Faculty." In *Online Teaching and Learning in Higher Education during COVID-19: International Perspectives and Experiences,* edited by Roy Y. Chan, Krishna Bista, and Ryan M. Allen, 167–80. New York: Routledge, 2021.

Parthasarathy, Rangarajan. "Emotional Intelligence and the Quality Manager: Beauty and the Beast?" *Journal for Quality and Participation* 31, no. 4 (2009): 31–34.

Pîrvu, Cătălin. "Emotional Intelligence—A Catalyst for Sustainability in Modern Business." *Theoretical and Empirical Researches in Urban Management* 15, no. 4 (2020): 60–69.

Poppa, Sofia, Vasiliki Ntella, Timoleon Giannakas, Vassilis G. Giannakoulis, Eleni Papoutsi, and Paraskevi Katsaounou. "Prevalence of Depression, Anxiety, and Insomnia among Healthcare Workers during the COVID-19 Pandemic: A Systematic Review and Meta-analysis." *Brain, Behavior, and Immunity* 88 (2020): 901–7. https://doi.org/10.1016/j.bbi.2020.05.026.

Sagherian, Knar, Linsey M. Steege, Sandra J. Cobb, and Hyeonmi Cho. "Insomnia, Fatigue and Psychosocial Well-Being during COVID-19 Pandemic: A Cross-sectional Survey of Hospital Nursing Staff in the United States." *Journal of Clinical Nursing*, online version of record, November 20, 2020. https://doi.org/10.1111/jocn.15566.

Schulte, Jennifer. "Professional Development for Communication Skills, Collaboration Skills, and Fostering Positive Connections in the Workplace." EdD diss., Arizona State University, 2021. ProQuest Dissertations and Theses (28410670).

Slaughter, Jerel E., Allison S. Gabriel, Mahira L. Ganster, Hoda Vaziri, and Rebecca L. MacGowan. "Getting Worse or Getting Better? Understanding the Antecedents and Consequences of Emotion Profile Transitions during COVID-19-Induced Organizational Crisis." *Journal of Applied Psychology* 106, no. 8 (2021): 1118–36. https://doi.org/10.1037/apl0000947.

Smyth, Ciara, Natasha Cortis, and Abigail Powell. "University Staff and Flexible Work: Inequalities, Tensions, and Challenges." *Journal of Higher Education Policy and Management* 43, no. 5 (2021): 489–504. https://doi.org/10.1080/1360080X.2020.1857504.

Stoker, Janka I., Harry Garretsen, and Joris Lammers. "Leading and Working from Home in Times of COVID-19: On the Perceived Changes in Leadership Behaviors." *Journal of Leadership and Organizational Studies* 29, no. 2 (2021): 208–18. https://doi.org/10.1177/15480518211007452.

Swanson, Paul. "Building a Culture of Resilience in Libraries." Editorial. *Information Technology and Libraries* 40, no. 3 (September 2021): 1–3. https://doi.org/10.6017/ital.v40i3.13781.

Tang, Chaoying, and Yunxia Gao. "Intra-department Communication and Employees' Reaction to Organizational Change: The Moderating Effect of Emotional Intelligence." *Journal of Chinese Human Resource Management* 3, no. 2 (2012): 100–17. https://doi.org/10.1108/20408001211279210.

Tranfield, M. Wynn, Doug Worsham, and Nisha Mody. "When You Only Have a Week: Rapid-Response, Grassroots Public Services for Access, Wellness, and Student Success." *College and Research Libraries News* 81, no. 7 (2020): 326–29, 336. https://doi.org/10.5860/crln.81.7.326.

Yue, Cen April, Linjuan Rita Men, and Bruce K. Berger. "Leaders as Communication Agents." In *Current Trends and Issues in Internal Communication: Theory and Practice*, edited by Linjuan Rita Men and Ana Tkalac Verčič, 19–38. Cham, Switzerland: Palgrave Macmillan, 2021.

CHAPTER 8

Side Effects
How the COVID Pandemic Helped Us Build a Healthier Library Organization

Amanda Nash, Joy Bolt, Timothy Daniels, and Austina Jordan

> "Culture does not change because we desire to change it. Culture changes when the organization is transformed; the culture reflects the realities of people working together every day."
>
> —Frances Hesselbein, former CEO of the Girl Scouts and organizational leadership expert[1]

Introduction

If asked to consider the range of difficult organizational experiences libraries might face, most library administrators would probably include a reorganization on their lists, perhaps near the top. Until recently, a pandemic likely would not have made the cut, but responding to a natural disaster would also rank highly among the possibilities. Imagine, then, the challenges and complexities that arise when a library embarks upon a complete reorganization and, just two months in, must react and respond to the turmoil of a global health crisis.

Within the life cycle of libraries, change is inevitable and comes in various shapes and sizes. One especially significant form of change is a reorganization, also referred to as a restructuring. A reorganization can come about for many reasons, and the literature points to several important catalysts—strategic plans, mergers, and new leadership.[2] Reorganization cannot happen overnight and requires thoughtful and diligent planning involving all members within the organization.[3] Key decisions are often made by leadership, but for organizational buy-in, it is essential that all levels of employees have an opportunity to provide feedback and insight into their experiences and understanding of their work.[4]

The University of North Georgia Libraries confronted these simultaneous challenges in 2020. In the case study that follows, four members of the administrative team will detail the structure and functional operation of the UNG Libraries before and after the reorganization and discuss the approaches taken to respond to pandemic-related closures and the shift to online operations. The authors will also detail how COVID-driven adjustments helped facilitate the adoption of a new organizational structure, which in turn helped the library weather the sudden upheaval. An explanation of the impact these tandem changes made to the libraries' culture across the authors' primary operational areas—technical services, access services, reference and instruction, and administration—is provided, along with a discussion of how the changes created a more resilient, inclusive, and collegial team of employees. This case study may assist other library teams who are contemplating restructuring by providing insight into the approaches taken and the challenges encountered and may aid libraries that are interested in adopting new approaches to team building and communication.

The Reorganization

Academic libraries are frequently stymied by the inertia of "but we've always done it this way." The UNG Libraries were no exception, but this organization's "always" goes back only to January 8, 2013, when the University of North Georgia was officially created through the consolidation of two vastly different institutions.

North Georgia College and State University was founded in Dahlonega in 1873 as North Georgia Agricultural College and is the second oldest public higher education institution in the state. The school originally offered both men and women degrees in agriculture and engineering, particularly mining, as it had been established in an area known for its gold deposits and on the site of a former United States mint. Because it was a land-grant institution, the college's male students participated in compulsory military training, which evolved into an ROTC program in 1916. With a decline in its agricultural programs over the next decade, the institution became North Georgia College in 1929. It gained university status in 1996, becoming North Georgia College and State University, a residential institution serving a largely traditional student population and maintaining a selective admissions process. Amid these changes, the college maintained its military identity, serving as a United States senior military college.

Gainesville State College began as Gainesville Junior College, established in 1964 and opening its first campus in 1966. The college offered the local community two-year degrees and certificate programs designed to prepare students to enter the workforce or to transfer to a four-year institution. Renamed Gainesville College in 1987, the college grew rapidly, and a second campus was added forty miles away in Oconee County in 2003. Continued growth led to the addition of limited baccalaureate degree programs, and the institution became Gainesville State College in 2005. Throughout its growth and expansion, Gainesville State College retained its identity as an access and commuter institution serving both traditional and nontraditional students.

When the consolidation was announced in January 2012, numerous working groups were created to develop new departmental policies, procedures, and organizational charts. The UNG Libraries chose to adopt a location-driven structure, with each of the four campuses (a fourth campus in Cumming had opened as a joint instructional site in 2012) being led by a head librarian who reported to the dean of libraries and served as a member of a library leadership team. Faculty and staff based at each location reported directly to their head librarian, with a few exceptions at the largest library facility in Dahlonega. The new UNG Libraries had no traditional academic library departments (e.g., access services, reference and instruction, etc.), and no one coordinated these functions; typical academic library services were the responsibility of various library faculty and staff located at each campus, and most personnel had responsibilities that cut across multiple functional areas.

While this location-driven arrangement was helpful for understanding and representing the various constituencies at each campus and for addressing facilities-related issues, its siloed nature created numerous communication challenges, and the lack of formally designated leadership for essential library activities greatly hampered function and effectiveness. All decision-making occurred at the library leadership team level, so a question regarding a circulation issue between two campuses, for example, would be directed up from a library assistant to their head librarian, then over to the other head librarian involved, down to their circulation staff member, with the chain reversed in reply. When problems arose, the head librarians would consult with the dean or with the entire leadership team to work toward a resolution. Despite a mission to provide equitable services across the campuses, many frontline activities, like instruction, continued to function independently at each location. Activities like circulation, which demanded more unified operations, sometimes undertook committee work to accomplish goals and were hamstrung by the cumbersome nature of conducting business meetings with members spread across a multi-county footprint at campuses located as far as 120 miles apart.

In 2018, the dean of libraries departed, and one of the head librarians stepped into the role, first as interim and then becoming dean in July 2019. With this change in management, the UNG Libraries were able to explore options for revamping the organizational structure to improve communication, provide clearer direction for operations and services, and better serve an institution that had grown over the previous six years to become a regional university serving nearly 20,000 students, with five distinct campuses, covering a geographic region spanning over 750 square miles (about half the area of Rhode Island).

There is no shortage of literature in the fields of management and business discussing change management within all kinds of for-profit and not-for-profit organizations. Libraries often turn to these fields to help guide their reorganization and merger efforts. One common tool that libraries use are frameworks that help give structure to the process of reshaping how the library operates with both internal and external constituencies.[5] The steps within these frameworks do not always happen in a linear pattern,[6] but they are useful tools to help individuals think through what they might anticipate along the way. Some of the pieces included in these frames are understanding why change is happening, considering the best steps forward, learning from mistakes, and the ever-important need to assess the change taking place.[7]

A pilot for a potential new structure began in 2018–2019, when it was decided to concentrate and streamline technical services operations by creating a division head position and centralizing operations at the Dahlonega campus library, the largest of UNG's library facilities with room for department personnel and materials. In fall 2019, plans were developed to fully adopt a traditional academic library operational structure. This structure seems instinctive, if not obvious, but the libraries' leadership would have to implement it with limited faculty and staff (roughly thirty-six FTE) scattered across multiple locations. Reflecting upon the input and concerns of the libraries' faculty and staff shared since consolidation, and drawing upon over 135 years of collective experience, knowledge, and expertise in developing a solution, the libraries' leadership team opted to create functional teams, or divisions, each with a single leader, as well as a location leader at each campus to address issues specific to that campus or facility and student body.

Two of the other former head librarians became assistant deans (a third retained the title of head librarian and served as a location lead until her retirement in December 2020), with one in charge of reference and instruction and the other in charge of online learning and assessment. The libraries received funding for a head of access services position, which was filled by an internal candidate, and revamped an existing position to become head of collection management. These faculty members, along with the special collections and digital initiatives librarian and head of technical services, formed a new leadership team (affectionately called the BLT, or best library team) that works together to provide overall administrative direction for the libraries. Each BLT member oversees their respective area, and each team has members from across the campuses, with representation determined by operational need, not by geography.

Once the structure was determined by the leadership team, the provost was updated as to the plans and gave full approval. With the reorganization plans finalized, the entire administrative team traveled among the campus libraries in late fall 2019 to hold town hall meetings where the new structure was shared and team assignments for each employee were explained. The new structure would become official with the start of the spring semester in January 2020. Expecting, as with any reorganization, that there would be confusion and challenges, the goal was to let each team leader develop and implement plans for their operations with their team members so that faculty and staff could adapt to the new structure incrementally.

In the best of circumstances, change is difficult. As quoted by John Kotter and Leonard Schlesinger, Niccolò Machiavelli aptly wrote, "There is nothing more difficult to take in hand, more perilous to conduct, or more uncertain in its success, than to take the lead in the introduction of a new order of things."[8] Kotter and Schlesinger go on to lay out a strategy for organizational change, including education, communication, involvement, and support. Unfortunately, the advent of COVID and the subsequent rapid shutdown of the university made it necessary to implement an emergency shift in services and operations.

The COVID-19 Response

While the libraries were settling into the new organizational structure, reports of a deadly new virus with pandemic potential began circulating in late January. While hoping it would never be needed, the BLT began the process of writing a continuity of operations plan (COOP). A COOP had been one of many policy and procedural items on the to-do list under the new leadership and structure, as a disaster response plan had never been fully developed and formally drafted, leaving the libraries vulnerable should a crisis arise. Now, developing a COOP was no longer something for the future; it moved to the top of the list. The timing was on point: by the time March rolled around, fears were becoming reality.

On Friday, March 13, the University System of Georgia announced a two-week shutdown for all institutions to prepare to transition to fully online instruction. The first order of business was to communicate with libraries' faculty and staff that this would be a hectic time while the libraries prepared for classes to resume in a virtual environment. There was quite a scramble to make sure that employees had the necessary technology and equipment to do their jobs at a distance.

With the COOP in hand, the BLT went into action, leading their direct reports through this transition period. The setup of the divisions and teams that came into being at the start of 2020 played a huge role in how the libraries were able to function and navigate changes and challenges successfully. One of the core elements to implementing this rapid and comprehensive change was communication.

Perhaps the most important aspect of the communication strategy during this time was the use of Microsoft Teams. As the leadership team was developing the organizational structure in 2019, the members discussed methods of communicating and working that would reinforce the organizational structure while also sharing information effectively across multiple campuses. As the institution was a subscriber to Office 365, the BLT landed on Teams as an option. The leadership team had introductory Teams training on February 28 and began discussions on what the use of Teams would look like for the libraries. Ideas flowed as to how to set up the team sites and channels. When the shutdown came, leadership threw this plan into action overnight. The dean set up a leadership team channel and a channel for each division or team and each location. The leadership team, while having only one training session, found that Teams was easy to manage and easy to use and met communication needs. It was quite a challenge, however, to get everyone else up and running at a distance without face-to-face training or support. Leadership continued to emphasize that the use of Teams was not temporary and it was not something being implemented strictly in response to COVID operations. Division heads set up regular Teams meetings with their direct reports to check in on work projects and encouraged everyone to contact each other over Teams, just to be sure their coworkers were doing OK.

Leading change requires the leader to effectively communicate with individuals and with the team as a whole. A study of organizational communications in the twenty-first century by Boris Groysburg and Michael Slind found that "Traditional corporate communication must give way to a process that is more dynamic and more sophisticated. Most importantly, that process must be *conversational*."[9] Further, Groysberg and Slind state that they "identified four elements of organizational conversation that reflect the essential attributes of interpersonal conversation: intimacy, interactivity, inclusion, and intentionality."[10] All four of Groysberg and Slind's elements can be accomplished in Microsoft Teams.

Rumors of budget issues were beginning to swirl along with the general fear of the virus. Morale was shaky. In the first week of the shutdown, leadership developed an idea for "Teams Tea Times" and held the first one on Thursday, March 19. This activity provided everyone an informal and casual way to try out the platform and become comfortable with Teams. It also was a boost to morale and allowed for some human interaction. Every libraries' faculty and staff member attended that first virtual event on Teams. The next week, libraries' employees continued coming together every afternoon Monday through Thursday, with different themed gatherings each day. Eventually, Tea Times were reduced to once a week, but they still provided a needed outlet for social interaction and educational exploration.

As the libraries' faculty and staff tried new methods of communication, the leadership team also worked on activating the COOP to continue services for students and faculty. The COOP reflected the new organizational structure in addressing how each of the following would function in a strictly virtual environment: physical collections, electronic resources, interlibrary lending, reference and informational questions, research consultations, library instruction, and collection development. The operational understanding according to the COOP outline was that all physical collections would be unavailable. However, near the end of the two-week shutdown, the dean was informed by the university administration that the libraries would be expected to have open hours in the facility at the university's residential campus in Dahlonega once virtual instruction resumed. This added an unexpected complication in the rollout, but, fortunately, some Dahlonega staff members were willing to be there in person, and they did excellent work setting things up in a way that kept everyone as safe as possible.

As an initial step in implementing the COOP's outline, the head of technical services took the lead on electronic resource support, managing troubleshooting and serving as a conduit to the state system, as many of the libraries' resources are provided through consortia. The head of technical services also served as the libraries' contact with the university's web team, which was important for providing patrons with information regarding library operations. Interlibrary lending, which included intercampus lending, GIL Express (a university system–wide lending program), and traditional interlibrary loan, fell under the purview of the head of access services. These services were all suspended indefinitely. Intercampus lending was halted in part to avoid bringing staff into closed facilities to process and check out books and because campus courier services had shut down. GIL Express and ILL, which rely upon the cooperation of other institutions to function, fell outside the UNG Libraries' control, a situation that proved extremely frustrating to patrons, particularly faculty. One of the assistant deans served as the lead for reference and informational questions, research consultations, and library instruction. These services proved to be quite challenging, requiring a huge shift from the former face-to-face model. Collection development did not completely shut down as the university was in the middle of the fiscal year, but the collection management division head decided to shift away from purchasing print materials due to lack of in-person staffing as well as a partial budget cut enacted by the university administration. The decision was also made to stop accepting donated materials during this time.

After three months of everyone being off campus, except for the skeleton staff in Dahlonega, it was decided to start bringing people back to the other campus libraries in June 2020, in preparation for face-to-face instruction resuming in August. Most entities within the institution planned to come back near the start of the fall semester, but library leadership was being encouraged by the university administration to make the library facilities more available across all campuses, even though virtual support services were working well. It was decided to open individual libraries on a gradual, rolling basis, allowing team leaders to pay attention to location-specific needs while also implementing the lessons learned at Dahlonega. To facilitate the openings, a working group was formed, composed of members of the leadership team and a contact person from each campus library. Once again, leadership used Teams to share real-time information and experiences that made for smooth reopenings. As the third location reopened, the BLT reinstituted intercampus lending. Statewide lending and interlibrary loan were still unavailable. All information desks reopened for in-person service, with online chat also remaining an option for patrons. Research consultations and library instruction remained virtual. The return was difficult for some as it was stressful to be back in the buildings working in person, but staggered shifts were implemented to allow for social distancing. All meetings were still held virtually, so Teams continued to play a significant role in how the libraries' teams communicated and functioned.

Impacts and Side Effects

With the sudden shift to online operations in March 2020, the old campus-based organizational structure was rendered moot. Library location was irrelevant. While the UNG Libraries have long been service-centered in principle, operating those services from off campus and delivering them to students and faculty working at a distance intensified their importance, and those services required agile leadership and prompt decision-making. The new organizational structure, with departmental teams populated according to need and expertise, not location, was ideally placed to respond to the challenges and helped to make the libraries more flexible and resilient.

Likewise, the COVID-driven operational changes that the libraries' leadership was forced to implement helped to advance the adoption of the new organizational structure. In part, the stress and uncertainty of those sudden changes eclipsed the ordinary discomfort of a reorganization. At the same time, team leaders took advantage of the opportunities created by the liminality of this experience to try new approaches, develop new procedures, and embrace new ways of working. Even aspects of the nascent team-based structure required revision; the online learning team was instantly dropped, as all students became distance students, and all libraries' faculty and staff members were focusing on meeting their needs virtually.

These concurrent changes—the reorganization and COVID operations—have reshaped the libraries' culture across all operational areas, in a surprising variety of ways.

Technical Services

For six years, the UNG Libraries were decentralized, including technical services. Library staff on three of the four campuses worked on various tasks that occupy a traditional technical services department. This dispersal of efforts created inefficient processes and confusion partly due to an evident resistance to change and centralization. Before the formal reorganization, the interim dean decided that establishing a centralized technical services department would be a practical step toward an efficient, consolidated organizational structure. A confluence of events, departures, and unfilled positions allowed for the creation of a head of technical services position and the formation of a technical services department at the Dahlonega location. This organizational change provided libraries' administration the opportunity to assess the process and consider how similar centralizations could be effective in other areas. The success of the technical services reorganization was influential in planning for the full reorganization in 2020.

The newly formed department included electronic resources, systems, serials, cataloging, and acquisitions. The new head of technical services began consolidating the department by reviewing operations, successfully lobbying to shift a shared staff position to the department full-time, and hiring a librarian cataloger. As a group, the department began to develop new workflows and procedures. The workflow assessment determined that all incoming materials would be delivered to the library on the Dahlonega campus for processing and then dispersed to their final destinations. It was also discovered that pockets of materials on other campuses needed some level of attention, and technical services staff would travel to the various libraries to help with those materials. Overall, the reorganization of the technical services department proved to be extraordinarily successful, primarily due to the willingness of the people who now make up the department to embrace change and try something new.

Other than suspending the processing of physical material, the COVID shutdown had the least dramatic impact on the technical services department. Before the shutdown, the team had identified several potential database cleanup projects for the coming year. With the decision to allow people to work from home, the team shifted focus to these projects and was able to continue working very effectively as a remote team. The technical services team members logged into Teams during work hours to replicate face-to-face communications that would normally be accomplished by stepping into each other's workspaces and to maintain department cohesion.

Access Services

As the largest division in the libraries, access services potentially had the greatest challenge in reorganizing. The shift to online operations and the projects the team tackled during the shutdown served as catalysts toward building a cohesive team of empowered staff members.

When shutdown occurred, the head of access services considered how to offer services from a distance in a teleworking environment while still offering limited in-person service at the residential campus. There was a good deal of anxiety among the staff because much of their work is forward-facing and in person. To begin, division staff received training in the use of the online chat service. This training freed librarians to focus on reference and instruction while access services handled informational and access inquiries. Many students left campus with library books, DVDs, and laptops in hand. Initial work was spent fielding questions from these students about returns, due dates, fines, and fees and working with graduating students to resolve their account issues. Staff members were assigned batches of students and corresponded with them individually, understanding each patron's circumstances, offering flexible policies, and giving them a contact for further questions.

The downtime in in-person service was also an opportunity to reexamine how the division did things during normal times, and several projects were begun. One of the team's projects was an evaluation of the division handbook. Staff members based at different campuses were assigned sections to review, comment on what the policy or procedure stated and what they perceived as policy at their locations, and identify missing elements. This effort allowed the division staff the space to take ownership of their work and the freedom to create a practical, up-to-date policy document. Access services staff also completed a significant ILS data cleanup project that had loomed since consolidation.

Some of the projects undertaken were completed by individual staff members who now have long-term responsibility for those divisional activities. Previously, all employees made new faculty and staff patron accounts on demand at the information desk via a paper form. The process is now automated, and one individual oversees it. Another staff member reconciled all student account holds in the ILS, Alma. At long last, when students inquire about holds, the libraries know the information is accurate.

The reorganization and the team's COVID response legitimized the work of the access services staff and shortened the communication channels between leadership and team members. Now, as a unified whole, staff can take proactive responsibility for key elements of the division's work. The staff understands their workflows fully, and the division head needs to communicate with only an individual about specific responsibilities, rather than a scattered group. The single most significant gain for the staff in this division is that their work now has focus; they have space to work out ideas and freedom to improve services, with someone in leadership to encourage progress.

Reference and Instruction

It is somewhat inconceivable that an academic library could function without a reference and instruction department. Before the reorganization, the UNG Libraries had ten reference librarian positions and several other librarians who worked limited hours at the information desks and occasionally taught classes. There was, however, no designated leader for those activities, and, as a result, no overarching plan or goal for those services. Aside from a centralized e-mail reference account and a come-when-you-can chat reference service, all activities were scheduled and delivered at the local level.

Every component of the libraries' reference and instruction work underwent some measure of lasting change that began during the shift to COVID operations and continued during the subsequent return to campus. Before the reorganization and COVID, research consultation appointments were delivered almost entirely face-to-face, and requests were scheduled independently at each campus. Online appointments were available only to students and faculty based at the newest campus where a librarian was not present. The shift to online operations fast-tracked centralized scheduling. A redesigned request form was implemented, the division moved from eight librarians involved in scheduling to three, and the schedulers began assigning requests based as much on expertise as availability. Because of these shifts, the division head was able to create workloads that are more equitable for the librarians while expanding the hours of appointment availability.

Instruction offerings before 2020 were also conducted almost exclusively in person. With COVID-related closures, the librarians shifted from delivering a steady drumbeat of fifty-minute one-shots to creating videos, online tutorials, and handouts for asynchronous instruction along with interactive online synchronous sessions.

None of the rapid implementation of online services could have been possible without the critical step of quickly training the librarians charged with instruction. During the two weeks when classes were suspended, the team focused its energies on developing three internal guides to online instruction for library faculty, identifying tools for building online library instruction resources, and outlining methods for conducting online sessions and research consultations. The team identified members who already had familiarity with certain tools or practices to serve as mentors, sharing their expertise with colleagues. The division head also built a communication space in Teams so members could discuss issues, share ideas, and vent frustrations. Even with the shock of the shift to online operations, there was only one instruction cancellation that semester out of the forty sessions initially scheduled for March 13 or later.

Administration

The libraries' administration had the most buy-in on the new organizational structure, as the administrators had all played a crucial part in creating it. The leadership team had taken the time to develop it, which meant more time to live with how things would work. As a result, the turmoil of 2020 for the administrative team became less about realizing the new team structure and more about managing the libraries' COVID response. The BLT continued bimonthly meetings as before, but they were held via Teams. From a practical standpoint, the travel time that was normally spent going to and from the different campuses was eliminated, along with the accompanying fatigue and stress. Leadership did away with written monthly division reports and began to rely on sharing information at the regular meetings, as well as at individual check-in meetings between the dean and division heads. In the beginning, these meetings were held every week because of the amount of information and questions being generated due to COVID operations. Some BLT members also had new responsibilities at the university level (e.g., working groups on providing for student technology needs, reopening working groups). The leadership team also took the opportunity to revisit certain policies and procedures (e.g., vendor contracts) that had been identified during reorganization planning.

The New and Improved UNG Libraries

Effective and frequent communication is a key way that leaders can help to build trust and reinforce a commitment to transparency.[11] When there is trust, there is generally thought to be more buy-in to the changes taking place.[12] As Elena Carrillo and Gwen Gregory note, "Sometimes, by sheer necessity, change does happen overnight, but effective and lasting change is the result of long-term consistency, communication, and collegiality."[13] Whatever the pace of the change, it is clear throughout the literature that communication is one of the most important elements.

One of the goals of the libraries' reorganization was to eliminate chain-of-command communications. In the planning discussions, leadership likened the libraries' communication patterns to the old telephone game. Information became muddled as it crossed up and over and down and back. The new structure and the use of Teams have both made an enormous difference, and leadership finds increasingly that library faculty and staff are reaching out directly to the right person to ask questions or share information. Being able to see each other while talking via webcams and not just talking on the phone or communicating via e-mail has helped build working relationships among the team members.

The use of Tea Times and the subsequent development of Library Learning and Leisure channels in Teams (devoted to hobbies and interests) has also allowed many employees to get to know each other on a much more personal level than the location-based structure had ever allowed. While some may see this as frivolous, leadership continues to see evidence that it does make faculty and staff more comfortable in reaching across divisions or campuses to work with their library colleagues. In late summer 2021, the libraries held their third annual retreat at an outdoor facility, with faculty and staff from all campuses attending. A marked change in how the faculty and staff interacted was obvious, with several employees from different campuses intermingling, many sitting by team rather than location, as they had done previously.

The efforts of the UNG Libraries' staff and faculty through the COVID crisis alone would be a testament to teamwork. Successfully navigating the flux of 2020 while undergoing a complete reorganization at a distance and accomplishing numerous projects demonstrates the completely new level of community that has been achieved. Confusion and misunderstandings occur, but because of the revamped structure and newfound skills developed in quick pandemic pivoting, the teams are more nimble and able to work together to get back on course. In the end, even if leadership had not implemented the reorganizational changes that were put forth in fall 2019, the organizational structure would have inevitably gone through some type of shift in response to online COVID operations. Fortunately, the reorganization was well-timed, and it helped the libraries not only weather the crisis but also begin to perform at a higher level than ever before.

As the libraries approached the two-year mark since the reorganization and the COVID transformation, the BLT reinforced earlier successes by undertaking new team projects. The reference and instruction team worked to update and expand the instructional guides first developed for COVID operations, and access services revisited its manual and adding procedures to the document. In 2022 the leadership team began reflecting upon the reorganization and considering what was learned to identify opportunities to further simplify and clarify the structure. As the libraries move forward into year four, leadership will continue to examine the organizational structure and make additional changes if they will benefit operations and cement the positive cultural transformation the UNG Libraries has undergone.

Notes

1. Frances Hesselbein, "The Key to Cultural Transformation," *Leader to Leader* 1999, no. 12 (Spring 1999): 6, https://doi.org/10.1002/ltl.40619991201.
2. Elena Carrillo and Gwen M. Gregory, "Change Management in Extremis: A Case Study," *Journal of Access Services* 16, no. 1 (2019): 21–33, https://doi.org/10.1080/15367967.2018.1560224; Ken Johnson, Susan Jennings, and Sue Hisle, "Ending the Turf War: Circulation, Reference, and Instruction on One Team," *Journal of Access Services* 8, no. 3 (2011): 107–24, https://doi.org/10.1080/15367967.2011.578 514; John Novak and Annette Day, "The Libraries They Are A-Changin': How Libraries Reorganize," *College and Undergraduate Libraries* 22, no. 3–4 (2015): 358–73, https://doi.org/10.1080/10691316.2 015.1067663; Jill Mierke and Vicki Williamson, "A Framework for Achieving Organizational Culture Change," *Library Leadership and Management* 31, no. 2 (January 13, 2017), https://doi.org/10.5860/llm.v31i2.7216; Petra Düren, "Leadership in Libraries in Times of Change," *IFLA Journal* 39, no. 2 (June 2013): 134–39, https://doi.org/10.1177/0340035212473541; Sarah Tusa, "Perspectives on Library Reorganization," *Serials Review* 45, no. 3 (2019): 163–66, https://doi.org/10.1080/00987913.2019.16444 83.
3. Mierke and Williamson, "Framework for Achieving Organizational Culture Change"; Novak and Day, "Libraries They Are A-Changin.'"
4. Irene Münster, "A Tale of Two Libraries: A Merger and Its Challenges. A Case Study," *Journal of Library Administration* 57, no. 2 (2017): 174–93, https://doi.org/10.1080/01930826.2016.1222119; Novak and Day, "Libraries They Are A-Changin'"; Johnson, Jennings, and Hisle, "Ending the Turf War"; Düren, "Leadership in Libraries in Times of Change."
5. Düren, "Leadership in Libraries in Times of Change"; Novak and Day, "Libraries They Are A-Changin'"; Mierke and Williamson, "Framework for Achieving Organizational Culture Change."
6. Novak and Day, "Libraries They Are A-Changin,'" 362.
7. Düren, "Leadership in Libraries in Times of Change"; Novak and Day, "Libraries They Are A-Changin'"; Mierke and Williamson, "Framework for Achieving Organizational Culture Change."
8. John P. Kotter and Leonard A. Schlesinger, "Choosing Strategies for Change," *Harvard Business Review* 86, no. 7/8 (July/August 2008): 130, EBSCOhost.
9. Boris Groysberg and Michaelk Slind, "Leadership Is a Conversation," *Harvard Business Review* 90, no. 6 (June 2012): 77, EBSCOhost.
10. Groysberg and Slind, "Leadership Is a Conversation," 78.
11. Johnson, Jennings, and Hisle, "Ending the Turf War."
12. Mierke and Williamson, "Framework for Achieving Organizational Culture Change"; Tusa, "Perspectives on Library Reorganization"; Düren, "Leadership in Libraries in Times of Change."
13. Carrillo and Gregory, "Change Management in Extremis," 30.

Bibliography

Carrillo, Elena, and Gwen M. Gregory. "Change Management in Extremis: A Case Study." *Journal of Access Services* 16, no. 1 (2019): 21–33. https://doi.org/10.1080/15367967.2018.1560224.

Düren, Petra. "Leadership in Libraries in Times of Change." *IFLA Journal* 39, no. 2 (June 2013): 134–39. https://doi.org/10.1177/0340035212473541.

Groysberg, Boris, and Michael Slind. "Leadership Is a Conversation." *Harvard Business Review* 90, no. 6 (June 2012): 76–84. EBSCOhost.

Hesselbein, Frances. "The Key to Cultural Transformation." *Leader to Leader* 1999, no. 12 (Spring 1999): 6–7. https://doi.org/10.1002/ltl.40619991201.

Johnson, Ken, Susan Jennings, and Sue Hisle. "Ending the Turf War: Circulation, Reference, and Instruction on One Team." *Journal of Access Services* 8, no. 3 (2011): 107–24. https://doi.org/10.1080/1536796 7.2011.578514.

Kotter, John P., and Leonard A. Schlesinger. "Choosing Strategies for Change." *Harvard Business Review* 86, no. 7/8 (July/August 2008): 130–39. EBSCOhost.

Mierke, Jill, and Vicki Williamson. "A Framework for Achieving Organizational Culture Change." *Library Leadership and Management* 31, no. 2 (2017). https://doi.org/10.5860/llm.v31i2.7216.

Münster, Irene. "A Tale of Two Libraries: A Merger and Its Challenges. A Case Study." *Journal of Library Administration* 57, no. 2 (2017): 174–93. https://doi.org/10.1080/01930826.2016.1222119.

Novak, John, and Annette Day. "'The Libraries They Are A-Changin': How Libraries Reorganize." *College and Undergraduate Libraries* 22, no. 3–4 (2015): 358–73. https://doi.org/10.1080/10691316.2015.1067663.

Tusa, Sarah. "Perspectives on Library Reorganization." *Serials Review* 45, no. 3 (2019): 163–66. https://doi.org/10.1080/00987913.2019.1644483.

CHAPTER 9

Managing Stakeholder Expectations during a Crisis

Jocelyn T. Tipton

For an academic library operating within the organizational structure of the larger institution, stakeholders, whose support is essential, are more than just users.

Introduction

Libraries want to be entwined and highly invested in the research and learning being done on their campuses. They strive to meet the academic needs of their students, faculty, and staff. The resources they provide, the services they offer, and the interactions with other campus units demonstrate the value they add to the mission of the university. In explaining this relationship to administrators, library team leaders often describe the library as the heart of the campus. This is an admirable goal and one that libraries take pride in accomplishing. This is a great position to be in when everything is running smoothly for the institution. However, when crisis hits, meeting the needs of various stakeholders requires greater focus and becomes more of a challenge.

During the COVID-19 pandemic in 2020–2021, universities were forced to send their students home, their faculty went to work remotely, and courses shifted to online learning. Libraries needed to be quick to respond to these changes. Many of the decisions that library managers made were reactive based on frequently changing information with little time to consult with users. Because of strong relationships with stakeholders before the crisis, they could be confident that their decisions were addressing needs. As the pandemic continued, additional decisions were made and original decisions were reevaluated as stakeholder needs continued to evolve.

Numerous articles and surveys were compiled to show what libraries did in response to the COVID-19 pandemic.[1] While the implementation of these decisions was, and is, important, equally important are the factors that influenced these decisions and the strategies leaders used to make them. Despite the fluidity of the situation, library directors were simultaneously autonomous in some decisions made while also hampered by limitations placed on them from outside entities and other factors. Internal and external stakeholders were exerting their influence to have their needs addressed; library teams often had to make painful decisions amid competing priorities.

Under normal operating conditions, libraries often choose to focus on users as the determining factor for decision-making. However, during a crisis additional groups exert their influence. One way of exploring these groups and their impact on decision-making is through the lens of stakeholder theory. Stakeholder theory stresses the interconnectedness of all those who have an interest in the organization and provides a framework for recognizing, prioritizing, and integrating their interests into the decision-making process.[2] Certain stakeholders may want more input or feel left out of the equation. Addressing the competing needs and managing expectations on tight budgets with effective communication is critical.

In response to COVID-19, library management made decisions and implemented services and procedures specific to each stakeholder group. During times of crisis, the relationship between stakeholder groups can shift, new stakeholders can emerge, and the needs of some stakeholders may take priority over those of others, and their expectations of the library can conflict. Library managers needed to take all of this into account as they maintained their essential role in their institutions. These decisions were made to reinforce the value that each stakeholder placed on the library. Using a midsize research library during the COVID-19 pandemic as an example, the chapter will explore various stakeholder expectations during a crisis, how a library responded, and the importance of knowing and communicating with stakeholders when implementing a response to the situation.

Stakeholders and Stakeholder Theory

Although stakeholder theory was developed for the corporate world, its underlying concepts are applicable to any organization, including libraries. Stakeholders are identified by their interest in the organization.[3] Freeman defines a stakeholder as any group or individual that can impact, or is affected by, an organization and without whose support the organization would cease to exist.[4] Stakeholder theory suggests that managers, therefore, have obligations to these stakeholders. For an academic library operating within the organizational structure of the larger institution, stakeholders, whose support is essential, are more than just users. Table 9.1 shows how library stakeholders have been classified in previous literature. Each list of stakeholders include more than just typical library users and acknowledge that academic libraries are influenced by groups outside of the library and the institution. Together these groups aid in accomplishing the mission of the library or are beneficiaries of its services and resources.

Table 9.1
Academic library stakeholders

Perel[a]	Cullen and Calvert[b]	Harland, Stewart, and Bruce[c]
Students, faculty, administration, and larger society	Resource allocators, senior library staff, other library staff, academic staff, graduate students, and undergraduates	All teaching, research, and administrative staff; undergraduate and graduate students; broad range of community groups, communities, and professional groups

a. W. M. Perel, "The Constituencies of Higher Education," *Educational Considerations* 14, no. 1 (1987): 12–14, https://doi.org/10.4148/0146-9282.1650.
b. Rowena J. Cullen and Philip J. Calvert, "Stakeholder Perceptions of University Library Effectiveness," *Journal of Academic Librarianship* 21, no. 6 (1995): 438–48. https://doi.org/10.1016/0099-1333(95)90087-X.
c. Fiona Harland, Glenn Stewart, and Christine Bruce, "Ensuring the Academic Library's Relevance to Stakeholders: The Role of the Library Director," *Journal of Academic Librarianship* 43, no. 5 (2017): 397–408.

A key component of stakeholder theory is the understanding that an organization is part of a larger system, and managers need to have a system perspective.[5] This was evident during the COVID-19 crisis, when decisions made at the federal and state levels were directly impacting businesses, organizations, and individual actions. Additionally, decisions made by campus departments were dictating library procedures. Specific examples of this will be shown later in the chapter. Freeman, Phillips, and Sisodia explain that "taking all stakeholders into account reflects a higher consciousness on the part of leaders, through which they are able to see the interconnectedness and interdependence."[6] As a matter of course, academic library managers navigate this interconnectedness in their decisions. Trying to achieve balance, fairness, and harmony within the entire system makes decision-making even more difficult during a crisis when stakeholders have disparate interests, new players enter the system, and expected outcomes conflict with one another.

Stakeholder Theory during a Crisis

Crisis research has shown that an organization's assumptions and understanding of its stakeholders' behavior affect that organization's success in managing crises.[7] In the context of crises, adopting the principles of a stakeholder model will lead companies to engage in proactive and accommodating crisis management behavior.[8] During a crisis, managers tend to make extra efforts to establish trusting and cooperative relationships with a broad set of stakeholders and increase their awareness of how different stakeholder may be affected by and respond to a crisis.[9] This is because in the stakeholder model they are concerned that the organization's decisions and actions may have a negative impact on particular stakeholders.[10] An efficient managerial approach to a crisis requires including as many stakeholders as possible in crisis preparation and response, allowing them to bring their perspectives, identity, and knowledge to analysis.[11] Sellnow and Sellnow warn that the urgency of the crisis, at the beginning phase, might complicate the organization's ability to maintain intensive forms of stakeholder communications because there is little time for stakeholder dialogue.[12] During the COVID pandemic, when decisions needed to be made quickly and information was constantly changing, it was not possible to always get feedback from stakeholders in advance. Library managers had to rely on what they already knew from previous stakeholder interactions.

Responding to Stakeholders during a Pandemic

In March 2020, like other higher education institutions around the world, the University of Mississippi needed to quickly react to the COVID-19 pandemic. The decisions that library administrators made were similar to those made at higher education institutions around the world. Using this school as an example, we can see how library managers applied stakeholder theory in their decision-making process. A major challenge for library managers who are focused on stakeholder interests is the diversity of stakeholders and their requirements.[13] Looking at five primary stakeholder groups (larger community, campus administrators, library employees, faculty, students) separately will show how their interests played a role in how the library responded to the crisis. In some cases, the stakeholder group had a greater effect on how the library administrators managed the crisis, and in other cases, they were the ones affected by the decision. Some examples will also show how the requirements of one stakeholder group conflicted with the interests of another. Qingchun points out that different stakeholders can have different and conflicting interests and there may be a variety of interests among similar stakeholders.[14]

Stakeholder Analysis

The larger community was one group of stakeholders who were external to the institution but extremely influential in setting policies and determining procedures. They included government officials (governors, mayors, health officials, etc.). They were the ones who conveyed the severity of the situation. They closed businesses, issued and repealed mask mandates, and set social distancing requirements. Academic institutions had few options but to go along with their regulations. This group would typically have little influence in the day-to-day operations of a library, but during the pandemic their input was prioritized. Stakeholder theory would classify this group as ones that had a greater effect on the organization than the reverse. The influence of these external entities demonstrates that powerful stakeholders can constrain the options available to other stakeholder groups.[15] At the same time the library looked at the community as a new stakeholder to see what it could do to help. Partnering with the local hospital the library was able to use its 3D printers to make face shields for the frontline health-care workers.

Campus administrators as stakeholders consist of the key decision makers for the university, and therefore those decisions impacted the library.[16] At the University of Mississippi, these stakeholders included the chancellor, provost, and deans as well as the Future Planning Task Force. The last group, along with its subcommittees, was formed to develop all aspects of the university's response. The library was fortunate to be included as a part of this decision-making group. Being included in this group was an acknowledgment by university leadership that the library is essential to the university's ability to accomplish its mission. These administrators and groups were the ones that established the protocols and procedures put in place for campus operations. The policies of university libraries were influenced by the decisions of university administration.[17] This powerful stakeholder limited how the library could address the needs of other groups. For example, they determined when employees could return to in-person work, when students could return to campus, how the library should arrange its furniture to meet social distancing guidelines, and what signage would be used throughout the building. Their decisions related to remote learning impacted how the library would deliver services to students. At the same time, library administrators were relying on them to provide guidance for us on how to respond to the crisis. This stakeholder group communicated the needs of some of our other stakeholder groups to the library, acting as proxy for those that we couldn't get input from directly.

Library employees are stakeholders who may be viewed as internal to the organization. Employees are an example of internal stakeholders. They are directly involved in the operational process and provide the services that address the concerns of other stakeholders. During the COVID crisis they became a group with their own set of needs and interests that had to be addressed by management. A survey of academic library directors pointed out that managers had to deal with tension between ensuring staff well-being and continuing to provide essential services.[18] Decisions about quarantining materials, offering contactless pickup of materials, and providing personal protective equipment prioritized the safety of employees and library users. A challenge for managers was how to equitably address where employees could work when the campus began to reopen. Most library employees were able to continue working remotely. However, some positions required staff to physically be in the building. An important aspect of using the stakeholder model for decision-making is realizing that there are differences within groups and a single solution may not be sufficient.

Faculty stakeholders as a group is one that academic libraries often see as a primary stakeholder. Services and collections are developed to support their research and teaching. In response to the rapid shift to online learning and remote work, the library was able to step in and demonstrate additional ways that it was able to assist them. Many faculty needed to learn how to transition their courses to online. The library became the go-to resource for answering copyright questions, providing access to digital course materials, and offering virtual library sessions. None of these services was new, but in the past they were often overlooked by faculty because there was no immediate need.

Managing expectations regarding access to resources for their research was more difficult. Most libraries had closed their buildings and were not loaning print materials—there was limited (or no) access to their print collections and no means of shipping materials, so interlibrary loan services were, in many instances, not possible. The library did expand its patron-initiated purchasing, and the requested items were shipped directly to the user.

Students are the largest group of stakeholders for the library—both graduate and undergraduate students. In order to remain available to them, the library was one of the last buildings on campus to close (waiting until there was a statewide stay-at-home order) and first to reopen. Students value the library space as a place to access technology, study, and collaborate with others. They also access resources and services in person and request assistance with their assignments, research, and personal interests. Those needs did not go away during the pandemic, and the library prioritized resuming normal operations while still adhering to the parameters and protocols set by other stakeholders. The library also expanded services to make it more convenient for students to get help. Besides providing space, the library created additional online tutorials, developed new topic and course LibGuides, and extended chat and e-mail reference hours. The library was familiar with the needs of this stakeholder group and was confident that it was meeting them despite difficult circumstances. It was a bit surprising when another group stepped in to speak for these stakeholders—their parents. Management needed to determine whether the requests being made were possible and what the students actually wanted. During a crisis it is essential to keep all stakeholders informed about the organization's response as the situation continues to unfold. Timely accurate information demonstrates that the stakeholder is valued.

Conclusion

As librarians settle into what is being referred to as the *new normal,* managers can reflect back on the importance of considering all stakeholder interests. Applying the stakeholder model is an important part of ensuring quality of academic library programs and services and remaining relevant to stakeholders.[19] Engaging with all stakeholder groups before, during, and after a crisis should be a priority for managers. Stakeholders can help librarians prepare for change and make better strategic decisions. Incorporating a stakeholder model as part of management decisions enables the library to find out the needs and how the library can meet those needs, and it allows the library to promote itself and its services, ensuring that it remains the heart of the university.

Notes

1. American Library Association, *Libraries Respond* (Chicago: American Library Association, 2020); Bradley P. Tolppanen, "A Survey of Response of Access Services in Academic Libraries to COVID-19," *Journal of Access Services* 18, no. 2 (2021): 65–76; Jennifer K. Frederick and Christine Wolff-Eisenberg, *Academic Library Strategy and Budgeting during the COVID-19 Pandemic* (New York: Ithaka S+R, 2020).

2. Ronald K. Mitchell, Bradley R. Agle, and Donna J. Wood, "Toward a Theory of Stakeholder Identification and Salience: Defining the Principle of Who and What Really Counts," *Academy of Management Review* 22, no. 4 (1997): 853–86.
3. Thomas Donaldson and Lee E. Preston, "The Stakeholder Theory of the Corporation: Concepts, Evidence, and Implications," *Academy of Management Review* 20, no. 1 (1995): 65–91.
4. R. Edward Freeman, "Stakeholder Theory," in *Wiley Encyclopedia of Management*, 3rd ed., vol. 2, *Business Ethics* (Hoboken, NJ: John Wiley and Sons, 2015), Wiley Online Library, https://doi.org/10.1002/9781118785317.weom020179.
5. Fremont E. Kast and James E. Rosenzweig, "General Systems Theory: Applications for Organization and Management," *Academy of Management Journal* 15, no. 4 (December 1972): 447–65.
6. R. Edward Freeman, Robert Phillips, and Rajendra Sisodia, "Tensions in Stakeholder Theory," *Business and Society* 59, no. 2 (2020): 221.
7. Ian I. Mitroff and Ralph H. Kilmann, *Corporate Tragedies* (New York: Praeger, 1984).
8. Can M. Alpaslan, Sandy E. Green, and Ian I. Mitroff, "Corporate Governance in the Context of Crises: Towards a Stakeholder Theory of Crisis Management," *Journal of Contingencies and Crisis Management* 17, no. 1 (2009): 38–49, https://doi.org/10.1111/j.1468-5973.2009.00555.x.
9. Thomas M. Jones, "Instrumental Stakeholder Theory: A Synthesis of Ethics and Economics," *Academy of Management Review* 20, no. 2 (April 1995): 404–37, https://doi.org/10.2307/258852.
10. Alpaslan, Green, and Mitroff, "Corporate Governance."
11. Maria L. Nathan and Ian I. Mitroff, "The Use of Negotiated Order Theory as a Tool for the Analysis and Development of an Interorganizational Field," *Journal of Applied Behavioral Science* 27, no. 2 (1991): 163–80, https://doi.org/10.1177/0021886391272002.
12. Tim Sellnow and Deanna Sellnow, "The Instructional Dynamic of Risk and Crisis Communication: Distinguishing Instructional Messages from Dialogue," *Review of Communication* 10, no. 2 (2010): 112–26.
13. Fiona Harland, Glenn Stewart, and Christine Bruce, "Ensuring the Academic Library's Relevance to Stakeholders: The Role of the Library Director," *Journal of Academic Librarianship* 43, no. 5 (2017): 397–408.
14. Yue Qingchun, "A Study of Crisis Management Based on Stakeholders Analysis Model," *IOP Conference Series: Earth and Environmental Science* 94 (2017): article 012042, https://doi.org/10.1088/1755-1315/94/1/012042.
15. Flore M. Bridoux and Pushpika Vishwanathan, "When Do Powerful Stakeholders Give Managers the Latitude to Balance All Stakeholders' Interests?" *Business and Society* 59, no. 2 (2020): 232–62.
16. Rowena J. Cullen and Philip J. Calvert, "Stakeholder Perceptions of University Library Effectiveness," *Journal of Academic Librarianship* 21, no. 6 (1995): 438–48, https://doi.org/10.1016/0099-1333(95)90087-X.
17. Muhammad Rafiq et al., "University Libraries Response to COVID-19 Pandemic: A Developing Country Perspective," *Journal of Academic Librarianship* 47, no.1 (2021): article 102280, https://doi.org/10.1016/j.acalib.2020.102280.
18. Frederick and Wolff-Eisenberg, *Academic Library Strategy*.
19. John B. Harer and Bryan R. Cole, "The Importance of the Stakeholder in Performance Measurement: Critical Processes and Performance Measures for Assessing and Improving Academic Library Services and Programs," *College and Research Libraries* 66, no. 2 (2005): 149–70; Fiona Harland, Glenn Stewart, and Christine Bruce, "Leading the Academic Library in Strategic Engagement with Stakeholders: A Constructivist Grounded Theory," *College and Research Libraries* 80, no. 3 (2019): 319–39, https://doi.org/10.5860/crl.80.3.319.

Bibliography

Alpaslan, Can M., Sandy E. Green, and Ian I. Mitroff. "Corporate Governance in the Context of Crises: Towards a Stakeholder Theory of Crisis Management." *Journal of Contingencies and Crisis Management* 17, no. 1 (2009): 38–49. https://doi.org/10.1111/j.1468-5973.2009.00555.x.

American Library Association. *Libraries Respond: COVID-19 Survey Results (May 2020)*. Chicago: American Library Association, 2020.

Bridoux, Flore M., and Pushpika Vishwanathan. "When Do Powerful Stakeholders Give Managers the Latitude to Balance All Stakeholders' Interests?" *Business and Society* 59, no. 2 (2020): 232–62.

Cullen, Rowena J., and Philip J. Calvert. "Stakeholder Perceptions of University Library Effectiveness." *Journal of Academic Librarianship* 21, no. 6 (1995): 438–48. https://doi.org/10.1016/0099-1333(95)90087-X.

Donaldson, Thomas, and Lee E. Preston. "The Stakeholder Theory of the Corporation: Concepts, Evidence, and Implications." *Academy of Management Review* 20, no. 1 (1995): 65–91.

Frederick, Jennifer K., and Christine Wolff-Eisenberg. *Academic Library Strategy and Budgeting during the COVID-19 Pandemic.* New York: Ithaka S-R, 2020.

Freeman, R. Edward. "Stakeholder Theory." In *Wiley Encyclopedia of Management*, 3rd ed., vol. 2, *Business Ethics.* Hoboken, NJ: John Wiley and Sons, 2015. Wiley Online Library. https://doi.org/10.1002/9781118785317.weom020179.

Freeman, R. Edward, Robert Phillips, and Rajendra Sisodia. "Tensions in Stakeholder Theory." *Business and Society* 59, no. 2 (2020): 213–31.

Harer, John B., and Bryan R. Cole. "The Importance of the Stakeholder in Performance Measurement: Critical Processes and Performance Measures for Assessing and Improving Academic Library Services and Programs." *College and Research Libraries* 66, no. 2 (2005): 149–70.

Harland, Fiona, Glenn Stewart, and Christine Bruce. "Ensuring the Academic Library's Relevance to Stakeholders: The Role of the Library Director." *Journal of Academic Librarianship* 43, no. 5 (2017): 397–408.

———. "Leading the Academic Library in Strategic Engagement with Stakeholders: A Constructivist Grounded Theory." *College and Research Libraries* 80, no. 3 (2019): 319–39. https://doi.org/10.5860/crl.80.3.319.

Jones, Thomas M. "Instrumental Stakeholder Theory: A Synthesis of Ethics and Economics." *Academy of Management Review* 20, no. 2 (April 1995): 404–37. https://doi.org/10.2307/258852.

Kast, Fremont E., and James E. Rosenzweig. "General Systems Theory: Applications for Organization and Management." *Academy of Management Journal* 15, no. 4 (December 1972): 447–65.

Mitchell, Ronald K., Bradley R. Agle, and Donna J. Wood. "Toward a Theory of Stakeholder Identification and Salience: Defining the Principle of Who and What Really Counts." *Academy of Management Review* 22, no. 4 (1997): 853–86.

Mitroff, Ian I., and Ralph H. Kilmann. *Corporate Tragedies: Product Tampering, Sabotage, and Other Catastrophes.* New York: Praeger, 1984.

Nathan, Maria L., and Ian I. Mitroff. "The Use of Negotiated Order Theory as a Tool for the Analysis and Development of an Interorganizational Field." *Journal of Applied Behavioral Science* 27, no. 2 (1991): 163–80. https://doi.org/10.1177/0021886391272002.

Perel, W. M. "The Constituencies of Higher Education." *Educational Considerations* 14, no. 1 (1987): 12–14. https://doi.org/10.4148/0146-9282.1650.

Qingchun, Yue. "A Study of Crisis Management Based on Stakeholders Analysis Model." *IOP Conference Series: Earth and Environmental Science* 94 (2017): article 012042. https://doi.org/10.1088/1755-1315/94/1/012042.

Rafiq, Muhammad, Syeda Hina Batool, Amna Farzand Ali, and Midrar Ullah. "University Libraries Response to COVID-19 Pandemic: A Developing Country Perspective." *Journal of Academic Librarianship* 47, no. 1 (2021): article 102280. https://doi.org/10.1016/j.acalib.2020.102280.

Sellnow, Tim, and Deanna Sellnow. "The Instructional Dynamic of Risk and Crisis Communication: Distinguishing Instructional Messages from Dialogue." *Review of Communication* 10, no. 2 (2010): 112–26.

Tolppanen, Bradley P. "A Survey of Response of Access Services in Academic Libraries to COVID-19." *Journal of Access Services* 18, no. 2 (2021): 65–76.

CHAPTER 10

When Change Management Is Not Enough

Cinthya Ippoliti

> *Planning for all contingencies is impossible; however, planning is an essential part of a leadership team's arsenal to address crises with preparedness.*

Introduction

The COVID pandemic has shifted focus on the ways in which libraries have provided services, advocated for resources, and supported staff. While the literature covers many aspects related to change management, there is an underlying assumption about a certain level of contextual stability that has not been present over the past year. Change management in the context of a crisis is even more challenging because the change itself is often unpredictable and usually detrimental, leaving supervisors to grapple with increased levels of anxiety, uncertainty, stress, and chaos. This chapter proposes to fill that gap by analyzing both the relational and the operational strategies that can provide a road map for library leaders in times of crisis and translate these concepts into actionable and practical applications. Now more than ever, library leaders have to work along parallel and often paradoxical tracks in order to blend these elements into a cohesive approach. This means that leaders may need to make difficult decisions that have both short- and long-term implications, or they may have to sacrifice resources in order to further reduce losses, postpone important initiatives, and reconcile library priorities with organizational ones that may result in increased tensions.

For the purposes of this chapter, the author will use the terms *leaders* and *leadership* to refer to individuals in formal capacities (managers, administrators, supervisors) who also have the positionality to effectuate changes in policies and operations, establish partnerships, and direct resources toward a specific set of actions or goals. The individuals in these roles have the responsibility and potentially the functional ability to mobilize the organization in its crisis response in ways that other employees may not. These roles are separate from the notion of leadership capacity, which is not role-specific and exists everywhere within an organization.

Defining Crises

Before analyzing how libraries can respond to a crisis, it's useful to frame and define it. Crises fall along a spectrum of scope and intensity, with an immediate crisis involving a natural disaster or situation that results in catastrophe. Emerging crises can be addressed sooner in their development while there are signs of impending problems; if they are caught early, their impact can be mitigated more easily. Finally, sustained crises involve issues that may linger for years and require long-term interventions.[1] The type of crisis facing a library will naturally influence the type and level of response. There are several key indicators that signal that there is a crisis-level situation occurring. These are especially important to understand in the case of emerging or sustained crises that may not be as readily obvious as events that pose a physical or infrastructural threat. According to Business Queensland, sample key indicators include these[2]:

- Employees may suffer from confusion, anxiety, and stress.
- It may be difficult to carry out typical operations and services.
- External support may be needed from the institution, the community, or governmental entities.
- There may be a lack of clear and timely information about what is happening.
- There may be limited time in which to make decisions.
- The organization may be under scrutiny and may need to respond in some public way.

Before a Crisis

Planning for all contingencies is impossible; however, planning is an essential part of a leadership team's arsenal to address crises with preparedness. There are a number of very helpful resources available to academic library leaders for crisis planning and preparedness. Many library associations, including the American Library Association, Public Library Association, and even the Library of Congress, in addition to groups such as Amigos Library Services, provide extensive resources for addressing various crises, covering everything from preserving collections, knowing what type of equipment might need to be stored on site, contacting local and federal organizations, and dealing with floods, fires, earthquakes, and so on.

It would be great if library leaders could forecast trends and predict the future with certainty so everyone could be ready for whatever may be ahead. But the reality is that even for crises that are ongoing, leadership can seldom determine in which direction a particular situation will evolve over time. Erica Hayes James and Lynn Perry Wooten state that in a "crisis situation, the individual leader's learning should happen in tandem with the organization's learning. At the core of this learning is the skill set for acquiring knowledge and implementing a behavioral change as a result."[3] Therefore, a proactive approach to each situation within a crisis is needed.

A leader may first gain an awareness that something is not going well either by their own observations or by observations that are shared with them; this awareness is then confirmed by gathering additional evidence. This serves several purposes: it allows for the collection of a wide variety of information, but more importantly, it also helps leaders model curiosity for employees as a way of understanding differing perspectives, acknowledging employee experiences and expertise, and inviting further input, all of which lend themselves toward fostering a much needed sense of community, trust, and stability in handling a crisis.

Once a leader has the needed information, they can then determine how to prepare the organization through scenario planning and resource allocation. Scenario planning is defined as "stories that describe alternative ways the external environment might develop in the future. Each scenario explores how different conditions might support or constrain completion of ...strategy objectives"[4] Scenarios can assist in challenging the status quo and testing assumptions about the future. In addition, scenarios can assist library leadership in determining how the group can bridge the gap between what is and what might be, in order to achieve that future state; or, in the case of a crisis, minimize damages. Fergnani underscores two types of scenarios that can be utilized.[5] Exploratory scenarios begin with the present as the starting point and move toward the future, either by extrapolating trends or potential causes, or simply by asking "what if?" questions to elicit developments that lie outside of these familiar boundaries. Normative scenarios start with a preliminary view of a possible future or set of futures that are of particular interest. They then look backward to see if and how these futures might evolve from the present—how they might be achieved or avoided given the existing constraints and resources within the organization. If a library already has a SWOT analysis in place, the SWOT can be used as the lens through which the planning for a scenario-based crisis could be reviewed. *SWOT analysis* is a term used for an examination of an organization's strengths, weaknesses, opportunities, and threats. Strengths are internal factors in the organization that will support moving the identified goals forward, such as particular expertise or a unique offering; weaknesses are internal components that might significantly delay implementation, such as lack of funding; opportunities are external advantages that will help achieve strategy in the form of partnerships or additional support; threats are external circumstances that may prevent implementation, for instance furloughs or layoffs.

The second area that leaders can consider is that of resource allocation, which is closely tied to supporting solutions identified in response to a particular scenario.[6] Going through needs using a detailed, critical analysis forces leaders to think through different options and may even prompt a preemptive request for additional support either in tangible assets or partnerships that might not have otherwise surfaced. For example, the library might be working with database vendors to provide expanded access to online resources for a certain period of time, or perhaps collaborate with companies to provide hot spots for users who could not otherwise afford an internet connection. Finally, there might be an opportunity for temporary funding to bring on additional coverage for services, such as chat or virtual consultations.

In the event that a crisis constitutes a loss of resources or services, as has occurred in recent history, and been observed during the COVID-19 pandemic, understanding the impact of these losses and being able to amortize it, however hypothetically, through a given scenario is critical. For example, assuming 5 percent, 10 percent, or even 15 percent reduction in across-the-board funding can assist a library in identifying both the criteria for determining where the cuts should be made and the decision-making mechanisms employed to effectuate them. While this does not make the process easier, it does provide some parameters around these difficult decisions.

Psychological Safety and Trust

While scenario planning and resource allocation address operational dimensions, leaders should also address relational ones. Felicity Menzies mentions that Amy Edmondson defines psychological safety as a "shared belief held by members of a team that the team is safe for interpersonal risk-taking."[7] Leaders can help set the stage for psychological safety as a way to support a thriving organization even before a crisis may be present. In general, psychological safety allows employees to hold differing views, discuss issues openly, and make mistakes without being penalized for taking a risk. An underlying tenet of psychological safety is that everyone should participate in establishing how the team wants to operationalize these actions. Leaders can create the figurative space where these conversations can occur and to model the behavior they wish to see. Psychological safety by extension relies on trust among individuals within an organization. If employees do not trust one another to behave in the ways described above, psychological safety can go only so far in supporting these actions. Trust is commonly defined as "a psychological state that comprises the intention to accept vulnerability based upon positive expectations of the intentions or behavior of another."[8] Gillespie and Dietz argue that employees' assessments of their organization's trustworthiness are based on the organization's characteristics that enable it to meet its goals and responsibilities (i.e., ability), the care and concern shown for the well-being of employees and other stakeholders (i.e., benevolence), and the organization's adherence to commonly accepted moral principles, such as honesty and fairness.[9] When the status quo is disrupted, it triggers an increased sense of vulnerability and uncertainty in the employee-employer relationship, which in turn reinforces the need to preserve it. Leaders can help employees understand why the status quo is potentially no longer viable, offer information on how the organization is likely to transition from the present uncertainty to a presumably more certain, if not entirely positive, future, and specify what the organization will potentially look like once that future is achieved.[10] Trust isn't about building rapport or team building. "It's making it clear why you're doing something, being honest about it, and then following through with it."[11]

Partnerships

Establishing and maintaining strong partnerships with key stakeholders across the institution is the final element that should be in place as part of building a solid foundation before a crisis hits. Being able to rely on those who can assist and advocate for the library may greatly increase the odds that the library will be more successful in dealing with the crisis. That being said, sometimes the very units or individuals who are usually able to help may be the ones who have to make tough decisions that will adversely impact the library. Difficult conversations may need to occur, but if the foundation has been laid, the library leader is more likely to mitigate the most damaging impacts.

Having shared goals helps to provide specific actionable direction for all parties, which helps to foster a sense of control, however minor, toward addressing the situation. These conversations also necessitate understanding the types and levels of resources that are available to the stakeholders. For example, when the pandemic first hit and most higher education institutions went remote, many students were left without adequate resources to complete their work from home, and many academic libraries stepped in to advocate for the students and to provide as much access to technology as possible with finite resources. Everyone should understand the role of each stakeholder in making decisions, which includes the types and levels of decisions, how input is sought and integrated into the process, and how to help individuals engage with a decision that they may not agree with.[12] This means that there may be times when partners are not all on the same page. It's important to understand where the areas of concern might remain—it could be that partners are fine with the overall direction of the decision but perhaps there are one or two elements that might need additional negotiation and compromise. If, however, this is a recurring issue, it could be that a lack of trust or a deeper problem is manifesting through resistance to the decision and will need to be addressed.

During the Crisis

As a crisis develops, it is critical that there be clear communication. One of the first things leaders can do is to communicate to the best of their knowledge what's happening and to let everyone know the limitations they are dealing with—be it limited time, a directive from somewhere else in the organization, or something else. Leaders must also be extremely aware of their personal limitations under pressure. What biases might they themselves harbor? Might they favor an approach that might not be appropriate in every instance? Do they have all of the information they need to make the best decision? Are they acting out of fear?[13] Another factor is that of ethics where aligning decision-making with organizational and personal values and being transparent will help employees understand how the leader is handling the crisis. With the understanding that not all decisions can be made collectively, defining what decisions should have everyone's complete agreement compared to those where folks can live with the decision even if they don't agree can mean the difference between a successful decision and a failed one. When dealing with a crisis, a leader should also encourage all employees to approach the situation from a problem-solving rather than a blaming perspective. Blaming refers to an emotion-filled process where responsibility is assigned for a past event, along with negative emotions tied to that responsibility. The blamer, who might be experiencing fear and anger, attempts to avoid responsibility and therefore abdicates control over the situation and any potential resolution by pointing to someone else. The receiver then becomes defensive and shuts down while the issue remains unresolved, leading to more frustration and stress for all parties. Problem-solving, on the other hand, focuses on understanding the problem and defining what should be happening as compared to what is happening, in order to determine how to close the gap by collectively crafting a solution that will address the issue in question.[14] A close companion to decision-making is communication. Internally, while the leader may not be able to manage everyone's emotions, it's fundamental for them to do as much as they can to minimize fear and be consistent in all aspects of communication.[15] To that end, leaders will have to be honest and provide as much information as quickly as possible and discuss what steps are being taken to address the crisis.[16] If a leader does not have the information or is waiting to hear back about something, that should be made clear as well. Showing sincerity and empathy especially is critical in establishing a structure that can help individuals feel supported even if there is bad news. One of the worst things a leader can do in this instance is to signal a lack of caring, even if unintentionally, because that can call into question all of the other actions being taken. Leaders should be actively involved and visible in the efforts of the organization to mitigate the crisis, which can include pitching in to support services, holding meetings to discuss issues, and generally being available to answer questions. Furthermore, there should be ample opportunities for employees to ask questions and offer feedback as needed through various methods such as Q&A sessions, open forums, online surveys, and individual and group meetings.[17]

Externally, a more formal communication plan might be needed. Once the scope of the situation has been understood, the first thing a leader can do is to acknowledge the issues and formulate a response that answers questions such as "Which issues should be addressed, and at what level of detail? Who should deliver the response, and through what channels?"[18] The answers to these questions can assist in the creation of a communication plan that has specific goals and is clear in terms of who is involved. This frequently means the communication may come from the larger organization instead of the library. For example, it may be easier to develop a PDF document outlining certain information that can be e-mailed to university communications and other stakeholders proactively as opposed to waiting for them to go to a website to find out the answer. Alternatively, perhaps a Twitter feed provides the most up-to-date information, but it is not considered an official channel of communication, and not many people may see it.

Tangible Employee Support

In addition to ensuring that employees feel supported emotionally during times of crisis and upheaval, it's imperative that leaders offer more tangible support as well. Tangible support can include offering flexible work schedules as policies allow; ensuring that everyone who wants to take leave feels that they can truly disengage from the office;

understanding where there is flexibility in taking personal time without having to formally request it; ensuring employees are aware of the mental health and wellness resources available to them; and finally, having adequate compensation. Knowing how to stretch certain policies is also up to the comfort level of managers, and as having some flexibility in work schedules makes sense, these policies should be applied as equitably as possible.

In the case of compensation, this is clearly a longer-term issue and may not even be within the purview of the leader to control. If there is an opportunity to offer even a temporary pay increase for taking on added duties or there is a reorganization resulting in a promotion or changes in responsibilities, it's important that the work be adequately compensated. Similarly, ensuring that student employees and temporary workers are taken into consideration as decisions are made (especially those related to layoffs, furloughs, etc.) shows that the organization cares about all employees, as it is often those who are paid the least and with the least amount of status who are most negatively affected by personnel decisions. Longer-term strategies would include conducting regular salary studies to identify equity and compression issues and developing a transparent compensation strategy that includes clear information about how employees can advance within the organization, how adjustments such as merit and cost-of-living increases are handled, and what the pay structures look like at each step. The University of Iowa offers a good example of this type of documentation.[19]

Advocacy

Developing an authentic way of advocating for personnel and resources is an essential tool in a leader's toolbox at any time, but especially during a crisis. Crutchfield and Grant explain an alternate perspective towards advocacy where the organization is leveraging collective strength to create impact towards addressing a systemic challenge.[20] What this means for the library is that it can position a request for resources within this context-of creating support that achieves institutional or organizational objectives. Reisman, Gienapp, and Stachowiak posit, "a theory of change typically addresses the set of linkages among strategies, outcomes and goals that support a broader mission or vision, along with the underlying assumptions that are related to these linkages"[21] which then lead to the creation of plan, and identifying needed resources and partners. In the instance of organizational changes, this could be a shift in mission and vision, being included in decision-making at a new level, or growing new partnerships. In terms of structural changes, this could mean anything from changes to policies, programs, services, or similar areas. One very specific example of advocacy is to request added funding or to prevent loss of funding using a narrative budget request. Rossman explains that there are several benefits of presenting a narrative budget within a library context, which include communicating complex financial information in a more understandable way; linking library mission, vision, values, and strategic plan with financial priorities; developing a deeper understanding of the library's stewardship of financial and human resources; inspiring support of the library because it is easier to see how funding makes a difference; and encouraging stakeholders and decision makers to discuss the needs of the community more deeply.[22] Rossman also outlines several steps needed in order to put a narrative budget together. The narrative itself should include specific examples of how the funds support activities, programming, and services and indicate varying levels of support that also connect to broadening circles of impact.[23] As an example, $5,000 would allow hiring three student employees who would assist in interlibrary loan functions, $10,000 would allow the hiring of students to support reference services as well as interlibrary loan, and an additional $5,000 on top of the other funding would allow for the development of an internship program to support creative technologies. Including both quantitative and qualitative data, user stories, and testimonials in a story-like format will strengthen the argument.

After the Crisis Is Over

Once a crisis has subsided, the organization needs plenty of time to process what happened, what lessons were learned, and how to move forward. It's important for leaders to offer time and a process for reflection. While this can center on operational and strategic issues, there may be a lot of emotions associated with what has happened, and some employees may have a difficult time looking ahead. People may be tired and burned out, and there may be a lack of interest or capacity to do anything new for some time. Leaders need to acknowledge and recognize all of these tensions and deal with them as openly as possible, using the tools we have discussed in this chapter. Offering resources and time to support mental wellness, sessions with counselors or the ombuds office, could be a part of this recovery as well. Once the crisis is concluded, leaders can couch lessons learned as opportunities to bridge the gap between the current state and the future state in a way that allows for flexibility as there may still be a lot of uncertainty about what that future state holds. This may entail developing smaller goals so that there is a feeling of progress without setting a vision that is so far removed from the current situation that it causes more anxiety and stress. It also entails ensuring, as before, that communication and decision-making around next steps are equally clear and inclusive and there is a sense of direction, but one that allows for variation as the organization emerges from this period and prepares for what's ahead.

Conclusion

Leadership is difficult under the best of circumstances, let alone during a crisis. Leaders are taxed to their personal and professional limits during difficult times that require them to use all of the tools at their disposal to ensure that the organization can effectively deal with the stressors and outcomes of these circumstances. One key to doing this well lies in harnessing the collective spirit, expertise, and energy of the entire organization to develop an environment where everyone is a part of the process. Internally, leaders can also help create the conditions necessary for success by ensuring that the organizational elements of communication, decision-making, and support foster transparency and inclusion. Externally, leaders can cultivate strong partnerships and advocate for resources by making a compelling case for support that highlights the impact of that support on organizational priorities and challenges. While no one person can truly handle all of the challenges that different crises may pose, leaders should prepare their team to proactively anticipate issues. While crises may uncover all of the hidden problems within an institution, they can also provide opportunities for teams to come together and work collaboratively with care and compassion.

Notes

1. Jessica Ruane, "How to Implement a Crisis Communication Plan," *Beekeeper* (blog), last updated September 6, 2022, https://www.beekeeper.io/blog/crisis-communication-plan/#:~:text=Emerging%20%E2%80%94%20Crises%20that%20can%20be,and%20require%0long%20term%20interventions.
2. Business Queensland. "Characteristics of a Crisis." Queensland Government, last updated May 21, 2021. https://www.business.qld.gov.au/running-business/protecting-business/risk-management/incident-response/crisis.
3. Erika Hayes James and Lynn Perry Wooten, "Crisis Leadership: Why It Matters," *European Financial Review*, December 2011, https://webuser.bus.umich.edu/lpwooten/PDF/TEFR%20decjan%202011%20Crisis%20Leadership.pdf (page discontinued).
4. Government Office for Science, *The Futures Toolkit*, edition 1.0 (London: Government Office for Science, November 2017), 11, https://assets.publishing.service.gov.uk/government/uploads/system/uploads/attachment_data/file/674209/futures-toolkit-edition-1.pdf.
5. Alex Fergnani, "Normative or Exploratory Scenarios: Use the Control Compass to Find Out," Medium, May 22, 2021, https://medium.com/predict/normative-or-explorative-scenarios-use-the-control-compass-to-find-out-d903c4e7183c.
6. Stephen W. Sawle, "Crisis Project Management," *PM Network* 5, no. 1 (January 1991): 25–29, https://www.pmi.org/learning/library/crisis-control-model-avoid-disasters-5185.
7. Amy Edmondson, quoted in Felicity Menzies, "How to Develop Psychological Safety and a Speak-Up Culture," *Include-Empower.com* (blog), October 3, 2018, https://cultureplusconsulting.com/2018/03/10/how-to-develop-psychological-safety/.
8. Rousseau, Denise M., Sim B. Sitkin, Ronald S. Burt, and Colin Camerer. "Not So Different After All: A Cross-discipline View of Trust." *Academy of Management Review* 23, no. 3 (July 1998): 393–404. https://www.jstor.org/stable/259285.
9. Nicole Gillespie and Graham Dietz, "Trust Repair after an Organization-Level Failure," *Academy of Management Review* 34, no. 1 (2009): 127–45. https://www.jstor.org/stable/27759989.
10. Stefanie Gustafsson et al., "Preserving Organizational Trust during Disruption," *Organization Studies* 42, no. 9 (September 2021): 1409–33, https://doi.org/10.1177/0170840620912705.
11. Claire Lew, "The 9 Leadership Mistakes You Don't Know You're Making as a New Manager," *Know Your Team* (blog), February 28, 2019, https://knowyourteam.com/blog/2019/02/28/the-9-leadership-mistakes-you-dont-know-youre-making-as-a-new-manager/.
12. National Education Association. *Collaborating in a Crisis* (Washington, DC: National Education Association, 2020), https://www.nea.org/sites/default/files/202010/Collaborating%20in%20a%20Crisis%20Guide%20.pdf.
13. James and Wooten, "Crisis Leadership."
14. Robert Bacal, "Exorcise Blame in Your Organization (Part 1)," part 1 of "Kill Blame in Your Organization: Switch to Problem-Solving," LinkedIn, November 5, 2014. https://www.linkedin.com/pulse/20141105171022-43127411-kill-blame-in-your-organization-switch-to-problem-solving-part-1/.
15. Paul A. Argenti, "Crisis Communication: Lessons from 9/11," *Harvard Business Review*, December 2002, https://hbr.org/2002/12/crisis-communication-lessons-from-911.
16. Rebecca Knight, "How to Talk to Your Team When the Future Is Uncertain," *Harvard Business Review*, April 20, 2020, https://hbr.org/2020/04/how-to-talk-to-your-team-when-the-future-is-uncertain.
17. Argenti, Paul A. "Crisis Communication: Lessons from 9/11." *Harvard Business Review*, December 2002. https://hbr.org/2002/12/crisis-communication-lessons-from-911.
18. Alice M. Tybout and Michelle Roehm, "Let the Response Fit the Scandal," *Harvard Business Review*, December 2009, https://hbr.org/2009/12/let-the-response-fit-the-scandal.

128 Chapter 10

19. University Human Resources, "Professional and Scientific Compensation Practices," University of Iowa, accessed August 3, 2021, https://hr.uiowa.edu/pay/compensation-classification/professional-scientific-compensation.
20. Crutchfield, Leslie R., and Heather McLeod Grant. *Forces for Good: The Six Practices of High-Impact Nonprofits.* San Francisco: Jossey-Bass, 2008.
21. Reisman, Jane, Anne Gienapp, and Sarah Stachowiak. *A Guide to Measuring Advocacy and Policy.* Baltimore, MD: Annie E. Casey Foundation, 2007.
22. Doralynn Rossmann, "Narrative Budgets: Telling the Story of Your Library's Value and Values," *Library Leadership and Management* 33, no. 4 (2019): 1–10, https://doi.org/10.5860/llm.v33i4.7384.
23. Rossmann, "Narrative Budgets."

Bibliography

Argenti, Paul A. "Crisis Communication: Lessons from 9/11." *Harvard Business Review*, December 2002. https://hbr.org/2002/12/crisis-communication-lessons-from-911.

Bacal, Robert. "Exorcise Blame in Your Company (Part 1)," part 1 of "Kill Blame in Your Organization: Switch to Problem-Solving." LinkedIn, November 5, 2014. https://www.linkedin.com/pulse/20141105171022-43127411-kill-blame-in-your-organization-switch-to-problem-solving-part-1/.

Business Queensland. "Characteristics of a Crisis." Queensland Government, last updated May 21, 2021. https://www.business.qld.gov.au/running-business/protecting-business/risk-management/incident-response/crisis.

Crutchfield, Leslie R., and Heather McLeod Grant. *Forces for Good: The Six Practices of High-Impact Nonprofits.* San Francisco: Jossey-Bass, 2008.

Fergnani, Alex. "Normative or Exploratory Scenarios: Use the Control Compass to Find Out." Medium, May 22, 2021. https://medium.com/predict/normative-or-explorative-scenarios-use-the-control-compass-to-find-out-d903c4e7183c.

Gillespie, Nicole, and Graham Dietz. "Trust Repair after an Organization-Level Failure." *Academy of Management Review* 34, no. 1 (2009): 127–45. https://www.jstor.org/stable/27759989.

Government Office for Science. *The Futures Toolkit: Tools for Futures Thinking and Foresight across UK Government,* edition 1.0. London: Government Office for Science, November 2017. https://assets.publishing.service.gov.uk/government/uploads/system/uploads/attachment_data/file/674209/futures-toolkit-edition-1.pdf.

Gustafsson, Stefanie, Nicole Gillespie, Rosalind Searle, Veronica Hope Hailey, and Graham Dietz. "Preserving Organizational Trust during Disruption." *Organization Studies* 42, no. 9 (September 2021): 1409–33. https://doi.org/10.1177/0170840620912705.

James, Erika Hayes, and Lynn Perry Wooten. "Crisis Leadership: Why It Matters." *European Financial Review*, December 2011: 60–64. https://webuser.bus.umich.edu/lpwooten/PDF/TEFR%20decjan%202011%20Crisis%20Leadership.pdf (page discontinued).

Knight, Rebecca. "How to Talk to Your Team When the Future Is Uncertain." *Harvard Business Review*, April 20, 2020. https://hbr.org/2020/04/how-to-talk-to-your-team-when-the-future-is-uncertain.

Lew, Claire. "The 9 Leadership Mistakes You Don't Know You're Making as a New Manager." *Know Your Team* (blog), February 28, 2019. https://knowyourteam.com/blog/2019/02/28/the-9-leadership-mistakes-you-I-know-youre-making-as-a-new-manager/.

Menzies, Felicity. "How to Develop Psychological Safety and a Speak-Up Culture." *Include-Empower.com* (blog), October 3, 2018. https://cultureplusconsulting.com/2018/03/10/how-to-develop-psychological-safety/.

National Education Association. *Collaborating in a Crisis: Ensuring Educator Voice When It Matters Most.* Washington, DC: National Education Association, 2020. https://www.nea.org/sites/default/files/2020-08/Collaborating%20in%20a%20Crisis%20Guide%20April%202020.pdf.

Reisman, Jane, Anne Gienapp, and Sarah Stachowiak. *A Guide to Measuring Advocacy and Policy.* Baltimore, MD: Annie E. Casey Foundation, 2007.

Rossmann, Doralynn. "Narrative Budgets: Telling the Story of Your Library's Value and Values." *Library Leadership and Management* 33, no. 4 (2019): 1–10. https://doi.org/10.5860/llm.v33i4.7384.

Ruane, Jessica. "How to Implement a Crisis Communication Plan." *Beekeeper* (blog), last updated September 6, 2022. https://www.beekeeper.io/blog/crisis-communication-plan/#:~:text=Emerging%20%E2%80%94%20Crises%20that%20can%20be,and%20require%20long%20term%20interventions.

Rousseau, Denise M., Sim B. Sitkin, Ronald S. Burt, and Colin Camerer. "Not So Different After All: A Cross-discipline View of Trust." *Academy of Management Review* 23, no. 3 (July 1998): 393–404. https://www.jstor.org/stable/259285.

Sawle, Stephen W. "Crisis Project Management." *PM Network* 5, no. 1 (January 1991): 25–29. https://www.pmi.org/learning/library/crisis-control-model-avoid-disasters-5185.

Tybout, Alice M., and Michelle Roehm. "Let the Response Fit the Scandal." *Harvard Business Review*, December 2009. https://hbr.org/2009/12/let-the-response-fit-the-scandal.

University Human Resources. "Professional and Scientific Compensation Practices." University of Iowa. Accessed August 3, 2021. https://hr.uiowa.edu/pay/compensation-classification/professional-scientific-compensation.

CHAPTER 11

When the World Shuts Down

Perspectives of Leading through Crisis and Strategies for Wellness, a Case Study

Kayleen Lam and Michele Whitehead

> *Employees and leaders often wonder what types of discussions are taking place outside of their awareness.... Leaders in these circumstances must make an extra effort to be transparent, provide context for difficult decisions, update the team with latest developments, devote time to meeting with team members individually, and give time between discussions to process what they have learned.*

Case Study Introduction: Public University Library Leaders in 2020–2021, Texas

Early in 2020, there was speculation about the outbreak of what was coming to be known as COVID-19, originating in Wuhan, China. Although The University of North Texas Health Science Center at Fort Worth (HSC), with its beautiful museum-district location, was over 7,500 miles from the outbreak origin, library administrators were already discussing ways to prepare if COVID continued to spread as was anticipated by public health and infectious disease experts. Two of the library leaders who were involved in these decision-making discussions were in very different places in their careers, which affected their perspectives and recommendations.

By late February, hand sanitizer and disinfectant wipes were out of stock. Two short weeks later, library administrators at Gibson D. Lewis Library sent staff home with needed equipment to begin remote work in preparation for what most expected to be a few weeks away from campus (see figure 11.1). Until this moment, the Research and User Experience (RUE) department's typical responsibilities were in person at traditional service points assisting with circulation and research needs. While at home, RUE staff members were asked to adapt these services online through tools like chat and a ticket system, which many had not previously used.

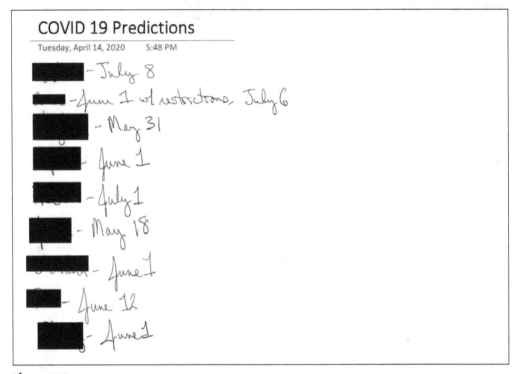

Figure 11.1
After a month into the pandemic, we took an informal poll of when staff thought they would be back in the library. This is a sampling of their answers.

Lewis Library's primary focus is serving a professional graduate health sciences campus where a main tenet of library education is information literacy. In addition to the campus audience, some librarians and staff work under a service agreement with a local hospital and clinic system. These librarians provide information support, such as in-depth literature searching, to these health-care partners, which has direct impact on patient care and outcomes. The COVID pandemic quickly became fraught with misinformation and presented endless challenges for health-care providers and information professionals alike.

The global pandemic also presented opportunities for team members to practice flexibility, learn new technologies, and innovate during a global crisis. This chapter is a case study of leading through rapid change from the perspective of the novice and seasoned professional leader of the RUE department.

Managers' Perceptions of Crisis, Change, and Responsibility

At the time of this writing, which is over a year and a half later, COVID continues to dominate the news headlines across the globe. The virus has mutated, and there is abundant medical misinformation circulating on social media, eroding faith in scientific research.[1] Vaccination and mask wearing have become politicized, creating additional challenges in navigating public service. The pandemic had and continues to have a far-reaching impact from medicine to the workplace.

Work at HSC has shifted to a more flexible model of remote and in-person services. This shift has provided positive outcomes as the library is currently enacting innovative ideas for reimagining library services, which better support our customers by providing access to resources and expertise with more convenience and ease. The past eighteen months have been challenging, and we are not collectively far enough removed to see if our ideas, leadership, and ability to handle crises are a success. However, by providing our pandemic operational strategies and wellness takeaways from the lessons we learned, the hope is these experiences will help prepare leaders for any future challenge.

Managing a Global Health Crisis and Natural Disasters in a Higher Education Setting

As work shifted to a work-from-home model, the primary consideration of library leaders was how to remotely sustain service for a campus that had traditionally operated in person. In most graduate biomedical sciences and medical school programs, portions of the curriculum require on-campus or hands-on activities. Clinical skills and laboratory activities, including the rotation of third- and fourth-year students in clinical sites across the United States, were not readily available at first in a virtual format. Even though the world was on lockdown, student learning was still a priority.

Library team members demonstrated exceptional resiliency, creativity, and growth to meet student needs. The library staff introduced and implemented new technologies, virtually met with students, and created online educational materials to support student learning and success. Examples of this are presented in the chapter, but include the creation of a remote service desk where customer support was available in a variety of ways during typical hours of operation, as well as an entire catalog of online learning opportunities using new tools for course design.

An additional complicating factor beyond the pandemic included a severe winter weather event in February 2021. This extreme storm shut down most of Texas and resulted in millions of dollars of damage, loss of power and safe water, increased food insecurity, and shelter concerns. The HSC campus was not spared from damage, and leaders were charged with making crucial decisions with multiple crises unfolding simultaneously.

The library addressed these issues by working with campus partners to safely reopen the building temporarily for students and their families who were without power or water. This example illustrates the reality for leaders that multiple crisis situations can occur concurrently and each situational need can be less compatible in some circumstances. In this example there was the need to socially distance from a disease mitigation perspective, while also opening a physical place people could come for safety from the record-breaking, harsh winter weather. Leaders must often make decisions with the best information they have at the time and critically weigh benefits versus risks.

Invoking and Revising Business Continuity Plans

Lewis Library developed a business continuity plan years prior to the COVID pandemic that detailed how operations would continue should there be any type of natural disaster that meant library operations would be carried out from a location other than the campus. The plan, originally written primarily for incidents like tornadoes or minor winter storms, was the first step for library administrators to review and revise when it became clear it would be prudent to anticipate transitioning to remote work. The business continuity plan included essential functions of each core area of work: administration, public services, technical services, special collections and records management, and the hospital. Detailed plans for communication between these functional areas also were a focus of maintaining operations.

The business continuity plan focused on needs related to making sure the library's website continued to be available and that library staff would need access to technology. It did not include planning to work with information technology services to support an entire campus with remote work needs. Seemingly overnight, leadership from academic programs and support units reached out expressing needs for internet access and laptop computers for some members of their team who traditionally worked on campus.

Equipped with knowledge of the university's plans and the latest research on an ever-evolving pandemic, the team leading the library's closing and later reopening planning knew there was a balance between providing the services needed for on-campus presence and safety. The return plan included a three-phase approach. The first phase prepared for student return twice a week by procuring cleaning supplies, creating assigned seating for twenty-five to fifty students, and minimal staff presence staggered two to three days per week. The second phase expanded services with circulation of physical items using curbside or locker technology, increased access to assigned seating for 100 to 150 students with a frequency of three to five days per week, and staff presence increased to match when students were on campus. The third phase would begin in January 2021, where there would be more access for students while restricting on-campus social and educational activities, and continued closure to nonaffiliated visitors.

Employee input was a vital contribution to decision-making. Creating an open dialogue with employees helped address any concerns and gave each member of the team ownership and control. Presenting possible outcomes, including contingencies, provided a more robust and thoughtful library reopening plan to university leadership.

Maintaining Flexibility for Implementing Decisions and Phased Return to On-Site Presence

Library administration initially planned for a return of staff to in-person operations with required face masks and social distancing by July 2020. When it became apparent that area hospitals were filling to capacity with COVID patients near that target date, the predicted surge required the university system to reconsider. A decision was made by the library administration to postpone Phase 1 return operations; unknown to campus at the time, a more complete return would not begin until almost a year later, during the summer and fall of 2021.

The timing of on-campus return was influenced by a myriad of political and public health conversations, education recommendations communicated by the state, and the availability of vaccines for the adult population. Decisions became more challenging for leaders because of increasingly alarming information about higher infection rates, particularly with the Delta variant in early 2021. Throughout the course of about fifteen months, the return to campus plans changed at least that many times. These changes highlight the necessity of remaining flexible and in a state of continuous learning, assessment, and nimble planning when the environment and preferred outcomes are rapidly shifting.

Opportunities for Shared Decision-Making and Distributed Leadership

Each member of Lewis Library's team offered a unique perspective related to their experience. A few library support staff members on the RUE team had more than twenty years of service to the institution. This organizational memory proved invaluable to decision makers and leaders to assess not only the effectiveness of the crisis triage response, but also in planning ahead for long-term service model revisions based on the lessons learned and retained.

Conversely, several of the newest team members began their employment a few short weeks before remote work began or were hired and onboarded entirely online, as was the case for one of the professional librarian positions. This fresh perspective on operations in other settings supplied the team and leaders with unique insight, encouraging alternative ideas. Lewis Library's entire team championed nontraditional solutions and assumed their own leadership roles, enacting numerous changes in operations, policies, and planning, from system support for low-touch lockers to contributing to space and service planning.

Responding to Change

For at least a decade, Lewis Library has operated with a continuous improvement culture, where all employees can provide input that shape practice. Emphasizing transparent communication and trust among team members has only increased during the pandemic and remote work. Strategically growing a caring, continuous improvement culture or improving on this foundation is especially important in change management.

World events unfolding in 2020, like the murders of unarmed black Americans including Breonna Taylor and George Floyd, highlighted long-standing systemic racial and social inequality and injustices. While this phenomenon was certainly not new, given more time to reflect further prompted interest of library team members in expanding their understanding of diversity, equity, and inclusion in addition to reimagining services and education provided by the RUE team. There are numerous health disparities the group wanted to explore related to the health sciences and related specifically to COVID. Members of the RUE team began facilitating conversations based on their own individual learning efforts, engaging with student leaders, and exploring ways to make improvements in the physical spaces of the library with inclusivity as a focus. One example reflected in the reopening of a newly renovated area of the building following the pandemic is an improved Student Food Pantry in collaboration with the Office of Care and Civility, as well as a Reflection Room for quiet meditation, yoga, prayer, and other well-being activities.

Rethinking Staffing for Public Services

Positions within some areas of public services saw higher rates of turnover before the COVID pandemic, particularly a former position for an access services librarian and their nine part-time hourly staff. Most of the part-time staff did not stay longer than a year as they were either students who finished classes or aspiring professionals. One of the goals of both the novice and the seasoned leader was to find ways to retain valuable employees by creating more full-time positions.

With the possibility of state-level budget cuts, the data from our virtual services provided a helpful narrative. The story clearly indicated staffing online chat and research request response was more than sufficient for the needs of our community and the nature of their requests. Operating hours with library staff present, both online and in person, could be shortened, which was one decision leaders easily made. Originally, the library was staffed ninety-nine hours a week, until 11 p.m., with part-time positions working weekends and evenings. The library building is accessible 24/7 for HSC affiliates, and the types of requests after 7 p.m. and on weekends were transactional in nature, like putting money on a printing account or managing community visitors. The transactional questions could be solved by implementing newer technologies like an online payment portal, lockers for item distribution, and a self-service storefront.

We had the option of keeping about half of our part-time positions or we could provide more meaningful work opportunities in the form of two full-time positions. During a time of layoffs and furloughs in other organizations, we carefully considered our budget constraints and service impacts. We determined that the value of providing full-time jobs with benefits was the best choice. This more fiscally sustainable model also meant staff had more time in their workweek to accomplish more in-depth projects, and supervising a smaller team would also result in enriched engagement between the novice manager and employee.

Challenges of Virtual Communication during Difficult Conversations

Communicating difficult news is never an easy task; however, having complex conversations in a digital environment proved to present additional challenges. For a novice manager, some of those first communications online, like conducting the first yearly performance review or having a disciplinary conversation, became even more challenging. Even from the perspective of an experienced manager, communicating difficult news from a distance felt impersonal and left little room for closure.

Reading the room for body language, anticipating emotional reactions, and creating a safe space for vulnerability can easily become hindered by shuttered webcams or, worse, the perceived pressure to stay on camera, mute buttons, and distractions when working in a remote environment. Regardless of the trust in leadership or colleagues, when employees are removed from one another outside of the office setting, there is a palpable disconnect. When return to work in person becomes an option, the disconnect may continue, and strategies for rebuilding the team's connections may be needed.

Employees and leaders often wonder what types of discussions are taking place outside of their awareness. Are there concerns or subtle issues that we would notice if we were in person? Leaders in these circumstances must make an extra effort to be transparent, provide context for difficult decisions, update the team with latest developments, devote time to meeting with team members individually, and give time between discussions to process what they have learned.

Building Connection and Creating Cohesion Virtually

Hiring for the new full-time positions occurred at the beginning of the new fiscal year. The library had been working remotely for five months, and staff members were more comfortable with newer online tools. Despite library administration's efforts to engage all staff in fun and interesting ways, there was a need for more direct interaction among RUE team members. This was made more apparent by the fully online nature where interactions with team members took place in a chat box and the only regular digital face-to-face connection was between supervisors and staff.

Weekly team huddles were a connection strategy employed by leaders as a new practice during the COVID remote work period. These full-team update sessions have continued to be invaluable even as more on-campus work has resumed. Huddles are intended to be brief discussions of work, pain points, challenges, and updates on progress, not full staff meetings. Library leaders continued to send periodic e-mails with bullet points for notable communications, created video updates, and incorporated personal touches like icebreakers to further enhance a sense of team togetherness.

Developing Ways to Be a Better Team through Training Opportunities

Leaders work to grow staff by identifying and providing training opportunities and professional development. In crisis scenarios, training may take on many forms. During the early triage of a situation, training may be more frantic or limited in time allocation and depth. Although not ideal, covering the basics of a new approach or operating procedure can serve to unite team efforts and instill a sense of control. One of the ways we maintained connection was by continuing standard operations training that would have occurred under more typical circumstances. An example of this was the decision to move forward with migrating our main integrated library system early in the pandemic-necessitated remote work.

For the RUE department, the pandemic also led to improvements that aligned with our goal to operate our educational offerings like an academic department, which involved developing courses and growing the skills of our team as professional educators. For Lewis Library's Education Team, this shift in operating procedures included a thorough examination of the development of courses, supplemental procedures, and accountability for educators. A course development guide was created and a peer review process was implemented. This allowed newer teaching librarians to practice giving and receiving constructive feedback on lesson planning, resource selection, alignment of assessments with learning objectives, and negotiating with faculty on course copyright.

Onboarding and Saying Goodbye in a Virtual Setting

Retirements, baby showers, engagements, job transitions, and even loss continued for library team members during the pandemic. Virtual games and funny backgrounds are not the same as in-person celebrations when saying goodbye to long-term employees or celebrating the arrival of a new family member. While online gatherings for these events allowed former team members in other states to participate, the disadvantage of not being able to share human interaction and celebration does diminish closure in some cases. For new employees, being welcomed to the team and onboarding from a distance does not provide a more immediate impression of the team's culture, where they fit, and the natural, beautiful rhythm of campus life.

For library leaders, one of the most important connections to maintain was with our student body and other stakeholders. Typical milestones, like Match Day for resident physician placements, research appreciation events, and graduations, have traditionally been exciting days on campus, but many of these celebrations occurred through social media posts or livestreaming instead. The library participated in these and other events by celebrating online via social media pos and attending virtual orientations and events (see figure 11.2).

Figure 11.2
Lewis Library team members celebrate and honor 2020 HSC graduates using social media.

Lessons Learned through Long-Haul Change

Related to our continuous improvement mindset, library leaders worked to encourage our team to approach all our decisions from a learning framework. The way we defined employee success prior to COVID rested largely on campus campaigns to build or enhance engagement, whether we had coverage for staffing schedules, and the institution's performance appraisal process. Like many institutions, the library was lacking data that truly measured the skills, abilities, and contributions of team members to the educational function of the university, as well as direct student impact. By operating a remote service desk and fully utilizing online tools, we now capture these contributions more thoroughly by qualitative analysis of online transcripts to supplement impressive statistics.

In communicating crisis response to campus administration, a library's ability to clearly articulate impressive wins are critical and can result in rewards for outstanding teamwork. One such example is the more than 1,200 percent increase we measured for in-depth research support from March 2020 to March 2021. Our revised service model is a substantial departure from a passive service point. Staff can now continue to engage with students and faculty in more meaningful ways resulting from our decision to adopt online tools as a longer-term solution, develop outreach through roving reference, and provide physical items using self-service delivery.

Rethinking Our Use of Defining Language Including "Normal" and Traditional Library Services

Rather than describing the inevitable changes in the long term with the cliché "new normal," we decided to adopt language as a tool to craft a compelling story. The way library leaders depict change to employees can have a major impact on morale or perception of the current situation and future direction. We give ourselves permission to fail, because we recognize this is realistically the best way to enact effective change and manage expectations in a sustainable way for library teams.

There were numerous silver-lining opportunities COVID provided for reanalyzing duties and tasks that may have been part of normal routines at one time but were misplaced in library operations. One example is in building access control. Prior to the pandemic, library staff spent an inordinate amount of time managing gate access, counseling students and faculty about forgotten access badges, and admitting visitors. These responsibilities for the rest of campus are managed by the university's police department. Looking at procedures and practices that seem more appropriately placed elsewhere can be one way to strategically set boundaries. For our library, located in a busy urban area, the potential exists for more traffic and additional security concerns. The campus police department have been incredible partners in controlling access and addressing safety concerns.

Communicating Boundaries and Strategic Goal Setting

When adopting a culture of caring paired with a drive for progress, our team recognized that boundary setting is a healthy practice. Even in a service-oriented profession, boundary setting enables teams to keep efforts aligned with vision and goals. In communicating new boundaries and expectations, we find greatest success when directly describing desired outcomes. When navigating a crisis, this intentional, succinct communication style becomes vital both within team situations and other university partners.

One tool our institution utilizes in strategic response and for situation-specific decision-making is the SBAR: situation, background, assessment, and recommendation (see figure 11.3). Originating in the military, this method was adopted in clinical and health practice. The goal when using SBAR is to help mitigate concerns about different communication approaches and to ensure message clarity when swift action is needed.[2] This is one tool available to leaders in crisis management scenarios.

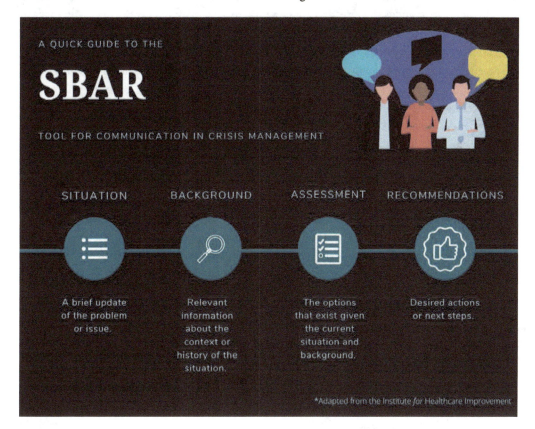

Figure 11.3
This simple graphic depicts the main components of SBAR, a process often used with interdisciplinary teams in clinical practice to ensure expectations and full scenarios are universally understood. This tool is often used related to patient safety, an area of expertise for HSC.

The library also began taking on longer-term strategic planning efforts during the pandemic. Overwhelmingly, library team members communicated that a priority in creating the vision should focus on empowerment of those we reach through education and resources. With this self-reliance, we are working to better prepare our students to navigate various crises, too.

Conversations in What Matters: Burnout and Long-Term Career Satisfaction

Turnover can be especially difficult during a crisis. Experience, memory, and understanding of the systems in an institution are lost every time someone makes a career move, even when that move results in improved outcomes for the employee and the organization. During long-haul crisis situations, employees may reach their limit in tolerance for change or other circumstances, like returning to work in person with high infectious disease rates. Doubts about the future in current roles can creep in and burnout becomes more prevalent at all levels of staffing.

As mentioned previously in this chapter, intentional professional development was one approach our team found to be particularly relevant to enhance career satisfaction while operating under crisis. Library staff were able to determine if their goals aligned with the path they were on when considering the future. For a novice manager, having a trajectory provides direction and enthusiasm to explore new venues and envision a future library career. For the experienced leader, these moments of enjoyable connection to others in the field served as an important reminder that personal and professional growth was still energizing. Interdisciplinary learning opportunities in public health, pharmacy, and education were invaluable in helping our team understand shared experiences and learn more about crisis operations from other perspectives.

Management Well-Being: Caring for Oneself before in Order to Care for Others

Leaders are often tasked with resource identification and explanation of benefits for their direct reports, but who cares for the leader? One of the greatest risks to crisis management, clear communications, and oversight of business continuity is the unwell leader. Whether experiencing crisis fatigue, career burnout, distraction, or feeling completely overwhelmed, leaders cannot perform their best without caring for themselves first. During any crisis, being available for your employees around the clock is not sustainable. Neuroscientists and psychologists agree; the human brain has only so much capacity for decision-making before this organ tries to protect itself from overstimulation.[3]

Work-life balance through flexible and remote work became a widely debated topic in early 2021. Organizational theorists had almost a year's worth of data about the impacts of early pandemic shutdown and extended remote work for employees that traditionally worked on-site. While there is an emerging body of literature showing employee preferences for a hybrid approach, one thing is clear: employees during and post-crisis demonstrate a need for better work-life balance.

As we conclude this chapter from the perspective of both the novice and experienced manager, we encourage you to consider what your team needs, but also to remember your own well-being. Figure 11.4 is a takeaway to remind you that you are seen, valued, and deserve to claim what you need to be at your best when leading through crisis.

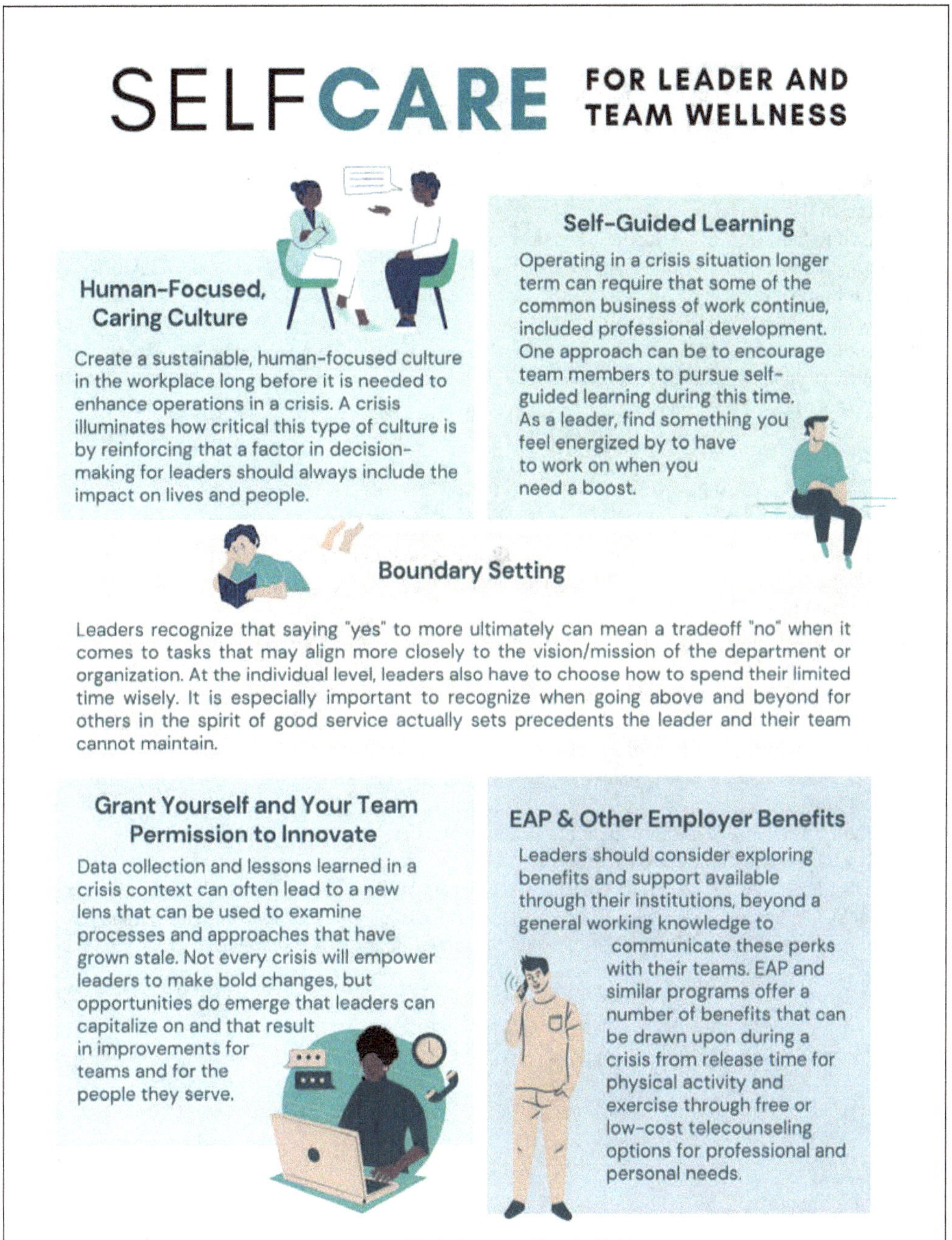

Image courtesy of Hayley Brunner and Lorraine Sheldon

Figure 11.4

Chapter takeaways for leader and team wellness. These are among the lessons learned by Lewis Library team members and leaders during the COVID pandemic.

Notes

1. Nelson A. Atehortua and Stella Patino, "COVID-19, a Tale of Two Pandemics: Novel Coronavirus and Fake News Messaging," *Health Promotion International* 36, no. 2 (April 2021): 524–34, https://doi.org/10.1093/heapro/daaa140; Justyna Obiała et al., "COVID-19 Misinformation: Accuracy of Articles about Coronavirus Prevention Mostly Shared on Social Media," *Health Policy and Technology* 10, no. 1 (March 2021): 182–86, https://doi.org/10.1016/j.hlpt.2020.10.007.
2. Kathryn R. Stewart, "SBAR, Communication, and Patient Safety: An Integrated Literature Review" (honors thesis, University of Tennessee Chattanooga, 2016), 7–10; Sin Yi Lee et al., "SBAR: Towards a Common Interprofessional Team-Based Communication Tool," *Medical Education* 50, no. 11 (November 2016): 1147–51, https://doi.org/10.1111/medu.13171.
3. Adrian F. Ward et al., "Brain Drain: The Mere Presence of One's Own Smartphone Reduces Available Cognitive Capacity," *Journal of the Association for Consumer Research* 2, no. 2 (April 2017): 140–54, https://doi.org/10.1086/691462.

Bibliography

Atehortua, Nelson A. and Stella Patino. "COVID-19, a Tale of Two Pandemics: Novel Coronavirus and Fake News Messaging." *Health Promotion International* 36, no. 2 (April 2021): 524–34. https://doi.org/10.1093/heapro/daaa140.

Lee, Sin Yi, Lijuan Dong, Yong Hao Lim, Chee Lien Poh, and Wee Shiong Lim. "SBAR: Towards a Common Interprofessional Team-Based Communication Tool." *Medical Education* 50, no. 11 (November 2016): 1145–72. https://doi.org/10.1111/medu.13171.

Obiała, Justyna, Karolina Obiała, Małgorzata Mańczak, Jakub Owoc, and Robert Olszewski. "COVID-19 Misinformation: Accuracy of Articles about Coronavirus Prevention Mostly Shared on Social Media." *Health Policy and Technology* 10, no. 1 (March 2021): 182–86. https://doi.org/10.1016/j.hlpt.2020.10.007.

Stewart, Kathryn R. "SBAR, Communication, and Patient Safety: An Integrated Literature Review." Honors thesis, University of Tennessee Chattanooga, 2016.

Ward, Adrian F., Kristen Duke, Ayelet Gneezy, and Maarten W. Bos. "Brain Drain: The Mere Presence of One's Own Smartphone Reduces Available Cognitive Capacity." *Journal of the Association for Consumer Research* 2, no. 2 (April 2017): 140–54. https://doi.org/10.1086/691462.

CHAPTER 12

More Change?!?
Developing a Strategic Plan during a Time of Crisis and Uncertainty

Bethany Wilkes

> *Moving forward with strategic planning during a time of uncertainty is risky, yet not doing so creates risks of its own.*

Introduction

Libraries around the world continuously grapple with balancing immediate challenges and responsibilities while also anticipating, forecasting, and planning for the future. It is crucial that academic libraries examine their strategies to align with their parent organizations while also anticipating the changing needs of their stakeholders. Strategic planning is one way in which libraries can do this; however, it is a time-consuming process that necessitates the involvement of employees and other stakeholders at all levels. Libraries may choose to postpone or ignore the necessity of strategic planning for a variety of reasons, such as uncertainty about the future or the need to keep pace with the everyday demands of business-as-usual activities. When a crisis arises, the temptation to defer planning can be intense; however, the crisis itself may reveal new opportunities worth pursuing.

Each one of these considerations was present prior to the move to engage in strategic planning at Singapore Management University Libraries in June 2021. The COVID-19 pandemic emerged in Singapore in early January 2020, necessitating a variety of measures that demanded immediate response. As months passed, the pandemic continued and presented ongoing challenges and concerns. The libraries, and the country, shifted between different phases and restrictions.

At the same time, there were several compelling factors that contributed to making this an opportune time for strategic planning, including recent changes in leadership across the university as well as the launch of the university's strategic plan, *SMU 2025: Growing Impact, Cultivating Change*. By deferring formal strategic planning, the libraries would risk missing an opportunity to closely align with the university's new strategic plan while also leveraging fresh perspectives.

This chapter explores Singapore Management University (SMU) Libraries' collaborative approach to fostering deliberate change through developing and launching its *Strategic Plan 2021–2025* while also managing imposed change resulting from the COVID-19 pandemic. It examines the approaches used to address the implications of, and changes brought by, the COVID-19 pandemic while concurrently preparing for the future during a time of uncertainty. It also highlights the collaboration, commitment, and creativity demonstrated by library employees as they navigated an unprecedented situation of forced change from within and without, while purposefully planning for change in the future.

Institutional Context

SMU is one of the six autonomous universities (AUs) in Singapore and is a young university, just celebrating a twenty-one-year anniversary. It is a vibrant city campus in the Bras Basah.Bugis precinct of Singapore, which is considered the arts and heritage centre of Singapore. It focuses on management, social sciences, technology, and their intersections, and comprises six schools (School of Accountancy, Lee Kong Chian School of Business, School of Economics, School of Computing and Information Systems, and Yong Pung How School of Law). As noted on its Overview web page, SMU's mission is "to create and disseminate knowledge. SMU aspires to generate leading-edge research with global impact ... [and] produce broad-based, creative and entrepreneurial leaders for the knowledge-based economy."[1] SMU offers a signature pedagogy in Singapore of interactive, personalized learning and seminar-style classes. SMU's Overview web page also states that it has a student population of about 11,500 students enrolled in bachelor's, master's, and PhD programs, and approximately 380 faculty members.[2]

In September 2020, SMU launched its strategic plan *SMU 2025: Growing Impact, Cultivating Change*. The strategic plan emphasizes three priorities: digital transformation, sustainable living, and growth in Asia. Alongside these priorities are the three strategies of "nurturing global citizens for tomorrow," "addressing societal challenges through cutting edge research," and "engaging with the city and world to make meaningful impact."[3] The university's strategic plan extends and enhances the previous strategic plan and provides focus and prioritisation for the university.

SMU Libraries have generally been closely integrated into the university. Their two libraries, Li Ka Shing Library and Kwa Geok Choo Law Library, are much loved by students and experience high foot traffic throughout the academic year. In 2019 SMU Libraries had a visitor-ship of just over 1.3 million. SMU Libraries have historically intentionally focused on developing a primarily digital collection, and almost 90 percent of their collections are currently in digital format. The libraries provide expertise and services in both the physical and digital environments. With the advent of COVID-19, digital interactions were expanded and enhanced, and foot traffic in the library buildings was reduced by almost half.

Addressing COVID-19: Early Days and Initial Steps

On January 23, 2020, the first case of COVID-19 was recorded in Singapore.[4] By late March, SMU had transitioned to online course delivery and work-from-home practices. Between April 7, 2020, and June 1, 2020, Singapore sustained a "circuit breaker," which necessitated the closure of campus facilities, including the physical libraries. Following the circuit breaker, universities across Singapore adhered to fluctuating government guidelines and worked closely with the Ministry of Education to operate in-line with the changing measures.

After the circuit breaker, first one, then both, of the physical libraries on campus were opened with a reduced capacity of approximately 50 percent. Staff were permitted to work on campus at varying percentage rates, ranging from 25 to 75 percent depending on regularly published government guidance. The libraries' dedicated staff consistently provided primary services on-site, while also expanding service delivery to the digital environment. Across the world, library workers have demonstrated great commitment, agility, and resilience during the COVID-19 pandemic, and the dedicated staff of SMU Libraries exemplified these traits as they navigated new modes of working; optimized use and acquisition of digital resources; transitioned services, teaching, and learning activities online; and negotiated the personal and professional impacts of the pandemic.

A Timely Opportunity

During these unprecedented circumstances and the changes that they imposed, library employees quickly addressed immediate needs: developing new skills, adjusting services and schedules, and engaging in different modes and ways of working to manoeuvre through the pandemic while keeping the needs of the SMU community at the forefront. Amidst this environment, there were significant factors present that indicated this was an opportune time for looking ahead and strategizing for the future. There was fresh leadership at varying levels across the university, including a new president in January 2019, a new provost in April 2019, and a new university librarian in March 2020. As noted earlier, the university announced its new strategic plan in September 2020. The libraries' previous strategic plan expired in 2018. Connecting the libraries' plans to the university's was crucial. As Boyce and colleagues state, "University libraries do not operate in isolation from their host institutions. Their development strategy needs to align closely to that of their institution and their vision of the future needs to fit that of their institution."[5]

Recently, Dempsey and Malpas have posited that models for library excellence will vary according to the type of parent institution and that "academic libraries will need to tune and refine their services to support diversifying institutional need."[6] While Dempsey and Malpas's work focuses on libraries and institutions in the United States, their insights are also relevant to the Singapore higher education environment, where the government-funded AUs have distinct roles and "provide a wide range of academic, research, work-learn and student life options to cater to students' diverse interests and learning styles."[7] Facilitating engagement with the university's strategic plan and early linkage to it would position the libraries advantageously in contributing to institutional needs and goals.

In addition to these changes across the university, library employees were enthusiastic about sharing their insights about SMU Libraries as well as exploring new opportunities. As Corrall states, "strategic planning has various functions" including "to clarify organizational purpose and objectives; to establish corporate directions and priorities; to assess environmental drivers and constraints" and more. She also notes that, significantly, one of the benefits of strategic planning is that "it creates a shared view of the future and commitment to doing new things, facilitating change by giving people a sense of ownership."[8] This aspect of strategic planning was particularly important to the libraries' leadership team, as the strategic planning process could demonstrate commitment to collaboration and inclusiveness as the team developed a shared vision and approach together. While the challenges of COVID-19 were certainly prevalent, there was a sense of momentum and enthusiasm about making strategic changes. Without leveraging these factors, an opportunity to provide future direction for the libraries would be lost. Furthermore, while colleagues were grappling with imposed change due to COVID-19, taking ownership of planned change could provide employees with a feeling of personal agency alongside shared purpose.

Planning While Navigating an Uncertain Present

During the months following the advent of COVID-19, leadership, communication, collaboration, preparation (as much as possible), and agility were crucial at all levels. Activities such as regular meetings and communications from and with the SMU Crisis Executive group, campus partners such as the Office of Safety and Security and Infrastructure Services, the libraries' own Emergency Preparedness Team, and student representatives contributed to optimal operations and service delivery while adhering to government advice. Working closely with these different partners and stakeholders ensured consistency with practices and in communications with the community, with health and safety a priority. The libraries' employees expanded digital offerings and transitioned to working from home. Physical services and enhanced digital services included "pick up and go" for print materials, augmented acquisitions of e-textbooks, copyright advisory relating to teaching materials, proactive virtual chat with additional hours, workshops to prepare students for online learning, the pivot of all of the libraries' information literacy teaching activities and other events online, and other innovations and adaptations. There was also attention to employees' well-being through institutional support programmes, including such things as care packs sent to staff members' homes, a mindfulness talk, and team-building activities.[9]

Alongside these endeavours and while navigating the myriad of arrangements and adjustments around COVID-19, engaging in strategic planning remained advantageous.

The libraries began the strategic planning process in June 2021. The approach and activities around planning were highly structured, although the ways in which colleagues chose to organise and work with one another and the topics were often flexible. The orderly approach allowed for steady progress and certainty in the pursuits and expectations of the process at a time when many of the libraries' workflows and services were in flux due to the pandemic.

The aim of the strategic planning venture was to design, develop, and implement an inclusive libraries-wide strategic plan for 2021–2025. The associated learning outcomes were that, by the end of the process, staff would be able to

- contribute their ideas in identifying the future direction of SMU Libraries,
- explain the process of developing the library's strategic plan, and
- communicate the library's new strategic plan to stakeholders.

The Library Planning Team (LPT), which is the libraries' leadership team, in collaboration with the university librarian, identified key elements of the strategic planning process, and the head, learning and engagement (then head, learning and information services, and also part of the LPT), first posited the aim and learning outcomes, oversaw the learning processes, interfaced with an external vendor, and kept the group on track. This emphasis on process and learning was central to the overall aim and in demonstrating that the value of the exercise resided not only in the output, but in the process as well.

The process necessitated considerable employee contributions and commitment to the overall strategy and planning. In addition to the aim and learning outcomes, there was the intent to look to the future and encourage blue-sky thinking (i.e., thinking and brainstorming freely, without limitations). The first activity was an Envisioning Survey, developed by the university librarian with input from the LPT and sent to all libraries' employees. The survey was the initial step in gathering staff input and building a vision together. A task force was established to conduct an environmental scan, and each unit in the libraries performed a variation of the SWOT (strengths, weaknesses, opportunities, and threats) analysis of their respective units. Rather than using the traditional SWOT format, each unit addressed guiding questions grounded in reflective practice, which were crafted by the LPT members:

- Think about the current services we provide. What area(s) are we doing well in and should continue to strengthen? What area(s) should we do less of or stop doing?
- As a team, what are we not doing that we should be doing, within SMU and externally within the larger environment (e.g., other libraries—local and international, organizations, industries)?
- For our team, who could be our potential partners within SMU and externally within the larger environment (e.g., other libraries—local and international, organizations, industries)? Who are our competitors?

The results of these activities were shared during a special staff meeting and used as a foundation for one of two workshops led by an external facilitator who also specializes in innovation. Following the first half-day workshop, which focused on vision, mission, and values, staff looked outward, exploring the three strategic priorities of the university (digital transformation, sustainable living, and growth in Asia) and differentiators (industry, innovation, internationalization, and integration).[10]

These priorities were expansive and needed careful consideration. Cross-unit teams investigated the different dimensions of the priorities and how the libraries fit into contributing to and advancing them. This gave staff the opportunity to critically consider the priorities and permitted them to creatively approach the priorities, differentiators, and strategies presented in *SMU 2025* to explore potentially relevant opportunities for the libraries from their perspectives. These findings were again integrated into a workshop by the same external facilitator, which was the culmination of the team-based work. The workshop included a variety of breakout sessions and activities around creating user profiles and identifying stakeholders needs, resulting in staff generating ideas that would meet stakeholders' needs (user profiles) relating to the SMU strategies of transformative education, cutting-edge research, and meaningful impact. Some feedback from staff highlighted that the process made them feel part of the organization and that working as a team could make the strategic plan a success.

Following the team activities, the external facilitator worked closely with the university librarian and the LPT in developing a draft of the strategic plan. The draft was then disseminated and addressed at the unit level to further engage staff and generate additional feedback, which was then taken into consideration by the LPT. In finalizing the draft, the key elements of alignment with the university's strategy and goals, evolving user needs and expectations, and a forward-looking viewpoint were kept at the forefront of conversations and the final document.

COVID-19 and Strategy Development

COVID-19 influenced different aspects of strategic planning, ranging from logistics and resilience to the actual strategy itself. On a logistical level, COVID-19 necessitated that strategic planning activities be held in the online environment, as staff were primarily working from home. The necessity of holding activities in the virtual environment informed the approach to them and the design. There was an emphasis on small-group activities and optimizing virtual collaboration tools. As Ceniza-Levine states, "The virtual environment is inherently siloed—be proactive in building an inclusive culture."[11] Tactics such as developing shared agreements and preassigning breakout rooms and facilitators allowed for a variety of voices to be heard and ensured colleagues were mixing across units and peer groups. LPT members worked closely with the external facilitator to identify and apply these tactics. Staff demonstrated resilience through their attentive participation and investment in the strategic planning process, even amid the evolving pandemic and related adaptations to their work roles and responsibilities. While at times demanding, both mentally and time-wise, participating in the strategic planning process provided opportunity for structured approaches and activities, cross-unit collaboration, and the ability to proactively set the future direction of the libraries at a time when many aspects of work were necessarily reactive or in flux. This provided team cohesion and clarity of purpose during a time of great uncertainty.

Of course, the advent and implications of COVID-19 extended beyond logistical arrangements and the need for flexibility and impacted elements of the strategy. As Cox, in a phrase borrowed from William Butler Yeats, proclaims, academic libraries will be "changed, changed utterly" by COVID-19.[12] These changes will not be to core library services and values, but in areas such as partnerships, service delivery, and spaces. While COVID-19 necessitated immediate changes in libraries, its consequences will also guide the way in which libraries approach the future, which relates directly to strategic planning. During the strategic planning process, attention was paid to those changes that were emerging that were germane to guiding strategy.

While the strategic planning activities did not specifically focus on libraries' responses and roles during COVID-19, the pandemic brought certain trends to the forefront and underscored those accelerated developments that were already underway. Elements of these trends informed the strategic plan; three are discussed next.

During COVID-19 and the quick pivot to digital, university libraries demonstrated that they were and can continue to be valuable partners in teaching and learning, providing a range of resources, services, and expertise in the digital environment. Libraries were well-positioned to address the needs of learners transitioning to the online environment.

> Academic libraries have been at the forefront of supporting the provision of flexible online learning resources, online services and training, positioning librarians to take on a leading role in supporting students and staff to develop information and digital literacy skills via online courses, tutorials, workshops and e-consultations.[13]

COVID-19 also emphasized the need for quick and easy access to reputable information for all communities, as well as individual university communities' demand for electronic resources amidst economic downturns around the world. This necessitated further advocacy and advancement of open scholarship, including open educational resources (OERs). While library closures happened at different intervals at various locations around the globe, the demand for, and the reopening of, physical libraries were reminders that library spaces continue to be a valuable service. In 2012, Dempsey wrote that

> a shift is underway in library space, from being configured around collections to being configured around research, learning and related social behaviors. In this way, space is an important aspect of how a library engages with its users; it is a service in itself.[14]

Libraries will continue to design spaces around these areas, yet spaces will also continue to change. Libraries' spaces will need to be flexible and address challenges such as social distancing to keep communities safe and healthy.[15] In fact, a contemporary Ithaka survey of library directors revealed that they

> expect that the physical library location will remain crucial to the library's mission.... With many students in particular struggling to access technology and find quiet spaces for coursework this year, it is no surprise that directors continue to see value in their in-person service provision for addressing these needs.[16]

These trends, while not explicitly examined as part of the planning process, influenced discussions around, and aspects of, the strategic directions and goals of SMU Libraries *Strategic Plan 2021–2025*, particularly the goals to "further digital competence" and

Chapter 12

to "empower information and knowledge discovery," in order to "cultivate connections, entrepreneurialism, and diverse learning experiences in sustainable spaces."[17] These goals would likely have been considered without the advent of COVID-19, yet the pandemic brought them to the forefront and altered the framing, focus, and positioning of each.

Conclusion

Moving forward with strategic planning during a time of uncertainty is risky, yet not doing so creates risks of its own. The forms of risk range from interference with daily operations to staff bandwidth and fatigue, to miscalculations of the strategy itself. During June 2021, the pandemic was impacting multiple aspects of life and society, and SMU Libraries were continually adjusting and repositioning, like other libraries around the world. Concurrently, several crucial factors arose that indicated the need to begin strategic planning. To ignore these factors, including a new university strategic plan, would also have been risky and could possibly leave the libraries open to even more uncertainty, potentially moving the libraries in directions not beneficial to their parent organization, without aligned and shared directions and goals.

Strategic planning was a collaborative process, involving the libraries' employees at all levels and requiring their investment in that process during dynamic times, when they were also juggling shifting responsibilities and requirements. Staff members' commitment to the strategic planning process was impressive, as was their attention to often-changing daily matters. Associated activities were varied and fruitful, fostering thoughtful team interaction during a time of physical separation. The pandemic and the changes it brought shaped conversations around the strategy, and resulting trends were infused into the libraries' strategy.

The SMU Libraries *Strategic Plan 2021–2025* was launched in January 2021. The pandemic was very much a factor in society and daily lives at that time and still is at the writing this chapter. The staff's investment in the plan has contributed to the team's cohesion and capability to work towards a shared vision and goals during a time of crisis and uncertainty which, unfortunately, continues. Without the strategy in place, it is likely that the libraries would not be as cohesive or aligned with university endeavours. Assessing and adjusting the strategy in its application as it is put into practice will be yet another opportunity to demonstrate agility and adaptability, hopefully without these terms also being associated with an ongoing pandemic.

Notes

1. "Overview," Singapore Management University, September 11, 2017, https://www.smu.edu.sg/about/overview (page discontinued).
2. "Overview."
3. "Vision 2025," Singapore Management University, September 4, 2020, https://www.smu.edu.sg/about/vision2025.
4. Timothy Goh and Ting Wei Toh, "Singapore Confirms First Case of Wuhan Virus; Second Case Likely," *Straits Times*, January 23, 2020, https://www.straitstimes.com/singapore/health/singapore-confirms-first-case-of-wuhan-virus.

5. Gavin Boyce et al., "Visions of Value: Leading the Development of a View of the University Library in the 21st Century," *Journal of Academic Librarianship* 45, no. 5 (September 2019): article 102046, p. 2, https://doi.org/10.1016/j.acalib.2019.102046.
6. Lorcan Dempsey and Constance Malpas, "Academic Library Futures in a Diversified University System," in *Higher Education in the Era of the Fourth Industrial Revolution*, ed. Nancy W. Gleason (Singapore: Springer Singapore, 2018), 67, https://doi.org/10.1007/978-981-13-0194-0_4.
7. "Autonomous Universities," Ministry of Education Singapore, accessed August 27, 2021, http://www.moe.gov.sg/post-secondary/overview/autonomous-universities.
8. Sheila Corrall, "Strategic Planning in Academic Libraries," in *The Encyclopaedia of Library and Information Science*, 2nd ed., ed. Miriam Drake (New York: Marcel Dekker, 2003), 2742.
9. Bethany Wilkes and Rajendra Munoo "Turning the COVID-19 Pandemic into Opportunities for Digital Transformation: Sharing the Singapore Management University Libraries Experience" (presentation, International Webinar: Librarians: Creativity and Opportunities in the Pandemic Era, Politeknik Internasional Bali, August 7, 2020).
10. "Vision 2025."
11. Caroline Ceniza-Levine, "How Inclusive Leaders Can Build a Collaborative Team in a Virtual Environment," *Forbes*, April 11, 2021, https://www.forbes.com/sites/carolinecenizalevine/2021/04/11/how-inclusive-leaders-can-build-a-collaborative-team-in-a-virtual-environment/.
12. Christopher Cox, "Changed, Changed Utterly," Inside Higher Education, June 5, 2020, https://www.insidehighered.com/views/2020/06/05/academic-libraries-will-change-significant-ways-result-pandemic-opinion.
13. Konstantina Martzoukou, "Academic Libraries in COVID-19: A Renewed Mission for Digital Literacy," *Library Management* 42, no. 4/5 (2021): 267, https://doi.org/10.1108/LM-09-2020-0131.267.
14. Lorcan Dempsey, "Two Things Prompted by a New Website: Space as a Service and Full Library Discovery," *LorcanDempsey.net* (blog), August 31, 2012, https://www.lorcandempsey.net/orweblog/two-things-prompted-by-a-new-website-space-as-a-service-and-full-library-discovery/.
15. Cox, "Changed."
16. Jennifer Frederick and Christine Wolff-Eisenberg, *Academic Library Strategy and Budgeting during the COVID-19 Pandemic* (New York: Ithaka S+R, December 9, 2020), 14, https://doi.org/10.18665/sr.314507.
17. SMU Libraries, *Strategic Plan 2021–2025*, Singapore Management University, accessed September 10, 2021, https://library.smu.edu.sg/sites/library.smu.edu.sg/files/library/pdf/StrategicPlan2021-25Web.pdf.

Bibliography

Boyce, Gavin, Angela Greenwood, Amy Haworth, Jacky Hodgson, Chris Jones, Gary Marsh, Maria Mawson, and Rosa Sadler. "Visions of Value: Leading the Development of a View of the University Library in the 21st Century." *Journal of Academic Librarianship* 45, no. 5 (September 2019): article 102046. https://doi.org/10.1016/j.acalib.2019.102046.

Ceniza-Levine, Caroline. "How Inclusive Leaders Can Build a Collaborative Team in a Virtual Environment." *Forbes*, April 11, 2021. https://www.forbes.com/sites/carolinecenizalevine/2021/04/11/how-inclusive-leaders-can-build-a-collaborative-team-in-a-virtual-environment/.

Corrall, Sheila. "Strategic Planning in Academic Libraries." In *The Encyclopaedia of Library and Information Science*, 2nd ed., edited by Miriam Drake, 2742–55. New York: Marcel Dekker, 2003.

Cox, Christopher. "Changed, Changed Utterly." Inside Higher Education, June 5, 2020. https://www.insidehighered.com/views/2020/06/05/academic-libraries-will-change-significant-ways-result-pandemic-opinion.

Dempsey, Lorcan. "Two Things Prompted by a New Website: Space as a Service and Full Library Discovery." *LorcanDempsey.net* (blog), August 31, 2012. https://www.lorcandempsey.net/orweblog/two-things-prompted-by-a-new-website-space-as-a-service-and-full-library-discovery/.

Dempsey, Lorcan, and Constance Malpas. "Academic Library Futures in a Diversified University System." In *Higher Education in the Era of the Fourth Industrial Revolution*, edited by Nancy W. Gleason, 65–89. Singapore: Springer, 2018. https://doi.org/10.1007/978-981-13-0194-0_4.

Frederick, Jennifer, and Christine Wolff-Eisenberg. *Academic Library Strategy and Budgeting during the COVID-19 Pandemic: Results from the Ithaka S+R US Library Survey 2020*. New York: Ithaka S+R, December 9, 2020. https://doi.org/10.18665/sr.314507.

Goh, Timothy, and Ting Wei Toh. "Singapore Confirms First Case of Wuhan Virus; Second Case Likely." *The Straits Times*, January 23, 2020. https://www.straitstimes.com/singapore/health/singapore-confirms-first-case-of-wuhan-virus.

Martzoukou, Konstantina. "Academic Libraries in COVID-19: A Renewed Mission for Digital Literacy." *Library Management* 42, no. 4/5 (2021): 266–76. https://doi.org/10.1108/LM-09-2020-0131.

McNicol, Sarah. "The Challenges of Strategic Planning in Academic Libraries." *New Library World* 106, no. 11/12 (January 1, 2005): 496–509. https://doi.org/10.1108/03074800510634982.

Singapore Management University. "Overview," September 11, 2017. https://www.smu.edu.sg/about/overview (page discontinued).

———. "Vision 2025." September 4, 2020. https://www.smu.edu.sg/about/vision2025.

Singapore Ministry of Education. "Autonomous Universities." Accessed August 27, 2021. http://www.moe.gov.sg/post-secondary/overview/autonomous-universities.

SMU Libraries. *Strategic Plan 2021–2025*. Singapore Management University. Accessed September 10, 2021. https://library.smu.edu.sg/sites/library.smu.edu.sg/files/library/pdf/StrategicPlan2021-25Web.pdf.

———. "Singapore Management University Libraries Strategic Plan 2021–2025." *IFLA Asia and Oceania Quarterly News*, May 15, 2021. https://www.ifla.org/news/singapore-management-university-libraries-strategic-plan-2021-2025-2/.

Wilkes, Bethany, and Rajendra Munoo. "Turning the COVID-19 Pandemic into Opportunities for Digital Transformation: Sharing the Singapore Management University Libraries Experience," Presentation, International Webinar: Librarians: Creativity and Opportunities in the Pandemic Era, Politeknik Internasional Bali, August 7, 2020.

CHAPTER 13

Continuity of Operations Planning (COOP) for Academic Library Crisis Management
A Case Study

Nancy Falciani-White and Kevin Butterfield

> The COOP ensures libraries can sustain their academic mission under all conditions by reducing or mitigating disruptions to operations.

Introduction

A crisis is a sudden, unexpected event that typically involves a high level of threat to life, safety, or the health of an organization.[1] Crises tend to disrupt routine processes, resulting in varying degrees of chaos and uncertainty. They are often characterized by time pressures, since delaying a response can result in more severe impacts; limited or no relevant information to inform decision-making; and an increased risk of failure. This can result in significant stress on those involved in crisis resolution.[2] In addition, crises are often unique to the people and campus cultures involved. Regardless of the crisis encountered, a continuity of operations plan (COOP) can provide practical and direct preparation to help an academic library deal with disruptive and unexpected events while minimizing harm to the organization and its stakeholders.

A COOP ensures that functions that are essential to the mission of an organization continue to be performed in the face of crises such as natural disasters, public health crises, accidents, and technological disruptions such as cyberattacks.[3] In addition to ensuring the performance of essential functions, a COOP should ensure employee safety and communication; protect essential equipment, vital records, and other assets; reduce disruptions to operations; and achieve an orderly recovery.[4] The Federal emergency management agency (FEMA) groups these components into four pillars of continuity planning: leadership, staff, facilities, and communications.[5]

Academic libraries have faced various crises over the years. Some, such as Hurricane Katrina, were somewhat localized events affecting a limited number of institutions, while others, such as the Great Recession that began in 2008 and the COVID-19 pandemic that began in 2019, have had widespread and long-term effects on many institutions.

Many academic libraries already have emergency or disaster plans detailing what to do in the event of clearly defined or anticipated occurrences such as a power outage, mold outbreak, medical emergency, or active shooter event.[6] Emergency and disaster plans are types of contingency planning.[7] Regardless of whether they realistically expect to experience the situations in their contingency plan, most libraries are able to identify possible threats and plan for them. Emergency planning in academic libraries often focuses on the safety of library staff and users and print collection preservation and recovery.[8] While a focus on print collections may be appropriate for special libraries or for specific special collections within academic libraries, the primary function of most academic libraries extends beyond simply providing access to their collections. For example, services, electronic resources, and equipment may be more important to users in the event of an unexpected situation.

While contingency plans are effective for anticipated disruptions, they are not sufficient for rare or complex crises.[9] For example, a terrorist attack, an active shooter event, or pandemic are each in themselves complex events to anticipate; but each can significantly and negatively impact library operations and should therefore be addressed with a more nuanced approach, such as a continuity of operations plan (COOP).

Continuity of operations planning looks at desired outcomes and puts systems and structures in place to ensure those desired outcomes are maintained in the face of a crisis that causes significant disruptions. Continuity planning requires an organization to prioritize its services, resources, and tools to address essentials quickly and to minimize disruption to those who rely on its services. COOPs include provisions for communication to staff as well as to external audiences that need to know how a crisis is being addressed (e.g., parents of college students). Clear communication can take on even greater significance during a crisis.[10] Using a COOP to focus recovery efforts on the essential functions of the academic library allows the library to prepare for and respond to any type of crisis more effectively. This chapter will use a case study to examine the authors' experiences with crises and crisis management at two liberal arts college libraries in Virginia. After reviewing the details of this case, the authors will propose a process for producing a COOP that aligns with the larger institution's goals and strategies and will outline the resources needed to ensure that the program remains viable and achievable.

Case Study

Randolph-Macon College, chartered in 1830, is a private liberal arts college of 1,543 undergraduate students located in Ashland, Virginia. The McGraw-Page Library sits near the center of campus. The original building, constructed in 1961, doubled in size with a 1987 addition, while a pavilion built in 2012 added a twenty-four-hour study space and classroom. In this case study, the library is 158,000 square feet and houses over 228,000 physical items.

The University of Richmond, also established in 1830, is a private liberal arts college of 3,147 undergraduates located in Richmond, Virginia. Libraries at the university are the Muse Law Library, Parsons Music Library, and the Boatwright Memorial Library. Boatwright Memorial Library consists of three sections: the original building, constructed in 1954, and two subsequent additions. At the time of our study, Boatwright Memorial Library held over 547,000 physical volumes within 127,533 square feet of total library space.

Randolph-Macon College completed no significant renovations to the library building after the large addition in 1987. The existing HVAC did not include humidity control, and the temperature was difficult to manage due to the age of the system. Temperatures in the building frequently fluctuated between too cold (60–65°F) and too hot (80+°F), and the relative humidity in the building was often above 60 percent.

In May 2019, employees discovered mold in the library's circulating collection during a routine search for a missing item. Over the next several days, a review of the area showed mold growth was widespread through almost half of the circulating collection. The emergency plan developed by the library several years earlier had a section on mold, but this primarily focused on identification. In addition, the emergency plan lacked remediation protocols and specific steps to take in the event of a mold outbreak. Also in May, the college was finishing spring semester classes and preparing for finals. The immediate concern for the library upon discovery of the mold bloom was student and staff safety. Was the mold dangerous, and should management close the library building, aggravating student stress levels that were already high with approaching finals?

The library director notified the college's physical plant department, which brought in a mycologist within one or two days. The mycologist determined that the mold was not airborne and presented no danger to users of the library. With the safety question resolved, the library updated in-library processes and began to work with the physical plant personnel to determine how to remediate the mold. The library's first step was to request that the special collections conference room, accessible from the second floor circulating collection, be removed from the college's room reservation system so that groups could no longer reserve the space for board meetings, end-of-semester presentations, and other events. This was done to keep mold spores away from special collections. The library also requested two large dehumidifiers for special collections to stabilize the humidity in that space. In addition, library staff made the following changes to other areas of the library while they worked to ascertain the extent of the mold outbreak:

- stopped shelving new or returned materials in sections containing mold;
- stopped lending books through interlibrary loan to prevent accidental contamination of other library collections;
- began checking books for mold before they were loaned to users and did not permit contaminated books to circulate; and
- began checking returned books for mold and quarantining any showing signs of growth away from books determined to be clean.

The college's physical plant staff decided to outsource mold remediation during the summer months so that it could be accomplished before most of the student body returned for the fall semester. The mycologist, library staff, and a consultant from Lyrasis partnered to develop a protocol, as no one on the library staff had expertise in mold remediation. After several weeks, we determined that a different approach was needed, as the initial contractors, used to dealing with mold discovered in homes and basements, were not well equipped to handle mold in a library collection. We revised the protocol and worked to locate and schedule another contractor. During this time, the temperature in staff work spaces reached 77°F, with humidity in the circulating collection at 64 percent.

While mold remediation was in progress, work had begun in late May, planned months prior, to replace the library roof. In early June, a Friday afternoon storm released 2.5 inches of rain on the town of Ashland over two hours. Library staff walking through the building in the morning found one leak near a window that was quickly addressed with a nearby trashcan to capture the water and dehumidifier to dry out the carpet. This incident was likely due to the ongoing roof replacement but did not affect any books in the circulating collection. However, later in the afternoon that same day, staff found water leaking through the ceiling of the mailroom on the first floor. Investigation revealed a quarter-inch of standing water on the floor of the special collections conference room and water pouring through HVAC vents in the conference room ceiling. We later learned that this was the result of improperly secured flashing during roof replacement. The water coming from the vents was falling in front of glass-fronted cabinets that housed the Virginia Methodist special collection and the Asian art history collection, as well as other rare materials displayed in that room, including an illuminated manuscript. While we saw no damaged materials initially, staff were unsure of the water source and whether water had compromised the wooden cabinets. Staff decided to empty the cabinets on the side of the room where the leak occurred to prevent any possible damage to the rare materials over the coming weekend.

Staff positioned containers under the largest leaks, and the team located all available book carts and storage containers. Staff wiped all book trucks with an antimicrobial solution before bringing them into special collections to prevent mold spores contaminating that space. Paper towels were put between the clean surface and the rare materials to protect those materials from the cleaning agent. Materials were carefully removed from the cabinets onto book trucks, keeping them clear of the rainwater continuing to come through the vents. As materials were relocated, the college's physical plant was notified of the leak and its staff came to assist. Because the cause and extent of the water issue were unknown at the time, physical plant staff covered the materials within the special collections vault with plastic sheeting to prevent damage to those materials. Materials removed from the conference room were taken into the vault for security purposes. Physical plant staff brought in fans and dehumidifiers to dry out the rug and floor of that space. The mycologist returned to the library the following week and determined that no mold was growing in the conference room due to the water incursion, and the wet drywall was removed and replaced quickly. The remaining materials in that room, which were located opposite the leak, were removed to the back room on carts as a precaution. The majority of the collections in the special collections and archives are stored on compact and regular shelving in the back room. While the space is not climate-controlled, it is separated from the known leak by a large office and is separately keyed from the conference room for additional security.

This event distracted from the process of identifying a new company to do mold remediation, a process completed in late June. During the intervening weeks, staff continued to review the collection, marking ranges where staff found mold growth. Finally, mold remediation began in earnest in early July. The second-floor classroom was reserved for the process, and cleaning the books took place in that space, removed from the circulating collection. Books were taken to the classroom, cleaned individually, put on a clean book cart, and brought back to the shelf, where they were put back more or less in the correct order.

While this work continued, temperatures in the building continued to reach uncomfortable levels. Staff spaces were over 80°F, and relative humidity in the circulating collection soared to 70 percent. Then during the third week of July, an HVAC condensate pan overflowed, drenching about 100 books in the circulating collection and the surrounding carpet. Mold remediation paused while the mold remediation contractor addressed this new crisis.

Library productivity was significantly affected during these crises, and staff postponed several summer projects. Managing mold remediation took a significant amount of staff time, primarily dedicated to identifying areas of the collections with mold and reviewing remediation work by contractors. Getting the mold growth under control was challenging, as water continued to enter a warm and humid environment. Staff were physically uncomfortable working in the building and, in some cases, worked in alternate locations on loaner laptops because their office spaces were unacceptably hot. These laptops often lacked the tools and software needed for them to work efficiently. Managing the physical environment became a significant component of the library director's job and that of several other employees. Morale dropped due to the number of events that occurred in quick succession and the prevailing feeling that so many of the summer's incidents were outside the library staff's ability to either prevent or resolve. Library staff entered the fall

2019 semester feeling burned out. As the coronavirus pandemic began to take shape early in 2020, the team had not fully recovered from the experiences of summer 2019.

Staff at the Boatwright Memorial Library at the University of Richmond found mold in late 2019. The mold was cleaned out of the archives collection storage room on B2 by a contractor over the summer after several severe HVAC issues occurred in late June and early July. This outbreak was part of a more extensive mold remediation service performed by this contractor, as mold was also discovered within extensive portions of the circulating collection on Levels B2 and B1. Within the archive collection storage room, mold was found in six document boxes and on many unboxed objects (primarily trophies and awards from the collection). All identified moldy material was moved into a 20.2 cubic foot freezer purchased for mold remediation of rare materials. These items filled the freezer. After freezing, the material was carefully cleaned using established best practices for rare materials, requiring specific tools (HEPA-filtered vacuum, HEPA-filtered fume hood, and cheesecloth).

While waiting for the appropriate tools to continue remediation, additional mold was identified in the processing office and workroom on Level B1. Active mold was found on materials in at least three collections within these spaces, comprised of two more document boxes and several unboxed items, including two plaster busts from the original university library and an oil painting of an alumnus. This outbreak brought the total number of document boxes with active mold to eight. Because the freezer was full of material awaiting further remediation, there was nowhere to move this material to stop the growth and prevent the mold from spreading.

All material in the three mold-affected rooms was at increased risk for mold growth due to this prolonged exposure and the increased temperatures as the building's heating system has turned on for the winter. Because these rooms were closed off for security and not on a separate HVAC system, the temperatures were well above industry standards and best practices for storage space (65°F-68°F) and above temperatures that would inhibit or prevent mold growth (70°F). While the Rare Book Room vault is on a separate HVAC system, the system cannot maintain appropriate temperatures, often sitting at or above the 70°F cutoff. For example, on Sunday, December 8th, 2019, the temperature was 71.6°F. After calling in Facilities to service the HVAC system the following Tuesday, the temperature on Thursday morning was 69.6°F. All materials currently sitting in rooms with active mold growth cannot be moved into the Rare Book Room vault because we risk infecting the materials currently housed there. Therefore, to mitigate the risk to the entire collection, a large portion of our holdings must be left in moldy rooms, increasing their continued chance of infection.

Discussion

The two academic libraries represented by this case study were in very different places regarding COOP and disaster preparedness when they encountered the crises described above. The McGraw-Page Library had a detailed but largely untested emergency plan and emergency kits on each floor of the building that included materials necessary to respond to common issues such as leaks. The emergency plan included some continuity elements, but others were either missing or loosely implied. The disasters that struck forced continuity to the forefront of the library's response, as it needed to analyze the impact that mold, high temperature and humidity, water damage, and later COVID-19 had on its ability to support the students and faculty relying on the library. These crises informed several areas of library management:

- The realization that building conditions had deteriorated to this state prompted improved HVAC equipment installed within the year.
- Staff realized that proper equipment was essential to continuity. When high temperatures and later COVID-19 forced staff away from their desktops, loss of hardware, software, and network access hampered their work. As a result, as staff desktops come up for replacement, they are being replaced with laptops, and we encourage staff to take these home in anticipation of long-term disruptions (e.g., approaching hurricanes or winter storms).
- Staff had practiced for leaks in the building, but not mold outbreaks, revealing the limitations of an untested emergency plan. As a result, employees learned that the path to recovery may look different depending on the crisis and how much preexisting knowledge there is among staff.
- The HVAC, mold, and temperature issues described above helped staff think about prioritization and function and provided some experience dealing with crises, all of which proved valuable when the coronavirus pandemic struck in spring 2020.
- The impact of crises on staff was cumulative. As crisis events continued to occur in quick succession, followed by the pandemic in 2020, stress among staff increased. However, staff tried to show grace to one another, and library leadership revisited goals and expectations based on these shared experiences.

Boatwright Memorial Library at the University of Richmond had a COOP for the libraries supported by the University of Richmond's crisis and emergency management plan (CEMP). While the plan helped focus energy and resources on the libraries' priorities, it also placed library staff in the correct mindset for addressing the problems that arose. In addition, collaboratively building the COOP made the campus aware of the facility's conditions that led to the mold outbreaks and better aligned the libraries with campus disaster preparation and capital project planning.

Continuity of Operations Plan Elements

A COOP should include the following elements, influenced by the size, type, and location of the institution and the library.

- **Essential functions.** Critical activities performed by your academic library for your institution and surrounding community. Critical activities are best identified by library staff and stakeholders.
- **Succession and authority.** Who will be responsible if key individuals are not available to respond to a crisis, what level of authority they will have, and for how long? How would a campus's emergency response team engage with library-specific elements of a crisis?

- **Continuity facilities.** Locations other than the existing buildings can be used to carry out essential functions. This could include circulating materials from a different site if materials are accessible but the building is not, developing partnerships with nearby libraries with similar resources, and remote work locations for staff.
- **Continuity communications.** Communication plans should include the contact information for staff and procedures for communicating with staff and stakeholders if a significant event disrupts internet or cell service. In addition, communications should provide the capability to perform essential functions in any crisis.
- **Vital records management.** The availability and security of electronic and physical documents, records, authentication information, protocols, and equipment that are needed to support essential functions during a crisis. This might include database and employee authentication information and copies of the COOP available off campus in hard copy. In addition, the institution's facilities or business offices may maintain some vital records.
- **Human capital.** Identify essential employees, ensure employees participate in COOP training, collaborate with human resources departments to prepare for how crises may impact employees, including leave time, pay, and mental health support.
- **Tests, training, and exercises (TT&E).** Build "muscle memory" by practicing with the plan regularly.
- **Reconstitution.** How the library returns to normal operations from the original or replacement location.[11]

The COOP should be informed by an assessment to identify any vulnerabilities that exist for the institution and the library, and essential functions and priorities should align with the larger institution's goals and strategies. Resources such as infrastructure and time are essential to ensuring the program remains viable and achievable. Infrastructure such as communication tools, file storage and backups, and alternate facilities plans should be maintained and tested at scheduled intervals. The plan itself should be reviewed and updated regularly to account for new resources, staff, and shifts to priorities. Elements of the plan related to safety or preservation, such as responding to a tornado warning, an active shooter event, or an active leak in the collection, should be practiced until they are second nature. If a crisis occurs, library staff should debrief lessons learned and improve their plan to ensure an improved response.

At the University of Richmond, all of these elements are included in the university's CEMP, with library-specific components incorporated into the libraries' COOP. For example, the university has identified essential functions, including provision of library services, in its CEMP. The libraries' COOP specifies essential library functions at a much more specific and detailed level, aligned with the library services identified by the university.

Producing a Continuity of Operations Plan

Developing a COOP for your library requires a shift in focus away from the salvage and preservation of print collections and toward essential library functions that your community would rely on in the event of a crisis. Library staff should develop a good plan in collaboration with campus risk management offices or in conversation with campus partners whose work would impact library functions, such as IT departments.[12]

The University of Richmond (UR) maintains a crisis and emergency management plan (CEMP) to address hazards. The CEMP provides the university with flexible, scalable guidance that applies to all phases of emergency management. It is compatible with the National Response Framework[13] and provides the structure for coordinating with local jurisdictions and external emergency response agencies.[14]

In collaboration with the Office of Emergency Preparedness, UR staff developed a building emergency plan (BEP) for each academic and administrative building on campus. Developed in partnership with Environmental Health and Safety to comply with OSHA 29 CFR 1910.38,[15] the BEPs at a minimum include the following information:

- procedures for reporting a fire or other emergency;
- systems for emergency evacuation, including the type of evacuation and exit route assignments;
- procedures to be followed by employees who remain to operate critical operations before they evacuate;
- procedures to account for all employees after evacuation;
- procedures to be followed by employees performing rescue or medical duties; and
- the name or job title of every employee who may be contacted by individuals who need more information about the plan or an explanation of their duties under the plan.[16]

The University of Richmond Libraries complemented the university CEMP with a COOP. The COOP

- ensures the University Libraries can sustain their academic mission under all conditions by reducing or mitigating disruptions to operations;
- helps achieve a timely and orderly recovery and reconstitution from an emergency (minimizing property and damage loss will ensure the University Libraries do not face extraordinary financial pressure in the wake of a crisis);
- protects personnel, facilities, equipment, records, and other assets in the event of a disruption; and
- may reduce the loss of life or injuries during an emergency or disaster.[17]

While much of the libraries' and university's plans focus on disaster relief and the safety of faculty, students, and staff, the libraries expanded their planning to include unique conditions impacting physical and digital collections. Mold, mildew, water leaks (both plumbing and resulting from incursions of stormwater), and rapid fluctuations in temperature and humidity have impacted our print collections. The library's COOP addresses each of these potential outbreaks by ensuring we maintain an adequate supply of emergency mediation tools ranging from simple plastic tarps to freezers, fans, and vacuums, allowing us to cope with small outbreaks quickly.

In addition, each unit within the library understands how these crises impact their operations and has developed plans for ensuring service to students and faculty continues uninterrupted while issues are addressed. Finally, in the case of larger problems, we have worked to educate campus facilities on the nature and consequences of these disasters and develop remediation plans that allow for the rapid response of outside contractors. This collaborative planning and the clear articulation of the financial impact a large-scale disaster would have on the print collection resulted in further long-term changes. The campus conducted a facilities condition assessment that evaluated the physical condition within which the libraries stored collections. This assessment resulted in improved lighting, HVAC, dehumidification equipment, and other changes that reduced risks to the print collection substantially.

Within the University Libraries, the CEMP and COOP create a structure we can follow when disaster strikes. Alignment between the two plans ensures that we remain on mission with the university and that the university understands the unique impacts disasters may have on library collections and staff.

Conclusion

Continuity of operations planning allows an academic library to respond to many crises and can improve the quality and coherence of crisis response, ensure critical functions continue, and calibrate allocation of personnel and resources for the most significant positive impact. It allows an academic library to proactively plan and prepare a response to many crises, from a weather event that leaves a library building without power for a week to a mold outbreak to truly unprecedented situations such as COVID-19, regardless of institution type, size, or resources. By preparing a proactive response, the library team is better equipped to address the challenges a crisis can bring. Library management and each unit within the library can better understand their individual and collective roles at such a time.

Notes

1. Lee Glendon, "A Winning Combination: The 3Cs of Business Continuity," *Journal of Business Continuity and Emergency Planning* 7, no. 1 (September 2013): 44–55.
2. Glendon, "Winning Combination"; Vener Garayev, "Crisis, Definition Of," in *Encyclopedia of Crisis Management*, ed. K. Bradley Penuel, Matt Statler, and Ryan Hagen (Thousand Oaks, CA: SAGE, 2013), 186–87, https://doi.org/10.4135/9781452275956.n64.
3. FEMA, *Federal Continuity* (Washington, DC: FEMA, July 2018), https://www.fema.gov/sites/default/files/2020-07/fema_brochure-continuity-ncp_082318_0.pdf; FEMA, *Continuity Plan Template and Instructions for Non-federal Entities and Community-Based Organizations* (Washington, DC: FEMA, August 2018), https://www.fema.gov/sites/default/files/2020-09/fema_non-federal-continuity-plan_template_08-31-18.pdf; FEMA, *Continuity of Operations: An Overview* (Washington, DC: FEMA, n.d.), https://www.fema.gov/pdf/about/org/ncp/coop_brochure.pdf.
4. Linda S. Hanwacker, "Continuity of Operations Plans: Simple or Detailed?" *Journal of Business Continuity and Emergency Planning* 12, no. 2 (Winter 2018): 133–49; FEMA, *Continuity of Operations*.
5. FEMA, *Federal Continuity*.
6. Rebecca Hamilton and Diane Brown, "Disaster Management and Continuity Planning in Libraries: Changes since the Year 2000," in *Handbook of Research on Disaster Management and Contingency Planning in Modern Libraries*, ed. Emily Nelson Decker and Jennifer A. Townes (Hershey, PA: IGI Global, 2016), 1–24, https://doi.org/10.4018/978-1-4666-8624-3.ch001; Kaitlin Kehnemuyi, "Effects of COVID-19 on Disaster Planning in Academic Libraries," *Journal of Library Administration* 61, no. 5 (2021): 507–29, https://doi.org/10.1080/01930826.2021.1924530; Jill Dixon and Nancy Abashian,

"Beyond the Collection: Emergency Planning for Public and Staff Safety," in *Handbook of Research on Disaster Management and Contingency Planning in Modern Libraries*, ed. Emily Nelson Decker and Jennifer A. Townes (Hershey, PA: IGI Global, 2016), 120–40, https://doi.org/10.4018/978-1-4666-8624-3.ch006.

7. Glendon, "Winning Combination."
8. Hamilton and Brown, "Disaster Management"; Mary Beth Lock, Craig Fansler, and Meghan Webb, "Emergency Planning (R)Evolution: Making a Comprehensive Emergency Plan for the Present and the Future," in *Handbook of Research on Disaster Management and Contingency Planning in Modern Libraries*, ed. Emily Nelson Decker and Jennifer A. Townes (Hershey, PA: IGI Global, 2016), 70–95, https://doi.org/10.4018/978-1-4666-8624-3.ch004; Dixon and Abashian, "Beyond the Collection."
9. Glendon, "Winning Combination."
10. Catherine Soehner, Ian Godfrey, and G. Scott Bigler, "Crisis Communication in Libraries: Opportunity for New Roles in Public Relations," *Journal of Academic Librarianship* 43, no. 3 (May 2017): 268–73, https://doi.org/10.1016/j.acalib.2017.03.003; Glendon, "Winning Combination."
11. FEMA, *Continuity of Operations*; FEMA, *Federal Continuity*; FEMA, *Continuity Plan Template*; FEMA, *Continuity Essential Records Management* (Washington, DC: FEMA, July 2018); Hanwacker, "Continuity of Operations Plans"; Hamilton and Brown, "Disaster Management."
12. Allison Galloup, "One Plan, Four Libraries: A Case Study in Disaster Planning for a Four-Campus Academic Institution," in *Handbook of Research on Disaster Management and Contingency Planning in Modern Libraries*, ed. Emily Nelson Decker and Jennifer A. Townes (Hershey, PA: IGI Global, 2016), 166–83, https://doi.org/10.4018/978-1-4666-8624-3.ch008.
13. FEMA, "National Response Framework," October 2020, https://www.fema.gov/emergency-managers/national-preparedness/frameworks/response.
14. University of Richmond, "Crisis and Emergency Management Plan," https://preparedness.richmond.edu/planning/emergency-operations.html.
15. Occupational Safety and Health Administration, "1910.38—Emergency Action Plans," accessed September 14, 2021, https://www.osha.gov/laws-regs/regulations/standardnumber/1910/1910.38.
16. University of Richmond, "Building Coordinators," Emergency Management, https://preparedness.richmond.edu/coordinators/index.html.
17. University of Richmond, "Business Continuity," Emergency Management, https://preparedness.richmond.edu/planning/continuity.html.

Bibliography

Dixon, Jill, and Nancy Abashian. "Beyond the Collection: Emergency Planning for Public and Staff Safety." In *Handbook of Research on Disaster Management and Contingency Planning in Modern Libraries*, edited by Emily Nelson Decker and Jennifer A. Townes, 120–40. Hershey, PA: IGI Global, 2016. https://doi.org/10.4018/978-1-4666-8624-3.ch006.

FEMA. *Continuity Essential Records Management*. Washington, DC: FEMA, July 2018. https://www.fema.gov/sites/default/files/2020-07/fema_brochure-essential-records-ncp_082418_0.pdf.

———. *Continuity of Operations: An Overview*. Washington, DC: FEMA, n.d. https://www.fema.gov/pdf/about/org/ncp/coop_brochure.pdf.

———. *Continuity Plan Template and Instructions for Non-federal Entities and Community-Based Organizations*. Washington, DC: FEMA, August 2018. https://www.fema.gov/sites/default/files/2020-09/fema_non-federal-continuity-plan_template_08-31-18.pdf.

———. *Federal Continuity*. Washington, DC: FEMA, July 2018. https://www.fema.gov/sites/default/files/2020-07/fema_brochure-continuity-ncp_082318_0.pdf.

———. "National Response Framework," October 2020. https://www.fema.gov/emergency-managers/national-preparedness/frameworks/response.

Galloup, Allison. "One Plan, Four Libraries: A Case Study in Disaster Planning for a Four-Campus Academic Institution." In *Handbook of Research on Disaster Management and Contingency Planning in Modern Libraries*, edited by Emily Nelson Decker and Jennifer A. Townes, 166–83. Hershey, PA: IGI Global, 2016. https://doi.org/10.4018/978-1-4666-8624-3.ch008.

Garayev, Vener. "Crisis, Definition Of." In *Encyclopedia of Crisis Management*, edited by K. Bradley Penuel, Matt Statler, and Ryan Hagen, 186–87. Thousand Oaks, CA: SAGE, 2013. https://doi.org/10.4135/9781452275956.n64.

Glendon, Lee. "A Winning Combination: The 3Cs of Business Continuity." *Journal of Business Continuity and Emergency Planning* 7, no. 1 (September 2013): 44–55.

Hamilton, Rebecca, and Diane Brown. "Disaster Management and Continuity Planning in Libraries: Changes since the Year 2000." In *Handbook of Research on Disaster Management and Contingency Planning in Modern Libraries*, edited by Emily Nelson Decker and Jennifer A. Townes, 1–24. Hershey, PA: IGI Global, 2016. https://doi.org/10.4018/978-1-4666-8624-3.ch001.

Hanwacker, Linda S. "Continuity of Operations Plans: Simple or Detailed?" *Journal of Business Continuity and Emergency Planning* 12, no. 2 (Winter 2018): 133–49.

Kehnemuyi, Kaitlin. "Effects of COVID-19 on Disaster Planning in Academic Libraries." *Journal of Library Administration* 61, no. 5 (2021): 507–29. https://doi.org/10.1080/01930826.2021.1924530.

Lock, Mary Beth, Craig Fansler, and Meghan Webb. "Emergency Planning (R)Evolution: Making a Comprehensive Emergency Plan for the Present and the Future." In *Handbook of Research on Disaster Management and Contingency Planning in Modern Libraries*, edited by Emily Nelson Decker and Jennifer A. Townes, 70–95. Hershey, PA: IGI Global, 2016. https://doi.org/10.4018/978-1-4666-8624-3.ch004.

Occupational Safety and Health Administration. "1910.38—Emergency Action Plans." Accessed September 14, 2021. https://www.osha.gov/laws-regs/regulations/standardnumber/1910/1910.38.

Soehner, Catherine, Ian Godfrey, and G. Scott Bigler. "Crisis Communication in Libraries: Opportunity for New Roles in Public Relations." *Journal of Academic Librarianship* 43, no. 3 (May 2017): 268–73. https://doi.org/10.1016/j.acalib.2017.03.003.

University of Richmond. "Building Coordinators." Emergency Management. https://preparedness.richmond.edu/coordinators/index.html.

———. "Business Continuity." Emergency Management. https://preparedness.richmond.edu/planning/continuity.html.

———. "Crisis and Emergency Management Plan." https://preparedness.richmond.edu/planning/emergency-operations.html.

CHAPTER 14

Professional Identity during COVID-19

Experiences of Academic Library Leaders in the United States

Erik Nordberg

> *The pandemic prioritized operational decision-making and organizational leadership, reducing bandwidth for professional scholarship and service. Pandemic isolation impacted the administrative and professional circles of most library leaders.*

The COVID-19 pandemic caused a quick, dramatic, and challenging shift in operations for academic libraries. With the pressures of suspending building operations, coordinating the departure of employees to remote work, and the transition of many services into virtual modalities, library leaders encountered significant limitations to their professional travel and service activities, as well as their individual research agendas. As COVID-19 increased operational management activity for library leaders, the resulting lack of bandwidth impacted opportunities for professional activity. In some cases, this resulted in suspension of such work altogether, while others pivoted to new areas of research and forms of virtual networking that created novel avenues for professional interaction and service.[1]

Structured interviews with a purposeful sample of twelve academic library deans and directors in the United States provide insights on their experiences during the pandemic. Additional information gathered through subsequent communication provided clarification and confirmed factual details. While the population interviewed was not intended to be statistically significant, this qualitative approach yields a richer understanding of the challenges encountered during COVID-19 and the responses made by academic library leaders. Informants were specifically selected from a range of institutions, large and small, public and private, to provide perspectives on their professional activity and changed expectations of their peers and executive reporting lines during the pandemic. The interview recordings were transcribed and then analyzed thematically.

The respondents were selected from academic libraries in eight states: Alabama, Kentucky, Michigan, Pennsylvania, South Carolina, Tennessee, West Virginia, and Wyoming. For ease of reference, all respondents are referred to as "dean" in this chapter. Although individual identities remain anonymous, a simple numeric system relates the size of their respective institutions: four of the deans (Dean 1–Dean 4) are employed at institutions with fewer than 5,000 students, three deans (Dean 5–Dean 7) work for universities between 5,000 and 15,000 students, and the remaining five deans (Dean 8–Dean 12) are located at campuses with more than 15,000 students.

Expectations of Academic Library Deans

The validity and value of systems of tenure and promotion for academic librarians has been a constant and consistent theme in the professional literature.[2] Critics claim that librarians, particularly those on twelve-month contracts, fail to maintain an active level of scholarship and publication comparable to teaching faculty in the academic departments. Debate continues as to whether the MLIS/MIS qualifies as a terminal degree. Advocates encourage professional academic librarians to improve their status by moving beyond simple reports of practice, pursue deeper quantitative and qualitative forms of inquiry, and report findings through peer-reviewed journals—including those outside their own literature. Little has been written, however, about expectations concerning tenure and scholarship for those in leadership roles as academic library deans. Few of the respondents to this survey reported that they are held to the same requirements for scholarship and service written into the bylaws of their tenure-track librarians. "I'm not tenure-track, so it's not required of me to publish or present," noted Dean 2. "I am motivating myself to do that, but there is no pressure from administration or my direct report." Smaller institutions seem less likely to extend faculty status to librarians, and some restrict such status to the primary library administrator. "This is the first school where I've held faculty status," noted Dean 4, "but I'm the only librarian here who is tenure-track." For those new to administrative positions, the learning curve for budget planning, personnel matters, facility concerns, and a crush of operational, peer, and executive meeting schedules often places lower priority on professional activity. Over time, the lack of clear expectations for research and publication can reinforce this de-emphasis on scholarship for academic library deans.

"The culture in higher education," reported Dean 3, "is that administrators administer, and faculty engage in the creative activities." Leadership roles in academic libraries place priority on strategic direction, operational efficiency, administrative management, fiscal control, and resource development, including grantsmanship, advancement, and donor relations. Several deans felt that their professional contributions were made in areas other than publication, including campus-wide strategic initiatives, leadership positions in national and international associations, and participation on blue ribbon panels exploring the wicked problems of academic libraries and higher education, such as the growing imbalance between open access and predatory vendor contracts, declining gate count and print circulation trends, and the role of the library in first-year retention and student success as campuses adjust to shifting student demographics. "Library deans support and advance the infrastructure of research and scholarship in other ways," noted Dean 6. "It is not as much about their individual contribution of scholarly content, but how their work to advance the use of open educational resources (OERs), to develop institutional repositories (IRs), their service on publication boards, and other activities advance the reputation of the institution." While not surprising, these responses indicate a divergence between the expectations for tenure-track librarians and the expectations for the library deans who direct, mentor, and evaluate these individuals—and, ultimately, have strong input on decisions for tenure and promotion.

Scholarship and Service

While most library deans aren't required to meet defined expectations from their provost or other campus administrators to publish, there is a sense of responsibility by the respondents to remain professionally active. Dean 3, who had ascended from a faculty position, missed a more active role in scholarship. "I have found some reward in encouraging others to pursue scholarship opportunities and have critiqued their work," he reported. "That is part of being an effective leader and mentor but does not replace the reward I felt previously in contributing to the scholarship in the field." Others expressed a self-imposed responsibility to remain professionally active. "I always view my role as leader of the faculty," said Dean 12. "I feel we need to lead a faculty life." Most of the respondents acknowledged a conscious desire to be "good" and "effective" leaders, with their decision to move into administrative roles with deliberate intent to improve the lives of their employees and increase the impact of their program on the institution. For those who traversed their own tenure processes before climbing into the leadership seat, the need to "model expectations" was strong. Some without a tenure experience earlier in their career were even more deeply committed to mentoring younger faculty and using their own professional activity as examples of positive outcomes.

Yet, the pandemic prioritized operational decision-making and organizational leadership, reducing bandwidth for professional scholarship and service. "When you're in a leadership position," noted Dean 10, "you're often working fifty to sixty hours to get everything done for your patrons and employees." With the increased number of COVID-related meetings, forums, and communication outputs, he noted, "there's not a lot of time for you to sit down and write scholarship." Many spring and summer conferences were canceled or rescheduled, greatly reducing opportunities for presentations and participation on scholarly panels.

Within a few months, however, some professional associations began to experiment with virtual conferences. As people acclimated to remote meetings, both internally and externally, professional service activities resumed and, in many cases, became even more necessary and energized. "Ironically, I think it actually spurred me to be more active," reported Dean 10. Work with associations and consortia provided a valuable network of peers and professional colleagues to compare responses to the public health crisis.

Provosts and campus administrators relaxed their expectations during the pandemic. "I have had nothing but support from my direct report," reported Dean 1. In many cases, pandemic response brought added responsibilities on campus-wide emergency response teams and additional assignments for library deans and directors. "My provost wouldn't be concerned right now if I was publishing, presenting, and engaging in service," noted Dean 8. "I think she's just glad that I'm able to do it." Library deans and directors with no formal expectation for service or scholarship pressed on regardless of requirements or the limitations imposed by COVID. Overall, the survey respondents remained surprisingly active during the pandemic. Dean 9 began service as president of a national library association, and Dean 10 was elected president of a large regional research library association. Several were invited to produce opinion pieces for national publications and local media. Some published peer-reviewed articles and coauthored book chapters, and many participated in virtual panel sessions or presented their research in other virtual settings. Time remained a challenging commodity, however, as the pandemic continued to prioritize operational matters. "The days and weeks seem to pass so quickly," noted Dean 1, "but I'm trusting we'll get back to a place where I can block out time for research and writing."

Stress-Impacted Bandwidth

Library deans are expected to juggle multiple demands on their time and attention. Everyday expectations for reporting, responding, and communicating may be affected by a crisis in the institution, or by external threats, such as that of the pandemic. When a crisis hits, expectations must be adjusted not only for the academic library dean, but also for the people working under them. Decisions must be made, and made quickly, when a crisis arises that affects the operations of the library and its ability to serve all stakeholders. One of the key expectations of leaders in any setting is to remain calm, level-headed, and reassuring in times of crisis.

COVID-19 presented one of the most serious challenges for library deans, both professionally and personally, to this core value. Several respondents reported that the additional work to manage the stress of employees—and of their own personal anxiety levels—further undermined and de-emphasized expectations of library deans for research and professional activity. Travel was suspended for professionals across the higher education sector, and most professional associations were slow to consider virtual options. "Our expectations of tenure-track library faculty for scholarship and service took a back seat to the public health crisis," said Dean 5. "In the past, I attempted to model this behavior for those who report to me, but it simply was not important as the situation worsened." Others agreed that the pre-COVID emphasis on scholarly activity and publication was rarely discussed. Dean 10 remembered one of the very first meetings to discuss closing his library: "People are looking at me for all the answers. I'm like, 'I don't have any more answers that the rest of you, but we'll work through this together.'" There was a genuine concern for the health of their employees. "I have fifty people's lives in my hands," recalled Dean 8 at the outset of the crisis. "I don't want a single one of them dead at the end of this. So, there was a lot of anxiety about people's health, their safety in the building, and whether what I was asking them to do was reasonable and safe." Nobody had confronted a pandemic before, there was no playbook and many, many unknowns. This lack of control was disturbing to many. "When is this going to end?" questioned Dean 7; "It's just not in my DNA not to have a plan." Several institutions suspended annual employee evaluations, and few deans closely tracked their employees' professional scholarship and service activities.

Respondents also noted increasing levels of exhaustion, as remote work extended into the summer and fall of 2020. "I'm really empathetic," said Dean 12, "and I became really worried about everyone." There was literal exhaustion from working in a highly charged, rapidly changing environment involving dozens of daily decisions. "I would have nights where I'm exhausted," recalled Dean 11. "I did not feel like I had stress or anxiety, simply tired from one busy day after another." Dean 3 characterized the net effect as "an emotional and spiritual vampire, just sucking all of the energy from you." Yet leaders realized the need to be the calm voice to move the library forward. "You have the same challenges they're facing," noted Dean 10, "but you have to be that stabilizing influence for the good of the organization." Many purposely turned to their traditional professional networks for personal support and, as tools for professional activity, sought opportunities for service, scholarship, and publication.

Pandemic protocols, including shelter-in-place orders, created initial difficulties to maintain professional networks. Individuals couldn't fly on planes, gather in large groups, attend conferences, participate in regional library meetings, or have coffee with a professional counterpart at a neighboring institution. Many spoke to a depression that accompanied the lack of routine contact with colleagues and friends. As with other professionals across the globe, the sudden disconnect from social structures was not only disconcerting but emotionally difficult. "Suddenly you can't do those things anymore," recalled Dean 3. "That hit me pretty hard in my personal life, and you know it's going to bleed into your professional life." Although some used vacation days to step away from the work, few were able to take "a normal vacation" or participate in the regular professional connections with their colleagues and research collaborators. Attention to mental health issues encouraged individuals to turn off their e-mail and Zoom screens. "I kept telling my leadership team to take a day off, a long weekend, or even a week," recalled Dean 12. Yet he himself hadn't taken a day off in nearly twelve months. "I guess I gotta start living what I'm talking about." The extra sense of responsibility many respondents felt toward their employees' stress levels allowed many respondents to play a more supportive role than what they may have played in the past, and also provided an opportunity for the deans themselves to explore their own emotional need to find an outlet for their stress. At their libraries, many redirected the time they previously committed to scholarship to operational work and new projects. Discussion about the long-range future of the institution helped to lessen some concerns about the current situation. Relaxed expectations for scholarship and publication allowed individuals to reconnect to personal hobbies like baking and gardening. "Time I would have spent in the evenings on reading and writing opened up for activities I hadn't done in years," reported Dean 5. Others had already developed personal coping mechanisms during previous challenging periods. "My well-being has not been terribly affected by this," reported Dean 2. "I had already established a foundational wellness practice before this happened. I was already equipped to respond to stress." Others reported the adoption of mindfulness practices, continuation of exercise regimens, and establishing firmer boundaries about e-mail and computer work to ensure a good work-life balance. One respondent revealed engagement with a counselor and their joint decision to begin a course of antidepressant medications.

Isolation and Support Networks

Health protocols dictated by the Centers for Disease Control and their institutions increased feelings of professional isolation for many library leaders. Although respondents reported strong (and often confidential) support from their immediate library leadership team, most accepted the tension inherent in establishing appropriate relationships with faculty and staff during a time of crisis. Unlike academic deans, sharing common activities in different disciplines, the academic library leadership position is unique on campus. Library deans usually manage larger groups of employees than deans of the academic colleges (often with a more complex mix of faculty, staff, and student positions), are responsible for large non-salary acquisitions budgets, and may have a more significant role in facilities management issues.

At a personal level, some continued to draw support from faith communities and other organizations that created virtual alternatives to group gatherings. Dean 5 organized socially distanced patio dinners and neighborhood "projector parties" to break from the isolation of the home office "Zoom tomb." Some individuals took advantage of remote work to spend more time with their immediate families. Dean 11 and her spouse maintain a long-distance marriage, so the pandemic lockdown allowed to them to live together for five months. Several also reported positive experiences working from home with spouses and their children. "You know, we didn't have a lot of friends over—we didn't have a lot of social anything," admitted Dean 9, "but it was time I had with my kids as adults I never would have had otherwise. They're so fun and they made me laugh when it was stressful." Both Dean 9 and Dean 11 also benefitted from their spouse's employment in academic libraries, for the ability to discuss responses and, occasionally, to vent frustrations about the crisis. The ability to make, broaden, or reconnect social networks during the time of crisis played an important role in coping with the isolation brought on by the work-from-home structures many institutions implemented.

Pandemic isolation impacted the administrative and professional circles of most library leaders. "It's a lonely position," said Dean 12, being the only dean *within* the library and the only library dean *across* campus. However, COVID response helped strengthen existing relationships with on-campus peers. Most were part of a formal "deans council" or an informal network of unit-level directors, though they continued to report pre-pandemic challenges as the only library person in the room. Kindred spirits were found in others with cross-institutional roles—directors for teaching and learning, information technology, and remote learning (one referred to their group as "the island of misfit toys"). But even in these supportive groups, it can be like "Oz working behind the curtain," Dean 11 reported. With other deans and campus leaders worried about classrooms, dorms, and dining halls, "they don't necessarily have the time or aptitude to deal with the library as it is foreign to them."

Interactions with professional colleagues and networks also changed during the pandemic. The lack of conferences and statewide meetings eliminated serendipitous meetings and a free exchange of ideas over coffee at a convention center. "My ability to build my network is limited to who I'm meeting through a screen now," lamented Dean 9, "not through some of those happenstance engagements at a professional meeting." It was most difficult for those who were new to positions just as the pandemic hit—or those who changed jobs. "I haven't had a chance to make a lot of work friends," noted Dean 1, who started their current position in July 2020. "I've reached out to a couple of the other library directors in the area, but we haven't really been going out for coffee or that kind of thing. So I have missed having those during my transition." However, most respondents reported that they also benefited as professional service work moved to remote settings and they reestablished interactions virtually with mentors, peers, and close friends across the profession. "My network has been my lifeline," noted Dean 7. "You're the leader, right? You can't necessarily go to your subordinates about some matters, so you turn to your peer colleagues around the nation. Honestly, I couldn't function without them." Respondents talked positively of the way that professional associations and consortia provided Zoom check-ins and remote committee meetings. "You would have thought if we're all at home we're not going to be as close," said Dean 10, referring to his work with a regional professional association. "What I found was the opposite."

Conclusion

In general, expectations for professional scholarship and service were already inconsistent for academic library deans and directors prior to the COVID-19 pandemic. The crisis further reduced individual leaders' limited time for scholarship and professional service beyond their primary strategic, administrative, and fiscal responsibilities.

An avalanche of decision-making concerning operational matters, both significant and minute, heightened levels of budgetary instability, and, in some cases, library leaders were confronted with furloughs, layoffs, and retirements, which further affected the provision of service. Library leaders also encountered heightened levels of anxiety, stress, exhaustion, and isolation in their employees and themselves. While few had been active researchers before the pandemic, COVID further reduced opportunities for service and other contributions to the profession.

Ironically, the pandemic increased the need for strong professional networks. The isolation of academic library deans on their campuses and regions (particularly those in smaller rural institutions) benefitted from the pivot to virtual engagement with consortiums and professional associations. It also had the effect of pushing some library leaders to seek creative outlets and new or broadened social networks, strengthening personal ties along the way.

As higher education emerges from COVID-19, library leaders should reexamine work-life balance, remote work, and the expectations for scholarship and service of the tenure-track librarians who report to them. A more nuanced understanding of the contributions each makes to the profession—as a librarian and as a library administrator—can affirm the differing and complementary impacts made collectively for students, institutions, and the profession.

Notes

1. A great variety of literature and news sources have considered the impact of COVID-19 on higher education and academic libraries. Ithaka S+R conducted surveys and gathered other resources: Ithaka S+R, "COVID-19 Resources for Higher Education and Academic Libraries, last updated December 9, 2020, https://sr.ithaka.org/our-work/covid-19/. Other examples include Alterline, *Supporting Academic Research: Understanding the Challenges* (Chicago: Ex Libris, 2020), https://page.exlibris-group.com/research-office-challenges-2020-report; Jennifer Frederick, Roger C. Schonfeld, and Christine Wolff-Eisenberg, "The Impacts of COVID-19 on Academic Library Budgets: Fall 2020," *Scholarly Kitchen* (blog), December 9, 2020, https://scholarlykitchen.sspnet.org/2020/12/09/academic-library-budgets-fall-2020/; and Mahnaz Dar, "How COVID-19 Has Transformed Reference Services for Public and Academic Libraries," *Library Journal*, November 10, 2020, https://www.libraryjournal.com?detailStory=how-covid19-has-transformed-reference-services-for-public-academic-libraries.
2. A good review of early scholarship on tenure in academic libraries is included in W. Bede Mitchell and Mary Reichel, "Publish or Perish: A Dilemma for Academic Librarians?" *College and Research Libraries* 60, no. 3 (May 1999): 232–43, https://doi.org/10.5860/crl.60.3.232. See also William Walters, "Faculty Status of Librarians at U.S. Research Universities," *Journal of Academic Librarianship* 42, no. 2 (2016): 161–71, https://doi.org/10.1016/j.acalib.2015.11.002, and Marcy Simons, *Academic Librarianship* (Lanham, MD: Rowman & Littlefield, 2021).

Bibliography

Alterline. *Supporting Academic Research: Understanding the Challenges*. Chicago: Ex Libris, 2020. https://page.exlibrisgroup.com/research-office-challenges-2020-report.

Dar, Mahnaz. "How COVID-19 Has Transformed Reference Services for Public and Academic Libraries." *Library Journal*, November 10, 2020. https://www.libraryjournal.com?detailStory=how-covid19-has-transformed-reference-services-for-public-academic-libraries.

Frederick, Jennifer, Roger C. Schonfeld, and Christine Wolff-Eisenberg. "The Impacts of COVID-19 on Academic Library Budgets: Fall 2020." *Scholarly Kitchen* (blog), December 9, 2020. https://scholarlykitchen.sspnet.org/2020/12/09/academic-library-budgets-fall-2020/.

Ithaka S+R. "COVID-19 Resources for Higher Education and Academic Libraries." Last updated December 9, 2020. https://sr.ithaka.org/our-work/covid-19/.

Mitchell, W. Bede, and Mary Reichel. "Publish or Perish: A Dilemma for Academic Librarians?" *College and Research Libraries* 60, no. 3 (May 1999): 232–43. https://doi.org/10.5860/crl.60.3.232.

Simons, Marcy. *Academic Librarianship: Anchoring the Profession in Contribution, Scholarship, and Service*. Lanham, MD: Rowman & Littlefield, 2021.

Walters, William H. "Faculty Status of Librarians at U.S. Research Universities." *Journal of Academic Librarianship* 42, no. 2 (2016): 161–71. https://doi.org/10.1016/j.acalib.2015.11.002.

CHAPTER 15

Overall Experience of Library Employees Working from Home during the COVID-19 Pandemic

Renee Gould, Amy Harris, Audrey Koke, Marissa Smith, Michelle Joy, and Delaney Rose

Implementing a work-from-home model for an institution would be quite valuable and needed not only for times of crisis but as an ongoing benefit for employees and employers.

Introduction

Working from home is not a new concept; however, its implementation on a mass scale due to the COVID-19 pandemic is unprecedented in American history. Many libraries needed to fully implement some type of work-from-home program for the safety of both employees and patrons. This chapter explores how library employees and their respective responsibilities were affected during the pandemic, focusing on those who worked from home. Originally, the investigators were interested solely in technical services employees due to their specialized needs for working with physical resources. The pilot data from the technical services area was so interesting that the researchers decided it justified distributing the survey to a wider array of library employees working in a variety of libraries. The investigators wanted to learn if working from home was a viable option for all library employees, rather than only those in technical services roles. They were also looking for clues about whether working from home would be a permanent future option for at least some of those surveyed.

The study concentrated on the months between March 2020 to June 2020. This period was chosen because the investigators felt it best characterized library personnel workflows pre-pandemic and the resultant changes after COVID-19 was declared a pandemic. The World Health Organization (WHO) officially recognized COVID-19 as a pandemic on March 11, 2020.[1] As a result of the declaration, many US states had issued various orders and declarations based on the Centers for Disease Control and Prevention's "15 days to slow the spread" guidance concerning this public health crisis to prevent hospitals from being overwhelmed and to protect the health and safety of the populace.[2] By mid-March, most US states "declared a state of emergency in response to COVID-19."[3] A few such measures implemented in the state of Florida, for example, were the following: the state adopted social distancing measures such as avoiding large gatherings of ten or more people, businesses were "encourage[d] to provide delivery, carry-out or curbside service outside," and lastly there was a strong urge for those "who can work remotely to do so."[4] During the months of March and April, many library employers implemented changes to conform with their state-level restrictions while also attempting to provide services to their patrons. Then, by May 20, 2020, "all 50 states [had] begun to partially lift restrictions."[5] Therefore, the investigators felt that June 1 would serve as a reasonable stopping point to the research. For consistency, the investigators will be defining the period March 1, 2020, to June 1, 2020, as the "lockdown." Anything prior to March 1, 2020, will be defined as "pre-COVID-19."

Technology, Society, and Telecommuting: A Literature Review

In July 1922, at the forty-fourth annual meeting of the American Library Association, presenter Mary Emogene Hazeltine described the ideal attitude of librarians toward service to their patrons. In one section she proclaimed:

> Our attitude toward the public should be that of a large understanding and eagerness to share our work and its methods; and as we meet the public halfway to receive the service we have to offer—this is the end and reward of our work.[6]

Nearly ninety years later, a similar attitude toward service seemed very familiar, yet the delivery of such assistance has drastically transformed. In all types of work environments, massive societal and technological changes led the way to novel approaches for conducting day-to-day operations. One avenue included the broader offering of work-at-home options for employees. In the library profession, particularly in cataloging and technical services, literature points to successful ventures into telecommuting as early as the mid-1990s. This practice was not widespread; it was mainly in a testing phase.[7] Numerous publications examined how telecommuting changed the dynamics of work. One such publication by Gainey, Kelley, and Hill likened the success of telecommuting to four underlying corporate cultures that were compared to the personalities of four Greek gods. For example, "Zeus" and "Athena" cultures relied on "extensive personal contact" and did not find work outside of the office walls as productive as the more laid-back "Apollo" or "Dionysus" cultures.[8] The authors also included that, overall, working from home provided many benefits, such as balancing work and family, reducing various costs of the workplace, and lessening or eliminating commute times, which in turn saved money on gas and was overall better for the environment. One drawback noted by Gainey, Kelly, and Hill, however, was the "isolation effect" from being physically away from the workplace and colleagues.[9]

Bathini and Kandathil also reported on how isolation was a negative factor for individuals working from home. Much of the literature they uncovered focused on the favorable, and not enough on the negative aspects. The authors provided evidence that working away from the office could be more stressful because employees felt "obligated and pressured" to work whenever possible and much longer than their regular office hours. This in turn resulted in mental and physical health issues as well as a disturbance of favorable work-life balance. They argued that safeguards should be legally implemented to dissuade employers from overworking their employees.[10] In 2000, Adrian Furnham predicted what work life would be like in twenty years by reviewing various trends and forecasts. He posited five "alternative work arrangements"—flextime, compressed weeks, increased part-time opportunities, temporary employment, and teleworking.[11] Furnham also examined the social reasons for these options becoming advantageous: environmental concerns, more attention paid to health and wellness, equality, and overall quality-of-life interests, many aspects of which have come sharply into focus in 2021. He continued by pointing out how rapid growth in technology facilitated the plan for greater telework opportunities and that "fortunate workers of the future may have more choice, flexibility and certain benefits than those of today."[12]

Ten years after Furnham predicted the future of the general workplace, Staley and Malenfant provided a forecast for academic librarians in 2025. The study included "26 possible scenarios based on an implications assessment of current trends" and examined what was most likely to occur.[13] There were glimpses of how online learning was growing and that "virtual service points" were becoming much more prevalent. This was paired with the fact that the new generations possessed "laptops in their hands since the age of 18-months old" and were "media savvy" by the time they reached college age. They also predicted that the brick-and-mortar college and library could potentially diminish completely and exist only virtually because of these factors.[14] In 2008, Jennifer Duncan proclaimed that telecommuting was increasingly becoming a solid option for technical and public services librarians. This was primarily due to the "explosion of technology."[15] In one section of her analysis, Duncan relayed research that working from home may increase happiness and lessen burnout. Furthermore, Lister and Harnish claimed it improved overall satisfaction by lessening stress and providing a stable work-life balance. It also resulted in better health and less illness[16]—but no research done by library personnel before 2020 predicted the need to work from home to avoid a global pandemic.

By the summer of 2021, numerous researchers had examined the impact of COVID-19 on various issues, including that of telecommuting. Anna R. Craft described how the pandemic "forced many libraries to make rapid changes that otherwise would have been given significant time and planning."[17] This chapter will examine the effects of COVID-19 and how mandatory work-from-home measures impacted the professional lives of library employees.

Background

The survey "Impact of COVID-19 Pandemic within the Library" was distributed to various e-mail distribution lists, forums, and social media platforms to reach a wide audience and in order to disseminate the survey to as many types of librarians as possible. Surveys that were not completed, or where the individual did not work at least one hour from home during lockdown, were removed from the data set. Of the 828 to respond to the survey, the investigators removed 187 responses that either were not completed or did not reflect at least one hour of working from home during the specified time period. It left the investigators a data set of 641 responses to work with. The most significant percentage of work-from-home respondents were from the following states: Florida (19.81 percent), New York (7.49 percent), California (6.55 percent), Illinois (6.24 percent), and Texas (4.99 percent). The investigators being based in Florida may have skewed response rates and contributed to a higher percentage of Floridian respondents. Although the sample was not highly representative of the library employee population in each state, there was at least one respondent from each state except Hawaii and Montana, and the response rate was sufficiently high to draw some conclusions.

The beginning of the survey requested common background data. Question 1 was the acknowledgment of consent to participate in research. Question 2 was to verify respondents were employees from the United States of America. Questions 3 and 4 focused on the locations of respondents. Most employees worked in their resident state. However, respondents from eighteen states and the District of Columbia indicated they resided in a state other than their place of employment. Most notably, one respondent moved across the country. They commented that "I moved in with my parents in NY to save money. When I return to on-site work …I will have to find another apartment to live in, and also I will drive across the country again." This information caused the investigators to wonder how many other respondents had moved during the pandemic. Additionally, it would have been interesting to incorporate commute time in the survey.

Question 5 focused on the type of library respondents worked in. Employees of four-year academic libraries led the work-from-home initiative with 53.98 percent, while public libraries followed second at 28.08 percent. The remaining respondents were from special libraries (9.98 percent), two-year academic libraries (7.49 percent) and K–12 school libraries (0.47 percent). Multiple respondents indicated that their format of instruction transferred from in person to online within educational settings. Comments that reflected a shift to online instruction included "all reference and instruction interactions went onto email or Zoom" and "all instruction done by Zoom." Overall, library employees seem to adapt to meeting their patrons' needs through finding alternative pathways.

Question 6 asked whether the respondent is considered a librarian, staff, administration, paraprofessional, or other within their library. Most respondents identified as librarian for a total of 68.95 percent, followed by staff at 15.29 percent, administration at 8.27 percent, paraprofessional at 5.30 percent, and other at 2.18 percent. The purpose of this data was to learn if there were any differences between roles. The investigators expected that library employees with higher ranks would experience higher levels of difficulty completing library jobs and duties while working from home, although no specific commentary was located to verify this concern. The roles held by each employee became more distinguishable in Question 8.

Question 8 asked what the respondents' primary roles were. Categories of response included Access and Delivery Services, Special Collections, Youth Services, Circulation, Administration, and Adult Services. The highest number of respondents identified their primary role to be Cataloging/Copy Cataloging/Metadata (21.53%), followed by Reference/Instructional Services (17.78%). Administration came in third at 11.86 percent, and Other was the fourth highest category at 10.45 percent. Most categories of positions fell below the 10 percent mark. Based on each respondent's primary role, the researchers could assume that they performed certain duties. In addition, depending on the specific duties assigned to each employee and their access to technology, the expected outcome of work completed at home was dissimilar. One comment that stood out claimed that many employees worked from home but could not do their job due to their "lack of computer or internet. This lead [sic] to a lot of bitter feelings between those that did work 40 hours, and those that had a 4+ month paid vacation." There were multiple comments throughout the survey concerning inadequate internet access for either the survey taker or their coworkers. Current literature is raising awareness of the inequity of internet access, especially in the wake of the pandemic. According to Lesley Choiou and Catherine Tucker, there is a direct correlation between income and having home internet access. In addition, their study showed

> that when states enacted directives encouraging people to stay at home, people living in high-income or high-Internet areas were more likely to increase their propensity to stay at home. We find also that the particular combination of a region having high-income and having more access to high-speed Internet, leads people to be far more likely to stay at home. In other words, the combination of high-income and high-Internet diffusion appears to be a large driver in observed inequality.[18]

It should be noted that there were roles within the library that required employees to be in the library at least once a week to handle physical media. One respondent stated that they needed to adjust their workweek to "come in on alternating Saturdays and focusing strictly on the physical materials allowed me to keep my head above the water, but I was contemplating coming in every Saturday because 8 hours every 2 weeks for physical was not quite enough." Furthermore, simply changing their job focus while working from home was not rare for library employees. One respondent stated that "I was unable to work with physical materials for cataloging new items and worked with surrogates. Performed a lot of clean-up projects that could be done without material." It appears that those who responded to the survey were able to adapt responsibilities and tasks in some manner to make the work from home possible.

For example, one advantage of cataloging is the ability to relocate most materials to an off-site work location. In the cases of materials that were either immovable or physically impossible to relocate due to size or weight limitations or other factors, catalogers used electronic databases to capture screenshots of item descriptors to avoid taking physical materials out of the library building. The efficiency of such technology allowed catalogers to work in various locations outside the library building anytime. For example, one commenter said that "they set up LogMeIn access, so we could access the catalog and our documents remotely."

For public services library employees, tools, technology, and media requirements were different than for technical services employees. Reference and instructional librarians leveraged new platforms and adapted to virtual teaching, reference, and patron-support tools. They were able to connect with patrons through telecommunication devices and platforms, such as Zoom and chat widgets, to either supplement or replace some in-person sessions. These applications allowed for capturing the interactions, which then became shareable with patrons and fellow library employees; one's work and interactions became much more visible and transparent; when further assistance was needed, one could access prior interactions as needed and provide better support in so doing.

Experience

While 100 percent of the respondents indicated that they worked from home for some period each week, there were respondents who had experienced something in addition to working from home during lockdown. Question 9 allowed respondents to indicate whether they had experienced something more than simply shifting their tasks to a work-from-home assignment. In addition to work from home, the choices were paid furlough or leave of absence, unpaid furlough or leave of absence, reduction in hours, pay cut, permanent layoff, temporary layoff, contract not renewed, quit, planned or forced retirement, and vacation. This question was intended to ascertain the overall experience, as the researchers knew from their own experience that there had not been a one-size-fits-all solution to the situation, and that experiences varied widely.

As depicted in figure 15.1, the vast majority—77 percent (494 people)—selected one response: the work-from-home option. However, 122 respondents, or 19 percent, indicated that they experienced not only work from home but at least one of the other listed choices. The remaining 25 respondents (4 percent) had experienced at least three or more of the listed conditions. The most common experience was working from home as well as having a vacation; 12.32 percent had experienced this during lockdown. A paid furlough or leave of absence combined with a work-from-home assignment was the second-most-common experience at 9.05 percent. Unpaid furloughs affected 2.96 percent, or 19 people. One person quit (0.12 percent), and 2 people (0.24 percent) experienced temporary layoffs during this period. A caveat of note concerning some categories is that these experiences and numbers may not accurately reflect the number of people who quit, as it is likely that people who left the profession were not aware of the survey and could not therefore respond.

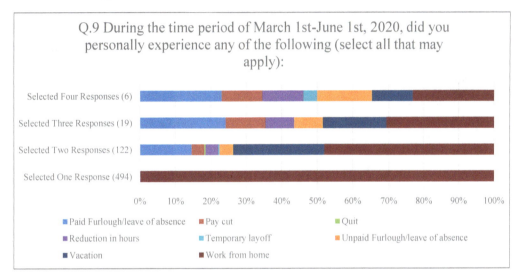

Figure 15.1
A depiction of what the respondents experienced during lockdown

Working Location

To avoid assuming that the option to work from one's residence was available to all respondents, and to take into account other locations where remote work may have been performed, the investigators defined "home" as "a location other than the address of your employment and does not necessarily mean the place where you reside." Question 12 asked about number of hours worked before and during lockdown. Perhaps unsurprisingly, there was a dramatic shift in where library personnel worked. As figure 15.2 shows, before the pandemic the majority of library employees averaged 37.70 hours per week at their library, while only 1.29 hours per week were at home. During lockdown, those hours flip-flopped. During lockdown, respondents spent on average 3.39 hours per week at their place of employment, but most of their working hours were at home (35.88 hours per week).

Question 13 asked which of five possible options best described the respondent's work-from-home situation: Mandated to work from home—full-time, Chose to work from home—full-time, Mandated to work part of the time at place of employment and part of the time at home, Chose to work part of the time at place of employment and part of the time at home, or Other. While the investigators were not surprised that the majority (72 percent) were mandated to work from home, they were surprised that 28 percent were given

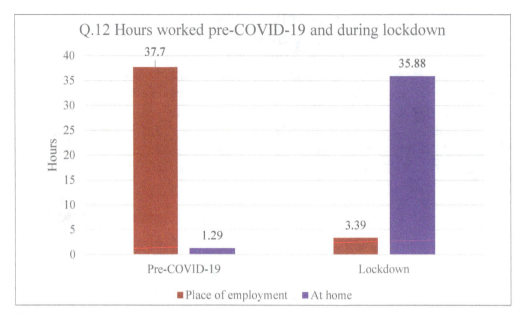

Figure 15.2
Comparison of working from home before and during lockdown

a choice as opposed to being mandated. Figure 15.3 illustrates that not all employees were mandated to work full-time. One area that will need additional exploration is the comments listed under the "Other" category. Although the respondents didn't feel as if their situation fell within the listed categories. What started out as a choice may have then become a mandate. One comment stated that they were originally mandated "to work at home, but choose [sic] to work part time at the library. I could have chosen to work full time at home. I was designated as essential but I was not forced to come in if I didn't feel comfortable."

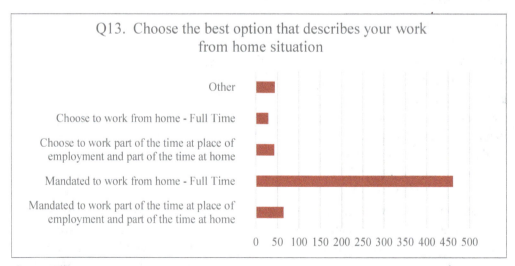

Figure 15.3
Having a choice in working from home

Access and Support

When asked how accessible their libraries were to them during the lockdown, 50 percent of surveyed participants stated that the libraries were open to them but on a limited basis. While 14 percent of respondents stated that their libraries were fully open with no restrictions in place, 30 percent of respondents had no access. Lastly, 7 percent selected the "Other" option when questioned. The investigators believed that the "Other" option was chosen due to the flux in status where libraries temporarily closed for a few weeks and then reopened to some extent.

When respondents were asked if they had the support of their employers to work from home, 59.44 percent stated that they strongly agreed. Of the 641 respondents, 11.39 percent somewhat agreed, and 23.24 percent agreed, while 3.90 percent disagreed with the statement. Overwhelmingly it appears that respondents, considering the circumstances, found themselves in a supportive environment.

Working from Home

Question 17 asked respondents what portion of their job they thought they could do at home prior to the pandemic, while Question 18 asked about changes after having to work from home after a period (see figures 15.4 and 15.5). Prior to the COVID pandemic, 50.54 percent of the survey respondents thought they could do only 50 percent or less of their job from home, and only 12.32 percent thought they could do 90 to 100 percent of their work from home. After working from home, 32.92 percent believed they could do 90 to 100 percent from home, with only 20.44 percent still believing they could do only 50 percent or less of their work from home. A strong 90.33 percent agreed that they were productive from home (figure 15.6), and 62.09 percent felt they had to alter their job only a little to a moderate amount to make working from home possible (figure 15.7).

Many things changed with the pandemic; for example, the investigators' library implemented reference assistance available through a chat service, which became extremely popular. This change allowed the investigators to be more available to all students than when previously staffing the physical reference desk. Though every library job varied, it appeared that most employees were able to make changes to their workflow or tasks. As a result, they were able to leverage technology so that they could accomplish more from home. Current themes in the professional literature are mixed about the productivity levels employees had from home, and as a result more research will be needed within the area of library employees. One study by Ferdinando Toscano and Salvatore Zappalà stated that because

> employees more concerned about COVID-19 show the need to feel as connected as possible to their colleagues when working remotely and those less concerned about the virus are less satisfied with remote work when their perceived productivity decreases, multiple pathways can be implemented to improve the wellbeing of these workers as much as possible.[19]

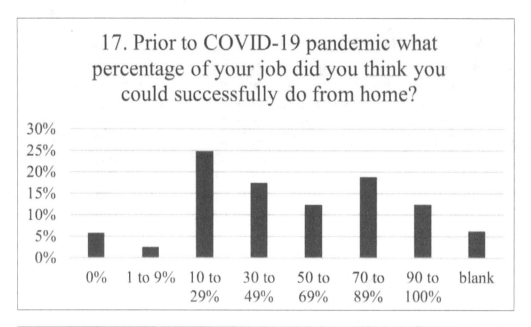

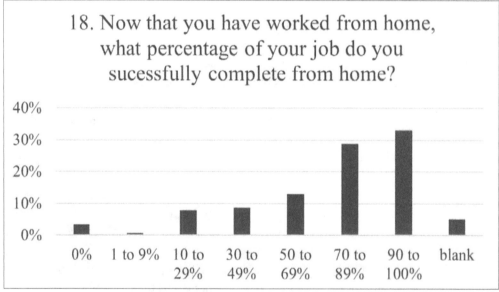

Figures 15.4 and 15.5
Depict the changes between life prior to lockdown and after based on questions 17 and 18 of the survey.

    The authors concluded that ideally the environment would emulate an experience like the "ordinary one" in regard to "connections with colleagues and providing tasks that sustain the feeling of working to the best of one's ability."[20] Although productivity was not the focus of the investigators' study, comments made throughout the study support a similar conclusion.

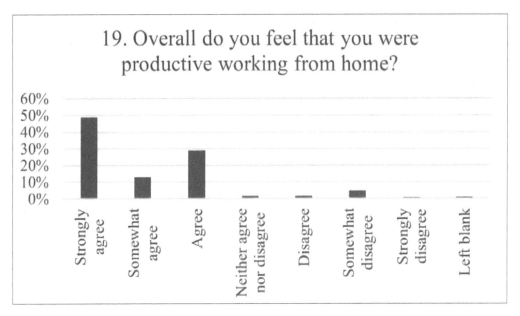

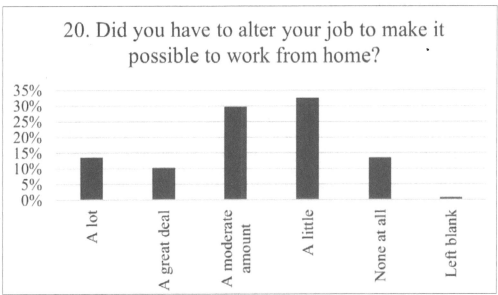

Figures 15.6 and 15.7
Two bar graphs depict how respondents felt while working from home. Respondents were asked if they felt productive and how much they had to alter their job to make it possible to work from home.

Working from Home in the Future

When participants were asked in Question 24 what they would do if they were offered the opportunity to work from home on a more permanent basis, 45.87 percent said they would strongly agree to that adaptation. This was followed by 33.54 percent agreeing or somewhat agreeing. A much smaller percentage was ambivalent or in disagreement at varying degrees with that option. These answers align well with pros and cons given regarding working from home in Questions 22 and 23. They also mirror what a variety of researchers have discovered. Working from home provides universal benefits for people, chiefly less commuting, more flexibility, and better work-life balance.[21] Some negative aspects that influenced people's responses are also reflected in the literature. One significant answer given for not wanting to work from home was that it increased the habit of being sedentary. This was supported by a study that claims working from home results in "greater time spent sitting and viewing screens."[22] Many other reasons, also reflected in the literature, point toward how isolating working from home can be and the importance of technological and supervisory support.[23] One comment captured how isolating working from home could be. The respondent stated that they were "very bored and lonely working from home. My answers may have been different if I didn't live alone and I knew I could do things with people or outside my home after/before work."

The final question of the survey was about how comfortable library employees would be with heading back to the physical workplace. A solid 50.08 percent said they would either be extremely or somewhat comfortable, while 13.73 percent declared neither comfortable nor uncomfortable. Another 25.73 percent claimed they would be somewhat uncomfortable, while the remaining 10.92 percent said they would be really uncomfortable. More research would be needed to learn precisely why going back to work would be uncomfortable to so many and if employers could do something additional to ease employees' comfort levels.

COVID-19 has transformed the lives of so many. For over a year now, many employees have worked from home to various degrees. Some respondents alluded to being elated about being physically reacquainted with their offices and colleagues. Comments included: "I enjoy being back at work on-site and being able to talk to co-workers in person," and "I'm so ready to work at work." Others may fear becoming exposed to COVID-19 variants (e.g., Alpha, Beta, Delta, etc.), even if vaccinated, due to herd immunity providing an uncertain safeguard. In addition, they may wonder how financially solid their work position is or, over the months, have pondered different employment opportunities. The responses received were surely tailored to individual qualms and hopes regarding a post-COVID-19 workplace.[24]

Conclusion

As a result of this study, the investigators learned that working from home appeared to be beneficial for all library employees. Throughout the survey respondents commented on heightened ability "to focus on projects and research … [it] made me feel much better about my contributions. We have limited staff but working from home allows us to meet with our students when they have time in the evening & on weekends." Another respondent commented that working-from-home had "a profound positive effect on my mental health." It is the intention of the investigators to produce future materials based on the qualitative data along with providing the tools and knowledge learned from this investigation to help generate future studies.

Once again to quote Mary Emogene Hazeltine in her speech at the forty-fourth ALA annual meeting, "we believe it is the mission of the library to offer to all the opportunity to reach out into the best world of thought which each individual is capable of entering."[25] From our data it is obvious that library personnel used the "best world of thought" to adapt to different working environments caused by the pandemic. As a result of the pandemic and with the feedback from the "Impact of COVID-19 Pandemic within the Library" survey, there is more evidence that many library roles do not need to be limited to a physical building anymore, something that has been discussed in the literature for years, but never operationalized.

In times of crisis, working from home was and is a viable option for many employees and employers who can no longer ignore this reality. Technology and the internet have made it increasingly evident that many jobs can have at least a partial work-from-home option. Therefore, implementing a work-from-home model for an institution would be quite valuable and needed not only for times of crisis but as an ongoing benefit for employees and employers. Digital platforms such as Teams and Zoom make it easier to create a sense of the office in an online environment; utilizing them effectively can enhance team connectedness even when dispersed geographically. In addition, it is evident that not all respondents would want to work from home full-time; a majority would prefer some type of hybrid model. Having the ability to work from home two or three days a week would be beneficial and an idea for institutions to keep in mind for their library employees. The investigators have concluded that library administrators should advocate that employers continue to offer a type of hybrid work schedule.

Appendix A: Impact of COVID-19 Pandemic within the Library

Impact of COVID-19 Pandemic within the Library

Q1. **IMPLIED CONSENT TO PARTICIPATE IN RESEARCH**

Principal Investigator: Renée Gould (Renee.Gould@saintleo.edu) 352-588-8265

Co-Investigator: Marissa Smith (Marissa.Smith@saintleo.edu) 352-588-7035; Michelle Joy (Michelle.Joy@saintleo.edu); Amy Harris (Amy.Harris03@saintleo.edu) 352-888-8412; Audrey Koke (Audrey.Koke@saintleo.edu) 352-588-8485; Delaney Rose (Delaney.Rose@saintleo.edu).

Title of Study: Working from Home: Impact of COVID-19 Pandemic within the Library

Purpose of Study: You are being asked to participate in a research study designed to examine how the COVID-19 Pandemic affected library employees that live and work within the United States of America. We are looking at the time period of March 1st through June 1st, 2020 and for those library employees who stayed with the same company during that time frame.
Procedures: You will be asked 25 questions relevant to working from home during the pandemic.
Benefits: There is no direct benefit to you but the results from this study will help develop new policies and incentives going forward.
Risks: None greater than those of daily life.
Costs/incentives: Participation in this study will cost nothing beyond 15 minutes of your time in filling out this survey.
Confidentiality: No information that can identify you personally will be collected as part of this research. The research is completely anonymous. The data you share will be saved in a password protected file ensuring its safety
Use of information: Findings from this study will be used to benefit the library community via means of publications in scholarly journal(s) and conference(s).
Voluntary Participation: The participants may withdraw from the study at any time, or decline to participate, without any penalty.

By clicking the I consent button below, you acknowledge:
- You have read the above consent statement and have had an opportunity to ask questions to your satisfaction.
- You understand that additional questions should be directed to Renee Gould (Renee.Gould@saintleo.edu) the Principal Investigator and Dr. Dr. Lisa Rapp-McCall, MSW, Ph.D (Dr. Lisa Rapp-McCall, MSW, Ph.D lisa.rapp-mccall@saintleo.eduD) the IRB Chair.
- You agree to participate in the study, under the terms outlined in this consent statement.
- You are aware that you may choose to terminate your participation at any time for any reason.

  ◯ I consent, begin the study

  ◯ I do not consent, I do not wish to participate

Overall Experience of Library Employees Working from Home during the COVID-19 Pandemic

Q2. Between March 1st -June 1st, 2020, did you work for a library within the United States of America?

- ○ Yes
- ○ No

Q3. In which state do you reside:

▼ Alabama ... Wyoming

Q4. In which state do you work:

▼ Alabama ... Wyoming

Q5. Indicate the library/organization affiliation:

- ○ Public Library
- ○ 4-year Academic Library
- ○ 2-year Academic Library
- ○ School Library (K-12)
- ○ Special Library

Q6. What are you considered?

- ○ Librarian
- ○ Staff
- ○ Administration
- ○ Paraprofessional
- ○ Other _____

Q7. What was your position title between March 1st - June 1st, 2020:

_____

Q8. What would you consider to be your primary role?

- [ ] Access and Delivery Services
- [ ] Acquisitions
- [ ] Administration
- [ ] Adult Services
- [ ] Assessment/User experience
- [ ] Cataloging/Copy Cataloging/Metadata
- [ ] Collection Development
- [ ] Circulation

- [ ] Information Technology
- [ ] Marketing/outreach/communications
- [ ] Reference/Instructional Services
- [ ] Special Collections
- [ ] Youth Services (Juvenile/Young Adult)
- [ ] Processing
- [ ] Other (please describe):

_____

Q9. During the time period of March 1st -June 1st, 2020, did you personally experience any of the following (select all that may apply):

- [ ] Paid Furlough/leave of absence
- [ ] Unpaid Furlough/leave of absence
- [ ] Reduction in hours
- [ ] Pay cut
- [ ] Permanent layoff
- [ ] Temporary layoff

- [ ] Contract not-renewed
- [ ] Quit
- [ ] Planned/Forced Retirement
- [ ] Work from home
- [ ] Vacation
- [ ] None of the above

Q10. Were you at the same job since the start of the pandemic to June 1st 2020?

- [ ] Yes
- [ ] No

Q11 Definitions going forward
Home will be defined as a location other than the address of your employment and does not necessarily mean the place where you reside.

Place of Employment will include your main work location before the pandemic. It may also include different physical branch locations if you were moved to a branch after March 1, 2020.

Q12. On average how many hours did you work in a typical week:

	Physically at your employment	Hours worked at home
Before March 1st, 2020:	_____	_____
Between March 1st -June 1st, 2020:	_____	_____

Q13. Choose the best option that describes your work from home situation during the time period of March 1st -June 1st, 2020.

○ Mandated to work from home - Full Time

○ Choose to work from home - Full Time

○ Mandated to work part of the time at place of employment and part of the time at home

○ Choose to work part of the time at place of employment and part of the time at home

○ Other _____

Q14. How accessible was the library to **you** during March 1st -June 1st, 2020? Such as: Were you able to go in it to retrieve work related items?

○ Completely closed off to you

○ Open to you but on a limited basis

○ Fully open to you with no restrictions placed

○ Other (please explain): _____

Chapter 15

Q15. Did you feel that you had the support of your employer to make your work from home possible?

○ Strongly agree

○ Agree

○ Somewhat agree

○ Neither agree nor disagree

○ Somewhat disagree

○ Disagree

○ Strongly disagree

Q16. Please elaborate on how you felt regarding having the support of your employer to make your work from home possible:

_____

_____

_____

_____

_____

Q17. Prior to COVID-19 pandemic what percentage of your job did you think you could successfully do from home?

	None	A little	A moderate amount	A lot	A great deal
	0 10	20 30	40 50 60	70 80	90 100

Q18. Now that you have worked from home, what percentage of your job do you successfully complete from home?

	None	A little	A moderate amount	A lot	A great deal
	0 10	20 30	40 50 60	70 80	90 100

Q19. Overall do you feel that you were productive working from home?

- ○ Strongly agree
- ○ Agree
- ○ Somewhat agree
- ○ Neither agree nor disagree
- ○ Somewhat disagree
- ○ Disagree
- ○ Strongly disagree

Q20. Did you have to alter your job to make it possible to work from home?

- ○ A great deal
- ○ A lot
- ○ A moderate amount
- ○ A little
- ○ None at all

Q21. If any, please explain some of the changes that you made to your job to make it possible to work from home:

_____

_____

_____

_____

_____

Q22. The following is a list of perks related to working from home. Please select your top three perks. The choices were inspired by: "Top 10 Advantages and Disadvantages of Working from Home."

ClickTime, https://www.clicktime.com/blog/top-10-advantages-disadvantages-working-from-home/. Accessed 22 July 2020.

- ☐ Flexible schedule
- ☐ Custom environment
- ☐ Cozy clothes
- ☐ More privacy to make phone calls
- ☐ Knock off some weekend to-do's
- ☐ No office distractions

- ☐ Zero commuting
- ☐ Save money
- ☐ Forget crowds and traffic
- ☐ More time with loved ones
- ☐ Other (please describe):
  _____

Q23. The following are a list of disadvantages related to working from home. Please select the top three disadvantages you found at work. The choices were inspired by: "Top 10 Advantages and Disadvantages of Working from Home." *ClickTime*, https://www.clicktime.com/blog/top-10-advantages-disadvantages-working-from-home/. Accessed 22 July 2020.

- ☐ Willpower
- ☐ Difficulty sticking to a routine
- ☐ Missing important calls or pings
- ☐ Naps are more inviting
- ☐ Boredom
- ☐ Working slowly
- ☐ No second monitor

- ☐ Connection issues
- ☐ Waiting for an answer
- ☐ More distractions
- ☐ Sedentary
- ☐ Lack of privacy with phone calls
- ☐ Other (please describe):
  _____

Overall Experience of Library Employees Working from Home during the COVID-19 Pandemic   195

Q24. Given the opportunity would you want to be able to work from home on a more permanent basis?

○ Strongly agree

○ Agree

○ Somewhat agree

○ Neither agree nor disagree

○ Somewhat disagree

○ Disagree

○ Strongly disagree

Q25. Please elaborate on why you would or would not want to work from home on a more permanent basis:

_____

_____

_____

_____

_____

Q26. After experiencing working from home, do you think you will comfortably transition back to work physically full time.

○ Extremely comfortable

○ Somewhat comfortable

○ Neither comfortable nor uncomfortable

○ Somewhat uncomfortable

○ Extremely uncomfortable

Q27 Overall feelings about returning to back to working physically at your library:

_____

_____

_____

_____

_____

Notes

1. "Archived: WHO Timeline—Covid-19," World Health Organization, April 27, 2020, https://www.who.int/news/item/27-04-2020-who-timeline---covid-19.
2. Florida Executive Order No. 20-91, April 1, 2020, https://www.flgov.com/wp-content/uploads/orders/2020/EO_20-91-compressed.pdf.
3. "Coronavirus: Timeline," US Department of Defense, accessed September 3, 2021, https://www.defense.gov/Explore/Spotlight/Coronavirus-DOD-Response/Timeline.
4. Florida Executive Order No. 20-91.
5. "Coronavirus: Timeline."
6. Mary E. Hazeltine, "The Librarian's Due to the Profession," *Bulletin of the American Library Association* 16, no. 4 (1922): 145, http://www.jstor.org/stable/25686047.
7. Anna R. Craft, "Remote Work in Library Technical Services: Connecting Historical Perspectives to Realities of the Developing COVID-19 Pandemic," *Serials Review* 46, no. 3 (2020): 228, https://doi.org/10.1080/00987913.2020.1806658.
8. Thomas W. Gainey, Donald E. Kelley, and Joseph A. Hill, "Telecommuting's Impact on Corporate Culture and Individual Workers: Examining the Effect of Employee Isolation," *SAM Advanced Management Journal* 64, no. 4 (Autumn 1999): 7, ProQuest.
9. Gainey, Kelley, and Hill, "Telecommuting's Impact," 4–5.
10. Dharma Raju Bathini and George Kandathil, "Work from Home: A Boon or a Ban? The Missing Piece of Employee Cost," *Indian Journal of Industrial Relations* 50, no. 4 (April 2015): 571–72, EBSCO.
11. Adrian Furnham, "Work in 2020: Prognostications about the World of Work 20 Years into the Millennium," *Journal of Managerial Psychology* 15, no. 3 (2000): 243, https://doi.org/10.1108/EUM0000000005321.
12. Furnham, "Work in 2020," 253.
13. David J. Staley and Kara J. Malenfant, "Futures Thinking for Academic Librarians: Higher Education in 2025," *Information Services and Use* 30, no. 1/2 (January 2010): 57, https://doi.org/10.3233/ISU-2010-0614.
14. Staley and Malenfant, "Futures Thinking," 66; 72–73; 75.
15. Jennifer Duncan, "Working from Afar: A New Trend for Librarianship," *College and Research Libraries News* 69, no. 4 (April 2008): 216, https://crln.acrl.org/index.php/crlnews/article/view/7972/7972.
16. Kate Lister and Tom Harnish, "Telework and its Effects in the United States," in *Telework in the 21st Century*, ed. Jon C. Messenger (Cheltenham, UK: Edward Elgar, 2019), 145.
17. Craft, "Remote Work," 228.
18. Lesley Chiou and Catherine Tucker, "Social Distancing, Internet Access and Inequality," working paper 26982, National Bureau of Economic Research, April 2020, 3, https://www.nber.org/papers/w26982.
19. Ferdinando Toscano, and Salvatore Zappalà, "Social Isolation and Stress as Predictors of Productivity Perception and Remote Work Satisfaction during the COVID-19 Pandemic: The Role of Concern about the Virus in a Moderated Double Mediation," *Sustainability* 12, no. 23 (2020): article 9804, https://doi.org/10.3390/su12239804.
20. Toscano and Zappalà, "Social Isolation and Stress," 12.
21. Balazs Aczel et al., "Researchers Working from Home: Benefits and Challenges," *PLoS ONE* 16, no. 3 (March 2021): e0249127, https://doi.org/10.1371/journal.pone.0249127.
22. Cillian P. McDowell et al., "Working from Home and Job Loss Due to the COVID-19 Pandemic Are Associated with Greater Time in Sedentary Behaviors," *Frontiers in Public Health* 8 (November 2020): article 597619, p. 5, https://doi.org/10.3389/fpubh.2020.597619.
23. Gainey, Kelley and Hill, "Telecommuting's Impact," 7; Craft "Remote Work," 229–30.
24. Iqbal Pittalwala and Holly Ober, "Anxious about Returning to Work? Psychologists Offer Insight and Tips," University of California, May 5, 2021, https://www.universityofcalifornia.edu/news/anxious-about-returning-work-psychologists-offer-insight-and-tips.
25. Hazeltine, "Librarian's Due to the Profession," 145.

Bibliography

Aczel, Balazs, Marton Kovacs, Tanja van der Lippe, and Barnabas Szaszi. "Researchers Working from Home: Benefits and Challenges." *PLoS ONE* 16, no. 3 (March 2021): e0249127. https://doi.org/10.1371/journal.pone.0249127.

Bathini, Dharma Raju, and George Kandathil. "Work from Home: A Boon or a Ban? The Missing Piece of Employee Cost." *Indian Journal of Industrial Relations* 50, no. 4 (April 2015). EBSCO.

Chiou, Lesley, and Catherine Tucker. "Social Distancing, Internet Access and Inequality." Working paper 26982. National Bureau of Economic Research, April 2020. https://www.nber.org/papers/w26982.

Craft, Anna R. "Remote Work in Library Technical Services: Connecting Historical Perspectives to Realities of the Developing COVID-19 Pandemic." *Serials Review* 46, no. 3 (2020): 227–31. https://doi.org/10.1080/00987913.2020.1806658.

Duncan, Jennifer. "Working from Afar: A New Trend for Librarianship." *College and Research Libraries News* 69, no. 4 (April 2008): 216–17. https://crln.acrl.org/index.php/crlnews/article/view/7972/7972.

Florida Executive Order No. 20-91. April 1, 2020. https://www.flgov.com/wp-content/uploads/orders/2020/EO_20-91-compressed.pdf.

Furnham, Adrian. "Work in 2020: Prognostications about the World of Work 20 Years into the Millennium." *Journal of Managerial Psychology* 15, no. 3 (2000): 242–54. https://doi.org/10.1108/EUM0000000005321.

Gainey, Thomas W., Donald E. Kelley, and Joseph A. Hill. "Telecommuting's Impact on Corporate Culture and Individual Workers: Examining the Effect of Employee Isolation." *SAM Advanced Management Journal* 64, no. 4 (Autumn 1999). ProQuest.

Hazeltine, Mary E. "The Librarian's Due to the Profession." *Bulletin of the American Library Association* 16, no. 4 (1922): 144–46. http://www.jstor.org/stable/25686047.

Lister, Kate, and Tom Harnish. "Telework and Its Effects in the United States." In *Telework in the 21st Century: An Evolutionary Perspective*, edited by Jon C. Messenger, 128–70. Cheltenham, UK: Edward Elgar, 2019.

McDowell, Cillian P., Matthew P. Herring, Jeni Lansing, Cassandra Brower, and Jacob D. Meyer. "Working from Home and Job Loss Due to the COVID-19 Pandemic Are Associated with Greater Time in Sedentary Behaviors." *Frontiers in Public Health* 8 (November 2020): article 597619, https://doi.org/10.3389/fpubh.2020.597619.

Pittalwala, Iqbaq, and Holly Ober. "Anxious about Returning to Work? Psychologists Offer Insight and Tips." University of California, May 5, 2021. https://www.universityofcalifornia.edu/news/anxious-about-returning-work-psychologists-offer-insight-and-tips.

Staley, David J., and Kara J. Malenfant. "Futures Thinking for Academic Librarians: Higher Education in 2025." *Information Services and Use* 30, no. 1/2 (January 2010): 57–90. https://doi.org/10.3233/ISU-2010-0614.

Toscano, Ferdinando, and Salvatore Zappalà. "Social Isolation and Stress as Predictors of Productivity Perception and Remote Work Satisfaction during the COVID-19 Pandemic: The Role of Concern about the Virus in a Moderated Double Mediation." *Sustainability* 12, no. 23 (2020): article 9804. https://doi.org/10.3390/su12239804.

US Department of Defense. "Coronavirus: Timeline." Accessed September 3, 2021. https://www.defense.gov/Explore/Spotlight/Coronavirus-DOD-Response/Timeline.

World Health Organization. "Archived: WHO Timeline—Covid-19." April 27, 2020. https://www.who.int/news/item/27-04-2020-who-timeline---covid-19.

CHAPTER 16

Crisis Management in Brazilian Libraries

Management Lessons Learned from the Pandemic of the Novel Coronavirus

Danielly Oliveira Inomata and Célia Regina Simonetti Barbalho

> Brazilian libraries have strategically examined their objectives and processes, their culture, and their relationships with users in search of the strengthening of their activities and services based on an understanding of the new dynamic of people's lives. It is certain that the effective understanding of the library's role in the face of the pandemic crisis compelled us to rethink how to serve the user.

Introduction

The effects of the global health crisis triggered by the spread of SARS-CoV-2 made libraries go through a challenging period due to the measures adopted globally to contain the pandemic's progress. Under these circumstances, crisis management, which aims at reducing the losses generated to fulfill the mission of the information units, constitutes an effective guideline to contain and mitigate the impacts caused by this moment of apparent imbalance in the supply of information products and services.

Facing the uncertain situations caused by the pandemic, academic libraries were urged to seek a balance so that the inevitable consequences of social isolation and the rapid disruption that this represented to people's daily lives would provide opportunities to connect or reconnect their users to the world through helping citizens face the circumstances that were overwhelmingly imposed on them.

Academic libraries have used diverse responses, based mainly on their institutional objectives, on the understanding of their service and product portfolio, and on local and institutional realities. Of course, an uncertain scenario does not allow the creation of a single response, equal for all libraries as well as for all users, especially because the circumstances are diverse, as well as the conditions to offer creative solutions that, in general, imply in behavioral changes as well as in the need to establish new learning aiming at increasing the chances of survival of the library.

To this end, Brazilian libraries have strategically examined their objectives and processes, their culture, and their relationships with users in search of the strengthening of their activities and services based on an understanding of the new dynamic of people's lives. It is certain that the effective understanding of the library's role in the face of the pandemic crisis compelled us to rethink how to serve the user, who started not to frequent the physical space and who, in his or her domestic environment and within the imposed limitations, started to conduct his or her life remotely.

Given the above, some questions demanded a reflection capable of pointing to the understanding of the performance of libraries under the circumstances described: Is there crisis management in libraries? Are library managers prepared to face a crisis? Is the staff able to respond efficiently? How does the learning process take place? What are the lessons learned?

In this context, this study aimed to examine crisis management in Brazilian libraries in times of pandemic. In particular, the following aspects are configured as specific objectives: (1) to characterize the role of the library manager in times of crisis; (2) to describe the behavior of the team as to positive and negative aspects; (3) to survey the practices adopted in the pandemic to perform the library's internal and external activities; (4) to map the lessons learned; and (5) to evaluate the process of execution of the measures adopted to face the crisis. This chapter is organized into a literature review on the central theme of the research—crisis management and libraries—exposure of the methodological path used to collect primary information that composed the research; and results and discussions of the data obtained and the conclusions.

Crisis in the Context of Libraries

The word *crisis* is related, according to Dictionary.com, to "a stage in a sequence of events at which the trend of all future events, especially for better or for worse, is determined."[1] In general, we speak of

> "crisis" in relation to subjects, to a life or a way of life, to a system or a "sphere" of action. Crises decide whether a thing endures or not. The paradigmatic case of crisis is the crisis of life, in which, if taken to the extreme, it is a matter of life or death. In every crisis those involved confront the Hamletian question: to be or not to be.[2]

Crises have negative connotations due to their close relationship with the existence of problems, bad situations, and difficulties. For the Institute for Crisis Management, a crisis is related to any issue, problem, or interruption that triggers negative reactions from stakeholders, involving situations that threaten or harm people and organizations, serious disruptions in operations, attacks on social networks, and highly negative media coverage, among other occurrences.[3]

For Deloitte Touche Tohmatsu Limited (DTTL) and the Brazilian Institute of Investor Relations (IBRI), it is initially necessary to understand and distinguish crisis from problem and incident/emergency, as shown in figure 16.1.[4]

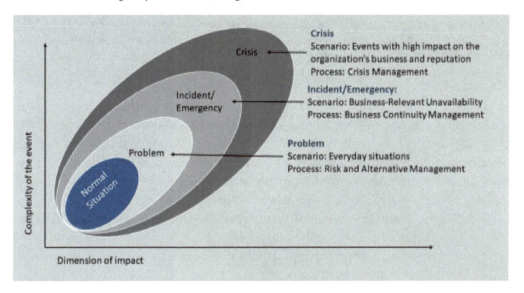

Figure 16.1
Problem, incident/emergency, and crisis. (Figure from Deloitte Touche Tohmatsu, *Manual de gestão de crise para relação com investidores: Comunicação e estratégia para preservação de valor* [London: Deloitte Touche Tomatsu, 2015: 4, https://www2.deloitte.com/content/dam/Deloitte/br/Documents/risk/Manual-Gestao-Crises-para-RI.pdf]).

Risk management consists of a way to identify and monitor the factors that may be a future threat, and crisis management is the process that assesses potential risks and seeks to solve the problems in case the crisis occurs; that is, they are sequential, yet distinct processes. To mitigate these effects and act proactively, it is necessary to understand how to act when faced with a crisis and, based on this understanding, provide the means to find the best alternatives to face it.

Salvador, Ikeda, and Crescitelli, when empirically verifying the application of the theories on brand crisis and recall, state that it is about a nonroutine, unexpected, and sudden event that creates uncertainty, threatens the organization's priority objectives, and may cause financial losses and erode the company's reputation.[5] Crises could harm stakeholders physically, financially, or emotionally.[6] Since a crisis is a nonroutine event, it is essential to seek and test possible solutions and plan for contingencies to contain the damage as much as possible, favoring recovery and organizational learning. The speed with which the organization reacts to the crisis scenario contributes to the possibility of a total interruption of operations or the threat to its reputation.

The evaluation of the threat involves the possibility of measuring whether a problem has the potential to become a crisis; adversity demands additional resources, effort, and attention. The Threat Grid model initially proposes to identify the type of threat—operational or reputational, which may intersect, creating the format of the grid employed by the prototype. Coombs and Holladay explain

> A Grid allows for each type of threat to be evaluated simultaneously. Each type of threat is arrayed along an axis of impact severity. Impact severity is concerned with how badly an event might hurt an organization. Impact severity is anchored by ability to thrive and ability to survive. The crisis managers must determine if the event reduces an organization's ability to thrive or is a danger to the very survival of the organization.[7]

The analysis of the crisis context is fundamental for the institution to deliberate on the measures that will be taken to promote the resumption of normalcy, leading to the continuity of organizational operations. In understanding that crises expose the levels of preparedness and responsiveness of an organization, Soehner, Godfrey, and Bigler further highlight Mallozzi's model for crisis communication and management, composed of four stages:[8]

1. crisis preparation, involving risk identification and assessment, scenario planning, and monitoring of information sources;
2. initial response to meet the expectations of customers and the community with which the institution is involved;
3. maintenance of corrective actions and continuous reactions during the crisis, implying a constant communication process designed to reduce the potential damage, protect the value of the organization, and minimize the impacts on the organizational reputation (this involves both internal and external communication); and
4. evaluation and follow-up in order to constitute elements that may favor the moment in which the organization must act in a coordinated way to solve the crisis.

Mallozzi's model has already been employed in libraries considering that these institutions need, as stated, to constitute elements that favor the facing of crises.

The discussions about the crisis and its impacts on libraries are collated by elements involving two meanings. The first meaning is related to the contribution that these agents can offer to face adversities of all kinds in order to ensure access to information, educational structures, and the fulfillment of their social role. This sense was the focus of the reflection promoted by the International Federation of Library Associations (IFLA) in 2019, whose content is gathered and disseminated in "Libraries in Times of Crisis,"[9] with a look aimed at dimensioning how the actions of the library are put to serve contemporary and future society in the face of situations of social impact. The second meaning, more pragmatic, is related to the impacts caused by economic issues and recessions, natural disasters, risks, emergencies, and public health issues, such as the most recent epidemic outbreak. Regardless of the nature of the crisis, libraries must adopt creative and innovative measures to maintain service quality and meet user needs.

This scenario faced by libraries is neither new nor groundbreaking. Libraries have long been confronted with troubled contexts of public calamity generated by economic downturns, wars, natural disasters, bioterrorist threats, or adversity motivated by health issues. In these circumstances, people seek answers to questions about the nature of the threats and how to respond to them. This has often led authorities to provide information designed to reassure society and minimize public reaction to the threat.[10]

The author further highlights that

> studies have shown that the public is more satisfied with the information they receive about a particular threat if they feel that this information is transparent and provides the facts, they need to make informed choices.... Lessons learned from these cases of health risk communication indicate that the public seeks "concrete, accurate, and consistent information about the actions needed to protect themselves and their family."[11]

Libraries are effectively reliable information providers, able to act proactively as a primary source in times of crisis. However, the various reports about the performance of libraries in the pandemic, in most cases, point to the actions of libraries based on the protection of their collections and the maintenance of their services in remote format in order to ensure they could meet their core mission, rather than as information portals concerning the pandemic.

Gomes, when prefacing the piece *The Role of Archivology, Librarianship and Museology Professionals at a Time of Pandemic*, states that the action of librarians and libraries facing a crisis scenario must be based on

> the challenge of finding the promising paths of an informational practice that can contribute to the construction of urgent alternatives for humanizing the encounter of social subjects with information in a time of struggle against COVID-19, in a time of struggle against false information, against misinformation and against the reduction of democratic access to knowledge, social knowledge and cultural production.[12]

It is in this sense exposed by the author that the core of the research was constituted, whose course and results are exposed below.

Methodological Process

As to the objectives, this is exploratory and descriptive research, with views to verifying the crisis management in Brazilian libraries at a time of pandemic. It was sought to describe both the elements that characterize the role of the manager concerning libraries and the behavior of the team in relation to positive and negative aspects, the practices adopted during the pandemic to execute the library's internal and external activities, the mapping of lessons learned, and the evaluation of the execution process of the measures adopted to face the crisis. This is qualitative approach research. The research population was composed of Brazilian libraries, regardless of their typology, by convenience sampling. The research established as subjects the librarian managers, for understanding that they (1) have the decision-making role and (2) in face of the turbulent scenario, had more information about the actions, the planning process of the biosafety protocols, and the guidelines for the team. Forty-seven library managers of seventy contacted participated in the survey.

Data was collected by means of an electronic form in the period from August to September 2020. The form was composed of two axes, namely: (1) descriptive statistics that provided a characterization of the manager and of the library to determine the time of performance and experience, in addition to the type of library and institution of attachment, and (2) diagnosis of crisis management in libraries to learn about the crisis management plan; the role of the manager in this context; the management practices of the team for sharing knowledge, to carry out both internal and external activities of the library; and finally, questions directed to the identification and evaluation of the lessons learned during the pandemic.

Results and Discussion

In order to favor a better understanding of the primary data collected, aiming at meeting the objectives proposed by the research, the results were presented in four sections: (1) identification of the subjects' profile; (2) crisis planning; (3) facing the crisis caused by the novel coronavirus; and (4) lessons learned.

Identification of the Subjects' Profile

With the purpose of understanding how the crisis caused by the COVID-19 pandemic was managed in Brazilian libraries, the survey was made up from the participation of forty-seven library managers of different types of libraries, most of the participants (77 percent = 36) being directors of university libraries (figure 16.2). Although it was not the objective of the survey, it was noted that most of the respondents were women (91 percent = 43).

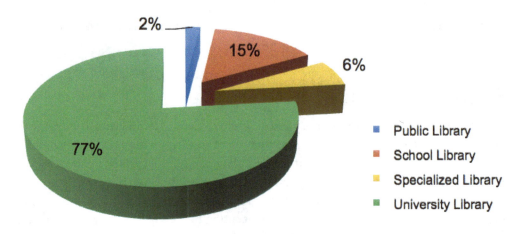

Figure 16.2
Types of libraries (Source: Field research, 2021)

In Brazil, university libraries, due to the remote services they offered before the pandemic, were the ones that more quickly transitioned to face the crisis with the determination of distancing. Moreover, these libraries support teaching, research, and extension activities, and, at first, the first ones were the ones that were completely paralyzed, and the two others kept running, even if at a slower pace, impacting the demand for information services.

It is noteworthy that 38 percent of the research participants indicated they had between one and five years of experience in the position (figure 16.3), while almost 50 percent indicated they had more than five years of managerial experience, which allowed us to infer that most respondents had sufficient experience in the function of library directors or managers to be comfortable in taking the lead and making decisions.

It was also observed that although some (13 percent) of the responding librarians had been working in the position of manager for less than one year, they indicated that they had more than five years of experience in libraries, which can be an important aggregating element when it comes to decisions that must be made in the face of a crisis, considering that time and experience contribute to greater discernment about the measures that must be taken.

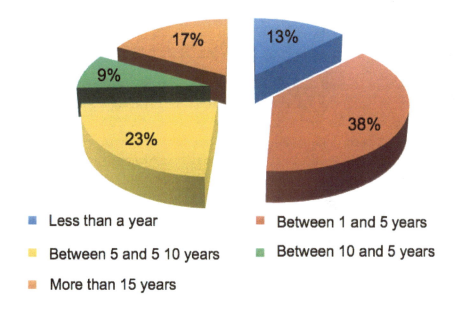

Figure 16.3
Time in leadership (or managerial) position (Source: Field research 2021)

In times of instability, two fundamental factors that directly impact the decision-making process in a crisis scenario are necessity and maturity. During a crisis, the need usually arises from the urgency for swift and decisive decision-making. It is in this sense that the maturity of the professional who is in charge of the library can mitigate the impacts through more assertive strategic decisions.

Crisis Planning

The research sought to find out if the libraries had crisis management plans concerning preparation, initial response, and maintenance of corrective actions and reactions, as well as evaluation and follow-up.

Of the institutions that participated in the survey, 32 percent indicated that they did not have crisis management plans, most of them being school libraries (table 16.1). The data suggests that university libraries were the ones that created crisis management plans, strengthening the statement that these information units were more responsive to the pandemic context.

Table 16.1 Existence of crisis plans in libraries (Source: Field research 2021)			
1. Does the library have a crisis management plan?	#	%	Observation
Yes. Approved by the institution.	21	45%	19 are university libraries. Two are school libraries.
Yes. In preparation.	11	23%	Eight are university libraries. One public, one specialized, and one school library.
Does not have.	15	32%	Four are school libraries.

As for the questions related to the role of the librarian manager regarding their perception of library staff, the internal and external practices adopted in time of pandemic, and the lessons learned, results were varied. However, there was transformation of various kinds through lessons learned in all types of libraries requiring of library managers the ability to act under three aspects: (1) leadership of people, (2) management of processes and environments, and (3) execution of the strategic vision. The librarians who participated in the research, in some degree, had these characteristics configured in their concern to keep the library providing its informational services with pandemic safety, for both employees and users, as can be observed in the following comments:

- "To create new ways of interaction and involvement with students, teachers and employees who are our target audience; to inform about new procedures in the face of the pandemic; and to be creative and innovative at this time." (Informant 13)
- "To attend [to] the academic community following the safety protocols." (Informant 17)
- "Define strategies for crises not foreseen in the Contingency Plan, such as COVID 19. These strategies are defined in conjunction with guidelines from the Higher Education Institution." (Informant 26)
- "Managing the remote activities so that the services are as close as possible to the face-to-face ones. Establish innovation parameters for service functionality." (Informant 35)

The open-ended responses point to the respondents' concern in meeting the demands, especially the necessary guidelines to prevent the spread of the contagion, whether by the library's rules or by its parent institution.

In addition to this initial question, the managers were asked to discuss their team, both the positive and negative points. According to the managers, in this period of crisis, it was perceived as positive that (1) the team was willing to contribute, as reported by Informant 19: "Team always attentive, available to collaborate with ideas, suggestions, actions," in addition to (2) the creativity of the team in adapting to telecommuting, which allowed (3) the collective learning.

Many survey respondents were more negative: (1) the team was affected psychologically by the fear of contagion and anxiety because it was an unknown situation, (2) the accumulation of work functions and domestic activities, as a result of telework, in addition to (3) "technological difficulties and setting of space for remote work" (Informant 44) because "some team members have difficulty in using technologies to carry out remote activities" (Informant 19).

The library's role amidst the pandemic transcended a space that preserves books and provides access to reading. It was, above all, a space of culture and dissemination of information; a welcoming and pleasant space that enabled people to live together, even at a physical distance; a space for representations that adapt to show social and human transformations while maintaining the identity and historicity of the subjects. In this sense, it is possible to highlight the response of one of the subjects, who stated:

> I think that as well as teachers, we are learning to use technologies and social media for interaction and communication with students. We started a Library Therapy pilot project so we can welcome our students and listen to their fears, concerns, and talk about the current moment. We chose literary texts that allow this meeting through [Google] Meet with the Industrial Apprenticeship classes. We are doing Database training.... The biggest difficulty is that the library [building] is closed, serving only for book returns and loans. The classes are still online and so we are identifying the users' needs in partnership with the Pedagogical Department and looking together for solutions to solve the problems that arise. (Informant 22).

Building new library practices to meet the needs of the users is an essential element to face a global crisis.

Coping with the Crisis Caused by the Novel Coronavirus

The Brazilian libraries that participated in the research showed intense willingness towards flexibility and adaptation by means of practices adopted during the pandemic period. All this effort was made by means of internal (table 16.2) and external (table 16.3) actions that offered an initial response.

Table 16.2

Map of internal practices adopted in the library during the pandemic period (Source: Field research 2021)

Internal practices	#	%
Brainstorming	26	55.30%
Consult biosafety manuals and protocols	37	78.70%
Consult specialists to find out how to proceed	20	42.60%
E-mail messages	36	76.60%
Meetings to evaluate and share lessons learned	26	55.30%
Mentoring	6	12.80%
Team training	32	68.10%
Virtual meetings with management (superior to the library)	32	68.10%
Virtual meetings with the team to align activities	37	78.70%
Others	10	21%

In the internal environment of the libraries, the main practices adopted were virtual meetings for the alignment of the strategies to be assumed (78.70 percent), considering the consultation of biosafety manuals and protocols (78.70 percent), and exchange of electronic messages with the team (76.60 percent), as well as team training (68.10 percent), and meetings with the library management (68.10 percent). It is observed that the construction of the actions occurred in a participative way, enabling the collective deliberations to support the work done.

In Brazil, the libraries followed the recommendations from the Brazilian Federation of Librarians, Information Scientists and Institutions Associations (FEBAB), especially the university libraries; they also followed guidelines from the Brazilian Commission of University Libraries (CBBU), which directed libraries to integrate the official plan of their institutions and follow general guidelines for the protection of workers. Specific recommendations for libraries included five areas: work teams, physical access to the library, collections, other technical services, and online services.

Table 16.3

Map of external practices adopted in the library during the pandemic period (Source: Field research 2021)

External practices	#	%
User training	25	53.20%
Development and offer of virtual service	44	93.60%
Implementation of digital technologies	29	61.70%
Use of information channels for access between users and the library	40	85.10%
Use of social media for dissemination and marketing	36	76.60%
Others	7	14.70%

As expected, due to the physical closure of libraries caused by the pandemic, the offer of virtual services (93.6 percent), use of information channels (85.10 percent), and use of social media to promote the library's marketing (76.60 percent) were the external practices most used during the pandemic. Lessa discusses the use of social media and the role of the library to maintain human relationships in the face of the COVID-19 pandemic, considering that social media can be characterized as an alternative space to make available the library's products and services, while enabling dialogue and collaboration, which facilitates the performance of information activities by libraries, among them the dissemination of information and sharing of content.[13]

Lessons Learned

As for the lessons learned, the managers indicated that they are related to having the ability to adapt (11), having the ability to communicate effectively with the team (10), developing competencies (6), having the ability to learn (4), having technological resources (2), maintaining the balance between work activities and personal life (2), and having the ability to innovate (2). To give voice to the managers, some of their inferences are shown in table 16.4.

Table 16.4
Key lessons learned during the pandemic (Source: Field research 2021)

Lessons Learned Category	Inferences
Have the ability to adapt	It is necessary to adapt to the new. Our profession is constantly changing and we need to keep up. You have to be open-minded about the situations that occur daily. (Informant 2).
	It is open to the changes in the ecosystem (library X user X community), innovating to continue serving the academic community. (Informant 4).
Have communication skills	[...] we are not prepared for emergencies and that the good dialogue with the team is fundamental for the solution of demands. (Informant 14).
	[...] despite the technological potential, the human potential is fundamental. Without the team's involvement, suggestions, competencies, it is difficult to achieve the proposed objectives. (Informant 19).
	I learned that it is extremely necessary to talk to the team, and try to create awareness of how important the information is—and that for this, it is not necessary to be inside the physical space of the library to be able to disseminate and make it available. It also made me think about how important it is to be in constant learning and development. (Informant 30).
Developing competencies	The need to develop the skills and attitudes of the employees, especially in communication and provision of virtual services and use of technology. Better administration of time and adequacy of processes developed exclusively in a face-to-face manner. The help and execution of team activities through the channels and shared tools. (Informant 1).
	[...] with Pandemic what I learned the most was that the union of the group is very important, because we are very connected and when one end is detached the whole team becomes fragile. I also learned that we have many abilities that we do not know we have and we develop them according to the need of the moment. (Informant 41).

Finally, considering the lessons learned, the managers were asked to indicate their level of agreement related to the following factors: preparation of the team, structure of the institution, information and communication technologies, current processes, processes in the new normal, training of the team, and new services (figure 16.4).

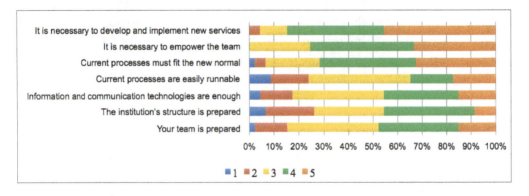

Figure 16.4
Level of agreement regarding the learning process during the pandemic (Source: Field research 2021)

Based on the managers' perspective, the teams were not prepared for this crisis; this may be related to the structure of the libraries and the information and communication technologies available in the pandemic period that are somehow related to the current processes of the libraries, designed for face-to-face service. Most managers agree that in the new normal there will be a need to adapt the processes, train the staff, and develop and implement new services.

Conclusion

Crisis management involves the recognition that an event is occurring that may be a destabilizing influence and it is necessary to find a solution for it that can be implemented. The culture of strategic management, with planning, execution, and follow-up, must be able to withstand crises in organizations, and the manager's role is fundamental. Brazilian libraries were not prepared for the pandemic of the novel coronavirus. Few libraries create crisis management plans. However, in times of crisis there are opportunities for improvement, by means of lessons learned.

For Santa Anna, "even going through challenges and countless changes, these institutions survive thanks to their ability to adapt to the constant transformations that occur over time."[14] Academic libraries in times of crisis such as the pandemic reflect that ability to respond and adapt.

With the results of the research, it was observed by the researchers that
- The ability to adapt to the constant changes in the knowledge and informational ecosystem into which libraries are inserted during a crisis involves resilience, a

term very present in the corporate world, also cited in the ambiance of libraries; adaptation to the provision of services in the remote modality.

- The internal communication process was cited as one of the main lessons learned. For the managers, in times of crisis, such as this novel coronavirus pandemic, keeping the team informed and trained was one of the most relevant aspects.
- The development of competencies is necessary, whether knowledge, skills, or attitudes to act in the virtual environment, for the development of new strategies.

The engagement and willingness of the team, the creativity to adapt services, and the compliance with biosafety protocols were positive outcomes. On the other hand, the accumulation of functions and the noise in communication, the difficulties in adapting traditional services that started to be mediated by information and communication technologies, were negatives for the team. The main knowledge-sharing practices were mediated by virtual meetings, team building, brainstorming, and the use of social media. The lessons learned are related to the resiliency of libraries in reacting to crisis, in the ability to adapt to the new and to be flexible.

Furthermore, it became evident that the information and communication technologies are great allies to the provision of services, to the management process. However, the human factor is still an essential element in the performance of libraries.

Notes

1. Dictionary.com, s.v. "crisis," accessed January 26, 2022, https://www.dictionary.com/browse/crisis.
2. William Outhwaite, ed., *The Blackwell Dictionary of Twentieth-Century Social Thought* (Oxford: Blackwell Reference, 1998), s.v. "crisis."
3. Institute for Crisis Management, "What Defines a Crisis?" 2021, https://crisisconsultant.com/.
4. Deloitte Touche Tohmatsu, *Manual de gestão de crise para relação com investidores: Comunicação e estratégia para preservação de valor* (London: Deloitte Touche Tomatsu, 2015), https://www2.deloitte.com/content/dam/Deloitte/br/Documents/risk/Manual-Gestao-Crises-para-RI.pdf.
5. Alexandre Borba Salvador, Ana Akemi Ikeda, and Edson Crescitelli, "Gestão de crise e seu impacto na imagem de marca," *Gestão & Produção* 24, no. 1 (January–April 2017): 15–24, https://doi.org/10.1590/0104-530x1668-14.
6. W. Timothy Coombs and Sherry J. Holladay, "Helping Crisis Managers Protect Reputational Assets: Initial Tests of the Situational Crisis Communication Theory," *Management Communication Quarterly* 16, no. 2 (2002): 165–86, https://doi.org/10.1177/089331802237233.
7. Coombs and Holladay, "Helping Crisis Managers," 340.
8. Catherine Soehner, Ian Godfrey, and G. Scott Bigler, "Crisis Communication in Libraries: Opportunity for New Roles in Public Relations," *Journal of Academic Librarianship* 43, no. 3 (May 2017): 268–73, https://doi.org/10.1016/j.acalib.2017.03.003; Cos Mallozzi, "Facing the Danger Zone in Crisis Communications." *Risk Management*, January 1994, Gale Academic OneFile.
9. Steve Witt and Kerry Smith, "Libraries in Times of Crisis," editorial, *IFLA Journal* 45, no. 1 (March 2019): 3–4. https://doi.org/10.1177/0340035219830549.
10. Lisl Zach, "What Do I Do in an Emergency? The Role of Public Libraries in Providing Information during Times of Crisis," *Science and Technology Libraries* 30, no. 4 (September 2011): 404–13, https://doi.org/10.1080/0194262X.2011.626341.
11. Zach, "What Do I Do?" 405.
12. Henriette Ferreira Gomes, preface to *Atuação dos profissionais da Arquivologia, Biblioteconomia e Museologia em época de pandemia*, ed. Daniela Spudeit and Claudia Souza (Florianópolis, Brazil: Rocha Gráfica e Editora, 2020), 11–14, http://biblio.eci.ufmg.br/ebooks/2021010004.pdf.

13. Beuna Lessa, "Acesso aos serviços e produtos da biblioteca em tempos de pandemia da covid-19: Possibilidades de uso do Facebook," *Informação & Informação* 26, no. 2: 333–53, https://doi.org/10.5433/1981-8920.2021v26n2p333.
14. Jorge Santa Anna, "O bibliotecário em face das transformações sociais: De guardião aum profissional desinstitucionalizado," *Revista ACB: Biblioteconomia em Santa Catarina Florianópolis* 20, no. 1 (January–April 2015): 138–157, https://revista.acbsc.org.br/racb/article/view/985.

Bibliography

Coombs, W. Timothy, and Sherry J. Holladay. "Helping Crisis Managers Protect Reputational Assets: Initial Tests of the Situational Crisis Communication Theory." *Management Communication Quarterly* 16, no. 2 (2002): 165–86. https://doi.org/10.1177/089331802237233.

Deloitte Touche Tohmatsu. *Manual de gestão de crise para relação com investidores: Comunicação e estratégia para preservação de valor.* London: Deloitte Touche Tomatsu, 2015. https://www2.deloitte.com/content/dam/Deloitte/br/Documents/risk/Manual-Gestao-Crises-para-RI.pdf

Institute for Crisis Management. "What Defines a Crisis?" 2021. https://crisisconsultant.com/.

Lessa, Bruna. "Acesso aos serviços e produtos da biblioteca em tempos de pandemia da covid-19: Possibilidades de uso do Facebook." *Informação & Informação* 26, no. 2 (2021): 333–53. https://doi.org/10.5433/1981-8920.2021v26n2p333.

Mallozzi, Cos. "Facing the Danger Zone in Crisis Communications." *Risk Management*, January 1994, Gale Academic OneFile.

Outhwaite, William, ed. *The Blackwell Dictionary of Twentieth-Century Social Thought.* Oxford: Blackwell Reference, 1998.

Salvador, Alexandre Borba, Ana Akemi Ikeda, and Edson Crescitelli. "Gestão de crise e seu impacto na imagem de marca." *Gestão & Produção* 24, no. 1 (January–April 2017): 15–24. https://doi.org/10.1590/0104-530x1668-14.

Santa Anna, Jorge. 2015. "O bibliotecário em face das transformações sociais: De guardião aum profissional desinstitucionalizado." *Revista ACB: Biblioteconomia em Santa Catarina, Florianópolis* 20, n. 1 (January–April 2015): 138–57. https://revista.acbsc.org.br/racb/article/view/985.

Soehner, Catherine, Ian Godfrey, and G. Scott Bigler. "Crisis Communication in Libraries: Opportunity for New Roles in Public Relations." *Journal of Academic Librarianship* 43, no. 3 (May 2017): 268–73. https://doi.org/10.1016/j.acalib.2017.03.003.

Spudeit, Daniela, and Claudia Souza, eds. *Atuação dos profissionais da Arquivologia, Biblioteconomia e Museologia em época de pandemia.* Florianópolis, Brazil: Rocha Gráfica e Editora, 2020. http://biblio.eci.ufmg.br/ebooks/2021010004.pdf.

Witt, Steve, and Kerry Smith. "Libraries in Times of Crisis." Editorial. *IFLA Journal* 45, no. 1 (March 2019): 3–4. https://doi.org/10.1177/0340035219830549.

Zach, Lisl. "What Do I Do in an Emergency? The Role of Public Libraries in Providing Information during Times of Crisis." *Science and Technology Libraries* 30, no. 4 (September 2011): 404–13. https://doi.org/10.1080/0194262x.2011.626341.

CHAPTER 17

Helping Readers Imagine the Past and Remember the Future

Calming Anxieties and Fostering Literacies during Crises

Lynn D. Lampert

> *Reading about pandemics, fictional or real, does more than just entertain or console during the outbreak of a dangerous new disease. Reading pandemic literature, both fiction and factual, also helps us recognize and combat the dangerous historic cycles of societal ills, such as racialized scapegoating and misinformation campaigns that have plagued communities during a disease outbreak.*

As the COVID-19 pandemic emerged in 2020, people searched for ways to cope with the frightening realities the novel coronavirus posed to daily life. The emotional trauma of the crisis motivated many to explore how others endured past epidemics. This chapter examines the increased interest in pandemic literature during the COVID-19 crisis and describes how libraries responded by recommending pandemic fiction and nonfiction titles through reader's advisory guides via LibGuides or other library-hosted platforms. These efforts to assuage readers' mounting anxiety and isolation gave students opportunities to investigate past pandemic narratives amidst the harmful "infowhelm" created

213

by inconsistent pandemic reporting.[1] Helping readers discover historical fiction and nonfiction chronicles of past pandemics also allowed students to consider how fact and fiction can combat anxiety, misinformation, and isolation during a crisis.[2] The promotion of pandemic literature through LibGuides, book clubs, author talks, or other academic library programming can increase students' historical and information literacy skills as outlined by the Association of College and Research Libraries' (ACRL) *Framework for Information Literacy for Higher Education*.[3] Why is this a great time to start a reader's advisory initiative or a book club? Because recreational reading has increased dramatically in the last two years; OverDrive, a major distributor of e-books, audiobooks, and streaming video to libraries, reported that more than 289 million e-books were checked out in 2020, "a 40 percent increase from 2019," presenting an opportunity for academic libraries.[4] While reader's advisory services and the marketing of fiction collections traditionally are public library specialties, these efforts can increase students' literacy skills and bolster student engagement with other academic library programming such as archival and special collection exhibits, book talks, and library-sponsored book clubs.[5] In this chapter, examples of how academic librarians might employ emerging reader's advisory tools to engage their community and foster critical thinking are also shared. The benefits of the paired promotion of pandemic fiction alongside recommended nonfiction studies to foster historical literacy as well as information and health literacies are also explored. Examples of popular pandemic literature titles promoted by academic libraries during the COVID-19 crisis, including historical fiction and nonfiction studies, are included in Appendix A: Bibliography of Pandemic Literature.

Pandemic Fiction and Its Impact on Readers

Published statistics reveal that Americans not only read more books during this pandemic, they also wanted specifically to read more pandemic fiction.[6] When the *Washington Post* asked subscribers what they were reading to cope with the pandemic in May of 2020, Albert Camus's 1947 novel *The Plague* emerged as the fifth most reported title.[7] Many readers attempted to escape their newfound isolation by reading recent bestsellers or older pulp novels about fictional pandemics like Stephen King's 1978 dystopian novel *The Stand*.[8]

As the pandemic dragged on, more obscure works of pandemic fiction were also discussed by library book clubs, including Daniel Defoe's 1722 *A Journal of the Plague Year*, which weaves fact with fiction to warn readers of future plagues. It chronicles the dangers posed by the Great Plague of London in 1655 and became a frequently recommended pandemic read in 2020.[9]

A partnership between the University of Iowa's famous writing workshop and Iowa City created the 100 Days of Decameron pandemic project, where students and the community met virtually to read and discuss Boccaccio's *Decameron* tales to celebrate "the remarkable resilience of the human spirit at times of global catastrophes."[10]

What was motivating people to read about past epidemics during the quarantine for a deadly new virus? What were readers hoping to discover by reading historical pandemic-themed novels? When analyzing the attraction that pandemic fiction in literature or film holds, Kathryn VanArendock posits that

> pandemic fiction is about how people behave in response to acute, sudden-onset helplessness. When we're confronted with that helplessness in real life…, some version of it—*any* version of it, and ideally one where at least some people survive—is comforting. It's a model for how we could respond.[11]

Reading about pandemics, fictional or real, does more than just entertain or console during the outbreak of a dangerous new disease. Reading pandemic literature, both fiction and factual, also helps us recognize and combat the dangerous historic cycles of societal ills, such as racialized scapegoating and misinformation campaigns that have plagued communities during a disease outbreak.

Pandemic fiction is not a new genre. It has resonated with readers for as long as books and other creative works have existed. From Homer's *Iliad* (850–750 BCE), which includes a plague wreaking havoc on the Greeks during battle at Troy, to Philip Roth's 2010 novel *Nemesis,* which shows how Americans reacted with fear, suspicion, and racial scapegoating during the polio virus outbreaks of the 1940s, fiction set during epidemics has shaped the trajectory of literature as much as the diseases that have occurred throughout history. From historical fiction to science fiction, narratives about deadly epidemics have enthralled readers for centuries. In fact, some of the best examples of pandemic literature were also written by authors who had real experiences with deadly illnesses. For example, Mary Shelley's *The Last Man*, considered by many to be the first science fiction–based apocalyptic novel set within a pandemic, was written in 1826, following the first great cholera epidemic in India and Asia between 1817 and 1824. That epidemic alerted Shelley and others to the dangers of cholera. Jack London's pandemic novel *The Scarlet Plague* is another example; it was written after he lived through the deadly bubonic plague epidemic in San Francisco, California, between 1900 and 1904. While neither of these fictional works are as well-known as some of the authors' other writings, they speak to the need of the human experience to process and document for others the effect of pandemics on society.

Scholars have long understood the impact that literary works focused on epidemics and illness have on readers. For example, Suzanne Keen and Neil Gaiman posit that reading disease- or apocalyptic-themed literature, or even general fiction, helps readers develop empathy for the fragility of the human condition.[12] Other scholars like Robert Wuthnow, Kathryn Shwetz, and Kerry Mallan suggest that pandemic fiction within the science fiction genre helps readers develop survivalist instincts to combat future health threats emerging from globalism, industrialization, or even climate change.[13] Whether fictional works prepare the reader to confront future diseases and their societal impact is a worthy subject to explore. As Neda Ulaby states, "by helping us make sense of the real world …books, TV shows and movies based on pandemics explore how people live upon and move around a planet defined by compromised ecosystems, borders and barricades."[14]

Assigning fictional works about epidemics is not a new trend within university courses. Ann Hudson Jones points out how medical students are regularly assigned novels discussing diseases to teach how illnesses and treatments impact patients.[15] Nationwide, specialized undergraduate courses also study diseases through literature. The work of Hawkins and McEntrye documents how these courses emerged as the medical humanities developed in the 1970s to help premed and humanities majors understand how illness and disease impact the human condition.[16] While these courses regularly read books on fictional and nonfictional accounts of past epidemics, university courses and classes outside literature or medical humanities programs are less likely to explore how epidemics impact people by examining literature. Researchers have studied undergraduates' health literacy and found wide variations in the formal knowledge students attain. Their findings suggest that it is not surprising that students not enrolled in public health education programs are less likely to formally study the historical roles that public health guidelines and medical interventions played in saving lives during disease outbreaks.[17] The existence of public health curricular gaps and health literacy disparities within undergraduate curricular settings outside public health programs, which were already noted as a growing concern in 2007, may still contribute to health illiteracy and impair some students' abilities to cope in a public health crisis.[18] Exploring the differences between historical and fictional pandemic narratives, and the impact that fictionalized reconstructions of disease outbreaks have on our ability to navigate public health crises, remains important for lifelong learning.

Readers Advisory Responses to the COVID-19 Pandemic

In response to the COVID-19 pandemic, faculty and librarians at Princeton University began developing course readings for students to discover how past societies dealt with outbreaks of novel deadly diseases. Princeton University's spring 2020 semester undergraduate course Literature and Medicine adapted its syllabus to focus on pandemic literature across genres and centuries to "bring the pandemic into focus …and delve into classic readings on epidemics 'as signifiers of a culture and its deep-seated values and fears.'"[19] This modification generated rich class discussions on how pandemics historically caused xenophobia and prejudice when people looked to blame a new disease's origins on other countries or groups to scapegoat or "pathologize a place along with is population and culture."[20] Other universities also brought the pandemic into the classroom; law students at the University of Washington explored literature examining how past epidemics posed legal challenges to societies. The law libraries supported students by creating LibGuides like the University of Washington's "Law in the Time of Covid-19."[21] Other universities offered less formal reading lists via blogs and clubs that went virtual, recommending a variety of topics for their readers, including pandemic-themed books such as *Love in the Time of Cholera* and *The Plague*.[22]

Around the country, faculty across disciplines began to crowdsource "#CoronavirusSyllabus" to plan lessons around the COVID-19 virus.[23] The results of the

#CoronavirusSyllabus project revealed academia's collective desire to accurately teach students about past epidemics like the great influenza outbreak of 1918, in order to expose the tragic consequences of unchecked pandemics. Prior to the COVID-19 pandemic, many Americans remained uneducated about the deadly influenza outbreak that the Centers for Disease Control and Prevention says infected over 500 million worldwide by 1920, killing between 20 and 50 million people.[24] When the popular television series *Downton Abbey* aired its second season's episode highlighting the deadly 1918 influenza outbreak in 2012, most younger Americans had not even heard of the historic pandemic, which was also labeled "the Spanish flu." As Leslie Gerwin noted when discussing this failed media education moment, "the general public's unwillingness to confront the reality of what a serious disease threat could look like in reality," even after viewing its devastation on a television show that averaged 9 million weekly viewers, supports the need to inform students about the likelihood of future public health threats.[25] Educating students about past epidemics to prepare them for future public health crises will require more than offering limited literature courses to premed students and literature majors. Entire academic communities, and their libraries, must create post-pandemic learning opportunities that strengthen the multiple literacies needed for critical thinking during public health crises. Critical-thinking skills can combat some of the effects of fake news during a crisis such as a pandemic, making these skills more important than ever.

More Than Reading: Reader's Advisory Services as Information Literacy Programming

While librarians were not teaching stand-alone courses on pandemic literature during the spring of 2020, many responded to the demand to identify pandemic literature during lockdown closures by curating online research guides, bibliographies, and other published reading recommendations. While the majority of COVID-19-themed LibGuides published by academic libraries since 2020 share published data and news from the Centers for Disease Control and Prevention and state and local public health authorities, a search of Google or the LibGuides community repository also retrieves large numbers of pandemic-themed recommended reading lists and subject guides.[26] Academic librarians have created similar guides showcasing authoritative information sources during previous national public health crises and traumatic events. Bibi Alajmi's work, examining the role that libraries can play during national crises, highlights library responses to crises like 9/11, Hurricane Katrina, and public health threats like HIV/AIDS, SARS, and the recent opioid health crisis.[27]

Noteworthy examples of academic libraries' LibGuides showcasing pandemic fiction and nonfiction reading suggestions include the University of West Florida's "A Scholar's Guide to Pandemics," Worcester Polytechnic Institute's "Pandemics and Intellectual Discourse," Claremont Colleges Library's "Pandemics and Epidemics: A Topic Resource

Guide," and Menlo College's "Coronavirus Racism."[28] These guides offer excellent paired recommendations of pandemic fiction and nonfiction titles. They also all delve deeper into pandemic topics by recommending titles that cover the history of diseases and vaccinations as well as the xenophobia and racial disparities in health care that plagued past public health crises. The creators of these resources all reported that these LibGuides were not formally tied to courses or assessed for impact beyond capturing LibGuide usage statistics. Therefore evidence of growth in critical-thinking skills, student knowledge of the topic, or other impacts of students viewing these highlighted resources are not known. The LibGuides created and launched closest to the outbreak of the COVID-19 pandemic have thus far received the most usage. Menlo College reports that its LibGuide, which was created for general use in the spring of 2020 and not connected to any courses, was surprisingly one its most heavily accessed guides during the fall semester of 2020, receiving 3,312 viewings on a campus with a student population of approximately 750 students. The University of West Florida Library reported that its LibGuide was viewed 1,000 times since it was launched in 2020. Worcester Polytechnic Institute's Library reported that its LibGuide was accessed 2,255 times since its launch in May of 2020. Claremont Colleges Library's LibGuide, created in 2021, reported that its captured analytics show 216 viewings.[29]

There are several important lessons to be learned from the collected reported experiences of these sample academic libraries' LibGuides showcasing pandemic readings. One is that stand-alone LibGuides that are not formally used within library instruction or tied to other programming often face difficulty in determining whether students discussed the recommended titles with peers or faculty after consulting these resource guides. Secondly, without running an assessment tied to reading recommendation promotions, it is difficult to measure impact beyond circulation statistics or LibGuide usage. Thirdly, it is helpful to establish a LibGuide launch and promotion time-line sequence. Closely timing the publication and marketing of reader's advisory LibGuides to the targeted crisis, current event, or shared societal issue may help drive initial student engagement with the resource. Sequencing the launch of related promotional tools, like tied-in book discussions, reading groups, or special speaker events, will also help ensure that reader's advisory LibGuides avoid becoming stand-alone resources with decreasing or limited viewings as time moves forward. Well-timed marketing instances, via library social media platforms and elsewhere, implemented after a LibGuide's publication are also recommended.[30]

Reader's advisory programming promoting leisure reading on high-interest topics should ideally be paired with library activities that will increase students' development of the concepts found in ACRL's *Framework for Information Literacy for Higher Education*. As Sanches, Antunes, and Lopes explain, "The analysis of literary reading promotion practices developed in an academic context points to a relationship between the information literacy and the skills associated with it…. With the different approaches to promoting literary reading, often mixing leisure and critical thinking."[31] The work of Sanches, Antunes, and Lopes supports the notion that ACRL's *Framework for Information Literacy for Higher Education's* six threshold concepts can be presented in effective cocurricular fashion through common library reader's advisory methods such as having students meet with an invited author to explore the concept of Authority Is Constructed and Contextual; using reading groups or book clubs to reveal Information Creation as a Process; promoting the discovery of an academic library's literary fiction or nonfiction collection dedicated to leisure reading, nonfiction titles, or other materials such as special collection holdings, using curated LibGuides to demonstrates the concepts of Information Has Value and Searching as Strategic Exploration; or lastly using group reading or discussion activities after author talks to investigate the Research as Inquiry and Scholarship as a Conversation framework concepts.

While most academic libraries promote their literary collections through new book title lists or dedicated leisure reading collections, more interactive efforts like those above would help academic libraries deliver more formal information literacy programming, while also promoting the value of their entire collections. Boston College's virtually hosted author talk with Emma Donoghue discussing her 2020 historical pandemic fiction novel, *The Pull of the Stars,* offers an example of an effective promotion of recent pandemic historical fiction that hits many of the information literacy framework's threshold concepts. This successful program saw 225 of the 310 people who registered attend this virtual-only event.[32] The author talk gave students a unique opportunity to learn about the writing and research process that Donaghue used to create her historical novel set during 1918 Spanish flu. While academic libraries previously struggled to fund bringing authors to campus, the successful pandemic use of Zoom and other virtual platforms to host live author discussions identified cost-effective ways to connect students with renowned authors worldwide. While academic librarians also previously feared that students would not attend leisure reading promotions, there is now ample evidence that suggests otherwise. Heightened interest in attending virtual book talks nationwide during the pandemic has caused publishers and authors to both embrace and see value in providing virtual book talks via Zoom and other platforms. As Hart and Nicolau note, "Authors are willing to do online events, and audiences are willing to show up—perhaps more willing than they had been before."[33]

The Promise of Reader's Advisory Programming during and after a Crisis

The scholarly literature of academic librarianship has long lamented the difficulties of promoting reading. As Pauline Dewan notes, "In the past fifty years, very few academic librarians have provided reader's advisory service, believing it to be a public library initiative" or an unpopular undergraduate activity.[34] Academic librarians may lack training in reader's advisory services, which is the process of making reading suggestions, typically fiction or nonfiction books, through direct or indirect methods to meet the information needs of their clientele. Subject specialists serving as discipline liaisons to academic departments are often best equipped to match titles to users' reading interests. But during a complex crisis like a pandemic, an entire staff of librarians may need to contribute to curated title lists to meet the full spectrum of information needs. For librarians unprepared to recommend pandemic literature or other public health titles, New York University's (NYU) Langone Health Center Library's freely available database Literature Arts Medicine (LitMed) offers annotations of both fictional and nonfictional works focused on diseases and past pandemics and other health topics.[35]

While interest in reading for pleasure may have been waning a decade ago, recent studies show that college-age students are increasingly readers outside of class. A survey analyzing the printed book reading population in the United States as of February 2019 "showed that 18 to 29-year-olds were more likely to have read a print book in the last year than their older counterparts."[36] The growing popularity of GoodReads, online celebrity book clubs, and #BookTok indicates that college-aged students are using online platforms to share reviews of books they read for pleasure. Student responses to 2020's multiple societal crises also show that interest in locating quality book recommendations on topics ranging from climate change to social justice exists. The myriad of anti-racist literature reading lists created by academic libraries and shared by students on social media following the murder of George Floyd in 2020 demonstrates that students were truly interested in these reading recommendations. Many students read and discussed these recommended titles in virtual reading groups at colleges and universities nationwide.[37] Mr. Floyd's tragic death and the powerful impact of the Black Lives Matter movement led to widespread calls for activism to promote social and racial justice and police reform. Historic protests and student activism inspired many campus libraries and reading groups to simultaneously discuss anti-racist and pandemic literature books. For example, the University of Maryland's Research Commons Interdisciplinary Dialogue speaker program, "Tale of Two Pandemics: Illuminating Structural Racism and COVID," explored the concurrent pandemics of racism and COVID-19 through a virtual discussion featuring faculty experts, students, and librarians.[38]

Interest in online reading groups and engagement with library-hosted talks also increased with the unprecedented move to remote learning and student isolation during pandemic lockdowns. Students joined virtual book clubs and Zoom reading circles to stay connected to others. In 2020, the Pandemic Book Club was founded at the University of California, Santa Barbara, in "hopes of creating a space where a remote community can grow around a love of reading …and weigh-in with their thoughts and opinions on the shared books or presentations via the online forum."[39] Over 160 students and faculty members participated in this reading group, which required only campus identification for participation. While this group initially read Emily St. John Mandel's popular pandemic-themed novel *Station Eleven*, its subsequent readings were not limited by genre or format. The University of Texas at San Antonio's (UTSA) peer virtual book club, which promoted the Big Texas Read Initiative through a partnership with Gemini Ink, a local literacy organization, was also lauded by the American Library Association's I Love Libraries initiative for its creative pandemic work. In this reading group, the library's peer student coaches mentored fellow students in research skills and technology while also promoting the book club to the UTSA community and providing technology support to guest authors.[40] Both these pandemic reading groups and others across the nation read a wide range of fiction, historical studies, and other nonfiction works, proving that student interest in reading and discussing books is strong.

Pandemics and Fear: How Reading History Helps Demystify Public Health Crises

Historians and history librarians can play a critical role during pandemics and other public health crises. The American Historical Association stressed how history and historians could help during the COVID-19 crisis by

> shedding light on the history of pandemics and the utility of that history to policy formation and public culture ...and explain[ing] social and cultural challenges met in crisis situations, epidemics and pandemics.... The fears, challenges, and permanent changes that will accompany this pandemic are both rooted in a historical context and have historical precedents themselves.[41]

While historical studies reveal how past generations dealt with other public health crises, most students are unlikely to explore this research without curricular interventions. Subjects like the fourteenth century's Black Death are typically only briefly covered in large western civilization survey courses. Most college graduates remain uneducated about the role that epidemics and other public health crises have played in American history. For example, few students probably ever learn that George Washington's soldiers faced a deadly outbreak of smallpox during the American Revolution, resulting in the controversial vaccination of soldiers in 1777.[42] Studying past events like these can provide critical historical understanding about important and historic public health literacy lessons.

To help readers learn more about past responses to public health crises, reader's advisory efforts in academic libraries ideally need to promote paired fictional and nonfictional recommendations and encourage the exploration of primary source holdings that support historical and information literacies. Recommended fiction title lists should include historical fiction and historical novels written during past disease outbreaks alongside related academic historical studies. Guest authors and scholars may also be invited to lead group discussions of curated titles and topics to improve students' historical thinking skills and increase awareness about the research process involved in creating accurate historical fiction or public history. Other programming possibilities include linking reader's advisory efforts to library special collections exhibitions or film showings.

While some academic librarians may not see a need for building up historical fiction collections, historians like Jessica Hower argue that historical fiction, in both print and film formats, fosters the development of critical-thinking skills in students.[43] Historical fiction is also highly effective at generating class discussions about past events and controversial crises. As Anna Diamond reminds us,

> History is a narrative after all, whether the information presented, or arguments made are in standardized textbooks or fictionalized accounts. The ability to decipher and interrogate historical assertions—by comparing, contrasting, and fact-checking them—is a vital tool, and one that it's never too early to start learning.[44]

Strong examples of academic libraries and history departments using library book clubs and joint programming to invite scholars to lead students in discussions about the creation, documentation, and preservation of historical research and other historical literacy skills during the COVID-19 pandemic can be found in the University of California Berkeley's Oral History Book Club and the Ohio State University's program Pandemics: Past, Present, Future. Many historians hope that more students will become interested in reading existing and future historical scholarship on pandemics that examines past pandemics and fosters reflection on our COVID-19 pandemic experiences.

Charity Anderson reminds educators interested in facilitating change in nontraditional academic settings during a crisis that humanistic texts promote reflection and change and build community. Rejecting the notion that COVID-19 did not offer fulfilling learning opportunities, Anderson writes that

> COVID-19, and all that encompassed 2020, re-shaped our country, hurting us deeply.... [It] has been an educational opportunity, a transformative one ...where humanistic texts and art can be incorporated across disciplines, giving students a chance to make interdisciplinary connections, question their beliefs and assumptions, and transform their perspectives.[45]

Before the historic and chaotic events of 2020, many in academia realized that films and television shows focused on fictional or real epidemics or even horrific historical events could inspire student class discussions and paper topics. Indeed, television shows like *Downton Abbey* or even *Watchmen* may potentially inspire some history majors to study the impacts of the Spanish flu or the Tulsa race riot of 1921. However, as most history librarians working in an academic library setting will attest, these same students will also need assistance in locating historical studies or primary sources that support studying these events. The success of reader's advisory programming during the COVID-19 pandemic proves that proactive library efforts can potentially inspire all students to learn more about historical events through the promotion of fictionalized or nonfiction narratives and work with research librarians. Post-pandemic reader's advisory programming in libraries must focus on helping students attain the critical-thinking skills needed to combat the most frustrating aspects of today's seemingly never-ending "infodemic."[46] An academic library's post-pandemic LibGuides, book clubs, hosted author events, and exhibitions must aim to balance fiction and nonfiction recommendations to foster the multiple literacies needed to understand Sir Lewis Namier's adage that we "imagine the past and remember the future."[47]

APPENDIX A
Bibliography of Pandemic Literature
Bubonic Plague
FICTION

Boccaccio, Giovanni, John Payne, and Charles S. Singleton. *Decameron*. Berkeley: University of California Press, 1982.

Brooks, Geraldine. *Years of Wonders: A Novel of the Plague*. New York: Penguin Publishing, 2002.

Camus, Albert, and Stuart Gilbert. *The Plague*. Translated. New York: Vintage Books, a division of Random House, Inc., 1991.

Chase, Marilyn. *The Barbary Plague: the Black Death in Victorian San Francisco*. New York: Random House, 2003.

Defoe, Daniel. *A Journal of the Plague Year Written by a Citizen Who Continued All the While in* London: J.M. Dent, 1957.

Marcus, Ben. *The Flame Alphabet*. New York: Vintage Books, 2012.

O'Farrell, Maggie. *Hamnet*. Knopf Doubleday Publishing Group, 2020.

Willis, Connie. *Doomsday Book*. New York: Bantam Books, 1994.

NON-FICTION

Cantor, Norman F. *In the Wake of the Plague: the Black Death and the World It Made*. New York: Free Press, 2001.

Kelly, John. *The Great Mortality: an Intimate History of the Black Death, the Most Devastating Plague of All Time*. New York: HarperCollins Publishers, 2005.

Mohr, James C. *Plague and Fire Battling Black Death and the 1900 Burning of Honolulu's Chinatown*. New York: Oxford University Press, 2005.

Tuchman, Barbara W. *A Distant Mirror: the Calamitous 14th Century*. New York: Knopf, 1978.

Cholera
FICTION

García Márquez, Gabriel, and Edith Grossman. *Love in the Time of Cholera*. New York: Alfred A. Knopf, 1988.

Giono, Jean. *The Horseman on the Roof*. San Francisco: North Point Press, 1982.

Holman, Sheri. *The Dress Lodger*. New York: Ballantine Books, 2001.

Mann, Thomas. *Death in Venice*. Cutchogue, N.Y: Buccaneer Books, 1986

Shelley, Mary Wollstonecraft and Anne McWhir. *The Last Man*. Ontario: Broadview Press, 1996.

NON-FICTION

Johnson, Steven. *The Ghost Map: The Story of London's Most Terrifying Epidemic—and How It Changed Science, Cities, and the Modern World*. New York: Riverhead Books, 2006.

Rosenberg, Charles E. *The Cholera Year: the United States in 1832, 1849, and 1866*. Chicago: University of Chicago Press, 1987.

Flu/ Influenza (1918)

FICTION

Cather, Willa. *One of Ours*. New York: Alfred A. Knopf, 1922.

Donoghue, Emma. *The Pull of the Stars: A Novel*. New York: Little, Brown and Company, 2020.

Maxwell, William. *They Came Like Swallows*. New York: Harper & Brothers, 1937.

Porter, Katherine Anne. *Pale Horse, Pale Rider: Three Short Novels*. New York: Harcourt, Brace and Company, 1939.

Steinbeck, John. *Cannery Row*. New York: Viking Press, 1963.

Wiseman, Ellen Marie. *The Orphan Collector: A Heroic Novel of Survival During the 1918 Influenza Pandemic*. La Vergne: Kensington Books, 2020.

NON-FICTION

Barry, John M. *The Great Influenza: the Epic Story of the Deadliest Plague in History*. New York: Viking, 2004.

Kolata, Gina Bari. *Flu: The Story of the Great Influenza Pandemic of 1918 and the Search for the Virus That Caused It*. New York: Simon & Schuster, 2001.

Spinney, Laura. *Pale Rider: the Spanish Flu of 1918 and How It Changed the World*. New York: Public Affairs, 2018.

HIV/AIDS

FICTION

Kushner, Tony. *Angels in America: a Gay Fantasia on National Themes*. New York: Theatre Communications Group, 1993.

Makkai, Rebecca. *The Great Believers*. New York, New York: Viking, 2018.

NON-FICTION

Shilts, Randy. *And the Band Played on: Politics, People, and the AIDS Epidemic*. New York, N.Y: Penguin Books, 1988.

Leprosy

FICTION

Brennert, Alan. *Moloka'i*. New York: St. Martin's Press, 2003.

Talarigo, Jeff. *The Pearl Diver*. Westminster: Knopf Doubleday Publishing Group, 2007.

NON-FICTION

Inglis, Kerri A. *Ma'i Lepera: Disease and Displacement in Nineteenth Century Hawai'i*. Honolulu: University of Hawaii Press, 2013.

Malaria

FICTION

Kingsolver, Barbara. *The Poisonwood Bible: A Novel*. New York: Harper Flamingo, 1998.

Shah, Sonia. 2011. *The Fever: How Malaria Has Ruled Humankind for 500,000 years*. New York: Picador.

Polio
FICTION
Roth, Philip. *Nemesis*. Boston: Houghton Mifflin Harcourt, 2010.

NON-FICTION
Oshinsky, David M. *Polio: an American Story*. Oxford: Oxford University Press, 2005.

Rabies
FICTION
García Márquez, Gabriel, and Edith Grossman. *Of Love and Other Demons*. New York: Penguin Books, 1996.
Hurston, Zora Neale and Jerry Pinkney. *Their Eyes Were Watching God*. Urbana: University of Illinois Press, 1991.

NON-FICTION
Wasik, Bill, and Monica Murphy. *Rabid: A Cultural History of the World's Most Diabolical Virus*. New York, New York: Viking, 2012.

Smallpox
FICTION
Donoghue, Emma. *Frog Music: A Novel*. New York: Little, Brown and Company, 2014.

NON-FICTION
Fenn, Elizabeth A. *Pox Americana: the Great Smallpox Epidemic of 1775-82*. 1st ed. New York: Hill and Wang, 2001.
Risse, Guenter B. *Driven by Fear: Epidemics and Isolation in San Francisco's House of Pestilence*. Urbana: University of Illinois Press, 2016.
Williams, Tony. *The Pox and the Covenant: Mather, Franklin, and the Epidemic That Changed America's Destiny*. Naperville, Ill: Sourcebooks, 2010.
Willrich, Michael. *Pox an American History*. New York, New York, U.S.A: The Penguin Press, 2011.

Tuberculosis
FICTION
Le Carré, John. *The Constant Gardener: A Novel*. New York: Scribner, 2001
Mann, Thomas, and John E. Woods. *The Magic Mountain: A Novel*. New York: Vintage International, 1996.

NON-FICTION

Bates, Barbara. *Bargaining for Life: A Social History of Tuberculosis, 1876-1938*. Philadelphia: University of Pennsylvania Press, 2015.

Daniel, Thomas M. *Captain of Death: The Story of Tuberculosis*. Rochester, NY, USA: University of Rochester Press, 1997.

Dormandy, Thomas. *The White Death: A History of Tuberculosis*. New York: New York University Press, 2000.

Ryan, Frank. *The Forgotten Plague: How the Battle Against Tuberculosis Was Won and Lost*. Boston: Little, Brown, 1993.

Typhus
FICTION

Mason, Daniel. *The Winter Soldier*. New York: Little Brown and Company, 2018

Pasternak, Boris Leonidovich. *Doctor Zhivago*. New York: Pantheon Books, 1960.

NON-FICTION

Allen, Arthur. *The Fantastic Laboratory of Dr. Weigl: How Two Brave Scientists Battled Typhus and Sabotaged the Nazis*. New York: W.W. Norton & Company, 2014.

Yellow Fever
FICTION

Anderson, Laurie Halse. *Fever, 1793*. New York: Aladdin 2002.

NON-FICTION

Crosby, Molly Caldwell. *The American Plague: the Untold Story of Yellow Fever, the Epidemic That Shaped Our History*. New York: Berkley Books, 2006.

General Pandemic Literature
FICTION

Atwood, Margaret. *Oryx and Crake*. London: Bloomsbury, 2003.

King, Stephen. *The Stand*. Garden City, N.Y: Doubleday, 1978.

Lewis, Sinclair. *Arrowsmith*. New York: Harcourt Brace Jovanovich, 1953.

London, Jack, and Tony Robinson. *The Scarlet Plague*. London: Hesperus, 2008.

Ma, Ling. *Severance: A Novel*. New York: Farrar, Straus and Giroux, 2018.

Mandel, Emily St. John. *Station Eleven: A Novel*. New York: Alfred A. Knopf, 2015.

Robinson, Kim Stanley. *The Years of Rice and Salt*. London: HarperCollins, 2002.

Saramago, José, and Giovanni Pontiero. *Blindness*. New York: Harcourt, 1998.

Walker, Karen Thompson. *The Dreamers: A Novel*. New York: Random House, 2019.

Wendig, Chuck. *Wanderers: A Novel*. New York: Del Rey, 2019

Whitehead, Colson. *Zone One: A Novel*. New York: Doubleday, 2011.

NON-FICTION

Diamond, Jared M. *Guns, Germs, and Steel: The Fates of Human Societies*. New York: W. W. Norton & Company, 1997.

Goldsmith, Connie. *Pandemic: How Climate, the Environment, and Superbugs Increase the Risk*. Minneapolis: Lerner Publishing Group, 2018.

Shah, Sonia. *Pandemic: Tracking Contagions, from Cholera to Ebola and Beyond*. New York: Sarah Crichton Books, Farrar, Straus and Giroux, 2016.

Quammen, David. *Spillover: Animal Infections and the Next Human Pandemic*. New York: W. W. Norton & Company, 2012.

Racism/Xenophobia During Pandemics or Disease Outbreaks

Cohn, Samuel Kline, and David Colacci. *Epidemics: Hate and Compassion from the Plague of Athens to AIDS*. Oxford: Oxford University Press, 2018.

Goldberg, Mark Allan. *Conquering Sickness: Race, Health, and Colonization in the Texas Borderlands*. Lincoln: University of Nebraska Press, 2007.

Hernández, Daisy. *The Kissing Bug: A True Story of a Family, an Insect, and a Nation's Neglect of a Deadly Disease*. Portland: Tin House. 2021

Mckiernan-González, John Raymond. *Fevered Measures: Public Health and Race at the Texas-Mexico Border, 1848-1942*. Durham, NC: Duke University Press, 2012.

Markel, Howard. *Quarantine!: East European Jewish immigrants and the New York City epidemics of 1892*. Baltimore: John Hopkins University Press, 1997.

Mohr, James. *Plague and Fire: Battling Black Death and the 1900 Burning of Honolulu's Chinatown*. New York: Oxford University Press, 2004.

Risse, Guenter B. *Plague, Fear, and Politics in San Francisco's Chinatown*. Baltimore: The Johns Hopkins University Press, 2012.

Roberts, Samuel. *Infectious Fear: Politics, Disease, and the Health Effects of Segregation*. Chapel Hill: University of North Carolina Press, 2009

Shah, Nayan. *Contagious Divides: Epidemics and Race in San Francisco's Chinatown*. Berkeley: University of California Press, 2001.

Notes

1. Heather Houser defines *infowhelm* as the phenomenon of being overwhelmed by a constant flow of sometimes conflicting information. See Heather Houser, "The COVID-19 'Infowhelm,'" *New York Review of Books*, May 6, 2020, https://www.nybooks.com/daily/2020/05/06/the-covid-19-infowhelm/.
2. Jamie Saxon, "Making Meaning of the Pandemic 'through the Lens of Literature,'" Princeton University, Office of Communications, May 15, 2020, https://www.princeton.edu/news/2020/05/15/making-meaning-pandemic-through-lens-literature.
3. Association of College and Research Libraries, *Framework for Information Literacy for Higher Education* (Chicago: Association of College and Research Libraries, 2016), https://www.ala.org/acrl/sites/ala.org.acrl/files/content/issues/infolit/framework1.pdf.
4. American Library Association, *2021 State of America's Libraries: Special Report: COVID-19* (Chicago: American Library Association, April 2, 2021), 17, https://www.ala.org/news/sites/ala.org.news/files/content/State-of-Americas-Libraries-Report-2021.pdf.
5. Tatiana Sanches, Maria da Luz Antunes, and Carlos Lopes, "Improving Information Literacy in Higher Education in an Unorthodox Way: The Literature Potential for ACRL Framework Application" (presentation, International Scientific Conference of Librarians, Western Balkan Information and Media Literacy Conference 2020, and 9th International Summit of Book, Bihac, Bosnia-Herzegovina, December 9-10, 2020, accessed on September 14, 2021, https://repositorio.ul.pt/

228 Chapter 17

bitstream/10451/47181/1/Sanches_Antunes_Lopes_Improving_information_literacy_in_higher_education.pdf.

6. See table 6 in Bureau of Labor Statistics. "American Time User Survey—May to December 2019 and 2020 Results," news release, July 22, 2021, https://www.bls.gov/news.release/pdf/atus.pdf. See also Kelly Jensen, "Americans Read Nearly 25% More Last Year, According to New Research," Book Riot, July 30, 2021, https://bookriot.com/american-pandemic-reading-habits/.

7. Stephanie Merry and Steven Johnson, "What the Country Is Reading during the Pandemic: Dystopias, Social Justice and Steamy Romance," *Washington Post*, September 2, 2020, https://www.washingtonpost.com/entertainment/books/2020-book-trends/2020/09/02/6a835caa-e863-11ea-bc79-834454439a44_story.html.

8. Ellen Gamerman, "Readers Binge on Books about Pandemics (Really); From Stephen King to Emily St. John Mandel, Here Are Five Books to Help You Lean into Coronavirus Fears," *Wall Street Journal*, Eastern edition, March 11, 2020. https://libproxy.csun.edu/login?url=https://www.proquest.com/newspapers/readers-binge-on-books-about-pandemics-really/docview/2375958946/se-2 (accessed December 17, 2022).

9. Lawrence Wright, "Five Best: Lawrence Wright on Pandemics in Fact and Fiction," *Wall Street Journal*, May 15, 2020,
https://www.wsj.com/articles/five-best-lawrence-wright-on-pandemics-in-fact-and-fiction-11589550822.

10. Iowa City UNESCO City of Literature, "100 Days of Decameron," 2020, accessed September 14, 2021, https://www.iowacityofliterature.org/decameron/ (page discontinued).

11. Kathryn VanArendonk, "Why Is Pandemic Fiction So Comforting Right Now?" *Vulture*, March 6, 2020, https://www.vulture.com/2020/03/contagion-coronavirus-pandemic-fiction.html.

12. See Neil Gaiman, "Why Our Future Depends on Libraries, Reading and Daydreaming," *Guardian*, October 15, 2013, https://www.theguardian.com/books/2013/oct/15/neil-gaiman-future-libraries-reading-daydreaming, and Suzanne Keen, *Empathy and the Novel* (New York: Oxford University Press, 2007).

13. See Katherine Shwetz, "Apocalyptic Fiction Helps Us Deal with the Anxiety of the Coronavirus Pandemic," Conversation, March 18, 2020, https://theconversation.com/apocolyptic-fiction-helps-us-deal-with-the-anxiety-ot-the-coronavirus-pandemic-133682; Kerry Mallan, "Dystopian Fiction for Young People: Instructive Tales of Resilience," *Psychoanalytic Inquiry,* 37, no.1 (2017): 16–24, https://doi.org/10.1080/07351690.2017.1250586; and Robert Wuthnow, *Be Very Afraid* (Oxford: Oxford University Press, 2010).

14. Neda Ulaby. "What Fictional Pandemics Can Teach Us About Real-World Survival," *All Things Considered*, NPR, February 10, 2020, https://www.kcrw.com/news/shows/all-things-considered/npr-story/803458265.

15. Ann Hudson Jones, "Why Teach Literature and Medicine? Answers from Three Decades," in *New Directions in Literature and Medicine Studies*, ed. Stephanie M. Hilger (London: Palgrave Macmillan, 2017), 31–48.

16. Anne Hunsaker Hawkins and Marilyn Chandler McEntyre, *Teaching Literature and Medicine* (New York: Modern Language Association, 2006).

17. Jehad A. Rababah et al., "Health Literacy: Exploring Disparities among College Students," *BMC Public Health* 19 (2019): article 1401, https://doi.org/10.1186/s12889-019-7781-2.

18. Susan Albertine, Nancy Alfred Persily and Richard Riegelman, "Back to the Pump Handle: Public Health and the Future of Undergraduate Education," *Liberal Education* 93, no. 4 (2007): 32–39.

19. Saxon, "Making Meaning of the Pandemic,".

20. Saxon, "Making Meaning of the Pandemic,".

21. University of Washington Libraries, "Law in the Time of Covid-19," LibGuide, April 20, 2020, https://guides.lib.uw.edu/law/covid19 (requires University of Washington Libraries login).

22. See Nicholas Alldred, "Classics for the Coronavirus," *Books We Read* (blog), March 11, 2020, https://sites.rutgers.edu/books-we-read/classics-for-the-coronavirus/; and Saint Leo University, "Recharge with Reading," LibGuide, accessed November 1, 2021, https://slulibrary.saintleo.edu/recharge.

23. Olivia B. Waxman, "Professors Are Crowdsourcing a #CoronavirusSyllabus. Here's the History They Think Should Be Used to Teach This Moment," *Time*, March 27, 2020, https://time.com/5808838/coronavirus-syllabus-history/.

24. Centers for Disease Control and Prevention, "History of the 1918 Flu Pandemic," last reviewed March 21, 2018, https://www.cdc.gov/flu/pandemic-resources/1918-commemoration/1918-pandemic-history.htm.
25. Leslie E. Gerwin, "Flu Season and Fiction: What *Downton Abbey* and *Contagion* Tell Us about Facing Reality," HuffPost, May 8, 2012, https://www.huffpost.com/entry/flu-season_b_1332409.
26. Springshare, LibGuides Community, https://community.libguides.com/.
27. Bibi Alajmi, "When the Nation Is in Crisis: Libraries Respond," *Library Management* 37, no. 8/9 (2016): 465–81.
28. See the following: University of West Florida University Libraries, "A Scholar's Guide to Pandemics," LibGuide, last updated May 28, 2020, https://libguides.uwf.edu/c.php?g=1015500&p=7356720; Worcester Polytechnic Institute, Gordon Library, "Pandemics and Intellectual Discourse: Art, Literature and Film," LibGuide, accessed September 14, 2021, https://libguides.wpi.edu/c.php?g=1038343&p=7572658; Claremont Colleges Library, "Pandemics and Epidemics: A Topic Resource Guide," LibGuide, last updated August 4, 2022, https://libguides.libraries.claremont.edu/pandemics; Menlo College, "Coronavirus Racism," in "Diversity, Equity, and Inclusion at Bowman Library, Menlo College," LibGuide, accessed September 15, 2021, https://menlocollege.libguides.com/c.php?g=1009931&p=7415257.
29. Benjamin Bell, University of West Florida University Libraries, e-mail to author, October 27, 2021; Paige Neumann, Lori Ostapowicz-Critz, Phil Waterman, and Karen Coghlan, Worcester Polytechnic Institute Library, e-mail to author, October 26, 2021; Randi Proescholdt, Tricia Soto, Valeria Molteni, Dr. Jodi Austin, Menlo College Library, e-mail to author, October 28, 2021; Adam Rosenkranz, Claremont Colleges Library, e-mail to author, October 28, 2021.
30. Bell, e-mail to author; Neumann et al., e-mail to author; Proescholdt et al., e-mail to author; Rosenkranz, e-mail to author.
31. Sanches, Antunes, and Lopes, "Improving Information Literacy."
32. Shaw, Chandler Boston College, e-mail to author, November 4, 2021.
33. Michelle Hart and Elena Nicolaou, "Authors Get Real about Going on a Book Tour …from Their Living Rooms," Oprah Daily, September 3, 2020, https://www.oprahdaily.com/entertainment/a33902384/authors-virtual-book-tour-experience/.
34. Pauline Dewan, "Reading Matters in the Academic Library: Taking the Lead from Public Librarians," *Reference and User Services Quarterly* 52, no. 4 (2013): 314.
35. New York University School of Medicine, Literature Arts Medicine Database: LitMed, accessed September 14, 2021, https://medhum.med.nyu.edu.
36. Amy Watson, "Penetration of Print Book Consumption in the U.S. 2019, by Age Group," Statista, September 28, 2020, https://www.statista.com/statistics/299794/printed-book-reading-population-in-the-us-by-age/ (page content changed).
37. Yvonne Kim. "Madison College to Welcome Ibram Kendi, Author of 'How to Be an Antiracist,'" *The Cap Times*, Madison, October 28, 2020, https://captimes.com/news/local/education/madison-college-to-welcome-ibram-kendi-author-of-how-to-be-an-antiracist/article_b7b1b0eb-e0a3-5e8b-b75b-602433b8c2d6.html#tracking-source=home-top-story-1
38. University of Maryland Libraries, "Interdisciplinary Dialogue Presents Tale of Two Pandemics: Illuminating Structural Racism and COVID," recorded November 18, 2020, YouTube video, 1:26:46, https://www.youtube.com/watch?v=XpAFzjN6pvo.
39. Linda Wang, "Pandemic Book Club Entering a Timeless World," University of California, Santa Barbara, Humanities and Fine Arts, October 28, 2020, https://www.hfa.ucsb.edu/news-entries/2020/10/28/the-pandemic-book-club-entering-a-timeless-world.
40. Lindsey Simon, "Library Book Clubs Go Virtual during Pandemic," I Love Libraries, American Library Association, May 18, 2020, https://www.ilovelibraries.org/article/library-book-clubs-go-virtual-during-pandemic.
41. American Historical Association, "AHA Issues Statement Regarding Historians during COVID-19," April 3, 2020, https://www.historians.org/news-and-advocacy/aha-advocacy/aha-statement-regarding-historians-and-covid-19-(april-2020).
42. Ciara O'Rourke, "George Washington Mandated Revolutionary War Troops Be Inoculated against Smallpox," Poynter, August 3, 2021, https://www.poynter.org/fact-checking/2021/george-washington-mandated-revolutionary-war-troops-be-inoculated-against-smallpox/.

43. Jessica S. Hower, "'All Good Stories': Historical Fiction in Pedagogy, Theory, and Scholarship," *Rethinking History* 23, no. 1 (2019): 78–125.
44. Anna Diamond, "Using Historical Fiction to Connect to Past and Present," *Atlantic*, February 21, 2017, https://www.theatlantic.com/education/archive/2017/02/using-historical-fiction-to-connect-past-and-present/516543/.
45. Charity Anderson, "'We Went through a Pandemic Together': Strategies for Facilitating Transformative Learning among Nontraditional Adult Learners during a Crisis," *Journal of Transformative Learning* 8, no. 1 (2021): 113.
46. Konstantina Martzoukou defines *infodemic* as the crisis brought on by the unrelenting amount of misinformation spread on social media during the COVID-19 pandemic. See Konstantina Martzoukou, "Academic Libraries in COVID-19: A Renewed Mission for Digital Literacy," *Library Management* 42, no. 4/5 (2021): 266–76.
47. Lewis Bernstein Namier. *Conflicts* (London: Macmillan, 1942).

Bibliography

Alajmi, Bibi. "When the Nation Is in Crisis: Libraries Respond." *Library Management* 37, no. 8/9 (2016): 465–81.

Albertine, Susan, Nancy Alfred Persily, and Richard Riegelman. "Back to the Pump Handle: Public Health and the Future of Undergraduate Education." *Liberal Education* 93, no. 4 (2007): 32–39.

Alldred, Nicholas. "Classics for the Coronavirus." *Books We Read* (blog), Rutgers University Libraries, March 11, 2020. https://sites.rutgers.edu/books-we-read/classics-for-the-coronavirus/.

American Historical Association. "AHA Issues Statement Regarding Historians during COVID-19." April 3, 2020. https://www.historians.org/news-and-advocacy/aha-advocacy/aha-statement-regarding-historians-and-covid-19-(april-2020).

American Library Association. *2021 State of America's Libraries: Special Report: COVID-19*. Chicago: American Library Association, April 2, 2021. https://www.ala.org/news/sites/ala.org.news/files/content/State-of-Americas-Libraries-Report-2021.pdf.

Anderson, Charity. "'We Went through a Pandemic Together': Strategies for Facilitating Transformative Learning among Nontraditional Adult Learners during a Crisis." *Journal of Transformative Learning* 8, no. 1 (2021): 110–14.

Association of College and Research Libraries. *Framework for Information Literacy for Higher Education*. Chicago: Association of College and Research Libraries 2016. https://www.ala.org/acrl/sites/ala.org.acrl/files/content/issues/infolit/framework1.pdf.

Bureau of Labor Statistics. "American Time Use Survey—May to December 2019 and 2020 Results." News release, July 21, 2021. https://www.bls.gov/news.release/pdf/atus.pdf

Centers for Disease Control and Prevention. "History of the 1918 Flu Pandemic." Last reviewed March 21, 2018. https://www.cdc.gov/flu/pandemic-resources/1918-commemoration/1918-pandemic-history.htm.

Claremont Colleges Library. "Pandemics and Epidemics: A Topic and Resource Guide." LibGuide. Last updated August 4, 2022. https://libguides.libraries.claremont.edu/pandemics.

Dewan, Pauline. "Reading Matters in the Academic Library: Taking the Lead from Public Librarians." *Reference and User Services Quarterly* 52, no. 4 (2013): 309–19.

Diamond, Anna. "Using Historical Fiction to Connect to Past and Present." *Atlantic*, February 21, 2017. https://www.theatlantic.com/education/archive/2017/02/using-historical-fiction-to-connect-past-and-present/516543/.

Gaiman, Neil. "Why Our Future Depends on Libraries, Reading and Daydreaming." *Guardian*, October 15, 2013. https://www.theguardian.com/books/2013/oct/15/neil-gaiman-future-libraries-reading-daydreaming.

Gammerman, Ellen. "Readers Binge on Books about Pandemics (Really); From Stephen King to Emily St. John Mandel, Here Are Five Books to Help You Lean into Coronavirus Fears." Wall Street Journal, Eastern edition, March 11, 2020. http://libproxy.csun.edu/login?url=https:www/proquest.com/newspapers/readers-binge-on-books-about-pandemics-really/docview/2375958946/se-2 (accessed December 17, 2022).

Gerwin, Leslie E. "Flu Season and Fiction: What *Downton Abbey* and *Contagion* Tell Us about Facing Reality." HuffPost, May 8, 2012. https://www.huffpost.com/entry/flu-season_b_1332409.

Hart, Michelle, and Elena Nicolaou. "Authors Get Real about Going on a Book Tour …from Their Living Rooms." Oprah Daily, September 3, 2020. https://www.oprahdaily.com/entertainment/a33902384/authors-virtual-book-tour-experience.

Hawkins, Anne Hunsaker, and Marilyn Chandler McEntyre. *Teaching Literature and Medicine*. New York: Modern Language Association, 2000.

Houser, Heather. "The COVID-19 'Infowhelm.'" *New York Review of Books*, May 6, 2020. https://www.nybooks.com/daily/2020/05/06/the-covid-19-infowhelm/.

Hower, Jessica S. "'All Good Stories': Historical Fiction in Pedagogy, Theory, and Scholarship." *Rethinking History* 23, no. 1 (2019): 78–125.

Iowa City UNESCO City of Literature. "100 Days of Decameron." 2020. Accessed September 14, 2021. https://www.iowacityofliterature.org/decameron/ (page discontinued).

Jensen, Kelly. "Americans Read Nearly 25% More Last Year, According to New Research." Book Riot, July 30, 2021. https://bookriot.com/american-pandemic-reading-habits/.

Jones, Anne Hudson. "Why Teach Literature and Medicine? Answers from Three Decades." In *New Directions in Literature and Medicine Studies*, edited by Stephanie M. Hilger, 31–48. London: Palgrave Macmillan, 2017.

Keen, Suzanne. *Empathy and the Novel*. New York: Oxford University Press, 2007.

Kim, Yvonne. "Madison College to Welcome Ibram Kendi, Author of 'How to Be an Antiracist.'" *The Cap Times*, October 28, 2020. https://captimes.com/news/local/education/madison-college-to-welcome-ibram-kendi-author-of-how-to-be-an-antiracist/article_b7b1b0eb-e0a3-5e8b-b75b-602433b8c2d6.html#tracking-source=home-top-story-1.

Mallan, Kerry. "Dystopian Fiction for Young People: Instructive Tales of Resilience." *Psychoanalytic Inquiry* 37, no.1 (2017): 16–24. https://doi.org/10.1080/07351690.2017.1250586.

Martzoukou, Konstantina. "Academic Libraries in COVID-19: A Renewed Mission for Digital Literacy." *Library Management* 42, no. 4/5 (2021): 266–76.

Menlo College Library. "Coronavirus Racism." In "Diversity, Equity, and Inclusion at Bowman Library, Menlo College." LibGuide. Accessed September 15, 2021. https://menlocollege.libguides.com/c.php?g=1009931&p=7415257.

Merry, Stephanie, and Steven Johnson. "What the Country Is Reading during the Pandemic: Dystopias, Social Justice and Steamy Romance." *Washington Post*, September 2, 2020. https://www.washingtonpost.com/entertainment/books/2020-book-trends/2020/09/02/6a835caa-e863-11ea-bc79-834454439a44_story.html.

Namier, Lewis Bernstein. *Conflicts: Studies in Contemporary History*. London: Macmillan, 1942.

New York University School of Medicine. LitMed: Literature Arts Medicine Database. Accessed September 14, 2021. https://medhum.med.nyu.edu.

O'Rourke, Ciara. "George Washington Mandated Revolutionary War Troops Be Inoculated against Smallpox." Poynter, August 3, 2021. https://www.poynter.org/fact-checking/2021/george-washington-mandated-revolutionary-war-troops-be-inoculated-against-smallpox/.

Rababah, Jehad A., Mohammed M. Al-Hammouri, Barbara L. Drew, and Mohammed Aldalaykeh. "Health Literacy: Exploring Disparities among College Students." *BMC Public Health* 19 (2019): article 1401. https://doi.org/10.1186/s12889-019-7781-2.

Saint Leo University. "Recharge with Reading." LibGuide. Accessed on November 1, 2021. https://slulibrary.saintleo.edu/recharge.

Sanches, Tatiana, Maria da Luz Antunes, and Carlos Lopes. "Improving Information Literacy in Higher Education in an Unorthodox Way: The Literature Potential for ACRL Framework Application." Presentation, International Scientific Conference of Librarians, Western Balkan Information and Media Literacy Conference 2020, and 9th International Summit of the Book, Bihac, Bosnia- Herzegovina, December 9-10, 2020. Accessed September 14, 2021. https://repositorio.ul.pt/bitstream/10451/47181/1/Sanches_Antunes_Lopes_Improving_information_literacy_in_higher_education.pdf.

Saxon, Jamie. "Making Meaning of the Pandemic 'through the Lens of Literature.'" Princeton University, Office of Communications, May 15, 2020. https://www.princeton.edu/news/2020/05/15/making-meaning-pandemic-through-lens-literature.

Shwetz, Katherine. "Apocalyptic Fiction Helps Us Deal with the Anxiety of the Coronavirus Pandemic." Conversation, March 18, 2020. https://theconversation.com/apocolyptic-fiction-helps-us-deal-with-the-anxiety-ot-the-coronavirus-pandemic-133682.

Simon, Lindsey. "Library Book Clubs Go Virtual during Pandemic." I Love Libraries, American Library Association, May 18, 2020. https://www.ilovelibraries.org/article/library-book-clubs-go-virtual-during-pandemic.

Springshare. LibGuides Community. https://community.libguides.com/.

Ulaby, Neda "What Fictional Pandemics Can Teach Us about Real-World Survival." *All Things Considered*, NPR, February 10, 2020. https://www.kcrw.com/news/shows/all-things-considered/npr-story/803458265.

University of Maryland Libraries. "Interdisciplinary Dialogue Presents Tale of Two Pandemics: Illuminating Structural Racism and COVID." Recorded November 18, 2020. YouTube video, 1:26:46. https://www.youtube.com/watch?v=XpAFzjN6pvo.

University of Washington Libraries. "Law in the Time of Covid-19." LibGuide. April 20, 2020, https://guides.lib.uw.edu/law/covid19 (requires University of Washington Libraries login).

University of West Florida University Libraries. "A Scholar's Guide to Pandemics." LibGuide. Last updated May 28, 2020. https://libguides.uwf.edu/c.php?g=1015500&p=7356720.

VanArendonk, Kathryn. "Why Is Pandemic Fiction So Comforting Right Now?" *Vulture*, March 6, 2020. https://www.vulture.com/2020/03/contagion-coronavirus-pandemic-fiction.html.

Wang, Linda. "Pandemic Book Club Entering a Timeless World." University of California, Santa Barbara, Humanities and Fine Arts, October 29, 2020. https://www.hfa.ucsb.edu/news-entries/2020/10/28/the-pandemic-book-club-entering-a-timeless-world.

Watson, Amy. "Penetration of Print Book Consumption in the U.S. 2019, by Age Group." Statista. September 28, 2020. https://www.statista.com/statistics/299794/printed-book-reading-population-in-the-us-by-age/ (page content changed).

Waxman, Olivia B. "Professors Are Crowdsourcing a #CoronavirusSyllabus. Here's the History They Think Should Be Used to Teach This Moment." *Time*, March 27, 2020. https://time.com/5808838/coronavirus-syllabus-history/.

Worcester Polytechnic Institute, Gordon Library. "Pandemics and Intellectual Discourse: Art, Literature, and Film." LibGuide. Accessed September 14, 2021. https://libguides.wpi.edu/c.php?g=1038343&p=7572658.

Wright, Lawrence. "Five Best: Lawrence Wright on Pandemics in Fact and Fiction." *Wall Street Journal*, May 15, 2020, https://www.wsj.com/articles/five-best-lawrence-wright-on-pandemics-in-fact-and-fiction-11589550822.

Wuthnow, Robert. *Be Very Afraid: The Cultural Response to Terror, Pandemics, Environmental Devastation, Nuclear Annihilation, and Other Threats*. Oxford: Oxford University Press, 2010.

CHAPTER 18

Quick and Precise
A Case Study of Flexibility and Strategy in the Time of COVID

Matthew Shaw, Michael Szajewski, and Suzanne Rice

> *The future invites and even requires innovation, and COVID-19 has emphasized the primacy of adaptability and responsiveness as characteristics of the effective academic library, which must increasingly become both quick and precise.*

Introduction

Disruption is often a catalyst for innovation and a springboard for creative approaches to immediate or emerging problems. The COVID-19 pandemic was one such catalyst at Ball State University Libraries. Ball State University is a public research university with an FTE of nearly 15,000 undergraduate and 3,200 graduate students and is designated a doctoral university: higher research. The University Libraries consists of Bracken Library, the main library, and three branch libraries: Architecture, Foundational Sciences, and Health. The libraries are an essential collaborator in student and faculty success and community engagement; they have, and will continue to, serve the university throughout the pandemic crisis.

    In March 2020, Ball State University pivoted to remote learning, and the University Libraries closed their physical spaces to the public. While the libraries were well positioned to provide virtual support through access to existing electronic collections, reference, instruction, and consultative services, the pandemic required fresh approaches to access, engagement, planning, communication, community programming, responsive staffing models, and work planning to continue achieving the libraries' mission, sustain advancement of strategic directions, and highlight the vitality and resilience of the academic library in a time of crisis.

This chapter will present several aspects of the libraries' COVID-19 response, emphasizing lessons learned and replicable strategies for approaching transformative moments from an administrative perspective. It also acknowledges the tension of uncertainties in an evolving situation and the necessity for agility and iterative responsiveness and planning throughout the ongoing crisis. Approaches cannot necessarily be characterized as crisis management as much as crisis responsiveness. New information was constantly reshaping protocols and plans, and it was important to cultivate through communication and other strategies a tolerance for fluidity and flexibility for both library personnel and users. The chapter examines both the period of physical closing and the challenges of reopening and operating during a pandemic.

Studies in disaster and crisis management in higher education institutions reveal a significant lack of organizational preparedness for global pandemics.[1] The scale and impact of the COVID-19 pandemic, unprecedented in this generation, necessitated new and inclusive approaches to planning and organizational communication. Universities learned new strategies for ensuring agility and responsiveness in a rapidly evolving environment. Fundamental to the Ball State University Libraries' effective response planning was the overarching work of campus task forces and communication teams, in which the libraries participated, to develop plans for remote operations and eventual reopening. In April 2020, the university created a new Task Force on the University's Strategic Transition (TRUST), whose charge was to strategically guide and coordinate the university's safe transition from the spring COVID crisis management response to a successful and sustainable operating environment. TRUST identified issues and made recommendations concerning a wide range of operational issues. Under the direction of the chief strategy officer, TRUST and its broad administrative membership consulted with external agencies and institutions to ensure contingency plans were consistent with emerging best practices, scientific research, and government directives. The broad representation in the task force provided a channel to identify critical issues, ensured the efficacy of proposed plans, and facilitated rapid coordination and consistent communication and actions across campus.

For the libraries, TRUST participation provided a critical channel throughout, from the early campus lockdown to the full reopening more than a year later, to share issues and participate in operational planning, solutions, and implementation. Direct contact with offices and individuals across campus aided in the collection and dissemination of information and rapid responses to meet operational needs on many levels even during the rapidly evolving situations of the pandemic crisis periods. Examples include sourcing and procurement of PPE, health and safety procedures, room occupancies and de-densification plans, communications, emergency response protocols, teleworking, and technical support, to name but a few. Communication to the campus was multichanneled with Ball State's coronavirus website (www.bsu.edu/coronavirus) providing the most up-to-date aggregation of publication of institutional information.

In early March 2020, as the pandemic took hold, the campus continued to function normally, but with what would become common safety protocols: social distancing, moving to online meetings, and enhanced cleaning. Consistent with guidance from the University Human Resources Services, the libraries immediately offered telework options to the following categories of employees: (1) vulnerable populations as defined by the Centers for Disease Control and Prevention (CDC); (2) those whose work-area adjacency prevented physical distancing; and (3) those with serious child- or elder-care challenges. The announcement of the campus pivot to remote operations came quickly in response to the countywide Disaster Emergency Declaration.[2] All university classes were migrated to virtual instruction beginning March 16, and the facilities of the libraries closed on March 21, 2020. University Libraries provided brief appointments to its users to retrieve physical materials and clear out graduate carrels and for staff to take essential items from workspaces that were needed to engage in effective telework and facilitate service and access continuity for campus constituents.

Nearly 90 percent of the libraries' staff was assigned to telework, with only a small cadre of personnel scheduled in the main library building to support essential services, such as scanning and curbside pickup. Periodic extensions of the original statewide Stay at Home executive order from Indiana Governor Eric Holcomb originally issued on March 23, 2020 and the subsequent development of a statewide Roadmap to Reopen executive order on May 1 ultimately led to a closure of the libraries to the general public through mid-August 2020.[3]

The majority of library professionals and staff were able to remotely continue work, which was highly central to their core job duties. However, the position functions and job duties of other employees, which mainly focused on services or workflows specific to an in-person environment necessitated alternative work assignments. The University Libraries leadership developed a project for staff to create typed-text transcriptions of historically and culturally significant archival resources in the Digital Media Repository, the libraries' repository of over 250,000 cultural heritage and local history items. Examples include nineteenth-century diaries, guest lectures by prominent architects dating from the 1970s to 1990s, archived public radio programs, and handwritten World War II correspondence.

Training staff to create transcript documents was generally a relatively straightforward process. Archives and Special Collections and Metadata and Digital Initiatives staff were already experienced in both creating transcripts and training students in transcription, and training documentation was in place to prepare libraries staff to conduct this work. However, others proved to be less proficient in the activity. Despite a spectrum of transcription skill levels among staff, nearly 500 archival items were transcribed during this time. Subsequent to ongoing quality control review, the addition of these transcripts to the repository will vastly improve discovery and access to these high-value digital collections for users and researchers.

Other barriers to telework included technology-related challenges that ultimately complicated supervision and professional engagement for some. Neither the libraries nor the university was fully equipped to provide staff with 1:1 computing access, and some staff with outmoded laptops lacked peripheral devices such as webcams and microphones, which hindered participation in online meetings, virtual professional conferences, and delivery of virtual instruction and consultative services. Others were without high-speed broadband internet at their homes. Fortunately, centralized Information Technology provided personal Wi-Fi hot spots and updated laptops for some library staff. The libraries continues to assess and investigate "next-time" approaches to minimize such disruptions for future events necessitating remote work. Remote work continued to be an important part of COVID-19 spread mitigation during the gradual reentry of library staff in the summer of 2020. Many staff were assigned remote/in-person rotations to maintain low density staffing in library work and service spaces. COVID-19-related telework arrangements did not completely expire until August 2021.

Responsive Service, Programming, and Resource Access Models

The rapid evolution of the pandemic demanded fluid and flexible approaches in all of these important areas. Ultimately, the University Libraries were ideally equipped to provide service, programming, and resource access continuity during the lockdown period. The libraries had mature virtual reference, research, and instructional services, digital repository and publishing platforms, and a breadth of electronic collections adequate to an R2 institution along with well-developed discovery solutions.

- **Course reserves.** Library staff concentrated efforts to quickly work with faculty in transitioning to online course reserves, open access or other alternatives such as Kanopy streaming video services, that could be seamlessly accessed by students using the Canvas course management system. The libraries developed workshops and online tutorials to guide faculty through the process of creating reading lists utilizing Leganto, a newly acquired course reserves platform that enabled the libraries' ability to integrate online course reserves into the Canvas environment.
- **Expanding access to online databases.** Many publishers generously responded to the sudden shift to remote teaching and learning by offering libraries temporary free access to their catalog of e-books, core collections, databases, and other research resources. Library personnel aggressively searched for these opportunities, updated access information, and kept faculty and students informed.
- **Expanding due dates and suspending fines.** The libraries proactively provided extended due dates for physical loans and suspended fines during the closure.
- **Ask-a-Librarian.** While a variety of forms of online research assistance were established long before the pandemic, teleworking librarians continued to provide research assistance via chat, e-mail, text, and videoconferencing, adding new communication platforms as needed. Individual online research consultations also saw increased usage.
- **Curbside pickup.** When the libraries closed their doors to the public, a curbside pickup/drop-off service was established enabling library personnel to conveniently provide touchless delivery and return of materials and digital equipment; initially

offered to faculty and graduate students, it was expanded to the entire campus and community members as it became apparent the closure would be for an extended period.

- **Interlibrary loan.** While not unique, the capacity to provide online ILL services and document delivery for locally held materials even during the campus closure was significant both in acquiring materials for students and faculty and in providing materials to other libraries. This was safely done by limiting on-site work to just a few staff members working in distanced silos, utilizing PPE, quarantining received materials, and engaging in frequent cleaning and sanitizing.
- **Research guides.** Research guides (LibGuides) tailored to specific courses and even specific course assignments increased in popularity for both undergraduate and graduate courses. Emphasis shifted to highlight resources available online, including further assistance via mini-tutorials and expanding staffing for reaching subject specialists via the embedded live chat widgets.

Available Web-Based Resources

Access to web-based resources was critical to delivering teaching, learning, and research support throughout the remote-access period. Fortunately, emphasis on 24/7/365 access to scholarly resources and the development of digitization initiatives began at the University Libraries in the early 2000s. Like many peer institutions, the Ball State University Libraries aggressively converted print subscriptions to online access, incrementally increased e-book purchasing, and invested heavily in the technologies, expertise, and platforms to advance digital open access publishing and repositories. Examples include access to:

- 297 electronic databases, over 147,000 unique electronic journals, and more than 380,000 e-books
- over 250,000 primary source materials in the Digital Media Repository, a cultural heritage repository and digital archive
- over 9,000 works of student and faculty scholarship in Cardinal Scholar, a DSpace-powered institutional repository

In recent years, the libraries have also expanded the portfolio of digital publishing and scholarship tools, representing a significant expansion of services, including

- Omeka digital exhibit–building platform, coupled with a Reclaim Hosting–based digital scholarship publishing solution offered via https://digitalresearch.bsu.edu.
- web-archiving solution powered by the Internet Archive used to preserve local and institutional web pages of historical and cultural significance.
- ArcGIS online digital mapmaking software, which is widely used across campus to support digital scholarship
- Open Journal Systems platform, which University Libraries use to publish nine open access journals edited by campus community members.

The gamut of electronic collections and services, as well as locally digitized cultural heritage and scholarly resources, provided researchers with much-needed access to research and archival materials during the remote operations period. This access, coupled with a strengthening reputation as a campus leader in digital research, scholarship, and creative solutions, effectively positioned the libraries to be seen as an intuitive collaborative partner to identify and deliver new, innovative support for the production and dissemination of research and creative work in an exclusively digital environment.

Student Symposium

During the 2020–2021 academic year, the libraries were asked to provide digital solutions to replicate in-person events canceled due to the pandemic, including: face-to-face symposia, conferences, and other research-oriented programming. One such event was the Ball State Student Symposium, organized annually since the 1990s. The event has given university students the opportunity to creatively visualize, present, and discuss their research to an audience of peers and faculty judges.

The event was migrated online in 2021, and symposium organizers in Sponsored Projects Administration collaborated with the University Libraries' Office of Digital Research and Publishing to use the Omeka platform to support the development of an online, asynchronous symposium, organizing content on a single site. Over 100 graduate and undergraduate students shared research as part of this online event, presenting their scholarship in a wide range of formats, including videos, interactive maps, digital research posters, infographics, and text. This online incarnation of the Student Symposium also provided an invaluable opportunity for students to share dynamic, interactive research with a global audience and to visually demonstrate their research and scholarship skills to potential future employers and graduate programs. While the university aims to return to holding such events on campus beyond 2021, event organizers remain committed to incorporate Omeka as a digital complement to the in-person symposium in the future.

Virtual Instruction and Workshops

In the wake of the pandemic, many academic libraries were able to quickly leverage and scale staff digital proficiencies to improve student engagement across many disciplines using new and innovative online delivery tools and methods for instruction. At Murray State University, librarians leveraged the Canvas Commons environment to deliver remote access to point-of-need information literacy and library instruction modules.[4] An Indiana University case study detailed the adaptive use of the Net.Create, an active learning digital scholarship network analysis tool, to effectively accommodate virtual engagement between students learning from home during COVID-19.[5] A University of Calgary case study highlighted heightened emphasis on the creation of narrated screen capture video tutorials to complement virtual instruction.[6]

Prior to COVID-19, the University Libraries provided information literacy and other forms of instruction in person, remotely, synchronously, or asynchronously to meet the needs of faculty and course delivery modes. However, in keeping with general on-campus academic course delivery methods, in-person library instruction was most common. Ongoing experience with virtual delivery systems greatly aided the libraries in making a very fast transition to virtual instruction when the campus moved to all-online courses, and libraries instruction professionals worked one-on-one with faculty to customize a virtual delivery approach best meeting classroom needs. This included:

- prerecorded videos and presentations
- live virtual sessions
- topic- or course-specific mini-tutorials, resource guides, and tool kits that could be embedded into a range of presentations or integrated into Canvas pages
- small-group sessions combining traditional instruction with research consultations

Early efforts to standardize instruction approaches and tools across library units proved unsuitable. Academic courses were offered through a variety of formats during the time period, and librarians also had proficiencies in a wide variety of tools and platforms for creating content with limited access to on-campus video production and broadcast services through University Media Services. As a result, University Libraries identified areas and opportunities for future growth and development, including:

- greater investment in video production hardware and studio space within the library to support prerecording and live delivery of virtual, video-based instruction
- additional skill development in the use of and access to screencasting and video editing software among library staff

Emphasis on Virtual Chat/Virtual Reference

During 2020 and 2021, University Libraries also leveraged existing experience with video conferencing, e-mail, and text-based chat to provide all-online consultations to researchers. Libraries staff increased the visibility of service access points through prominent placement on libraries web pages and research guides. Librarians further emphasized the availability of these contact points through presentations and outreach to faculty, students, and other campus and community collaborators.

Streaming Media Review

The University Libraries' Copyright and Scholarly Communications Office collaborates with University Media Services to manage a streaming media request approval and delivery workflow whereby faculty request access to copyrighted video and audio to incorporate in face-to-face and online classroom environments. As faculty faced the daunting task of redeveloping in-person instruction for remote and hybrid online learning environments, the office provided expanded collaborative and consultative services. In the year prior to the outbreak of COVID-19, the office fielded just over four streaming media requests per month. In the year following the outbreak, this figure increased to just over thirty requests per month.

Maintaining Momentum toward Key Strategic Priorities

The University Libraries launched a Strategic Alignment Plan in 2019 focused on student and faculty success, community engagement, and institutional and inclusive excellence.[7] COVID-19 delayed some important initiatives related to physical spaces in library facilities and created barriers for many types of community engagement and support. However, library professionals adapted programming and discovered new audiences. Examples include those discussed below.

Community Programs

At the University Libraries, as in many academic libraries, the importance of community outreach and events that are open to the public are part of the culture of the institution. Central to many academic libraries' mission is creating a culture of learning and curiosity as well as community. Scholars like LaFlamme have highlighted the immense value of libraries in generating social capital to empower reciprocal community building.[8] In the years preceding the COVID-19 pandemic, the libraries were highly successful in engaging with local audiences of learners through in-person, off-campus community education programs that focused on local history and cultural heritage. During the COVID-19 pandemic, University Libraries worked closely with community partners including the Muncie Public Library, Delaware County Historical Society, and Minnetrista Cultural Center to deliver these programs in a synchronous, online environment. These virtual programs were dynamic, emphasizing local history stories through primary sources and engaging community members in discussion of shared history and culture. During the 2020–2021 academic year, these programs averaged twenty-eight attendees per session, a marked increased over prior in-person-only participation.

The online programs removed access barriers for several unique population sectors, expanding inclusive access to our programs as a means of diversifying participation and engagement. Interested community members whose schedules, home care responsibilities, or travel and mobility limitations would not allow travel to physical community venues were easily able to engage and participate in these online programs from home. Furthermore, individuals living outside of the immediate geographic vicinity could easily participate. Libraries personnel were also able to engage with audiences beyond Delaware County by developing virtual community education programming in collaboration with the Peru, Indiana, and Carmel, Indiana, public library systems. This emphasis on inclusivity was especially critical during COVID-19 as the necessary restrictions required to slow the virus spread prevented many from accessing physical community spaces and supportive community networks, leaving many to face a stark sense of isolation.

Digital Scholarship Workshops

The pandemic also significantly impacted the delivery of campus-focused research workshops and programs. During the 2019–2020 academic year, University Libraries planned a new digital scholarship workshop series to launch during the fall 2020 semester. In addition, the libraries' GIS Research and Map Collection coalesced its existing workshops into a more streamlined, sequenced GIS workshop series. Between these two series, thirteen hour-long workshops were planned.

Though the workshops were originally conceived as in-person programs, the University Libraries pivoted to deliver all thirteen of these workshops in a synchronous, online environment in response to COVID-19. Recordings were made of workshop sessions and disseminated to interested parties who were not available to attend synchronously. These workshops were attended by 101 faculty, staff, and students during the fall 2020 semester, a total well outpacing expectations for the initial offering of these series. The online format widely expanded the base of potential participants to include

- students in online programs living outside of Muncie
- individuals whose schedules did not conveniently allow them to be present at Bracken Library during the scheduled workshop time
- faculty who might typically work off campus during a portion of the week

Strong attendance and engagement with these workshops encouraged University Libraries to continue to use the synchronous, online format in 2021, even as campus policies and protocols allowed for in-person gatherings at pre-pandemic capacities.

Reopening Plan Development

Reopening plans for the libraries across the United States were iterative and based on a multitude of factors. State and county governments, government and health authority guidelines, and prevailing best practices in library operations all played a role in the decision-making process. For this institution in particular, the TRUST committee set the guidelines, and reentry began in July 2020, as acrylic barriers were installed in high-traffic service and reception areas and sufficient PPE became available. On-site staffing levels began to gradually increase, and the libraries, including branches, began offering collection access and services to the Ball State community of students, faculty, and staff Monday through Friday, 8 a.m. to 5 p.m.

From August 2 to August 15, the libraries opened more generally to the public, including community users, with Bracken Library further operating during evening and weekend hours. The libraries resumed regular hours of operation on August 16, just prior to the beginning of fall semester. During the 2020–2021 academic year, certain smaller public services spaces with enclosed reading rooms or service areas remained accessible by appointment only. These included units such as Archives and Special Collections, the Seager Archives of the Built Environment, and the GIS Research and Map Collections.

To encourage compliance with physical distancing and room capacity limitations, furniture was reconfigured throughout the libraries, and public computer access was reduced through removal from service of alternating machines throughout the buildings. Masks were required to be worn at all times, except in designated eating areas.

Every effort was made to engage users in the work of the Ball State community to mitigate spread of the virus. Signage was ubiquitous. Table tents were designed for study tables, and room capacity signs were placed in each area and on study room doors. Library staff in public services areas were trained in strategies to bring users into compliance through friendly conversations and appeals to university and community values rather than direct, decontextualized enforcement. However, compliance rates seemed to decrease over the course of the semester, and students and other users were not always receptive to continual reminders, requiring administrative action, which generally involved conversations with a user conducted by senior managers or the dean. In no case was any user ultimately banned from the libraries.

Staff and student assistants were also responsible for rigorous cleaning activities, sanitizing study tables, computer keyboards and peripherals, and personal workstations.

Following up-to-date research from the Reopening archives, libraries and museums (REALM) project sponsored by the Institute of Museum and Library Services, OCLC, and Battelle, the libraries developed quarantine protocols for circulating materials and established low-contact workflows for handling items. Circulating digital equipment was carefully sanitized after each return. Virtual meetings of staff members continued, and the libraries suspended staff social gatherings and use of a lounge area in Bracken Library for breaks and meals. Through these efforts, the libraries successfully avoided any hot spots or concentrated outbreaks in library facilities as determined by university contact tracers.

Considering the Future

COVID-19 has significantly altered the access, service, and business models of the academic library, and questions remain concerning the long-term impacts on user behaviors and expectations. At Ball State, the University Libraries continue service approaches such as curbside pickup and synchronous/asynchronous delivery of online programming to good effect. However, it is unclear if a lagging gate count is the effect of COVID or the availability of more modern and appealing study and collaboration spaces in several new academic buildings and residence halls on the Ball State campus.

Ultimately, nationwide lockdowns resulting in restricted access to public spaces on campuses were disruptive to the central "third place" value proposition narrative carefully cultivated and communicated by academic libraries, which have almost universally invested in the transformation of library spaces to promote collaboration, social learning, technology access, and focused study. Campus *hubs, living rooms,* and *commons* defined by gathering and often measured by attendance metrics became vacant. Even after reopening, safety protocols such as physical distancing and room capacity limits created new barriers for students working in groups and new challenges for library staff, who assumed the uncomfortable role of policy compliance promotion—a strange shift from the customer service ethos of the pre-COVID library environment.

The disruptions of COVID also brought into sharp focus the vulnerabilities of collection access and reliance on resource sharing for academic libraries. While physical materials were still available for pickup, this is useful only to local users with transportation who successfully navigate discovery layer functionality. Further, interlibrary loan became impossible as libraries around the world shut down and statewide and interstate courier systems suspended operations. Support levels have only recently returned to pre-COVID levels as more and more states have reopened campuses, and libraries have increased staffing levels. These issues highlight the critical importance of achieving greater access to open access content, e-content with favorable licensing to allow e-book lending, and well-established controlled digital lending approaches.

The future invites and even requires innovation, and COVID-19 has emphasized the primacy of adaptability and responsiveness as characteristics of the effective academic library, which must increasingly become both quick and precise. All learning organizations recognize that assessment is essential to this process, and libraries must proactively investigate, understand, and implement strategies that directly and measurably impact student success, retention, and resilience and advance faculty research, publication, scholarship, and teaching excellence. On the other side of lockdowns, this must include development and refinement of new and expanded virtual services, access, environments, and expertise. Also, there is a need for thought work and planning around creation of more flexible public and workspaces easily adapted to accommodate the need for physical distancing, as we consider the likelihood of future public health crises.

Notes

1. Takako Izumi et al., "Managing and Responding to Pandemics in Higher Educational Institutions: Initial Learning from COVID-19," *International Journal of Disaster Resilience in the Built Environment* 12, no. 1 (2021): 51–66, https://doi.org/10.1108/IJDRBE-06-2020-0054.
2. Delaware County, Indiana, "Disaster Emergency Declaration 2020-02," March 20, 2020, https://www.co.delaware.in.us/egov/documents/1584746863_77816.pdf.
3. State of Indiana Executive Department, "Executive Order 20-08: Directive for Hoosiers to Stay at Home," State of Indiana official website, March 23, 2020, https://www.in.gov/gov/files/Executive_Order_20-08_Stay_at_Home.pdf; State of Indiana Executive Department, "Executive Order 20-26: Roadmap to Reopen Indiana for Hoosiers, Businesses, and State Government," State of Indiana official website, May 1, 2020, https://www.in.gov/gov/files/Executive%20Order%2020-26%20Roadmap%20to%20Reopen.pdf.
4. Katherine Farmer et al., "Using Canvas Commons to Transform Information Literacy Instruction," in *Handbook of Research on Library Response to the Covid-19 Pandemic*, ed. Barbara Holland (Hershey, PA: Information Science Reference, 2021), 231–47.
5. Kalani Craig et al., "Increasing Students' Social Engagement during COVID-19 with Net.Create: Collaborative Social Network Analysis to Map Historical Pandemics during a Pandemic," *Information and Learning Sciences* 121, no. 7/8 (2020): 533–47, https://doi.org/10.1108/ILS-04-2020-0105.
6. James E. Murphy et al., "Expanding Digital Academic Library and Archive Services at the University of Calgary in Response to the COVID-19 Pandemic," *IFLA Journal* 48, no. 1 (March 2022): 83–98, https://doi.org/10.1177/03400352211023067.
7. "Strategic Alignment Plan," Ball State University Libraries, accessed November 22, 2021, https://www.bsu.edu/-/media/www/departmentalcontent/library/new%20website%20pdfs/university%20libraries%20strategic%20alignment%20plan.pdf.

8. Katherine A. LaFlamme, " The Intersection of Community Engagement and Library Science," *Library Philosophy and Practice*, 2021, DigitalCommons@University of Nebraska–Lincoln, 5574, https://digitalcommons.unl.edu/libphilprac/5574.

Bibliography

Ball State University Libraries. "Strategic Alignment Plan (2019–2024)." Accessed November 22, 2021. https://www.bsu.edu/-/media/www/departmentalcontent/library/new%20website%20pdfs/university%20libraries%20strategic%20alignment%20plan.pdf.

Craig, Kalani, Megan Humburg, Joshua A. Danish, Maksymilian Szostalo, Cindy E. Hmelo-Silver, and Ann McCranie. "Increasing Students' Social Engagement during COVID-19 with Net.Create: Collaborative Social Network Analysis to Map Historical Pandemics during a Pandemic." *Information and Learning Sciences* 121, no. 7/8 (2020): 533–47. https://doi.org/10.1108/ILS-04-2020-0105.

Delaware County, Indiana. "Disaster Emergency Declaration 2020-02." March 20, 2020. https://www.co.delaware.in.us/egov/documents/1584746863_77816.pdf.

Farmer, Katherine, Jeff Henry, Dana Statton Thompson, Candace K. Vance, and Megan Wilson. "Using Canvas Commons to Transform Information Literacy Instruction." In *Handbook of Research on Library Response to the Covid-19 Pandemic*, edited by Barbara Holland, 231–47. Hershey, PA: Information Science Reference, 2021.

Izumi, Takako, Vibhas Sukhwani, Akhilesh Surjan, and Rajib Shaw. "Managing and Responding to Pandemics in Higher Educational Institutions: Initial Learning from COVID-19." *International Journal of Disaster Resilience in the Built Environment* 12, no. 1 (2021): 51–66. https://doi.org/10.1108/IJDRBE-06-2020-0054.

LaFlamme, Katherine A. "The Intersection of Community Engagement and Library Science." *Library Philosophy and Practice*, 2021. DigitalCommons@University of Nebraska–Lincoln, 5574. https://digitalcommons.unl.edu/libphilprac/5574.

Murphy, James E., Carla J. Lewis, Christena A. McKillop, and Marc Stoeckle. "Expanding Digital Academic Library and Archive Services at the University of Calgary in Response to the COVID-19 Pandemic." *IFLA Journal* 48, no. 1 (March 2022): 83–98. https://doi.org/10.1177/03400352211023067.

State of Indiana Executive Department. "Executive Order 20-08: Directive for Hoosiers to Stay at Home." State of Indiana official website. March 23, 2020. https://www.in.gov/gov/files/Executive_Order_20-08_Stay_at_Home.pdf.

———. "Executive Order 20-26: Roadmap to Reopen Indiana for Hoosiers, Businesses and State Government." State of Indiana official website. May 1, 2020. https://www.in.gov/gov/files/Executive%20Order%2020-26%20Roadmap%20to%20Reopen.pdf.

CHAPTER 19

Testimony and Tenacity
Rapid-Response Collecting the Pandemic

Sean D. Visintainer, April W. Feldman, Pamela Nett Kruger, and Christopher B. Livingston

---

> *Rapid-response COVID-collecting efforts by archivists have created research collections and opportunities for future scholars; provided a means for patrons to reflect on, interpret, and grieve their experiences; engaged communities at a time when everyone has been distanced from them; and given the team focus during uncertain and foreboding times.*

Introduction

Once the novel coronavirus made North American landfall in winter and spring of 2020, the lives of librarians and archivists of the California State University (CSU) were upended. First, rumors of campus and state shutdowns percolated through our workplaces, soon followed by the Chancellor's Office instituting a March 20 system-wide campus closure. While preparing our individual departments for the looming shutterings and shifting to our new work-from-home realities, a conversation fermented at the CSU Archives and Archivists Roundtable (CSUAAR), a community of practice centered around the CSU Libraries' twenty-three campus archives and special collections departments.[1] Needing additional support during this shared trauma and stress, our virtual meetings doubled to twice monthly, and many felt as connected to the previously established online community as to colleagues at home institutions. Naturally, discussion of our lived experiences arose:

246 Chapter 19

the coping and adapting to changing workplaces and uncertain futures. And, importantly from an archivist's perspective, discussions of professional obligations during this rapidly developing, highly stressful, and historically significant situation arose, and of how to collect as much of the extraordinary events unfolding around us as was feasible.

Historical Pandemic Collections

In building COVID-19 archival collections, evaluation of related documented crises—such as the 1918 influenza pandemic—is instructive. Accountings of the 1918 flu are often contained in larger, less-focused collections documenting the era. With the records buried in larger collections with little information in their catalog or finding aid descriptions, discovery is currently quite difficult. Local staff's familiarity with their holdings makes them the authoritative source of knowledge within their institutions, and they can offer researchers assistance with discovery, alternative approaches of inquiry, and appropriate sources.

Historian Sean Wempe notes that while there is a large volume of archival material related to the 1918 flu pandemic, "the problem is that none of it is effectively or efficiently centralized and may not be filed just under 'pandemic.'"[2] A relationship with the researcher bolsters archivists' knowledge of collections, both inside and outside their institutions, and guides collection development strategies. Conversation concerning what the researcher has already discovered and what they are still seeking can be instructive of other institutions' collections, and there is no better measure of the needs of the research community than researchers themselves. Further complicating the matter is that some, and perhaps many, collections are unprocessed, even though the 1918 pandemic occurred a century in the past.

An example search reveals the complex nature of discovery of 1918 pandemic archival holdings. A query of the Online Archive of California (OAC) using the search term "Influenza Epidemic, 1918-1919—California" returns forty-two collections, seventeen of which mention the pandemic in the collection's front matter description, most frequently noting that someone related to the materials died during the pandemic.[3] The remaining twenty-five results include the term *influenza* in a box list or scope and content note.[4] Just five are narratives consisting of materials like correspondence, diaries, and family papers, illustrating a noticeable gap in the record. One sole collection contains items exclusively relating to the 1918–1919 influenza pandemic.

To illustrate Dr. Wempe's comments, the records of UCLA's Los Angeles Unified School District Board of Education total 1,300+ linear feet. The finding aid notes there are two boxes pertaining to the pandemic.[5] Potentially more common is the Alton L. Flanders World War I Correspondence Collection at CSU Northridge (figure 19.1).

The entirety of the collection consists of four letters, one which includes a brief note regarding Flanders's sickness, which hospitalized Flanders while in France with the 5th Marines. There is no mention of influenza in the collection's finding aid. Also illustrative is CSU Chico's Robson Papers, an unprocessed collection containing photographs of people wearing masks as they travel by boat. Because this collection is unprocessed, discovery by

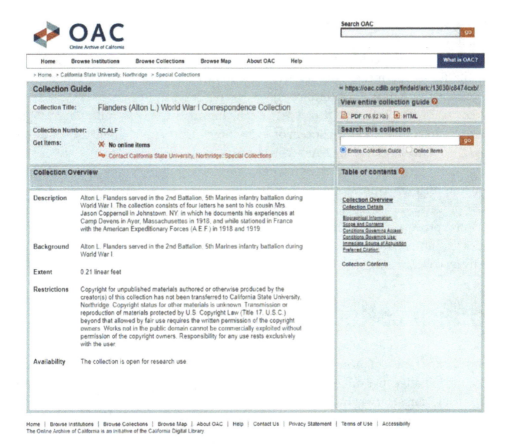

Figure 19.1
Finding aid for the Alton L. Flanders World War I Correspondence Collection at CSU Northridge. Screenshot of the Online Archive of California.

researchers can occur only in conversation with the archives' staff. This is not an uncommon occurrence; staffing models for libraries, and archives in particular, are less than ideal and collections can languish for decades awaiting processing.

Researchers often incorrectly assume that everything is available online and therefore accessible with a few searches and a few clicks. This assumption recently occurred at CSU Northridge, where a few faculty believed that the archives were intentionally withholding access to issues of the campus newspaper, due to a chronological gap in the materials' online surrogates. Archives staff resolved this misconception by verifying sequential issue and volume numbers that showed the paper was not printed during summer and winter breaks during the period in question.

Efforts are underway to resolve these issues of access and visibility of records for the 1918 flu pandemic, as there is a renewed interest in these records because of the current pandemic. The University of Michigan's 1918 Influenza Digital Archive has aggregated sources from several memory institutions, including the National Archives and Records Administration, the Allentown Public Library, and the Vermont Historical Society.[6] The

National Library of Medicine has also made some of its 1918 flu pandemic records available in its digital collections.[7]

The 1918 pandemic collections serve as an example of how, like the COVID-19 coronavirus, the diseases permeate many aspects of life and are documented using a wide variety of approaches by various institutions. However, collection strategies appear to be quite different when comparing the two events. While the opportunity to collect born-digital documentation now exists, the concept of "everything" being available and the bandwidth to capture it remains a challenge. As archives and special collections departments attempt proactive and thematic collection development, lessons from 1918 pandemic collections reveal and further emphasize that documenting these events remains a complex and murky process. The 1918 pandemic and related incidents can inform contemporary descriptive practices for current and future crises. It can also reveal collaborative opportunities to centralize the discovery of the current pandemic experience, an approach aided directly by collaborating with the affected communities themselves.

Modern Collecting Initiatives

The ability today to collect via automated and virtual means gives rise to projects facilitated through (almost) instantaneous and seamless connectivity with community collaborators. Collecting initiatives use online platforms to gather community reflections about events such as Hurricane Harvey in Houston, Texas, and the uprising in the aftermath of the murder of Mike Brown in Ferguson, Missouri.[8]

These projects employ "rapid-response collecting," defined by Dr. Meredith Evans as "a strategy where cultural institutions engage and collect content that document a current event in a timely manner."[9] Rapid-response collecting often takes place in response to a specific crisis, disaster, or event,[10] such as a shooting, protest, hurricane, or disease. This institution-led approach is usually centralized, with a heavy reliance on professionals to determine the scope and depth of the project.

However, collecting that draws on community awareness, engagement, and collaboration has also been used to create participatory archives, where nonprofessional community members draw on their lived experiences and recollections to participate in the curation of their pasts.[11] Examples of participatory archives include the Mass. Memories Road Show, which aims to document Massachusetts history through family photographs and stories contributed by community members, and VT Stories, an oral history project collecting stories of Virginia Tech's students, alumni, and employees via "Hokies interviewing Hokies."[12]

Rapid-response collecting and especially participatory archives are less reliant on archivists, librarians, or curators to appraise materials and describe and contextualize objects in comparison to more "traditional" archival collection development models. These initiatives instead decentralize and recenter expertise away from professionals and into the community, which draws on its lived experience. These initiatives also remove profit models from the equation and scatter provenance from single donors, sellers, or institutions, engaging the collection's constituent community directly, a radical reimagining of user orientation and contextualization of both the records and the collection, and the curation process.[13]

Figure 19.2
#Thankanurse painting by Marilyn Huerta, 2020. Image courtesy of Special Collections, University Library, California State University San Marcos.

Campus Projects

The CSU is the largest four-year public university system in the nation. The twenty-three individual campuses vary in size, educational scope, and student demographics. The CSU spans 800 miles from Humboldt to San Diego, with enrollments from 900 students (the Maritime Academy) to 41,000 (CSU Fullerton). Some campuses are in rural areas surrounded by farmland, like CSU Chico and Bakersfield, while others, such as CSU Northridge and San Marcos, sit within large metropolitan areas. Almost one-third of the CSU student population are first-generation college students, and nearly half of CSU students are underrepresented minorities.[14] The CSU has the most diverse student population in the nation:

financially, demographically and academically.[15] These differences dictate that campus collecting strategies vary accordingly. Four campus-level initiatives are highlighted here.

CSU Bakersfield COVID-19 Community Archive

Located on a campus of roughly 11,000 students, the Historical Research Center (HRC) at CSU Bakersfield (CSUB) is staffed by an archivist, a paraprofessional, and two student assistants. With the HRC's limited staffing, the approach to rapid collection and documentation of the pandemic necessitated a highly focus approach. The HRC prioritized the following areas:

- **Local.** Campus communications (including memos, e-mails, and training modules) and programs, community information (including newspaper articles, infection and death tallies), and government response
- **State.** Reports and California's pandemic response
- **National.** CDC reports and select news stories
- **Worldwide.** WHO reports and country infection/death tolls
- **Social media.** Selected social media posts
- **Testimonials.** Oral and written student experiences

While the above areas continue to be the focus, HRC now also incorporates suggestions from students, faculty, and community.[16] As news and social media posts are constantly created and updated, the HRC staff have woven collecting into daily routines. As the pandemic shifts, strategies shift. For example, with vaccine development and deployment, the HRC has begun collecting related local and national information. With social justice issues thrust to the forefront of a volatile political climate, the HRC is also gathering material related to the "Summer of Racial Reckoning." The two events are intertwined.

Figure 19.3
Black Lives Matter activists at a rally in Bakersfield, California September 25, 2020. Photo by Donato Cruz. Image courtesy of the Historical Research Center, University Library, California State University, Bakersfield.

Looking forward, staff will check the integrity of the digital files and bring them into ADA compliance. This review will also assess gaps regarding content. Although it is believed the strategies employed are developing a diverse and complex collection, with only two people curating the collection, it is possible there is bias concerning the collections.

The switch to remote working paused the processing and maintenance of physical collections and it was easy to focus on collecting and organizing digital content. With campus repopulation underway amid the ebb and flow of COVID, employees are contemplating how to resume normal operations while maintaining pandemic collecting efforts. The HRC is a small department within a small library, and the archivist also has reference, liaison, and teaching duties, diminishing dedicated time for collections development and management.

The NorCal Pandemic Diary Project (CSU Chico)

California State University, Chico, popularly known as Chico State, is located within Northern California's Sacramento Valley. The university's regional service area includes the twelve northeastern counties of California, though most students come from the state's Los Angeles and Bay Areas.[17] Because of this large geographic spread and the university adopting predominately online classes,[18] it was anticipated students would be returning home with the campus shutdown, including many moving beyond Chico State's regional service area. This necessitated a broad scope of participant inclusion in the pandemic diaries project. Collecting focuses on the experiences of student, faculty, staff, community members, and alumni, including those scattered to other areas of the state, documenting how remote learning and pandemic life are unfolding in different environments. The pandemic diary project is also viewed as an opportunity for students to remain connected to campus while physically separated.

Students lack proportional representation in archival holdings, and documenting their voices is a priority. At the start of the project, beginning March 2020, faculty were encouraged to offer extra credit for their students' participation. The student writing center was also approached and engaged for assistance with outreach via social media and inspirational writing prompts.

Once a group of roughly 100 participants committed to the project, employees periodically checked in via e-mail with encouragement.

For the project's collecting scope, the Diary Project accepted textual formats, submitted online, and encouraged participants to curate social media posts and submit them as PDFs. As the library reopens in fall 2021, the Diary Project will also collect printed and handwritten formats. This community has not been affected by the pandemic alone; it has also recently experienced a series of horrific natural disasters. In 2017, 180,000 people were evacuated due to a potential dam failure. In 2018, the Camp Fire, the deadliest fire in US history, destroyed the neighboring town of Paradise, killing eighty-five people. The year 2020 brought the North Complex fire, killing sixteen people, and the August Fire Complex, which destroyed over a million acres in Northern California.[19] The collective

Figure 19.4
Instagram post, Meriam Library, Writing Center, California State University, Chico. Image courtesy of Special Collections, California State University, Chico.

trauma of these events exacerbated the stress and disruption wrought by the pandemic and necessitated diverting focus from other activities. Equally impactful, the library is relatively understaffed; serving roughly the same number of students as CSU San Marcos with half of the staff at San Marcos. Though eager to document the pandemic in the region, employees also must to be mindful of our own collective trauma and bandwidth and are taking a modest approach when compared to other CSU library efforts.

Collecting COVID @ CSUN (CSU Northridge)

University Archives and Campus History (UACH), located in the University Library, is one of six units comprising Special Collections and Archives. UACH collects the records of university administration, schools, departments, and official auxiliary organizations and documents the student, faculty, and staff experience at CSU Northridge. UACH staff consists of one archivist and two student assistants.

Early in the lockdown, the conversation within the CSUAAR and the larger archival community regarding pandemic collecting facilitated conversations in Special Collections and Archives gauging the viability of collecting the community's reflections. Decisions regarding scope, submission method, and legal issues were foremost in these discussions. CSUN is located within a large urban center, and several COVID collecting projects are already in place in Los Angeles City and County, so it was decided to limit the project scope to CSUN students, faculty, staff, and community partners.

The web page and submission form went live May 4, 2020. Unfortunately, the submission form was the target of an exploit attack in June 2021. The hacker or hackers submitted a PDF file containing a hidden script via the web form and subsequently contacted and activated the malicious script. They then uploaded approximately 10,000 files in six hours, with the goal of getting their clickbait onto a high-traffic website in order to generate statistics to sell advertising services. It is also likely that the hackers activated cookies to collect user data. The attack necessitated closing the submission form and implementing alternative submission methods.[20]

CSUN faculty participating in the project now add the archivist to the class Canvas page as a TA. The archivist can then download submissions directly without needing further action by students or instructors. Donors submitting materials outside of participating classes upload their submissions to Dropbox upon receipt of the completed deed of gift.

The greatest challenge in this initiative has been, and continues to be, outreach. Given the timing of the spring 2020 campus closure, followed by the annual summer lull in campus activity, finding the institutional bandwidth for outreach has proven difficult. Faculty, librarians, and students focused on shifting in-person instruction and learning online. Administration, faculty, and staff created new web content to keep students informed while the web team delivered this new content. Previously relied-upon strategies became increasingly untenable.

While the marketing setbacks have hampered collecting efforts, success has been found by collaborating with freshman orientation classes. The faculty coordinator and UACH began collaborating during summer 2020, providing significant time to finalize guidelines and details of the online submission process. The collaboration has been both remarkable and fruitful. However, it has resulted in the bulk of the collection being course assignments, unfortunately limiting the voices represented in the collection to approximately 180+ distinct donors from a pool of roughly 5,000 first-year students.

Heading into fall 2021, UACH will engage the library's subject specialists in outreach to instructional faculty; the subject specialists plan to inform instructors of the project and provide referral for further information. In order to collect other voices, a questionnaire was added for those who want to participate but do not know what to contribute; in addition, an instructional PDF file was created and made available online for instructors from other institutions should they wish to create pandemic-related assignments for inclusion in the collection.

UACH will continue collecting COVID reflections: What it is like coming back from lockdown and returning to campus? What has changed, and what has stayed the same? Feelings, stories, and memories shift as time passes, and the project plan is to document that as well.

Together/Apart (CSU San Marcos)

Given the abruptness of the virus's arrival and the upheaval that followed, we desired to start collecting immediately for a few reasons: collecting the pandemic's early days would yield raw perspectives heightened by new realities, perspectives that would otherwise grow more reflective over time; by contributing to the project, participants would be able to gain some sense of control over their own trauma and uncertainty; and the project was envisioned as a means to engage with students, staff, faculty, and region as everyone navigated the liminality of being a library with no physical, open place.

The project Together/Apart: The COVID-19 Community Memory Archive was built, as the dean put it, as if building a plane while airborne.[21] Confident in the team's ability and flexibility, and conscious of the need to treat ourselves with compassion, the team adopted an iterative approach, refining the project as it progressed. Components of the project were identified: the submission site's infrastructure and language; terms and conditions; outreach; and collecting mission. Stakeholders were given ownership over these components, with relevant staff working on their aspects and touching base via Zoom.

Within a couple of weeks of campus closure, the team built a simple website, allowing for participation by filling out a guided questionnaire or submitting a digital file. The site is intuitive enough to enable participation and not serve as a roadblock, an important consideration in participatory projects in the age of Archives 2.0.[22] The site's architecture allows for anonymous submitting and directs submissions to an in-house server, protecting personal information from big tech. Together/Apart's terms and conditions allow submitters to retain their copyright and provide the library a license to display, reproduce, and utilize contributions for nonprofit educational and promotional purposes. The terms also elucidate the collecting scope, providing participants with guidelines for what will be included in the archive.

While the website underwent design, the outreach team publicized the project, because as Palmer notes, building something doesn't ensure use.[23] This important outreach placed the archive into local news stories and into campus consciousness, greatly increasing early participation.

After Together/Apart ran for a few weeks, the team began tinkering with the "plane," designing spin-off projects geared to specific communities important to the collecting mission. Craft brewing professionals were targeted with a Glass Half-Full Memory Project, and the Telling Our Stories initiative focused on putting Together/Apart into classrooms as assignments or extra credit.[24] Instructors created assignments geared around personal narrative, short films, and podcasting, and ethnic studies and border studies classes provided contributions from members of campus communities underrepresented in the special collections holdings, an important departmental directive.

The team designed a digital exhibition in winter 2020, built in house using Omeka as the exhibit's architecture.[25] We launched Stories and Snapshots in February 2021 with a panel discussion featuring employees from CSUSM's Special Collections as well as participants from other regional institutions also collecting the pandemic. The panel was attended by ninety-five individuals, making it one of the more successful events the library has hosted. The exhibition features about one-quarter of Together/Apart's submissions to date and can be explored by map, linked data, and search bar. The team will build out the exhibition to reflect every digital submission to the collection, scaffolding the exhibition into the project's future digital access portal.

Figure 19.5
Stories and Snapshots exhibition home page. Image courtesy of Special Collections, University Library, California State University San Marcos.

To date, 235 individuals have contributed 472 items to Together/Apart. The team will continue collecting in the near term, with on-campus oral history interviews coinciding with a return to campus for students, staff, and faculty and a spin-off project where students will create messages to their future selves describing this juncture in their lives, which will be unveiled in a future digital exhibition.

Lessons

These four rapid-response collecting projects are the first of their kind by the authors' institutions. Given the United States' political situation, global climate change, and massive cultural shifts brought about by automation, civil rights, mis/disinformation, and of course the pandemic—the COVID-collecting projects will be useful models for future initiatives.

Today, technology allows for instantaneous capture of events and emotions and widespread dissemination of information at the click of a button. A dearth of resources as for previous worldwide disasters like the 1918 pandemic collections likely won't be an issue. Instead, questions will arise around curatorship, and answers to these questions will define what the rapid-response collections of the future will look like. As Schwartz and colleagues note around their efforts collecting in the wake of the Pulse Nightclub massacre, these questions will be ethical and legal in nature. Who owns the items collected? How will the community react? When is too soon to collect traumatic incidents? To exhibit? To interpret?[26] The answers will depend on the specifics of the events collected and the communities affected, as well as the nature of the grief and trauma, if any, associated with collected events.

While these participatory projects have increased community engagement and awareness, management issues specific to their participatory natures have arisen. File names, for example, are created by nonprofessionals with no understanding of how their submissions fit into a larger collection's context. Each institution's collections include multiple files with redundant and nonsensical names.

These files—and their metadata—need to be normalized and contextualized in a way that is intuitive within their larger collections. In this way participatory archives are no different from traditional collections, where an archivist imposes order on a body of records to make them accessible to researchers.

Our COVID collections are digital, and preservation of these resources will be a long-term issue. While there is not consensus within the profession about whether we are entering a digital dark age,[27] there are technical, staffing, and funding needs for unique digital resources regardless. The CSU's Digital Archives Working Group recently released recommendations for our digital preservation programs, including commitments to responsible storage, file integrity, security, metadata, and file format standardization.[28] However, most CSU libraries are in the nascent stages of creating their digital preservation programs, including conducting essential institutional outreach and education regarding the costs, skills, and funding necessary for such work.

Challenges with departmental bandwidth and competing priorities also occur. Archival labor is often invisible to all but those doing the work. As Hillel Arnold notes, profession-wide salaries are low and collection maintenance work—the arrangement, description, and preservation work foundational to creating discovery and access of our resources—is undertaken by understaffed programs, unpaid interns, and temporary employees.[29] Within the discipline there's an expectation that we "will work without complaint, for very little and if we are lacking resources, we will hire volunteers or unpaid interns to do the work."[30] Reliance on unpaid and low-paid labor perpetuates a cycle; each person takes on more work, doesn't

Figure 19.6
COVID collection filenames. Image courtesy of Special Collections, University Library, California State University San Marcos.

say no, and doesn't advocate for monetary and staffing needs. This approach is detrimental to the work and mission itself—and there are an increasing number of needs.

The pandemic was just one disruptive event. The murder of George Floyd by Minneapolis police and resultant nationwide unrest commanded necessary diversion of attention and resources, and continuing unrest will certainly bring more. Regional disasters, such as those plaguing CSU Chico's service area recently, also necessitate focus and funding to collect—perhaps even more so than larger scale events, as there are fewer institutions documenting them.

Conclusion

Rapid-response COVID-collecting efforts by archivists have created research collections and opportunities for future scholars; provided a means for patrons to reflect on, interpret, and grieve their experiences; engaged communities at a time when everyone has been distanced from them; and given the team focus during uncertain and foreboding times. Communities are still processing their experiences; as with other projects collecting grief and trauma, the library will certainly receive donations long after the pandemic ends and proactive collecting stops.[31] In the work of corporations, profit motive may compete with the public good. Archives, which lack the profit motive of corporations competing with the public good, are the perfect places for pandemic collections, and archivists are integral and committed stewards of public memory. The libraries are blessed with a robust community—both through the CSUAAR and through our larger work and social networks—that help resolve impediments, bounce ideas around, and provide working models, as everyone navigates through the herculean task of collecting this slowly unfolding crisis. For this community, we should be—and are—are abidingly grateful.

Notes

1. Communities of practice, as defined by Etienne and Beverly Wenger-Trayner, are "groups of people who share a concern or a passion for something they do and learn how to do it better as they interact regularly." Etienne Wenger-Trayner and Beverly Wenger-Trayner, "Introduction to Communities of Practice: A Brief Overview of the Concept and Its Uses," June 2015, https://wenger-trayner.com/introduction-to-communities-of-practice/. See also Berlin Loa and Pamela Nett Kruger, "Community of Practice at the California State University Special Collections and University Archives," *Journal of Western Archives* 12, no. 1 (2021): article 1, https://digitalcommons.usu.edu/westernarchives/vol12/iss1/1.
2. Sean Wempe, e-mail message to author, June 8, 2021.
3. "The Online Archive of California (OAC) provides free public access to detailed descriptions of primary resources collections maintained by more than 200 contributing institutions including libraries, special collections, archives, historical societies, and museums throughout California and collections maintained by the 10 University of California (UC) campuses." Online Archive of California, "About OAC," accessed September 1, 2021, https://oac.cdlib.org/about/.
4. Search conducted August 16, 2021.
5. Los Angeles Unified School District Board of Education Records, Online Archive of California, LSC 1923, https://oac.cdlib.org/findaid/ark:/13030/c80r9nr7/.
6. Center for the History of Medicine, "1918 Influenza Digital Archive," University of Michigan Medical School, http://chm.med.umich.edu/research/1918-influenza-digital-archive/.

258 Chapter 19

7. National Library of Medicine, "Digital Collections," https://collections.nlm.nih.gov/.
8. Harvey Memories Project home page, https://harveymemories.org/; Documenting Ferguson home page, http://digital.wustl.edu/ferguson/, respectively.
9. Meredith Evans, "Modern Special Collections: Embracing the Future While Taking Care of the Past" (accepted manuscript, *New Review of Academic Librarianship*), Washington University in St. Lewis University Libraries, Open Scholarship Institutional Repository, April 18, 2015, pp. 12–13, https://openscholarship.wustl.edu/lib_papers/2.
10. Sean Visintainer and Judith Downie, "Real Time Collecting and the COVID-19 Pandemic: The *Together/Apart* Archive at California State University San Marcos," *Journal of San Diego History* 67, no. 1 (Spring 2021): 6, https://sandiegohistory.org/wp-content/uploads/2022/02/SDHC-JOSDH-Spring-2021.pdf.
11. Ana Roeschley and Jeonghyun Kim, "'Something That Feels Like a *Community*': The Role of Personal Stories in Building Community-Based Participatory Archives," *Archival Science* 19 (March 2019): 29, https://doi.org/10.1007/s10502-019-09302-2.
12. Mass. Memories Road Show, Digital Collections, Joseph P. Healey Library, UMass Boston, https://openarchives.umb.edu/digital/collection/p15774coll6; VT Stories home page, http://vtstories.org/; VT Stories, "About Us," accessed August 8, 2021, http://vtstories.org/about-us/.
13. Isto Huvila, "Participatory Archive: Towards Decentralized Curation, Radical User Orientation, and Broader Contextualization of Records Management," *Archival Science* 8 (September 2008): 25, https://doi.org/10.1007/s10502-008-9071-0.
14. California State University, *Fact Book 2021* (Long Beach: California State University, 2021), 2, 14, https://www2.calstate.edu/csu-system/about-the-csu/facts-about-the-csu/Documents/facts2021.pdf.
15. California State University, "Diversity," accessed August 30, 2021, https://www2.calstate.edu/impact-of-the-csu/diversity.
16. Most suggestions have been about collecting specific items, such as campus signage.
17. California State University, Chico, "Chico Facts," accessed July 15, 2021, https://www.csuchico.edu/about/chico-facts.shtml.
18. Gayle Hutchinson, "COVID-19: Critical Campus Updates," Office of the President, California State University, Chico, March 18, 2020, https://www.csuchico.edu/pres/pres-messages/2019-2020/march-18-2020-covid-critical.shtml.
19. Mike Wolcott, "The Crises Keep Coming—Fortunately, So Do the Heroes," *Chico (CA) Enterprise-Record*, July 25, 2021, https://www.chicoer.com/2021/07/25/the-disasters-keep-coming-fortunately-so-do-the-heroes/.
20. Elizabeth Altman, e-mail message to author, August 30, 2021.
21. Together/Apart's collecting site may be found at https://together-apart.csusm.edu/. The corresponding digital exhibition, Stories and Snapshots, can be found at https://together-apart.csusm.edu/omeka-classic/.
22. Joy Palmer, "Archives 2.0: If We Build It, Will They Come?" *Ariadne*, no. 60 (July 30, 2009), http://www.ariadne.ac.uk/issue/60/palmer/.
23. Palmer, "Archives 2.0."
24. Together/Apart, "Submit to SCUSM Brewchive®: A Glass Half Full," California State University San Marcos, University Libraries, https://together-apart.csusm.edu/submit_brewchive (closed to new submissions); California State University San Marcos, University Library, "Telling Our Stories in the Age of COVID-19," LibGuide, last updated February 18, 2021, https://libguides.csusm.edu/stories, respectively.
25. Omeka is an open-source web-publishing platform used by memory institutions for display of digital materials and surrogates. Omeka home page, https://omeka.org/.
26. Pam Schwartz et al., "Rapid-Response Collecting after the Pulse Nightclub Massacre," *Public Historian* 40, no. 1 (February 2018): 106, https://doi.org/10.1525/tph.2018.40.1.105.
27. The digital dark age is a feared loss of knowledge as our accelerating digital evolution obsoletes the hardware and software necessary to digital records' accessibility and as the ephemeral nature of some born-digital resources prove difficult to find, collect, and preserve. See the following citations for perspectives on the impending (or not) digital dark age. Vint Cerf, at the time of the article's writing a vice-president at Google, takes a predictably capitalist perspective on the issue, believing that a dark age can be avoided if companies create a form "digital vellum," a way to embed emulation of

obsolete software and hardware in a file. Vint Cerf neglects to mention that libraries, archives, and other memory institutions are also working on this issue, despite being omitted from the public narrative, as Lyons points out. Lyons and Tansey are more concerned with the issues of the erasure of archival labor, archival silences, and records management practices bringing about a digital dark age than with technological issues such as obsolescence. Pallab Ghosh, "Google's Vint Cerf Warns of 'Digital Dark Age,'" BBC News, February 13, 2015, https://www.bbc.com/news/science-environment-31450389; Bertram Lyons, "There Will Be No Digital Dark Age," *Archivists on the Issues* (blog), Issues and Advocacy Section, Society of American Archivists, May 11, 2016, https://issuesandadvocacy.wordpress.com/2016/05/11/there-will-be-no-digital-dark-age/; Eira Tansey, "Institutional Silences and the Digital Dark Age," *Archivists on the Issues* (blog), Issues and Advocacy Section, Society of American Archivists, May 23, 2016, https://issuesandadvocacy.wordpress.com/2016/05/23/institutional-silences-and-the-digital-dark-age/.

28. Eric Milenkiewicz et al., "Guidelines and Resources for Digital Preservation at the CSU Libraries," white paper, March 2021.

29. Hillel Arnold, "Critical Work: Archivists as Maintainers," *Hillelarnold.com* (blog), August 2, 2016, https://hillelarnold.com/blog/2016/08/critical-work/.

30. Stacie Williams, "Implications of Archival Labor: If We Want Respect for Our Labor, We Need to Value It More," *On Archivy* (blog), Medium, April 11, 2016, https://medium.com/on-archivy/implications-of-archival-labor-b606d8d02014.

31. As the authors note, "the field collecting has been suspended, but donations still come in, a year and a half after the event." Schwartz et al., "Rapid-Response Collecting," 112.

Bibliography

Arnold, Hillel. "Critical Work: Archivists as Maintainers," *Hillelarnold.com* (blog), August 2, 2016. https://hillelarnold.com/blog/2016/08/critical-work/.

California State University. "Diversity." Accessed August 30, 2021, https://www2.calstate.edu/impact-of-the-csu/diversity.

———. *Fact Book 2021*. Long Beach: California State University, 2021. https://www2.calstate.edu/csu-system/about-the-csu/facts-about-the-csu/Documents/facts2021.pdf.

California State University, Chico. "Chico Facts." Accessed July 15, 2021. https://www.csuchico.edu/about/chico-facts.shtml.

California State University San Marcos, University Library. "Telling Our Stories in the Age of COVID-19. LibGuide. Last updated February 18, 2021. https://libguides.csusm.edu/stories.

Center for the History of Medicine. "1918 Influenza Digital Archive." University of Michigan Medical School. http://chm.med.umich.edu/research/1918-influenza-digital-archive/.

Documenting Ferguson home page, http://digital.wustl.edu/ferguson/.

Evans, Meredith. "Modern Special Collections: Embracing the Future While Taking Care of the Past." Accepted manuscript, *New Review of Academic Librarianship*. Washington University in St. Lewis University Libraries, Open Scholarship Institutional Repository, April 18, 2015. https://openscholarship.wustl.edu/lib_papers/2.

Ghosh, Pallab. "Google's Vint Cerf Warns of 'Digital Dark Age.'" BBC News, February 13, 2015. https://www.bbc.com/news/science-environment-31450389.

Harvey Memories Project home page, https://harveymemories.org/.

Hutchinson, Gayle. " COVID-19: Critical Campus Updates." Office of the President, California State University, Chico. March 18, 2020. https://www.csuchico.edu/pres/pres-messages/2019-2020/march-18-2020-covid-critical.shtml.

Huvila, Isto. "Participatory Archive: Towards Decentralized Curation, Radical User Orientation, and Broader Contextualization of Records Management." *Archival Science* 8 (September 2008): 15–36. https://doi.org/10.1007/s10502-008-9071-0.

Loa, Berlin, and Pamela Nett Kruger. "Community of Practice at the California State University Special Collections and University Archives." *Journal of Western Archives* 12, no. 1 (2021): article 1. https://digitalcommons.usu.edu/westernarchives/vol12/iss1/1.

Los Angeles Unified School District Board of Education Records. Online Archive of California, LSC 1923. https://oac.cdlib.org/findaid/ark:/13030/c80r9nr7/.

Lyons, Bertram. "There Will Be No Digital Dark Age." *Archivists on the Issues* (blog), Issues & Advocacy Section, Society of American Archivists, May 11, 2016. https://issuesandadvocacy.wordpress.com/2016/05/11/there-will-be-no-digital-dark-age/.

Mass. Memories Road Show. Digital Collections, Joseph P. Healey Library, UMass Boston. https://openarchives.umb.edu/digital/collection/p15774coll6.

Milenkiewicz, Eric, Erik Beck, Alyssa Loera, Stephen Kutay, Azalea Camacho and Elizabeth Blackwood. "Guidelines and Resources for Digital Preservation at the CSU Libraries." White paper. March 2021.

National Library of Medicine. "Digital Collections." https://collections.nlm.nih.gov/.

Omeka home page. https://omeka.org/.

Online Archive of California. "About OAC." Accessed September 1, 2021. https://oac.cdlib.org/about/.

Palmer, Joy. "Archives 2.0: If We Build It, Will They Come?" *Ariadne*, no. 60 (July 30, 2009). http://www.ariadne.ac.uk/issue/60/palmer/.

Roeschley, Ana, and Jeonghyun Kim, "'Something That Feels Like a Community': The Role of Personal Stories in Building Community-Based Participatory Archives." *Archival Science* 19 (March 2019): 27–49. https://doi.org/10.1007/s10502-019-09302-2.

Schwartz, Pam, Whitney Broadaway, Emilie S. Arnold, Adam M. Ware and Jessica Domingo. "Rapid-Response Collecting after the Pulse Nightclub Massacre." *Public Historian* 40, no. 1 (February 2018): 105–14. https://doi.org/10.1525/tph.2018.40.1.105.

Tansey, Eira. "Institutional Silences and the Digital Dark Age," *Archivists on the Issues* (blog), Issues and Advocacy Section, Society of American Archivists, May 23, 2016. https://issuesandadvocacy.wordpress.com/2016/05/23/institutional-silences-and-the-digital-dark-age/.

Together/Apart. "Stories and Snapshots: Documenting a Year of the Pandemic." California State University San Marcos, University Library. https://together-apart.csusm.edu/omeka-classic/.

———. "Submit to SCUSM Brewchive®: A Glass Half Full." California State University San Marcos, University Libraries. https://together-apart.csusm.edu/submit_brewchive (closed to new submissions).

Together/Apart: The COVID19 Community Memory Archive home page. California State University San Marcos, University Library. https://together-apart.csusm.edu/.

Visintainer, Sean, and Judith Downie. "Real Time Collecting and the COVID-19 Pandemic: The *Together/Apart* Archive at California State University San Marcos." *Journal of San Diego History* 67, no. 1 (Spring 2021): 1–22. https://sandiegohistory.org/wp-content/uploads/2022/02/SDHC-JOSDH-Spring-2021.pdf.

VT Stories. "About Us." Accessed August 8, 2021. http://vtstories.org/about-us/.

VT Stories home page. http://vtstories.org/.

Wenger-Trayner, Etienne, and Beverly Wenger-Trayner. "Introduction to Communities of Practice: A Brief Overview of the Concept and Its Uses." June 2015. https://wenger-trayner.com/introduction-to-communities-of-practice/.

Williams, Stacie. "Implications of Archival Labor: If We Want Respect for Our Labor, We Need to Value It More." *On Archivy* (blog), Medium, April 11, 2016. https://medium.com/on-archivy/implications-of-archival-labor-b606d8d02014.

Wolcott, Mike. "The Crises Keep Coming—Fortunately, So Do the Heroes." *Chico (CA) Enterprise-Record*), July 25, 2021. https://www.chicoer.com/2021/07/25/the-disasters-keep-coming-fortunately-so-do-the-heroes/.

CHAPTER 20

Libraries Making Lemonade

Technical Services Work Roles

Emily Szitas and Melissa Brooks

> The Technical Services unit could not have planned for all the drastic changes about to occur.... What the unit had to accept is that the events that happened were not within its control. What each person learned was that they were stronger for having weathered the situation.

Introduction

This case study examines the Indiana University of Pennsylvania (IUP)—a mid-regional university that is a part of the Pennsylvania State System of Higher Education (PASSHE), which is a conglomerate of fourteen Pennsylvania commonwealth-owned universities—and how the IUP Technical Services unit handled its staffing issue pre-, during, and post-pandemic.

Adequately staffing a Technical Services unit is a challenge many academic libraries face. Data gleaned from EBSCO's 2011 library and collections survey shows that library Technical Services units would see the largest decrease in personnel if positions were cut during the period after the Great Recession. The data indicated that 62 percent of libraries would choose to eliminate Technical Services positions over other library departments.[1] This trend is continuing during the COVID-19 pandemic, with data provided from the Ithaka S+R US Library Survey 2020 showing staffing cuts occurred in Access Services and Technical Services over other library units.[2] During the pandemic, the unit reconsidered job roles and responsibilities and how their work impacted the overall structure of the workflows and what staff completed each work component. This book chapter will discuss how library faculty and staff in the unit took on additional job responsibilities and how the unit analyzed job functions and redistribution of responsibilities.

261

The Ingredients (Pre-2019)

In the fall of 2019, the Technical Services unit at IUP consisted of four library staff and three faculty librarians, all of whom were represented by collective bargaining units. University staff are represented by the American Federation of State, County, and Municipal Employees (AFSCME). Librarians hold faculty status and are represented by the Association of Pennsylvania State College and University Faculties (APSCUF) bargaining unit. Since faculty and staff are represented by different bargaining units, there must be coordination of job descriptions, eliminating as much as possible any gray areas in responsibilities. The focus is that neither a faculty member's nor a staff member's job description can overlap in duties assigned.

Library staff fall into three ranks—library technician (cataloging/metadata), library assistant II (serials, acquisitions), and library assistant I (acquisitions/collection development)—and are supervised by the three Technical Services librarians. The unit's two staff members at library assistant II rank report to the acquisitions librarian, a library technician reports to the metadata and discovery librarian, and a library assistant I reports to the collection development librarian. All staff and faculty positions are full-time. Another librarian (reference/cataloging librarian) worked with the unit part-time to complete copy cataloging. To coordinate activities, the assistant dean for Technical Services led monthly meetings with departmental employees (see figure 20.1).

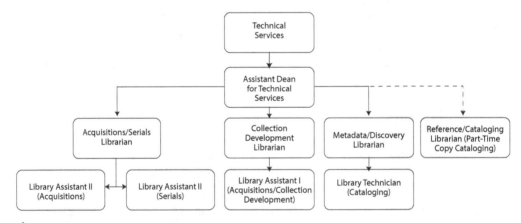

Figure 20.1
Pre- 2019 Technical Services organizational structure

Commonwealth, University, and Library Financial Problems

In January 2017, a discussion about a PASSHE redesign for all fourteen schools began as a system-wide cost savings plan. On February 13, 2020, Chancellor Daniel Greenspan sent a memorandum from the Pennsylvania Board of Governors to the PASSHE university presidents. It described a five-year sustainability plan to balance each school's budget. Actions insisted upon by the chancellor included eliminating academic programs with low enrollment and ensuring "effective use of evidence-based practices in supporting and retaining students." A reduction of the workforce was also one of Greenspan's action items. Vacant staff and faculty positions were not to be filled whenever possible, according to the memorandum. In July 2020, the sustainability plan moved from balancing the university budget to consolidating six PASSHE universities into three and finally two entities.[3] Of the fourteen schools, only six would be consolidated. IUP was not one of these six institutions. The change in tenor from the chancellor's office from before the COVID shutdown (February 2020) to post-shutdown (July 2020) was drastic, and uncertainty loomed large. It was not the first time that IUP or the other thirteen schools in the PASSHE system had declining enrollments and were considering how to deal with slowing cash flows.[4] Before the consolidation plan, several capital projects were completed at IUP, including the $53.49 million Kovalchick Convention and Athletic Complex that opened with much fanfare in spring 2011, and over $19 million in costs were covered through fundraising. The remainder, over $30 million, was subsidized through loans.[5] New, luxury dormitories were raised between 2006 and 2010 with costs of nearly $250 million. Dormitory construction costs were secured with bond debt. Dorm occupancy in 2021 had declined to 68 percent, but the debt on these suite dorms still needed to be paid. The debt resulting from this building boom at IUP is only a tiny portion of the $1.39 billion building debts incurred by the fourteen PASSHE schools.[6]

In fiscal year 2019 (FY19), IUP Libraries' acquisitions budget was over $2 million. However, funding to the libraries budget was cut significantly in the FY20 and FY21 school years, with $420,000 in total reductions. The loss of funding was a symptom of the university- and state-wide fiscal problems. Enrollment at IUP fell from 15,000 students in 2010 to 10,000 students in 2020. As enrollment fell, so did the proportion of funding for the universities from the commonwealth. Governor Tom Corbett, who served from January 2011 to January 2015, reduced funding to PASSHE schools by 20 percent ($82.5 million) in 2012, and funding during his tenure thereafter remained flat.[7]

As an immediate consequence of the libraries' collections budget cuts, cancellations and spending cuts became the norm for IUP Libraries. Database subscription cancellations were considered at every faculty and management budget committee meeting. Cost per use and overlap analyses were pored over. Determining how academic programs would be affected was at the forefront of meetings with faculty. Long lists of cancellations to serials and standing orders were managed by staff. When the spring 2020 shutdown occurred due to the COVID-19 pandemic, university management met for budget planning to determine how finances and budgeting would look for the next fiscal year in such uncertain times.

On Friday, March 13, 2020, the IUP president, Dr. Michael A. Driscoll, sent out a campus-wide e-mail notifying all personnel that in-person instruction would not occur for the following two weeks. This decision was made in alignment with Pennsylvania Governor Thomas Wolf's closing of all K–12 schools from March 16 to 29. On March 13, libraries administration notified personnel that their work would be completed remotely during the shutdown period. Each employee organized hard copies of documentation and packed them up as preparations were made for short-term remote work. When the shutdown period extended past the end of the spring 2020 semester and into the summer months, the Technical Services unit faced transformative changes in its workflow structure relating to staff responsibilities.

Pre-COVID-19 Staffing Changes

In the months prior to the March 2020 pandemic shutdown, the Technical Services unit workforce decreased. The assistant dean accepted an offer from another university in fall 2019. Also, during this time, both APSCUF and ASCME unions offered employees early retirement incentives throughout the 2019 year. The serials and acquisitions librarian took advantage of this offer and retired in January 2020. The remaining full-time Technical Services faculty (collection development and electronic resources librarian and metadata and discovery librarian) then temporarily divided the work from that position evenly. After some thoughtful conversation, acquisition responsibilities became part of collection development, and electronic resources and serials fell to the purview of the metadata and discovery librarian. The reference/cataloging librarian was not asked to assume any Technical Services responsibilities, due to their other job duties. Even though the Technical Services faculty had reassigned the work among themselves, they coordinated with all library faculty using a committee structure and developed new job descriptions. Documentation and justification for rehiring the serials and acquisitions librarian were submitted to libraries administration, at which time it was determined by the administration that the libraries would not fill the position and the reallocated serials and acquisitions librarian job duties changes became permanent.

As the Technical Services unit was dealing with the loss of the serials and acquisitions librarian, the acquisitions library assistant II also retired, in June. These duties were more challenging to reassign, as the remaining staff members each held different job ranks. Library administration could not promote to a higher grade, nor could they authorize a new hire to replace the retiree. This posed a problem in establishing level of responsibility and pay scale.

Developing the job roles based on the organization's needs and not the aptitudes or preferences of the person already serving in those roles meant that Technical Services unit personnel needed to consider new tasks in their daily work. Resetting responsibilities meant that staff would be evaluated on the new duties in their annual reviews. The implication of accepting the new roles for the staff indicated that they added more to their already extensive workloads. The administration could not offer further compensation either. However, the unit could not continue functioning otherwise. By developing each job role and adding more responsibility to each of the three remaining staff positions, the unit's work objectives would be met indefinitely. By developing job roles that were configured around specialization, the unit would have a permanent framework to use in the future if more changes were to occur. The proposed framework would stand the test of time.

Rearranging the Ingredients: Implementation of New Technical Services Workflows

To facilitate the needed changes in the unit, the Technical Services librarians reviewed all aspects of the work. They looked at each function that needed to be completed and how it could be done more efficiently. To visualize the work processes, the librarians created several flowcharts. These flowcharts did not look at the work based on the person. It instead looked at how the work accomplished the end goal, accessibility of materials to patrons. This work prompted meetings with libraries administration and Technical Services staff as the unit reorganized the work. The flowcharts caught missing workflow components and were color-coded to show where in the department the work should be completed. These workflows are included as an appendix.

After workflows were determined, the Technical Services unit completed a staffing reassignment. The library technician (Cataloging/Metadata) and library assistant II (Serials, Acquisitions) reported to the metadata and discovery librarian, and the library assistant I (Acquisitions/Collection Development) reported to the collection development and electronic resources librarian (see figure 20.2).

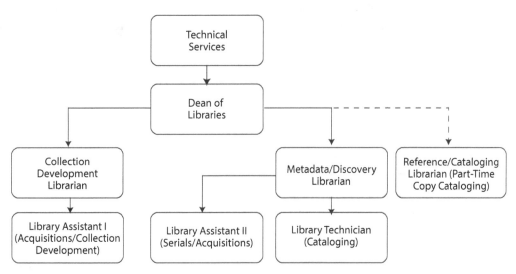

Figure 20.2
February 2020 Technical Services organizational structure

As a result of these changes, the Technical Services librarians created assignments to meet the challenges of the unit's new staffing levels. The unit recognized that some colleagues were more strongly challenged in their new roles than others in the short term. However, with a spirit of camaraderie, the unit personnel accepted their new roles. The steep learning curve was particularly notable for the library assistant II. Her responsibilities evolved from solely managing the serials processing and public services desk to include accounts payable. In addition, the COVID-19 pandemic made training a challenge as both librarians and staff needed to complete all work, and to train for these new responsibilities remotely. With health and safety as a pressing concern, communication consisted of videoconference calls (Zoom and Microsoft Teams), instant messaging, e-mail, and phone calls. Microsoft Teams and Zoom also became the standard in the University Libraries for one-on-one and departmental meetings.

Training for these new roles was delivered through online tutorials via the Ex Libris Alma Knowledge Center, virtual meetings, and, if possible, through socially distanced in-person meetings. Ex Libris's training tools were extremely valuable in providing a baseline understanding of Alma and the configurations of each module. However, each library can configure back-end workflows to meet institutional needs in Alma, so learning new processes was a challenge, and changes could not be made in isolation. Each person in the unit had to contribute to their colleagues' learning and understanding of the system. An exceptional level of teamwork came from the library assistant I; she and the library assistant II partnered together for many pieces of training on the Alma Acquisitions module.[8]

The timing of when the new job roles were implemented is significant. Most of the budget had already been spent in the final quarter of a university's fiscal year—April through June—with most print serial and database subscriptions already paid and book selection deadlines completed. This meant few practice items were available. However, some foundation accounts had purchase orders open. Remitting payments for foundation accounts was also reviewed and reconfigured when remote work started. The process was documented and solidified during this period.

As part of the training process, the unit also reviewed the Technical Services manual. Revisions of the manual were already underway in preparation for librarian and staff retirements. Due to limited staffing on-site, these revisions occurred online over the university's network drive. Revision and reorganization of the manual made sense as the unit managed remote work and new job roles. It was vital for the manual to be available electronically and perpetually. Lastly, reviewing and revising the manual as a team allowed the unit to consider workflows that were already in place and adjust them as needed. For example, purchasing of materials was not a one-size-fits-all process. Instead, the libraries have multiple custom processes for each scenario, including through a McNaughton lease program, firm orders, standing orders, and serials. Each has a different workflow. One of the other added benefits of staff training and document review was the discovery of orphan documents. This informed the unit of places where the manual had been missing sections and needed additional information.

During the spring 2020 shutdown period, the unit was charged with a redistribution of work responsibilities that required a forward-thinking, work-centered design. The Technical Services unit reorganization created opportunities for staff trading duties to meet workflows better. With the serials library assistant II taking on more acquisition duties, some serials work needed to be handled in other areas of Technical Services. It was determined that bindery management needed to become a function of cataloging. This change in responsibility moved a hands-on, time-intensive task, allowing for better use of time and staff. The training for this change in workflow was handled by both in-person and virtual training. These trainings were conducted over several months and involved both serial and monographic binding. Overall, this move allowed for a more streamlined process with less handling of materials.

The Technical Services unit worked well together. Their shared goal was to make sure patrons had access to the materials needed for their success. Each member of the unit was dedicated to working collaboratively and helping their community with their information needs. During the challenges of the COVID shutdown, the unit learned that coordination and timely communication between people is essential to success and that each person's role is interdependent on their colleagues. They shared triumphs and losses. The unit also learned that documentation is key to understanding and running efficiently as a department. The unit was lucky enough to start these processes in a useful trajectory, understand their importance, and communicate the significance of their work to libraries administration and to their colleagues throughout other library departments. During the examination of roles, the unit also discovered that the person does not determine the completed work. Instead, the work that needs completing defines the role.

Shaken, Not Stirred: Faculty Retrenchment and Staff Furloughs at IUP

The decisions made by the Technical Services faculty when faced with workforce reductions in 2020 were intentional. Looking toward a long-term framework and implementing a plan to put it into effect, the unit was in a position for success. In fall 2019, the unit had an assistant dean, four staff, and three-and-one-half FTE faculty serving Technical Services.

In May 2020, after several months of unknowns in the IUP budget, a letter of intent for retrenchment due to financial exigency was issued as per the APSCUF collective bargaining agreement. A financial exigency clause allows the university to lay off both tenured and tenure-track faculty to keep the university financially solvent. Once a letter of intent is issued, the university has several deadlines to continue with the retrenchment process. Each deadline is based on the tenure process. Tenured faculty are notified earliest in this process, followed by tenure-track based on years of service.

Retrenchment had not occurred at IUP in the past. Retrenchment is a process that terminates faculty employment through no fault of the employee. University administration determines the total number of retrenched faculty and how the retrenchments are divided among the academic departments. Retrenchment terminates the employees with the least amount of seniority first in each academic department; as a result, the junior faculty are terminated first. There were eighty-one letters of retrenchment sent out on October 30, 2020. In the libraries, where twelve faculty served, five letters of retrenchment were issued. Both full-time Technical Services faculty received retrenchment letters, with an effective date of June 4, 2021. The AFSCME (staff) bargaining unit was also hit with staffing losses. The library assistant I was furloughed through their staffing reductions from the IUP Libraries, with an effective date of May 14, 2021. This new retrenchment further reduced this unit to two staff and one-half FTE faculty. Through the retrenchment and furlough processes, each person still did their job to the best of their abilities while also supporting their colleagues' learning their new roles. With only seven months to complete any outstanding tasks, to train other employees to take on new responsibilities, and to determine their own future employment prospects, it was a very difficult time of transition for all.

Spilled Lemonade: What Is the Future of Technical Services in a Mid-regional University?

Unfortunately, the additional faculty retrenchments halted the new workflows and the efforts to continue functioning effectively as a unit. Libraries administration recognized that the unit, so diminished, was unrecognizable and inoperable. The remaining library faculty, along with the libraries administration, which included an interim dean, determined a new organizational structure must be put into place to carry out the work of Technical Services. The new organizational structure, developed just before the authors separated from the university, proposed four different areas for IUP Libraries functions: Content, User Experience, Learning/Research/Enrichment, and Administrative Groups. Much of the Technical Services work would now fall under Content (figure 20.3). The employees affected could react to the situation and cope only by choosing the best options available to continue to complete their work accurately and professionally, as each of the employment terminations took place.

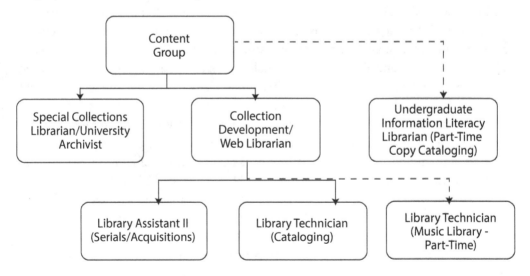

Figure 20.3
June 2021—Content group organization structure

Life after Technical Services

After June 2021, the furloughed library assistant I staff member transferred to a different position at another university. She is not currently working in a library. The metadata and discovery librarian found a new opportunity as head of technical services at a different university before the retrenchment date. The collection development and electronic resources librarian was retrenched on June 4, 2021. She accepted a full-time position outside of higher education, working for an engineering firm. The remaining employees in Technical Services were also affected. Before the new organizational chart was put into effect, the library assistant I's duties were already allotted out to other staff. Some of her duties remain with the two Technical Services staff and a third library technician from the Orendorff Music Library. The library technician (Cataloging/Metadata) moved his office to accommodate his new duties, and the library technician from the music library has her time split between two offices. Notably, there were no resignations.

Lessons Learned: How to Make a Better Lemonade

The Technical Services unit could not have planned for all the drastic changes about to occur after the unit's reorganization was completed in summer 2020. The unit could not have made appropriate succession planning documents to solve the gaping holes in workflows knowing that three vital positions would be terminated within the year. The unit was no longer a unit, but a collection of random functions disconnected from the workflows by the retrenchments and gaps in staffing caused by them. At that point, what the unit had to accept is that the events that happened were not within its control. What each person learned was that they were stronger for having weathered the situation. Even though the new workflows were not implemented for very long, the authors would continue to advocate for examining workflows and tasks not by rigid structures and past practices, but by looking at trends in Technical Services, determining staff strengths, and finding ways to automate processes that allow for better efficiency. The methodological approach described here avoided some potential pitfalls, specifically office politics, but cannot guarantee other negative side effects of workforce reductions. A mistrust of management and a loss of loyalty from the remaining employees is likely. The effects from the loss of institutional and technical knowledge will not be immediately quantifiable either, and the combined effect of these two factors will not be positive for IUP Libraries or the university in the long run.

APPENDIX 20A.
Workflows

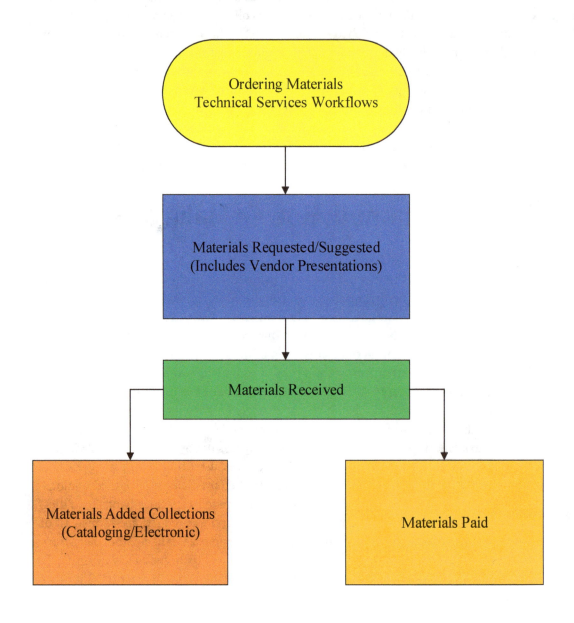

Libraries Making Lemonade 271

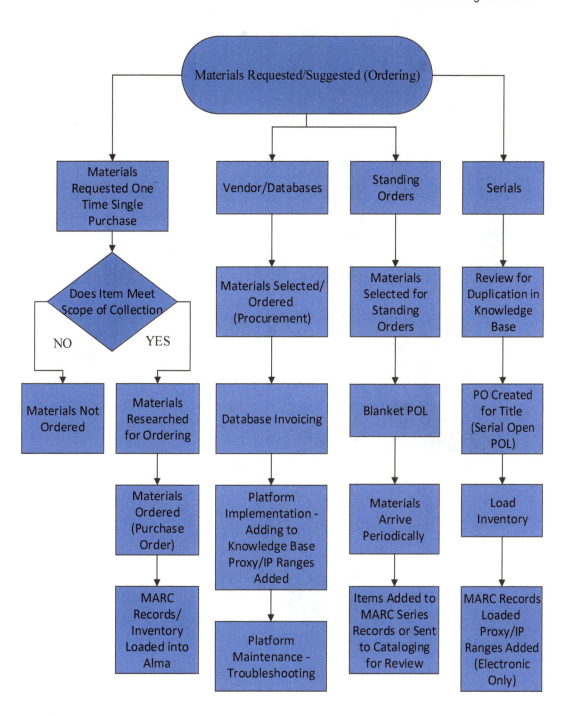

Chapter 20

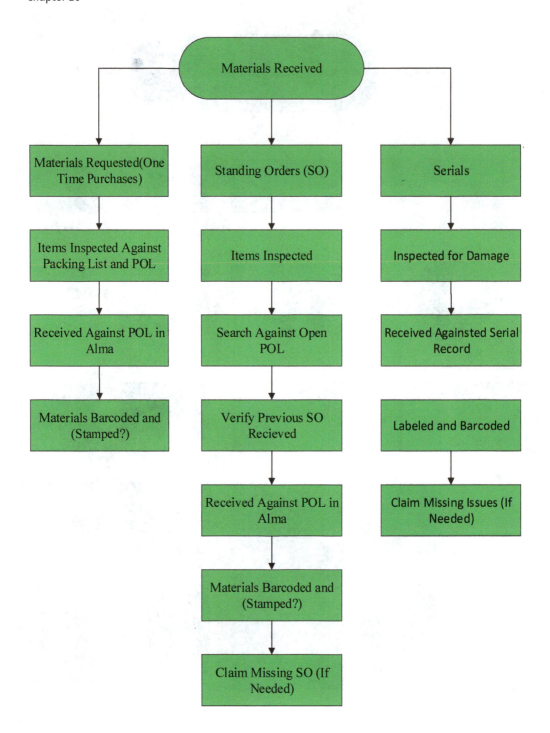

Libraries Making Lemonade

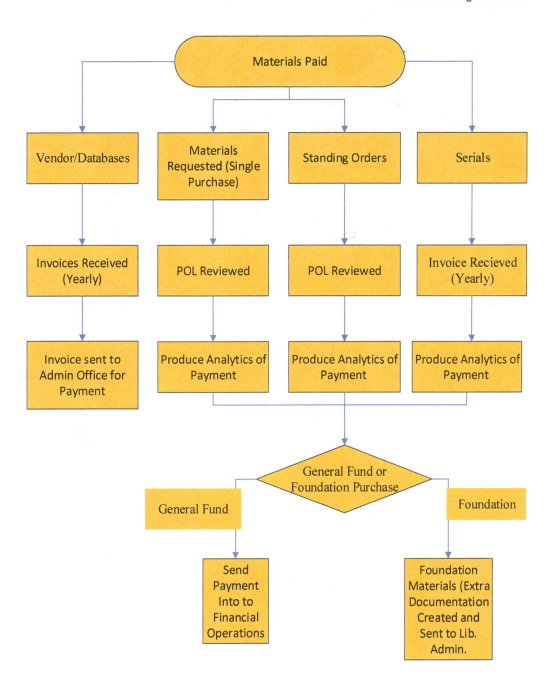

Chapter 20

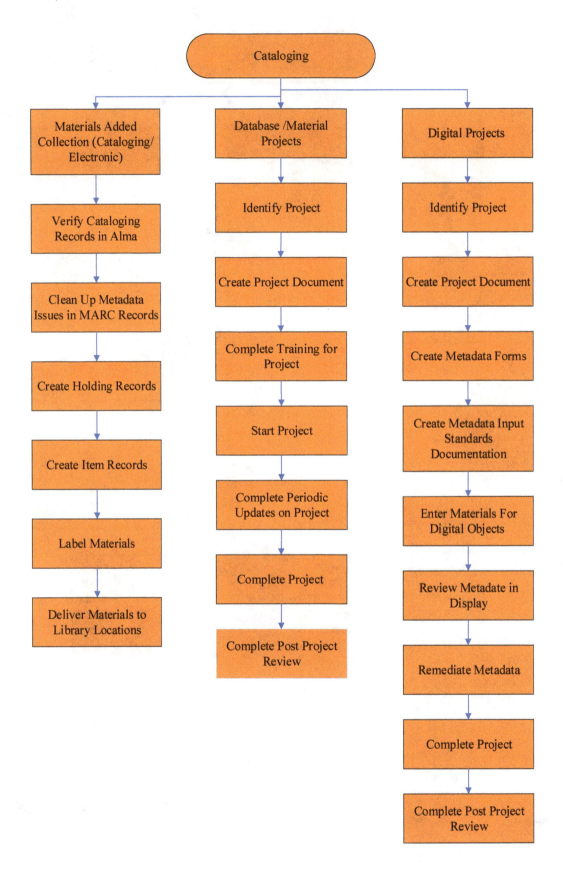

Notes

1. Tim Collins, "The Current Budget Environment and Its Impact on Libraries, Publishers and Vendors," *Journal of Library Administration* 52, no. 1 (January 2012): 18–35, https://doi.org/10.1080/01930826.2012.630643.
2. Jennifer K. Frederick and Christine Wolff-Eisenberg, *Academic Library Strategy and Budgeting during the COVID-19 Pandemic* (New York: Ithaka S+R, December 9, 2020), https://doi.org/10.18665/sr.314507.
3. Dan Greenstein, "Giving New Meaning to Sharing," *Chancellor's Blog*, Pennsylvania's State System of Higher Education, July 16, 2020, https://chancellorgreenstein.blogspot.com/2020/07/.
4. Susan Snyder, "Pennsylvania's State Universities Record Biggest One-Year Enrollment Decline in More Than a Decade," *Philadelphia Inquirer*, October 11, 2021, https://www.inquirer.com/news/pennsylvania-state-university-enrollment-drop-pandemic-20211011.html.
5. Indiana University of Pennsylvania, "Kovalchick Center Construction Under Way," *IUP News* (blog), February 17, 2009, https://www.iup.edu/news-events/news/2009/02/kovalchick-center-construction-under-way.html.
6. Deb Erdley, "Empty Dorm Rooms Pose Financial Problems for Pennsylvania Public Universities," Trib Live, August 1, 2021, https://triblive.com/local/regional/empty-dorm-rooms-pose-financial-problems-for-pennsylvania-public-universities/.
7. Association of Pennsylvania State College and University Faculties, "Governor Corbett's Budget Cuts to Public Higher Education Jeopardize Pennsylvania's Future," February 7, 2012, https://www.apscuf.org/govenor-corbetts-budget-cuts-to-public-higher-education-jeopardize-pennsylvanias-future/.
8. Ex Libris, "Alma," Ex Libris Knowledge Center, 2021, https://knowledge.exlibrisgroup.com/Alma.

Bibliography

Association of Pennsylvania State College and University Faculties. "Governor Corbett's Budget Cuts to Public Higher Education Jeopardize Pennsylvania's Future." February 7, 2012. https://www.apscuf.org/govenor-corbetts-budget-cuts-to-public-higher-education-jeopardize-pennsylvanias-future/.

Collins, Tim. "The Current Budget Environment and Its Impact on Libraries, Publishers, and Vendors." *Journal of Library Administration* 52, no. 1 (January 2012): 18–35. https://doi.org/10.1080/01930826.2012.630643.

Erdley, Deb. "Empty Dorm Rooms Pose Financial Problems for Pennsylvania Public Universities." Trib Live, August 1, 2021, https://triblive.com/local/regional/empty-dorm-rooms-pose-financial-problems-for-pennsylvania-public-universities/.

Ex Libris. "Alma." Ex Libris Knowledge Center, 2021. https://knowledge.exlibrisgroup.com/Alma.

Frederick, Jennifer K., and Christine Wolff-Eisenberg. *Academic Library Strategy and Budgeting during the COVID-19 Pandemic: Results from the Ithaka S+R US Library Survey 2020.* New York: Ithaka S+R, December 9, 2020. https://doi.org/10.18665/sr.314507.

Greenstein, Dan. "Giving New Meaning to Sharing." *Chancellor's Blog*, Pennsylvania's State System of Higher Education, July 16, 2020. https://chancellorgreenstein.blogspot.com/2020/07/.

Indiana University of Pennsylvania. "Kovalchick Center Construction Under Way." *IUP News* (blog), February 17, 2009. https://www.iup.edu/news-events/news/2009/02/kovalchick-center-construction-under-way.html.

Snyder, Susan. "Pennsylvania's State Universities Record Biggest One-Year Enrollment Decline in More Than a Decade." *Philadelphia Inquirer*, October 11, 2021. https://www.inquirer.com/news/pennsylvania-state-university-enrollment-drop-pandemic-20211011.html.

CHAPTER 21

Planning through a Pandemic
A Case Study of Miami University

Kimberly Hoffman, Rachel Makarowski, and William Modrow

> Even in a time of crisis, the libraries remained focused on pivoting to provide the academic community with the resources and services they needed to succeed in the suddenly virtual environment.

Introduction

The COVID-19 pandemic has triggered far-reaching challenges and changes to daily operations in academic libraries, regardless of resources and staffing levels. At the start of this pandemic, Miami University, a public, midsize university in rural Oxford, Ohio, had a library staff of eighty-eight, with one main library facility and three on-campus branches. The university serves a student population of approximately 18,000 undergraduates and 2,000 graduate students.[1] The Carnegie Classification designates Miami as an institution with high research activity.[2] During the onset of the pandemic, the Miami University Libraries' disaster response team, composed of representatives from every department throughout the library, began planning for a probable university-wide shut down, with no knowledge of how long to expect the shutdown to last. As with many other libraries, rapid assessment and action were needed in a matter of days or weeks, not months.

This chapter discusses a series of policies, actions, and initiatives taken in response to the pandemic through the case study of Miami University, focusing on the response of the Miami University Libraries. The authors will review the process of rapidly planning, executing, and iterating on emergency response at an academic library during a global pandemic. In the early days of the pandemic, upper management made many decisions based on other institutions' responses, as well as recommendations from state and federal governments and the Centers for Disease Control and Prevention. This chapter investigates the roles of library staff in planning and executing emergency procedures. This chapter also examines lessons learned throughout the process and includes suggestions on how to handle crises.

Phase 1: Emergency Preparation

In early March of 2020, the potential for a devastating global health crisis affecting the Miami University campus became increasingly certain. Library leadership and staff began to observe the response of other universities and businesses across the country, notably Ohio State University, Indiana University, and the University of Cincinnati,[3] and consider how the Miami University Libraries might decide to follow the process. Staff predicted interruptions to facilities and services, whether due to an outbreak or due to preventative measures such as quarantines and extended closures.

Response planning commenced quickly, though there was still some facade of normalcy at the libraries. Effective Tuesday, March 10, 2020, the university suspended all in-person classes for students.[4] Faculty were given one day to convert their classes into an online format. Student employees were still allowed to work in person; however, students living on campus were directed to return home March 21, giving them less than two weeks to pack and arrange to leave campus and return to their homes.[5] During this period, the libraries hosted two scheduled in-person events: a digital storytelling workshop on March 10 and 11, and on March 13, the annual Women's History Month lecture on the history of women's suffrage.[6] Candidate interviews for a new digital discovery librarian were also taking place in early March. An on-site candidate interview and presentation were held on Friday, March 13. The successful candidate from this on-site visit, however, did not physically return to the library until July 6, 2021. The new hire orientation, training, and onboarding, along with all meetings, were conducted virtually.[7] The nature of the position enabled the discovery librarian to begin working immediately, even in a remote work setting. The evolving situation required staff to constantly reevaluate event safety and consider measures that had not yet become common, such as reducing capacity, avoiding food, and introducing a virtual component. These events served as an early warning signal to library team members to expect further disruptions in their workplace and jobs.

As a campus closure became increasingly expected, two major concerns for library management were avoiding layoffs or furloughs and establishing remote work. Library leadership, including department heads and assistant deans, worked to identify staff members who might struggle to complete their job duties from a remote work location. Staff across the library developed project lists suitable for remote work. The Walter Havighurst Special Collections and University Archives staff generated a list of projects that would benefit from assistance outside the department and could be suitable for someone with limited internet access or prior training. This collaboration resulted in a pool of work projects for those staff members whose main duties were accomplished only while working in the physical library building, for example, circulation staff. Systems staff and librarians provided additional equipment, training, and technological support on short notice. Because of careful planning, there were no layoffs or furloughs during the pandemic.

The preservation librarian and the facilities coordinator, cochairs of the library's Continuous Operations and Disaster Response Committee, worked together during this time to prepare for an extended facilities closure. Their primary goal was to mitigate risk due to aging buildings and environmental systems, as well as making recommendations to leadership that would minimize service interruptions, which became a command center for documentation, updates, and discussion regarding the evolving response to the pandemic. To allow for efficient collaboration, they created a shared "Outbreak and Extended Shutdown" folder in Google Drive.[8] Prior to the COVID-19 pandemic, the library had no existing protocol for pandemics or infectious disease outbreaks. However, the library's disaster response committee already had plans in place to respond to flooding and other disasters,[9] in part because the library buildings suffer known issues with plumbing and roof leaks. The disaster response plans and policies in place at Miami were developed using American Library Association resources and best practices as a model.[10] Over the past ten years, the library disaster response team had already needed to respond to flooding, seeping leaks, and water damage to collections and office materials that have occurred regularly in all four libraries. Each time, the preservation librarian made recommendations to alleviate these issues. Some repairs have been attempted by the university; however, water leaks persist in all four libraries. Fortunately, some of the preexisting protocols for responding to floods and other disasters were applicable in this unprecedented situation. As a result, the cochairs were able to use some of the previously developed resources as starting points for drafting new policies and procedures.

With the campus closed and no staffing in the buildings, the disaster response committee knew that there would be an increased likelihood that adverse incidents such as leaks, pests, or HVAC failures could go undetected, creating an elevated risk of loss or damage to the collections, including circulating materials, archives, and special collections. In the days before the shutdown, the preservation librarian and facilities coordinator created policies and procedures and updated the existing emergency response binders and immediate action guides.[11] These binders and guides, containing reference information and key contact information necessary during emergent situations, are available to staff both online and at points of service and other key locations across the libraries. It was especially important to ensure that staff and vendor contact information in these binders was up to date before any campus closure in order to mitigate potential confusion around whom to contact during an emergency during the shutdown.

The team also took other steps to prepare collection spaces. Library employees were instructed to bring all food, including packaged and refrigerated items, home each night to avoid spoilage or attracting pests. Materials stored on the floor due to shelving issues, such as archival boxes, were moved to carts or tables to protect from any possible water damage. Several shelf ranges throughout the four libraries known to be vulnerable to leaks due to recurring plumbing issues were covered with plastic sheeting. Any areas with known prior water damage or other maintenance issues were documented through photographs to allow for tracking change over time.

A key factor in the preservation strategy for facilities and collections was scheduling inspections or walk-throughs of the four library buildings and collection areas, as recommended by the American Alliance of Museums.[12] Regular walk-throughs would allow emergent issues such as plumbing or building leaks, pest infestations, mold, HVAC environmental issues, breakdowns, or other problems to be addressed before they escalated in seriousness due to inaction. The disaster response committee cochairs successfully championed the decision that a walk-through team would function as essential staff during a facilities closure and be allowed to retain card access to buildings and spaces in the event that other staff members were locked out and asked to stay home. These essential staff were charged with patrolling the buildings regularly, which would also provide an opportunity to empty book drops and collect mail. Using a VPN, remote access to office telephones was available via Cisco Jabber, the voice-over-IP application utilized by Miami University. The VPN also allowed access to security cameras for remotely monitoring the library spaces. This team were trained on the new walk-through procedures and what to do in response to potential disasters during the approaching shutdown.

Phase 2: Executing Emergency Preparations

Starting on March 16, all departments at Miami University, including the University Libraries, were required to shift to remote work. As part of this shift, the disaster committee cochairs and the walk-through team began to implement the procedures and policies they had designed in the previous weeks. Walk-throughs of the buildings began on the second day of remote work and continued on a weekly basis. The initial walk-through was used to establish a routine, check known issues, and clear away any remaining trash or food that might attract pests during the shutdown. Using a spreadsheet developed in the Outbreak and Extended Shutdown shared folder,[13] the four staff members trained on walk-throughs kept records on the condition of each of the buildings and potential problems that could arise. The staff communicated with the members of the walk-through team to prevent them from escalating. Record logs were kept, though not as often as planned; the team members using this system caught several leaks in the different buildings before the water caused irreparable damage to the materials.

The walk-through team also maintained an existing environmental monitoring program for archival and special collections materials housed across multiple library facilities. The special collections department had three museum-quality PEM2 data loggers to measure temperature and relative humidity in collection storage areas, as well as seven lower-quality Accu-Rite temperature and humidity readers with minimal data storage. During walk-throughs, team members recorded temperature and humidity readings from the Accu-Rite units on a paper log. The preservation librarian periodically downloaded the PEM2 data and transferred it to environmental monitoring software for analysis. These steps gave the team an overview of environmental conditions in the spaces and alerted them to any potential HVAC issues.

The walk-through team was not in charge of just the buildings during the first few months of remote work. An unforeseen duty of this group included caring for both communal and individual plants that staff did not bring home with them due to the unexpectedly fast closure and the rapid switch to remote work. The walk-through team members served as intermediaries for the rest of staff. Personnel who needed materials from their office or a book from the collections would inform one of the staff on the walk-through team, who would then page the item and hand it off to the staff member outside. Walk-through staff also were in charge of collecting books from the return bins at each location, taking them inside if necessary, and putting them on carts for quarantining. Miami quarantine periods were determined and adjusted in accordance with ongoing findings by the REopening Archives, Libraries, and Museums (REALM) project,[14] which was launched by OCLC, the Institute for Museum and Library Services, and Battelle to investigate the impact of COVID-19 on collections and library services to help keep library staff and patrons safe.

During the shutdown of physical library spaces, the libraries' staff sought new ways to stay connected with one another. The Share + Showcase Department, which encompasses library communications, facilities, and strategic planning, created a library-wide instance of Slack. This informal application allowed staff to communicate with each other on a larger scale. They compiled staff newsletters, which were sent three times a week to allow for more formal announcements, though some of the content was purposefully lighthearted to provide staff with much needed levity during the ongoing crisis. These newsletters were e-mailed to library employees. They consisted of a mixture of content designed by Share + Showcase alongside submissions shared by library staff members. The library staff events team held weekly lunch hour trivia over Slack to boost morale. Library departments also held virtual celebrations for important milestones and individual accomplishments. Library management also made sure to celebrate these accomplishments on a larger scale at all-staff meetings.

Even in a time of crisis, the libraries remained focused on pivoting to provide the academic community with the resources and services they needed to succeed in the suddenly virtual environment. Within two weeks of the students' classes shifting to a remote environment, the coordinator of scholarly communications created an on-demand digitization service, Limited Online Library Access Lending Service (LOLA), that satisfied copyright law while providing faculty and students with the texts they needed for their classes and research.[15] Library circulation moved to renew items and dismissed any late fees accrued during this time.

By August 2020, employees were slowly able to start returning on a limited basis. Circulation staff launched two new services: curbside pickup for those who lived in town and mail delivery for those who lived out of town.[16] Library instruction and reference services were maintained in the virtual environment. Many instruction librarians began to explore and share new tools that could be incorporated into the virtual classroom and also created new teaching videos and modules that could be uploaded into different courses on Miami's learning management system, Canvas. Special Collections and University Archives moved its instruction services online and worked to expand its current online offerings.[17] It also tackled the task of updating its outdated finding aids and inputting the newly updated finding aids into its local instance of ArchivesSpace.

Phase 3: Surfacing from Emergency Status

As the summer of 2020 progressed, the library struggled with the problem of reopening without endangering students, faculty, or staff. In July 2020, the library began preparing for the fall semester and the arrival of students and the public. Leadership needed to decide who would return, which responses were working, and what were the potential fail points of having staff, faculty, and students both in person and virtual. Although the pandemic crisis had not ended, the library forged a path to provide services under a new normal.

By late July 2020, library staff were allowed to begin returning to work. Some staff members returned to working in the office full-time if their roles required it, while others were permitted to return for occasional days on campus as needed. Services and job duties could be maintained in this new hybrid approach. On August 17, 2020, special collections staff returned to campus on a cohort basis. Staff were divided into two groups, with the exception of the department head, who maintained a flexible schedule to fill in where needed, and one fully remote staff member. Working on an alternate schedule, each group spent one week in the office, followed by one week remote. This solution reduced staff density in the department and helped minimize the risk of exposure to the virus. To prepare for this arrangement, the library associate in special collections and the preservation librarian worked together to create cleaning procedures for the department. They used established disinfecting and sanitizing practices. Everyone who was in the office that week for the department was expected to contribute to the daily cleaning in accordance with these new protocols.[18]

To ensure that library staff coalesced around a standardized approach, the facilities coordinator planned a library-wide "COVID Camp," which served as a COVID frontline training workshop of best practices. This session, held over Zoom on August 28, 2020, covered disinfection protocols, mask policies, materials quarantine, and how to approach compliance issues and policy breaches.[19] The training addressed a need for clear communication and leadership on COVID expectations. An earlier COVID Camp would have been prudent, as staff had already returned to the building and the semester had commenced. By late August, the libraries had already reopened to the public, leaving a communication gap where policies were misunderstood, enforcement lacking and confusing, and staff discomfort levels mounting.[20] Many staff members remained confused about how to enforce policies among patrons and who would be charged with cleaning the more open, public spaces.

The COVID Camp session coincided with a strong desire for public messaging inside the libraries. The communications team, following university recommendations, created signage to remind visitors of the university's mask policy and other guidelines with videos on new safety procedures.[21] Signs also advised patrons that food and drink would be restricted to the ground floor café area to limit mask removal and reminded them about spacing and social distancing requirements. To set the stage for health and safety, staff removed and rearranged furniture to space out seating in compliance with social distancing. When removal was not feasible, space was created by taping off or blocking off areas. Despite the early push and continued efforts to convey these policies, an emphasis on being welcoming of students who were in the library took precedence, leading to unevenly enforced COVID safety policies based on staff comfort levels with both confrontation and COVID risk.

While the COVID Camp training served as a shared starting point, individual departments found the need to develop specific, tailored plans for the upcoming semester. In anticipation of having to reopen the libraries to researchers and students, the library associate in special collections and the preservation librarian worked together to create a set of policies for their student employees.[22] These policies were designed to minimize students' risk of exposure while in the department and reduce the risk they posed of exposing full-time staff to the virus.

Preparations for the fall semester took place against the backdrop of evolving CDC recommendations, university policy, and state and local regulations. The City of Oxford passed a face-covering ordinance on July 14, 2020, requiring masks indoors or outdoors when unable to maintain a social distance of six feet.[23] Miami University addressed the upcoming semester by launching a COVID dashboard, announced on August 21, 2020, to track positive results from tests conducted at the Employee Health Center and Student Health Services.[24] Staff and faculty members could receive tests if they had symptoms or a confirmed contact with a positive case, while students were incorporated into a larger surveillance-testing program.[25] Miami also applied a color-coding system to describe the infection rate of dormitory buildings and floors, with purple-level dorms requiring two-week isolation. The university also designated select dormitories to quarantine students.

In spring 2021, vaccines became available to some Miami community members. On May 19, the university announced updated guidelines that allowed fully vaccinated members of the Miami community to go mask-less both indoors and out. Unvaccinated staff and students were still required to continue wearing masks.[26] However, the university policy update prohibited staff and faculty from inquiring whether any student or staff member had received the vaccine and from requiring that they get the vaccine.

Phase 4: "The New Normal"

In April 2021, in what the university administration termed a "return to normal," the university president announced that each division on campus was expected to make a full return to in-person work by July 6.[27] In anticipation of this return, many of those who remained fully remote began to return to the libraries to reacclimate to their former routines. Those who had already returned to in-person work before July 2021 kept to their routines, though some started to add more on-site days. However, after having experienced successful remote work, employees across the university sought an official remote work policy from the university administration, which did not exist beyond the emergency permission that had been granted the year prior. University administration began to work on creating an official remote policy for salaried staff. Hourly staff already had an existing flexible work policy that allowed them to work ten-hour days for a four-day workweek. Because of this existing policy, there are no current options for hourly staff to work remotely nor are there current plans to allow them to do so. Few hourly staff in the libraries use their option of flexible work beyond summer scheduling.

The initial return to campus went smoothly, with many individuals excited to be back in person. On June 2, 2021, the City of Oxford relaxed mask regulations, allowing fully vaccinated individuals to stop wearing masks, but still asked that those who remained unvaccinated wear masks indoors or outdoors when social distancing would not be possible.[28] The university followed suit on these policy changes, allowing in-person meetings to resume, and celebrated bringing the community of students, staff and faculty back together. Staff who worked remotely throughout the pandemic were nervous and unsure about returning to campus, but quickly established their former routines. Zoom meetings were still popular despite the ability to meet in person. With the numbers of infections declining and the eased restrictions on social distancing, people slowly became more comfortable being near each other.

However, concerns rose in July and August with the rise and surge of the Delta variant, particularly as more students returned for the semester and COVID cases rose to new levels among the younger age groups and the unvaccinated in Butler County.[29] In an effort to slow the spread, Miami University mandated masks again starting on August 9, 2021.[30] Signage about indoor mask requirements, taken down the previous month, was replaced throughout the library. Staff discomfort at being in person rose again, although there were few affordances given to them as space to social distance became a commodity. While staff were asked to ensure students wore their masks, there was little effort to ensure staff followed the masking requirement in open work spaces.

The second week of August also brought restrictions on any catered food at events unless the food was served outdoors.[31] This required a quick pivot for the committees that were in charge of planning library orientations for students and faculty. Both events were successfully held but required last-minute additional space and resources that were not a part of the original plan. The ban on indoor food at events highlighted the need to develop contingency plans for any events that were being held in person.

The library's orientations originally planned for undergraduate students evolved from the traditional three-hour, full-library event prior to the first week of classes to a much more sedate resource fair consisting of three tables set up on the first floor during the first week of classes.[32] Each table featured one to two departments and was staffed by a single representative of each department. It was spread out over five days to distance potential attendees. Unlike previous years, which featured snacks and drinks for students, there was no food at this event. There was an emphasis on how each department could serve students both virtually, with the new services that had been developed during remote work, and in person, with the traditional services that were being provided again.

COVID positive cases have continued to rise slowly since the date of move-in, though the degree to which that data is reliable is questionable.[33] Students who are unvaccinated or have yet to provide proof of vaccination are required to be tested. Staff, faculty, and vaccinated students are tested upon proof of contact with someone who has tested positive.[34] Miami anticipates that cases will eventually fall a month after student move-in and rise again upon return from breaks.

Staff, faculty, and students are expected to wear masks indoors at all times regardless of vaccination status. Prior to September 1, vaccines were not required, though the university had a supply of vaccines to administer and encouraged everyone to be vaccinated and report their status. Staff, faculty, and students have since been mandated to show proof of vaccination or apply for an exemption with a deadline of November 22, 2021.[35] Since many students need constant reminding to wear their masks in the 2020–2021 academic year, staff anticipate facing this problem in the following academic year. Public announcements reminding staff and students of the guideline are more regular and timely compared to the previous year, when they were made on an irregular basis. Even with a vaccine mandate for Miami University campuses, consistency and reminders to mask up and social distance when possible will remain key in continuing to manage the COVID crisis.

Best Practices in Application

After nearly two years of pandemic restrictions and adjustments, some experimental endeavors have proved unhelpful, unsuccessful, or irrelevant, while other practices have become mainstays of our new normal. The library continues to function with in-person staff and the measures necessary to ensure their safety, but a new remote work component supports those efforts. Both elements are necessary to ensure a safe environment while providing the library services that support our student population.

Social distancing and wearing a mask were key to slowing the spread of outbreaks, particularly when paired with proper support from upper administration and enforced policies. Following CDC guidelines ensures that library policies and procedures are backed by science and align with the best outbreak-specific authority available to us as a US-based institution. Some practices can evolve rapidly depending on the state of the pandemic. For example, banning food at events during surges helps to support the mask policy while discouraging behavior that is risky during periods of high transmission. In all outbreak phases, staff and student employees should quarantine after exposure in order to stop the spread of disease. A robust remote work policy allows staff to quarantine without taking vacation or sick days.

Implementing practices that allow for greater equity between those working remotely and in person have been crucial. Remote work arrangements allowed for a staggered return to in-person work, which decreased the physical footprint of staff in the libraries, making social distancing easier for those in the buildings. Continued remote work has served the same purpose. Meetings are now virtual or held in spaces that allow for a hybrid modality so that those who are remote are not excluded. To support this, the university has extended a paid subscription to Zoom and invested in other types of technology support. A formal policy, outlining the expectations of remote work and guidelines for how to communicate to other members on staff about work modality, clarifies potential miscommunications and provides structure to those who qualify to use remote work.

These practices and policies will provide the basis for potential future pandemic responses. They will also continue to serve the libraries as the current pandemic changes and progresses with time. The ability to present an evidence-based, flexible response to an infectious outbreak will prove to be a critical skill to the future of the libraries and their parent institutions.

Notes

1. Miami University, "Miami University Report Card 2020–2021," accessed August 7, 2020, https://miamioh.edu/about-miami/recognition/report-card/index.html.
2. Miami University, Research and Innovation, "Carnegie Classification," last modified October 29, 2021, https://miamioh.edu/research/proposal-prep/institutional-data/carnegie-classification/index.html.
3. Laura Robel, "A Letter to Hoosiers," Indiana University Bloomington, Office of the Provost and Executive Vice President, March 19, 2020, https://provost.indiana.edu/statements/covid/for-students/march-19.html; Michael V. Drake, "Coronavirus Updates: Classes, Work Arrangements, Travel, and Events," Ohio State University, Office of the President, March 9, 2020, https://president.osu.edu/story/coronavirus-update-march-9; Neville G. Pinto, "COVID-19 Update: March 16, 2020," University of Cincinnati, UC News, March 16, 2020, https://www.uc.edu/news/articles/2021/01/covid-19-update--march-16-2020.html.
4. Jason Osborne, e-mail to the community, March 10, 2020.
5. Jason Osborne, "3-18-20 Message to Community," Miami University, Academic Affairs, March 18, 2020, https://www.miamioh.edu/academic-affairs/news/2020/03/3-18-20-message-to-community.html.
6. Miami University, University Libraries, "Digital Storytelling: Workshop," last modified March 13, 2020, https://libguides.lib.miamioh.edu/digital_storytelling/workshop; William Modrow, "Celebrating Women's History Month—Dr. Carolyn Jefferson-Jenkin's Lecture," *Walter Havighurst Special Collections and University Archives Blog*, February 24, 2020, https://spec.lib.miamioh.edu/home/celebrating-womens-history-month-dr-carolyn-jefferson-jenkins-lecture/.
7. A copy of Miami University Libraries' onboarding documentation is available from the authors by request.
8. A copy of Miami University Libraries' "Disaster Planning Documents" is available from the authors by request.
9. A copy of Miami University Libraries' "Response Team Handbook" is available from the authors by request.
10. American Library Association, Issues and Advocacy, "Disaster Preparedness and Recovery," accessed November 30, 2021, https://www.ala.org/advocacy/disaster-preparedness.
11. A copy of the Miami University Libraries "Immediate Action Guide (IAG)" is available from the authors by request.
12. American Alliance of Museums, "Preparing for Closures or Re-closures," accessed March 20, 2020, https://www.aam-us.org/programs/about-museums/preparing-for-closures/.
13. A copy of the Miami University Libraries' "Walkthrough Checklist & Notes" is available from the authors by request.
14. Institute of Museum and Library Services, "REopening Archives, Libraries, and Museums (REALM)," accessed December 2, 2021, https://www.imls.gov/our-work/partnerships/reopening-archives-libraries-and-museums.

15. Miami University, University Libraries, "Limited Online Library Access Lending Service," last modified September 1, 2021, https://www.lib.miamioh.edu/use/borrow/lola/.
16. Miami University, University Libraries, "Home Delivery," last modified September 1, 2021, https://www.lib.miamioh.edu/use/borrow/home-delivery/; Miami University, University Libraries, "Curbside Pickup," last modified September 1, 2021, https://www.lib.miamioh.edu/use/borrow/curbside/.
17. Miami University, University Libraries, "Special Collections and Archives Online Instruction," last modified August 16, 2020, https://libguides.lib.miamioh.edu/c.php?g=1063089&p=7730729.
18. A copy of the Walter Havighurst Special Collections and University Archives' "Cleaning Protocols & Checklist" is available from the authors by request.
19. A copy of the slide deck for and a recording of the "COVID Camp" training session is available from the authors by request.
20. Miami University Libraries (@miamiohlib), "King library is opening today for the first time since March! We welcome you to visit as we stay #HealthyTogether by wearing a mask and following social distance guidelines," Instagram photo, August 3, 2020, https://www.instagram.com/p/CDbk4AVDSzV/.
21. Miami University, University Libraries, "Healthy Together @ the University Libraries," accessed December 2, 2021, https://www.lib.miamioh.edu/libraryhealthy/.
22. A copy of "Special Collections, Archives & Preservation (SCAP) COVID Response: Policies, Procedures, and FAQs" is available from the authors by request.
23. Abby Bammerlin, "'Our Fate Is in Our Hands': Oxford Mandates Masks in Public and Bans Police Chokeholds," *Miami Student*, July 15, 2020, https://www.miamistudent.net/article/2020/07/our-fate-is-in-our-hands-oxford-mandates-masks-in-public-and-bans-police-chokeholds.
24. Miami University, "COVID-19 Campus Updates," accessed November 29, 2021, https://miamioh.edu/covid19/index.html.
25. Jayne Brownell, "Miami's COVID-19 Testing Strategy, 3:41 p.m.," Miami University, COVID-19 Campus Updates, August 28, 2020, https://www.miamioh.edu/covid19/campus-announcements/2020/08/08-28-20.html.
26. COVID Response Team, "COVID-19 Campus Update | 2:23 p.m.," Miami University, COVID-19 Campus Updates, May 19, 2021, https://www.miamioh.edu/covid19/campus-announcements/2021/05/campus-update-may19.html.
27. Gregory P. Crawford, e-mail to Miami University staff members, April 20, 2021.
28. Enjoy Oxford Ohio, "Safety Measures during COVID-19," accessed November 29, 2021, https://enjoyoxford.org/article-archive/covid-safety-measures/ (page discontinued).
29. Butler County General Health District, "COVID-19 Cases on the Rise in Butler County," news release, July 19, 2021, http://health.bcohio.us/news_detail_T6_R182.php.
30. Miami University, Policy Library, "COVID-19," accessed October 20, 2021, https://www.miamioh.edu/policy-library/employees/general-employment/miscellaneous/covid-19.html .
31. Miami University, Student Activities, "Health and Safety Guidelines for Fall 2021," last modified August 24, 2021, https://www.miamioh.edu/student-life/student-activities/student-org-resources/covid-19-faq/index.html (page discontinued).
32. Miami University, "Explore King Resource Fair at King Library," accessed December 3, 2021, https://events.miamioh.edu/event/explore_king_resource_fair_at_king_library#.YaT-CNDMKUk.
33. Butler County General Health District, "Butler County General Health District's 91st COVID-19 Update (11/20/2021)," November 24, 2021, http://health.bcohio.us/CovidReportButlerCounty%2011.20.21.pdf.
34. Miami University, COVID-19 Campus Updates, "Testing," last modified November 16, 2021, https://www.miamioh.edu/covid19/testing/.
35. Gregory P. Crawford, "Vaccine Requirement Announcement | 11:40 a.m.," Miami University, COVID-19 Campus Updates, August 31, 2021, https://www.miamioh.edu/covid19/campus-announcements/2021/08/vaccine-requirement-announcement.html.

Bibliography

American Alliance of Museums. "Preparing for Closures or Re-closures." Accessed March 20, 2020. https://www.aam-us.org/programs/about-museums/preparing-for-closures/.

American Library Association, Issues and Advocacy. "Disaster Preparedness and Recovery." Accessed November 30, 2021. https://www.ala.org/advocacy/disaster-preparedness.

Bammerlin, Abby. "'Our Fate Is in Our Hands': Oxford Mandates Masks in Public and Bans Police Chokeholds." *Miami Student*, July 15, 2020. https://www.miamistudent.net/article/2020/07/our-fate-is-in-our-hands-oxford-mandates-masks-in-public-and-bans-police-chokeholds.

Brownell, Jayne. "Miami's COVID-19 Testing Strategy, 3:41 p.m." Miami University, COVID-19 Campus Updates, August 28, 2020. https://www.miamioh.edu/covid19/campus-announcements/2020/08/08-28-20.html.

Butler County General Health District. "Butler County General Health District's 91st COVID-19 Update (11/20/2021)." November 24, 2021. http://health.bcohio.us/CovidReportButlerCounty%2011.20.21.pdf.

———. "COVID-19 Cases on the Rise in Butler County." News release, July 19, 2021. http://health.bcohio.us/news_detail_T6_R182.php.

COVID Response Team. "COVID-19 Campus Update | 2:23 p.m." Miami University, COVID-19 Campus Updates, May 19, 2021. https://www.miamioh.edu/covid19/campus-announcements/2021/05/campus-update-may19.html.

Crawford, Gregory P. E-mail to Miami University staff members. April 20, 2021.

———. "Vaccine Requirement Announcement | 11:40 a.m." Miami University, COVID-19 Campus Updates, August 31, 2021. https://www.miamioh.edu/covid19/campus-announcements/2021/08/vaccine-requirement-announcement.html.

Drake, Michael V. "Coronavirus Updates: Classes, Work Arrangements, Travel, and Events." Ohio State University, Office of the President, March 9, 2020. https://president.osu.edu/story/coronavirus-update-march-9.

Enjoy Oxford, Ohio. "Safety Measures during COVID-19." Accessed November 29, 2021. https://enjoyoxford.org/article-archive/covid-safety-measures/ (page discontinued).

Institute of Museum and Library Services. "REopening Archives, Libraries, and Museums (REALM)." Accessed December 2, 2021. https://www.imls.gov/our-work/partnerships/reopening-archives-libraries-and-museums.

Miami University. "COVID-19 Campus Updates," Accessed November 29, 2021. https://miamioh.edu/covid19/index.html.

———. "Explore King Resource Fair at King Library." Accessed December 3, 2021. https://events.miamioh.edu/event/explore_king_resource_fair_at_king_library#.YaT-CNDMKUk.

———. "Miami University Report Card 2020–2021." Accessed August 7, 2020. https://miamioh.edu/about-miami/recognition/report-card/index.html.

Miami University, COVID-19 Campus Updates. "Testing." Last modified November 16, 2021. https://www.miamioh.edu/covid19/testing/.

Miami University Libraries (@miamiohlib), "King library is opening today for the first time since March! We welcome you to visit as we stay #HealthyTogether by wearing a mask and following social distance guidelines." Instagram photo, August 3, 2020. https://www.instagram.com/p/CDbk4AVDSzV/.

Miami University, Research and Innovation. "Carnegie Classification." Last modified October 29, 2021. https://miamioh.edu/research/proposal-prep/institutional-data/carnegie-classification/index.html.

Miami University, Student Activities. "Health and Safety Guidelines for Fall 2021." Last modified August 24, 2021. https://www.miamioh.edu/student-life/student-activities/student-org-resources/covid-19-faq/index.html (page discontinued).

Miami University, University Libraries. "Curbside Pickup," last modified September 1, 2021, https://www.lib.miamioh.edu/use/borrow/curbside/.

———. "Digital Storytelling: Workshop." Last modified March 13, 2020. https://libguides.lib.miamioh.edu/digital_storytelling/workshop.

———. "Healthy Together @ the University Libraries." Accessed December 2, 2021. https://www.lib.miamioh.edu/libraryhealthy/.

———. "Home Delivery." Last modified September 1, 2021, https://www.lib.miamioh.edu/use/borrow/home-delivery/.

———. "Limited Online Library Access Lending Service." Last modified September 1, 2021. https://www.lib.miamioh.edu/use/borrow/lola/.

———. "Special Collections and Archives Online Instruction: Instruction Options." Last modified August 16, 2020. https://libguides.lib.miamioh.edu/c.php?g=1063089&p=7730729.

Miami University, University Policy Library. "COVID-19." Accessed October 20, 2021. https://www.miamioh.edu/policy-library/employees/general-employment/miscellaneous/covid-19.html.

Modrow, William. "Celebrating Women's History Month—Dr. Carolyn Jefferson-Jenkin's Lecture." *Walter Havighurst Special Collections and University Archives Blog*, February 24, 2020. https://spec.lib.miamioh.edu/home/celebrating-womens-history-month-dr-carolyn-jefferson-jenkins-lecture/.

Osborne, Jason. E-mail to the community, March 10, 2020.

———. "3-18-20 Message to Community." Miami University, Academic Affairs, March 18, 2020, https://www.miamioh.edu/academic-affairs/news/2020/03/3-18-20-message-to-community.html.

Pinto, Neville G. "COVID-19 Update: March 16, 2020." University of Cincinnati, UC News, March 16, 2020. https://www.uc.edu/news/articles/2021/01/covid-19-update--march-16-2020.html.

Robel, Laura "A Letter to Hoosiers." Indiana University Bloomington, Office of the Provost and Executive Vice President, March 19, 2020. https://provost.indiana.edu/statements/covid/for-students/march-19.html.

CHAPTER 22

Hunker Down, Anchor Town!

How the University of Alaska Anchorage Consortium Library Responded to COVID-19, March 2020 to May 2021

Lorelei Sterling

> *The library was one of the only buildings on campus to remain open during the larger campus lockdown. In fact, during the entire time covered by this chapter, the library closed for only two days: one day for completely non-COVID-related reasons (a windstorm caused a power outage) and one day because a student used a study room the day after testing positive. The students using the library during this time were precisely the ones the library was staying open to support.*

Introduction

The COVID-19 crisis significantly changed policies and procedures at the University of Alaska Anchorage/Alaska Pacific University's Consortium Library (CL) and, in turn, affected students, staff, faculty, and community patrons. The management of COVID-19 restrictions in the Access Services department is the central focus, but this chapter will also briefly discuss Instruction and Research Services, Archives and Special Collections, Systems, Technical Services, Collection Development, and the Alaska Medical Library.

The novel coronavirus is not the first pandemic to strike the world; there have been documented events leading to crisis response recorded in China and Europe as far back as 429 BCE.[1] Mask wearing, social distancing, and other measures are recorded for the Black Death of 1347–1352 and the 1918 flu pandemic. While these crises echo through history and may provide some insight as this pandemic works its way into the history books, the immediate need for addressing the current crisis was evident.

The head of access services/building manager (interim) worked closely with the library dean, fellow department heads, and the university's risk management team to figure out how to keep the library open to serve the University of Alaska Anchorage (UAA) and the Alaska Pacific University (APU) community. The team continually had to ask themselves: How will this impact building access for users? How will this impact the collections? Most importantly, how do we keep people safe while in the building? The library never closed its doors because of COVID-19, but every day brought new changes, new ways of doing things, and the possibility of new university policies. As a result, policies became living documents that continually evolved as new information based on science emerged and the university reacted to the information. These decisions had significant consequences; library employees quit over fears for their safety, yet the library was needed to provide students with a place to participate in newly created online classes. This chapter is about how the COVID-19 crisis changed the responses, responsibilities, and experiences of students, staff, faculty, and community patrons at the CL.

The CL serves both the communities of UAA, a public institution, and APU, a private nonprofit institution.[*] These institutions have a combined student head count of just over 16,000. Anchorage, Alaska, contains some of the most diverse neighborhoods in the United States and the CL provides support to both a highly diverse student body and the broader community population. In addition, the CL belongs to the Alaska Library Catalog (ALC), a cooperative program of the Alaska Library Network. The ALC is a consortium of eighty-seven public, academic, special, and K–12 libraries that serve 92 percent of the population of Alaska. The shared catalog has 3.2 million titles.[2]

The CL building itself is three stories tall and includes over 200,000 square feet. There are over 210 tables, 480 chairs, multiple open areas for group collaboration and quiet individual study, and 18 group study rooms, as well as 12 individual study rooms. Prior to the pandemic, average daily usage measured around 12,000 patrons per week, or about 1,700 patrons per day. The library was open to the general public until 8:00 p.m. every day of the week and restricted to current UAA/APU students, staff, faculty, and alumni for late-night study until midnight. The library is on major bus lines and is located across the street from the largest hospital in the city, near the library there is also a juvenile detention center, and a psychiatric institute. Given the library's urban location, community patrons were frequent users, and there were often issues with intoxication, drug use, and aggressive patron behavior, particularly in the winter months, as patrons experiencing homelessness tried to escape the frigid temperatures of an Alaskan winter.[3] The CL's policies addressed some of these issues with community patrons by limiting access hours, designating specific computers for their use, and developing a robust code of conduct that was general enough to be applied to a variety of disruptive behaviors.[4]

---

[*] Although the CL supports both universities, UAA policies and procedures take precedence over operational decisions.

Alaska's experience and management of the COVID-19 crisis has been unique in many ways. From March 2020 to May 2021, the period covered by this chapter, Alaska maintained incredibly low case and death rates, but the state's geographic size, rural population, and limited health care system complicate national comparisons. Alaska is physically isolated from the rest of the United States, and indeed the world, so when Canada closed its borders on March 15, 2020, it left Alaska accessible only by air or sea. In some ways, this simplified the state of Alaska's response in that visitors to the state were entering through controlled borders that allowed for health screening and quarantining similar to that experienced by Hawaii and New Zealand. However, because universities are places where people gather to learn, study, work, and socialize, UAA's COVID-19 policies have been much stricter than those of the state or even the municipality of Anchorage.

Everything began to change at the CL on Thursday of spring break week, March 12, 2020. Spring break was extended by a week, with classes set to resume Monday, March 23, 2020. At first, this was the only change, but things started snowballing quickly. The mayor of Anchorage ordered a "hunker down" period on March 22, 2020, and soon after, the university canceled all on-campus activities, including graduation events and in-person lab classes, through the end of the semester.[5] All university buildings were closed, and everyone was sent home to work remotely. The exception was made for essential workers, including facilities and maintenance, university police, janitorial staff, and, importantly, the Access Services department at the library. All other library workers were told to work remotely if at all possible. The next significant change was the library cutting its hours, closing at 8:00 p.m. instead of midnight, and soon after cutting them again from 102.5 hours per week pre-pandemic to 54 hours during the height of the restrictions. Library hours were diminished to only 9:00 a.m. to 5:00 p.m. Monday through Friday and 10:00 a.m. to 5:00 p.m. Saturday and Sunday. This cut in hours lasted from March 2020 to August 2020, when the hours were increased to 78 hours a week for the 2020–2021 academic year. In-person usage averaged 210 patrons per day, or about 12 percent of the norm. Wi-Fi remained available twenty-four hours a day, seven days a week, for those who did not want to be in the building. Also, the virtual reference desk was open an additional two hours after the building closed to help support students.

The CL closed to community patrons when COVID restrictions in Alaska went into effect, and as of this writing, they are still not allowed in the building except by special appointment for research needs only. This includes alumni, who have been the most upset by the lack of access to the physical building. The library was very fortunate in that there was a card swipe access system prior to the pandemic, whereas most buildings on the UAA campus were locked, and no access was possible without a key. The card swipe system makes it possible to provide contact tracing information as the system notes every person who entered the building and at what time. It also allowed for monitoring the capacity of the building. The library was one of the only buildings on campus to remain open during the larger campus lockdown. In fact, during the entire time covered by this chapter, the library closed for only two days: one day for completely non-COVID-related reasons (a windstorm caused a power outage) and one day because a student used a study room the day after testing positive. To date, there have been no documented cases of COVID contact spread within the building.

Before the pandemic, a fully staffed Access Services department consisted of seven circulation clerks, a student supervisor, an income manager, an interlibrary loan clerk, a department head, and fifteen to eighteen student workers. Maintaining a full staff proved extremely difficult. Within the first two weeks, two circulation clerks quit over health and safety concerns. Six student workers quit: four because they did not feel safe in the library and two because they lived in on-campus housing and were not allowed to return to the dorms as they were shut down as well. Those two student workers left the Anchorage area altogether but returned to work at the library in fall 2020. Fortunately, the loss of these workers was tempered at the time by the reduction in the library's hours. Fewer hours meant fewer staff members were needed; at this time, the CL had dropped to five full-time workers and nine student workers. The student supervisor and income manager positions have been merged into one.

When the UAA campus closed down in late March 2020, Access Services staff wanted to know why the library remained open when all other campus buildings were closed and why they had to come to work when all other library staff could work from home. When these questions were brought to the library dean, his response was that the library was remaining open for the students, staff, and faculty who did not have adequate access to the technological resources needed to transition to an online learning or remote work environment, and in order to keep Access Services staff employed, the building needed to remain open.[6] Before the pandemic, there was a perception that everyone had access to the internet and owned a smartphone or a computer. This quickly changed, and national news highlighted the digital inequities that were already well known in Alaska.[7] The students using the library during this time were precisely the ones the library was staying open to support. These students often lacked the basic technology needed, including computers and a robust internet connection, and struggled with some of the basic computer skills to handle online classes. Access Services staff and student workers performed over 150 hours of troubleshooting with these students to ensure they could access their online classes using the learning management platform, instructing them on the finer details of Zoom, and teaching them how to upload and print assignments.

Quite a few physical changes to the building were required to accommodate patrons. The group study rooms were transitioned quickly into individual study rooms to allow for social distancing. Furniture was rearranged to six feet between patrons, chairs at tables were removed, computer stations were spread out, plexiglass was installed at the staff desks, caution tape was placed on couch seats to limit folks sitting next to each other, and the most helpful thing of all was the clean/dirty signs provided by the Risk Management team. These signs had been used in emergency preparedness drills; one side read "Clean" on a green background, while the other side read "Dirty" on a red background. They were made of a nonporous material that could be easily cleaned. As not enough were available, more were created in house using a lamination machine. These signs went on every surface that could be cleaned: computer keyboards, tables, chairs, and benches. They were in study rooms, the computer lab, and even at the circulation staff computer stations to remind folks to clean between uses.

Student workers and staff were assigned cleaning shifts throughout the day and could see which spaces had been used and could focus on cleaning those. This protocol was based on university guidelines for frequent cleaning;[8] before using these signs, a full sweep of the entire building was taking place with all surfaces cleaned multiple times a day. It was exhausting and impossible to maintain. These signs allowed for targeted cleaning and reassured patrons that the areas they were using were clean. Patrons were educated on the use of the signs and given reminders to flip them over if necessary, but the signs helped. In addition, cleaned chairs were leaned up against the tables or faced away from the tables to make it clear that they had not been used. This made it obvious which chairs needed to be wiped down. The cleaning product the library used is Virex, produced by Diversey. According to Virex's website, it is a "ready-to-use, quaternary-based, disinfectant that provides excellent cleaning and deodorizing in one step. Bactericide, tuberculocide, virucide, fungicide."[9] The facilities department provided Virex and microfiber rags for use in cleaning the furniture. It also provided cleaning wipes for computer keyboards, mice, and monitors, as the Virex spray could harm the electronic equipment.

Some of the changes made will continue as they are practices that are good for public health. These include frequent cleaning of high-touch-point areas like doorknobs and elevator buttons, cleaning workstations between staff uses, and encouraging library workers to stay home if they feel sick. This has been one of the most profound changes to the work culture at the CL. Four years ago, a library staff member had pneumonia twice within six months and missed only three days of work. It is no longer considered acceptable to come to work if one is even slightly ill. Now, if anyone has even a mild case of the sniffles, they stay home from work and get tested to make sure it is not COVID. This has become the standard expectation based on CDC guidelines,[10] and no one comes into work if they are not feeling well. It has, however, caused some staffing issues over the last year and a half as the circulation desks require staffing for all the hours the library is open. Staff must be able to enforce the mask policy and also ensure community patrons do not enter the building.

For the first few months of the pandemic, Access Services staff were instructed to stop all patrons entering the library and ask them a series of health-related questions: Have you had a fever of 100.0 or greater? Do you have a new cough or shortness of breath? Are you feeling sick at all, even with symptoms that are cold- or flu-like? Has anyone in your immediate housing group shown the above symptoms? If the patron answered yes to any of these questions, staff were to deny access to the building and help the student make alternative arrangements for meeting student learning objectives. In addition, staff had to explain the use of the Clean/Dirty signs, encourage social distancing, and explain the new study room capacity (i.e., only one person per room). Near the end of this phase of the pandemic, patrons would barely slow down to listen, and everyone, including staff, was very frustrated with the amount of gatekeeping taking place.

Fortunately, by the beginning of fall 2020, the health screening questions were no longer required, and signage had been placed to inform users about the study room capacity change. However, over the Labor Day weekend, everything changed again. The chancellor of the university received numerous complaints from faculty and students regarding the lack of enforcement of the mask mandate within the library. Whereas staff had previously been enforcing the mask mandate only as patrons entered the building and if there were complaints, the new directive was for library staff to actively patrol the building to enforce compliance with the mandate. To this point, library leadership, including all department heads and the library dean, had strenuously advocated for staff not to become "mask police" as no one had been hired with this expectation, and masking was and remains a politicized issue in the state of Alaska. The CL was provided with both cloth and disposable masks that were given to patrons who entered the building without a mask. Having a ready supply of masks helped support this effort tremendously.

Developing the new enforcement mechanism had to be done quickly, but it also had to be done right. The policy had to be clear, and it had to be easy to explain to everyone while also being straightforward and without a lot of wiggle room. Masks had to be worn at all times and had to cover both nose and mouth. Masks could be removed briefly to eat or drink but needed to be put back on between bites and sips. Consequences of noncompliance also needed to be clear and easily explained. Library leadership ultimately decided on a three-strikes policy. The first time someone was seen without a mask on, it was a warning. The second time, the person was told they would be asked to leave for the day if it happened again. The third time, the person was asked to leave.

The whole situation felt completely overwhelming. To help prepare the Access Services staff for this new policy enforcement, role-playing exercises were developed to practice what to say, how to say it, and how to deal with aggressive behaviors and escalating tensions. Staff also started tracking mask violation warnings using a simple grid on a whiteboard. This allowed everyone to visually track how often warnings were given. Prior to this tracking, everyone involved in the enforcement efforts was very stressed out about this new role, but fortunately, the problem was not as prevalent as feared. Although it felt as if there were constant warnings, once staff started tracking them, they soon discovered that first warnings were averaging under five a day and second warnings under ten a month. In fact, only five people were asked to leave the building because of a third mask policy violation. Nor were people as aggressive or resistant to the policy as was unfortunately seen across the Lower 48.[11]

The mask enforcement policy was one of the final policies developed in the ever-evolving world of the pandemic. One of the first was the ALC holds policy. The state of Alaska is unique in that there is a shared catalog for nearly all libraries in the state, whether academic, public, school, or special. Patrons using this shared catalog can request items from almost any library in the state using the same mechanism to place a local hold rather than an interlibrary loan request. Before the REopening Archives, Libraries, and Museums (REALM) studies had come out,[12] it was unclear how the virus spread. It was believed that it might be from physical contact with the virus from surfaces. Even before libraries shut down around Alaska, they suspended holds as no one wanted to take the chance of spreading the virus that may have existed on book surfaces to others around the state. As items returned, a quarantine system was established. First, books were left stacked in the bins they were delivered in, but the REALM studies proved pretty definitively that if the virus was on books and they were left stacked, it could take up to six days for it to die.[13] A new system was developed to track when items came in, how long they had been in quarantine, and when they could be processed back into the collection. Spreading out returned items required a lot of shelf space, and bookends were utilized to keep items separated from each other, allowing the most exposure to air, hastening the virus's death. A separate area and process were created for ILL items as the end processing was different and was handled by a different team of student workers.

The risk management team provided thousands of non-latex gloves in all sizes, from extra small to extra large, as well as disposable and cloth masks. Student workers who were cleaning with the highly irritating Virex were pleased to have hand protection. Risk management took the gloves from the labs on campus as there were no longer in-person classes. They also donated personal protective gear to the local hospitals dealing with shortages at the beginning of the pandemic when supply chain and production problems were happening. It was especially critical in Alaska as the state receives most of its goods via twice-weekly barge deliveries. If a delivery does not happen, there is no way to get materials up here quickly. Port issues on the West Coast and a lack of goods coming from China also caused delays.[14]

Physical course reserves needed to be changed because of the quarantine requirements as well. Pre-pandemic checkout times included two or four hours, and one, two, or three days. While quarantining items, everything was moved to a two-day checkout with a two-day quarantine. If a student needed an item before the quarantine was over, they were informed of the situation and staff let the individual make their own risk assessment about checking out the material. Informing professors about the change was done through announcements in the daily newsletter, UAA's *Green and Gold,* and the faculty e-mail distribution list.

Interlibrary loan usage skyrocketed during the first six months of the pandemic because the CL was one of only a few libraries nationwide that continued to lend materials. This branch of the Access Services department had only one full-time staff member and two part-time student workers. In addition, circulation student workers were asked to perform some of the more routine tasks to allow the interlibrary loan student workers to concentrate on the more advanced portions of these tasks. The staff member worked from home 60 percent of the time, but the students were needed in the building. The increase in lending requests was not just for physical items, but for the delivery of electronic journal articles and excerpts from books. It was not only other libraries' patrons, but also CL patrons making more requests, particularly for items in the physical collection, as they did not want to come to the library in person to pick them up.

Within the other departments of the library, there was a range of changes. The Instruction and Research Services department's reference librarians were moved to remote work almost immediately. Rather than working the reference desk, all of their work became virtual. Phone calls became audio files sent to a personal home or cell phone, Zoom instructional sessions became the norm, and reference questions were asked and answered using e-mail, chat, and text services. Without the reference librarians in the building, circulation staff and student workers became the default for initial support for printing problems, finding books in the stacks and in the catalog, and the basic directional questions typically handled by the reference desk. This caused a lot of stress and tension for patrons as they were used to having direct access to reference librarians, who usually answer those kinds of questions.

However, remote work proved impractical for quite a few positions. Department heads were mainly in the building as they needed to be available to their staff members working on campus. Technical Services staff who handled physical collection materials needed to be in the office to process the new acquisitions. They created a hybrid schedule, while others in the department worked solely from home. Two staff members within the Systems department started alternating weeks working in the office and at home. Another staff member continued to come into the building every day as that work required hands-on updates to staff and student-use computers. The Archives and Special Collections staff had to create new procedures to support researchers. In-person access to collections became by appointment only, and archives staff began offering virtual appointments over Zoom for people who could not come in. They also purchased new equipment to more easily display documents during these virtual appointments.

Collection Development staff worked hard to keep up with the vast offerings from publishers and database vendors to acquire new online resources for patrons. Early on, it was determined to highlight only items that were extensions of current holdings. A decision was made to purchase e-books almost exclusively, particularly ones with perpetual access and unlimited simultaneous users. Print items were purchased only when an e-book was unavailable or prohibitively expensive. This was a marked change from pre-pandemic even split between purchasing print and electronic resources.

The Alaska Medical Library (AML), housed within the CL, supports the College of Health and provides information and research assistance for health-care practitioners, researchers, and administrators across Alaska. Usage of its services soared with the need for current and accurate information about COVID-19. In addition, because of travel restrictions, an effort to bring health-care information to health-care practitioners in urban and rural areas of the state moved online. Unfortunately, this became problematic as the internet in rural areas of the state is exceedingly expensive and often cannot handle the video and audio requirements. To help mitigate this issue, AML sent out postcards to communities to advertise its services, including interlibrary loan and prerecorded videos.

The changes made at CL to protect everyone impacted how every department of the library functioned and how patrons utilized the library. Strikingly, there were positive outcomes from some of these changes. Cleaning procedures have improved, which will help public health measures beyond COVID-19. Computers are spaced apart, allowing for a more comfortable working environment. Purchasing a greater percentage of resources in electronic format will remain the priority. The CL is seen now more than ever as a critical component in supporting student success. The CL's experience during the COVID-19 pandemic was unique in many ways. There were no other libraries in the state that remained open throughout the entire pandemic. No other library kept its interlibrary loan services active. Most importantly, there were no layoffs due to the pandemic, and there were no COVID-19 outbreaks at the CL. Keeping library staff healthy and employed is perhaps the most remarkable result of this incredibly challenging time.

Notes

1. Joshua J. Mark, "Plague in the Ancient and Medieval World," *World History Encyclopedia*, March 23, 2020, https://www.worldhistory.org/article/1528/plague-in-the-ancient--medieval-world/.
2. Alaska Library Network, "Alaska Library Catalog," accessed October 3, 2021, https://jlc-web.uaa.alaska.edu/.
3. Michelle Theriault Boots, "City Aims Services at a Place That's Already an Unofficial Refuge for the Homeless—the Loussac Library," *Anchorage (AK) Daily News*, June 19, 2016, last updated July 20, 2016, https://www.adn.com/alaska-news/anchorage/2016/06/19/city-aims-services-at-a-place-thats-already-an-unofficial-refuge-for-the-homeless-the-loussac-library/; Lex Treinen, "23-Year-Old Arrested at UAA Library after Allegedly Stealing Police Officer's Rifle," NBC—2 KTUU (Anchorage, AK), January 8, 2020, Alaska's News Source, https://www.alaskasnewssource.com/content/news/23-year-old-arrested-at-UAA-library-after-allegedly-stealing-police-officers-rifle--566828021.html.
4. Consortium Library, "Code of Conduct," University of Alaska Anchorage and Alaska Pacific University, accessed December 8, 2021, https://consortiumlibrary.org/about/policies/conduct.php.
5. Aubrey Wieber, "Anchorage Mayor Issues 'Hunker Down' Order to Curb Spread of Coronavirus," *Anchorage (AK) Daily News*, March 20, 2020, last updated March 22, 2020, https://www.adn.com/alaska-news/anchorage/2020/03/21/anchorage-mayor-issues-hunker-down-order-to-curb-spread-of-coronavirus/.
6. Tyler Cooper and Julia Tanberk, "Best and Worst States for Internet Coverage, Prices and Speeds, 2020," BroadbandNow Research, accessed October 10, 2021, https://broadbandnow.com/ research/best-states-with-internet-coverage-and-speed (2020 information deleted from page).
7. Cailyn Nagle, "A Survey of College Students and Textbook Affordability during the COVID-19 Pandemic," in *Fixing the Broken Textbook Market*, 3rd ed. (U.S. PIRG Education Fund, February 2021), https://studentpirgs.org/2021/02/24/fixing-the-broken-textbook-market-third-edition/.
8. Green and Gold News, "Access to UAA Campus Buildings Currently Restricted," University of Alaska Anchorage, March 25, 2020, https://www.uaa.alaska.edu/news/archive/2020/03/access-campus-buildings-restricted.cshtml.
9. Virex, "Products," accessed October 20, 2021, https://www.virexdisinfectant.com/products.
10. Occupational Safety and Health Administration, "Control and Prevention," US Department of Labor, accessed December 7, 2021, https://www.osha.gov/coronavirus/control-prevention.
11. Bill Hutchinson, "'Incomprehensible': Confrontations over Masks Erupt amid COVID-19 Crisis," ABC News. May 7, 2020, https://abcnews.go.com/US/incomprehensible-confrontations-masks-erupt-amid-covid-19-crisis/story?id=70494577.
12. OCLC,"REALM Project: REopening Archives, Libraries, and Museums Research," accessed October 5, 2021, https://www.oclc.org/realm/research.html.
13. OCLC, "How Long the Virus Survives on Commonly Used Library, Archives, and Museum Materials," accessed October 5, 2021, https://www.oclc.org/content/dam/realm/documents/visual-aid.pdf.
14. Keith Bradsher and Niraj Chokshi, "Virus Disrupts China's Shipping, and World Ports Feel Impact," *New York Times*, February 20, 2020, ProQuest.

Bibliography

Alaska Library Network. "Alaska Library Catalog." Accessed October 3, 2021. https://jlc-web.uaa.alaska.edu/.

Boots, Michelle Theriault. "City Aims Services at a Place That's Already an Unofficial Refuge for the Homeless—the Loussac Library." *Anchorage (AK) Daily News*, June 19, 2016, last updated July 20, 2016. https://www.adn.com/alaska-news/anchorage/2016/06/19/city-aims-services-at-a-place-thats-already-an-unofficial-refuge-for-the-homeless-the-loussac-library/.

Bradsher, Keith, and Niraj Chokshi. "Virus Disrupts China's Shipping, and World Ports Feel Impact." *New York Times*, February 20, 2020. ProQuest.

Consortium Library. "Code of Conduct." University of Alaska Anchorage and Alaska Pacific University. Accessed December 8, 2021. https://consortiumlibrary.org/about/policies/conduct.php.

Cooper, Tyler, and Julia Tanberk. "Best and Worst States for Internet Coverage, Prices and Speeds, 2020." BroadbandNow Research. Accessed October 10, 2021. https://broadbandnow.com/ research/best-states-with-internet-coverage-and-speed (2020 information deleted from page).

Green and Gold News. "Access to UAA Campus Buildings Currently Restricted." University of Alaska Anchorage, March 25, 2020. https://www.uaa.alaska.edu/news/archive/2020/03/access-campus-buildings-restricted.cshtml.

Hutchinson, Bill. "'Incomprehensible': Confrontations over Masks Erupt amid COVID-19 Crisis." ABC News, May 7, 2020. https://abcnews.go.com/US/incomprehensible-confrontations-masks-erupt-amid-covid-19-crisis/story?id=70494577.

Mark, Joshua J. "Plague in the Ancient and Medieval World." World History Encyclopedia, March 23, 2020. https://www.worldhistory.org/article/1528/plague-in-the-ancient--medieval-world/.

Nagle, Cailyn. "A Survey of College Students and Textbook Affordability during the COVID-19 Pandemic." In *Fixing the Broken Textbook Market*, 3rd ed. U.S. PIRG Education Fund, February 2021. https://studentpirgs.org/2021/02/24/fixing-the-broken-textbook-market-third-edition/.

Occupational Safety and Health Administration. "Control and Prevention." US Department of Labor. Accessed December 7, 2021. https://www.osha.gov/coronavirus/control-prevention.

OCLC. "How Long the Virus Survives on Commonly Used Library, Archives, and Museum Materials." REALM Project. Accessed October 5, 2021. https://www.oclc.org/content/dam/realm/documents/visual-aid.pdf.

———. "REALM Project: REopening Archives, Libraries, and Museums Research." Accessed October 5, 2021. https://www.oclc.org/realm/research.html.

Treinen, Lex. "23-Year-Old Arrested at UAA Library after Allegedly Stealing Police Officer's Rifle." NBC—2 KTUU (Anchorage, AK), January 8, 2020. Alaska's News Source, https://www.alaskasnewssource.com/content/news/23-year-old-arrested-at-UAA-library-after-allegedly-stealing-police-officers-rifle--566828021.html.

Virex. "Products." Accessed October 20, 2021. https://www.virexdisinfectant.com/products.

Wieber, Aubrey. "Anchorage Mayor Issues 'Hunker Down' Order to Curb Spread of Coronavirus." *Anchorage (AK) Daily News* (AK), March 20, 2020, last updated March 22, 2020. https://www.adn.com/alaska-news/anchorage/2020/03/21/anchorage-mayor-issues-hunker-down-order-to-curb-spread-of-coronavirus/.

CHAPTER 23

Mold Mitigation during a Pandemic
Accessible Strategies for Archivists

Kayla Van Osten and Jill M. Borin

> *Although we were prepared to confront the next mold discovery, no one anticipated the global COVID-19 pandemic and how it would affect the conditions in storage areas.*

Introduction

As librarians and archivists, we are no strangers to managing crises and are always prepared to meet any crises that may affect our collections. Environmental monitoring is essential to preserving collections and is therefore always a concern. This concern is compounded by the fact that we, like many other archivists, work in a building that lacks adequate temperature control and ventilation. Unfortunately, these conditions provide the perfect breeding ground for mold, which has forced us to be more vigilant. Mold needs two things to germinate: organic material and moisture. It can grow on various surfaces, such as wood, carpet, and insulation. According to the US Environmental Protection Agency, "it is impossible to eliminate all mold and mold spores in the indoor environment. However, mold growth can be controlled indoors by controlling moisture indoors."[1] In this chapter, we will discuss the strategies we used to manage the mold outbreaks that occurred both before and during the COVID-19 pandemic. Because closed, dark, and undisturbed areas that are lacking sufficient environmental monitoring create the perfect conditions for mold growth, the team was concerned this would lead to another outbreak.[2] Additionally, mold outbreaks can occur due to other crises, such as power outages during natural disasters, unexpected roof leaks, or mechanical failures. The affordable and accessible strategies that

301

we developed will aid others who are facing similar situations even with limited budgets and resources.

The Wolfgram Memorial Library houses the University Archives and Distinctive Collections at Widener University. The mission of the archives is to collect, preserve, and make available to researchers the institution's print and digital materials. These include papers, photographs, audiovisual items, and memorabilia related to the history of Widener and its predecessor institutions, as well as the history of the city of Chester, Pennsylvania, where the institution is located. Although the archives did not start collecting archival materials until 1952, the materials in our physical collections trace back to the founding of the institution around 1821. As archivists, the team strives to follow archival best practices and standards, especially environmental monitoring due to past crises from roof leaks and resultant water damage.

In December 2016, the University Archives acquired 300 volumes of leather-bound copies of the *Delaware County Daily Times*, a local newspaper that would have been an asset to our history of Chester collection. Due to limited storage space, these copies lived in our ground floor storage room within the library, on the floor against a concrete wall. About two years went by while we discussed ideas around what to do with these newspapers. In October 2018, the curator of the Sexuality Archives (Molly Wolf), discovered mold on the books shelved in her storage area located on this floor as well. To our knowledge, this was the first instance of mold in the library. When Archivist Jill Borin and Assistant Archivist Kayla Van Osten went to look at the bound newspapers to give them to the Delaware County Historical Society, we discovered that they were covered in mold as well. Unbeknownst to the archivists, mold can grow on concrete,[3] and it is recommended that all storage racks should be freestanding to increase air flow.[4] It is therefore not surprising that mold was found on these bound newspapers, which were stored against a concrete wall. Thus, the mold mitigation journey began.

Figure 23.1
Wolfgram Memorial Library, Widener University Chester, PA

The triangle-shaped Wolfgram Memorial Library building was built in 1970. Originally, the first floor had an open concept plan. Since then, renovations segmented the space into smaller rooms for different purposes, without consideration of proper ventilation or air handling. Due to limited space and the odd shape of the building, today the archives storage spaces are spread throughout the building, with two storage spaces on the ground floor, both of which lack adequate temperature control and an inconsistent air handling system. Ideally, the room temperature should be 65°F or lower for paper materials, with little to no temperature fluctuation to ensure the integrity of the artifacts.[5] The storage room affected by mold houses approximately 651 linear feet of shelves. Because of limited resources and budget, we had to initially use resources at hand to manage the mold outbreak. Many institutions may face a similar situation with low budgets and few to no resources, especially as the COVID-19 pandemic led to furloughs and budget cuts. Though our first mold outbreak occurred prior to COVID-19, the steps we took to mitigate mold are accessible to those institutions that may have experienced these cuts. Developing an action plan prior to a crisis can help identify steps needed to mitigate potential damage. A mold outbreak is an example of an ongoing invisible crisis that is always lurking in the background. Additional factors, such as loss of power or temperature controls from mechanical failure, could also escalate the problem. Archivists must be prepared to confront these potential issues, which the COVID-19 pandemic could have exacerbated.

The leather-bound copies of the *Daily Times* stored against a concrete wall and the humid room created the perfect breeding ground for mold in our collections. Ideally, the relative humidity (RH) for archival storage locations should remain at 65 percent or lower.[6] In our building, RH is impossible to adjust and could only be monitored. The prior archivist tracked the RH using a hygrothermograph, but without buy-in from the University or the budget to renovate, nothing else could be done to lower the relative humidity. No doubt, many institutions will face a similar situation where a full renovation or installation of better environmental controls is impossible. Yet some accessible remediation steps can mitigate these environmental hazards.

When discovering mold, the first step is to contact your maintenance or facilities department. It can help evaluate the situation and determine any next steps. Due to the large-scale mold outbreak, our facilities department hired a mold mitigation team to clean the archive storage rooms. If this is unavailable to you, there are some simple steps archivists can take. Dry brushing the affected items and sweeping the mold into a vacuum nozzle is an appropriate alternative to cleaning the items. This will not eliminate the mold, but it will decrease the chance of new growth. Providing sufficient air circulation is also an important preventative step and, on a limited budget, can be established by installing fans within the room.[7] Contacting regional organizations with expertise in mold mitigation is also an accessible and beneficial step because these organizations have a depth of experience with managing mold. They can provide free online resources and welcome any questions. Sexuality Archivist Molly Wolf consulted with the Conservation Center for Art and Historic Artifacts, a local conservation center in Philadelphia, for advice on how to preserve the artifacts. The center advised us to clean, isolate, and discard the affected items. We used these recommendations for our mold mitigation strategies.

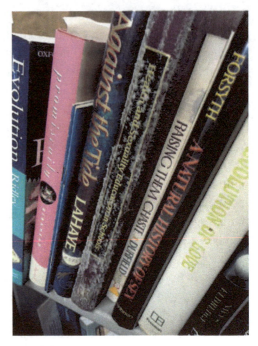

Figure 23.2
Mold on archival box

Figure 23.3
Mold on Sexuality Archives books

After discovering the mold on the bound newspapers, the team spot-checked other items in the collection that we thought might attract mold. When doing this, we discovered mold on book covers, wooden picture frames, trophies, leather-bound papers, and binders.

Using the steps recommended by the Conservation Center for Art and Historic Artifacts, we separated these moldy items into sealable plastic storage containers to isolate them from the other items in the collection. In her book *Fungal Facts*, Mary-Lou Florian recommends the use of "inexpensive packing materials that can be disposed of after one use."[8]

Our suggestions to other institutions facing similar situations are to begin by reviewing each affected item for its content, historical significance, and rarity. Consider if the artifact should be reformatted, replaced, or cleaned and rehoused. This approach will determine the next actions for preservation. The New York City Department of Health and Mental Hygiene states that nonporous materials such as metal, glass, and hard plastic can be cleaned, while semi-porous materials such as wood can be cleaned as long as they are structurally sound. All porous materials, such as ceiling tiles and insulation, should be discarded.[9] Using an alcohol disinfectant to clean nonporous items is recommended, and it is very important to keep the disinfecting area clean.

> The greatest threat to mold-free objects or objects that have been decontaminated is cross-contamination.... Contaminated materials include anything that may have come in contact with moldy objects, such as packing cases or boxes, packing materials, gloves, brushes, and other tools used during cleaning, and even the surfaces they are put on for cleaning.[10]

Using disinfectant wipes already housed in the library, the team wiped down items such as trophies and medals. There were several leather-bound scrapbooks and binders that could not be cleaned. For these items, the team removed the outer binding, and rehoused the photos and print documents in acid-free folders. Fortunately, the historical content of the artifacts could still be preserved despite discarding the damaged casings. The steps taken to clean and rehouse these items were all relatively simple and affordable, and therefore accessible to most archives.

In addition to cleaning the individual items, the team also worked with the campus facilities department to quickly get a mold remediation company to the library. The mold remediation company sealed off the room with plastic and cleaned all of the archival boxes, and shelves. The bound newspapers were not salvageable and were discarded. Knowing that mold does not really go away, it was not surprising to find more mold on other items several weeks later. After this second discovery, the mold mitigation company came back and cleaned the room a second time. After analyzing, cleaning, and rehousing the affected items, it was concluded that many of the moldy items were originally stored in older untreated classic record storage cartons with cutouts for handholds. These boxes are commonly used for record storage because they are affordable and can hold a large amount of records. While these cartons may be acid-free, they lack the laminate or acrylic coating that helps protect against moisture and, of course, do not fully seal against other environmental concerns such as dust.

DocuDry flip-top document cases were purchased from Gaylord Archival as a replacement; these moisture-resistant storage containers replaced around 100 older untreated archival boxes. The team recommends that institutions replace untreated archival boxes, especially those with cutouts, with treated, enclosed boxes to help lower the risk of a mold outbreak. Beyond preventing mold, this process had other indirect benefits, such as forcing the team to become more familiar with certain collections. Another added benefit was space consolidation; when rehousing items from the larger classic storage cartons, which fit into about three DocuDry flip-top cases, we were able to consolidate them and gain shelving space. This also made the collections more accessible because the smaller flip-top cases are easier to lift and manage due to their lighter weight. Finally, sensitive items were moved to another archival storage room on the third floor, which never had a visible mold outbreak. Each DocuDry case was given a temporary box number on a Post-it Note to expedite the process.

During the process of reshelving and organizing the archival boxes, a new building maintenance project began. The facilities department suddenly notified the archives team that it planned to hire outside contractors to remove and replace the carpet with tile in the ground floor storage areas. Although unrelated to the mold outbreak, this project was beneficial for the archives in assisting with our mold prevention goals. According to the National Collaborating Centre for Environmental Health, porous materials such as carpet cannot be effectively cleaned. Instead, carpet should be removed and discarded. Therefore, tile is preferred in archival spaces.[11] While this development was unanticipated, it was a beneficial step in addressing a potential mold "incubator" and prevent future mold outbreaks. The carpet removal and tile installation process required the relocation of over 903 linear feet of boxes in two storage areas, making this a daunting project.

Figure 23.4
Temporary Post-It Note labels on archival boxes

At this point in the mold remediation journey, the team rehoused many materials into new DocuDry flip-top document cases, but the boxes still had temporary box numbers on Post-it Notes. The National Archives and Records Administration recommends not using Post-it Notes on archival paper materials due to the residue that is left behind and the potential to cause damage over time,[12] but because these notes were affixed only to the boxes themselves, we were not concerned. While they were very useful in keeping us organized, we feared that they would fall off the boxes during the moving process. Therefore, the team quickly noted which boxes needed permanent labels, printed them, and affixed them to the boxes. The team even labeled some empty boxes as place holders to maintain the order and correct shelf spacing.

To accomplish a smooth transition, it was essential to provide guidelines that the contractors would follow to ensure that the collections were safely moved to temporary storage and returned with the order of the boxes maintained. These guidelines included a detailed explanation of how the boxes were organized, as well as a visual map to aid the contractors. The visual map would ensure that the original order was preserved, as we did not want to face a long process of reshifting and reshelving. To create the map, the archivists took pictures of each shelf and created a document with each image labeled with the shelf number and the box number range. We shared this document with the facilities department and contractors. The contractors put the archival boxes in large cardboard boxes for ease of moving and replicated the designated numbering system on these boxes. Once the tile was installed, the contractors accurately put the boxes on the correct shelves and in the correct order, a welcome surprise, as it was unclear that this would happen. The team's detailed planning contributed to this surprising and beneficial outcome. This process reinforced for everyone that careful planning and detailed guidelines for outside contractors are essential to the success of a recovery project.

Mold Mitigation during a Pandemic 307

Shelf 32: Box 770-923

Shelf 33: Box 924-1098

Figure 23.5
One section of the visual map

Figure 23.6
Labeled facilities boxes containing our archival boxes in a temporary storage room

After the tile was installed and the shelves were reassembled with the boxes now in place, the team could take advantage of the surprising benefits this ordeal provided. Archives storage increased, gaining about twenty-six linear feet of space. Along the way the team had the opportunity to learn more about the collections, especially those materials not often viewed. A short period of relative calm occurred, which allowed the team to rehouse more items into the new DocuDry flip-top document cases and devote their energies to other preservation activities. This period of relative calm was unfortunately brief and lasted only until more mold was discovered in other boxes not previously assessed. It was impossible to determine if this was the result of new mold growth or existing contaminated items that had not previously been evaluated. The discovery of mold on the same type of cultural objects, including wooden frames, cardboard encasings, and plastic notebook coverings, was not a welcome occurrence. As mold growth in archives remains a constant threat, vigilant monitoring and assessment activities are essential. The Conservation Center for Art and Historic Artifacts recommends daily walk-throughs to spot signs of mold growth,[13] which the team was doing infrequently due to additional work priorities.

Once again, the archivists followed the treatment protocols by first separating the affected items and isolating them in sealable plastic storage containers. Then the affected casings were removed, materials rehoused in acid-free folders, placed into the new DocuDry flip-top document cases, and reshelved. This new mold outbreak led to the conclusion that constant monitoring was still needed.

One of the steps for preventing an infestation of mold, requires "controlling the environment to prevent the development of the fungal structures that may be on or in the material."[14] In a building with an inconsistent HVAC system and the inability to control humidity levels, an environmental reality shared by many archives housed in university libraries, one must anticipate the inevitable discovery of more mold.

Although we were prepared to confront the next mold discovery, no one anticipated the global COVID-19 pandemic and how it would affect the conditions in storage areas. The library shut down in mid-March 2020, and most employees were unable to reenter the building for about four months. During that time, portable dehumidifiers were installed in the storage areas, and the team relied on custodial staff to monitor and empty them. According to the *Guidelines on Assessment and Remediation of Fungi in Indoor Environments*, dehumidifiers can lower humidity levels in basement storage areas during prolonged vacancy in a building.[15] This remained the only preventative approach available at the time due to the shutdown. Even with a running dehumidifier, mold on book covers was discovered during a brief visit gathering materials to answer a research question. When the university prepared to reopen the building for restricted student and staff use in the fall of 2020, an air quality study revealed poor air circulation in the building. This resulted in an upgrade of the HVAC system, which certainly benefited the environmental conditions in all storage areas, though it is not a perfect solution. Yet without access to and control of regular environmental monitoring, the team knew that future mold growth could still occur. Widener was not alone with this concern. The Conservation Center for Art and Historic Artifacts conducted a survey in August 2020, to which over 180 institutions responded. The survey found that 55 percent of the institutions reported the inability to ensure regular environmental monitoring, which was one of the concerning challenges of the shutdown caused by the pandemic.[16]

From this prolonged, arduous experience, the archivists learned that constant monitoring of archival collections is imperative to ensure swift mitigation of any future mold outbreaks. Though the initial appearance of mold in archival collection areas can seem overwhelming, institutions do not need a large budget to have successful remediation strategies. Freely available online resources from conservation centers provide guidelines and techniques to help during the remediation process. Remember the primary goal is to preserve the content of the archival materials to the best of your ability. This may require discarding any casings affected by mold that do not have any intrinsic historical value. Additionally, clear communication with the facilities department and any contractors involved is essential when an outbreak occurs to ensure proper archival procedures are followed. Mold is ever-present and a common crisis archivists need to manage. Larger crises, such as the COVID-19 pandemic, can impact the everyday threats that affect archival collections, especially when steps such as constant monitoring are unavailable. Yet by implementing simple remediation solutions, archival institutions can effectively manage these environmental hazards.

Resource List

- Conservation Center for Art and Historic Artifacts (CCAHA), https://ccaha.org/
- Gaylord Archival, https://www.gaylord.com/
- Society for American Archivists (SAA), https://www2.archivists.org/
- US Environmental Protection Agency, https://www.epa.gov/

Notes

1. US Environmental Protection Agency, *Mold Remediation in Schools and Commercial Buildings*, EPA 402-K-01-001 (Washington, DC: US Environmental Protection Agency, September 2008), 2, https://www.epa.gov/sites/production/files/2014-08/documents/moldremediation.pdf.
2. Emma Ziraldo, "Learning in the Present to Prepare for the Future: A Greater Understanding of the Impact of COVID-19 on Collections Preservation in the US," Conservation Center for Art and Historic Artifacts, August 2020, https://ccaha.org/sites/default/files/attachments/2020-12/Emma%20Ziraldo%202020%20Survey%20Data%20Analysis.pdf.
3. New York City Department of Health and Mental Hygiene, *Guidelines on Assessment and Remediation of Fungi in Indoor Environments* (New York City Department of Health and Mental Hygiene, November 2008), http://www1.nyc.gov/assets/doh/downloads/pdf/epi/epi-mold-guidelines.pdf
4. Agnes W. Brokerhof, Bert van Zanen, and Arnold den Teuling, *Fluffy Stuff*, trans. Jennifer Barnett, (Amsterdam: Netherlands Institute for Cultural Heritage [ICN], 2007), 12.
5. William K. Wilson, *Environmental Guidelines for the Storage of Paper Records* (Bethesda, MD: NISO Press, 1995), 1-2, http://www.niso.org/sites/default/files/2017-08/tr01.pdf.
6. New York City Department of Health and Mental Hygiene, *Guidelines*, 6.
7. Brokerhof, van Zanen, and den Teuling, *Fluffy Stuff*, 10; Conservation Center for Art and Historical Artifacts, *Managing a Mold Infestation* (Philadelphia: Conservation Center for Art and Historical Artifacts, September 20, 2019), https://ccaha.org/resources/managing-mold-infestation-guidelines-disaster-response.

8. Mary-Lou E. Florian, *Fungal Facts* (London: Archetype Publications, 2002), 87.
9. New York City Department of Health and Mental Hygiene, *Guidelines*, 6.
10. Mary-Lou Florian, "Aseptic Technique: A Goal to Strive for in Collection Recovery of Moldy Archival Materials and Artifacts," *Journal of the American Institute for Conservation* 39, no. 1 (2000): 114, https://doi.org/10.2307/3179967.
11. Chrystal Palaty, *Mold Remediation Recommendations*, rev. Mona M. Shum (Vancouver, BC, Canada: National Collaborating Centre for Environmental Health, October 2010, rev. March 2014), 3, https://ncceh.ca/sites/default/files/Mould_Remediation_Evidence_Review_March_2014.pdf.
12. Kristin Tyree, "To Post-it or Not to Post-it," *Smithsonian Institution Archives* (blog), September 5, 2013, https://siarchives.si.edu/blog/post-it-or-not-post-it.
13. Conservation Center for Art and Historical Artifacts, "Collections Housekeeping Guide," accessed August 12, 2021, https://ccaha.org/resources/collection-housekeeping-guide.
14. Florian, *Fungal Facts*, 115.
15. New York City Department of Health and Mental Hygiene, *Guidelines*, 23.
16. Ziraldo, "Learning in the Present."

Bibliography

Brokerhof, Agnes W., Bert van Zanen, and Arnold den Teuling. *Fluffy Stuff: Integrated Control of Mould in Archives*, Trans Jennifer Barnett. Amsterdam: Netherlands Institute for Cultural Heritage (ICN), 2007.

Conservation Center for Art and Historical Artifacts. "Collections Housekeeping Guide." Accessed August 12, 2021. https://ccaha.org/resources/collection-housekeeping-guide.

———. *Managing a Mold Infestation: Guidelines for Disaster Response*. Philadelphia: Conservation Center for Art and Historical Artifacts, September 20, 2019. https://ccaha.org/resources/managing-mold-infestation-guidelines-disaster-response

Florian, Mary-Lou E. "Aseptic Technique: A Goal to Strive for in Collection Recovery of Moldy Archival Materials and Artifacts." *Journal of the American Institute for Conservation* 39, no. 1 (2000): 107–15. https://doi.org/10.2307/3179967.

———. *Fungal Facts: Solving Fungal Problems in Heritage Collections*. London: Archetype Publications, 2002.

New York City Department of Health and Mental Hygiene. *Guidelines on Assessment and Remediation of Fungi in Indoor Environments*. New York City Department of Health and Mental Hygiene, November 2008. http://www1.nyc.gov/assets/doh/downloads/pdf/epi/epi-mold-guidelines.pdf.

Palaty, Chrystal. *Mold Remediation Recommendations*. Revised by Mona M. Shum. Vancouver, BC, Canada: National Collaborating Centre for Environmental Health, October 2010, rev. March 2014. https://ncceh.ca/sites/default/files/Mould_Remediation_Evidence_Review_March_2014.pdf.

Tyree, Kristin. "To Post-it or Not to Post-it." *Smithsonian Institution Archives* (blog), September 5, 2013. https://siarchives.si.edu/blog/post-it-or-not-post-it.

US Environmental Protection Agency. *Mold Remediation in Schools and Commercial Buildings*. EPA 402-K-01-001. Washington, DC: US Environment Protection Agency, September 2008. https://www.epa.gov/sites/production/files/2014-08/documents/moldremediation.pdf.

Wilson. William K. *Environmental Guidelines for the Storage of Paper Records*. Bethesda, MD: NISO Press, 1995. http://www.niso.org/sites/default/files/2017-08/tr01.pdf.

Ziraldo, Emma. "Learning in the Present to Prepare for the Future: A Greater Understanding of the Impact of COVID-19 on Collections Preservation in the US." Conservation Center for Art and Historic Artifacts, August 2020. https://ccaha.org/sites/default/files/attachments/2020-12/Emma%20Ziraldo%202020%20Survey%20Data%20Analysis.pdf.

CHAPTER 24

Utilizing Library Storage Facilities in Crises and Disasters

Charlotte M. Johnson and Sharon Jasneski

> Plans for transferring material to off-site storage should be well established in order to be prepared for a sudden crisis, especially if the campus climate, like ours, is one of downsizing or reusing space for other purposes.

Introduction

When disaster hits, the academic library may have several tools at its disposal, from preservation departments to third-party restoration companies to intense weeding projects. What may be overlooked, however, is the utility of the off-site storage facility in cases of crisis and disaster. In this chapter, the authors will make the case that not only do off-site storage facilities serve as an emergency resource in crises and disasters, but they should also be considered and closely integrated into libraries' disaster plans to use them most effectively. As knowledge management and institutional history are an integral part of planning and policy making,[1] the authors will recall past scenarios, describe how they have learned from them, and make recommendations based on these lessons.

When talking about crises, it is important to distinguish between crisis and disaster. This chapter considered definitions of disasters throughout library literature[2] and defined *disaster* as an incident that causes damage to the materials. *Crisis* is more broadly defined as an event or series of events that rapidly change how the library functions.

Off-site storage is defined as a facility separate from the main and departmental libraries, usually in a location removed from campus. The authors will focus mostly on high-density remote storage facilities (the Harvard model), which Walker describes as a facility where items are shelved by size, not by call number, and each item has a unique barcode.[3]

Off-Site Storage at the University of Pittsburgh

The University of Pittsburgh's off-site facility is formally called ULS-Thomas Boulevard, but internally referred to as LCSU (library collections storage unit). The original building was constructed in 2002 and holds three million items. It is a stark upgrade from the previous facility, known as UPARC, which was prone to flooding and other environmental factors that made it subpar for storing library materials.

This chapter is rooted in the knowledge management model outlined in Islam, Agarwal, and Ikeda.[4] The authors capture the institutional knowledge, share it in this chapter, and then use these stories to synthesize general suggestions for library managers to use in including off-site storage in their disaster and crisis policies. Sharon Jasneski, the operations manager, and head of LCSU, has worked in library storage for over twenty years and has a wealth of experiences and stories to share, which will help the reader to better understand the potential and additional resilience offered by off-site storage for libraries. She will provide the stories in this chapter. Charlotte M. Johnson, LCSU's librarian, will contextualize these stories within the broader literature and provide commentary and suggestions for other library managers.

Disasters and Prevention

Disasters in libraries take many forms: water (from burst pipes, heavy rains, hurricanes, or other sources), earthquakes, sinkholes, fires, civil unrest, and more. An abundance of literature exists about how libraries handle disasters. Less common is literature illustrating the role off-site facilities play in these situations. For example, when Hurricane Katrina ravaged New Orleans and surrounding areas, Tulane University's off-site storage facility became the headquarters for the material recovery efforts.[5] Calvert writes of shared storage in New Zealand, "[dividing up the collection among several facilities] also helps spread the risk of loss, simply because multiple stores rather than one reduces the risk of losing everything in a single disaster."[6] Finally, Teper and Pilette discuss research done in high-density storage disaster prevention for fire-prone regions.[7]

Not only do off-site facilities play reactive roles during disasters, but with the proper planning and measures, they also play a preventative role. Concerns like theft, vandalism, mold, and material decay are examples of disasters that can be prevented with well-designed off-site storage. Off-site storage also lessens the chances of human-related disasters such as theft and vandalism by restricting physical access to the collections behind a security system, thus making sure every item that leaves the facility is accounted for.

Climate-controlled facilities with proper HVAC prevent mold spores from flourishing that may have appeared on materials before they went to storage. Off-site facilities' environmental controls, when designed properly, also provide the best climate for the preservation of materials, slowing the deterioration of materials over time.[8] These preventative measures are especially important if the facility stores archival or special collections, as the facility at the University of Pittsburgh does. Scenarios like these can happen at any time. Here, Sharon recalls the disasters the team has responded to and how they have impacted best practices.

The Thomas Boulevard Flood of 2018

Sharon: "Many libraries have experienced water disasters, especially those located in older buildings with older pipes and leaky windows. In January 2018, the Library Resource Facility, a building housing several library and university departments, experienced a massive flood caused by a broken pipe on the roof. This caused water to pierce the roof in the early hours of the morning when the first employees were arriving, pouring water onto the mostly vacant fifth floor, as well as the fourth floor, which housed archival collections in various states of processing and the University of Pittsburgh Press; several office areas on the third floor, where Technical Services and the Digital Research Library were located; and the Preservation Lab on the second floor. Massive amounts of water poured into these spaces, and water could be seen shooting through a crack on the outside of the building.

"As a member of the Disaster Response Team and a unit head, I was notified early in the morning of the disaster and asked to come in immediately. Each department gathered as many employees as possible and scrambled to move materials, computers, and printers, beginning the clean-up process as University Facilities employees turned off the water. The building manager was able to contact the preservation coordinator, who was (of course) out of town on vacation, and relayed instructions to the people who worked to remove and salvage damaged collections.

"Unlike most of the departments in the building, LCSU was not directly affected by the disaster. However, the preservation coordinator knew that her department, which consisted primarily of students who had not yet arrived to work, was flooded and had no one to work on clearing out the lab and cleaning up the nearly two inches of water that pooled on the floors. The archivists were busy moving their own collections on the fourth floor and assisting the press. Technical Services had many areas impacted on the third floor. IT worked with Technical Services because, in addition to collections, computers and printers were located under small waterfalls. Therefore, several of the LCSU staff and I jumped in and led the cleanup of Preservation.

"I had been a member of the Disaster Response Team for many years because historically where we stored our older material was frequently the home of water tragedies. Having dealt with several of my own at UPARC, I was well versed in the art of interleaving paper towels in wet pages and setting them up with fans for drying. I also had my own cache of preservation materials, like absorbent pads for standing water, plastic sheeting to shield materials from active leaks, fans, paper towels, and a wet/dry vacuum. I also had several 100-foot extension cords on hand. Because our lengthy extension cords needed to accommodate the size of the high-density warehouse, the cords allowed the cleanup crew plenty of mobility.

"At the time, the LCSU consisted of five employees, including me. Two people remained in the department to fulfill the requests for the morning while the other three of us grabbed our wet/dry vacuum, mops from the cleaning closet, and plastic sheeting and headed for the second floor. The wet/dry vacuum we had was the only one available at the time since the two Preservation had were in use on the third and fourth floors. The cleanup ended up taking the better part of that day, and other staff did end up coming to help as we went on.

"There were a few lessons learned. Having a formalized disaster response plan and a team with training or experience is crucial. We benefited from having many people with experience, so the cleanup and recovery started immediately, saving collections and office equipment from further damage. It is also important to have a disaster cache of equipment and tools readily available to anyone. We were fortunate that the disaster happened in the same building as our Preservation Department, but all our libraries have at least a small cache. We could have certainly used more wet/dry vacuums, so more have been purchased."

Recovery at LCSU

Sharon: "There have been times when LCSU assisted Archives and Special Collections with materials in damaged condition, such as books that were encased in vellum and degrading film. One summer, the temperatures on the fourth floor of Thomas Boulevard, where we kept much of the Archives and Special Collections materials during a renovation project, rose to over eighty degrees and the humidity was so terribly low that the vellum books started to warp and twist. Fortunately, at LCSU, we have an environment perfect for paper materials, with a consistent sixty-five degree temperature and a humidity range of 40 to 45 percent, so the books were moved there temporarily until they relaxed and were able to be returned to their department. Additionally, the size of the warehouse means that even if the HVAC is turned off or power is lost for a time, the building's temperature and relative humidity are not going to shift quickly, preventing any mold spores from activating and materials from degrading faster. A shelf of film from a recently acquired collection was suffering from "vinegar syndrome," (a term for when film begins to degrade, releasing a vinegar-like smell) and Archives and Special Collections wanted to put it in a much more stable environment, so LCSU also housed that for a while. We had a lot of available space that we were able to utilize for setting up fans and segregating materials."

As with the first story, water may be the most common culprit of library disasters. Sharon mentions her expertise from other water damage disasters at our previous facility. As this older facility was not built for good storage practices, we suffered from water damage. This is something to keep in mind during facility construction or retrofitting. Administrators need to balance the need for cost saving with the need for preservation and disaster prevention. Poor storage conditions may end up costing more in recovery efforts or loss of materials. A space less prone to disaster also makes off-site storage an ideal place to stage materials during their recovery, as we see both in Sharon's example of rescuing the vellum books and in the case of Tulane University's hurricane recovery.

While in our case, the water damage at Thomas Boulevard did not extend to our storage facility, our team was well situated to help. If LCSU itself were to experience any disasters, it would likely be heavy water damage from pipes, smoke hatches in the roof required by city fire code, or fire suppression measures. To prevent these kinds of disasters, staff should constantly monitor for leaks and other signs of damage to the facility, especially during heavy rain or snow melt, and report all leaks immediately to the appropriate building managers. Have the personal contact information of all pertinent parties for when they are not at the site. They should also monitor the facility's temperature and relative humidity to maintain the ideal storage environment: between 50 and 70 degrees Fahrenheit and 30 to 50 percent relative humidity.

Since LCSU holds most of the general collection as well as Archives and Special Collections materials, it is imperative that we take preventative measures against water and other forms of damage. Managers of off-site facilities need to develop good working relationships with those responsible for the building so that early warning signs of damage can be addressed and that when disaster strikes, the culprit is addressed as quickly and effectively as possible. It is also useful to work closely with library preservation staff, who can answer questions about non-paper materials or best practices in stemming disaster-related damage. To that end, managers and their partners also need to have a disaster plan specifically designed for the high-density storage environment if applicable. Pilette points out, after all, that high-density off-site library storage is different from a typical warehouse environment.[9]

Crises

The issue of running out of space to shelve collections has long been referred to as a space crisis, and this is the foundational reason for the invention of off-site storage facilities. For example, Iowa State's facility was built expressly for the emergency of too rapidly increasing collection sizes and not enough places to put them.[10] It was an alternative to compact shelving or building another library. Other crises have also called for the use of off-site storage. During World War II, items had to be moved from the Harvard College Library to the New England Deposit Library in order to make space for training army and navy recruits.[11] Snowman describes how Penn State's Annex proved useful when books had to be removed from the main library due to unsafe conditions and explicitly argues:

> The availability of space controlled by the Libraries to facilitate phased renovations or rapid response to a structural emergency greatly reduced the expense of these initiatives while maintaining access to the collections. Though not the prevailing reason for implementing a storage program, this has been perhaps one of its most significant benefits.[12]

Even a renovation can be considered a crisis if the deadline is close enough. Take, for example, the four months Duke University Medical Center Library and Archives had to clear off an entire floor for other use by the university.[13] One of its main strategies was to move materials to storage. Sharon can recall two such crises in recent memory.

Hillman Library Renovation

Sharon: "In 2018, the University of Pittsburgh's Hillman Library began a major multiphase, multiyear renovation project. By the time contracts were signed and schedules were solidified, the contractors were ready to start working, leaving the libraries six months to move 210,000 items before the top floor of Hillman closed for construction. To get as much material out of Hillman as possible, ten to fifteen transport trucks a day were dispatched, each truck holding twelve to sixteen linear feet of material, regardless of whether we could process that quantity. Even with five temporary workers, we couldn't receive, measure, and scan enough items into trays before the next batch came. Approximately 20,000 books ended up being temporarily shelved in a side room until they could be processed.

"At that time, catalog maintenance for transferred materials was not completed by catalogers and metadata librarians, but by Hillman service desk staff who were not formally trained in cataloging. Despite training efforts, we found error rates were around 1 percent—still a large number, considering the 200,000+ items the team processed. Unfortunately, I was the only person providing quality control, and I could not fix all the errors and still get the materials accessioned and shelved in time for the next batch. Many errors persist to this day.

"After the first year, I was placed on the renovation-move team, which enabled us to address some of the problems that we were experiencing. I was able to communicate with the renovation team to reinforce what I thought LCSU could accomplish in a day: how fast could we turn around transport trucks. We also asked Technical Services experts to complete the transfers in the catalog, greatly reducing the number of problems and ensuring a more accurate catalog.

"By the end of the first phase of the Hillman renovation, we accessioned 350,000 items in just over sixteen months. Without the high-density storage facility, we would have had to withdraw a lot of material, including titles that potentially would be used.

"We were not always able to respond like this, though. At our previous facility, UPARC, transferring books to storage was easier and faster. We weren't a high-density storage facility, so processing meant we assigned books an accession number based on the order we received them and placed them on warehouse shelves. Staff didn't need order-picker training, so we could have temporary staff assist with shelving materials. In our current facility, that is not the case. Items are sorted by size, which increases processing time but allows for the storage of much more material. More catalog processing is also required so that books are easily requestable online and retrievable. In addition, we did not previously house special collections at UPARC, but when we moved to Thomas Boulevard, we began collecting special collections and archival materials, and accessioning became a lot more complicated. Suddenly there were more sizes, formats, and types of boxes to store that required different handling procedures.

"Still, the move to the Harvard high-density storage model from the UPARC model was critical because being able to house more and different material while being able to easily request and use collections is necessary. UPARC was a place that the libraries sent materials that they didn't have the heart to withdraw, but that they didn't want people necessarily requesting either. After all, UPARC was fifteen to twenty miles off campus, and there was only one courier run a day. Things were not going to come back to campus quickly. Naturally, it was going to be a fairly dead collection.

"Finally, we could not accomplish as much as we did without our silver transport trucks (figure 24.1). They were designed specifically for use in storage (modified from the wooden carts used at the University of Minnesota), which was the best thing we ever did. Shipping materials in these trucks via a courier with a small moving truck has been key to moving large numbers of materials and keeping them out of the elements. Some of those trucks are now fifteen years old, and they're still working well. It's probably one of the things we've created that I'm most proud of. In UPARC days we boxed everything, which was time-consuming and expensive, as the boxes wear down over time. The trucks can also lock, which is good for transporting special collections safely and securely."

As we see in this story, planning for a transfer project can take much longer than administration may expect: from selection to the logistics of moving off campus to cataloging to accessioning and shelving. We're experiencing the same crunch at the time of writing this chapter, as we move into our next phase of the Hillman renovation. If our libraries didn't have an off-site storage facility, we might be spending a small fortune on commercial storage that would not allow us to provide our patrons with access to the collections.

Thanks to Sharon's institutional knowledge, LCSU has developed a new cataloging and accessioning process and changed our transfer team roster since the first move, and already we are seeing an improvement in efficiency and accuracy. Plans for transferring material to off-site storage should be well established in order to be prepared for a sudden crisis, especially if the campus climate, like ours, is one of downsizing or reusing space for other purposes. As space needs change in the on-campus libraries, we will end up storing most of our collections off-site, and it's important that they remain in good condition and

Figure 24.1
Metal transport trucks are an invaluable part of moving collections to storage

accessible to our patrons. Off-site storage's accessioning process should account for the location of every item, ensuring that patrons can still request materials.

Additionally, when constructing or renovating an off-site storage facility, it is useful to build in staging areas, where large numbers of books can sit on bookshelves or carts while waiting to be accessioned. Having proper equipment, such as the aforementioned silver trucks, on hand for sudden moves is also an invaluable resource, saving money that would be spent on large numbers of plastic bins or cardboard boxes.

The COVID-19 Pandemic

Sharon: "In the early days of the pandemic, the campus libraries closed their doors to patrons, but we kept filling scanning requests and ILL requests, following COVID-19 safety protocols. At LCSU, we were well situated to take on this new way of working, being that we had more space than anywhere else. Staff can easily socially distance in storage, unlike elsewhere on campus. We didn't interact with the public face-to-face and were able to easily shut ourselves off from the rest of the Thomas Boulevard building. It really worked out well: we were slowly able to increase staffing on-site to scan materials as time passed, and we had at least half the collection right there at our fingertips.

"One bonus of being at Thomas Boulevard is that we share a building with our acquisitions department and university mailroom. This meant that all new books being purchased were coming into our building. Faculty needed these books digitized for course reserves, and we had a great overhead scanner. We had never scanned material for reserves before, but it was something that I think we were eager to do because, at least for me, we wanted to feel useful in some way during a trying time. The COVID-19 pandemic can certainly be classified as a crisis since it severely interrupted staff workflows and required a rapid response. The pandemic also contributed to sudden space changes in the libraries. For LCSU, that meant clearing collections from another part of the building to accommodate the University of Pittsburgh's increased shipping and surplus materials activities. This resulted in LCSU installing ranges of "person-height" shelving in our high bay and moving our miscellanea there until they can be addressed."

Pandemic-related literature has already started being published and presented, but none yet specifically about off-site storage. As Sharon says, off-site storage is uniquely situated to provide service during this time of limited services because of it has enough space to remain socially distanced and lacks face-to-face interaction with patrons. Ellero credits the uninterrupted service to patrons at her library in part to the off-site storage facility.[14] While the pandemic still goes on, we are learning what works and how to best move forward.

Conclusion

These stories provide examples of practical application of the benefits of having off-site storage facilities. During a crisis or disaster, off-site storage is invaluable for its separation from the main library, its environmental conditions, and the amount of space available.

For those libraries that already have off-site storage facilities, it is important to consider how these potential benefits will fit into current disaster plans and to plan space usage strategically so these benefits are not lost. For libraries considering off-site storage, the benefits outlined in this chapter cannot be overlooked in the decision-making process. The more libraries can identify their resources and integrate them into their planning, the more smoothly crisis aversion and disaster recovery will go.

Notes

1. Md Anwarul Islam, Naresh Kumar Agarwal, and Mitsuru Ikeda, "Effect of Knowledge Management on Service Innovation in Academic Libraries," *IFLA Journal* 43, no. 3 (2017): 266–81, https://doi.org/10.1177/0340035217710538.
2. Michael Ahenkorah-Marfo and Edward Mensah Borteye, "Disaster Preparedness in Academic Libraries: The Case of the Kwame Nkrumah University of Science and Technology Library, Kumasi, Ghana," *Library and Archival Security* 23, no. 2 (2010): 117–36, https://doi.org/10.1080/01960075.2010.501417; Bibi Alajmi, "When the Nation Is in Crisis: Libraries Respond," *Library Management* 37, no. 8/9 (2016): 465–81, https://doi.org/10.1108/LM-05-2016-0043; Promise Ifeoma Ilo et al., "Challenges of Disaster Training: Implication for Federal and State University Libraries in Nigeria," *Disaster Prevention and Management* 28, no. 3 (2019): 332–42, https://doi.org/10.1108/DPM-05-2018-0175; Yeni Budi Rachman, "Disaster Preparedness of Academic Libraries: A Case Study from Indonesia," *Preservation, Digital Technology and Culture* 49, no. 2 (2020): 67–74, https://doi.org/10.1515/pdtc-2020-0002; Catherine Soehner, Ian Godfrey, and G. Scott Bigler, "Crisis Communication in Libraries: Opportunity for New Roles in Public Relations," *Journal of Academic Librarianship* 43, no. 3 (May 2017): 268–73, https://doi.org/10.1016/j.acalib.2017.03.003.
3. Ben Walker, "Drafting Recommendations for a Shared Statewide High-Density Storage Facility: Experiences with the State University Libraries of Florida Proposal," *Resource Sharing and Information Networks* 19, no. 1–2 (2008): 51–62, https://doi.org/10.1080/07377790802427381.
4. Islam, Agarwal, and Ikeda, "Effect of Knowledge Management."
5. Andy Corrigan, "Disaster: Response and Recovery at a Major Research Library in New Orleans," *Library Management* 29, no. 4/5 (2008): 293–306, https://doi.org/10.1108/01435120810869084; Elisa F. Topper, "After Hurricane Katrina: The Tulane Recovery Project," *New Library World* 112, no. 1/2 (2011): 45–51, https://doi.org/10.1108/03074801111100445.
6. Philip Calvert, "A Low-Cost National Cooperative Store: The CONZUL Experience," *Journal of Interlibrary Loan, Document Delivery and Electronic Reserve* 28, no. 1–2 (2019): 29, https://doi.org/10.1080/1072303X.2019.1655513.
7. Roberta Pilette and Jennifer Teper, "Preparing for the Worst: Disaster Planning for High Density Storage," webinar, ALCTS Continuing Education, recorded February 22, 2012, YouTube video, 59:29, posted August 22, 2012, https://www.youtube.com/watch?v=FVybdyz7bJ8.
8. Catherine Murray-Rust, "Library Storage as a Preservation Strategy," in *Advances in Librarianship*, vol. 27, ed. Frederick C. Lynden, (Bingley, UK: Emerald, 2009), 159–83, https://doi.org/10.1016/S0065-2830(03)27006-9.
9. Pilette and Teper, "Preparing for the Worst."
10. Charles E. Friley and Robert W. Orr, "A Decade of Book Storage at Iowa State College," *College and Research Libraries* 12, no. 1 (January 1951): 7–10, https://doi.org/10.5860/crl_12_01_7.
11. Francis X. Doherty, "The New England Deposit Library: Organization and Administration," *Library Quarterly* 19, no. 1 (1949): 1–18.
12. Ann MacKay Snowman, "The Penn State Annex: The Life and Times of an Off-Site Storage Facility," *Collection Management* 30, no. 1 (2005): 51, https://doi.org/10.1300/J105v30n01_05.
13. Patricia L. Thibodeau, "When the Library Is Located in Prime Real Estate: A Case Study on the Loss of Space from the Duke University Medical Center Library and Archives," *Journal of the Medical Libraries Association* 98, no. 1 (January 2010): 25–28, https://doi.org/10.3163/1536-5050.98.1.010.

14. Nadine Ellero, "An Unusual Story of Perseverance, Privilege and Prosperity during a Pandemic," *Christian Librarian* 64, no. 1 (2021): article 10, https://digitalcommons.georgefox.edu/tcl/vol64/iss1/10.

Bibliography

Ahenkorah-Marfo, Michael, and Edward Mensah Borteye. "Disaster Preparedness in Academic Libraries: The Case of the Kwame Nkrumah University of Science and Technology Library, Kumasi, Ghana." *Library and Archival Security* 23, no. 2 (2010): 117–36. https://doi.org/10.1080/01960075.2010.501417.

Alajmi, Bibi. "When the Nation Is in Crisis: Libraries Respond." *Library Management* 37, no. 8/9 (2016): 465–81. https://doi.org/10.1108/LM-05-2016-0043;

Calvert, Philip. "A Low-Cost National Cooperative Store: The CONZUL Experience." *Journal of Interlibrary Loan, Document Delivery and Electronic Reserve* 28, no. 1–2 (2019): 25–33. https://doi.org/10.1080/1072303X.2019.1655513.

Corrigan, Andy. "Disaster: Response and Recovery at a Major Research Library in New Orleans." *Library Management* 29, no. 4/5 (2008): 293–306. https://doi.org/10.1108/01435120810869084.

Doherty, Francis X. "The New England Deposit Library: Organization and Administration." *Library Quarterly* 19, no. 1 (1949): 1–18.

Ellero, Nadine. "An Unusual Story of Perseverance, Privilege and Prosperity during a Pandemic." *Christian Librarian* 64, no. 1 (2021): article 10. https://digitalcommons.georgefox.edu/tcl/vol64/iss1/10.

Friley Charles E., and Robert W. Orr. "A Decade of Book Storage at Iowa State College." *College and Research Libraries* 12, no. 1 (January 1951): 7–10. https://doi.org/10.5860/crl_12_01_7.

Ilo, Promise Ifeoma, Margaret Ngwuchukwu, Happiness Chijioke Michael-Onuoha, and Chidi Segun-Adeniran. "Challenges of Disaster Training: Implication for Federal and State University Libraries in Nigeria." *Disaster Prevention and Management* 28, no. 3 (2019): 332–42. https://doi.org/10.1108/DPM-05-2018-0175.

Islam, Md Anwarul, Naresh Kumar Agarwal, and Mitsuru Ikeda. "Effect of Knowledge Management on Service Innovation in Academic Libraries." *IFLA Journal* 43, no. 3 (2017): 266–81. https://doi.org/10.1177/0340035217710538.

Murray-Rust, Catherine. "Library Storage as a Preservation Strategy." In *Advances in Librarianship*, vol. 27, edited by Frederick C. Lynden, 159–83. Bingley, UK: Emerald, 2009. https://doi.org/10.1016/S0065-2830(03)27006-9.

Pilette, Roberta, and Jennifer Hain-Teper. "Preparing for the Worst: Disaster Planning for High Density Storage." Webinar, ALCTS Continuing Education. Recorded February 22, 2012. YouTube video, 59:29. Posted August 22, 2012. https://www.youtube.com/watch?v=FVybdyz7bJ8.

Rachman, Yeni Budi. "Disaster Preparedness of Academic Libraries: A Case Study from Indonesia." *Preservation, Digital Technology and Culture* 49, no. 2 (2020): 67–74. https://doi.org/10.1515/pdtc-2020-0002.

Snowman, Ann MacKay. "The Penn State Annex: The Life and Times of an Off-Site Storage Facility." *Collection Management* 30, no. 1 (2005): 45–53. https://doi.org/10.1300/J105v30n01_05.

Soehner, Catherine, Ian Godfrey, and G. Scott Bigler. "Crisis Communication in Libraries: Opportunity for New Roles in Public Relations." *Journal of Academic Librarianship* 43, no. 3 (May 2017): 268–73. https://doi.org/10.1016/j.acalib.2017.03.003.

Thibodeau, Patricia L. "When the Library Is Located in Prime Real Estate: A Case Study on the Loss of Space from the Duke University Medical Center Library and Archives." *Journal of the Medical Libraries Association* 98, no. 1 (January 2010): 25–28. https://doi.org/10.3163/1536-5050.98.1.010.

Topper, Elisa F. "After Hurricane Katrina: The Tulane Recovery Project." *New Library World* 112, no. 1/2 (2011): 45–51. https://doi.org/10.1108/03074801111100445.

Walker, Ben. "Drafting Recommendations for a Shared Statewide High-Density Storage Facility: Experiences with the State University Libraries of Florida Proposal." *Resource Sharing and Information Networks* 19, no. 1–2 (2008): 51–62. https://doi.org/10.1080/07377790802427381.

CHAPTER 25

Task Sharing in Academic Libraries

Creating Opportunities for Professional Growth and Community during Times of Crisis

Yuki Hibben, Laura Westmoreland Gariepy, and M. Teresa Doherty

---

> Both early in the pandemic and later once buildings were reopened, task sharing allowed the library to improve discovery and usability of library resources, respond to users' needs more quickly, and advance or complete projects that had been on the back burner, which otherwise may not have been addressed for some time.

Introduction

In 2018, Virginia Commonwealth University (VCU) Libraries accepted an invitation to join the Association of Research Libraries as its 125th member. That same year, VCU Libraries received the Association of College and Research Libraries' prestigious Excellence in Academic Libraries Award. Library employees were thrilled to be recognized for their work and filled with optimism about the future. The budget was relatively stable, several new positions were established, and organizational growth was on the horizon. This positive momentum was to be derailed by unforeseen circumstances.

Unfortunately, 2020 brought unprecedented challenges to the VCU library system. COVID-19 affected all operations at the university and introduced extraordinary stressors into the workplace. Amid evolving and unpredictable circumstances, the dean of libraries proceeded with his planned retirement after twenty-one years of service.

Although a few additional retirements were also anticipated, an unexpected number of library employees decided to retire or leave the university, possibly due, at least in part, to concerns and uncertainties related to the pandemic and impending leadership changes. In an effort to provide flexibility for the incoming dean, VCU Libraries senior administration deferred rehiring of library positions except in the most critical instances. Anticipating a budget shortfall, the university also instituted a soft hiring freeze that required extra layers of approval to hire even essential positions.

When the VCU Libraries' buildings closed temporarily in 2020 due to COVID-19, teleworking employees contributed to the organization in new and innovative ways, but also exacerbated issues related to short staffing. After the buildings reopened, employees continued teleworking or returned to work on-site depending on their essential job functions and individual circumstances. The continuing vacancies and affordance of telework often placed a disproportionate burden on employees responsible for frontline in-person services and on-site operations.

A year before the pandemic, the Special Collections and Archives (SC&A) department at VCU Libraries struggled to staff its service desk due to unexpected vacancies. The department head of SC&A reached out to the head of the Information Services and Learning Spaces department (IS&LS)—both of whom were serving in interim leadership roles—and learned that a staff member was interested in learning more about archival work. After several discussions, the two departments embarked on a task-sharing pilot arrangement: the staff member from IS&LS would work several hours each week on the SC&A service desk while learning more about the role of an archivist. The temporary task sharing began as a voluntary arrangement intended to benefit everyone involved. To articulate the objectives and expectations of the arrangement, the department heads and staff members collaborated to draft a memorandum of understanding (MOU) including specifics such as the hours of work, schedule, and dates for evaluating the arrangement. An MOU is a written document that outlines the responsibilities of each party in the agreement.[1] Criteria used to evaluate the arrangement included the degree to which it benefitted the respective employees and the departments and whether they continued to meet the business needs of the organization.

As an experimental measure, the task-sharing initiative succeeded—it met operational needs while also providing an opportunity for cross-training and career development, inspiring other managers and employees to discuss other comparable ideas for more staff integrations and to develop similar arrangements. Designed to redistribute responsibilities and develop talent, task sharing can also foster cooperation, mentoring, and community support.[2] Task sharing prior to the pandemic set the stage for a collaborative spirit and flexible work approach. When the pandemic hit, the libraries embraced task sharing more extensively as a strategy to address staffing and operational challenges.

What Is Task Sharing?

Task sharing emerged in the health professions in the mid-2000s as a strategy to mitigate critical staffing shortages and expand services to underserved communities.[3] By cross-training cadres of health-care workers to perform tasks that are typically handled by a different group of professionals, the number and categories of personnel who can provide certain services are increased.[4] For example, the World Health Organization recommends that tasks typically handled by nurses and midwives, such as contraceptive injections, can be shared with pharmacists and well-trained health-care workers to increase access to family planning in localities and countries where essential services are constrained due to a shortage of health-care workers.[5] The Centers for Disease Control and Prevention suggests that task sharing can reduce the workload of overburdened health-care workers and safeguard providers in high-risk health categories from exposure to COVID-19, particularly in low-resource settings outside of the United States.[6] The benefits of task sharing as seen in the health-care professions include sharing the workload in a more equitable manner, expanding tasks that employees can perform, increasing skill sets of employees through cross-training and career development, and filling gaps in services.[7] While not as common in larger academic libraries given the high degree of specialization employees often assume, the concept of cross-training and task sharing is not new to libraries, especially in smaller academic libraries where employees tend to wear multiple hats by necessity.[8]

As a pilot initiative, VCU Libraries introduced task sharing as a voluntary work arrangement in which an employee assumed temporary responsibility for functions outside of their primary job responsibilities in order to develop career goals and meet organizational needs. Task sharing arrangements at VCU Libraries differ from interim appointments. An employee in an interim role assumes responsibility for most or all of a vacant full-time position at an administrative level above their permanent role. Interim appointments are usually initiated by management or administration and include compensation in the form of a salary adjustment. In task sharing at VCU Libraries, the employee or manager can initiate the arrangement, responsibilities may be limited to specific tasks, and primary job duties generally take priority. Task sharing is a part-time arrangement in which the employee dedicates relatively few hours to work outside of the scope of their normal duties while continuing their primary responsibilities at a reduced percentage. The work is typically at the same level of responsibility as the employee's regular duties and does not require a salary adjustment. It also differs substantially from a job reassignment, which involves an administrative decision to transfer an employee to another position based on operational or strategic needs.

Task sharing should not be confused with the similar-sounding but distinct work arrangement known as job sharing. According to the United States Department of Labor, job sharing is when "two (or more) workers share the duties of one full-time job, each working part-time, or two or more workers who have unrelated part-time assignments share the same budget line."[9] Job sharing developed in the 1970s as women became an increasingly vital part of the labor force and desired greater flexibility to balance their work and home lives.[10] Unlike task sharing, where employees assume specific responsibilities in a temporary arrangement, employees in a job-sharing arrangement collaborate to fulfill the overall objectives of one permanent position, each receiving a prorated portion of the full-time salary.[11] COVID-19 has led to a resurgence in flexible work arrangements such as job sharing, which is available at many academic institutions.

Pilot Initiatives

VCU Libraries embarked on its first task sharing initiative in January 2019. As described in the introduction, the arrangement was initiated by the department managers as a strategy to address the staff shortage in SC&A. The IS&LS department was fully staffed at the time, and its staffing model required some redundancy to allow for desk rotations and staff leave. In addition to their primary responsibilities of providing research support and user assistance at the library's main service desk, IS&LS staff devoted a percentage of their hours each week to other duties, providing some flexibility for staff to consider task sharing. VCU had also launched a new human resources initiative in 2018 that required all staff to create an annual career development plan with goals and learning objectives. According to VCU Human Resources,

> Career planning is a collaborative process between the employee and their manager and allows employees to focus on their needs for growth and development. Managers provide support, resources, guidance, and other assistance so that employees have the opportunity to grow in their careers.[12]

The combination of employee-centered career development expectations, an environment supporting mentoring and learning, and the capacity for staff to devote a percentage of their time to duties outside of their primary roles made it possible for IS&LS staff to participate in the task-sharing pilot.

In addition to its potential to address staff shortages, SC&A saw task sharing with IS&LS as an opportunity for frontline staff who respond to different but frequently overlapping research inquiries to share their skills and knowledge. Not only would task sharing facilitate cross-training and staff development, but it could also enhance consistency and service quality between the IS&LS and SC&A service desks. Following initial conversations regarding task sharing, the head of IS&LS identified a staff member who was interested in the pilot and had the capacity to participate. The staff member was a recent graduate of the history program at VCU, had some experience using archival collections, and was interested in learning more about working in SC&A. As a voluntary arrangement aligning with the employee's career development plan to learn about archival work, the pilot promised to be a positive and beneficial experience for all involved.

Following two weeks of formal training including materials handling, patron registrations, reading room rules, and the use of ArchivesSpace and other resources, the IS&LS staff member worked alongside SC&A staff before working independently on the service desk. The arrangement gave staff in two different departments the opportunity to work closely together, share experiences, and develop a greater understanding and appreciation of their respective roles. The department head also arranged for the IS&LS staff member to meet with archivists to learn about their work. Once trained to work on the service desk, the IS&LS staff member began assisting with inventorying and other collection management projects. Whenever possible, the IS&LS staff member attended SC&A meetings and social events and was perceived as a member of the SC&A team. Hearing positive reports about the task sharing pilot, another IS&LS staff member expressed an interest in participating in a similar arrangement, helping the library's conservator. Again, the arrangement was possible because the staff member had the capacity to perform other duties while meeting their primary responsibilities. The task sharing also met the staff member's career development plan to build on their previous book repair experience and to develop new preservation skills. The conservator needed assistance and was amenable to training the staff member, but recommended that an MOU be drafted to articulate expectations and outline tasks. She had used an MOU form for similar purposes at another institution and agreed to adapt it for use at VCU Libraries (see figure 25.1).

October 22, 2019
Memorandum of Understanding

Information Associate X will assist the Collections Care Librarian and Conservator in the preservation of VCU Libraries' materials for 4-5 hours per week beginning on Tuesday October 22, 2019 as part of their work at VCU Libraries.

Tasks may include: Repairing and caring for materials from VCU Libraries' circulating collections: mending paper, rebinding books, re-sewing, spine repairs, making enclosures to house materials, and assisting with other collections care tasks in a variety of formats. There are also projects that come up that include (but are not limited to): collection surveys, environmental monitoring, outreach/education, and emergency preparedness. The ability to work independently and maintain a record of work will be required as well as the ability to collaborate and share space in a workshop environment. Training sessions with the student worker Collections Care Technicians are held on Tuesday afternoons so it is important that *Information Associate X* is able to attend these as much as possible so that they can learn how to treat the materials that come to Preservation for repair.

Collections Care Librarian and Conservator
Signature: _____ Date: __Oct. 22, 2019___

Interim Head, Information Services & Learning Spaces
Signature: _____ Date: __Oct. 22, 2019___

Information Associate X
Signature: _____ Date: __Oct. 22, 2019___

Figure 25.1
Memorandum of understanding for a task-sharing arrangement in preservation, VCU Libraries, 2019.

While drafting this task sharing MOU with the conservator, the head of IS&LS invited SC&A to follow suit. The department heads and staff member worked together to draft an MOU specifying the following:

> [Staff member name] will assist Special Collections and Archives (SC&A) by providing research support on the service desk 3 hours per week beginning January 9, 2019. Their hours will be Wednesdays from 2:00 to 5:00 p.m. The purpose of this arrangement is two-fold: to provide this Information Associate with a meaningful professional development opportunity as part of their work for VCU Libraries, and to assist SCA with essential business functions.

The MOU also outlined tasks that the staff member would be trained to accomplish: registering patrons, recording patron interactions, paging materials, monitoring the reading room, instructing patrons on the proper handling of rare books and manuscripts, and using tools such as ArchivesSpace, ArchiveGrid, and local indexes.

As new task sharing arrangements developed, MOUs also evolved to provide more clarity about the nature and requirements of the working relationships (see figure 25.2). Provisions outlined in various MOUs across the organization include but are not limited to the following:

- The employee, supervisors, and project managers will maintain open lines of communication regarding employee workload, performance, and how the task sharing is working for all parties.
- The ability to work independently and maintain a record of work will be required, as well as the ability to collaborate and communicate in an online environment.
- The work of the employee's home department will take priority over this task sharing when research support/desk hours, patron appointments, and instruction are needed. Adjustments may need to be made to the employee's goals to allow for this regular work.
- Evaluations of (employee)'s work will be conducted by (manager of the department in which the task sharing is happening). Feedback should be shared regularly, and a summary of (employee)'s performance should be shared with the employee's supervisor during the performance evaluation cycle.
- The employee or manager can end this agreement at any time.

Job-sharing/Shared Project Memorandum of Understanding
April 5, 2021

[Staff Name] will assist [Supervisor Name] in [Metadata and Discovery (MAD)] for [X] hours per week beginning on [date] as part of their work at VCU Libraries. Hours will be evaluated after 1 month and may be increased to allow for additional training and greater responsibilities. The primary purpose of this job-sharing arrangement is to fill a need by providing additional staff support in MAD while providing a learning experience for [Staff Name]. The desired end goal is for [Staff Name] to develop the skills to flexibly move between MAD and Special Collections and Archives (SC&A) to provide copy-cataloging for both departments according to VCUL priorities.

Tasks and details include:

1. Book sorting: Before the start of the training on cataloging, [Staff Name] will learn how to sort new receipts of books into 2 categories of books based on cataloging level in associated bibliographic records: 1) somewhat more complete records created by the Library of Congress and 2) brief/incomplete records created by OCLC member libraries. The latter group of books will be kept in the backlog to be cataloged by trained catalogers. This sorting activity is a good opportunity to help the trainee become familiarized with MARC records prior to learning how to perform "easy" copy cataloging.

2. Train under the supervision of [Supervisor Name] with the goal of acquiring simple copy cataloging skills. Training will cover:

- Introduction to bibliographic record format (MARC record): fields, subfields, indicators
- Practice with searching in Connexion for records describing purchased / gift books in Connexion
- Descriptive and subject cataloging (classification)
- Authority control concept
- Introduction to Alma cataloging module (old metadata editor)
- Various cataloging learning sites at LC and MAD's training documentation

3. Search OCLC Connexion for matching cataloging records for standing order books.

Evaluations of [Staff Name]'s work will be conducted by [Supervisor Name]. Feedback should be shared regularly, and a summary of [Staff Name]'s performance will be shared with the employee's supervisor during the performance evaluation cycle.

The work of the employee's home department will take priority over this job share when research support/desk hours, patron appointments, and instruction are needed. Adjustments may need to be made to the employee's goals to allow for this regular work.

The employee, supervisors, and project managers will maintain open lines of communication regarding employee workload, performance, and how the job-share is working for all parties.

The ability to work independently and maintain a record of work will be required as well as the ability to collaborate and communicate in an online environment.

The employee or managers can end this agreement at any time.

Employee signature: _____
Date: _____

Employee's supervisor's signature: _____
Date: _____

Project manager's signature: _____
Date: _____

Figure 25.2
Draft memorandum of understanding for a task sharing arrangement in cataloging, VCU Libraries, 2021.

Projects and Tasks-Sharing during COVID-19 and Beyond

In March 2020, VCU closed its campuses in response to COVID-19; students, faculty, and staff moved to a fully online environment. Although many library employees, such as the digital engagement and academic outreach librarians, were able to transition from on-site to remote work with only moderate disruptions due to the nature of their work, those working at service points faced different challenges. A key function of staff at service desks is to support researchers, students, and guests in the libraries' physical spaces, and it thereby revolves heavily around their on-site presence; working at service points consumed the majority of frontline staff members' time before the pandemic. This was true of employees in the IS&LS department, who are responsible for staffing all frontline services at James Branch Cabell Library, including the service desk with combined circulation and research assistance, in addition to chat and text support. While the library was closed, IS&LS employees expanded chat and text to meet the increased demand for virtual services, but many needed additional projects to replace duties normally conducted in the library building to make the best use of their time during this period of working off-site.

The libraries' management council, composed of department heads across all functional areas, recognized the need to create meaningful opportunities for IS&LS and Health Sciences Library Operations employees responsible for working the main service desks at VCU's two libraries. Working with their teams, the department heads quickly created a shared document of projects appropriate for remote work and facilitated task sharing that could be taken on by staff in these departments. Almost every department in VCU Libraries had projects that had been simmering on the back burner for lack of time or staffing; it was believed that with appropriate training, some of these projects could be transferred to a library worker with the capacity for additional work as a result of the libraries' closure of the buildings. The shared projects list included a summary of the project, the contact information of the project coordinator, and an estimate of the time needed to complete the project. Supervisors reached out to project coordinators to connect staff with projects. Staff also reviewed the projects list to choose work that interested them. Many were excited to participate in these projects, which offered opportunities far different from traditional service desk work. Staff maintained project time logs to document their work, and project coordinators provided input and feedback throughout the projects. Throughout the pandemic, we heard from staff that their opportunity to engage in tasks or projects outside of their normal responsibilities helped them remain engaged at work, while the project coordinators were grateful for the additional assistance.

Some projects were relatively small, requiring just a few hours of work from one person, while other projects were large enough for multiple employees to work on simultaneously for longer durations of time. Once matches were made between projects and employees, managers and employees worked together to more fully define the nature of the project. Projects that could be accomplished within a fairly brief period could typically be arranged via discussions and e-mail, while more complex or time-consuming projects, such as facilitated task sharing, often resulted in the development of an MOU.

Examples of smaller projects include the following:

- reviewing subscription database landing pages for VCU Libraries branding (or lack thereof)
- checking links in Alma and Primo from a spreadsheet of specific journal titles to identify those needing updates
- participating in crowdsourcing initiatives such as those offered by the Library of Congress, the Library of Virginia, and the National Archives and Records Administration

Examples of larger projects include the following:

- reviewing closed-captioning transcripts for audio and video files of oral histories and video tutorials using Verbit, VCU Libraries' captioning partner, to increase accessibility (MOU, average of eight hours per week)
- enhancing accessibility for materials in VCU Libraries' institutional repository, Scholars Compass, by generating abstracts for items in the University History Books collection; reviewing abstracts for findability, search engine optimization, and accuracy, and enhancing these as needed (MOU, average of six hours per week)
- developing a plan to map the information architecture of the Silver Stallion webspace, a website dedicated to author James Branch Cabell, the namesake of one of our libraries; inventorying the contents and updating spreadsheets to note all the website's pages, internal and external links, and images (MOU, average of ten hours per week)
- proofreading content for the Social Welfare History Portal, researching and writing articles for this collaborative site, and creating image descriptions for items in the image portal for increased accessibility (MOU, average of ten hours per week)

Impact of Task Sharing in Crisis

One of the most immediate and obvious benefits of task sharing early in the pandemic was VCU Libraries' ability to effectively steward library resources so that employees had meaningful work to do from home while all campus buildings were closed due to COVID-19. It was important to ensure that we, as a public university, were fulfilling our responsibility to effectively use state resources, even in a time of crisis. Both early in the pandemic and later once buildings were reopened, task sharing allowed the library to improve discovery and usability of library resources, respond to users' needs more quickly, and advance or complete projects that had been on the back burner, which otherwise might not have been addressed for some time. Although most projects and task sharing in March 2020 were initially intended to provide work for employees without sufficient duties that could be completed from home, a number of projects were sustained even as employees returned to on-site work. Because building traffic and engagement with library services and collections overall were lower than usual once buildings reopened due to a large number of classes continuing to be offered virtually, some employees who returned to work on-site continued to have the bandwidth to participate in task sharing. For example, the public services staffer who proofread content for the Social Welfare History online portal continued that work from March 2020 through August 2021, more than a year after library buildings had reopened.

As the pandemic has continued longer than anyone could have imagined, task sharing has continued to play a role in the organization at VCU Libraries. The acceleration of task sharing opportunities during the pandemic served as a foundation for a nimbler organization that is now better prepared and able to work beyond divisional and departmental silos. After seeing several successful task sharing and project-sharing initiatives, department heads and associate deans are now more open to asking peers in other units if someone with the appropriate skills, interests, and abilities may be able to assist with a particular project or task outside of their normal responsibilities. For example, at the time of this writing and more than eighteen months after the pandemic began, staff members from several departments are preparing to assist VCU Libraries' stacks management team with shelving and shifting physical materials. This will provide support for an understaffed department and offers a welcome change of pace for some staff members. MOUs will be prepared to reflect the nature of the work and the percentage of an employee's time that will be assumed in these arrangements. Another benefit of task sharing is the added understanding and increased transparency of work happening through the libraries.

Task sharing can also improve the institution's resilience in terms of staffing and business continuity. By assuming a flexible posture in which employees and managers are encouraged to explore how different departments and divisions can formalize collaborations to support each other, the library has been better able to cope with temporary absences when an employee departs or is on temporary leave. Instead of automatically assuming that every position vacated must be immediately rehired, employees who have the capacity to take on additional tasks have sometimes been able to do so with no increased expense to the organization (although it should be noted that this is not always an appropriate strategy). In addition, some task sharing arrangements have served as useful test scenarios for permanent changes and have even provided ideas for departmental or divisional reorganizations in the future. Finally, task sharing at VCU Libraries has dovetailed well with a VCU-wide initiative focused on career development for employees, in which managers are expected to actively support employees' exploration of new skill sets and professional growth opportunities in their future careers. Task sharing allows employees to sample types of work beyond their regular job assignments and build their skill sets.

At VCU Libraries, MOUs have been critical in establishing that understanding for sustained task sharing. However, it can be difficult to discern when or if an MOU is needed. For example, in instances when someone is working on a fairly brief project, it may suffice to arrive at a shared understanding of how the work will be accomplished via discussion. That said, the authors recommend that one err on the side of formalizing an MOU as the surest way to enhance understanding. In instances where library leaders have seen task sharing not work well, it is usually a result of unclear expectations or limited understanding of the expectations. Additionally, articulating the terms of the MOU can clarify whether or not a task sharing arrangement is truly feasible and may prevent unsustainable arrangements from being established.

It is also important that managers and supervisors be careful to make adjustments to task sharing employees' regular workloads when needed to enable their success in task sharing. At VCU Libraries, this sometimes meant making adjustments to individuals' job-related goals for the year, adjusting the percentage of time devoted to regular duties, or adding a goal that reflects the task sharing arrangement.

Another challenge that has been occasionally encountered with cross-departmental or cross-divisional task sharing is developing a plan to ensure that the employee's new responsibilities be reasonably prioritized. The MOUs generally articulate that the work of the employee's primary department takes precedence over the task sharing arrangement. For example, if a service point in the employee's primary department needs to be covered due to short staffing, that person's task sharing responsibilities in another department may not be executed. While this is an easy enough thing to articulate in a memo, it's another thing to ensure that the task sharing arrangement results in the work being accomplished in the secondary department or division most of the time. In some instances, managers and employees may discover that the task sharing arrangement as originally envisioned is not feasible. For this reason, current MOUs reflect the fact that the nature of the task-sharing setup can be reviewed or terminated by either party at any time.

Conclusion

Task sharing played an important role in weathering the COVID-19 crisis at VCU Libraries, increasing organizational resilience and flexibility while enhancing employee growth. Task sharing before and during the pandemic has also enhanced the sense of community at VCU Libraries and fostered a collaborative culture. It has sparked discussions across the organization about new ways to work together and make the most of the library's talented workforce, and it has served as a test bed for leadership to consider alternative work arrangements on a permanent basis. The library team expects task sharing to continue to play an important role in our ability to accomplish our mission for the remainder of the pandemic and beyond.

Acknowledgment

We would like to thank our many colleagues who have played critical roles in establishing a culture and practice of task sharing at VCU Libraries. There are too many to name individually, but we offer special thanks to Laura Crouch, Nora Bloch, Erin Bragg, and Katie Condon, all of whom significantly influenced the way or the frequency with which we have been able to embrace task sharing.

Notes

1. Jackie Nytes, "MOU: A Tie That Binds," *Library Journal* 143, no. 14 (September 1, 2018): 25.
2. Barney Olmsted, "Job Sharing: An Emerging Work-Style," *International Labour Review* 118, no. 3 (May– June 1979): 283–98, HeinOnline.
3. Centers for Disease Control and Prevention, "Sharing and Shifting Tasks to Maintain Essential Healthcare during COVID-19 in Low Resource, Non-US Settings," last modified October 14, 2020, https://www.cdc.gov/coronavirus/2019-ncov/global-covid-19/task-sharing.html.
4. Global Health Learning Center. "Task-Sharing.". https://www.globalhealthlearning.org/taxonomy/term/3838.
5. World Health Organization, *Task Sharing to Improve Access to Family Planning/Contraception*, summary brief (Geneva, Switzerland: World Health Organization, 2017), http://apps.who.int/iris/bitstream/handle/10665/259633/WHO-RHR-17.20-eng.pdf?sequence=1.
6. Centers for Disease Control and Prevention, "Sharing and Shifting Tasks to Maintain Essential Healthcare during COVID-19 in Low Resource, Non-US Settings," last modified October 14, 2020, https://www.cdc.gov/coronavirus/2019-ncov/global-covid-19/task-sharing.html.
7. Emilia Ngozi Iwu and William L. Holzemer, "HIV Task Sharing between Nurses and Physicians in Nigeria: Examining the Correlates of Nurse Self-Efficacy and Job Satisfaction," *Journal of the Association of Nurses in AIDS Care* 28, no. 3 (2017): 395–407. https://doi.org/10.1016/j.jana.2017.02.005; Barbara Janowitz, John Stanback, and Brooke Boyer, "Task Sharing in Family Planning," *Studies in Family Planning* 43, no. 1 (March 2012): 57–62, https://doi.org/10.1111/j.1728-4465.2012.00302.x; David J. Olson, "Task Sharing, Not Task Shifting: Team Approach Is Best for HIV Care," *Vital* (blog), IntraHealth International, August 8, 2012. https://www.intrahealth.org/vital/task-sharing-not-task-shifting-team-approach-best-bet-hiv-care; Giuseppe Raviola, John Naslund, Stephanie Smith, and Vikram Patel, "Innovative Models in Mental Health Delivery Systems: Task Sharing Care with Non-specialist Providers to Close the Mental Health Treatment Gap," *Current Psychiatry Reports* 21 (2019): article 44. https://doi.org/10.1007/s11920-019-1028-x.
8. Bruce Massis, "Academic Libraries Break Down Silos," *Information and Learning Science* 119, no. 1/2 (2018): 135–38, https://doi.org/10.1108/ILS-11-2017-0111.
9. US Department of Labor, "Job Sharing," https://www.dol.gov/general/topic/workhours/jobsharing.
10. Barney Olmsted, Willie Heller, Susie Ruggels, and Suzanne Smith, *Job Sharing in the Public Sector* (Palo Alto: New Ways to Work, 1979), 1–3; Angela Spencer, "Job Sharing: A Primer," *Journal of Hospital Librarianship* 17, no. 1 (2017): 80–87, https://doi.org/10.1080/15323269.2017.1259471.
11. Julie Nicklin Rubley, "Job Sharing on the Tenure Track," *Chronicle of Higher Education*, February 3, 2004, https://www.chronicle.com/article/job-sharing-on-the-tenure-track/.
12. Virginia Commonwealth University, "Career Development Planning," last modified August 25, 2021, https://insidehr.vcu.edu/guidelines/career-development/career-development-planning/.

Bibliography

Centers for Disease Control and Prevention. "Sharing and Shifting Tasks to Maintain Essential Healthcare during COVID-19 in Low Resource, Non-US Settings." Last modified October 14, 2020. https://www.cdc.gov/coronavirus/2019-ncov/global-covid-19/task-sharing.html.

Global Health Learning Center. "Task-Sharing." Accessed August 10, 2021. https://www.globalhealthlearning.org/taxonomy/term/3838.

Iwu, Emilia Ngozi, and William L. Holzemer. "HIV Task Sharing between Nurses and Physicians in Nigeria: Examining the Correlates of Nurse Self-Efficacy and Job Satisfaction." *Journal of the Association of Nurses in AIDS Care* 28, no. 3 (2017): 395–407. https://doi.org/10.1016/j.jana.2017.02.005.

Janowitz, Barbara, John Stanback, and Brooke Boyer. "Task Sharing in Family Planning." *Studies in Family Planning* 43, no. 1 (March 2012): 57–62. https://doi.org/10.1111/j.1728-4465.2012.00302.x.

Massis, Bruce. "Academic Libraries Break Down Silos." *Information and Learning Science* 119, no. 1/2 (2018): 135–38. https://doi.org/10.1108/ILS-11-2017-0111.

Nytes, Jackie. "MOU: A Tie That Binds." *Library Journal* 143, no. 14 (September 1, 2018): 25.

Olmsted. Barney. "Job Sharing: An Emerging Work-Style." *International Labour Review* 118, no. 3 (May–June 1979): 283–98. HeinOnline.

Olmsted, Barney, Willie Heller, Susie Ruggels, and Suzanne Smith. *Job Sharing in the Public Sector*. Palo Alto, CA: New Ways to Work, 1979.

Olson, David J. "Task Sharing, Not Task Shifting: Team Approach Is Best for HIV Care." *Vital* (blog), IntraHealth International, August 8, 2012. https://www.intrahealth.org/vital/task-sharing-not-task-shifting-team-approach-best-bet-hiv-care.

Raviola, Giuseppe, John Naslund, Stephanie Smith, and Vikram Patel. "Innovative Models in Mental Health Delivery Systems: Task Sharing Care with Non-specialist Providers to Close the Mental Health Treatment Gap." *Current Psychiatry Reports* 21 (2019): article 44. https://doi.org/10.1007/s11920-019-1028-x.

Rubley, Julie Nicklin. "Job Sharing on the Tenure Track." *Chronicle of Higher Education*, February 3, 2004. https://www.chronicle.com/article/job-sharing-on-the-tenure-track/.

Spencer, Angela. "Job Sharing: A Primer." *Journal of Hospital Librarianship* 17, no. 1 (2017): 80–87. https://doi.org/10.1080/15323269.2017.1259471.

US Department of Labor. "Job Sharing." Accessed August 10, 2021. https://www.dol.gov/general/topic/workhours/jobsharing.

Virginia Commonwealth University. "Career Development Planning." Last modified August 25, 2021. https://insidehr.vcu.edu/guidelines/career-development/career-development-planning/.

World Health Organization. *Task Sharing to Improve Access to Family Planning/Contraception*. Summary brief. Geneva, Switzerland: World Health Organization, 2017. http://apps.who.int/iris/bitstream/handle/10665/259633/WHO-RHR-17.20-eng.pdf?sequence=1.

CHAPTER 26

Deconstructing the Team

Using Documentation and Cross-training to Maintain Coverage during Times of Crisis

Renna T. Redd and Mason Smith

> *Reorganization into a more decentralized structure based on goals and priorities gave the team a chance to redistribute the various duties of the unit based on location and not necessarily on any one person's skill set; cross-training was provided as needed.*

Introduction

No one academic library is capable of housing and providing access to all of the resources sought by its patrons, making the supplementation of collections through consortia and broader borrowing partnerships, or resource sharing, a vital part of library services. Yet despite the importance of the service, libraries often struggle to determine where the department best fits in an organizational structure. A 2018 survey of academic libraries in the Association of Research Libraries found resource sharing as a part of access services, reference, collection services; as a stand-alone department; or as part of the library records center.[1]

Because resource sharing may be part of a variety of larger units, it is unsurprising to find that the department may cover a wide range of responsibilities at different institutions and may be in constant flux as duties and employees are added or removed from the core bundle of services typically expected from resource sharing. In addition to interlibrary loan and consortial lending and borrowing, resource sharing may offer scanning services from a print collection, purchase-on-demand programs, library mail or courier services, or reserves services.

Though Clemson Libraries has made only one change to the resource sharing department within the organizational structure—transitioning it from a stand-alone department to part of a larger unit—the responsibilities of the department have changed considerably since its creation and especially during the last few years. Despite these changes, and the implementation of new software, *and* the recent upheaval in academia due to the COVID-19 pandemic, the Clemson Libraries resource sharing team has developed a robust cross-training system, built trust among team members old and new, and continually offered patrons high-quality service.[7]

Background

Clemson University

Founded in 1889, Clemson University is a public land-grant institution located in the foothills of the Blue Ridge Mountains in northwest South Carolina. The university occupies the traditional and ancestral land of the Cherokee people.[2] Enslaved African people worked the land for the Pickens, Clemson, and Calhoun families, and African American convict laborers transformed the land into the campus of Clemson.[3] According to the university's "Interactive Factbook," in 2019, the institution served 20,195 undergraduate and 5,627 graduate students.[4] Clemson offers 119 degree programs from seven different colleges[5] and recently received a Research 1 status from the Carnegie Classification of Institutions of Higher Education.

Clemson Libraries

Clemson Libraries operates six locations: the Robert Muldrow Cooper Library, which is the main library; the Emory A. Gunnin Architecture Library, the Education Media Center and Digital Media Learning Lab, and the Special Collections and Archives, which are branch libraries; the Library Depot, an off-site storage facility; and the Clemson Design Center, a satellite location in Charleston, South Carolina. As of this writing, the libraries employ twenty-eight faculty, fifty-five staff, and over ninety student workers. As stated in a recent presentation to the board of trustees, with a budget of $18,200,000, the libraries hold over 1.5 million print titles, over 500,000 e-books, over 82,000 electronic journal subscriptions, over 26,400 items in their institutional repository, and over 12,000 cubic feet of materials in the Clemson Special Collections and Archives.[6] Additionally, as included in the 2019 annual report to the board of trustees, the libraries cover more than 200,000 square feet of space combined, offering over 2,100 seats across locations, and boast an annual gate count of over 1.5 million.[7]

The current administrative structure of the libraries is relatively flat: a dean of the libraries and four unit heads oversee five functional divisions: Information and Research Services, Library Information Technology, Technical Services and Collection Management, Special Collections and Archives, and Administrative Services. Workflow and procedural changes are implemented somewhat informally, with stakeholders being consulted via e-mail. Policy changes affecting patron services go through a multilevel review, beginning with a public services council (made up of employees who oversee public service points, such as circulation, resource sharing, special collections, and makerspaces) and, after approval, to a library leadership team (which consists of the dean, unit heads, and members of the Administrative Services unit). A plan is currently underway to reorganize the libraries into three divisions (Collections and Discovery; Organizational Performance and Inclusion; and Teaching, Learning, and Research) managed by three associate deans. Multiple cross-functional teams (Collections Strategy, Discovery, and Instruction) will be charged with reviewing and implementing policy changes.

Clemson Libraries Resource Sharing

The Resource Sharing department of the Clemson Libraries was established in 1990; at that time it included copy services, interlibrary loan, document delivery, and PASCAL (Partnership among South Carolina Academic Libraries) Delivers services; however, the department was dismantled in 2011, leaving only interlibrary loan lending and interlibrary loan borrowing services within it scope of services. The libraries added an off-site storage facility, known as the Library Depot, in 2012, which houses both high-density storage and the Technical Services and Collection Management unit. In 2015, library administration opted to bring interlibrary loan borrowing, interlibrary loan lending, document delivery, and PASCAL Delivers back under a single umbrella, with the team using ILLiad and Millennium software packages to process all resource sharing requests and make them available for users. Because an increasing amount of library materials were being moved to off-site storage to make room for more student study space, it was decided in January 2018 that both high-density storage management and services would also be transferred to the Resource Sharing team. This streamlined the team's increasing interactions with off-site storage personnel to provide document delivery scans. In 2020, library mail and courier services were also moved to the Resource Sharing team due to the fact that the majority of incoming and outgoing mail was generated through interlibrary loan transactions.

Cross-training

Cross-training for Large Projects

Cross-training is key to maintaining services in a changing environment that may include working with employees new to, or outside of, Resource Sharing. From 2012 to 2018, high-density storage functioned as part of a small group of staff whose only commonality was being based at the Library Depot. Once Resource Sharing began offering document delivery services again as part of its core function in 2016, interactions between employees in off-site storage and Resource Sharing increased; training was provided to the off-site storage manager on how to use the ILLiad interlibrary loan software to process and deliver requests for scans of material located off-site. Prior to this, Resource Sharing staff e-mailed the off-site storage manager with citation information pertaining to the requested item and the material's barcode. The off-site storage manager would then enter the barcode into the GFA (Generation Fifth Applications) LAS (Library Archival Solutions) software system to determine where the material was located. The material was retrieved and scanned, then the scan was e-mailed back to Resource Sharing staff. With all parties now using ILLiad, no data is missed in the e-mail request, and off-site storage personnel can use the software to deliver scans directly to patrons, increasing efficiency, supporting better communication, and cutting processing time significantly.

The Resource Sharing team's communication and teamwork was put to the test in the summer of 2019. Library administration made the decision to move nearly 74,000 items from Cooper Library to off-site storage to make more room for student study space. The majority of Q–Z bound serials were relocated, the remaining collection was shifted to one floor rather than two, and the rest of the bound periodicals not selected for shifting were relocated to off-site storage and accessioned into high-density storage and shelved. The project was an all-hands-on-deck affair: Technical Services staff worked remotely in the ILS (Millennium) to change locations and statuses of materials that were either slated for relocation or were discarded, and, because off-site storage was part of the Resource Sharing team, Resource Sharing staff coordinated the physical processing of the materials for the move. The interlibrary loan librarian coordinated the barcoding of each item that did not have a barcode on the front cover (necessary for quick accessioning and retrieving); coordination efforts included the interlibrary loan borrower covering Resource Sharing office functions, while the interlibrary loan lender barcoded materials, and the document delivery and PASCAL Delivers coordinator pulled oversized materials, managed communications among different parties, and coordinated the search and cleanup of items that had gone missing in action, while the off-site storage manager did all of the aforementioned as well as triaging catalog records in need of extended work and acting as a liaison with the contract moving company.

Cross-training for Service Turnaround

With the majority of bound serials now located off-site, the Resource Sharing team needed to reexamine the balance of staffing. In order to maintain timely services, the interlibrary loan lender relocated off-site to work with the off-site storage manager at the Library Depot so that there were now two FTE staff at the off-site facility to retrieve materials from high-density storage, process scan requests for interlibrary loan lending and document delivery, and process monograph lending requests for PASCAL Delivers and interlibrary loan lending.

This reorganization into a more decentralized structure based on goals and priorities gave the team a chance to redistribute the various duties of the unit based on location and not necessarily on any one person's skill set; cross-training was provided as needed. Rather than one person working on document delivery requests and another person working on interlibrary loan lending requests, duties were rearranged so that one person at the Library Depot pulled items for PASCAL Delivers, interlibrary loan lending, document delivery, and scanned materials, while another individual worked at Cooper Library to pull materials for PASCAL Delivers, interlibrary loan lending, document delivery, and scanned materials there. The individual at the Library Depot also retrieved and reshelved materials in high-density storage, while the individual at Cooper Library coordinated the processing of monographs to be sent out for interlibrary loan lending and PASCAL Delivers services. Also, the team elected to hire additional student workers to assist in processing records in ILLiad and to run materials to and from all of the branches.

Figure 26.1
Evolution of workflow changes as the resource sharing team expanded from 2017 to 2021

Cross-training for Force Majeure

In mid-March 2020, due to the increasing threat of the COVID-19 pandemic, Clemson University pivoted to an online learning model; subsequently, the libraries suspended in-person services. With a sharper focus on online services, the Resource Sharing team created a plan to determine which interlibrary loan functions would continue and from where team members would work to accomplish tasks. Library courier services ceased with the suspension of in-person services; PASCAL Delivers services were turned off by the consortium; and university mail services, which previously delivered to departmental mailrooms, began holding mail at Central Receiving and asking departments to pick up their own items. With this in mind, the Resource Sharing team:

- opted to stop interlibrary loan lending of physical materials;
- continued offering interlibrary loan borrowing when possible, concentrating on e-books and articles or book chapters; and
- continued offering document delivery of articles and chapters from both print and online sources.

While interlibrary loan borrowing can be managed solely from home, interlibrary loan lending requires that a team member be physically present on-site to print, pull books, and scan incoming requests. While the interlibrary loan lender processed incoming requests from home, the PASCAL Delivers and document delivery coordinator worked half-days on-site at Cooper Library and the off-site storage manager worked half-days at the off-site storage facility to scan and send those requests. The mail and courier operation manager worked on-site to retrieve and unpack campus mail. The interlibrary loan librarian worked some days on-site and some days from home, serving as backup to all duties as needed.

With the cases of COVID-19 in South Carolina on the rise, the Resource Sharing department also considered a plan for the potential sickness or quarantine of a team member. With four team members cleared for work on-site, two team members cleared for backup duty if necessary, and ample cross-training completed already, the team was able to easily flex schedules should someone fall ill. In the event of a possible quarantine of an on-site employee, team members switched duties for two weeks: the team member typically working on-site stayed home and processed requests in ILLiad, while the team member typically at home traveled to campus to physically process and finish those requests. This flexibility was possible because of the cross-training. On-site team members also took the opportunity afforded by a change in routine processes to cross-train in areas new to the department so as to provide even more extended backup in the future, when needed.

Cross-training Equals Change Insurance

Having staff who were cross-trained ensured that processes were able to be completed with minimal disruption in service to patrons. Scholarship about library cross-training usually discusses it within the context of covering essential services in the instance of position vacancies.[8] Academic librarianship is often described as functioning within silos and cross-training across different departments and units may be considered "threatening as it brings into question the viability of their current titles and responsibilities."[9] Within the context of an existing small unit or team, however, cross-training can be utilized as a way to discover individuals' strengths and add increased satisfaction with work through increasing the variety of tasks and responsibilities available. The nuts and bolts of implementing this cross-pollination project for the team included documentation, communication, informal observations, and job shadowing.

Documentation and Communication

Communication prior to commencing cross-training and shifts in responsibilities is essential. Preparing the individuals to carry out their responsibilities while also underscoring the value of each employee's contribution to the team effort will make this transition easier. It is important to emphasize when commencing a cross-training program that individuals' jobs are not being taken from them; in fact, they are being made process owners of the tasks they oversee (to use Six Sigma parlance[10]), meaning that at the end of the day they are still the most knowledgeable person about their job. By documenting the workflow and processes and sharing the unique elements of those processes, staff are able to demonstrate to their colleagues the importance of what they contribute to the team and the organization. Additionally, their colleagues gain a more complete understanding of how various services and functions interact to create a positive library user experience in a complex and technology-rich environment. Beyond the benefits of team building and increased internal understanding of library functions, having a group that is cross-trained means that if someone is out sick, or if there is a large-scale library project, or even a global pandemic, services can be covered with less stress to those stepping in to provide it, and the potential disruption to services patrons rely on is minimized.

The first step of implementing an effective cross-training program lies in having sufficient documentation available to work from. Even without cross-training as the end goal, having supporting documentation is essential in case a library employee is suddenly unable to come to work (also known at Clemson University Libraries as the abducted-by-aliens rule for the sake of levity). It is important to acknowledge that there are few life-and-death emergencies in libraries and that a culture of vocational awe has instilled within many in the profession a sense of having to work at the risk of endangering their own mental, physical, and emotional health.[11] That said, having some sort of documentation at hand when an employee has to miss work means less confusion on the whole when another individual is tasked with covering duties.

One key element to observe when creating documentation is to consider the audience for whom it is written. Ideally, write for someone who works in a different department; they know basic library concepts (e.g., the difference between a holding and an item record) but might not know concepts germane to the task at hand. What are the essential duties to be covered, and what can wait to be completed? What jargon is used that could be clarified? Are there acronyms that should be spelled out at least once? Are there log-ins and passwords that need to be shared? Screenshots are essential to this documentation as well. While some individuals are able to read written instructions and follow them without illustrations, providing images of what screens and processes *should* look like will create an additional resource for the individual accessing the documentation.

Communication is key for teams to function in any instance; however, when discussing shared procedures and services that affect patrons, it is essential. While we live in an age of too much screen time and too many e-mail messages, e-mail does have the capacity to function as another form of somewhat quick-and-dirty documentation of procedures—especially as it is searchable and time-stamped. Do not be shy when e-mailing; consider whether it's better to be copied on something one does not need to know or not copied on something one does need to know. Other tools are available for increased communication, such as shared calendars showing student worker schedules or who will have the shared library vehicles when.

Observation and Shadowing

The second element of cross-training involves two individuals spending time together to discuss the work at hand. Unit management determines which team members will be pairing up to share processes (note that sharing does not have to be on a one-to-one basis). While the interlibrary loan lending coordinator learns about the processes of the PASCAL Delivers coordinator, the PASCAL Delivers coordinator could be learning about the processes of off-site storage; the off-site storage manager might be learning about document delivery operations.

Rather than having pairs of employees together for extended amounts of time, consider implementing a shadowing and observing stage that mimics a circular process as illustrated in Figure 26.2; this gives members of the team a chance to view the team's functions in a more holistic manner.

Once personnel pairings are decided, the first meeting or two should be short, low-stakes, and informative—for example, a process owner talking through or demonstrating their workflow while the observer asks questions and eventually tries out the workflow themselves. Starting small creates an open environment for discussion and some socializing,

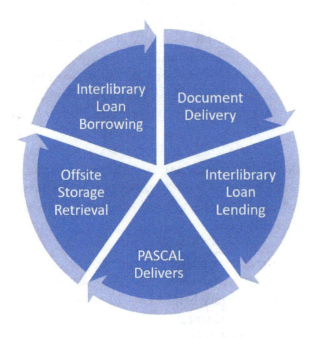

Figure 26.2
Cycle of shadowing and observation across multiple workflows and functions

which might take a bit of pressure out of the meeting. After the meeting, a copy of the documentation should be provided to the observer, and they can watch the process owner going through each step as written. This opens the door to questions and observations: Is something the trainer is doing not clear on the page? This is the chance to further clarify, amend, and improve what is recorded. Once the documentation is clear to the observer, they should try performing the processes themselves to see if they are able to do the basics if the incumbent has to be out of work. It is also important to emphasize that this stage of training is just to cover the essential elements of a process, not to cover all of the nuances involved in any given position. This is meant to be low-stakes, and anyone can make mistakes. If they do, add how to correct them in the documentation!

Conclusion

Cross-training acts as an insurance policy when times of crisis arise; however, it can also serve as a way to help a team of individuals think about their processes holistically, see how those fit together to create a standard of service, and also imbue a sense of ownership and investment in the work performed. In the instance of the practice of resource sharing, services are scattered throughout library organizational charts and organizational charts are being updated fairly frequently. Hence there is no one standard bundle of services offered under the umbrella term.

Cross-training and documentation are key to maintaining services in a changing environment that may include working with employees new to, or outside of, resource sharing. It is vital to look at developing workflows as an iterative process. This approach permits the creation of a cross-training program that is ongoing rather than a one-time event.

Software changes; staff leave and new staff are hired; libraries change, so why should workflows and processes remain stagnant? The Clemson Libraries Resource Sharing team was able to develop a holistic training program during the COVID-19 pandemic by scaling up our previous practice into a more robust cross-training and documentation system that has built trust among team members, created a more cohesive unit, allowed us to easily step up for each other in times of need, and avoid disruptions in service to our patrons.

Notes

1. Renna Redd, "Where Do We Belong? Where Does Resource Sharing Fit in an Academic Library?" (lightning talk, Southeastern Resource Sharing Conference, Charlotte, NC, October 11–12, 2018).
2. Clemson University Historic Properties, "The Cherokee Nation," accessed August 7, 2020, https://www.clemson.edu/about/history/properties/hopewell/native-americans.html.
3. Clemson University Historic Properties, "Fort Hill: National Historic Landmark," accessed August 7, 2020. https://www.clemson.edu/about/history/properties/fort-hill/.
4. Clemson University Office of Institutional Research, "Clemson University Interactive Factbook," accessed August 7, 2020, https://www.clemson.edu/institutional-effectiveness/oir/factbook.
5. Clemson University, "Degree Programs," accessed August 7, 2020, https://www.clemson.edu/degrees/index.html.
6. Christopher Cox, "Clemson Libraries Annual Report 2019" (presentation to board of trustees, Clemson University, Clemson, SC, October 10, 2019).

7. Christopher Cox, "Clemson University Libraries Annual Report to the Board of Trustees Data Book" (all-employee meeting presentation, R. M. Cooper Library, Clemson University, Clemson, SC, September 30, 2019).
8. Xuan Pang and Teresa E. Maceira, "We See a Rainbow: Resource Sharing and Reference Services Working Together," *Journal of Interlibrary Loan, Document Delivery and Electronic Reserves* 28, no. 1/2 (2019): 13–23, https://doi.org/10.1080/1072303X.2019.1650156; Cori Wilhelm, "'That's Not My Job': Developing a Cross-training Process in an Academic Library," *College and Research Libraries News* 77, no. 7 (2016): 342–46, https://doi.org/10.5860/crln.77.7.9523; Simone L. Yearwood, "Putting the 'I' Back in Team," *Journal of Access Services* 14, no. 3 (2017): 146–52, https://doi.org/10.1080/15367967.2017.1350583.
9. Emy Nelson Decker, "Encouraging Continuous Learning for Librarians and Library Staff," *Library Management* 38, no. 6/7 (2017): 286, https://doi.org/10.1108/LM-10-2016-0078.
10. Basem El-Haik, and Raid Al-Aomar, *Simulation-Based Lean Six-Sigma and Design for Six-Sigma* (Hoboken, NJ: Wiley-Interscience, 2006), 383
11. Fobazi Ettarh, "Vocational Awe and Librarianship: The Lies We Tell Ourselves," *In the Library with the Lead Pipe*, January 10, 2018, https://www.inthelibrarywiththeleadpipe.org/2018/vocational-awe/.

Bibliography

Clemson University. "Degree Programs." Accessed August 7, 2020. https://www.clemson.edu/degrees/index.html.

Clemson University Historic Properties. "The Cherokee Nation." Accessed August 7, 2020. https://www.clemson.edu/about/history/properties/hopewell/native-americans.html.

———. "Fort Hill: National Historic Landmark." Accessed August 7, 2020. https://www.clemson.edu/about/history/properties/fort-hill/.

Clemson University Office of Institutional Research. "Clemson University Interactive Factbook." Accessed August 7, 2020. https://www.clemson.edu/institutional-effectiveness/oir/factbook/.

Cox, Christopher. "Clemson Libraries Annual Report 2019." Presentation to board of trustees, Clemson University, Clemson, SC, October 10, 2019.

———. "Clemson University Libraries Annual Report to the Board of Trustees Data Book." All-employee meeting presentation, R. M. Cooper Library, Clemson University, Clemson, SC, September 30, 2019.

Decker, Emy Nelson. "Encouraging Continuous Learning for Librarians and Library Staff." *Library Management* 38, no. 6/7 (2017): 286–93. https://doi.org/10.1108/LM-10-2016-0078.

El-Haik, Basem, and Raid Al-Aomar. *Simulation-Based Lean Six-Sigma and Design for Six-Sigma*. Hoboken, NJ: Wiley-Interscience, 2006.

Ettarh, Fobazi. "Vocational Awe and Librarianship: The Lies We Tell Ourselves." *In the Library with the Lead Pipe*, January 10, 2018. https://www.inthelibrarywiththeleadpipe.org/2018/vocational-awe/.

Pang, Xuan, and Teresa E. Maceira. "We See a Rainbow: Resource Sharing and Reference Services Working Together." *Journal of Interlibrary Loan, Document Delivery and Electronic Reserves* 28, no. 1/2 (2019): 13–23. https://doi.org/10.1080/1072303X.2019.1650156.

Redd, Renna. "Where Do We Belong? Where Does Resource Sharing Fit in an Academic Library?" Lightning talk, Southeastern Resource Sharing Conference, Charlotte, NC, October 11–12, 2018.

Wilhelm, Cori. "'That's Not My Job': Developing a Cross-training Process in an Academic Library." *College and Research Libraries News* 77, no. 7 (July 2016): 342–46. https://doi.org/10.5860/crln.77.7.9523.

Yearwood, Simone L. "Putting the 'I' Back in Team." *Journal of Access Services* 14, no. 3 (2017): 146–52. https://doi.org/10.1080/15367967.2017.1350583.

CHAPTER 27

Difficult Decisions in Downsizing:

A Library Management Perspective and Case Study

Alison S. Gregory

> *When employees have an active choice in leaving or staying, remaining employees are often more committed and engaged in their work. The library's downsizing happened within a matter of weeks, precluding opportunity for voluntary departures, and there was little time for employees to adjust to the idea or to have closure with departing colleagues*

Introduction

In the summer of 2020, the library at a medium-sized private university was swept into a perfect financial storm. In addition to the stressors of a global pandemic, projected undergraduate enrollment was in decline and fewer students had opted to live on-campus, resulting in decreased auxiliary services revenue, and the overall financials were not performing as anticipated. The university hired a consulting group to assist in identifying potential budgetary savings and one main area recommended for reduction was the library's budget. The result was that the library was directed to reduce its budget by 30% and to accomplish that reduction in less than six weeks. This necessitated reducing personnel and resource budgets dramatically. The University Librarian (UL) was entrusted to approach the situation with a "common good" mindset and was empowered to use her expertise to make the cuts in the most appropriate way.

While cases are typically selected to support the study of a predetermined research question or topic, in this instance, the events that transpired allowed the author to compare

345

and contrast the University Librarian's experiences with established research in change management, evaluating best practices and lessons learned in downsizing.

Review of the Literature

Change Management

Organizational changes to processes, hierarchy, infrastructure, or culture can fall into two categories: adaptive changes that are minor and gradual, and transformational changes that are larger in scale and can be sudden or dramatic. Change management is the process of preparing for, implementing, and cementing these changes.[1] Optimal adaptation to change requires multiple phases, including gaining early buy-in from employees by raising their awareness of the situation and the need to make changes; creating a shared vision for change—including goals, scope, stakeholders, and performance indicators; empowering employees to implement the changes; and embedding the new processes and culture to minimize the risk of reverting to old practices.[2]

Sudden widespread layoffs are considered to be "the most virulent form of downsizing," leading employees to feel undervalued and insecure.[3] When leaders show concern for employees' well-being, communicate openly to reduce rumors or misinformation, and engage remaining employees in restructuring post-downsizing, resistance to change can be reduced.[4] When previous tasks and responsibilities have to be eliminated or scaled back, it is important to acknowledge the legacy work and those who conducted it. Afterwards, work should be reassigned in a way that plays to remaining employees' strengths, and leaders should ensure that employees have the training to take on the new duties.[5]

It is essential that leaders determine the right tempo for making changes, and that "should be based on the quickest speed that the group with the most difficult part can play."[6] When organizations are making changes on their own terms, the pace tends to be slower and more thoughtful, whereas when change is imposed there is less time for deliberation and detail, and leaders have to move things forward while supporting the employees who will have the most difficult changes to make.[7] In times of transition, leaders should identify allies "who can help to create a momentum" to move through the change process.[8] Allies can be process helpers who are excellent communicators, able to influence others; solution givers who are well-versed in industry-specific best practices, and stabilizers who understand the big picture and can help reestablish group dynamics.[9]

Communication

Early communication is important for employees to understand downsizing, especially in giving "a sense of necessity …to increase efficiency [as] a matter of survival."[10] Frequency of communication is important and leaders should provide continuous updates as situations evolve.[11] Additionally, communications from leadership should share the rationale for necessary changes and decision-making criteria.[12]

Workplace communication between leaders and employees is best done synchronously when a "mutual understanding and agreement" needs to be reached, whereas asynchronous communication channels are better for conveying new information that needs time to be processed by employees.[13] Synchronous communication allows for better clarity and shared understanding; asynchronous channels provide flexibility for revisiting the information repeatedly.[14] When making the decision of the best means of communication, library leaders should keep in mind that employees have been found to prefer face-to-face communication, which is perceived to be more effective and is positively correlated to employee job satisfaction.[15] In all cases, leaders should consider "the fit between communication situation and channel."[16]

There is risk in communicating bad news early, before all details are known.[17] However, communicating transparently with as accurate a description of the situation as possible can counteract some of the fear exacerbated by the unknown.[18] In addition to clarity, it is also important that communications give "a hopeful vision of the future toward which people can direct their energy," describing what can be achieved post-change.[19] Leaders should be succinct, direct, and deliver all of the bad news at once, address the rationale driving the change, and reassure those who will remain in the organization that the "changes...prepare a way forward."[20]

Survivor's Guilt and Employee Commitment

Those who retain their employment sometimes experience survivor's guilt, which can manifest in behaviors such as anger, decreased productivity, distrust of the organization and supervisor, anxiety about job security, decreased willingness to innovate, and low morale and job satisfaction.[21] Downsizing can lead to survivor's guilt because layoffs break the psychological contract between employer and employees, where the "sense of reciprocal obligation" is disrupted.[22] The impact on morale can be minimized if colleagues depart through voluntary reduction opportunities, if the decisions are made fairly and without bias, and if those laid off receive appropriate severance packages.[23]

When employees have an active choice in leaving or staying (despite additional demands and stress that may result from reorganization), remaining employees are often more committed and engaged in their work, a sort of "reversed survival syndrome."[24] Involving employees, either via labor unions or other subgroups, in decision-making can increase perceptions of fairness and transparency, though the risk of involving select stakeholders in decision-making processes is that of information being shared prematurely, which could lead to increased anxiety among other personnel.[25]

Some employees will resist change on principle, and reasons can range from fear of the unknown future state, lack of understanding of the need for change, anticipated loss of security or status, and disinclination to take on additional work.[26] Leaders can moderate resistance by encouraging stakeholder engagement in the process, introducing the changes respectfully, and enumerating the support for and benefits of the coming change.[27] In a study of academic librarians' resistance to change, it was found that levels of resistance are higher with (1) increasing age of the librarian, (2) increasing years of experience, (3) the more supervisory duties the librarian has, and (4) if the change is driven from outside of the library.[28] Those who are resistant to change may engage in sabotage behaviors such as ongoing insistence on full consensus on all decisions, repeatedly revisiting decisions they did not agree with, or derailing conversation in order to delay decision-making.[29]

The Case

Like most institutions of higher education, the author's university faced innumerable challenges spurred by the COVID-19 pandemic. The university was also in the unfortunate position of compounding financial factors, which led to careful evaluation of costs across the institution in an effort to realign expenses. A consulting group identified areas that appeared to have excess resources; the data seemed to indicate an over-resourced library relative to the university's benchmarking institutions. As a result, the university administration instructed the library to make unfathomable reductions of 30% within less than six weeks. No directives were given for how to reach the savings, and the UL had the discretion to meet the goal in the way she felt most appropriate.

Reductions on this scale could only be accomplished through a combination of decreased spending on the collection and a downsizing of personnel. Cuts in both print and e-resources were difficult decisions to make, as all of the resources showed usage and were important to the programs they supported, and it required the liaison librarians to quickly identify remaining resources to support student and faculty research needs. However, the decisions in reducing the workforce headcount were far more difficult and emotionally charged.

The UL had the opportunity to meet with the consulting group and discuss their preliminary analysis of the library. The UL provided additional data and requested reevaluation of their recommendation, in an effort to better align the recommendation with the context of the university-wide services included in the library's budget; the consultants declined to reevaluate their findings. Throughout the process of working with the consultants, the UL solicited input from the library's advisory council, which included the leaders of each of four service groups (access, education, collections, and technology) who worked collaboratively with the UL to consider solutions.

In addition to the input from the library's advisory council, the provost appointed a small group of faculty to assist the UL in evaluating data. Having this group to advise parameters for resource elimination was invaluable for its outside perspective and for its eventual role in messaging the situation to faculty. The group evaluated data and asked thoughtful questions throughout the process, as they came to understand library resources and operations. Among countless other facets, the group looked at database cost per usage data, resource allocations by academic program, services usage data, and job descriptions.

While these groups were meeting multiple times each week, the UL also communicated regularly with all library personnel. There were weekly meetings (held virtually due to pandemic conditions), weekly updates in a newsletter, and countless email communications. These served to update library personnel on the discussions taking place, the additional data needs, the ongoing list of savings identified to date, and the emerging criteria

Difficult Decisions in Downsizing   349

for how reductions would be decided upon. Personnel were given notice at the beginning of the process that it was extremely unlikely that the library could achieve its reduction goal through resource cuts alone, and that positions were likely to be eliminated as well. This transparency was a double-edged sword, where having advance notice of pending changes allowed people to mentally prepare and plan accordingly, but also caused a great deal of anxiety.

During this time, the library's collections team met frequently, to identify and discuss possible resource cuts. The team leader communicated with the consortia with whom the library had pooled access to resources in order to determine the options for withdrawing from those agreements if needed, and also reached out to vendors to negotiate prices. All library personnel were given updates on the collection cuts in progress and had the opportunity to comment and make suggestions. The collections meetings were challenging, as each librarian simultaneously wanted to do what was best for the situation overall, and also wanted to ensure that their liaison areas were supported. The collection team approached its task in a data-driven manner, but it was not always a peaceful process.

Throughout the six weeks, the UL met frequently with the university's human resources professionals and with a faculty member with industry expertise in human resource reorganizations. Salary information was not shared with members of the advisory groups, but they were involved in discussions to prioritize the library's core work and eliminate any overlap of job functions. Making data-driven decisions regarding personnel meant that an employee might have been providing the data that resulted in their own position elimination. All positions in the library were evaluated for elimination, including that of the UL; the library had managed with an interim UL previously, so no position was sacred in this process. The UL continually communicated to all personnel that decisions on downsizing would be made based entirely on maintaining essential library functions, and not on length of employment service or performance evaluations.

Ultimately, the library advisory council's work, combined with the recommendations from the faculty group, led to a recognition that in order to meet the reduction goal, the library would have to reduce its personnel by one-third and would have to cut e-resource spending by 50% and the print resource budget by 90%. In communicating final plans to library personnel, the UL made it explicitly clear that while many people had input in the process, all final decisions were the responsibility of the UL. This was done in hopes of minimizing negative sentiments toward anyone on the faculty group or the library's advisory council.

The e-resource reduction was complicated by the lack of alignment between subscription year and fiscal year in many cases. The library was able to achieve some immediate savings, while other savings would be realized more gradually. Print resource spending for the fiscal year was limited solely to support the library's heavily used textbook reserves collection. There were some instances of teaching faculty objecting to resource cuts, but the reductions were communicated by the faculty advisory group in such a way that most of their peers understood and accepted the situation.

Personnel reductions included eliminating three full-time staff positions, three part-time staff positions, as well as the loss of a full-time library faculty line following a fortuitously timed retirement. The library went from a headcount of 24 to 16.5 in a matter of weeks. Layoffs were communicated to each downsized employee by the UL, with the position's service group leader and a representative from human resources present. The UL delivered the news in a straightforward manner, emphasizing that the *position* was being eliminated, and that it was not a reflection on the person's performance or contributions. The UL and service group leaders offered to serve as references for the person's future job search, and the UL informed departing colleagues of the severance packages being offered. While severance packages were not required by the university, the UL felt strongly that it was appropriate to provide these as a way to acknowledge that the departing colleagues were not at fault in any way. The severance packages were paid through the library's budget, which meant that the entire wage savings could not be realized, which further complicated calculations of reductions.

The three part-time positions were eliminated first, only two weeks into the process. The service group leaders and the UL agreed those were the least essential positions based on the nature of the work and service hours provided. Three full-time positions were eliminated three weeks later, after a more in-depth evaluation of the library's *essential* services. The library dissolved the faculty position vacated by a retirement as part of the savings gained. The work of each position had to be eliminated or redistributed quickly, leading to additional responsibilities for many employees with no increase in compensation, which negatively impacted morale.

The downsizing also prompted a reorganization of the library's structure, resulting in a more agile organization with two departments (access/education and resources/systems) instead of four service groups, improving communication and efficiency.

However, after the initial upheaval, some behaviors aligned with survivor's guilt began to manifest amongst the remaining employees, which delayed the library's ability to fully embrace its new structure. Additionally, there was discontent expressed by some library personnel concerning selection of long-time employees for termination as part of the restructuring and downsizing, which they perceived to be grossly unfair. Employees who had given significant portions of their professional lives to the library's success did not reap any perceived benefit from that loyalty because the reduction was mandated by the university administration and length of tenure was not part of the criteria for position eliminations. This was an understandable reaction and was addressed as much as possible.

From the UL's perspective, it was affirming to be entrusted to lead the process of analysis and decision making. This speaks to the need to establish trusting relationships, where there was no doubt from the administration that the UL would make decisions with the institution's best interests in mind, regardless of personal interests. The UL envisioned the process as having to amputate digits and limbs, and while that would be difficult to adapt to under the best of circumstances, the UL preferred to have agency in deciding which elements would be cut in an effort to minimize the pain. Of course, not all library personnel agreed with the decisions and even many months after the downsizing and reorganization, there was dissension voiced in an evaluation survey for the UL, with an expressed sentiment that "the library has been gutted and it's the UL's fault."

Discussion and Lessons Learned

Change Management

The best practices for phases of change management were challenging to implement in the library's case. Setting the stage and creating buy-in were difficult because the reduction was mandated by the university administration, which was not a rationale that all personnel could accept. It is essential to implement change at an appropriate pace, and the imposed deadline accelerated decision-making. Given a more standard timeframe, the UL would have slowed the process down for two groups in particular: the collections team would have benefited from additional time to evaluate resource usage data, and the circulation team would have had additional time to determine options for service points. Change management also necessitates deliberate effort to cement the new normal into the practices and culture of the organization, and the compressed time frame for making changes collided with the beginning of the academic year and its inevitable chaos.

Layoffs can cause employees to feel resentment towards the leadership, anxious, undervalued and insecure. Leaders can mitigate this with open communication, engaging employees in implementing new structures. In the library's case, the UL was able to give all personnel advance notice of the scope of pending changes, as well as the ultimate budget reduction number. The processes of developing the criteria for cuts involved key stakeholders in the collections team and the service group leaders, though it did not involve all library personnel. In hindsight, the discussions would have benefited from involving additional library stakeholders, including student employees.

At the conclusion of the reductions, the library's organizational structure was revamped and essential work was redistributed. Work that was eliminated or scaled back needed to be recognized as important, though it was deemed nonessential to the library's operations. The UL publicly acknowledged individuals' contributions and strengths, and openly thanked and offered support to downsized employees. As work was reassigned, the UL encouraged adequate training for newly assigned duties, but was unable to provide professional development funds to further that. Work reassignments should play to the strengths of remaining employees; the UL and service group leaders attempted to do this, though some changes were driven solely by which employee had the bandwidth to take on the duties, regardless of strengths, which was detrimental to long-term success.

Allies are important in transition and can help to influence and implement change at both the logistical and organizational culture levels. The UL was able to capitalize on allies in the library's service group leaders, each of whom had different strengths as process helpers and solution givers. Additionally, the faculty group were allies as solution givers and as stabilizers for reseating the library within the larger academic affairs context.

Communication

Continuous and frequent communication is essential during times of change. The UL provided multiple communications to provide updates on decision-making and planning. Best practices indicate that synchronous communication between leaders and employees is important when mutual agreements need to be reached. Much of the communication during the library's downsizing process was synchronous via a video conferencing platform, though not face-to-face due to remote work. Information was also shared asynchronously via email and weekly news updates. Unfortunately, the UL was not able to meet and share information in person, though the position elimination meetings were face-to-face with the UL.

There is risk in communicating bad news before all details are known and this was the case in the library, where advance notice of likely position eliminations caused anxiety across the library, as each employee feared that their position would be lost. It is important to communicate a vision for the future so that employees can see a path toward better conditions. In the turmoil of the process, the UL neglected to present a compelling vision or silver lining, though this later began to emerge after the library's reorganization was completed and the UL was able to demonstrate that the "new normal" included improvements over past practices.

When communicating difficult news, particularly at the magnitude of the library's situation, leaders should be direct and forthcoming with the extent of the changes, rather than doling it out gradually. In the library's case, the UL was blunt in communicating that both resource and personnel reductions would be unavoidable; the extent of the reductions evolved as the process progressed and the UL continually updated employees on progress toward the target budget. This transparency was positive in allowing all employees to see the status of the changes, and negative in increasing anxiety of the unknown.

Survivor's Guilt and Employee Commitment

Those who retain their employment sometimes experience survivor's guilt and declines in morale. If colleagues depart voluntarily, employees perceive that decisions were made fairly, or severance packages were satisfactory, negative impacts can be minimized. The library's downsizing happened within a matter of weeks, precluding opportunity for voluntary departures, and there was little time for employees to adjust to the idea or to have closure with departing colleagues. The circumstances caused a palpable decline in employee morale. The UL involved the library's service group leaders in decision-making, which did help to create a sense of fairness, but this was little consolation to remaining personnel.

It is not uncommon for employees who are resistant to change to engage in sabotage behaviors such as insistence on full consensus on all decisions or revisiting decisions already finalized. The library's timeline for making decisions and changes did not allow for revisiting decisions nor making all decisions by consensus, and the UL had to make many decisions unilaterally. This was not an optimal approach, and given adequate time, more decisions would have been given fuller consideration and discussion with all library stakeholders.

While the budget reduction directive came from the top down, its implementation was at the discretion of the UL, who was making rapid-fire difficult decisions while attempting to manage the change for personnel, keeping the library's core operations intact, and making unpopular choices to eliminate or reduce services and operations. Change management is an integral part of leadership, but that does not eliminate the human element of managing through such crises and the process took an emotional toll on the UL. Downsizing under duress required keeping library personnel well-informed throughout the process and continually communicating the rationale behind each decision, which helped everyone to see the overall situation and unavoidable nature of the changes, even if not all were in agreement with the decisions made.

Based on best practices and lessons learned in this case, an optimal approach to large-scale downsizing would have had additional time to allow for voluntary employee departures, inclusion of additional stakeholders in discussions, fuller evaluation of data, and the collaborative creation of a long-term vision for resultant positive outcomes. Communication was early, often, iterative, transparent, and face-to-face whenever possible. Departing colleagues need to be recognized for their valuable contributions, and personnel need time to grieve the loss of colleagues and to the accept the new practices and structures. Work reassignment needs to be done based on strengths and aptitudes, and ample training and development opportunities are essential to employee success and morale. While some of the practices were followed in this case, all would have benefited from a more moderated pace to change.

Limitations and Future Research

Literature and best practices in change management are well studied, and have been applied to this case study. However, chronicling a single case may have limited applicability, as does its reflective nature and personal bias from the university librarian who was responsible for the downsizing of both resources and personnel.

In addition to comparative analysis from multiple cases of downsizing in academic libraries, future studies could specifically address employee morale and survivor's guilt in higher education. There are few studies or works on the impact of downsizing decisions on the leader's psyche, which also presents opportunities for further study.

Notes

1. Ibid.
2. Ibid.
3. Brian Harney, Na Fu, and Yseult Freeney, "Balancing tensions: Buffering the impact of organizational restructuring and downsizing on employee well-being," *Human Resource Management Journal* 28 (2018): 237, 239.
4. Ibid., 240.

5. Elena Carillo and Gwen M. Gregory, "Change management in extremis: A case study," *Journal of Access Services* 16, no. 1 (2019): 32-33.
6. Corey Seeman, "Squirreling Away: Managing Information Resources & Libraries—Finding Your Beat: Rapidity and Change Management," *Against the Grain* 32, no. 3 (June 2019): 52.
7. Ibid., 52, 55.
8. Gisela von Dran, Gisela, "Human Resources and Leadership Strategies for Libraries in Transition," *Library Administration & Management* 19, no. 4 (2005): 182.
9. Ibid., 183.
10. Ola Bergström and Rebecka Arman, "Increasing Commitment After Downsizing: The Role of Involvement and Voluntary Redundancies," *Journal of Change Management* 17, no. 4 (2017): 310.
11. Michaela J. Kerrissey and Amy C. Edmondson, "What Good Leadership Looks Like During This Pandemic," *Harvard Business Review* (2020): https://hbr.org/2020/04/what-good-leadership-looks-like-during-this-pandemic.
12. Bergström and Arman, "Increasing Commitment," 306.
13. Stephan Braun et al., "Emails From the Boss—Curse or Blessing? Relations Between Communication Channels, Leader Evaluation, and Employees' Attitudes," *International Journal of Business Communication* 56, no.1 (2019): 54.
14. Ibid., 56, 66.
15. Ibid., 62.
16. Ibid., 74.
17. Kerrissey and Edmondson, "What Good Leadership Looks Like."
18. Ibid.
19. Kerrissey and Edmondson, "What Good Leadership Looks Like"; Bård Norheim and Joar Haga, *The Four Speeches Every Leader Has to Know* (Switzerland: Palgrave/Macmillan/Springer Nature, 2020).
20. Norheim and Haga, *Four Speeches*, 62, 60, 68.
21. Leon Grunberg, Richard Anderson-Connolly, and Edward S. Greenberg, "Surviving Layoffs: The Effects on Organizational Commitment and Job Performance," *Work and Occupations* 27, no. 1 (2000): 8.
22. Ibid., 10.
23. Bergström and Arman, "Increasing Commitment," 298; Grunberg, Anderson-Connolly, and Greenberg, "Surviving Layoffs," 10, 21.
24. Bergström and Arman, "Increasing Commitment," 313.
25. Ibid., 307.
26. Brian Young and Ashley Dees, "From Saboteurs to Change Management: Investigating the Correlation between Workplace Behavior and Change Resistance," Paper presented at *Association of College & Research Libraries Conference: At the Helm: Leading Transformation, Baltimore, MD, March 2017*, http://hdl.handle.net/11213/17736, 247-48.
27. Ibid., 248.
28. Ibid., 249-50.
29. Ibid., 251.

Bibliography

Bakker, Arnold B., and Evangelia Demerouti. "The Job Demands-Resources model: state of the art." *Journal of Managerial Psychology* 22, no. 3 (2007): 309-28.

Bakker, Arnold B., Evangelia Demerouti, and Martin C. Euwema. "Job Resources Buffer the Impact of Job Demands on Burnout." *Journal of Occupational Health Psychology* 10, no. 2 (2005): 170-80.

Bergström, Ola, and Rebecka Arman. "Increasing commitment after downsizing: The role of involvement and voluntary redundancies." *Journal of Change Management* 17, no. 4 (2017): 297-320.

Braun, Stephan, Alina Hernandez Bark, Alexander Kirchner, Sebastian Stemann, and Rolf van Dick. "Emails From the Boss—Curse or Blessing? Relations Between Communication Channels, Leader Evaluation, and Employees' Attitudes." *International Journal of Business Communication* 56, no.1 (2019): 50-81.

Carillo, Elena, and Gwen M. Gregory. "Change management in extremis: A case study." *Journal of Access Services* 16, no. 1 (2019): 21-33.

Grunberg, Leon, Richard Anderson-Connolly, and Edward S. Greenberg. "Surviving Layoffs: The Effects on Organizational Commitment and Job Performance." *Work and Occupations* 27, no. 1 (2000): 7-31.

Harney, Brian, Na Fu, and Yseult Freeney. "Balancing tensions: Buffering the impact of organizational restructuring and downsizing on employee well-being." *Human Resource Management Journal* 28 (2018): 235-54.

Hendrix, Dana. "Emotional Intelligence and the Winds of Change in Academic Libraries." Paper presented at *Association of College & Research Libraries Conference: Imagine, Innovate, Inspire, Indianapolis, IN, April 2013*, 172-80. https://www.ala.org/acrl/sites/ala.org.acrl/files/content/conferences/confsandpreconfs/2013/papers/Hendrix_Emotional.pdf

Hernon, Peter, and Nancy Rossiter. "Emotional Intelligence: Which Traits Are Most Prized?" *College & Research Libraries* 77, no. 6 (2006): 260-74.

Kerrissey, Michaela J., and Amy C. Edmondson. "What Good Leadership Looks Like During This Pandemic." *Harvard Business Review*. April 13, 2020. https://hbr.org/2020/04/what-good-leadership-looks-like-during-this-pandemic

McLean, Jaclyn, Diane (DeDe) Dawson, and Charlene Sorensen. "Communicating Collections Cancellations to Campus: A Qualitative Study." *College & Research Libraries* 82, no. 1 (2021): 19-43.

Miller, Kelsey. "5 Critical Steps in the Change Management Process." *Harvard Business School Online*. March 19, 2020. https://online.hbs.edu/blog/post/change-management-process

Norheim, Bård and Joar Haga. *The Four Speeches Every Leader Has to Know*. Switzerland: Palgrave/Macmillan/Springer Nature, 2020.

Seeman, Corey. "Squirreling Away: Managing Information Resources & Libraries—Finding Your Beat: Rapidity and Change Management." *Against the Grain* 32, no. 3 (June 2019): 51-52, 55.

von Dran, Gisela. "Human Resources and Leadership Strategies for Libraries in Transition." *Library Administration & Management* 19, no. 4 (2005): 177-84.

Young, Brian, and Ashley Dees. "From Saboteurs to Change Management: Investigating the Correlation between Workplace Behavior and Change Resistance." Paper presented at Association of College & Research Libraries Conference: At the Helm: Leading Transformation, Baltimore, MD, March 2017, 247-254. http://hdl.handle.net/11213/17736.

CHAPTER 28

Saying No to Say Yes

Mediating Student Technology Needs in Times of Crisis

Catherine Fonseca, Rita Premo, and Hilary Smith

Enacting boundaries proved essential in getting to a decisive space.

Introduction

Sonoma State University (SSU) is a public, master's-level, liberal arts–focused institution of approximately 8,600 students as of fall 2019 (93 percent undergraduate) located in Rohnert Park, California,[1] a 1960s-era suburban community less than an hour north of San Francisco. SSU is one of twenty-three campuses in the California State University (CSU) system, which educates nearly 500,000 ethnically, economically, and academically diverse students annually.[2] As of March 2020, the library employed eight full-time librarians and twenty administrators and staff members, plus student assistants.

Within the CSU, librarians are faculty. Various researchers have discussed the relative merits of academic librarians receiving faculty or quasi-faculty status.[3] At SSU, a central benefit to librarian faculty status is that the library has full voting representation in faculty governance, including seats on all regular committees and subcommittees, as well as the Academic Senate. While university service must be optimized and decided upon collectively by the faculty because of our small size, such involvement situates librarians in many places where issues relevant to the entire campus are discussed and decided. Thus, we have a high-level understanding of university operations broadly and possess deeper opportunities for advocacy based on our professional expertise, union protection, and faculty status.

357

At the same time, as an academic services provider, we partner and collaborate with other campus entities, such as student advising, information technology, and facilities. This liminal status helps the library faculty bridge gaps between student services staff, administrators, nonlibrary faculty, and students themselves.

Meanwhile, crisis experiences at SSU starting in fall 2017—including multiple regional wildfires, air quality issues, and fire-related power outages—primed the SSU library faculty and staff to anticipate how typically siloed portions of campus would react in a crisis, what challenges might arise, and how faculty concerns would likely differ widely from student concerns. As each of these events impacted our university, we learned important lessons: Regional power shutdowns informed us that not all students, staff, and faculty have internet access at home. Power outages on campus, with multiple failures of backup resources, might affect university systems such as websites, learning management systems, online library authentication, doors, and so on. Wildfires and evacuations demonstrated that students do not always feel agency regarding their own safety, instead relying on campus to advocate for their safety; however, campus often leaned on resiliency narratives rather than proactively protecting student health and safety. A unified support center in response to disasters was located within the library because space elsewhere on campus was unavailable. The Emergency Operations Center was also housed in the library due to limited space in its original location for the necessary body of individuals and equipment. In general, we learned that people turn to the library during an emergency for many things—technology, spaces, and so on—including some that are outside our scope of work and responsibility.

This chapter details the mediating role embraced by the SSU Library in managing university-wide technology and learning challenges during an unanticipated pivot to remote instruction and is organized according to lessons we learned. Responding to COVID disruptions in real time. we identified key areas where our expertise and relationships allowed us to advocate for and support students, while also saying no or limiting our participation in others. Limiting the services provided during a crisis to only those that fit within the core scope of our mission was a powerful tactic that libraries should exercise often and widely communicate. Rather than answering every call to service and overextending ourselves, libraries must embrace saying no and exercise transparency around decision-making. In doing so, libraries conserve energy and resources to deliver core services, thereby ensuring that primary services are thriving, robust, and able to withstand instabilities wrought by crises.

Core mission work included a technology-lending program that prioritized support of underserved populations. In addition, we leveraged our position in the campus community to underscore students' remote learning challenges, including privacy, surveillance technology, and the interplay of basic needs and student success. During this process, we quickly learned that we would have to establish and enforce boundaries to ensure a focus on the students most in need of learning resources and empathetic approaches to remote instruction. Saying no to different stakeholders—in the administration, peers in the university such as faculty or staff, and students—when we felt it was appropriate, was difficult and possibly politically problematic, but necessary in the pursuit of equity.

Saying No to Performative Equity

As COVID-19 cases began to climb in the US in March 2020, one of the librarians' earliest instances of exercising equity-informed pushback came as the campus pivoted toward physical closure and remote instruction. On March 12, 2020, SSU suspended face-to-face classes, thereby giving instructors a week plus the short spring break to move course content to online modalities, anticipating a worsening public health crisis. Initially, campus decision makers intended to resume classes remotely for the remaining seven weeks of the spring term, while still providing access to essential on-campus resources, such as residential halls, dining locations, the health center, and the library.

The library had concerns regarding this long-term plan for maintaining physical access, even at reduced hours, despite the equity justifications for this arrangement. The rationale supplied by administrative powers primarily rested on the need to supply students with the technology necessary to complete their coursework online. Discipline-specific faculty also expressed concerns around shutting down the library. However, despite classifying the library as an essential campus resource, SSU leadership originally issued no additional custodial support, no guidance around cleaning or distancing protocols, conflicting internal communications, and incorrect or incoherent campus-wide messaging regarding library services between what was on the library website versus the university's electronic communications. Examples include messaging that technology was provided on a first-come, first-served basis or that the library was responsible for hot spots, using the library's laptop request form for a separate nonlibrary effort and distributing widely the laptop request form during a period when it was to be distributed only to prioritized student groups. Much of the university-led communications worked from a set of assumptions about library practices without consulting the library, creating inconsistent messaging and more work for the library. After some advocacy from the library, these issues were largely ameliorated by the campus simply linking to the library's service page rather than trying to restate information about library offerings.

The lack of institutional support for ensuring the health and well-being of all persons in the building prompted library faculty to petition SSU's cabinet to close the building. On March 20, 2020, two days after the Sonoma County health officer ordered a shelter-in-place,[4] library faculty sent a letter to the university president and provost—patterned after similar statements at other CSU libraries—strongly urging the closure of the library building as long as shelter-in-place directives remained. Aside from outlining plans for continuing service in a remote capacity, our letter cited as a rationale the undue burdens placed on campus populations with the least amount of leverage, namely students and library employees. Indeed, the letter ended with a distinct denunciation of the campus plan as one that propagated disparities, stating

> We pride ourselves on supporting those within our communities who are often overlooked and underserved. We recognize that the students who would continue to use our facilities during this time constitute our most vulnerable populations. However, we refuse to perpetuate further inequities by upholding the university's current stance requiring

> vulnerable students to use shared facilities and forcing them to weigh their and their families' safety against their grades.

Remaining open meant putting at risk those employees and students without further recourse—soliciting employees to choose between their livelihood and their wellness and students to prioritize their education above their health. Instead of supporting these scenarios for the sake of access and casting the library as a savior for those interested in using the facilities, library faculty refused campus administration. Rejecting the role of library savior necessitates that service delivery first focus on internal capacity, resisting the pressure to promise a library solution. While emergencies certainly heighten the urgency to respond and relieve, libraries must strike a healthy balance between timely reaction and taking time to lessen the gap between expectations and the complexity of outcomes. By enacting our stated commitment to equity while exercising our privileges as a largely tenured or tenure-track faculty to advocate for those without the same influence and protections, we framed our refusal to offer in-person services as equity over access, which proved compelling enough for campus administrators to close the library building as of March 25.

The rapid initial measures taken to protect public safety proved prescient in light of the ensuing closures and intermittent re-closures adopted by libraries across the country, as well as the subsequent mass gathering guidelines established at state and federal levels. In addition to bringing our library into prevailing best practices, the closure of our library's physical doors hastened the opening of other, remote opportunities. The library team immediately shifted to the planning and adoption of remote reference, contactless borrowing, and virtual instruction services. Moreover, framing the library's closure as a means of protecting our most vulnerable populations necessitated a conscientious, prioritized effort toward replacing in-person access for those most impacted by lack of access to our physical resources. Refusing to acquiesce to the university's planned response allowed the library to develop an equitable and student-focused approach.

Leveraging Connections to Enact Boundaries

Responding to the building closure, the library quickly adapted to providing innovative, off-site services to accommodate changing user needs. Among these was the rollout of a laptop mailing program to connect students dispersed across California with the tools necessary to complete online coursework. This project entailed reconfiguring our pool of more than 100 MacBook laptops (from either in-house instruction or short-term circulation pools) for semester-long use. Given the immediacy of digital learning support further exacerbated by unavailability of in-person library technologies, the library laptop lending program was more of an impromptu, on-the-spot process as opposed to the more methodical, slow bureaucratic planning normally reserved for launching library initiatives. As a result, policies, workflows, marketing, and logistics were developed concurrently with the rollout of the program.

Enacting boundaries proved essential in getting to a decisive space. Early on, the small internal working group tasked with overseeing the library's emergency laptop delivery program refused certain user groups in an effort to conserve resources for those deemed most in need. First, our task force determined that only students would be eligible to receive a laptop loan, thereby declining to fill technology access gaps among faculty and staff. As further demands on library technology arose—including those from junior college students in the region, supervisors looking to support telework, faculty seeking equipment for student research assistants, students requiring technology for non-curricular purposes, and so on—we further narrowed eligibility only to students currently enrolled in SSU courses requiring technology for course-related learning.

The evolution of the emergency program's eligibility criteria reflects the largely improvised nature of any disaster response. Yet it also reveals the nature of disaster planning as a largely local matter, requiring flexible solutions that can be properly tailored or pivoted to address cultural, regional, and community considerations. A strong sense of institutional identity and values can also ease the process of saying no when establishing or managing emergency services. Our student-focused, course-bound eligibility parameters aligned well with the library's strong identity as a teaching organization whose collections and service models already prioritized curricular support and student learning first, above faculty research.

Additionally, the strong culture of university service and strategic campus partnerships intentionally cultivated by SSU's library faculty as part of our liaison role allowed us to anticipate that student learning would likely be left out of campus considerations for remote technology, bringing clarity to decisions about the purpose and mission of the library technology lending program and eligibility criteria. Prior to the pandemic, SSU had not attempted to comprehensively survey technology access across campus. The library lacked such local empirical data; yet given our service positions in relevant committees, we understood that campus information technology (IT) likely did not envision student technology fulfillment as part of its central mission and anticipated that IT would instead allocate much of its efforts toward outfitting and supporting employees for telework. In this way, embedded librarianship in campus governance helped inform and bolster our decision-making around the core value of equity, identifying students as the user group with the highest level of unmet needs during the coming months.

Faculty status for librarians ultimately allowed us to proactively place ourselves in governance positions and participate in conversations that likely otherwise would have taken place without our being able to advocate for those most likely to be left out of the equation. Our limited faculty librarian cohort necessitates that we be quite selective in our service commitments, opting for committees focused on administrative policies and programs as opposed to advisory bodies or curricular matters. Our pre-pandemic placement of library representatives on high-level governance groups proved to be an effective strategy in helping shape our own crisis response within the library. Beyond simply using these service commitments as opportunities for gathering information, librarians also used our committee platforms to be transparent about library emergency measures, share challenges and obstacles in supplying provisional services, mediate the gap between

Student Affairs and Academic Affairs via our liminal position as an academic unit with a student-oriented service model, and ultimately advocate for equitable, long-term planning around student technology support.

A community-focused approach to emergency preparedness, then, entails cultivating a seat at the table before the crisis hits, building rapport with community stakeholders, and demonstrating the library's value and expertise in joint activities and non-LIS contexts—all prior to the onset of an emergency.

Opting for Restorative over Broad Access

Saying no to equipment requests from faculty, staff, and community to instead prioritize student needs reflected the scarcity mentality that should be integral in any library's emergency response. While "serving all" and "equity of treatment" are common messages across library institutions, crises often create contexts where deliberately providing access to some while refusing service to others is, in fact, the more equity-minded path. With limited capacities and supplies, libraries must make intentional choices to allocate resources to their most vulnerable users, even if that may be at the expense of other user cohorts. The SSU library found itself in this very situation when launching our emergency technology lending program.

Where the library had previously provided a larger number of short-term laptop loans and served a more expansive patron pool, circulating our limited number of laptops on a long-term basis rendered obsolete our previous definition of equity. The campus closure and the wide diffusion of our student population to their places of origin during remote instruction meant we could no longer provide a larger quantity and faster turnaround of loans via shorter checkout periods. In reimagining equity in our new contexts, we shifted from an inclusive service model with higher volume to a triage approach focused on high-impact, user-targeted service. Rather than asking "How can we better serve?" or "Whom are we not serving?" our focus turned to questions such as "How many can we serve?" and "Whom should we serve first?"

Thus, we arrived at a measure of equity that shifted from equal distribution to restorative access—that is, centering those users at the far edges of social privilege. At the onset of the emergency laptop delivery program, we introduced a priority period in which underserved students would be able to request laptops before the general student population. This priority mechanism relied on sharing an unpublished link to the online request form with Student Affairs departments specifically dedicated to serving undocumented, first-generation, low-income, Latinx, foster, and disabled students. Rollout of this strategy benefited from relationships and strategic infusion of librarians across campus committees prior to the pandemic: One librarian was the chair of the Student Affairs Committee, while another had cultivated an informal liaison relationship with cocurricular campus units. In this way, the library pivoted from a more traditional sense of equity—that is, access for the masses—to service delivery that contributes to countering prevailing hierarchies of race, ethnicity, socioeconomic status, physical ability, and citizenship. This approach proved particularly salient during a pandemic that exacerbated and laid bare these very inequalities.

Yet even among these priority student populations, saying no was still necessary to sustainably improve access to library technology during a time when so much was unknown about the longevity of pandemic measures. For example, the library limited the priority loan period to this underserved constituency to two weeks only, after which requests were opened up to the remainder of eligible students. Another boundary enacted was to limit loans and require students to return their laptops at the end of the term, without exception. While this return mandate allowed library personnel to conduct repairs and system reimaging necessary for longer term circulation, it also allowed for more frequent circulation to a broader range of students. Though a remnant of the broad access mentality, limiting laptops to a single-semester loan bridged our previous model of broad service to the more restorative focus of our emergency lending program.

Predictably, the library faced some pushback in the face of these restrictions, albeit relatively infrequent and restrained in nature, including students requesting renewals for subsequent semesters and entities serving underrepresented students wanting to extend the priority request period. However, library measures proactively anticipated and ameliorated concerns, including prepaid mail return slips to eliminate barriers for end-of-semester returns, as well as early and consistent communications regarding priority requests. Ultimately, political capital formed from our relationship building with students and student-serving departments prior to the pandemic enabled us to generally obtain buy-in around prohibitory policies and ease instances when the library chose to say no.

Rejecting Library Saviorism

In addition to our laptop lending program, the library partnered with campus stakeholders to facilitate additional technology lending programs, including Wi-Fi hot spots and noise-cancelling headsets. While the headsets were a library initiative, the hot spot program was managed by IT—at the insistence of the library. The library also embarked on measures to support faculty in their delivery of online learning, namely the introduction of emergency digitization services in lieu of physical reserves. While each of these new services presented its own unique challenges, one emergency initiative owes its relative success over the other in large part to the mentality adopted by the library: one of pragmatism over saviorism. Indeed, our approach to the laptop program is revealing of this tactic. Our decision to pivot our laptop lending program for a finite period of time was ultimately shaped with what was feasible under current conditions rather than what was desired by the university. Rather than promise a long-term solution to the digital divide and scramble to launch a new permanent service, the SSU library instead offered a makeshift program that was functional yet imperfect: a winning combination for the rapid response required. In offering a stopgap only, the library largely met a major need, conserved resources for other emergency programs, and bought the university some valuable time for arriving at a wider, more sustainable solution to the digital divide on campus. On the whole, our emergency programs were more fully realized when the library clearly voiced reluctance and inserted itself in a provisional capacity, rather than offering solutions that cast the library in a savior light.

In defining library saviorism, it is useful to draw on the work of Fobazi Ettarh and her concept of vocational awe.[5] Ettarh describes how a prevailing narrative around academic librarians has emerged: one that portrays them as "priest and savior" whose work is to singularly uphold and defend age-old institutions of democracy, freedom, access, lifelong learning, and the civic good. This savior archetype contributes to a "vocational awe": a "set of ideas, values, and assumptions" librarians hold about themselves that contributes to their aggrandized self-image. Notions about the profession then portray the library as an inherently sacred site of societal improvement and librarianship as a divine calling. While vocational awe insulates the library and its attendant profession from critique or reproach, it does so at the expense of the individual worker, who is perpetually held to an insatiable occupational "purity test." Therein lies the trap of vocational awe: veneration of the institution itself ultimately leads to low morale, depreciation, and burnout among library professionals. Altruism and self-sacrifice characterize the labor of the individual librarian, whereas self-preservation is left behind in fulfillment of our hallowed mission. Going above and beyond to serve the needs of our users is not as innocuous as it first appears, then. As Schlesselman-Tarango notes, under the guise of service, we diminish our users as "deficient, inherently needy, or in need of saving," which renders the library-patron relationship lopsided, denies the agency of our users, frames the librarian as the evangelizing missionary, and activates the vicious cycle of exhaustion and stress so prevalent within our profession.[6]

The urge to promise beyond our means, a common symptom of library saviorism, hindered both the hot spot and headset lending programs and, in the case of the building and facilities, could have had detrimental effects if the library had attempted to stay physically open. In the cases of the hot spots and the headphones, the library was unable to resist this temptation, resulting in inefficiencies in the program rollouts, user confusion, and even failure to launch, as in the case of noise-cancelling headsets.

With the fall 2020 semester about to begin and students clamoring for support, tremendous pressure existed to reassure students that help was on the way. Almost as soon as funding was identified, administrators asked that we implement programs and create request forms. Yet in respect to both headsets and hot spots, we had to contend with supply chain and purchasing issues that were and remain endemic. Despite SSU's notoriously idiosyncratic procurement process and the broader uncertainty of supply chains, request forms went live on the library's website before the hot spots or headsets had been purchased. As students began populating these request forms, we continued to face significant setbacks in locating suppliers, heightened by pandemic-induced demand spikes and shipping delays. As a result, we spent considerable time responding to student queries about their request status or arrival times for sought-after equipment.

While IT eventually procured hot spots and delivered them to students, the library was unable to acquire noise-cancelling headphones and deliver the goods on the student requests that were, in hindsight, prematurely solicited. In retrospect, particularly during a crisis, it's far easier to say no at the outset when solutions are not certain than it is to say yes and then have to retract it. By going above and beyond to provide service in the face of anticipated pitfalls, libraries contribute to the fallacy that systemic problems can be sustainably solved with singular, and not multifaceted, solutions.

Another major failure of library saviorism is the concealment of those problems we seek to mitigate. When a library steps up to offer solutions, it must not obscure associated costs, potential pitfalls, or an issue's intricacies from key stakeholders. For the SSU library, perhaps the use of equipment waiting lists most clearly demonstrates this lesson. Funding for the hot spot lending program covered IT's purchase of 180 devices and a one-year service plan for each. IT did not plan to provide access beyond the 2020–2021 academic year, uncertain that more devices or plans could be purchased if needed. It was suggested that we could utilize a waiting list for the request form so that if additional hot spots became available, those requests could be filled. The headset lending program also incorporated a waiting list while the library futilely shopped around for equipment.

We strongly advised against using waiting lists, suggesting that instead we institute or reopen a request form and market availability after acquiring the necessary devices. We had two concerns: that students would take from the existence of a waiting list the hope that devices would become available soon and their request was likely to be filled, and that campus stakeholders would come to believe from the continued availability of a request form that student needs for adequate internet access or other technology were being adequately addressed. Despite our concerns, the waiting lists were enabled. Eventually, we had to notify students on the initial list and in the wait-listed group that headset supplies were unavailable. And, as anticipated, because the request form for hot spots and its lengthy waiting list remained live on the library website long after all hot spots had been distributed, a prevailing false narrative began to emerge on campus that student connectivity needs had been amply met. Waiting lists in this context, then, only served to set up an unfulfillable expectation, sow confusion among patrons, and insulate ongoing student requests on a spreadsheet restricted to a handful of operational personnel and largely neglected once the supply of devices ran dry.

Our wait-list system attempted to expedite lengthy pre-circulation processes (i.e., procurement, delivery, systems integration, technical services, and funding additional equipment). But in this case, waiting lists presented the appearance of activity and momentum in service delivery while library personnel scrambled behind the scenes. The pursuit of seamless service hid the expansive work of creating and sustaining library lending. However, this emphasis on frictionless service ultimately hurt our users as much as it set up our organization for failure and diverted attention away from the seemingly solved problem via assurances of a forthcoming solution.

Though the library limited its involvement in the hot spot program, we did partner with IT to help provide a more consistent user experience, finding a middle ground. Given that students and faculty already identified the library as a source of technology support, the library hosted the request form on our site and worked with IT to develop a process that aligned with the laptop lending program and thus would be somewhat familiar to students. After some negotiation, we were able to draw firm boundaries around ultimate responsibility for hot spot management.

In this way, the library rejected the savior ethos to instead opt for a secondary, supporting role to IT's lead. Beyond our consultative work at the program launch, the library's meaningful contributions to hot spot lending have largely occurred on the sidelines, via continued advocacy within faculty governance for extending the service beyond its one-time, emergency scope and pushing for an institutional solution to bridging the digital divide.

That is not to say that libraries should not experiment, pivot, and potentially expand service during times of crisis. If a library identifies sufficient capacity and resources to address a pressing need that was either surfaced or worsened by a present crisis, it should move forward with a healthy dose of skepticism and hesitancy. The SSU library found itself better positioned when it stepped into a service arena with the expectation at the outset that we would eventually step out of that emergency function once the crisis had abated. Our emergency digitization service illustrates this process.

When we closed our building, we were acutely aware that online learning would require renewed reliance on digital copies of print materials. Given the pressing needs of disciplinary faculty while pivoting to online environments, we opted to provide a more rapid, makeshift response rather than seek a long-term, more sustainable alternative. At the outset, we also communicated definitive boundaries regarding practical and copyright constraints and offered information via virtual workshops and targeted messaging dedicated, in part, to providing insight on how the library was managing copyright compliance under this new paradigm.[7]

We also successfully emphasized the impermanence of the effort through consistent branding as an emergency service that would sunset eventually (later determined to be spring 2022). The success of our crisis response with respect to offering short-term digitization largely rested on our ability to precipitously look ahead and identify an exit point. Beyond simply filling a need, we were able to communicate our limited capacity and gained valuable insight into an uncharted service area; a path we intend to investigate post-pandemic when our organization is better positioned to consider an established digital reserve system.

Maintaining Lines of Communication in Crisis

Libraries have long been hampered by our impulse to be all things to all users, to repeatedly demonstrate our worth to our users and administrators, and to advocate for our position in the academy. Saying yes is the easy response and certainly appeals to our users, but as Douglas notes in her plea to push back against "library magic," "We need to get into complex explanations and uncomfortable conversations and we need to assume that our students and faculty can handle it."[8] For a no to be successful, however, uncomfortable conversations cannot end discussion completely. When further communication shuts down, the siloed decision-making that seems to permeate academia fills the void. The library's decision to purchase smart lockers, such as those used to allow secure pickup of packages held at an apartment complex, for contactless pickup exemplifies how such situations might occur and play out.

Smart lockers were proposed early during pandemic response planning as a means to offer safe contactless pickup services. The library's COVID response working group, charged with developing protocols and establishing priorities evaluated the proposal. (Although a number of the CSU libraries had implemented or were in the process of implementing a contactless pickup program via lockers, our library had not previously considered this technology.) After much research and discussion, the group recommended against the purchase due to bureaucratic challenges with the procurement process, the immediate and ongoing costs, uncertainties about workflow implementation and technology compatibility, and concerns about the time line.

We communicated our no and our reasoning to decision makers; however, the locker project moved forward without further consultation with the working group or the stakeholders responsible for implementation. Although sound reasons existed for exploring the use of lockers to facilitate contactless pickup, our concerns about this project have been borne out. More than a year after their purchase and weeks after the library reopened, the lockers were finally operational and thus were of little benefit in our pandemic response.

The peril of the no also was evident in another decision-making process. Libraries walk a thin line between gathering data that can inform and improve our practice and protecting user information and privacy.[9] The desire to demonstrate our worth through data collection goes hand in hand with the impulse to say yes to users, and quantitative data is a highly prized means of communicating this value. As a library, we are aware of the potential for harm in our data practices. While ensuring that library services meet our goals and user needs, we must also be mindful to not place additional burdens on our students.

Our faculty status within the university and our focus on programs and services in the library give us a unique perspective on both university priorities and student needs. As noted earlier, the library faculty are active in governance, have strong relationships with disciplinary faculty, and work closely with student services and cocurricular programs. As a result, we are attuned to both student and faculty concerns as well as administrative priorities and initiatives.[10] Our laptop lending program filled a critical, urgent need in the pandemic crisis and was a clear success for the library, and the program offered an obvious opportunity to quantify our impact on student success. Lee, Jeong, and Kim found that significant numbers of students suffered from moderate to severe stress, anxiety, or depression and that these experiences were most common in vulnerable populations.[11] Indeed, our laptop lending program was designed to alleviate some of the stressors by providing access to adequate technology.

But despite ample data about the laptop program, a further survey to provide data for use in garnering future support for the program was suggested. While we consider the opportunity to gather qualitative feedback from students as a chance to learn more about student needs during the pandemic, as well as what was and was not working in our laptop lending program, multiple stakeholders across campus had expressed concern that students were being over-surveyed. Library faculty within the laptop lending working group noted that such a survey would be counter to student interests at that time. Nevertheless, a survey was created with no further input from the faculty and disseminated to all students who had received a laptop. The resulting data provided no new information or insights yet undermined a library and university commitment to streamlining communication and preserving student bandwidth during a period of crisis.

Meanwhile, the library was particularly successful in forging clarity around our capacity to support hot spot lending in large part due to consistent, clear communication across campus. From the outset, the library pushed back on any suggestion that we take on the hot spot program as a whole. While laptop lending was a logical extension of the significant services and technology we offered prior to COVID—which also included desktop computers, printing and scanning capacity, and extensive Wi-Fi access—hot spot loans and the technology support required were not. We have long advocated that university IT take a more prominent role in supporting student technology needs in addition to faculty and staff support. The issues that have surfaced during the pandemic have highlighted the need for a holistic and university-wide approach. Libraries must be protective of their labor and capacity whenever considering mounting additional programs, particularly those that come without additional funding or resources, and communicate that to campus stakeholders. These examples highlight the need to maintain communication with stakeholders across the library and across campus, especially when disagreement about priorities exists.

Looking Forward

The SSU library faculty are considering how our response to the COVID crisis and recurring crises of wildfire threats will inform our future practice. We recognize that the normal structures of communication in the university, which tend to be both hierarchical and siloed, are ineffective and often detrimental in crisis response. To respond nimbly in a crisis, units across campus must be prepared to manage laterally in addition to managing up and down. Our experiences in the library responding to a succession of crises reinforced the value of our liminal role in the university structure as both faculty members and service providers. The pandemic and the preceding disasters highlighted the importance of aligning our service work and relationships with our own strategic goals and priorities. Moreover, present and other crises reveal the tangible harm caused by an ecosystem that praises library professionals who provide an excess of service despite insufficient means while failing to criticize the organizations demanding these very excesses. Moving forward, we are committed to using our relative power as faculty to draw attention to and disrupt these lopsided expectations.

Beyond the lessons of flexibility, collaboration, self-advocacy, and communication in uncertain times, the pandemic has foregrounded structural inequities and gaps within the university, particularly in the area of student technology. Though the landscape of higher education today requires consistent and reliable access to a wide range of technologies, the approach to providing that access has oftentimes been haphazard. The COVID crisis has revealed the need for a coherent, comprehensive, and sustainable system to support student technology in the university. Our experience providing a bridge between student needs and university expectations has demonstrated that such a program is beyond the library's current resources. We continue to both advocate strongly for the university to take on this issue and reject calls to convert our temporary program to a permanent service.

While advocating for student access to technology, we have also identified a need to push back against many of the surveillance technologies that have been hastily adopted during the pandemic. We are aware that, as the university considers a pivot to increased online instruction post-pandemic, such efforts will likely come with an increased use of this type of surveillance. Plagiarism detectors, proctoring software, and indeed the learning management system all raise significant privacy and data collection concerns in addition to issues of bias, the unequal impact on marginalized student groups, and the exacerbation of inequities already present in the system. As conversations and consciousness around technological surveillance emerge on our campus, librarians are bracing to enter these dialogues and amplify our practiced noes on behalf of our affected students.

Finally, we recognize that, for our institution and others contending with climate change, crisis response is the new normal. Although the circumstances of each new challenge may differ, our experiences have highlighted for us that our mission and our core values do not change. We have recognized the importance of setting boundaries and saying no while working to maintain communication. Going forward we are prepared to respond in ways that support our students, promote equity, and make clear that we are neither saviors nor magicians.

Notes

1. Sonoma State University, "Facts: Students," accessed September 15, 2021, http://sonoma.edu/about/facts.
2. California State University, *The California State University Fact Book 2021*, accessed September 15, 2021, https://www2.calstate.edu/csu-system/about-the-csu/facts-about-the-csu/Documents/facts2021.pdf.
3. Elise Silva, Quinn Galbraith, and Michael Groesbeck, "Academic Librarians' Changing Perceptions of Faculty Status and Tenure," *College and Research Libraries* 78, no. 4 (2017): 428–41, https://doi.org/10.5860/crl.78.4.428; Nathan D. Hosburgh, "Librarian Faculty Status: What Does It Mean in Academia?" *Library Philosophy and Practice*, 2011: article 572, https://digitalcommons.unl.edu/libphilprac/572; Danielle Bodrero Hoggan, "Faculty Status for Librarians in Higher Education," *portal: Libraries and the Academy* 3, no. 3 (July 2003): 431–45, https://doi.org/10.1353/pla.2003.0060; Association of College and Research Libraries, "ACRL Joint Statement on Faculty Status of College and University Librarians," accessed September 15, 2021, https://www.ala.org/acrl/standards/jointstatementfaculty; Bruce R. Kingma and Gillian M. McCombs, "The Opportunity Costs of Faculty Status for Academic Librarians," *College and Research Libraries* 56, no. 3 (1995): 258–64, https://doi.org/10.5860/crl_56_03_258; Catherine Coker, Wyoma vanDuinkerken, and Stephen Bales, "Seeking Full Citizenship: A Defense of Tenure Faculty Status for Librarians," *College and Research Libraries* 72, no. 1 (2011): 406–20, https://doi.org/10.5860/crl-54r1.
4. County Administrator's Office, "Health Officer Orders County Residents Shelter in Place," news release, County of Sonoma, March 17, 2020, https://sonomacounty.ca.gov/CAO/Press-Releases/Health-Officer-Orders-County-Residents-Shelter-in-Place.
5. Fobazi Ettarh, "Vocational Awe and Librarianship: The Lies We Tell Ourselves," *In the Library with the Lead Pipe*, December 10, 2018, https://www.inthelibrarywiththeleadpipe.org/2018/vocational-awe.
6. Gina Schlesselman-Tarango, "The Legacy of Lady Bountiful: White Women in the Library," *Library Trends* 64, no. 4 (Spring 2016): 681, https://scholarworks.lib.csusb.edu/library-publications/34.
7. Rita Premo and Kaitlin Springmier, "Connecting Students to Course Materials: Getting Help from Sonoma State University Library," webinar, July 15, 2020, YouTube video, 28:36, https://youtu.be/75G0Wfl26mQ.
8. Veronica Arellano Douglas, "Pulling Back the Curtain on Library Magic," *ACRLog*, February 25, 2021, https://acrlog.org/2021/02/25/pulling-back-the-curtain-on-library-magic/comment-page-1/.
9. Andrew D. Asher, "Risk, Benefits, and User Privacy: Evaluating the Ethics of Library Data," in *Protecting Patron Privacy: A LITA Guide*, ed. Bobbi Newman and Bonnie Tijerina (Lanham, MD: Rowman

& Littlefield, 2017): 43–56, https://scholarworks.iu.edu/dspace/bitstream/handle/2022/22035/Asher--Risk_Benefits_User_Privacy_Final.pdf.

10. Jacob Berg, Angela Galvan, and Eamon Tewell, "Responding to and Reimagining Resilience in Academic Libraries," *Journal of New Librarianship* 3 no. 1 (2018): 1–4, https://doi.org/10.21173/newlibs/4/1.

11. Jungmin Lee, Hyn Ju Jeong, and Sujin Kim, " Stress, Anxiety, and Depression among Undergraduate Students during the COVID-19 Pandemic and Their Use of Mental Health Services," *Innovative Higher Education* 46 (2021): 519–38, https://doi.org/10.1007/s10755-021-09552-y.

Bibliography

Asher, Andrew D. "Risk, Benefits, and User Privacy: Evaluating the Ethics of Library Data." In *Protecting Patron Privacy: A LITA Guide*, edited by Bobbi Newman and Bonnie Tijerina, 43–56. Lanham, MD: Rowman & Littlefield, 2017. https://scholarworks.iu.edu/dspace/bitstream/handle/2022/22035/Asher--Risk_Benefits_User_Privacy_Final.pdf.

Association of College and Research Libraries. "ACRL Joint Statement on Faculty Status of College and University Librarians." Accessed September 15, 2021. https://www.ala.org/acrl/standards/jointstatementfaculty.

Berg, Jacob, Angela Galvan, and Eamon Tewell. "Responding to and Reimagining Resilience in Academic Libraries." *Journal of New Librarianship* 3 no. 1 (2018): 1–4. https://doi.org/10.21173/newlibs/4/1.

California State University. *The California State University Fact Book 2021.* Accessed September 15, 2021. https://www2.calstate.edu/csu-system/about-the-csu/facts-about-the-csu/Documents/facts2021.pdf.

Coker, Catherine, Wyoma vanDuinkerken, and Stephen Bales. "Seeking Full Citizenship: A Defense of Tenure Faculty Status for Librarians." *College and Research Libraries* 72, no. 1 (2011): 406–20. https://doi.org/10.5860/crl-54r1.

County Administrator's Office. "Health Officer Orders County Residents Shelter in Place." News release, County of Sonoma, March 17, 2020. https://sonomacounty.ca.gov/CAO/Press-Releases/Health-Officer-Orders-County-Residents-Shelter-in-Place.

Douglas, Veronica Arellano. "Pulling Back the Curtain on Library Magic." *ACRLog*, February 25, 2021. https://acrlog.org/2021/02/25/pulling-back-the-curtain-on-library-magic/.

Ettarh, Fobazi. "Vocational Awe and Librarianship: The Lies We Tell Ourselves." *In the Library with the Lead Pipe*, January 10, 2018. https://www.inthelibrarywiththeleadpipe.org/2018/vocational-awe.

Hoggan, Danielle Bodrero. "Faculty Status for Librarians in Higher Education," *portal: Libraries and the Academy* 3, no. 3 (July 2003): 431–45. https://doi.org/10.1353/pla.2003.0060.

Hosburgh, Nathan D. "Librarian Faculty Status: What Does It Mean in Academia?" *Library Philosophy and Practice*, 2011: article 572. https://digitalcommons.unl.edu/libphilprac/572.

Kingma, Bruce R., and Gillian M. McCombs. "The Opportunity Costs of Faculty Status for Academic Librarians." *College and Research Libraries* 56, no. 3 (1995): 258–64. https://doi.org/10.5860/crl_56_03_258.

Lee, Jungmin, Hyn Ju Jeong, and Sujin Kim. "Stress, Anxiety, and Depression among Undergraduate Students during the COVID-19 Pandemic and Their Use of Mental Health Services." *Innovative Higher Education* 46 (2021): 519–38. https://doi.org/10.1007/s10755-021-09552-y.

Premo, Rita, and Kaitlin Springmier. "Connecting Students to Course Materials." Webinar, July 15, 2020. YouTube video, 28:36. https://youtu.be/75G0Wfl26mQ.

Schlesselman-Tarango, Gina. "The Legacy of Lady Bountiful: White Women in the Library." *Library Trends* 64, no. 4 (Spring 2016): 667–86. https://scholarworks.lib.csusb.edu/library-publications/34.

Silva, Elise, Quinn Galbraith, and Michael Groesbeck. "Academic Librarians' Changing Perceptions of Faculty Status and Tenure." *College and Research Libraries* 78, no. 4 (2017): 428–41. https://doi.org/10.5860/crl.78.4.428.

Sonoma State University. "Facts: Students." Accessed September 15, 2021. http://sonoma.edu/about/facts.

CHAPTER 29

Interim Leadership in a Crisis

Livia Piotto

> The interim head librarian assumed the role of reassuring the staff that the library was not left rudderless and that someone was ready to step in and move the library forward. At the same time, she had to acknowledge that a period of mourning was necessary for everyone in the team and that everyone was coping with grief in different ways.

Introduction

Periods of disruptive change, such as the COVID-19 pandemic, have invariably had a great impact in the world of the libraries, challenging the library staff in many unexpected ways to embrace chance and resilience and to step up in confronting the difficulties. Disruption also offers opportunities. Managing change in libraries has always been quite a challenge under normal circumstances, and the 2020 pandemic proved to be an extraordinary crisis for managing any library. The challenge became even bigger when the disruptive moment of change needed to be managed with only interim leadership.

The role of the library manager in critical situations is essential for any library to effectively function with minimum disruption in services and staff. The director of the library is like the captain in a ship. What happens when the library faces a crisis within a crisis and loses the library leader first to illness and then to a sudden and unexpected death? In case of sudden loss, there are grief and emotions to deal with, and even more so when library staff are already affected by the increased fatigue caused by the pandemic. Nevertheless, it was, and is, necessary to keep the library running as smoothly as possible, and the role of interim director becomes even more important when faced with two severe upheavals at once.

In this chapter, based on personal experience, the author will discuss how the sudden loss of the library manager can impact the work of all involved, but mostly of the person who is called to take over the director's responsibilities—especially during a crisis. The COVID-19 pandemic hit John Cabot University library in the same way it hit every other library in Italy and other countries around the world. The March 2020 lockdown dictated by the Italian government forced everyone to work remotely and to transfer all library services online.

Following the directives of the Italian government to plan on slowly reopening the country, the university started planning its reopening in the summer 2020, and the then-head librarian was naturally the person in charge to make all decisions related to library services and operations. When we all went back to work in person in September 2020, the head librarian had to take a sudden leave to take care of her health. At first, operations and services, including the work of the library staff, continued normally, especially because the head librarian was consulting from home and directing the regular operations. However, her prolonged sick leave required the university administration to take action to continue to ensure all operations proceeded smoothly. Legally, in Italy, while a person is on sick leave, that person is bound to not do any type of work, and official decisions on behalf of the head librarian were required while she was away. After almost fifteen years as a loyal collaborator, the reference and instruction coordinator was called to act on behalf of the head librarian while still performing her regular duties. The distinction between *acting* and *interim* is subtle, and, in many contexts, the two terms are used interchangeably,[1] but in this situation it is a distinction that is worth making, although officially the temporary job title that was given to the reference and instruction coordinator always remained interim head librarian.

For the purposes of this chapter, the initial temporary position, which was only a way to work on behalf of the person who was on sick leave, will be referred to as *acting head librarian*, while *interim head librarian* will be used for the second, longer period, when the author assumed control in a more official capacity after the sudden and unexpected death of the head librarian until a decision was made to officially replace the position.

The Unexpected Interim Leadership

As Irwin and deVries point out, there is a gap in the literature related to interim leadership in libraries; most of the articles that discuss the issue examine how the interim leaders can prepare themselves for the role, providing personal experiences as examples.[2] Irwin and deVries compile a very comprehensive literature review on interim leadership in librarianship, but the literature they include refers mostly to the typical situation that sees the retirement of library directors or their move to a different position as the principal cause that starts the process of searching for and appointing an interim director. Not much has been written on how interim leaders can prepare themselves for the case of the sudden death of the person they are going to replace.

With the awareness that every library is different and understanding that the same situation could be handled in an entirely different way in another institutional context, this chapter examines one experience, or a case study, of an interim head librarian called in to temporarily replace the former library leader in a highly stressful period of profound crisis, comparing it with what the literature considers recommended practices and trying to assess what was learned from the situation.

All studies on interim leadership recommend that those willing to accept such a temporary appointment clarify expectations and responsibilities prior to the appointment itself, as well as the compensation, length of the appointment, and clearly outlined goals of the position.[3] In this situation at John Cabot University, there was no time for these initial discussions or decisions. The administration needed a person to step into the role fast, to keep all the operational procedures in place without any further disruption, given that the circumstances were already very complex due to the COVID-19 pandemic and new decisions needed to be made almost daily to respond to the constantly changing external circumstances. The administration called for a person who could become the acting head librarian and help run the library in a critical moment while maintaining a sense of stability in the transition. Subsequently, the presence of a person already invested in the interim role helped minimize as much as possible the emotional stress created by the unexpected loss of the library leader. Having worked at John Cabot University for over a decade, the reference and instruction coordinator knew the institution, the people, and the library staff and, most importantly, had an awareness of the expectations and demands of the job under the current pandemic conditions.

As Munde points out, "the library director is a difficult vacancy to fill on an interim basis"[4] because the person who is appointed as interim director usually does not have significant leadership or management training or specific preparation to do the job,[5] but the expertise of the retiring or leaving director might still be available. In the extreme case of the sudden loss of the director, there is no official means of passing the baton, as might normally happen. In this situation, while during the initial phase there was constant contact and exchange between the head librarian and the acting head, after the sudden passing of the official leader, not only there was no time for an official handover of the responsibilities, but also all the aspects of the job itself needed to be reconstructed from scratch and rapidly, especially under the conditions caused by the pandemic. By utilizing teamwork and by doing a lot of digging in past documentation, some processes, policies, and procedures could be modified for current circumstances. The position might be immediately filled with the presence of an interim director, but the specific contribution provided by the former director remained a vacuum. Therefore, the interim head librarian needed to rely on staff's expertise to make some basic decisions, collecting knowledge about the job from library colleagues who worked closely with the previous director or colleagues in other university areas that had close relationships with the former director.[6]

As Matthews notes in her description of the stages of the Nicholson and West Transition Cycles Model through which a new library leader should normally expect to transition when assuming the role,[7] becoming interim director after a precipitous termination does not allow for the first stage of the model, preparedness, to happen. The interim director usually jumps into the encounter stage without much preparedness for the job, and it becomes essential to accelerate the process of learning new job competencies. Additionally, as Sandra Shell notes, being an interim director involves a lot of stress and more difficulties than one might expect.[8] This is certainly what happens in normal circumstances. The level of stress and the difficulties undoubtedly increase when the interim position happens without a period of transition or formal succession planning. Given the lack of a formal handover, it was critical for the newly appointed interim head librarian to build up current and new relationships and find a way to get many questions answered. This was possible only with the help and support of other library staff members. Even if the new role was formally as a superior, asking for help was indeed a successful strategy to access the knowledge and the training needed and to allow former colleagues to feel empowered to be part of the change. As Thomson notes, "loss, grief and trauma are profoundly personal, but they are also *community* issues,"[9] and the fact that the interim head librarian relied a lot on the expertise of the staff made them feel that they were contributing to the change process that the circumstances forced upon them. Decisions were not just made, they were discussed collegially, and they became part of the learning process of the interim head librarian, who could start reconstructing her new job responsibilities that the former head librarian never had the time to formally hand over. Trusting the library staff to take ownership of their job responsibilities and duties created a sense of community that allowed them to embrace the grieving process as a group and not to feel left alone dealing with their grief and sense of abandonment. When change has a lot of emotions behind it—loss and grief in this circumstance—it can trigger strong responses, but grief can also be "transformational"[10] and become the trigger for allowing the staff to grow in their professional roles and to build a deeper commitment to the team and the job.

However, despite the trust that the administration put in the interim head librarian, this remained a temporary position until an official decision to replace the library director was made. As normally happens in similar circumstances, it is difficult to make long-term decisions because of the uncertainty of the appointment itself,[11] but at the same time, the interim director has to act with the same mindset and accountability the permanent position requires,[12] while also coping with the stress a new position creates, especially when the replacement is entirely unexpected.[13] The uncertainty of the duration of the appointment makes planning and organizational change more difficult, as the majority of the scholarship, not only in academic librarianship but also in management, around interim leadership positions concurs.[14] That same uncertainty, however, can also protect the interim director from making important decisions too quickly in a highly stressful situation like the loss of the previous director, compounded by the pandemic, which is in itself an uncertain moment that requires fast decision-making to respond to the institution's plans that vary day by day.

The uncertainty created by the pandemic and by the unexpected loss of the head librarian required the library staff to find a way to make sense of their working lives after the traumatic events. The biggest challenge in this situation is that both the interim director and the senior administrators, who will also be grieving the loss of an esteemed colleague and coping with the general anxiety created by the pandemic, have to "exercise great sensitivity and diplomacy"[15] toward the other employees, who may express difficulties in handling the circumstances—sudden loss of their manager, confusion regarding leadership, and a sense of abandonment, but also uncertainty about what was happening in the world—which can result in lack of concentration and focus in the workplace. The same difficulties were experienced by the interim head librarian as well, but the uncertain duration of the job also protected the interim leader from rushing into the new role without preparation. As is common in many similar cases, other university constituencies proved respectful of the grief and did not demand that important decisions be made, especially if decisions were not time-sensitive and could be postponed. For this to happen, however, the senior administration must be able to fully trust the interim director.

The shield of the uncertainty also offers the possibility of buying more time to better understand the dynamics of the new role, especially since the person appointed to be the interim director sees a sudden role shift from being an expert in the previous job to being a neophyte in dealing with managerial responsibilities. The literature about interim positions often stresses that the interim role for a person appointed internally frequently means wearing the old hat while managing the new role, thus aggravating an already complicated situation.[16] Therefore, while the interim appointee has little more than a vague idea of what the new job takes, the two concurrent jobs must be accomplished with "equal attention."[17] There will be mistakes, but skills can be transferred from the previous job, and although it is perfectly reasonable to feel unsure about being able to do the new job and to feel unprepared for the challenge, this "sense of difficulty"[18] can be overcome by relying on the support of the rest of the staff and by trusting them and feeling comfortable in delegating tasks.

Being in this uncertain role for a while and trying to decide whether to apply for the permanent position or not, the interim head librarian found it helpful to seek professional development and training opportunities to learn leadership and managerial skills. The position itself created the conditions for a great learning experience that ended up facilitating the development of new skills and the possibility of flexing new muscles.[19] Even beginning to understand that a person in a leadership position does not have to be flawless was essential to understanding that being the interim director did not mean knowing everything; rather, it meant empowering the staff to take more ownership, with less supervision, and allowing them to become more accountable for their work.[20] While the interim head librarian had just lost her mentor at work, she sought advice from other colleagues at different institutions, and they soon became essential mentoring figures for her growth as a new leader. Coaching and mentoring are to be considered key tools for anyone in an interim position, independently of whether one wants to apply for the permanent position or not, because the advice from experienced colleagues is always vital for putting things in perspective. A mentor can help you see potential pitfalls that can be encountered while leading a library and that are simply not taken into consideration due to lack of experience.[21]

What is obvious is that, when a librarian is asked to step in and become the interim director after the sudden passing of the former director, no effective succession planning can be put into place because of the unexpected event. It is true that typically succession planning in academic libraries tends to be a minor priority,[22] even in institutions that are getting ready to fill positions that are close to being vacant due to a planned retirement.

Following Singer and Griffith's definition of *succession planning* as "a systematic effort by the library to ensure continuity in key positions, retain and develop intellectual and knowledge capital for the future, and encourage individual advancement,"[23] this process means also identifying potential employees who can be trained for key leadership positions when needed, but this concept is in contrast with the forced training imposed by the interim appointment as library director. Usually, for an interim director selected internally, "workplace learning is a major source of leadership growth."[24]

Grief and Emotions in Interim Leadership

There is a dearth of publications dealing with sudden loss and grief in the library as a workplace, and even less can be found describing what happens after the sudden and unexpected death of the library director. In general, the death of a member of the work family can have a long-lasting impact both in terms of coping with grief, which is a different process for each member of the work family, and in terms of how the work is then reorganized.[25] Any death in the workplace brings an "emotional toll on the staff, but there is also an issue of compromised productivity."[26] Vacancies in leadership positions always bring disruption in the regular operational workflow, and they often leave staff members with a sense of uncertainty. If the vacancy is abrupt, the feeling of being left with no direction is clearly amplified by the other feelings that might overwhelm the staff, who also need to process the sudden void. Therefore, the interim director must take on the unique and challenging opportunity to "simultaneously [comfort] people and [motivate] them to continue doing their jobs."[27]

As Topper notes, when an employee dies, the rest of the staff will look to the supervisor to set an example on how to deal with the situation.[28] When the person who dies is the supervisor, the staff will look at the newly appointed leader, who might be struggling with the same emotional issues but also must quickly learn how to become the leader and set the example. Moreover, sudden loss does not allow any planning, and intense emotions may also appear months after the death, when specific projects or tasks were previously set to be accomplished.[29]

The quick transition provided by the interim director can help minimize potential disruption, but how does it leave the interim director? Besides being intrigued and excited by the idea of trying something new and possibly advancing in one's career, *vulnerable* is the term that comes to mind, and it is definitely how the interim head librarian felt when asked to transition from acting to interim director. *Vulnerability* is defined by Brené Brown as "the emotion that we experience during times of uncertainty, risk, and emotional exposure,"[30] and it is essential for library leaders because it helps to create trust in two directions, in the others, the colleagues, and in ourselves: being vulnerable requires being able to trust.[31] While grieving the loss of a colleague, even if one is superior in rank, it is easy to feel, for quite a long time, a sense of vulnerability mixed with deep emotional displacement for having unjustly taken a job that might not feel rightfully taken.

For a long time and even until this day, emotions have been considered out of place in the working environment, but not only do they perfectly belong to the workplace, but they also lead to actions.[32] Allowing oneself to grieve and to use that grief in one's daily tasks can help the person deal with the situation and start the healing process. It can also help in making sense of the loss and beginning to move on. Nevertheless, these circumstances require a wise use of emotions. The interim head librarian had to quickly learn how to respond to emotions in the new job role because "too little emotion and a leader runs the risk of looking like a robot, but showing too much emotion can make a leader appear to not be in control of the situation or themselves."[33] Being in control of emotions in the critical moment that followed the death of the director, who was also a dear friend and a mentor, during a pandemic that disrupted all the normal library operations, not to mention the entire world, was one of the most difficult things the interim head librarian had to experience in her working life. In similar circumstances it is easy to feel the pressure to maintain control when things fall apart, but sometimes it is essential to show one's vulnerable side.[34] "By showing [the staff] there is no shame in authentic emotion, you're giving them a platform to experience their own processes of grieving"[35] because the unexpected change in leadership leaves the staff undoubtedly confused about their identity and, in some cases, profoundly hurt.

While the interim head librarian became the point person to lead the library, all she wanted and needed to do was process her grief and cry. She lost a mentor and a friend, after all. Admitting her own vulnerability and sadness was the way to establish a new bond with the rest of the staff, one based on trust and empathy. However, as always happens with internally appointed interim directors, it is impossible not to "carry some existing perceptions"[36] due to the preexisting relationships with the rest of the staff, but also depending on the "perceptions related to the predecessor.... When perception of the predecessor is positive, everyone will want the [interim director] to work in the same style."[37] Independently of how the rest of the staff had perceived the former director, the interim head librarian had to acknowledge that each member of the staff was grieving in their own way, but they were all also grieving as a group, like children who lost a parent.[38]

As Klare suggests, using emotional intelligence and empathy to focus on yourself and on others can help keep the staff as a cohesive group.[39] The interim head librarian assumed the role of reassuring the staff that the library was not left rudderless and that someone was ready to step in and move the library forward. At the same time, she had to acknowledge that a period of mourning was necessary for everyone in the team and that everyone was coping with grief in different ways. It is important for the interim director to support the staff in a highly stressful moment, but at the same time the interim director needs to learn how to reframe the relationship with those who used to be peers and to adjust the personnel dynamics, overcoming the awkwardness of suddenly being the boss and acknowledging that the new relationship demands isolation from the same people who were colleagues.[40] Kobulnicky describes the new dynamics with a sad but realistic image: "the library director is the loneliest job in the university."[41]

Being asked to fill her late supervisor's role felt as if the interim head librarian was taking that role away from the former director or that she did not deserve it. Taking the place of a person she had worked with for almost fifteen years created a sense of guilt for filling the vacant position not for her own merits but because the necessities and the circumstances required her to do so. This survivor's guilt can last for a long time,[42] and at present the author still feels that she is filling this position only temporarily because the rightful owner will eventually come back. The sense of abandonment created by the sudden death caused, and still causes, the interim director to be constantly thinking how the former director would have handled specific situations or trying to make the right decision that she would have approved. There is also a twinge of guilt in seeing that some processes have developed in a more effective way than they would have had following the directions of the former director. But there is also a sense that the library team has grown stronger having gone through this tough moment together.

Conclusion

Any crisis, as a moment of unexpected change, adds new layers of complexity to the role of the leader. The fast-changing nature of the crisis brings more complexity to the decision-making process, given that it increases the speed at which decisions, even the simplest ones, need to be made. A crisis creates uncertainty and disruption, and "leading during a crisis requires leaders to be agile and resilient, and open to the challenges that the crisis brings."[43] Every crisis is unique; what John Cabot University Library faced were three overlapping crises: the COVID-19 pandemic, the need for someone to take over managerial responsibilities to support the head librarian who was on sick leave, and then the grief caused by her unexpected death and transitioning to interim leadership. The uncertainty of the situation created by these three critical intersecting circumstances predictably created sudden, unexpected, and unfamiliar problems. Any leader in a critical situation must be agile in making decisions and responding to the fluidity of the situation. The interim leader who takes the job in a similarly critical situation needs to quickly learn how to respond to the challenges posed—which in this case were the pandemic and the consequent fluctuating institutional situation, but also the emotional trauma created by the effect of pandemic on staff members and the sudden death of a leader. The need during the pandemic "to work concurrently and collaboratively in order to achieve leadership outcomes"[44] was institutionalized by the interim role. "Having someone with these new responsibilities who demonstrates they are ready to stretch themselves in the interest of the library will provide better reassurance in times of uncertainty"[45] for the entire staff and the senior administration. It became necessary to use compassion and empathy to step in and lead. But at the same time the interim director needed to take care of her own emotions, vulnerabilities, and insecurities. In this context, more than ever, showing vulnerability helped validate the interim role, and it was essential to learning how to lead with "mind, heart, gut and soul."[46]

Any expertise derived from interim leadership comes from experience. There are few if any other guidelines to follow for similar circumstances, but reflecting on the experience and reviewing the professional literature have helped to make sense of the experience from which others may also be able to learn. Reflecting on and writing about the experience could be helpful to others in the same or similar situations. Many people left the profession unexpectedly during the pandemic; some for personal reasons, others for health reasons.

In the future, it is likely there will be additional sudden disruptions in the workplace, and those interim leaders may find this case study to be helpful.

We still have to find a way to honor our former head librarian, but her memory is still very much alive in everything the library does because she built most of it. The library has become a thriving part of the university thanks to what she created, and even the staff members who had different opinions on operational matters now often refer to what she wanted for the library and how she wanted it to be accomplished. Her legacy is the simple fact that the library exists.

Notes

1. John E. Chapman, Judy J. Chapman, and John O. Lostetter, "The Acting or Interim Leadership Position: Expectations, Perceptions, Realities," *Health Care Management Review* 13, no. 4 (1988): 81–88; Norm Medeiros, "Training Ground: The Role of Interim Library Director," *OCLC Systems and Services: International Digital Library Perspectives* 26, no. 3 (2010): 153–55, https://doi.org/10.1108/10650751011073580; Pat A. Newcombe and James M. Donovan, "Becoming Director: An Internal Candidate's View," *Library Management* 34, no. 3 (2013): 188–99, https://doi.org/10.1108/01435121311310888.
2. Kathy M. Irwin and Susann deVries, "Experiences of Academic Librarians Serving as Interim Library Leaders," *College and Research Libraries* 80, no. 2 (2019): 238, https://doi.org/10.5860/crl.80.2.238.
3. Maggie Farrell, "Interim Leadership," *Journal of Library Administration* 56, no. 8 (2016): 990–1000, https://doi.org/10.1080/01930826.2016.1231547; Paul J. Kobulnicky, "Between the Acts: The Interim or Acting Director of a Research Library," *Journal of Library Administration* 24, no. 3 (1997): 3–29; Sandra J. Weingart, "Costs and Benefits of Interim Managerial Assignments in an Academic Library," *Library Management* 24, no. 4/5 (2003): 237–42, https://doi.org/10.1108/01435120310475338; Cynthia J. Boyle et al., "The Influence of Interim Deans: More Than Keeping the Ship Afloat and Warming the Captain's Seat," *American Journal of Pharmaceutical Education* 80, no. 7 (2016), https://doi.org/10.5688/ajpe807112; Farrell, "Interim Leadership"; Cynthia L. Fountaine, "Stepping In: The Unique Challenges Faced by Interim Law Deans," *University of Toledo Law Review* 40 (2009): 343–55; Kobulnicky, "Between the Acts"; Gail Munde, "My Year as Interim," *College and Research Libraries News* 61, no. 5 (2000): 416–17, 420, https://doi.org/10.5860/crln.61.5.416; Weingart, "Costs and Benefits."
4. Munde, "My Year as Interim," 417.
5. Farrell, "Interim Leadership"; Munde, "My Year as Interim"; Eric Shoaf, "Suddenly Directing: An Interview with Florence Doksansky," *Library Administration and Management* 19, no. 3 (2005): 116–18; Mark Stover, "From Reference Librarian to Interim Dean: A Journey of Comparisons and Contrasts," *Reference and User Services Quarterly* 50, no. 4 (2011): 322–24.
6. Tom Bielavitz, Dawn Lowe-Wincentsen, and Kim Read, "In the Interim: Leadership Shorts from Three Interim Library Directors," *PNLA Quarterly* 82, no. 2 (2018): 26–30; Fountaine, "Stepping In"; Rochelle Logan, "Executive Transitions: My Time as an Interim Director," *Public Libraries* 53, no. 6 (November/December 2014): 17–19; Medeiros, "Training Ground."
7. Catherine J. Matthews, "Becoming a Chief Librarian: An Analysis of Transition Stages in Academic Library Leadership," *Library Trends* 50, no. 4 (Spring 2002): 578–602.
8. Sandra Shell, "My Experience as a Bridge," *Virginia Libraries* 57, no. 2 (2011): 17, https://doi.org/10.21061/valib.v57i2.1157.
9. Neil Thompson, *Loss, Grief and Trauma in the Workplace* (New York: Routledge, 2017), 125.
10. Thompson, *Loss, Grief and Trauma*, 132.
11. Boyle et al., "Influence of Interim Deans"; Kobulnicky, "Between the Acts"; Munde, "My Year as Interim"; Shoaf, "Suddenly Directing."
12. Bielavitz, Lowe-Wincentsen, and Read, "In the Interim"; Farrell, "Interim Leadership"; Kobulnicky, "Between the Acts"; Elisa F. Topper, "Dealing with Death of an Employee," *New Library World* 109, no. 11/12 (2008): 584–86, https://doi.org/10.1108/03074800810921386.

13. Lynn Chmelir, "Here Today, Gone Tomorrow: Observations of an Interim Academic Library Director," *OLA Quarterly* 18, no. 1 (2012): 6–7, https://doi.org/10.7710/1093-7374.1346; Medeiros, "Training Ground"; Munde, "My Year as Interim"; Shell, "My Experience as a Bridge"; Shoaf, "Suddenly Directing."
14. Bielavitz, Lowe-Wincentsen, and Read, "In the Interim"; Rebecca Knight, "How to Step in as an Interim Manager," *Harvard Business Review*, March 1, 2021, https://hbr.org/2021/03/how-to-step-in-as-an-interim-manager; Christine H. Mooney, Matthew Semadeni, and Idalene F. Kesner, "Interim Succession: Temporary Leadership in the Midst of the Perfect Storm," *Business Horizons* 56, no. 5 (2013): 621–33; Weingart, "Costs and Benefits," 238.
15. Fountaine, "Stepping In," 347.
16. Claire-Lise Benaud and David G. Null, "Acting Positions: The Good, the Bad, and the Ugly," *College and Research Libraries News* 52, no. 1 (1991): 30–33, https://doi.org/10.5860/crln.52.1.30; Boyle et al., "Influence of Interim Deans"; Farrell, "Interim Leadership"; Logan, "My Time as an Interim Director"; Gregory MacAyeal and Marianne Ryan, "Surviving and Thriving in an Acting Leadership Position," *Reference and User Services Quarterly* 56, no. 4 (2017): 228–31; Shell, "My Experience as a Bridge."
17. MacAyeal and Ryan, "Surviving and Thriving," 228.
18. Kobulnicky, "Between the Acts," 6.
19. Farrell, "Interim Leadership"; Logan, "My Time as an Interim Director."
20. Deborah Ancona et al., "In Praise of the Incomplete Leader," *Harvard Business Review*, February 1, 2007, https://hbr.org/2007/02/in-praise-of-the-incomplete-leader.
21. Farrell, "Interim Leadership"; Kobulnicky, "Between the Acts."
22. Quinn Galbraith, Sarah Smith, and Ben Walker, "A Case for Succession Planning: How Academic Libraries Are Responding to the Need to Prepare Future Leaders," *Library Management* 33, no. 4/5 (2012): 222, https://doi.org/10.1108/01435121211242272.
23. Paula M. Singer and Gail Griffith, *Succession Planning in the Library* (Chicago: American Library Association, 2010), 1.
24. Gabrielle K. W. Wong, "A Tool for Academic Libraries to Prioritize Leadership Competencies," *College and Research Libraries* 80, no. 5 (July 2019): 599, https://crl.acrl.org/index.php/crl/article/view/18156.
25. Topper, "Dealing with Death of an Employee."
26. Sian Brannon et al., "Managing Sudden Loss," *Journal of Library Administration* 59, no. 1 (2019): 88, https://doi.org/10.1080/01930826.2018.1549413.
27. Fountaine, "Stepping In," 347.
28. Topper, "Dealing with Death of an Employee."
29. Brannon et al., "Managing Sudden Loss," 89.
30. Brené Brown, *Dare to Lead* (New York: Random House, 2018), 19.
31. Jason Martin, "Daring Librarianship: What Library Leaders Can Learn from Brené Brown," *College and Research Libraries News* 81, no. 2 (2020): 87, https://doi.org/10.5860/crln.81.2.87.
32. Jason Martin, "Emotional Intelligence, Emotional Culture, and Library Leadership," *Library Leadership and Management* 33, no. 2 (2019): 2, https://doi.org/10.5860/llm.v33i2.7329.
33. Martin, "Emotional Intelligence," 3.
34. Arielle Dance, "Working Through the Death of a Colleague," *Harvard Business Review*, November 5, 2020, https://hbr.org/2020/11/working-through-the-death-of-a-colleague.
35. Dance, "Working Through."
36. MacAyeal and Ryan, "Surviving and Thriving," 230.
37. MacAyeal and Ryan, "Surviving and Thriving," 230.
38. Anna Ranieri, "How to Handle Shared Grief at Work," *Harvard Business Review*, May 26, 2015, https://hbr.org/2015/05/how-to-handle-shared-grief-at-work.
39. Diane Klare, "The Accidental Director: Critical Skills in Library Leadership," *Library Leadership and Management* 31, no. 2 (2017): 4, https://journals.tdl.org/llm/index.php/llm/article/viewFile/7191/6407.
40. Boyle et al., "Influence of Interim Deans"; Farrell, "Interim Leadership"; Kobulnicky, "Between the Acts"; Logan, "My Time as an Interim Director."
41. Kobulnicky, "Between the Acts," 12.
42. Xan Goodman, Susan Wainscott, and Samantha Godbey, "Grief in the Library: Coping with the Loss of a Colleague," *College and Research Libraries News* 77, no. 4 (2016): 202–3, https://doi.org/10.5860/crln.77.4.9481.

43. Nita Lawton-Misra and Tyrone Pretorius, "Leading with Heart: Academic Leadership during the COVID-19 Crisis," *South African Journal of Psychology* 51, no. 2 (2021): 207, https://doi.org/10.1177/0081246321992979.
44. Lawton-Misra and Pretorius, "Leading with Heart," 208.
45. Klare, "Accidental Director," 4.
46. Lawton-Misra and Pretorius, "Leading with Heart," 209.

Bibliography

Ancona, Deborah, Thomas W. Malone, Wanda J. Orlikowski, and Peter M. Senge. "In Praise of the Incomplete Leader." *Harvard Business Review*, February 2007. https://hbr.org/2007/02/in-praise-of-the-incomplete-leader.

Benaud, Claire-Lise, and David G. Null. "Acting Positions: The Good, the Bad, and the Ugly." *College and Research Libraries News* 52, no. 1 (1991): 30–33. https://doi.org/10.5860/crln.52.1.30.

Bielavitz, Tom, Dawn Lowe-Wincentsen, and Kim Read. "In the Interim: Leadership Shorts from Three Interim Library Directors." *PNLA Quarterly* 82, no. 2 (2018): 26–30.

Boyle, Cynthia J., Renae Chesnut, Michael D. Hogue, and David P. Zgarrick. "The Influence of Interim Deans: More Than Keeping the Ship Afloat and Warming the Captain's Seat." *American Journal of Pharmaceutical Education* 80, no. 7 (2016). https://doi.org/10.5688/ajpe807112.

Brannon Sian, Kevin Yanowski, Taylor Evans, and Julie Leuzinger. "Managing Sudden Loss." *Journal of Library Administration* 59, no. 1 (2019): 86–96. https://doi.org/10.1080/01930826.2018.1549413.

Brown, Brené. *Dare to Lead: Brave Work. Tough Conversations. Whole Hearts*. New York: Random House, 2018.

Chapman, John E., Judy J. Chapman, and John O. Lostetter. "The Acting or Interim Leadership Position: Expectations, Perceptions, Realities." *Health Care Management Review* 13, no. 4 (1988): 81–88.

Chmelir, Lynn. "Here Today, Gone Tomorrow: Observations of an Interim Academic Library Director." *OLA Quarterly* 18, no. 1 (2012): 6–7. https://doi.org/10.7710/1093-7374.1346.

Dance, Arielle. "Working Through the Death of a Colleague." *Harvard Business Review*, November 5, 2020. https://hbr.org/2020/11/working-through-the-death-of-a-colleague.

Farrell, Maggie. "Interim Leadership." *Journal of Library Administration* 56, no. 8 (2016): 990–1000. https://doi.org/10.1080/01930826.2016.1231547.

Fountaine, Cynthia L. "Stepping In: The Unique Challenges Faced by Interim Law Deans." *University of Toledo Law Review* 40 (2009): 343–55.

Galbraith, Quinn, Sarah Smith, and Ben Walker. "A Case for Succession Planning: How Academic Libraries Are Responding to the Need to Prepare Future Leaders." *Library Management* 33, no. 4/5 (2012): 221–40. https://doi.org/10.1108/01435121211242272.

Goodman, Xan, Susan Wainscott, and Samantha Godbey. "Grief in the Library: Coping with the Loss of a Colleague." *College and Research Libraries News* 77, no. 4 (2016): 202–3. https://doi.org/10.5860/crln.77.4.9481.

Irwin, Kathy M., and Susann deVries. "Experiences of Academic Librarians Serving as Interim Library Leaders." *College and Research Libraries* 80, no. 2 (2019): 238–59. https://doi.org/10.5860/crl.80.2.238.

Klare, Diane. "The Accidental Director: Critical Skills in Library Leadership." *Library Leadership and Management* 31, no. 2 (2017). https://journals.tdl.org/llm/index.php/llm/article/viewFile/7191/6407.

Knight, Rebecca. "How to Step In as an Interim Manager." *Harvard Business Review*, March 1, 2021. https://hbr.org/2021/03/how-to-step-in-as-an-interim-manager.

Kobulnicky, Paul J. "Between the Acts: The Interim or Acting Director of a Research Library." *Journal of Library Administration* 24, no. 3 (1997): 3–29.

Lawton-Misra, Nita, and Tyrone Pretorius. "Leading with Heart: Academic Leadership during the COVID-19 Crisis." *South African Journal of Psychology* 51, no. 2 (2021): 205–14. https://doi.org/10.1177/0081246321992979.

Logan, Rochelle. "Executive Transitions: My Time as an Interim Director." *Public Libraries* 53, no. 6 (November/December 2014): 17–19.

MacAyeal, Gregory, and Marianne Ryan. "Surviving and Thriving in an Acting Leadership Position." *Reference and User Services Quarterly* 56, no. 4 (2017): 228–31.

Martin, Jason. "Daring Librarianship: What Library Leaders Can Learn from Brené Brown." *College and Research Libraries News* 81, no. 2 (2020): 87–89. https://doi.org/10.5860/crln.81.2.87.

———. "Emotional Intelligence, Emotional Culture, and Library Leadership." *Library Leadership and Management* 33, no. 2 (2019). https://doi.org/10.5860/llm.v33i2.7329.

Matthews, Catherine J. "Becoming a Chief Librarian: An Analysis of Transition Stages in Academic Library Leadership." *Library Trends* 50, no. 4 (Spring 2002): 578–602.

Medeiros, Norm. "Training Ground: The Role of Interim Library Director." *OCLC Systems and Services: International Digital Library Perspectives* 26, no. 3 (2010): 153–55. https://doi.org/10.1108/10650751011073580.

Mooney, Christine H., Matthew Semadeni, and Idalene F. Kesner. "Interim Succession: Temporary Leadership in the Midst of the Perfect Storm." *Business Horizons* 56, no. 5 (2013): 621–33.

Munde, Gail. "My Year as Interim." *College and Research Libraries News* 61, no. 5 (2000): 416–17, 420. https://doi.org/10.5860/crln.61.5.416.

Newcombe, Pat A., and James M. Donovan. "Becoming Director: An Internal Candidate's View." *Library Management* 34, no. 3 (2013): 188–99. https://doi.org/10.1108/01435121311310888.

Ranieri, Anna. "How to Handle Shared Grief at Work." *Harvard Business Review*, May 26, 2015. https://hbr.org/2015/05/how-to-handle-shared-grief-at-work.

Shell, Sandra. "My Experience as a Bridge." *Virginia Libraries* 57, no. 2 (2011). https://doi.org/10.21061/valib.v57i2.1157.

Shoaf, Eric. "Suddenly Directing: An Interview with Florence Doksansky." *Library Administration and Management* 19, no. 3 (2005): 116–18.

Singer, Paula M., and Gail Griffith. *Succession Planning in the Library: Developing Leaders, Managing Change*. Chicago: American Library Association, 2010.

Stover, Mark. "From Reference Librarian to Interim Dean: A Journey of Comparisons and Contrasts." *Reference and User Services Quarterly* 50, no. 4 (2011): 322–24.

Thompson, Neil. Loss, Grief and Trauma in the Workplace. New York: Routledge, 2017.

Topper, Elisa F. "Dealing with Death of an Employee." *New Library World* 109, no. 11/12 (2008): 584–86. https://doi.org/10.1108/03074800810921386.

Weingart, Sandra J. "Costs and Benefits of Interim Managerial Assignments in an Academic Library." *Library Management* 24, no. 4/5 (2003): 237–42. https://doi.org/10.1108/01435120310475338.

Wong, Gabrielle K. W. "A Tool for Academic Libraries to Prioritize Leadership Competencies." College and Research Libraries 80, no. 5 (July 2019): 597–617. https://crl.acrl.org/index.php/crl/article/view/18156.

Author Bios

Braegan Abernethy is the Department Head for Resource Acquisitions at the Georgia State University Library. She manages the library collections budget and provides leadership for the acquisitions, electronic and continuing resources, and interlibrary loan units. Previously, Braegan served as the Technical Services Librarian at the University of West Alabama, where she oversaw content management and discovery and library acquisitions. Her research interests include the future of library acquisitions and budget forecasting, emerging trends in library-publisher agreements, and copyright practices in interlibrary loan. Braegan has previously published on mentoring and community service in academic librarianship. She earned her Master's in Library and Information Studies from the University of Alabama.

Marlowe Bogino holds a MSLS from Clarion University of Pennsylvania, a BS of Allied Health from Widener University and AAS degree in Respiratory Care from Delaware Technical and Community College. She has worked as the Director of Medical Libraries at Christiana Care hospital in Delaware and is currently the Clinical Reference Librarian with Rowan University/Cooper Hospital in New Jersey.

Jill Borin has worked at Widener University for nearly 20 years as an archivist and Research and Instruction Librarian. Currently, Jill is Head of Archives & Distinctive Collections at Widener. Jill received an MLIS from Rutger's University, an MA in History from the University of Delaware, and a BA in History from Muhlenberg College.

Stephanie Brasley is the Dean of the University Library at California State University, Dominguez Hills, in Carson, California. Previously, she served as Dean of Academic Affairs at Los Angeles Southwest College. Prior to that, she managed systemwide information literacy initiatives for the California State University system. She received her MLS and BA in Spanish Literature from the University of California, Los Angeles. Her doctorate, from Brandman University, focused on organizational leadership. She has written and presented on information literacy, assessment, and Open Educational Resources. Her current research interests relate to the promotion of Open Educational Resources, organizational leadership, and diversity, equity, and inclusion in academic libraries.

Laureen P. Cantwell-Jurkovic, MSLIS, is the Head of Access Services & Outreach at Colorado Mesa University's Tomlinson Library. She oversees their Checkout + Reserves service point and staff, as well as their Resource Sharing/ILL staff. Laureen is pursuing a PhD in Information Science from University at Buffalo – SUNY. She also co-edited *Memphis Noir* (Akashic Books, 2015), *Finding Your Seat at the Table: Roles for Librarians on Institutional Regulatory Boards and Committees* (Rowman & Littlefield, 2022), and has published book chapters and articles on topics ranging from librarians on IRBs to MOOCs to curbside pickup services, from chat reference to library printing to digital badging, and more.

Tim Daniels is the Head of Technical Services at the University of North Georgia Libraries. He is currently enrolled at Valdosta State University, pursuing an Ed.D. in Leadership focusing on Higher Education. His research interests include leadership development programs for academic librarians, managing organizational change, staff development, and core competencies, data governance in higher education, and technology in higher education. Tim is a graduate of Appalachian State University and the University of North Carolina at Greensboro.

M. Teresa Doherty Teresa Doherty leads VCU Libraries' undergraduate student success initiatives, with a specific focus on first- and second-year undergraduates, students who identify as first-generation or underrepresented minorities, and low-income students. She graduated from VCU with a BA in English and Comparative Literature, and from the University of Wisconsin-Milwaukee with an MS in Library and Information Science.

Jessica Epstein is a reference librarian at the Atlanta University Center's Robert W. Woodruff Library, where she also heads the library's Online Learning & Technology Services unit. She earned her Master's in Library and Information Science from the University of Illinois at Urbana-Champaign and has a Master's in Public Policy from the University of Southern California. Jessica has a Bachelor of Arts in English Literature from American Jewish University. She currently serves as a member on ALA's Committee on Legislation as well as ACRL's Politics, Policy and International Relations Section, and is incoming convener for ACRL's History Librarians Interest Group.

Nancy Falciani-White (Randolph-Macon College, Ashland, VA) has worked in liberal arts college libraries for more than twenty years. She received her MSLIS degree from the University of Illinois at Urbana-Champaign and her Ed.D in Instructional Technology from Northern Illinois University in Dekalb, Illinois. Her research interests include creativity, the intersection of research and technological innovation, and academic library leadership.

April W. Feldman has worked in Special Collections & Archives at California State University, Northridge for over a decade and has been responsible for the University Archives and Campus History Collections since 2016. She holds an MA in History from Cal State Northridge, and an MLS from the University of North Texas.

Author Bios 385

Laura W. Gariepy is Associate Dean for Research and Learning at Virginia Commonwealth University's James Branch Cabell Library. Gariepy oversees undergraduate and graduate education and outreach; information and research services; assessment; emergency planning and response; and the physical spaces of the nationally renowned library. She holds a Ph.D. in Educational Research, Assessment, and Evaluation from Virginia Commonwealth University; an M.S. in Library Science from the University of North Carolina-Chapel Hill; and a B.S. in Sociology from Appalachian State University.

Joy Garmon Bolt is the Dean of Libraries at the University of North Georgia. Having worked in libraries since high school, she has held several positions in both academics and private law firms. Her professional interests include library administration, management and leadership as well as accessibility and advocacy. She currently resides in Flowery Branch, GA with her artist husband Don and their two cats, Hex and Fillister.

Renee Gould is an Assistant Professor/Collection Development Librarian for Saint Leo University. She holds a M.L.I.S. from the Palmer School of Library and Information Science (Long Island University). She has published in peer-reviewed journals including *Journal of Academic Librarianship* and *Internet Reference Services Quarterly*. In addition, she has presented at both national and state conferences on topics involving various areas of technical services, marketing, and accessibility.

Alison S. Gregory has been in academic libraries since 2005 and in leadership roles since 2013. Her professional passions are discipline-integrated information literacy, mentorship, and organization development. With masters' degrees in library science as well as leadership and management, Alison strives to merge theory with real-world applications in strengthening academic libraries and the people who make them work. Outside of libraries, Alison is a mom, a sucker for rescue dogs, an art historian wannabe, and a voracious reader of historical fiction set in the Renaissance.

Amy Harris has been working in academic libraries for over 20 years. She has presented at multiple conferences including the International Conference on Information Literacy, the Association of Christian Librarians Conference, and the Florida Library Association Conference. After earning her MLS at Indiana University, she worked in various librarian positions at Gainesville University, Southwestern Baptist Theological Seminary, Sinclair Community College, and Southeastern University. She is the Instruction and Assessment Librarian at Saint Leo University.

Yuki Hibben serves as the Senior Curator of Special Collections and Archives at Virginia Commonwealth University Libraries where she oversees the collection development and management of rare books and manuscripts including nationally significant collections of comic arts and contemporary artists' publications. She holds an M.L.I.S. from the Catholic University of America, an M.F.A. in Sculpture from Temple University's Tyler School of Art, and a B.A. in Fine Arts from the College of William and Mary. She is a member of the Academy of Certified Archivists.

Kim Hoffman is the Preservation Librarian at Miami University in Oxford, Ohio. Her responsibilities include maintaining both the circulating and special collections as well as the digital preservation program. She received her MS in Library and Information Science and her MA in Museum Studies in 2019 from Syracuse University in New York, where she also earned a Certificate of Advanced Studies in Cultural Heritage Preservation. Her research interests include centering diversity, equity, and inclusion in library preservation work. She holds volunteer positions in the American Institute for Conservation (AIC), the Academic Library Association of Ohio (ALAO), the Ohio Preservation Council (OPC), and the Society of American Archivists (SAA), where she is the current Vice-Chair/Chair Elect of the Preservation Section.

Cinthya Ippoliti has been a librarian for over 20 years and has held roles at a wide variety of academic institutions. Most recently, as director of the Auraria Library, Cinthya provides direct administrative leadership for library services, spaces, partnerships, and programming on the tri-institutional Auraria Campus which includes the University of Colorado, Denver; Metropolitan State University of Denver, and Community College of Denver and serves approximately 35,000 highly diverse students in an urban setting. In collaboration with the Library's administrative team, she sets a strategic vision to develop new services, foster creativity and collaboration, and provide professional development and mentorship opportunities for all library employees. Prior to joining the Auraria Library she was the Associate Dean for Research and Learning Services at Oklahoma State University and Head of Teaching and Learning at the University of Maryland Libraries. Her research interests include leadership, organizational development, and managing change.

Sharon Jasneski is the Head of Operations for ULS-Thomas Boulevard at the University of Pittsburgh's University Library System, where she runs the facility's daily operations. She has worked in library storage since 1999.

Charlotte M. Johnson, MLIS, is the Research Collection Coordinator at the University of Pittsburgh's University Library System and the librarian for ULS-Thomas Blvd. She has been working in library storage since 2016. Her research interests include library storage, collections, and library leadership and management. She is a graduate of the University of Maryland iSchool.

Michelle Joy earned her BA in English and Creative Writing and her MA(LIS) at the University of South Florida. She has worked as a librarian at several institutions, including as an Undergraduate Online Services Librarian at Saint Leo University, at Moffitt Biomedical Library, at Hillsborough Community College, and at Polk State College.

Kristina Keogh is the Dean of the Nelson Poynter Memorial Library at the USF St. Petersburg campus. Previously, she was Director of Library Services at Ringling College of Art and Design, where she managed operations including budget planning, facilities, user services, and personnel in the Alfred R. Goldstein Library. She has over 15 years of experience in library management, public services, and teaching roles. She was the Head of the Fine Arts Library and the Director of the Art Librarianship Specialization at Indiana University Bloomington. She holds an MLS from Florida State University and received a PhD in Art History from Virginia Commonwealth University. Her professional interests include the study and assessment of outreach and research services for art and design constituencies.

Audrey Koke is the Serials, E-Resources, and Instructional librarian at Saint Leo University. Her research interests include serials and technical services best practices as well as explorations into psychological and historical aspects of librarianship. Prior to her current position, Koke was a reference librarian for 15 years in Massachusetts and Florida. She has also worked for eight years as a reference librarian in the public sphere in Rhode Island and New York.

Kayleen Lam is a Research and User Experience Librarian who began working for The University of North Texas Health Science Center at Fort Worth in 2017. As a new librarian and manager, she is driven by a desire to engage with her team and the larger campus community. She takes pride in the collaborative process to deliver quality resources and services at HSC. Kayleen also supports the research and education efforts for the Graduate School of Biomedical Sciences. She has a Masters in Music Theory from Texas Christian University and a Masters in Library Science from Texas Woman's University. Her research interests include information literacy, evidence-based practice, hiring and management practices, as well as music theory.

Christopher B. Livingston is the director of the Historical Research Center housed at California State University, Bakersfield. He holds a MA in History from CSUB and a MLIS from San José State University. He teaches courses in Archives and Special Collections and Oral History where he exposes students to the role of diversity and power in shaping archival collections and the historical record.

Rachel Makarowski is the Special Collections Librarian at Miami University. In her position, she is responsible for many of the functions for special collections, including instruction, outreach, reference, cataloging, curation, and collection management. She graduated from Indiana University Bloomington with an MLS, specializing in Rare Book and Manuscript Librarianship, and worked in numerous positions at the Lilly Library. She previously worked at the Rare Book School during her time as an undergraduate at the University of Virginia. Her research interests focus on teaching with primary sources, including the intersection of primary source instruction with other responsibilities in special collections. She has actively volunteered in a number of professional organizations, including the Rare Book and Manuscripts Section (RBMS) of the Association for College and Research Libraries (ACRL), Teaching with Primary Sources (TPS) Unconference Planning Group, and Academic Library Association of Ohio (ALAO).

Austina McFarland Jordan is the Head of Access Services at The University of North Georgia Libraries. She is currently enrolled in the University of West Georgia Ed.D.

program in Higher Education Administration. Her research interests include student employment as a path for student learning and success and staff professional development. She and her husband David live in Royston, GA with their dog Molly and cat Buddy. When not doing homework for her Ed.D. she enjoys running, baking, and trying out new restaurants.

William Modrow is Head, Walter Havighurst Special Collections & University Archives, Miami University. He has spent over twenty years in libraries where he has experience creating new departments to meet the changing demands of library services and resources. He has been developing library professionals and programs to meet the changing needs of researchers and patrons. An active advocate for all things library related he received an MA & MLIS The Florida State University where his focus was library leadership and staff development and the information needs of underrepresented groups. His professional involvement has been in ALA CORE (formerly LLAMA) mentorship and leadership committees, Association for College & Research Libraries, Association of Research Libraries & The Society of American Archivists.

John Mokonyama, MS, MBA, MSLS, AHIP-S, is the Medical Librarian at Penn Medicine, Chester County Hospital's Healthcare Library. He manages and runs all operations of the library, including acquisitions, cataloging, circulation, reporting, bibliographic instruction, reference and research. Mokonyama has recently completed a post-baccalaureate certificate program in Healthcare Informatics from Drexel University. He collaborates with physicians, nurses and hospital staff on various research projects. He recently helped design the first Physicians' Annual Competency Education in Knowledge Link at his hospital. Mokonyama has published topics such as diversity equity, inclusion. He has also co-authored on how Librarians meet the challenges of the COVID-19 pandemic. Mokonyama is a proponent of evidence based practice (EBP) and clinical research.

Amanda Nash is the Assistant Dean of Libraries at the University of North Georgia, where she leads the libraries' Reference and Instruction division. In addition to reference services and information literacy, her professional interests include library administration, pedagogy, faculty development, and instructional design. Amanda received her BA in English Literature from Dickinson College and her MLIS from the University of South Carolina. When she's not at the library, you'll most often find her walking her 60-pound lapdog, Bodhi.

Pamela Nett Kruger is the Institutional Repository Librarian at California State University, Chico Meriam Library. She has an MA in Anthropology from California State University, Northridge, and an MLIS from San José State University. Her research interests include communities of practice, and inclusive and constructivist pedagogies.

Dr. Erik Nordberg is Dean of the Paul Meek Library at the University of Tennessee at Martin. He holds an MPhil from Trinity College Dublin, an MSLS from Wayne State University, and a PhD from Michigan Technological University. He was employed as a professional archivist at Indiana University of South Bend, Michigan Tech, and is former director of the Walter Reuther Library at Wayne State. Nordberg was dean of libraries at Indiana University of Pennsylvania before beginning his current role in February 2021. In addition to serving as board member and executive director of the Michigan Humanities Council, he has served as principal investigator, project director, and a significant participant in projects funded by NEH, NHPRC, the American Library Association, and the W.K. Kellogg Foundation.

Stephen Patton [ORCIDID# 0000-0002-2840-0597] is the Chair of the Library Systems Department at Indiana State University, where he provides strategic leadership in all aspects of information technology, digital strategies, and scholarly communication in a teaching and research environment. Through his current and previous roles, he also has extensive experience in library operations, facilities management, and data-gathering and assessment. Previously, he was the head of library systems and Electronic Services Librarian at Delta State University in Mississippi. He holds an MLS from Florida State University, the M.S. in Applied Computer Science from Columbus State University, and is a PhD candidate in Technology Management at Indiana State University. His research interests include privacy equity, digital and object preservation, research participant protections, and regulatory compliance.

Livia Piotto is the Head Librarian at John Cabot University (Rome, Italy), where she started working in 2006 first as Reference Librarian and then as Reference and Instruction Coordinator, after receiving her MLS from the University of Rome "La Sapienza". In her role at John Cabot University, she manages the library operations and coordinates all instruction activities, especially in her capacity of library liaison for business and social sciences.

Adriana Popescu is Dean of Library Services at California Polytechnic State University (Cal Poly), in San Luis Obispo, California. Previously, she served as Director of Science, Business and Engineering Services at Hesburgh Libraries, University of Notre Dame. She has a Master of Engineering from the Technical University of Civil Engineering in Bucharest, Romania and received her MLS from Rutgers University. Her current research interests include planning, designing, and implementing innovative academic services that connect people; and developing library organizations that embody the academic and cultural values of their communities.

Christina Prucha, MLIS, EdD, is the Head of Collection Services at University Portland's Clark Library. She manages technical services, special collections, and digital initiatives and is also responsible for electronic resource management and collection development. She has published on topics such as teaching information literacy to English language learners and lone-arranging in archives and is currently interested in the roles academic librarians play on college and university campuses.

Delaney Rose holds an M.S. in Library and Information Science from Florida State University and a B.A. in English from the University of South Florida. She specializes in research on disability accommodation and the information needs of people with Autism Spectrum Disorder.

Christine F. Smith, MLIS is the Head, Acquisitions & Serials at Concordia University (Montreal, Canada). Smith holds diverse experience across the library and information sector and has sat on committees, working groups and boards of directors of provincial, national, and international library associations.

Marissa Smith is the Library Technology Specialist at Saint Leo University. As an undergraduate, she served as an associate editor for The Crime and Justice Institute Northeastern State University's Contemporary Law and Justice Journal. This experience greatly encouraged her editing and writing skills. She gathered library experience through volunteering at local elementary school's libraries. She holds a Master of Science in Information from Florida State University. In addition to her technology position, she assists patrons with research inquiries.

Emily Szitas earned her BA in Journalism from the Pennsylvania State University. Ms. Szitas earned her MLIS from the University of Pittsburgh (2005) and her MBA from Indiana University of Pennsylvania (2021). She is an active member of the Pennsylvania Library Association. She worked full-time in academic libraries for 16 years advancing information literacy, furthering collection development, and improving electronic resource access across the college campuses. On June 4, 2021 Ms. Szitas was retrenched from her faculty position. She currently lives in Western PA with her husband and daughter and works in business development at Northwind Engineering LLC.

Jocelyn Tipton is the Assistant Dean for Public Services at the University of Mississippi Libraries. In this role she provides leadership for Access Services (composed of circulation and ILL), Library Information Technology, Research and Instruction, and the Science Library by advocating to ensure that the library operations and services respond to the current and future needs of the user community. She previously served as Head of Reference Services at Eastern Illinois University. Jocelyn holds an M.L.S. from the University of Maryland, an M.A. in political science from Eastern Illinois University and a Ph.D. in higher education from the University of Mississippi. Her dissertation focused on faculty use of open educational resources. Additional research interests relate to the academic library's involvement in the higher education ecosystem.

Renna Tuten Redd (she/her/hers) is the Interlibrary Loan Librarian at Clemson University Libraries, where she oversees a team of five employees who perform resource sharing duties, including interlibrary loan, document delivery, consortial print delivery services, offsite storage, and mail delivery services. Her current research focus is on middle management issues in academic librarianship and participates in service work relating consortial sharing, continuing education initiatives, and equity, diversity, and inclusion. She holds an MLS from the University of South Carolina, an MA in Southern Studies from the University of Mississippi, and a BA in Art History from the University of Georgia.

Doris Van Kampen-Breit, M.A. (LIS), MBA (HR), Ed.D. (C&I), is currently the University Librarian and chief academic officer of the library at Saint Leo University. During her 20+ years at Saint Leo, she has been on both sides of the table as a faculty member with tenure and as an administrator.

Kayla Van Osten has worked at Widener University for nearly 5 years as a Research and Instruction Librarian & Assistant Archivist. She received a BA of Arts in English and Communications from Albright College and received her MLIS from Drexel University.

Alicia Virtue is the Dean of Library and Learning Resources at CSU Channel Islands (CSUCI). Prior to joining CSUCI, she most recently served as Senior Dean of Learning Resources and Educational Technology at Santa Rosa Junior College. She received her BA in Linguistics from the University of California at Santa Barbara, her MLS from the University of California at Los Angeles, and a Doctorate in Organizational Leadership from Brandman University. Alicia's current research interests are in the areas of equity access to information and data privacy protection in the digital age. She has published works on innovative applications of educational technology for use in information discovery and learning environments.

Sean D. Visintainer has worked in Special Collections for over a decade, in St. Louis, Missouri, Texas's Rio Grande Valley, and since 2019 at California State University San Marcos, where Sean is the Head of Special Collections. Sean holds an MLS from the University of Missouri Columbia. His research interests include community and participatory archives and collaborative community archival partnerships.

Michele Whitehead joined the Gibson D. Lewis Health Science Library at the University of North Texas (UNT) Health Science Center at Fort Worth (HSC) in 2011. She is the Director of Research, Education, and Engagement. Michele also serves as a faculty member at Tarleton State University in the Department of Criminology, Criminal Justice, and Public Administration. Michele previously served as a faculty member at the University of Texas at Arlington (UTA) and began her education career in K-12 with Lubbock ISD. She holds two Masters degrees: the first in Criminology and Criminal Justice from UTA and the second in Library Science from UNT. She was also a member of the first cohort to complete the Graduate Certificate in School Management and Leadership at Harvard.

Bethany Wilkes has worked in libraries for almost 20 years, and her most recent position was as the University Librarian at Singapore Management University (SMU). Bethany has a fondness for islands and has worked in leadership positions and roles advancing information literacy in university libraries in several parts of the world, including Hong Kong SAR, Alaska, and the US Virgin Islands. Her diverse international experiences contribute to her commitment to collaboration and international librarianship.